AF736241

Relational Identity in International, Comparative and European Union Law

Antonio Lazari

Relational Identity in International, Comparative and European Union Law

palgrave
macmillan

Antonio Lazari
Derecho Público
Universidad Pablo de Olavide
Seville, Spain

ISBN 978-3-031-59481-6 ISBN 978-3-031-59482-3 (eBook)
https://doi.org/10.1007/978-3-031-59482-3

This monograph was supported by the grant *Estancias de personal docente y/o investigador senior en centros extranjeros 2023, no. PRX23/00031*, awarded by Spanish Ministry of Science, Innovation, and Universities.

© The Editor(s) (if applicable) and The Author(s), under exclusive license to Springer Nature Switzerland AG 2026, corrected publication 2026

This work is subject to copyright. All rights are solely and exclusively licensed by the Publisher, whether the whole or part of the material is concerned, specifically the rights of translation, reprinting, reuse of illustrations, recitation, broadcasting, reproduction on microfilms or in any other physical way, and transmission or information storage and retrieval, electronic adaptation, computer software, or by similar or dissimilar methodology now known or hereafter developed.
The use of general descriptive names, registered names, trademarks, service marks, etc. in this publication does not imply, even in the absence of a specific statement, that such names are exempt from the relevant protective laws and regulations and therefore free for general use.
The publisher, the authors and the editors are safe to assume that the advice and information in this book are believed to be true and accurate at the date of publication. Neither the publisher nor the authors or the editors give a warranty, expressed or implied, with respect to the material contained herein or for any errors or omissions that may have been made. The publisher remains neutral with regard to jurisdictional claims in published maps and institutional affiliations.

Pattern © Melisa Hasan

This Palgrave Macmillan imprint is published by the registered company Springer Nature Switzerland AG.
The registered company address is: Gewerbestrasse 11, 6330 Cham, Switzerland

If disposing of this product, please recycle the paper.

The original version of the book has been revised. Funding information has been included in the frontmatter. A correction to this book can be found at https://doi.org/10.1007/978-3-031-59482-3_14

To Ale, Dani, and Marián,
who helped me discover the essence of relational identity in life. This book is but a testimony to our relationship.

And now what will become of us without barbarians?
Those men were some kind of solution
C.P. Cavafy, "Waiting for Barbarians" (1898)
Confines prevent the poor from entering, not the rich from leaving.
(Eero Suilehto)

Acknowledgements

My first thanks go to the professors of the Universidad Pablo de Olavide in Seville and, in particular, to my colleagues in the Area of Public International Law and International Relations, especially Lucía Millán Moro and Luis Pérez-Prat Durbán, who have always shown me closeness and support at every moment.

I would also like to thank all the colleagues I met during my research stay (Estancias de personal docente y/o investigador senior en centros extranjeros 2023) at the Scuola Superiore Sant'Anna in Pisa, with whom I had inspiring and open conversations, and in particular my friend Peppe Martinico, without whose constant support many things would not have been possible.

I am also deeply grateful for the support I have always received from my colleagues Gian Antonio Benacchio, Jacques Ziller, Francesco Donato Busnelli and Gianluigi Palombella.

My thanks also go to my friends MCarmen and Agustín, and to my entire extended family in Italy and Spain. My special thanks go to my dear brother Gianluigi, and to my beloved mother and my father, whose memory, with time, becomes clearer and filled with beautiful colours.

Finally, to Dani, Ale, and Marián: the meaning of this monograph is our living together.

Competing Interests The author has no competing interests to declare that are relevant to the content of this manuscript.

Contents

CHAPTER 1

Prologue

Abstract In this introductory chapter we will deal with tracing the contours of the old and new epistemological glasses necessary to read a new identity reality. The first moment of identity is that of abandonment from the usual thought, that is of bewilderment. We have to lose our cognitive habits through an écart, a reckless movement. Collective identity, in fact, must flee both from the deception of the universalisation of time ("we have always been like this") and from the pitfall of geographical isolation ("only we are like this"). Another way of conceiving identity comes to us precisely from Jullien's écart, which should not be translated as gap: it is not identity separation from Others. It is the opening of a distance that puts things in a reflective relation to one another. It is tension between them.

Keywords Identity • Écart • Separation • Tension • Epistemology

1.1 Prodromes: Old and New (Conceptual) Frameworks

The present work is the fruit of reflections which have unfolded throughout my personal academic experiences, the first of which dates to a visit to the Prado Museum exhibition entitled "Velázquez, Rembrandt and Vermeer. Similar views". Visitors were invited to enjoy not only the quality

© The Author(s), under exclusive license to Springer Nature Switzerland AG 2026
A. Lazari, *Relational Identity in International, Comparative and European Union Law*,
https://doi.org/10.1007/978-3-031-59482-3_1

and significance of the seventy-two works (by some of the most reputed seventeenth-century European painters), but also to establish points of comparison between them. But the question is: What comparison were the creators of the exhibition referring to?

It long seemed logical to believe that art diverged considerably across the European continent: Velázquez, for example, was the "very Spanish" representative of the pictorial art of his era while Rembrandt was "very Dutch". This appreciation results from the excessive influence of nineteenth and twentieth century nationalist sensibility and ideology regarding our understanding of art. The scholars of the time attached great importance to the differences between nations, to their belligerent phases of exclusion and expulsion (or even elimination) of the Other. And the belief that these differences were naturally expressed through art was widespread. Moreover, the distance sometimes created a gap between some national authors and others. Such a perspective narrows the focus down to the sole belonging to a nation, overlooking the common traits shared by European artists, as well as their interactions, mutual infiltrations, and their inextricable knot of influences. Rather than reasoning in terms of exclusivity, recent scientific epistemologies emphasise the relational nature of art and culture, woven around the tangle[1] of complex interactions that reality is made of. The most illustrative work in this sense is perhaps the Spinners or The Fable of Arachne of 1657, owing to its artistic interactions or meta-painting characteristic. Indeed, Velázquez alludes here to Rubens' fresco elaborated between 1628 and 1629, and which had been inspired, in turn, by Titian's 1544 painting.

A "common ground of the epoch" exists, together with the contributions and fruits of the artists of course, in our case, of the jurists. This is the idea of *écart* put forward by Jullien, the French philosopher. "*Je ne me demanderai plus en quoi la pensée d'Aristote est différente de celle de Plato, ni en quoi elle en diffère; je me demanderai plutôt en quoi la pensée d'Aristote ouvre un écart – se nourrit d'une distance – par rapport à celle de Platon. D'abord, jusqu'à quel point peut-il s'éloigner de cette pensée ? Aristote prend ses distances avec la célèbre théorie des idées, mais il ne peut cependant pas s'écarter du statut formalisant de l'*eidos".[2] We could similarly compare the painters Velázquez, Rubens and Tizzano based on their *écart* within the

[1] The reference is to F. *Remotti's concept of* "groviglio" (tangle), *Somiglianze. Una vía per la convivenza*, Editori Laterza, Bari, 2019.

[2] F. Jullien, *L'écart et l'entre*, Galilée, Paris, 2012, pp. 48–49.

framework of the common ground of their era. This latent dialogue between European painting and the painting in Europe materialises in the myth of Arachne, in the action of weaving comparative strands between masters which, in later years, would be considered the products of nationalism.[3]

The latter was the goal of the art exhibition, and it is also one of the objectives of the present volume. On the other hand, for early twentieth-century formalist Russian philosophers,[4] art was the epitome of "*ostranenie*", that is, of the distancing from one's own identity. Yet, to decipher this complex reality, to view these paintings from another perspective, we must adopt new "epistemological lenses".[5] No longer should we use the instruments manufactured in periods of compartmentalisation of reality to promise inclusion and to exclude de facto: on the contrary, we should employ tools which enable us to read complex identities.

Remaining in the pictorial sphere, another preliminary question concerns the outlining of identity. No subject is depicted using a single colour only.[6] Most studies on this subject inevitably tend to conceive identity in monolithic terms, including the works which criticise the very existence of identity.[7] Nuances will be applied here to the subject contours in order to avoid encapsulating the complexity of identity into a single container. "*Identities are complex, and complexity is the hallmark of twenty-first*

[3] A. Hernández-Gil, *El rapto de Europa*, in *ABC* 3 April 2017: "Despite the contemporaneity of the figures, The Spinners represents another ancient myth: that of Arachne who, equally following the Metamorphoses, wove a tapestry about the abduction of Europa. Velázquez paints an old and humble Arachne behind the spinning wheel, in the shadowy corner of the studio. In the background, placed behind women in sumptuous attire and bathing in an air-piercing light hangs a tapestry of The Rape of Europe by Rubens, whom Velázquez admired. The Spinners tells the story of two myths: that of Arachne, whom we see weaving in the foreground, and that of Europa, weaving behind her. Velázquez is referring to Rubens, who copied Titian, who illustrated Ovid, whose poetry, in turn, illuminates the whole, in an infinite regression, all intertwined through a mise en abyme which, connecting times and places, sorts history and unites it into a single image" (author's translation).

[4] V. Shklowsky, *Art as Artifice*, in Todorov, T. (ed.), *Teoría de la literatura de los formalistas rusos*, Mexico, Siglo XXI, 1991, pp. 55–70.

[5] As we shall see below, essential here is the contribution of L. Wittgenstein, *Philosophical Investigations,* Blackwell, 1974, § 129, p. 50.

[6] Pivotal in this regard in the historical sphere is E. Manzano Moreno, *España diversa. Keys to a plural history*, Crítica, Barcelona, 2024.

[7] F. Remotti, *Contro l'identità*, Editori Laterza, Rome-Bari, 2001, who maintains, however, in the last work Idem, *Somiglianze. Una vía per la convivenza*, Editori Laterza, Bari, 2019, a more open-minded stance on the existence of collective identity.

century law".[8] When analysing a historical period, as well as state, supra-state, and epistemic identity, I shall "complexify" the results obtained from confronting apparently contradictory data. This is the comparative operation of the *écart*.[9] Yet there is a difference between knowing and appreciating the paintings and self-knowledging.

Thus, the first question we must ask ourselves is of a Pirandellian nature: Is a state's identity (re)recognisable? Can a supranational identity truly exist? Pirandello introduced this question at the beginning of his "*Uno, nessuno e centomila*",[10] much to the confusion of the central character Vitangelo Moscarda.

There has been a lot of talk recently of the (threatened) identity of Western law, and, within Europe's legal realm, of the Member States' constitutional identity. Identity, even in terminological terms, is understood as exclusive, almost as if it were a legal effrontery or a populist heritage.[11] How is so much unease created? A sudden movement, "*una scoperta improvvisa e inattesa*", caused almost inadvertently by a sentence pronounced by his wife.[12]

The core question of our research is, after all, very simple: can the collective identity that is spoken of daily in an exclusive sense at the social, political and legal levels be defined in a relational way? Can state or supranational identity only be conceived by exclusion?

Foreigners, aliens, disturbing strangers, *tremendum et fascinans*, exposed entirely before our eyes, perceived as barbarians who must be

[8] M. Graziadei, *Obviously European?*, in *Persona e Mercato*, 2021/2, p. 243.

[9] Rather than being trapped by identity and difference, where one's own identity is presumed and a tendency towards it is cultivated in a sterile fashion, the *écart* opens a realm of fecundity. In the controversy over Europe's Christian roots in the preamble of the Treaty establishing a Constitution for Europe, a difference became evident between the defenders of Christianity and secularism. "What are we?" An underlying idea of exclusionary identity leads to a dead end. In Jullien's perspective, European culture is space, the tension that subsists between these two poles. Cf. F. Jullien, *Contro la comparazione. The 'scarto' and the 'tra'. Un altro accesso all'alterità*, Mimesis, Milano, 2014, pp. 46–47.

[10] L. Pirandello, *Uno, nessuno e centomila*, Mondadori, 1987, p. 8.

[11] For example, R. Spano, *The rule of law as the lodestar of the European Convention on Human Rights: The Strasbourg Court and the independence of the judiciary*, in *Eur Law Jour.*, 2021, p. 17: "*Attempts to legitimise relativistic conceptions of the rule of law, quite often tied to politics of national identity and parochial definitions of the common good, defined by the closed circle of the powerful, must be rejected*". Cf. G. Martinico, *Contro l'uso populista dell'identità nazionale. Per una lettura "contestualizzata" dell'art. 4.2 TEU*, in *DPCE online*, 2020/3, p. 3968.

[12] L. Pirandello, *Uno, nessuno e centomila*, Mondadori, Rome, 1987, p. 8.

educated and civilised or, in the worst case, who need to be fought and annihilated if they do not let themselves be reduced to the We. Such foreigners open a relational space, based on questioning, exchange and responsibility. Yet, the very concept of the Other has varied over time. Inescapable, however, and almost indispensable is the variable but indispensable theoretical reflection on identity and otherness, as well as legal research on respect, equality, and difference. An encounter with the Other affects both our knowledge and our relationships. It leads us not only to reconfigure the meaning and value of the life associated with it, but also to rethink the essence of what is human and its distinctive feature: identity in relation to belonging, inserted in a codified and shared system of norms and values.[13] I shall delve into the genealogy of the Encounter with the Other in legal terms, qualifying some theories developed in various historical moments while avoiding a hypostatic and granitic approach to Western responses.

Human sociability indeed implies that we can never completely isolate the narratives constructed by the Other about Us. The identities of the Others are built within these cultural frameworks, never outside of them. These networks of meanings, however, are not univocal and indisputable.[14] They are therefore part of the conceptual framework within which (collective and individual) subjects are immersed and where they build their identity by contributing to the construction of subjects, in their capacity to configure the identities of individuals and collectives.[15] Law is a way of imagining the subject and its relationship with the world: the modern legal world is composed of complex and interrelated conceptual fabrics.[16] However, the current identity of the Law is highly sectionalised, atomised into separate and watertight legal sciences.[17]

In particular, the two law sciences (international law and comparative law) which have addressed the relationship with the Other and continue to do so today emerged almost at the same time at the end of the

[13] C. Pépin, La rencontre, une philosophie, Allary Editions, Paris, 2021.

[14] D. Bonilla Maldonado, *Los bárbaros jurídicos: Identidad, derecho comparado moderno y el Sur global* (Filosofía política y del derecho), Siglo del Hombre Editores, Bogotá, 2020.

[15] Finally, A. Maalouf, *La labyrinthe des égarés: L'Occident et ses adversaires*, Edition Grasset & Fasquelle, 2023, speaks to us of a clear sense of loss.

[16] M. Koskenniemi, *Histories of International Law: Dealing with Eurocentrism*, in *Rechtsgeschichte—Legal History*, 2011, pp. 152–176.

[17] Cf. A.B. Rozo, *La interdisciplinariedad horizontal. Las formas económica, social, política y jurídica de construir realidades*, in *Co-herencia*, 2016, pp. 43–58.

nineteenth century. They developed within the same exclusive positivist *episteme* and, contrary to what we have been led to believe, they were linked to pursuits which were considerably more concrete than universal. An ontological incompatibility has always been proclaimed and has been presumed to exist between the two disciplines: internationalist law science was concerned with the set of rules governing relations between states. Comparative law science, on the other hand, sought exclusively to measure the legal differences between the legal systems of the (pre-eminently Western) States. This compartmentalised vision is also based on a Law worldview loaded with typically Western divisive connotations.[18] "*In qualunque contesto o livello si posizioni, ogni noi comporta un qualche grado di violenza dovuto alla distinzione originaria, al gesto di separazione che lo costituisce e lo fa esistere*".[19] This *actio finium regundorum* operation resembles the conception of *Closure* or *Separation* characterising Glenn's comparative law research or Derrida's *force de loi* mysticism.[20] The conceptual tools developed particularly at the end of the nineteenth century further developed an exclusive and isolated vision of state identity regarding aspects of both comparative and internationalist law. "The 'otherness' of the third world has been instrumental in constructing the 'I' of international law, an 'I' that is blatantly Eurocentric and directed towards excluding the 'other'.[21] The first part of this work will focus on various encounters with the Other and how the latter have led to the creation of epistemological legal lenses in Europe which still contribute to an exclusionary identity approach in the legal world vision.

The second part is dedicated to unravelling the movement against classification, distancing and normative exclusion: that is, the tendency towards integrative and relational identity at the state and scientific levels.[22] As can already be observed, these two conceptual strata interact with

[18] T. Makkonen, *Identity, Difference and Otherness [:] The Concepts of "People", "Indigenous People" and "Minority"* in *International Law*, Helsinki, Forum Iuris, Faculty of Law, University of Helsinki, 2000, specifically p. 43 (both notions of race and culture are based on "the proto-racist belief in the existence of insurmountable natural, cultural, or biological differences").

[19] Cf. F. Remotti, *L'ossessione identitaria*, Laterza, cit., p. 50.

[20] J. Derrida, *Force of Law: The Mystic Foundation of Authority*, in 11 Cardozo Law Review, 1990, esp. p. 921.

[21] A. Bianchi, *International Law Theories: An Inquiry into Different Ways of Thinking*, Oxford University Press, Oxford, 2017, p. 123.

[22] On the subject, H. Muir Watt, *Alterity in the Conflict of Laws: An Ontology of the In-Between,* in *Rabels Zeitschrift für Auslandisches und Internationales Privatrecht*, 2023, pp. 7–8.

each other: to read a complex identity, one needs to equip oneself with new epistemological lenses. "International law has always been involved in the 'constitution' of the world order and has invariably carried with it a methodology of interpretation that would provide the modalities through which that order is shaped. In this process, ideology plays a leading role, since it provides the particular ways to frame and shape the world".[23]

Both (state and scientific) traditional identities stemmed from an initial stage of imposition and were even enforced by their universality. The new identity, conversely, consists of acknowledging our incompleteness and how the Others are indispensable to preserve our very We. The new paradigm recognises a communication between identities and the dialectical communicative technique.[24] As Jullien[25] and Remotti suggest, "*l'identità è per sua natura definitoria, separatoria e oppositiva: rifugge dalle sfumature e dalle implicazioni reciproche è un prodotto di un pensiero che non sa fare altro che classificare e ordinare, distinguere e separare, ovvero imporre le proprie categorie rigide alla realtà, mortificando la realtà stessa*".[26] In this reflection, reality is composed of a web of relationships. And fed by transformation dynamics and fabric-weaving, an intellectual shift regarding the very idea of identity eventually unfolds (in both scientific and supranational terms). In the face of a growing and dangerous evolution of authoritarism in Russia, China and the United States—albeit differently structured, yet grounded in a clear nationalist conception of identity—there emerges a political, social and legal need to conceive and implement a concept of relational identity.

However, this epistemic change in identity would not be possible without the creation and consolidation of a European or international *communitas*, conceived along the same lines traced by the philosopher Roberto Esposito.[27] Unlike the mercantilist and individualistic *societas*, governed by a merely synallagmatic contractual relationship, "[t]he community is not a property, a plenitude, a territory that must be defended and separated

[23] Idem.

[24] Especially J. Habermas, *The Inclusion of the Other: Studies in Political Theory*, Polity Press, 1998.

[25] In particular in F. Jullien, *L'écart et l'entre. Leçon inaugurale de la Chaire sur l'altérité*, Galilée, Paris, 2012.

[26] Cf. F. Remotti, *L'ossessione identitaria*, Laterza, Bari, 2010, pp. 48–49.

[27] R. Esposito, *Communitas. Origin and destiny of the community. Protection and denial of life*, Amorrortu, Buenos Aires, 2005.

from those who are not part of it, but a void, a debt, a gift (these are the meanings of *munus*) in relation to others, which at the same time refers us to our constitutive otherness also with respect to ourselves".[28] This is appropriately integrated with the thesis of the *écart* as a continuous tension with the Law of the Other. Both conceptions imply the necessary existence of the Law of the Other for the existence of Western identity law. It is a theme that runs through the entire plot of this work.

1.2 Objectives and Structure of the Study: How to Read New Identities Through New Lenses

Can a supranational identity truly exist? The second objective of the work is concrete and limited to a mainly European and legal domain. The question, nevertheless, refers to a previous subject and will be addressed in the last part.

Is it possible to truly know and talk about our own selves, about our very own identity? Such self-awareness becomes possible when an *écart* is verified, a *scarto* between our idea of ourselves and reality. But how can the *écart* be applied in the sphere of Law? I believe that we can address the subject of identity and observe our world by simply refocusing the lenses through which we observe legal reality. Indeed, the narrative about our identity is closely linked to the epistemological tools fabricated to create and reinforce the Western world's subjectivity. Comparative and international law were viewed through these divisive lenses until a few decades ago. And today, they are being reworked to reinterpret the sovereignty aspirations mainly advanced by certain political parties or national constitutional courts. The phantoms of the *arcana imperii* of past sovereignty are re-emerging.[29] The question, therefore, is as follows: Can the world be contemplated through distinct lenses?

The present monograph gives a positive answer to these questions. But it also offers a new epistemological identity of comparative law, one that is based no longer on civilising instruments of hegemony (legal taxonomies and transplants, among others), ethnocentric demarcation, and international law. The latter centre on the idea of sovereign States, juxtaposed

[28] R. Esposito, *Communitas. The origin and Destiny of Community*, Stanford University Press, Stanford, 2009, p. 4.

[29] Enlightening in this regard is L. Niglia's article, *The New Transformation of Europe: Arcana Imperii*, in *The American Journal of Comparative Law*, 2020, pp. 151–185.

within an assumed international community, opening the scientific gates to a greater inclusion of the Others within normativity.[30] The monograph objectives are thus of an epistemological and practical nature. To address the question of how scientific and supranational identity conceptions were born, the genealogy of the Encounters with the Other will be studied. The analysis runs from the first contacts with South America's indigenous people, until the gradual shaping of two legal sciences which both created gaps, dividing civilised and non-civilised peoples. Before this, however, the mechanism of exclusion itself will be investigated. First, the subject of "**how**" these epistemological lenses of exclusivity work will be tackled, following by the question of the "**when**" they were manufactured—bearing in mind they are still being held in tension in other identity models.

"*We will not escape from thinking about ourselves and our society in identity terms. But we need to remember that the identities dwelling deep inside us are neither fixed nor necessarily given to us by our accidents of birth. Identity can be used to divide, but it can and has also been used to integrate*".[31] The first part of the book, which could be defined *as destruens* or deconstructive, consists of a historical study of the modern elaboration of current legal epistemology and national identity, all embedded in the idea of separation. This tendency emerged with the first reflections on the Other back in the sixteenth, seventeenth and eighteenth centuries. The advent of scientific-legal identities would later definitively separate them.

In the second part, *construens*, we will study what the movement against classification, distancing and normative exclusion consists of: that is, the tendency towards integrative and relational identity at the state and scientific levels.[32] As can be seen from the beginning, these two conceptual levels interact: in order to be able to read a complex identity, it is necessary to equip oneself with new epistemological glasses. We will therefore move from the identity need to exclude the (Law of) the Other to affirm oneself to the need for the (Law of) the Other to affirm relational identity. A powerful tension will emerge between new conceptions of national

[30] B. Rajagopal, *International Law from Below: Development, Social Movements and Third World Resistance*, Cambridge University Press, 2003, p. 295.

[31] F. Fukuyama, *Identity. Contemporary Identity Politics and the Struggle for Recognition*, Profile Book, London, 2018, pp. 182–183.

[32] Sobre el tema cfr. H. Muir Watt, *Alterity in the Conflict of Laws: An Ontology of the In-Between,* en *Rabels Zeitschrift fur Auslandisches und Internationales Privatrecht*, 2023, pp. 7–8.

identity and the incipient origin of a supranational identity, which could be defined as interfacial, held in place by inter-systemic architectural knots.[33]

I shall begin by addressing how the difference resulting from encounters between civilisations is managed. Yet, to fully understand the chronology of these episodes, the underlying exclusion/inclusion mechanism must be approached based on philosophical and sociological studies. Derrida's theory of traces and *différance* contributes to understanding this foundational mechanism of violence. I propose to analyse the major stages of the exclusionary convergence between the two disciplines which have addressed the relationship with the Other in the legal domain: comparative law and international law. To do so, I shall only partially follow the new decolonising theories of international law and keep in line with the most critical doctrinal branch of comparative law. The subsequent move will thus be the diachronic analysis of the milestones of this relationship: from the theories of Francisco de Vitoria, via the theories of Grotius, Pufendorf, De Vattel, Kant, Montesquieu and Maine, to the positivist period of creation of the international law and comparative law sciences to the present day. Through these Encounters with the Other, I shall examine the Foucauldian *épistémès* which unite the two disciplines to achieve the—rather overt—goal of promising to include the Other according to universalist parameters and then excluding it from the normative regulation of relations between cultures.[34]

[33] "*Europe now shares a set of institutions and norms that were established in the after- math of the Second World War as a guarantee against the risks of aggressive nationalism, authoritarian regimes, and the suppression of fundamental freedoms and rights. An anthropology of law that locates its fieldwork in the law and policies promulgated by European institutions is taking shape, showing what the moving target of European integration has meant in terms of building a new* ***composite identity****, putting pressure on the national and local levels of government, and devising new subjectivities*"; and M. Graziadei, *The Anthropology of European Law*, in *The Oxford Handbook of Law and Anthropology*, published by M.C. Foblets, Oxford University Press, Oxford, 2020, p. 273.

[34] This conceptual continuity is emphasized in *Introducción* a *Imperialismo y Derecho internacional*, published by A. Anghie, M Koskenniemi, A. Orford, University Library, Universidad de los Andes, 2016, p. 7: "Their establishment as central international law figures owed to the readings given by later authors – from Grotius to James Brown Scott and many Latin American internationalists – of the works of sixteenth and seventeenth century jurists based on their own interests, and the way in which they refer to (and continue to refer to) the classical authors as the founders of a humanist natural tradition in the conduct of global relations, overlooking the role they played in the imperial expansion" (author's translation).

However, within the exclusionary episteme, all periods under study present nuances, which we will be unravelled through *écarts*. The major criticism advanced by the fascinating deconstructivist theories is that the very idea of identity is called into question while it is also made one's own. Moreover, the periods corresponding to De Vitoria, Grotius, or Vettel are regarded as a monolithic ensemble. In this way, the *nuances* are lost, and they shall be reconstructed here by means of *écarts* (for example, between Herodotus and Plato, between de Vitoria and de las Casas). The idea is to understand the Other through a complex *scientific* episteme.

Certain key points, that is, some basic principles of intersection exist between these two legal branches, and they stem from the conceptual triptych "*classificare, separare, escludere*".[35] It was mainly at the end of the nineteenth century and at the beginning of the twentieth century that in its taxonomic efforts, comparative science tended to shape and sort legal reality through Western lenses, whether directly or subliminally, thereby annulling or despising the Other. International law emerged over the same period, headed by its epistemic community. It crystallised this relationship of exclusive force with its legal apparatus of separation and distance from legal subjects, both disciplines leading to the clear exclusion of the Other. These dynamics unfolded mainly within the period referred to, yet they had cropped up over the previous centuries in the legal reflections of a number of thinkers on the relationship with the Other. We are not witnessing here merely a dusty historical inquiry, since "*the past remains the present, albeit in a different form, and the historical relationship with the Empire continues to inform the way in which relations of subordination and domination, inclusion and exclusion, play out in the contemporary period*".[36]

To illustrate this conceptual arsenal, I propose to study the protection of cultural property in the field of internationalist law, which will address the main intersections under study. Cultural property represents a significant part of a community's identity. The superiority manifested by European Empires, and then States, was a determining factor in the systematic plundering of the cultural heritage of the Other: "*humans and things constitute each other and that materiality matters for identity*".[37]

[35] M. Aime, *Classificare, separe, escludere. Razzismi e identità*, Einaudi, Torino, 2020.

[36] R. Kapur, *Erotic Justice: Law and the New Politics of Postcolonialism*, Glass. House Press, 2005, p. 20.

[37] C. Stahn, *Confronting Colonial Objects: Histories, Legalities, and Access to Culture*, Oxford University Press, Oxford, 2023, p. 7. As Martin Skydstrup has argued, the idea that an "intrinsic identity" is catalysed in an object, "being always attached to a social entity—

Therefore, the first period shall be explored, running from the theories of De Vitoria to the nineteenth century, characterised by a substantial annihilation of the Other through the systematic plundering of identity goods based on the *ius praedae*. By means of *écarts* with respect to the main theories of the following periods, a constant and contrasted consolidation of Western identity shall be witnessed through the annulment of the Other's identity goods. In the encounter with the Other, this time the African Other, and coinciding with the Berlin Congress of 1878, the proposal to return illegally appropriated cultural property and to protect identity property during the war was substantially implemented by the most civilised nations. Major regulations on cultural property protection were approved in the second post-war period, and their enforcement was thereafter strongly conditioned by the circulation dynamics between destination and origin countries. The final section of the chapter is dedicated to recent hybridising trends regarding cultural good identity conceptualisations in the direction marked by indigenous culture.

The second part explores these new inclusive lines further, this time in the European sphere. After the tragedy of the Second World War, moving towards a new idea of the relationship with the Other, a relational theory is advanced in the *construens* section. This latter theory is applied not only to the cognitive connections between these two branches—which have long been in interaction in the most thorough doctrinal proposals—but also to the very conception of national identity in the two illustrative fields selected above. I shall steer clear of any linear legal vision of today: indeed, transnationalism and nationalism, or globalising and localising processes are mutually constitutive, since they create and shape each other, unlike nineteenth-century identities surreptitiously classified as exclusive.[38]

whether a group, a community, a region, or a nation—is compromised by the simple fact that an object's status is constantly subject to continuous processes of cultural redefinition." (uthor's translation) Cf. M. Skrydstrup, '*Righting Wrongs? Three Rationales of Repatriation and What Anthropology Might Have to Say About Them*' in G. Mille and J. Dahl (eds.), *Utimut. Past Heritage: Future Partnership. Discussions on Repatriation in the 21st Century*, Greenland National Museum and Archives & International Work Group for Indigenous Affairs, Copenhagen 2008, pp. 56–63.

[38] Cf. M. Graziadei, *What Does Globalisation Mean for the Comparative Study of Law?*, in *The Journal Of Comparative Law*, 2021, p. 573; H. Muir Watt, *Globalization and Comparative Law*, in M. Reimann and R. Zimmermann (eds.), *The Oxford Handbook of Comparative Law*, 2nd ed. Oxford University Press, Oxford, 2019, p. 499.

The novelty of limiting national sovereignty by transferring the exercise of certain competences has gradually created a relational or connective scientific identity,[39] both in the State's constitutional doctrines, which are increasingly concerned with European Union law, and in the interpretation of European law through the Court of Justice's comparative methodology (Weiler,[40] Ziller,[41] von Bogdandy,[42] Martinico,[43] Scholtes,[44] among others). This new identity paradigm indeed permeates other realities, national parliaments[45] for example, as well as the institutional declarations of senior state officials.[46] Yet, considering the importance of the first vector, the study shall precisely be limited to the interactions between judges, where a departure from the "identity of the European Union" has started to occur.[47]

[39] Cf. R. Drayton and D. Motadel, *Discussion: the futures of global history*, in *Journal of Global History*, 2018. pp. 1–21.

[40] *Ex multis* J.H.H. Weiler, "*Federalism without Constitutionalism: Europe's Sonderweg*", in K. Nicolaidis and R Howse (eds), *The Federal* Vision, Oxford University Press, 2001, esp. pp. 54–68.

[41] *Ex multis* J. Ziller, *Comparison within Multi-Level Polities and Governance Regimes*, in *The Oxford Handbook of Comparative Administrative Law* (P. Cane, H. C. H. Hofmann, E. C. Ip, and P.L. Lindseth eds.), Oxford University Press, 2018, esp. pp. 4–10.

[42] *Ex multis* A. Von Bogdandy, *La transformación del derecho europeo: el concepto reformado y su búsqueda de la comparación*, en *Revista de Derecho Comunitario Europeo*, 2016, 54, spec. p. 460.

[43] *Ex multis* G. Martinico, *The Tangled Complexity of the EU Constitutional Process. The Frustrating Knot of Europe, Routledge, Second Edition, 2023.*

[44] J. Scholtes, *The Abuse of Constitutional Identity in the European Union*, OUP, 2023.

[45] Cf. P. Faraguna, *Taking Constitutional Identities Away from the Courts*, in *Brook. J. Int'l L.*, 2016, pp. 41–68; Idem, *The Constitutional Identity of the EU as a Counterbalance for Unconstitutional Constitutional Identities of the Member States*, in *European Yearbook Of Constitutional Law*, 2023, pp. 342–351; Idem, *Unconstitutional Constitutional Identities in the European Union*, in R. Hirschl, Y. Roznai (eds), *Deciphering the Genome of Constitutionalism. The Foundations and Future of Constitutional Identity*, Cambridge University Press, 2024.

[46] The idea expressed by Fabbrini is thought-provoking– O. Pollicino, *Constitutional Identity in Italy. Institutional Disagreements at a Time of Political Change*, in *Constitutional Identity in a Europe of Multilevel Constitutionalism*, C. Calliess and G. van der Schyff (eds.), Cambridge University Press, 2019, pp. 201–221, according to which the President of the Republic Mattarella expressed in several official statements the Europeanist idea of Italian constitutional identity: "Constitutional republican Italy only exists in the European Union".

[47] They refer to the European identity in the judgments of the Court of Justice (Full Court), respectively, both of 16 February 2022, delivered in the cases *Hungary v European Parliament and Council of the European Union* (C-156/21) and *Republic of Poland v European Parliament and Council of the European Union* (C-157/21).

Naturally, the struggle for (relational, according to Cartabia[48]) law has only just begun: in fact, it is on the contrary synonymous with tension. A tension between the new relational community paradigm, which has recently appeared in the Court of Justice jurisprudence and that of some Italian and French constitutional courts *in primis*, and the return to the "Ulysses unleashed" without limits.[49] The state's limitations, previously understood as absolute, are intertwined: this network of constitutional and supranational limits is the essence of the relationality of European identity. The very reality of EU law cannot be understood without the contributions of comparative law[50]: its mode of transmission is interfacial.[51] "[T]he in-between can be seen as a mode of existence that weaves through different life-worlds and cultural forms, crossing borders, changing shape, creating hybridity. Significantly for the conflict of laws, it has been argued that such complex interweaving (*cum plessis*) constitutes an ontology of the frontier itself".[52]

In this sense, the *écart* represents an essential contribution to methodology: a Luxembourg Court decision cannot be understood without holding it in tension with the judgments of the national constitutional courts. To approach the debate from a different angle, let us recall an incisive question posed by Robert Lecourt[53]: "What would have become of the protection of fundamental rights in the European Union without the judicial disagreements raised by the Italian and German constitutional

[48] M. Cartabia, *Editorial. Courts' Relations*, in *Intern. Rev. Const. Law*, 2020, p. 7.

[49] J. Elster, *Ulysses Unbound: Studies in Rationality, Precommitment, and Constraints*, Cambridge University Press, 2000.

[50] Cf. Michele Graziadei, *The European Court of Justice at Work: Comparative Law on Stage and Behind the Scenes*, in *J. Civ. L. Stud.*, 2020, pp. 2–32.

[51] Borrowed from literary criticism, the term *in-between* is now used as a significant conceptual category in multiple fields of knowledge spanning linguistics, political theory, history, anthropology, sociology, psychology, art, gender studies and philosophy. For example, it serves to underline that the forms through which we understand the empirical world and confer meaning on it—artistic forms; landscape design; narratives in terms of chains of events; linguistic styles; configurations of time and space—are not necessarily linear, stable and one-dimensional, but multifaceted, mobile and ephemeral.

[52] H. Muir Watt, *Alterity in the Conflict of Laws: An Ontology of the In-Between*, in *Rabels Zeitschrift für Auslandisches und Internationales Privatrecht*, 2023, pp. 7–8.

[53] L. Burgorgue-Larsen, *Sobre un acercamiento dialógico al Derecho Constitucional Europeo*, en *ReDCE núm. 25. Enero-Junio de 2016*, available in http://www.ugr.es/~redce/REDCE25/articulos/05_BURGORGUE.htm

courts?".[54] Could the state Constitution defenders be required to firmly renounce a fundamental rights protection system in favour of a supranational order that could potentially violate the national constitution protection standard? If the reproduction of a binary mechanism is inconceivable, judicial dialectics is logical and desirable, in so far as it has made it possible to transfer the indispensable contribution of national constitutional orders to the Union's legal order, while respecting the Community law structure and objectives.[55]

An answer to the questions initially posed will therefore be advanced: Is it possible to construct a porous supranational identity and a dialogical expression of national identities? Can a non-exclusive legal subjectivity be constructed, as built in the past by comparative and international law epistemology?

This comparative methodology can serve mutatis mutandis to broaden the scope of inclusion of international law,[56] for example, in the reform of the aforementioned article 38 of the Statute of the Court of Justice, currently before the International Law Commission. In this case, identity could be porous and complex, the product of continuous "interfacial" operations with primary state identities, and not a means of imposing international contract law, as in the case of legal transplants for example. The incipient epiphany of a European identity is possible provided it consists of a common "identity reservoir", as we shall observe with the example of personal data circulation extraterritoriality. If the latter brings about undue impositions on other legal systems, and no counter-situations take place—i.e. if foreign regulations are in some cases applied *in melius* in European territory—a hegemony attempt would again be before us.

[54] R. Lecourt, *Quel eût été le droit des Communautés sans les arrêts de 1963 et 1964?*, in *L'Europe et le droit. Mélanges en hommage à Jean Boulouis*, Dalloz, Paris, 1991, p. 359.

[55] G. Martinico, *Lo spirito polemico del diritto europeo Studio sulle ambizioni costituzionali dell'Unione*, Arachne, Rome, 2011, in particular the fourth chapter on the necessary and desired tension between legal systems and judges.

[56] M. Koskenniemi, *The Gentle Civilizer of Nations. The Rise and Fall of International Law 1870–1960*, Cambridge University Press, Cambridge, 2009, spec. pp. 232 ff.

1.3 The Methodology and Two *Caveats*: Another Identity Is Possible

A methodological digression is necessary to understand how the objectives set out above can be achieved. The first is to reconstruct the dynamics of state identity creation linked to the exclusion of the Other and the tension with the promises of inclusion, to the philosophical theses of Derrida,[57] Foucault[58] and Ricoeur,[59] *in primis*. In the introductory phase, I will present Jullien's theory of *écart* to propose a new philosophical approach: by moving away from the classical operation of comparison and subsequent classification, it is possible to know the Other without assimilating or annihilating this Other. The operation of applying philosophical ideologies into the legal sphere is not new, but in the present work, this prior knowledge is a propaedeutic for understanding the modalities of epistemological exclusion. The scenario is also enriched with proposals drawn and extrapolated from the discipline of anthropology, such as the theses put forward by Remotti,[60] Appiah[61] and Aime.[62] Thus, relations with the Other will later be addressed through the filter of a number of theories coming from certain currents of thought which tend to deconstruct the major lines of the internationalist and comparative law sciences: it will draw from the works of Koskenniemi,[63] the *Third World Approach*

[57] Among many others, J. Derrida, *La Différance*, in *Márgenes de la filosofía*, Cátedra, Madrid, 1998; Idem, *Force of Law: The "Mystical Foundation of Authority"*, in *Cardozo Law Review*, 1990, pp. 920–102.

[58] Among many others, M. Foucault, *Les mots et les choses*, Gallimard, Paris, 1966, Idem, *L'archéologie du savoir*, Gallimard, Paris, 1969.

[59] I extrapolate the concept of identity mainly in the sense of ipseity and sameness. Cf. P. Ricoeur, *Soi-même comme un autre*, Éditions du seuil, Paris, 1990.

[60] Mainly F. Remotti, *Somiglianze. Una* via *per la convivenza*, Editori Laterza, Bari, 2019; F. Idem, *Contro l'identità*, Editori Laterza, Rome-Bari, 2001.

[61] K.A. Appiah, *Rethinking Identity: The Lies that Bind*, Profile Books, Devon, 2018.

[62] M. Aime, *Classificare, separe, escludere. Razzismi e identità*, Einaudi, Torino, 2020.

[63] Mainly Koskenniemi *The Gentle Civilizer of Nations. The Rise and Fall of International Law 1870–1960*, Cambridge University Press, Cambridge, 2009; Idem, M. Koskenniemi, *Histories of International Law: Dealing with Eurocentrism*, in *Legal History*, 2011, p. 23.

to International Law,[64] the *Critical Legal Studies*,[65] as well as authors such as Legrand,[66] Muir Watt[67] or Maldonado Bonilla.[68]

It is worth specifying, however, in this preliminary phase, that there is no intention in this monograph to stigmatise or condemn certain so-called Western world behaviours on an ideological level. As pointed out at the beginning, while most studies set out new epistemological horizons allowing to improve our understanding (of the legal culture) of the Other, they tend to demonise the Western world as a whole, overlooking other authors' stances of resistance or objections. Although they individualise certain rejection scenarios of the Other, critical studies of exclusionary Western identities precisely fall into the same essentialism which they attribute to classical internationalism and comparative law.[69] The *écart* method allows advancing towards a more nuanced picture.[70] This book sets out to probe the layers, contractions, tensions which are beyond the scope of simplified identity. In this way, a step is taken away from the growing

[64] On the TWAIL current of thought, cf. M.W. Mutua, *What Is TWAIL?*, in *Proceedings of the ASIL Ann. Meeting*, n. 312,000, p. 36; B. S. Chimni, *Third World Approaches to International Law: A Manifesto*, in *International Community Law Review*, 2006, pp. 3–27; J. Thuo Gathii, *TWAIL: A Brief History of its Origins, its Decentralized Network, and a Tentative Bibliography*, in *Trade L. & Dev.*, 2011, p. 26.

[65] On *Critical Legal Studies*, see J. Gilchrist Stewart, *The Rise and Fall of Critical Legal Studies: Law, Politics, Culture*, Oxford University Press, Oxford, 2024; J. A. Pérez Lledó, *"Critical legal studies"* in a nutshell, in *Teoría & Derecho. Revista De Pensamiento jurídico,* 2020, pp. 251–264.

[66] P. Legrand, *Jameses at Play: A Traction on the Comparison of Laws*, in *Am. J. Comp. L. (Special Issue)*, 2017, p. 19, also available at. http://www.pierre-legrand.com/jameses-at-play.pdf; Idem, *The impossibility of 'Legal Transplants'*, in *Maastricht J. Eur. & Comp. L.*, 1997, p. 123.

[67] H. Muir Watt, *Alterity in the Conflict of Laws: An Ontology of the In-Between*, in *Rabels Zeitschrift für Auslandisches und Internationales Privatrecht*, 2023, p. 9; Idem, *La fonction subversive du droit comparé*, in *Revue international de droit comparé*, 52, 3, 2000, pp. 503–527.

[68] D. Bonilla Maldonado, *Los bárbaros jurídicos: Identidad, derecho comparado moderno y el Sur global*, Siglo del Hombre Editores, Bogotá, 2020.

[69] In the historiographical domain, E. Manzano Moreno *signals this same problem* mutatis mutandis. *España diversa, Claves de una historia plural*, cit., p. 18.

[70] F. Jullien himself, *Il n'y a pas d'identité culturelle, Éditions de l'Herne*, Paris, 2016, p. 46, offers us a paradigmatic example of *écarts* that nuance and offer resources with respect to closed values or identities. In postcolonialist critique, see the work of R.J.C. Young, *Postcolonialism. An Historical Introduction*, Blackwell, London, 2001, p. 74, which closely links colonialism to its critical components.

self-centred approach to identity, adopted by both its open defenders and by its fighters who have subliminally reproduced it.

Although powerful Marxist works will be frequently cited due to their undeniable proximity to the ideas I put forward, I did not intend here to define a conceptual framework of general Western stigmatisation: the focus is on hegemonic behaviours, or even violent behaviours, in terms of human behaviours.[71] "[M]*any – if not all – legal systems through time and space have performed some function of 'othering' and ideas of civilisational superiority have not been unique to the West*".[72] Having demonstrated how certain conceptions and lexemes still structure and permeate part of the consciousness of international law and comparative law, the next step will be to address the *pars construens* concerning the study of new and still weak scientific and legal identities. "*The Euro-centric perspective that privileged the state (legocentrism) and territoriality (nationalist concern) is not only quite parochial, but an idiom based on lost memory which does not lead towards a globally acceptable method of understanding law and its many pluralities, mixed manifestations, and commonalities*".[73]

The second part of the work, nevertheless, will inevitably approach complexity in philosophical, sociological, as well as legal terms. The proposal I advance, however, departs from any previous reference, since it attempts to recognise a new model of a relational type of supranational and legal identity. The point is not to argue that this incipient European identity paradigm—which is secondary because it depends on a continuous interaction with state legal cultures—is replacing the states' exclusionary identities. Rather, these identity models are held in tension: they mutually sustain each other through this network of *écart* or *in-between*.[74]

[71] Relevant, once again, is the *caveat* by E. Manzano Moreno, *España diversa. Keys to a plural history*, cit., p. 20: "If the past only serves to search for ourselves, we will tend to repudiate those who represent values and beliefs which are different from ours: we will tend to portray the 'others' as alien and driven by an irrationality that never exists in the events led by the 'Us'"(author's translation). This statement is addressed to the historians critical of Spain's traditional history.

[72] N. Tzouvala, *Capitalism as civilisation: a history of international law*, Cambridge University Press, Cambridge MA, 2020 p. 86.

[73] W.F. Menski, "*Comparative Law in a Global Context: The Legal Systems of Asia and Africa*", Cambridge University Press, 2009, p. 198.

[74] Cf. H. Muir Watt, *Alterity in the Conflict of Laws: An Ontology of the In-Between*, in *Rabels Zeitschrift für Auslandisches und Internationales Privatrecht*, 2023, pp. 7–8; J. Klabbers, G. Palombella, *The Challenge of Inter-Legality*, Cambridge University Press, Cambridge, 2019.

To fully understand it, as mentioned, the time has come to build new epistemic binoculars: "*comparative lawyers must learn to harmonize local influences with emerging global pattern of thought, avoiding the current mental cul de sacs that dismiss local cultures as obstacles to the implementation of international laws and globally uniform human rights principles. In the age of localised globalisation, a new phase of diversity-conscious identity construction has become necessary*".[75]

Of note, the study of identities also draws on a twofold methodological exploration "with an ethnographer's sensitivity"[76]: the temporal and spatial coordinates.

1.3.1 The Space Factor and Identity: Wittgenstein's *Familienähnlichkeiten*[77]

On the one hand, identity understood in monolithic terms (let us call it arborescent), blinds our vision of the forest of multiplicity, and, even more so, of the tangle of similarities that exist in Us. On the other, a monolithic view eliminates the similarity/difference relationships that unite us to others. "*Da un lato trasforma illusoriamente i soggetti (i noi) in entità piene, compatte, compiute, dall'altro trasforma la rete delle relazioni intersoggettive in un vero e proprio deserto, in uno spazio in cui si profila un unico tipo di relazione, ovvero la relazione che oppone noi agli altri*".[78] The *pars construens* differs from—and follows—the *pars destruens* precisely on this crucial point: today's comparative law and internationalist law sciences can still strive to detect these hybridisations resulting from *cross-fertilisation* mechanisms in order to broaden the inclusion of other international law systems conceived as a legal framework.

A highly relevant component regarding this first aspect of identity refers to the desinence of number at the synchronous-spatial level, ultimately affecting our world vision. These epistemological categorisations today disturb our worldview, preventing us from seeing the kaleidoscope-type

[75] W.F. Menski, "*Comparative Law in a Global Context: The Legal Systems of Asia and Africa*", Cambridge University Press, 2009, p. 210.

[76] A. Bianchi, *Las Teorías Del Derecho Internacional. Un estudio sobre diferentes maneras de pensar*, cit., p. 222.

[77] L. Wittgenstein, *Philosophische Untersuchungen*, Oxford, Blackwell, 1968; translated into Spanish in L. Wittgenstein, *Investigaciones filosóficas*, second edition in Spanish, trans. by C. Ulises Moulines, UNAM Mexico, 2017.

[78] F. Remotti, *L'ossessione identitaria*, cit., p. 28.

atlas before us, that is, the comparative legal taxonomies, or one could even say Law in general.

In Amartya Sen's theory, a "singularist" approach (which can be defined as reductionist) represents a simple or rather simplistic way of misinterpreting almost all cultures and individuals in the world.[79] Both at the collective and literary levels,[80] as well as in anthropological spheres,[81] identity, given its multifaceted connotation, should be referred to in its plural form. Michaels expresses the idea categorically: "*Plurality is built into the very reality of law*".[82] Reducing a complex being or a complex collective to a single angle of identity can lead to a hegemonic or even violent position.[83]

Wittgenstein suggests how to extend our beliefs through the mechanism of comparison: the operation is much more refined than a simple mechanical conceptual expansion which would therefore consist of a somewhat uncritical assimilation of new types of experiences, a sort of pile-up. In fact, our concept of number [or family, for example] is expanded in the same way that strands are tangled to make a rope. And the strength of the rope does not come from a single strand running along the entire length, but by the weaving of many fibres together.[84] The rope strength, i.e. the "power" of comparison, depends on the fabric. The idea of "weaving", of "interlacing", which then corresponds to the "network" of resemblances therefore plays a pivotal role. It is, moreover, the opposite of the spasmodic search for the *Platonic reductio ad unum*, which shall be addressed later. In fact, the operation is counter to and complements the idea of delimiting concepts in order to define them: while we proceed to "cut off" (and deny) the similarities using adjacent phenomena to define concepts or to draw their limits, we use similarities—which are intertwined like strands to make the rope robust—to expand the concepts. One could argue that for Wittgenstein, we are always bathing in the coil of inclusive

[79] A. Sen, *Identity and Violence: The Illusion of Destiny*, Penguin Books 2007, London, p. 45.

[80] For example, A. Maalouf, *Identidades asesinas*, Alianza Madrid, 2012.

[81] K.A. Appiah, *Rethinking Identity: The Lies that Bind*, Profile Books, Devon, 2018.

[82] R. Michaels, *Law and Recognition: Towards a Relational Concept of Law*, in *In Pursuit of Pluralist Jurisprudence*, ed. by Nicole Roughan, Andrew Halpin, 2019, Cambridge University Press, Cambridge, p. 107.

[83] A. Sen, 2007, p. 23: "Violence is encouraged when the feeling that we have a supposedly unique, inevitable identity is cultivated [...]. The imposition of an assumed unique identity is often a basic component of the 'martial art' of promoting sectarian strife" (author's translation).

[84] L. Wittgenstein, *Philosophische Untersuchungen*, cit., p. 47.

comparisons, both in cultured thought (philosophy, science) and in everyday life. A classificatory and identity order, composed only of identities and not of otherness, mentally suppresses the jungle of similarities and differences, which contaminate and disturb the lines of separation and the categories of belonging. "*The clear political message of these alternative ontological modes and their accompanying aesthetic is that the only adequate response to our late-modern obsession for division, closure, classifications and hierarchies is to inhabit the in-between. By the same token, it also signifies a radical reversal of coloniality as an attitude towards alterity*".[85] When properly prepared and woven, the bonds of relationality are robust and tenacious: let us remember that "the rope strength"—"the strength of identity"—derives from the "intertwining of numerous strands".[86] It can be maintained that "*la persona coincide non con un individuo a sé, ma con il fascio di relazioni in cui egli è inserito*".[87] All borders, in fact, define an identity only because they link them to a difference, as we will see in the following chapter. The legal implications of all this are as follow: the traditional paradigm of the Law of State and identities which isolate themselves by looking inwards and by recognising themselves only, must be integrated into a different, open and complex paradigm. The latter will be addressed in the third chapter.

1.3.2 The Time Factor and Identity: Tacitus and the Universalisation of Identities

Universalisations, Platonic and Aristotelian conceptualisations can ultimately annihilate differences in their pursuit of an abstract Idea, of general principles built around the sub *specie aeternitatis* projections of our *nomoi*. From this second viewpoint, the universality inaugurated by Rome unfolded in the juridical sphere: a single norm was imposed in such a vast empire. Universal citizenship, *civitas universalis*, begins its journey in Rome: according to juridical parameters, universality stems from Platonic-Aristotelian philosophy and its logical accoutrement in order to define a

[85] H. Muir Watt, *Alterity in the Conflict of Laws: An Ontology of the In-Between*, in *Rabels Zeitschrift für Auslandisches und Internationales Privatrecht*, 2023, p. 9.

[86] Ludwig Wittgenstein, *Philosophische Untersuchungen*, Oxford, Blackwell, 1968, p. 47.

[87] F. Remotti, *Noi, primitivi. Lo specchio dell'antropologia*, Torino, Bollati Boringhieri (I ed. 1990, 2009, p. 333.

unity of status and condition. Yet, here too emerged a historian who counteracted this absolutist-oriented vision.

In the *Discourse of the Emperor Claudius on Roman Citizenship*, Tacitus clarifies that "Everything, Senators, which we now hold to be of the highest antiquity, was once new. Plebeian magistrates came after patrician; Latin magistrates after plebeian; magistrates of other Italian peoples after Latin. This practice too will establish itself, and what we are this day justifying by precedents, will be itself a precedent".[88] With brilliant clairvoyance, Claudius affirms that Athens and Sparta were ruined because of their outright refusal to incorporate the subjected populations into the citizenship, while Rome used to "make [foreign peoples] Romans". Roman citizens could be of Italian, Gaul, Hispanic, Germanic or African origin and maintain their identity: indeed, the fact of being a Roman citizen was completely unrelated to origin, language, or beliefs. "Thus, anyone can be a Roman citizen regardless of what their identity is".[89] The error of aspiring to universalising or hypostatising a continually shifting identity is tantamount to the mistake of reducing an identity to a single one only. Identity cannot be pure, nor can it be universal; nor can it be in the present of its own self. " [I]*t is only on the basis of différance and its 'history' that we can allegedly know who and where 'we' are, and what the limits of an 'era' might be*".[90] A wide range of legal systems contribute to our conception of identity and they are mutually interacting continuously. Identity, therefore, is an open system. That is why Derrida points out that while identity is sustained in this network of interactions, it dies when one tries to petrify it, or to identify it.

And when exploring the time factor, I will not claim to extract *a* science, *a* rationality, *a* mentality, *a* culture. On the contrary, when I delve into the diachronic analysis of legal and extra-legal theories concerning the Other, I will attempt to unravel a weaving of inter-positivity whose limits and meeting points cannot be fixed at the same point in time. In this sense, Foucauldian archaeology provides the inspiration to conduct a comparative analysis aimed not at reducing the diversity of discourses and

[88] Gaius Cornelius Tacitus, *Annals*, Akal, 2007, XI, 23, 25: Emperor Claudius' speech on Roman citizenship.

[89] G. Pereira Menaut, *Ciudadanía romana clásica* vs. *ciudadanía europea. Innovaciones y vigencia del concepto romano de ciudadanía*, in *Historia Actual Online*, 2005, p. 143.

[90] J. Derrida, *La Différance*, in *Márgenes de la filosofía*, Cátedra, Madrid, 1998, p. 42.

outlining their unity, but rather at breaking down their diversity into different figures.[91]

1.3.3 Jullien's Proposal: The Écart

But how can cultural diversity be managed while preventing the *uniform* from being standardised and avoiding *common* from being confused with *assimilated*? I am referring here to Jullien's argument: "I propose to address the diversity of cultures in terms of *écart*; instead of identity, in terms of resources or fertility".[92] To the extent that difference functions through distinction, difference separates one space from other spaces and establishes its specificity through comparison. At the same time, it presupposes a close category within which the difference is marked and an identity is determined. [...] In the *écart*, on the contrary, the two separate terms remain subject to a dynamic comparison. But what does 'hold in tension' mean exactly? In the case of difference, once the comparative relation is complete, each term steadily returns to its place, withdrawing into its own specificity. In the *écart*, on the other hand, the distance keeps both in confrontation with each other. The comparison remains standing, alive, intense. In other words, in the difference, each compared term retreats back to its purity after allowing its essence to be discerned through opposition. In the *écart*, on the other hand, the two separate terms are constantly held in tension, constantly discovering themselves in the other, exploring and thinking through it. There is no foundational moment of Law: there is no *prius*. Each depends on the other to learn about each other and cannot retire into what their identity would be. Owing to the open distance between one and the other, the *écart* exposes the 'between': this 'between', therefore, is always active.[93] In the *écart*, thanks to the *gap* opened by the distance that has appeared, each remains before the other, in tension, rather than pulling back and returning into oneself, or basing

[91] M. Foucault, *L'archéologie du savoir*, Gallimard, Paris, 1969.

[92] F. Jullien, *Il n'y a pas d'identité culturelle, Éditions de l'Herne*, Paris, 2016, p. 46.

[93] J. Klabbers, G. Palombella expose a similar vision in the legal domain, *The Challenge of Inter-Legality*, Cambridge University Press, Cambridge, 2019, p. 58–59: "*The premise for inter-legality reasoning is that the law of one single legal regime might not have unconditional primacy in given circumstances, not if the issue it regulates is also controlled by the law of another entitled and recognized legal regime. Consequently, inter-legality draws the path on which the search for a legal solution can be started. The point to note is that this solution is embedded within the law and justified by the law*".

oneself on oneself. These interfaces undergo constant interaction. This vision is analogous to the tradition defined by Glenn in terms of Lan, referring to telematic jargon. Indeed, the *between* is neither one nor the other and has no essence in itself or anything of its own. In reality, the between "is" not.[94] It is a fertile tool that liberates belonging and property built over centuries through difference, which is then undone by classical identity.

If defining comparisons creates profound trenches, the 'between' is always left open by the *écart* which does not let itself be closed, thus opening the doors of belonging and freeing property built through difference. The classic canons of identity are thereby undone. The *écart* liberates us from the traditional perspective of identity, since rather than an identity, it sheds light on what I would call a fecundity, i.e. a resource. That is why it is fruitful: it does not give rise to knowledge by classification but provokes reflection through the tension it creates. "And, above all, because adopting the perspective of difference to consider the diversity of cultures inevitably leads to an impasse. An impasse that is on both sides, since in difference we always find identity."

In addition, we must evaluate the danger of addressing cultural diversity in terms of differences and identity. Indeed, it comes at a cost, not only in terms of thought, but also history. In this regard, it is worth recalling here Samuel Huntington's book The Clash of Civilisations. The fact of describing what would be the world's major cultures in terms of differences (the 'Chinese', the 'Islamic', the 'Western'), and therefore of identity, of having established their features and then organising them by typology in a table, was indeed what made the book successful—despite the stance being comfortable indeed. Of course, this procedure did not disturb anything, it did not open any *écart* with respect to convention. Whoever fails to recognise the heterogeneity present in each culture (its internal 'heterotopia') falls into the easy posture of classification, which comes with a feeling of relief. "*It is tempting to assume that what is European has its roots on European soil, but then not all that is Italian or German originates in Italy, or in Germany, and not all that is European*

[94] Cf. A. Riles, *Representing In-between: Law, Anthropology and the Rhetoric of Interdisciplinarity*, in *University of Illinois Law Review*, 1994, pp. 597–611.

originates in Europe. To understand what Europe is, it is also necessary to look elsewhere, beyond European borders".[95]

Assuming that such a 'hard core' exists, Huntington lets the interesting dimensions of these cultures slip away, reducing them to banalities, isolating them from each other, enclosing them in presumed specificities, in their identity, which then leads them to 'clash' as referred to in the title of the book. We must therefore clearly specify that: "*Écart* translates into English as gap. Yet *écart* means the opposite. Gap designates the trench that separates; *écart* designates a distance that opens up and establishes a comparison, makes a *between* appear which holds in tension what has been set apart and allows each term to understand itself with respect to the other".[96]

Difference, associated with identity, is what isolates and 'essentialises' cultures. In this case, cultural difference is presented as second and identity as first. Yet this unitary-identity principle is projected from my own cultural perspective, that is, it is merely the result of ethnocentrism.

Unlike difference, which leads each term to fall back into its original place and in isolation, the *écart* can effectively produce the common by comparing and also holding in tension what it has separated: and this common is not impoverished, it is alive, intense, and active. In the *in-between* opened by the *écart,* each term, placed in relation to the other, loses its self-sufficiency, stepping out of the prison of its *as-it-is*.[97] It is worth remembering that *common* and *similar* have distinct meanings and this differentiation should be applied at the political level: *integration* is not *assimilation*. "If the idea of universal is imposed as a requirement, cultures will remain – *held in tension* – directed towards other cultures, other languages and other ways of thinking rather than retreating into their 'differences' and enjoying what would be their 'essence'".[98] When applied to the concept of identity, this reflection means that the essence of identity either does not exist or is a hegemonic concept. Certain dialogical resources hold different cultures in tension on a constant basis. Let us remember these

[95] M. Graziadei, *Obviously European?*, in *Persona e Mercato*, 2021/2, p. 231; Idem, *The European Court of Justice at Work: Comparative Law on Stage and Behind the Scenes*, in *J. Civ. L. Stud.*, 2020, pp. 2–32.

[96] Author's translation of F. Jullien, *Il n'y a pas d'identité culturelle, Éditions de l'Herne*, Paris, 2016, p. 86.

[97] In this epistemological sense, see J. Klabbers, G. Palombella, *The Challenge of Inter-Legality*, Cambridge University Press, Cambridge, 2019.

[98] F. Jullien, *Il n'y a pas d'identité culturelle*, cit., p. 42.

considerations regarding the necessary complexity of identities, both understood as fruitful resources. Indeed, they will be useful when delving deeper into the same themes in the field of law. The grammar will be complex and relational. Moreover, contrary to watertight Western compartments, they will be represented as the *quipu*[99] knot (a *com-plex* identity at the heart of a set of webs), which the Inca seem to have employed to build their own language.[100]

[99] J. Acosta, *Historia Natural y Moral de las Indias*, Seville, Atlas, 1994, pp. 189–190.

[100] On the anthropological change of perspectives cf. D. Graeber and D. Wengrow, *The Dawn of Everything: A New History of Humanity*, Allen Lane, 2021.

PART I

Pars Destruens: The Creation of an Exclusionary Western Identity

CHAPTER 2

The Genealogy of Mechanisms for Excluding and Including the Other

Abstract Exclusionary mechanisms directed towards the Other have been apparent since the initial engagement between European thinkers and indigenous cultures in the sixteenth century. Despite the principle concerning indigenous peoples as Imago Dei, the theories under discussion share a central theme: the evangelisation of the Other. The construction of difference is predicated upon a perceived incompleteness of the Other relative to criteria established by Western philosophers, primarily revolving around concepts such as private property and the associated notion of Catholic *communitas*. Nonetheless, through comparative analysis, it becomes clear that varied perspectives exist within Western thought, challenging the perception of it as a monolithic exclusionary entity. Consequently, an evolving concept of *ius gentium*, positioned as the universal norm among States, is beginning to take shape.

Keywords Francisco de Vitoria • Bartolomé de Las Casas • Hugo Grotius • Catholic *Communitas* • Ius gentium

The emergence of a Western identity with scientifically verifiable characteristics is fundamentally attributable to the development of a scientific identity in both International Law and Comparative Law, which significantly coincides with the rise of positivism in the late nineteenth century.

© The Author(s), under exclusive license to Springer Nature Switzerland AG 2026

A. Lazari, *Relational Identity in International, Comparative and European Union Law*,
https://doi.org/10.1007/978-3-031-59482-3_2

Prior to this period, the management of legal and cultural differences did not assume a definitive value articulated in scientific terms, as we understand them today in the Kuhnian paradigm. Rather, comparative legal reasoning was frequently intertwined with international legal doctrine. In the writings of thinkers such as Francisco de Vitoria, Grotius, Pufendorf and Vattel, one finds a fusion of considerations that would now be categorised separately as pertaining to International Law and Comparative Law. Our current understanding of what International Law is, what it does, or what it ought to do, rests upon a series of theoretical assumptions and presuppositions. These are not always explicitly disclosed, yet they continue to shape the discipline in a manner that suggests they are best left unexamined. We may observe, mutatis mutandis, a comparable structure of thought in the Scholastic approach adopted by the theologian Francisco de Vitoria regarding the Spanish conquest of the Americas.

2.1 The Evangelising 'Communality' of Spanish Scholasticism

Commissioned by the Habsburg Emperor Charles V to examine the legitimacy of Spanish claims over the lands of the New World, De Vitoria advanced the argument that the Indigenous peoples possessed rightful dominion over both their persons and their property. On the one hand, like the masses of any Christian community, the Indigenous populations pursued, however imperfectly or inchoately, the goal of *eudaimonia*. On the other hand, De Vitoria repeatedly stressed what he regarded as the cowardly, irrational and ignorant character of Indigenous life, alongside their rudimentary political organisation.[1] As a consequence, De Vitoria advised that appropriate governance should be established over the Indigenous peoples by the Spanish, who were to govern in the capacity of fiduciary administrators on behalf of the "uncivilised" Indigenous populations.

These populations are thus rendered as children in need of a guardian. A conceptual **gap** therefore emerges between the ontologically 'universal' human subject presumed to exist in the Indigenous peoples of the Americas, and their historically and socially 'particular' condition. The

[1] F. De Vitoria, *Relectio de indis o libertad de los indios*, Consejo Superior de Investigaciones Científicas, 1967, p. 78.

conclusion reached was that this gap could only be bridged through the intervention of the Spanish, who were conceived as agents of Natural Law.

On another level, moreover, their 'savage' society had not yet been shaped by the disciplining influence of ethical principles, nor had it established a civic structure capable of cultivating its members through normative ethical systems. And without such ethical discipline, the Indigenous peoples could never fulfil their true potential—could never become what they ought to be. "*The ability of the Indians to reason like their European counterparts was not enough to include them in the family of nations. The difference in cultural practices also played a role in such exclusion. The cultural practices of the non-European world, which were not in conformity with the practices of Christian Europe, were regarded as 'barbaric'*".[2]

De Vitoria explained that the imparting of ethics (that necessary bridge between uncultivated human nature and virtuous human nature) was provided by means of *jus gentium*. By adhering to this 'law of nations', the Indigenous peoples of the Americas would realise their *telos* and become what they were 'naturally' destined to be. And should these communities fail to comply with the norms of International Law and the cultivation of virtue, the Spanish would, consequently, acquire just cause to wage war against them.[3] As previously noted, however, we cannot equate proto-Western thought exclusively with De Vitoria's theory. Such a typology of identity would be both reductive and historically misleading. The deployment of arguments grounded in Natural Law ought to apply to "*los hombres que viven en paz en sus tierras, sin deber nada a nadie y gobernados por sus señores naturales*":[4] they cannot legitimately be compelled to obey a foreign king of whom they have never heard. Bartolomé de Las Casas likewise continues to make use of the just war theory, and for him as well, a just cause is defined by *injuria*, specifically, the violation of a legal right (*jus*). As he states: "*ninguna guerra es justa si no hay causa para declararla, es decir, que el pueblo, contra el que se va a mover, la merezca a causa de*

[2] J. Chinwe Okubuir, *Application of Hegemony to Customary International Law: An African Perspective*, in *Global Journal of Comparative Law*, 2018, p. 241.

[3] J. Chinwe Okubuir, *Application of Hegemony to Customary International Law: An African Perspective*, cit., p. 243.

[4] B. de Las Casas, *Obras completas*, Fundación "Instituto Bartolomé de Las Casas" de los Dominicos de Andalucía, Alianza Editorial, Madrid, 1989–1999, p. 54; Idem, *Brevísima relación sobre la destrucción de las Indias*, Editorial Universidad de Antioquia, 2006, pp. 41–42.

una iniuria *que ha cometido contra el otro pueblo.*"[5] However, he eventually effects a volte-face in his stance. The position ultimately reached by De Las Casas is summarised in the account provided in *Brevísima relación de la destrucción de las Indias*: "*Sé por ciencia cierta e infalible que las guerras de los indios contra los cristianos han sido siempre muy justas, mientras que ninguna de las que han hecho los cristianos contra los indios ha sido justa. Por el contrario, todos eran diabólicos e injustos, mucho más que los movidos por cualquier tirano de todos los tiempos.*"[6] In his latterly held view, it is solely the Spanish conquistadors who have committed *iniuria*, consistently violating the legitimate rights of the native populations.[7] Existing frameworks were being challenged, and new theoretical approaches were clearly emerging. "*L'utilizzazione della teoria della guerra giusta da parte di Las Casas deve molto alla messa a punto compiuta da Vitoria. La discussione sull'entità dell'influenza del secondo sul primo è ancora aperta, e alcuni interpreti hanno sostenuto che è piuttosto la difesa lascasiana degli indigeni ad aver costituito uno dei punti di riferimento per la Relectio de Indis del 1539*".[8] An analysis of the tension between these two prominent Spanish thinkers allows us to trace the intellectual communality of their time.

2.2 Incompleteness in Francisco De Vitoria's Theory[9]

As shown previously, Vitoria's view of cultural difference and of the identity of Indigenous peoples played a key role in shaping his theory.[10] From the very beginning, it is clear that the idea of cultural difference has had a strong influence on how International Law—in this case, *jus gentium*—was understood and applied. "*The problem confronting Vitoria, then, was not the problem of order among sovereign states, but the problem of creating a system of law to account for* ***relations between societies which he***

[5] B. de Las Casas, *Obras completas*, cit., 12, p. 496.

[6] B. de Las Casas, *Obras completas*, cit., 10, p. 40.

[7] B. de Las Casas, *Obras completas*, cit., 9, p. 526.

[8] L. Baccelli, *Bartolomé de Las Casas. La conquista senza fondamento*, Feltrinelli Editore, Milano, 2016, p. 121.

[9] G. Cavallar, *The rights of strangers: Theories of international hospitality, the global community and political justice since Vitoria*, Routledge, London, 2002.

[10] A. Anghie, *La evolución del derecho internacional: realidades coloniales y poscoloniales*, in *Imperialismo y Derecho internacional*, edited by A. Anghie, M Koskenniemi, A. Orford, Biblioteca universitaria, Universidad de los Andes, 2016, p. 113.

understood to belong to two very different cultural orders*, each with its own ideas of propriety and governance*" [emphasis added].[11] This dynamic is already present in Columbus' account of his "taking possession" of the New World. At that time, the doctrine of sovereignty had not yet been formulated. It is in Vitoria's writings that we begin to see the emergence of this doctrine, developed in response to the challenge posed by cultural difference.[12] More narrowly, it becomes a matter of identifying certain contradictory features within his thought that ultimately served to legitimise a form of discrimination. Vitoria's *jus gentium* can be broadly summarised as a set of qualities that he believed were most clearly embodied in the life of the idealised Spaniard. "*Thus, in order for the Indians to "realize" their natural potential, what International Law apparently required was for the Indian to no longer be Indian, but to become* Spanish".[13] All human beings are equal before God, yet the completeness of the human person is treated as a conceptual *prius*, a necessary precondition that can lead to the potential negation of the Other, should the latter fail to acknowledge their own perceived incompleteness. Viewed in this light, recognition of the humanity of Indigenous peoples produces ambiguous outcomes. While it ostensibly serves to include them within the framework of natural law, despite its claims to universality, this law derives from an idealised European worldview grounded in European identity.[14] As a result, Indigenous peoples, by virtue of their mere existence, their distinct identity and their cultural practices are almost inevitably positioned as violators of a legal order that formally treats Spaniards and Indigenous peoples as equals, but in practice generates unequal effects due to the profound asymmetries between them. Cultural difference turns into violence when the right of Spaniards to migrate is undermined. "*The encounter is then engaged in only insofar as law can be expressed in terms of European sovereignty*".[15]

[11] A. Anghie, *Imperialism, Sovereignty and the Making of International Law*, Cambridge University Press, 2005, p. 67.

[12] A. Anghie, *Hacia un derecho internacional poscolonial*, in Derecho y Crítica Social, 2015, pp. 71–99.

[13] J. Desautels-Stein, *The Right to Exclude: A Critical Race Approach to Sovereignty, Borders, and International Law*, Oxford University Press, Oxford, 2023, p. 33.

[14] A. Anghie, *Imperialism, Sovereignty and the Making of International Law*, Cambridge Studies in International and Comparative Law, Cambridge University Press, 2005, p. 56.

[15] S. Pahuja, *Laws of encounter: a jurisdiction account of International Law*, in *London Review of International Law*, Volume 1, Issue 1, 2013, p. 64.

Following these Thomistic natural precepts, all of humanity might be said to have the potential to reach its highest *telos*: the practice of virtuous sociability. A first and immediate question arises: virtuous sociability according to whom? Crawford responds: "*Thus Spanish identity or, more broadly, an idealised Western identity, is projected as universal in two different but connected dimensions of Vitoria's system; Spanish identity is both externalized, in that it acts as the basis for the norms of jus gentium, and internalized in that it represents the authentic identity of the Indian*".[16]

De Vitoria reclaims the Aristotelian theoretical tradition of the *respublica sibi sufficiens* within a framework that appears to prefigure the modern concept of sovereignty as *superiorem non recognoscens*. For De Vitoria, there is only one legitimate cause for war: the experience of *injuria*. Notably, the term *in-juria* carries the precise legal meaning of a violation of a *jus*, that is, a subjective right. Importantly, De Vitoria does not use the term *culpa*, which would have also encompassed sin, and he explicitly excludes violations of Natural Law, such as idolatry or moral perversion, as just causes for war. In this way, *jus* and *bellum justum* become mutually reinforcing. De Vitoria upholds the existence of a set of *universal jura* (again understood as subjective rights) that underpin the law of nations and are grounded in Natural Law. These include *jus peregrinandi et degendi*, *jus commercii*, *jus communicationis*, and the right to citizenship. All of these rest upon the Aristotelian principle of *naturalis societas et communicatio*. To these natural law principles is added the right to preach and proclaim the Gospel.[17] If these rights are denied, *injuria* is committed, which constitutes a just cause for war.

2.2.1 The Écart *with Bartolomé de Las Casas*

The *écart* opens up perspectives and deploys interpretative resources. The deployment of Aristotelian arguments by Bartolomé de Las Casas leads to different corollaries. This indicates that Western identity *in fieri* can be considered tendentially exclusionary, but it reveals clear tensions that are rarely recognised by deconstructivist doctrine.[18]

[16] J. Crawford, *Foreword*, in A. Anghie, *Imperialism, Sovereignty and the Making of International Law*, Cambridge University Press, Cambridge, 2005, p. 6.

[17] In the same vein, M. Koskenniemi, in *To the Uttermost Parts of the Earth*, cit., p. 110, speaks on this matter of *The Political Theology of Ius gentium. The Expansion of Spain 1526–1559*.

[18] L. Baccelli, *Bartolomé de Las Casas. La conquista senza fondamento*, cit., p. 143.

Despite explicit and implicit references to the work of the master of Salamanca, De Las Casas questions the theoretical core of his argument: the legitimisation of conquest based on universal human rights. For De Las Casas, man is also *zoon politikon*. However, whereas De Vitoria derives from natural society and communication a series of rights that ultimately legitimise the Spanish presence in the Americas (the appropriation of common goods, their claim to trade, reside permanently and reproduce), De Las Casas holds that the true dominions and legitimate natural lords (the native peoples) have the right to prevent or regulate the presence of foreigners on their lands, without prejudice to natural duties of hospitality and assistance. Thus, if the attribution of universal status to the *jus peregrinandi in illas provincias et illic degendi* was the foundation for one of the legitimate titles of conquest, De Las Casas counters with the card of particularism in defence of the natives.[19] De Las Casas adopts from De Vitoria the idea that the right to wage war (*jus belli*) is a necessary condition for the self-sufficiency of the political community, which, as we have seen, anticipates the modern connection between sovereignty and the law of war. However, applying this argument in favour of the Indigenous peoples, he rejects it insofar as it defends the limits of the community, effectively challenging the universality and absolute character of the right to migrate and reside. Territory is a function of the *jus imperandi*, and the *respublica* must be *sibi sufficiens*. Indeed, violating the boundaries of others is forbidden '*per divinam legem*', as attested since Deuteronomy. It is here maintained that resistance to the mere presence of Christians is legitimate.

It is in the oppressed Indigenous peoples, victims of violence, that De Las Casas sees the poor of the Gospel, from which arises a Christology that extends to the present day through Liberation Theology.[20] To adopt the perspective of the natives, to think "as if we were indigenous", and to judge events through this lens is inseparable from the process of evangelisation. And precisely in relation to the *casus belli* of Herodotus' *nomos basileus*, De Las Casas apprehends the religious significance of practices that scandalise his contemporaries, such as human sacrifices, even if he does not approve of them: because of his commitment to the conversion

[19] D.R. Brunstetter, *Sepúlveda, Las Casas, and the Other: Exploring the Tension Between Moral Universalism and Alterity*, cit., p. 429.

[20] Cf. G. Gutiérrez, *En busca de los pobres de Jesucristo. El pensamiento de Bartolomé de Las Casas*, Instituto Bartolomé de Las Casas / CEO, Lima 1992.

of the Indigenous peoples, he respects their freedom in matters of religion. Gradually, he comes to argue that non-Christians have the right to reject those who seek to impose their religion upon them.

On the other hand, citing the testimony of Isidore of Seville and Pompeius Trogus, De Las Casas writes that "*los hispánicos eran llamados bárbaros y salvajes.*"[21] Should Saint James, then, have evangelised the fellow citizens of Sepúlveda through servitude?[22] Ultimately, among the seminal contributions to the critique of colonialism must also be counted the questioning of one of its most powerful theoretical tools, namely, the theory of just war. Hence the *écart* that must be unpacked in relation to De Vitoria's theories.[23]

2.3 The Evangelising *Epistemé* of the School of Salamanca

Drawing on the tools of theological tradition, scholastic philosophy, and canon and civil law, De Las Casas developed a perspective that enabled him to produce a pioneering analysis of Indigenous cultures.

The three volumes of his *Apologética Historia Sumaria* are dedicated to the study of the geography of the West Indies and, in particular, the customs and traditions of the native peoples. His objective, as the title openly declares, is laudatory: to construct a counter-narrative to the early descriptions of the Indies that supported the project of conquest. In this comparison, it goes without saying, he highlights the virtues, gentleness and courage of the native peoples, who prove capable of living in peace and administering justice. De Las Casas emphasises that their realms were by no means *magna latrocinia* in the Augustinian sense, and therefore constituted legitimate political communities. The capacity to adopt the perspective of the Other extends to the point of recognising the reasons behind it, of seeing the Other as the bearer of their own values and truths, and, moreover, of acknowledging them as an equal and free subject. The remainder of the *Apologética Historia Sumaria* is dedicated to

[21] B. de Las Casas, *Obras completas*, cit., p. 106.

[22] L. Mora Rodríguez, *Bartolomé de Las Casas. Conquête, domination, souveraineté*, Presses Universitaires de France, Paris 2012, pp. 23–44.

[23] L. Baccelli, *Bartolomé de Las Casas. La conquista senza fondamento*, Feltrinelli Editore, Milano, 2016, p. 176.

demonstrating that the Indigenous communities fulfilled the sixth requirement of a well-ordered republic: the existence of rulers, judges and justice.[24]

The proto-anthropological analysis of De Las Casas, therefore, shows that the Indigenous institutions express the political prudence of the inhabitants and are fully framed within the *jus gentium* developed from the respect for native identity. This "*demuestra plenamente la racionalidad de los habitantes de las Indias y constituye la base más sólida de sus derechos.*"[25] Indeed, it is precisely on the question of human sacrifice that De Las Casas' contextualist approach reaches its most mature expression: such practices are neither justified nor accepted and clearly constitute a violation of the seventh commandment as well as a form of idolatry. However, De Las Casas argues that the native peoples were not in a position to understand that they were committing an unlawful act. In fact, on the basis of the information available to them, they could have believed they were fulfilling a sacred duty to the divine. Vitoria addresses the issue of human sacrifice under the fifth 'legitimate title' in his *Relectio de Indis*. In the preceding discussion, the universality of natural rights is framed from a distinctly European perspective: while the holders of rights derived from natural sociability, communication and the right to proclaim and preach the Gospel are ostensibly all human beings, what is specifically at stake in this context is the exercise of such rights by the Spanish, and their violation by the Indigenous peoples, a violation deemed a grave *injuria* and thus a just cause for war. By contrast, here the violation of natural rights to life and liberty, which are likewise universal, is committed to the detriment of the so-called 'barbarians' and takes place "*propter leges tyrannicas in iniuriam innocentium*".[26] Moreover, authors such as Strabo, Jerome and Herodotus recount that cannibalism was once practised in France, Spain, England and Scotland, as well as among the Scythians, the Massagetae and the Tartars, in Pontus and in India. Therefore, the custom of the inhabitants of the Caribbean, while representing a grave form of savagery, was not unique: "*esta gente no estaba sola en este pecado.*"[27]

De Las Casas' treatment of the issue is significant for his complex reflection on the customs of the native peoples, and in particular on human

[24] B. De Las Casas, *Obras completas*, cit, pp. 1454–1463.

[25] B. de Las Casas, *Obras completas*, cit., p. 1574.

[26] Cf. T. Todorov, *La conquête de l'Amérique. La question de l'autre*, Seuil, Paris 1982.

[27] B. De Las Casas, *Obras Completas*, cit., 8, p. 1323.

sacrifice, as it introduces an anthropological approach that ultimately rejects the supposed universalism of the Western legal and theological worldview, thus clearing the way for the recognition of a non-aprioristic form of comparison.[28] The question returns of the greatest possible distance between the civilised and the barbarian, which occasioned the already-mentioned episode of the *nomos basileus* in Herodotus.[29] These two key concepts are capable of indicating the differences that Viveiros identifies as existing between Western and Amerindian cosmologies. They emerge from an analysis of the "metaphysics of predation", that is, the cannibalistic and anthropophagous practices of the Amerindian peoples. This is curious, given that cannibalism and anthropophagy represent the most extreme hypotheses of the 'moral' distance between Western and Amerindian thought. Perhaps, however, 'the most extreme case' is precisely the one that best allows us to observe the vast cosmological distances, though it is often invoked specifically to block any form of intercultural transition or even contact with otherness and difference.[30]

What is truly unacceptable about the cannibal hypothesis lies, rather, in a model of understanding the colonisation process that focuses on the incessant becoming of bodies. This Western Catholic idea allows for the positing of transhistorical identities and denies the existence of pure territories untouched by hybridity. Indeed, we might consider that the colonised subject becomes Other "*a través de la incorporación de las formas de subjetivación, los modos de producción y los arquetipos deseantes del colonizador.*"[31]

[28] B. De Las Casas, *Brevísima relación de la destrucción de las Indias*, Madrid, 2020.

[29] In relation to this point, the reflections made by S. Muñoz Machado are particularly insightful: *Civilizando a los bárbaros*, reception speech at the Real Academia de Ciencias Morales y Políticas, 22 May 2012, Madrid, particularly, pp. 63–68.

[30] About "*multiculturalismo emancipatório*", cfr. Boaventura de Sousa Santos (ed.), *Reconhecer para Libertar. Os Caminhos do Cosmopolitismo Multicultural*, Civilização Brasileira, Rio de Janeiro, 2003. A perspective on the rights of the other can be found in E. Costas Douzinas, *O Fim dos Direitos Humanos*, Editora Martins Fontes, São Paulo, 2009, especially pp. 349–374. Giacomo Marramao discusses the 'cosmopolitanism of differences' in the book *Passaggio a Occidente*, Bollati Boringhieri, Torino, 2003. The notion of interculturality is developed by Flavia Stara, Massimo Meccarelli, Héctor Samour, Raúl Fornet-Betancourt et al. in the volume curated by Flavia Stara, *La costruzione de pensiero e delle strategie interculturali*, cit.

[31] A. Chaparro Amaya, *Pensar caníbal. Una perspectiva amerindia de la guerra, lo sagrado y la colonialidad*, Katz, Madrid, 2013, p. 268.

On the other hand, it is worth noting that De Las Casas' reflections are not far removed from the methodological approach to understanding cultural diversity discussed above. Naturally, in considering these *écarts*, we must take into account what Jullien himself describes as the common historical ground, that is, the historical context. And of course, Las Casas' conceptions cannot be abstracted from the teleological framework of evangelisation.[32]

Although we cannot speak of true epistemological ruptures, since De Las Casas always operates within the Aristotelian-Thomistic paradigm, his intellectual trajectory is nonetheless marked by a series of theoretical and political distancings. His writings clearly reveal a determination to intervene, to prevent the extermination of the native peoples, to make evangelisation possible and thus save them from eternal damnation, to improve their condition and to liberate them from slavery and servitude. Moreover, one refrain remains constant throughout: "***Todos los reynos de las Indias tenemos usurpados.***"

2.4 Jus Gentium, Catholic *Communitas* and Private Property

Across different historical contexts, we have examined the underlying dynamics in "the seams of the shrouds of identities",[33] that is, the use of a universal trait as a shroud that conceals frameworks with ethnocentric features. Thinkers such as De Las Casas, who instead wove comparative frameworks incorporating the reality of the Other's Law, were able to conceive of identities that were tendentially non-exclusionary.

In light of the reflections in the previous paragraph, two key axes are identified to unveil the exclusionary identity of this initial Encounter with the Other: the (early germs of the) idea of European national *communitas*, the imposition of the concept of private property in commercial contexts beyond national territories, and the (emerging) conception of State sovereignty.

[32] Cf. L. Iglesias Ortega, *Bartolomé de Las Casas: Cuarenta y cuatro años infinitos*, Fundación José Manuel Lara, Sevilla, 2007; L.A. Clayton, *Bartolomé de las Casas. A Biography*, Cambridge University Press, New York 2012.

[33] G. Vizenor and R.A. Lee, *Postindian Conversations*, University of Nebraska Press, Lincoln, 1999, p. 79.

From the perspective of private law, the image of a *communitas* is strongly shaped by its legal articulation in contractual terms, "*expresión de un credo en el que se enfatizan, en clave holística, los vínculos del individuo con la colectividad.*"[34]

2.4.1 The Idea of Communitas

It is essential for our research to emphasise that the phenomenology of European hegemony in the initial Encounter is consummated primarily through commercial jurisdiction and essentially by the imposition of the idea of private property, accompanied by the logical exclusion of other forms of social organisation. This mechanism of imposition was later recognised by Rousseau in his writings concerning the Western capital sin of private property.[35]

The State community is created out of fear in Hobbes' philosophy and with early capitalist traits in Locke, while it is founded on guilt in Rousseau's theses. Indeed, we will adopt the definition of *communitas*, closely linked to its counterpart, which is collective, State-centred and supranational identity: "*la idea filosófica de comunidad no se refiere a las pequeñas patrias a las que dirigen la mirada nostálgicamente los viejos y nuevos comunitarismos. La comunidad no es una propiedad, una plenitud, un territorio que se debe defender y separar de los que no son parte suya, sino un vacío, una deuda, un don (estos son los significados de* munus*) en relación con los otros, que nos remite a la vez a nuestra constitutiva alteridad también respecto de nosotros mismos.*"[36] True *communitas* arises only within the State sphere or within Indigenous collectives. Thus, even in the realm of *communitas*, a relational canon can be established. The very history of the "Conquest" could be viewed through the lens of an encounter between a relational *communitas* (Indigenous) and an exclusionary, hegemonic *communitas* (Western), which had already violently expelled the Other from within itself. On the other hand, a mercantile *societas* underlying the *jus gentium*, marked by strong commercial features, gradually took shape, as we will see below. In contrast to this reality, Indigenous communities might be seen

[34] A. Somma, *Introducción crítica al Derecho comparado*, Ediciones Jurídicas Olejnik, 2017, p. 187.

[35] J. J. Rousseau, *Discours sur l'origine et les fondements de l'inégalité parmi les hommes in collection complète des oeuvres*, Genève, 1780–1789.

[36] R. Esposito, *Communitas. Origen y destino de la comunidad. Protección y negación de la vida*, Amorrortu, Buenos Aires, 2005, p. 4.

to have maintained "*un circuito de donación recíproca cuya peculiaridad residía justamente en su oblicuidad respecto de la frontalidad de la relación sujeto-objeto, y por comparación con la plenitud ontológica de la persona.*"[37] This last aspect was abundantly emphasised, albeit in different words, by De Las Casas in his accounts. Faced with these Indigenous realities was a religious *communitas* and, consequently, an evangelising mission towards the Other, which persists with different, non-religious features to this day. It is important to reiterate that these religious ideas should not be seen merely as a veneer or justificatory cover for deeper capitalist hegemonic practices: in some cases, they have acted as a restraint on indiscriminate exploitation, as exemplified by the position taken by De Las Casas.[38]

2.4.2 The Idea of Private Property

However, the most enduring idea that drove European expansion was neither religious righteousness (although this also contributed indirectly to the imposition of Spanish identity) nor the mere assertion of European civilisational superiority. Rather, it was the belief that States, and indeed humanity itself, could only be preserved through the exploitation of the Earth's resources, to which all peoples held a common right, but to which some populations acquired superior rights by exploiting natural resources.[39] "Thus, occupation introduced an understanding of property in terms of the exploitation of nature. This process of exploitation is what drove society from one step in history to the next. Moreover, these early modern authors stressed that occupation could not simply be a taking of something 1with the hands, as it had been for medieval authors. Rather, they argued that occupation was only achieved by use or, in modern's terms, improvement".[40]

While De Vitoria's discourse implicitly justified incompleteness in relation to a more organised society, later authors we will analyse justify land appropriation through an interweaving of the principle of State sovereignty and the optimal use of natural resources.

[37] R. Esposito, *Communitas. Origen y destino de la comunidad*, cit., p. 31.

[38] A. Fitzmaurice, *Sovereignty, Property and Empire*, Cambridge University Press, Cambridge, 2014, p. 13.

[39] A. Fitzmaurice, *Sovereignty, Property and Empire*, cit., p. 12.

[40] A. Fitzmaurice, *Sovereignty, Property and Empire*, cit., p. 19.

Western exclusionary identity is shaped in tune with increasing economic exploitation by seventeenth- and eighteenth-century philosophers, alongside the progressive sophistication of the concept of State sovereignty.[41]

For Schmitt, International Law, and to a large extent modern political thought, centres on the creation of an empire and the hegemony of European states. In words echoed by many contemporary historians, he argued that the "discovery of a new world [...] did not occur by chance. It was an achievement of newly awakened Occidental rationalism, the product of an intellectual and scientific culture".[42] The occupation of space was an idea employed to legitimise Empire, not to oppose it, and in this sense Schmitt is followed by many more recent thinkers. The concept of occupation, he argued, suited the emerging order of inter-State competition for territory, as it did not allocate new lands to Europeans collectively, but only to those who physically appropriated them. The ***Nomos of the Earth*** is the foundational order that governs the distribution of space and power in the world at a given historical moment. From the sixteenth to the nineteenth century, the *Jus Publicum Europaeum* was based on a balance between European States and a distinction between just war within Europe and colonial expansion beyond it. In fact, the seed of a possible European *communitas* had already been sown by Hobbesian fear.

In the modern world, property is an omnipresent institution and, alongside contracts, one of the foundational pillars of the economy.[43] Locke's philosophy, in particular, contributes to the formation of a modern identity centred on the individual as an agent endowed with rights and capacities, including self-responsibility and autonomy.[44] This conception of the "punctual self" underscores an individualist approach and the capacity for self-determination as central elements of identity.[45] As we shall see

[41] For a study of a non-European *jus gentium* cf. A. Becker Lorca, *Mestizo International Law: a global intellectual history 1850–1950*, Cambridge University Press, Cambridge, 2012.

[42] C. Schmitt, *The Nomos of the Earth in the International Law of the Jus Publicum Europæum*, Telos Press Publishing, London, 2003, p. 132.

[43] S. Weil, *Echar raíces*, cit., p.10.

[44] Cf. B. Bhandar, *Colonial Lives of Property Law, Land, and Racial Regimes of Ownership*, Duke University, 2018. Bhandar challenges Locke's notion of property, as well as the broader liberal tradition, which presents property as a universal and neutral right. Instead, she demonstrates how Western legal doctrines have been employed to justify the appropriation of land in colonial contexts such as Canada, Australia and South Africa.

[45] For further reading on this subject, see the essential text by C. Taylor, *Sources of the Self: The Making of the Modern Identity*, Harvard University Press, Cambridge, 1989, p. 139.

shortly (and beyond the economic sphere), liberal thinkers in the West, from Locke to Kant and Hegel have defined modernity and modern individuality in terms of property. In this sense, property has come to stand in opposition to nature, conceived as an object of appropriation through the establishment of rights over it by human action. "According to this mode of thought, nature is considered as an entity that has no agency, no intentionality of its own, and is thus subject to appropriation through human industry. A bright line is therefore drawn between the inert natural world and humanity: humanity stands apart from nature, and is morally superior to it".[46]

2.5 The Structuring of Sovereignty and the Law to Exclude in the Formation of the New *Jus Gentium*

"The law of nations was not a coherent body".[47] Before the nineteenth century, *jus gentium* was part of a broader body of literature on the governance of States, specifically those aspects that dealt with their foreign relations. As already indicated in the discussion surrounding the *communitas totus orbis* of De Vitoria, one of the central points of debate was whether the rules of the law of nations applied exclusively to relations between European nations, or whether other peoples were also subject to them.[48] In post-Conquest and post-*Reconquista* Spain, a dynamic of difference began to emerge, generally denoting the ongoing process of creating a divide between two cultures. One was deemed supposedly universal and civilised, while the other was regarded as "particular" and uncivilised. There were attempts to close the gap through the development of techniques, including religious derivation, aimed at normalising the so-called aberrant society.[49]

During the seventeenth and eighteenth centuries, this dynamic of difference was translated into normative terms, primarily through the very concept of sovereignty itself. With the following philosophical theories, we enter the thorny terrain of asserting State sovereignty. Two elements

[46] M. Graziadei, *On Universalizing 'Nature' and 'Property': the Unravelling of a Master Narrative*, in *Journal of Interdisciplinary History of Ideas*, 2023, p. 27.

[47] A. Fitzmaurice, *Sovereignty, Property and Empire*, cit., p. 19.

[48] Cf. N. Mull, *Divine law divided: Francisco de Vitoria on civil and ecclesiastical powers*, in *Intellectual History Review*, 2021, pp. 201–223.

[49] M. Koskenniemi, *To the Uttermost Parts of the Earth*, cit., p. 145.

will be examined before we turn to the influence these conceptualisations have had on the formation of an exclusionary Western identity: firstly, the gradual articulation of sovereignty in exclusionary terms; and secondly, the consequent universalisation of a specifically European *jus gentium*. These two poles constitute what Jouannet insightfully identifies (though she defines it in antithetical terms) as an *écart* in Western legal identity.[50] Here, we describe it as an intrinsic tension within both past and present International Law.

2.5.1 The Concepts of Property and Sovereignty

The sovereignty of the State and private property form a true knot. As recognised in the nineteenth century, "*la cuestión de la propiedad y la de la soberanía siempre son dos caras de la misma moneda.*"[51] To think through the history of the relationship between sovereignty and property is to think about the "*formación de un pensamiento político del dominio (individual exclusivo o colectivo)*".[52] This idea of exclusivity is central to the formation of State identity. Ultimately, sovereignty entails both a monopoly over enjoyment and the power to exclude third parties.

From a commercial perspective, *dominium* has a dual meaning: on one hand, it refers to the power exercised by the sovereign over their territories and subjects, but it also denotes a sphere of economic freedom for individuals, which includes private property, an element that cannot be limited by sovereigns, as it derives from a title that is both equivalent and universally applicable. This individual *dominium* is not a prerogative granted by the sovereign or public power, but rather a horizontal justice between individuals, each of whom holds their own *dominium*.

The idea of *dominium* expands to the colonies through *jus gentium*. In De Vitoria, it does not take on precise contours. It is not that *jus gentium* is a natural law, nor that it is the law imposed by a sovereign on the territories under their control. Rather, it serves as a vehicle: the 'private' idea of *dominium* was universalised through international 'human' law. War is, rather, the consequence that arises from the violation of *jus gentium*, and

[50] E. Jouannet, *Universalism and Imperialism: The True-False Paradox of International Law?* in *The European Journal of International Law*, p. 392–399.

[51] See P. Dardot and C. Laval, *Dominar. Estudio sobre la soberanía del estado de Occidente*, Gedisa, Barcelona, 2021, p. 56.

[52] See P. Dardot and C. Laval, *Dominium: Essai sur la souveraineté de l'État en Occident*, La Découverte, Paris, 2020, p. 66.

in this case, ***jus gentium*** entails the private concept of ***dominium***, which in turn involves the idea of commercial liberty and private property. But there is more. "In other words, the sovereign's right to exclude is more capacious than the private owner's right of the same name. For both individual owners and sovereigns, the territorial dimension of the right to exclude connects mastery over things with the production of the state's legal personality. It is only for sovereigns, however, that the generative dimension gives a right to set the rules for the international system, and vitally, creating that system through the delimitation of its borders".[53]

This dynamic of difference is exponentially amplified in normative terms, primarily through the concept of sovereignty. "There was, however, a fundamental paradox in the first law of peoples, which was adopted by the European powers and theorised by the jurists from the natural law school (Grotius, Pufendorf, Wolff, Vattel): while being a direct product of European thought, and thus of a narrowly regional vision of International Law, from one specific culture and civilisation, it was conceived by its founders as being composed of norms that were abstract, neutral and universally applicable to all states, whatever their legal cultures or traditional ways of understanding law".[54] Naturally, the universalism projected onto the international stage through Eurocentric conceptions is not a new development. What is novel, however, is the *quomodo*: the safeguarding of International Law as a direct expression of the Westphalian State system.

The very emergence of the State as a fundamental concept in modern European culture, and the resolution of the complex dialectical relationship between civil and religious power, gave rise to the idea of sovereignty, a conceptual element necessary to overcome the Emperor's supremacy over the Pope.[55] The international society resulting from the Peace of Westphalia was, and in many ways still is, defined by the emergence of the sovereign State as the only relevant social actor on the international stage, leading to the enshrinement of the principle of *superiorem non recognoscem*, which in turn brings with it the corollary of independence and

[53] J. Desautels-Stein, *The Right to Exclude: A Critical Race Approach to Sovereignty, Borders, and International Law*, Oxford University Press, Oxford, 2023, p. 45.

[54] E. Jouannet, *Universalism and Imperialism: The True-False Paradox of International Law?* cit., p. 382.

[55] F. Mariño Menéndez, *Derecho Internacional Público (Parte General)*, IV^{a} ed., Trotta, Madrid, 2005, p. 30.

individualism in international relations.[56] The birth of new European kingdoms was also accompanied by a colonial experience and the related goal of eradicating any trace of civilisation distinct from that of the metropolis. The classics of the Spanish School of the Law of Nations focused on the human being, rather than the State, as the foundation of the then international (Catholic) community as a form of human sociability, drawing on Aristotelian influences[57].

2.5.2 *Sovereignty and Exclusion*

The pivot, therefore, lies in the right to exclude, which is shared within these interconnected domains.[58] It forms the third element of our conceptual triptych: classify, separate, exclude.

In the sixteenth, seventeenth and eighteenth centuries, principles of the incipient *jus gentium* emerge, or are reinforced, which reveal this abyssal gap: the principle of sovereignty, the principle of recognition, the prohibition of interference in the internal affairs of States, etc. They are all corollaries of the "law of exclusion"[59] or, as Pizzorno would say, the absence of communication.[60] They form the conceptual and legal foundations of society and the law of separation, which Glenn refers to in his notion of *closure*. The exercise of the principle of sovereignty isolates States and cre-

[56] Cf. A. Marín López, *El principio de igualdad soberana de los Estados en el ámbito de las Naciones Unidas*, in *AHLADI*, 1967, pp.89 ss.; J. A. Carrillo Salcedo, *Soberanía del Estado y Derecho Internacional*, Tecnos, Madrid, 1976; Idem, *Soberanía de los Estados y Derechos humanos en Derecho Internacional contemporáneo*, Tecnos, Madrid, 2001.

[57] It is remarkable to see the efforts made by Natural Law theorists and the early codifiers to elevate, almost as something sanctified, the right to private property. This is precisely emphasised by Hans Kelsen in his Pure Theory of Law, where he seeks to demonstrate the contradictions inherent in the arguments of Natural Law proponents, who argue that one of the primary functions of the State (that is, of positive law) is to protect the right to property, which they claim is established by nature itself. In this context, Kelsen illustrates how a metaphysical narrative of law progressively developed with the aim of safeguarding the concept of dominion that underpins capitalism and, ultimately, the modern State. Cf. H. Kelsen, *Teoría pura del derecho*, Eudeba, Buenos Aires, p. 111.

[58] Cf. J. Desautels-Stein, *The Right to Exclude: A Critical Race Approach to Sovereignty, Borders, and International Law*. Oxford University Press, Oxford, 2023, especially Chap. 'Imperium and Dominium', pp. 25–61.

[59] J. Desautels-Stein, *The Right to Exclude: A Critical Race Approach to Sovereignty, Borders, and International Law*, Oxford University Press, Oxford, 2023.

[60] A. Pizzorno, *Il velo delle diversità. Studi su razionalità e riconoscimento*, Feltrinelli, Milano, 2007, pp. 371–387.

ates a breakdown in communication. Within what was then Western Law, the foundational and mythical moment is not merely consumed as territorial appropriation—Schmitt's *Landnahme*[61]—but in a philosophical key as a radical cognitive separation of the thinking subject from the *res extensa*, developed between the seventeenth and nineteenth centuries.[62] Western Law of the time, and in particular International Law, is also built on this abyssal line: it is the **Law of Separation and Exclusion**.[63] In other legal cultures there is a *continuum* between man and nature, and nature as a living entity is not simply subordinated to man's needs or desires. This leads to the recognition of a non-dualistic anthropology, which does not separate what is human and what is non-human into two distinct ontological domains. This separation is characteristic of Western societies and is largely ignored in other parts of the world. The modern worldview of the Western world, therefore, is the exception rather than the rule in many ways.

This view, which arises from the need to shield the new Westphalian creation from secular and religious influences, began to take shape through two significant principles: the principle of recognition and the immunity of the State and its representatives.[64]

The Principle of Recognition: The Creation of *Communitas*

Hobbes' *communitas* implies a social contract born out of fear of the Other: *homo homini lupus*. Hobbes' solution to the crisis of human

[61] C. Schmitt, *The Nomos of the Earth*, 1950, cit., Parte2: "*El Ius Publicum Europaeum*", p. 89. See also R. Nichols, Theft Is Property! Dispossession and Critical Theory, Duke University Press, 2020.

[62] For a completely different view on property, see H. Selin (ed.), *Nature Across Cultures: Views of Nature and the Environment in Non-Western Cultures*, Springer, Dordecht, 2013.

[63] As for the structuring of International Law in these exclusive terms, I refer *ex multis* to the works of E. Jouannet, *Universalism and Imperialism: The True-False Paradox of International Law?* in *The European Journal of International Law*, p. 394; and J. Desautels-Stein, *The Right to Exclude: A Critical Race Approach to Sovereignty, Borders, and International Law*. Oxford University Press, Oxford, 2023. From a comparative point of view, we should not overlook the essential study by H. P. Glenn, *The Cosmopolitan State*, Oxford University Press, Oxford, 2013, p. 63.

[64] In relation to this point, see V. Bou Franch, *Inmunidad del Estado y violación de normas internacionales de ius cogens: el asunto Al-Adsani contra Reino Unido*, in *Anuario de Derecho Internacional*, 2002, p.17; J. Ferrer Lloret, *La inmunidad de jurisdicción del Estado ante violaciones graves de los derechos humanos*, in *Revista Española de Derecho Internacional*, 2007, pp. 29–63.

relations is absolute dissociation. Individuals associate only in the form of their reciprocal withdrawal to exorcise the fear of human contact[65]. The Hobbesian social contract is understood as that which is not a gift, an absence of *munus*, a bond that implies the need for the Other. On the contrary, it means the neutralisation of fear due to its presence. The Hobbesian State is presented as the de-socialisation of the community bond. Any association within the State is considered a threat to sovereignty, which ends up coinciding with dissociation. The expression "political body"[66] in Hobbes does not mean concord, but the union of many men. The Leviathan, that biblical monster, composed of segments of men, is its ultimate expression. Social glue, as Hume already asserted, lies in the notion of a "balance of powers", which seems to logically derive from the existence of distinct sovereign political entities.[67]

This division is what immunises against the inherent risk of death within the community, in the opposition between *immunitas* and *communitas* that underpins the entire modern project.[68] The logic of the Hobbesian pact is reformulated in the idea of exoneration or exemption (*Entlastung*), where the modern individual disconnects from prior obligations or encloses themselves in an institutional environment that excludes any communal figure, characterised by the equal diversity of self-interests.[69]

Recognition is also a form of (in)communication with the Other, constructing both an identity for oneself and for the Other through delimitation.

Firstly, the right to exclude is territorial separation: it is essentially about keeping foreigners away from a defined territory. This first aspect draws from the theories of occupation and possession, which have been defined in Cartesian terms.[70] Evidently, the principle of non-intervention in the internal affairs of other States made little sense within the *jus commune* of the *Respublica Christiana*, a society conceived as a unity governed by the

[65] Cf. G. Palombella, *Filosofia del Diritto*, Cedam, Padova, 1996.

[66] T. Hobbes, *De cive*, cit., p. 101. Cf. G. Agamben, *Homo sacer. El poder soberano y la nuda vida*, Editorial Pre-Textos, Valencia, 2006.

[67] D. Hume, *Of Balance of Power*, in *Political Essays*, Cambridge University Press, Cambridge, 2012, pp. 154–160.

[68] M. Foucault, *Histoire de la sexualité, tome I: La volonté de savoir*, Gallimard, Paris, 1976, p. 126.

[69] Cf. J. Rawls, *Justicia como equidad*, Tecnos, Madrid, 1999.

[70] Cf. S. Wiessner, *Indigenous sovereignty: A reassessment in light of the UN declaration on the rights of indigenous peoples*, in *Vanderbilt Journal of Transnational Law*, 2008, p. 1141.

Emperor of the Holy Roman Empire as ***dominus mundi*** and by the Roman Pontiff as Christ's earthly representative, under whose name the vicars administered their lands.[71] The feudal system, in essence, was open to influences from external elements beyond its territory. In this way, the Emperor's vassals could call upon his assistance when threatened by other vassals or by popular uprisings. Princes, republics and free cities also did not have exclusive control over their territories and populations internally. Different social groups (clergy, Jews, non-believers, etc.) were subject to different rules, and certain privileges could be exercised by one prince in a territory formally governed by another.[72] As a result, no matter was truly internal.

Secondly, the right to exclude is also constitutive, as it helps to define the contours of a legal system's identity by creating boundaries. This process forms the subjectivity of those on the outside (foreigners) and those on the inside (subjects and later citizens), who come first. This second aspect draws from theories of property. In the conceptual realm of sovereignty, the territorial dimension of the right to exclude generates both dominion over things and the creation of a legally individualised state subjectivity. That is, within the context of sovereignty, the territorial dimension of the right to exclude results in two complementary and overlapping perspectives on possession and personality. The first reflects the sovereign's right to prohibit intervention within their territory and internal affairs, while the second pertains to the right to self-determination as a subject of International Law, which is later corroborated by the related principle of State recognition by pre-existing subjects.[73]

The role played by the principle of recognition in this context is also of interest for our purposes, as it is in the works of Natural Law theorists and

[71] The principle of continual interference governed relations in the previous period, as noted by R. Ward, *An Enquiry into the Foundation and History of the Law of Nations*, vol I, Butterworth, 1795, p. 367: "*the right to interfere with one another, which the states of Europe mutually assumed in consequence of the divisions and subdivisions into which they had fallen*".

[72] Cf. A. Nussbaum, *A Concise History of the Law of Nations*, rev. edn, Macmillan 1954.

[73] In other words, the sovereign's law of exclusion is broader than the corresponding law of the private owner. For both individual owners and sovereigns, the territorial dimension of the law of exclusion connects the domination of things with the production of the State's legal personality. However, the generative dimension only gives sovereigns the right to establish the rules of the international system and, more importantly, to create such a system by defining their borders. On the powerful analogy between Western State civil law and International Law, see T. E. Holland, *The Elements of Jurisprudence*, 13 edn, Clarendon Press, Oxford, 1924, pp. 393–394.

the early positivists of the eighteenth century that the first separate treatment of this subject appears. What emerges from their works is that, both under natural law and the law of nations, it was considered that sovereignty originated from within the State, not from the outside. In other words, the title and rank of hereditary and elective sovereigns did not depend on recognition by other States or, even less so, on a universal authority (at least when the rules of succession were respected). The refusal to recognise a legitimate monarch was, in fact, a criminal act, as it contradicted the principle of the sovereign equality of States. Thus, the period following medieval universalism was characterised by the consolidation of absolute monarchies and a pluralistic community of States with exclusive jurisdiction over their own territorial spheres.

The Principle of State Immunity: The Creation of *Immunitas*

The principle of immunity is established as the sole channel of communication between emerging sovereign States in isolation. It is a customary principle of International Law, a norm of *jus gentium*, whose roots can be traced back to the origins of the modern State. Although there is evidence of earlier precedents, this doctrine has a Christian root: 'all authority comes from God' (John 19:11 and Romans). 13.1). Therefore, "authority cannot be judged by any court."[74] That is why Ushakov asserts that the essence of the principle of State immunity is "the non-subordination of one State to the power of another State" (*par in parem non habet imperium*). However, the claim of immunity to avoid such undue subordination can be made only before a *domestic* court of another State. Precisely as a consequence of sovereign equality, a State may demand from another State that its judicial bodies respect that sovereign equality, refraining from prosecuting it when it acts as a sovereign State. From the perspective of *jus gentium* and current International Law, that court is considered to be an organ of that other State, however independent it may be from the latter's Executive in the performance of its duties. The foundation of immunity must be sought in the correlate notions of sovereign equality and reciprocity. In 1812, the famous judge Marshall, president of the American Supreme Court, in the case of *The Schooner Exchange* argued thus: "*Since the world is composed of distinct sovereignties possessing equal rights and equal Independence.* [...] *All sovereigns have accepted, in practice and under*

[74] A.L. Calvo Caravaca and J. Carrascosa González, *Tratado de Derecho Internacional Privado*, Tirant Lo Blanch, 2ª ed., Valencia, 2022, p. 337.

certain circumstances, a limitation of the absolute and complete jurisdiction conferred on them by sovereignty within their respective territories".[75] However, one must ask whether it is merely mutual respect for the independence of others that serves as the driving force behind States' willingness to accept and respect this legal concept. All States have a shared interest in upholding this institution of immunity and separation. Thus, this legal concept involves the recognition by domestic courts of a privilege inherent to the status of a State: the privilege of not being obliged to submit to their jurisdiction. Especially with De Vattel, this customary principle is systematised within a context of increasing state separation, a trend that, as we shall see, continues to this day.

2.5.3 **Jus Gentium** *as a Universal Norm of States*

Steiger points out that, from antiquity to the Middle Ages, *jus gentium* was always conceived as *jus commune* (*jus commune omnium hominum*), rather than as a law of peoples understood as distinct groups, separate from one another.[76] Following the Catholic ideal developed by De Vitoria (see below), it was only with the gradual formation of the system of States, purged of its religious features, that *jus gentium* would take the form of a legal order between peoples, rulers, or states (*civitates*).[77] Cicero understood *jus gentium* as Natural Law, and it was this link between *jus gentium* and *jus naturale* that shaped legal thinking about the law of nations up until the Middle Ages. Thus, Thomas Aquinas based *jus gentium* on Natural Law, much like De Vitoria, while other jurists (such as Bartolo da Sassoferrato) emphasised the shaping influence of custom (*usus*, understood as *nomoi*), as did De Las Casas.

Vázquez, in effect, also offers a theory of the law of nations. By understanding this type of right as a historical development, he is, in fact,

[75] U.S. Supreme Court Judgement, The Schooner Exchange v. MacFaddon, 1812, which addressed the claim by United States nationals of a vessel requisitioned by Napoleon's navy. Cf. A. Lazari, *Jurisprudencia española en materia de Derecho Internacional Público. Section 3.7: Inmunidad de jurisdicción del Estado*, Revista Española de Derecho Internacional, vol. 67, 2, 2015, p. 177.

[76] H. Steiger, *Völkerrecht*, in O. Brunner, W. Conze, R. Koselleck (eds.), *Geschichtliche Grundbegriffe: Historisches Lexikon zur politisch-sozialen Sprache in Deutschland*, Klett-Cotta, Stuttgart, 1992, vol. 7, pp. 99–100.

[77] G. Gozzi, *Rights and Civilizations: A History and Philosophy of International Law*, Cambridge University Press, 2019, especially pp. 33–44.

announcing a future in which a positivised system of peoples will form the basis of interaction with the Other. However, unlike De Vitoria, Vázquez delimits its scope arguing that it cannot be universalised, since it cannot be applied to peoples who are not governed by "honest" laws and customs, removed from Spanish customs.[78] *Jus gentium* is the definition that Hugo Grotius returns to in the seventeenth century.[79] Steiger highlights the new rationalist meaning that the concept of *jus gentium* acquired from the sixteenth century onwards[80], alongside its progressively more State-oriented nature.

The Theory of Hugo Grotius

In the development of a fundamental (proto)international interstate Law, the theoretical contribution of Hugo Grotius[81] has been crucial. In 1609, in *Mare Liberum*,[82] he presented a defence of the freedom of the seas that would gain widespread fame. In making his case, Grotius was inspired by De Vitoria, particularly the arguments put forward in *De Indiis* regarding the justifications for the Spanish conquest of the Americas. Among these justifications, as we have already seen, was the principle of free trade. If the Indigenous people rejected the natural freedom to trade peacefully in goods, then it was up to the Spanish to persuade them to do so.[83] If this

[78] "*Ius autem gentium negavit totum mundum amplexum fuisse, nam primum excepit eas gentes, quae sine legibus & moribus honestis reguntur, quas innumeras esse apparuit, postquam nos hispani novum orbem indorum reclusimus ac invenimus* [...]. *Ergo si ipsum ius gentium universum mundum non complectitur, quanto minus illum complectetur ius civile, quod est longe angustius*"; also F. Vázquez de Menchaca, *Controversiarum illustrium aliarumque usu frequentium libri tres*, Rampazetus, Venezia, 1564, I, 26, § 14, p. 5.

[79] Grotius in *De Jure Belli ac Pacis* (1625) writes: "*ius illud, quod inter populos plures aut populorum rectores intercedit, attigerunt pauci [...] Cicero praestabilem hanc dixit scientiam, in federibus, pactionibus, conditionibus populorum, regum exterarumque nationum, in omni denique belli iure & pacis.*" Hugonis Grotii, "*En tres libros De jure belli ac pacis prolegomena*", in *De Jure Belli et Pacis Libri Tres*, Cambridge University Press, Cambridge, 1853), vol. 1, pp. xxxvii–xxxviii.

[80] G. Gozzi, *Rights and Civilizations: A History and Philosophy of International Law*, Cambridge University Press, 2019, especially pp. 33–44.

[81] M. Koskenniemi, *EJIL Foreword: Imagining the Rule of Law: Rereading the Grotian "Tradition"*, in *European Journal of International Law*, p. 17.

[82] Hugonis Grotii, *De jure praedae commentarius, Ex Auctoris Codice descripsit et vulgavit* H.G. Hamaker, Litt. Dr., Hagae Comitum, Apud Martinum Nijhoff, 1868. Cf. I. Pizza, *Antropologia e fondazione dello Stato nel De Jure praedae di Ugo Grozio*, in *Storia del pensiero politico, Rivista quadrimestrale*, 3/2020, pp. 447–465.

[83] Hugonis Grotii, *De jure praedae commentarius*, cit.

attempt failed, the Spanish were legitimised in conquering their lands. Grotius took advantage of this declaration of principles to argue that, by the same reasoning, the Spanish and Portuguese could not legitimately prevent the Dutch from participating in free trade.[84] *Mare Liberum* of 1609 was the revised version of the twelfth chapter of a broader work that Grotius wrote between 1604 and 1606, titled *De Jure Praedae Commentarius*,[85] in which he defended Dutch colonial enterprises.

Following De Vitoria and Vázquez, Grotius recognises as universal the right to travel (*jus peregrinandi*), the right to trade and the right to appropriate common property[86]. Building on these legal principles, he rejects the Portuguese claim to a monopoly and addresses the issue of freedom of the seas and the rights of Indigenous populations. It is on this same basis that he makes an assessment of Western colonial expansion. Regarding the issue of free trade, Grotius draws on several classical sources (Ulpian, Aristotle, Seneca) to support his assertion that this freedom "springs from primary law of nations, which has a natural and permanent cause, so that it cannot be abrogated. Moreover, even if its abrogation were possible, such a result could be achieved only with the consent of all nations."[87] And since this norm is universal—continues Grotius—it cannot be limited by discovery (*inventio*) or occupation (*occupatio*), or by the fact that one nation (the Portuguese) was the first to establish trade relations with another (the East Indies).[88] The attempt by the Portuguese and the Spanish to establish an overseas monopoly over the East Indies must not be tolerated in the society of humanity, and thus, concludes Grotius returning to De Vitoria, "*cum igitur supra Victoriae auctoritate et exemplis*

[84] Hugonis Grotii, *De jure praedae commentarius*, cit.

[85] Hugonis Grotii, *De jure praedae commentarius*, cit.

[86] I.M. Porras, '*Constructing International Law in the East Indian Seas: Property, Sovereignty, Commerce and War in Hugo Grotius' De Iure Praedae—The Law of Prize and Booty, or "On How to Distinguish Merchants from Pirates*"', cit., p. 745.

[87] "Commercandi igitur libertas ex iure est primario gentium, quod naturalem et perpetuam causam habet, ideoque tolli non potest, et si posset nisi omnium gentium consensus". H. Grotii, De Jure Praedae, Hugonis Grotii, De Jure Praedae Commentarius: Ex Auctoris Codice Descripsit et Vulgavit, ed. Hendrik Gerard Hamaker, Martinum Nijhoff, The Hague: Apud, 1868, chap. XII, pp. 244–245.

[88] Cf. M.J. van Ittersum, *Hugo Grotius in Context: Van Heemskerck's Capture of the Santa Catarina and its Justification in De Iure Praedae (1604–1606)*, in *Asian J. Soc. Sci.*, 2003, pp. 500–529.

demonstratum sit iustam esse belli causam, cum libertas commerciorum vindicatur adversus prohibentes".[89]

So even Grotius, like De Vitoria before him, foregrounded the question of managing diversity. In fact, Grotius fully accepted and recognised the existence of other cultures that were not compatible with Western civilisation, and emphatically denounced any attempt to exploit that diversity as a means to advance Western strategy. The systematic architecture of *De Jure Praedae* (or *De Indis*) was certainly designed to defend the commercial expansion of Dutch enterprises, and its argument in favour of the right to property for the peoples of the East Indies was, therefore, instrumental for this purpose. The aim was to ensure the Dutch could trade freely with these peoples without the Portuguese monopoly getting in the way.

[89] H. Grotii, *De Jure Praedae*, cit., chp. XII, p. 249.

CHAPTER 3

The Consolidation of State *Communitas* and International Exclusionary *Societas*

Abstract The consolidation of a *communitas* of States is once again examined through a series of distinctions (écarts) between Hobbes' concept of mercantilist *societas* and Rousseau's communitarian perspective. Similar tensions emerge in the property theories advanced by Locke and Pufendorf. Understanding the progressive development of exclusionary identity relies on examining the emergence of private property, particularly as it relates to land exploitation. The establishment of ius gentium as a body of law governing States is further illustrated through De Vattel's framework. However, these theoretical positions are not uniform; notable divergences can also be observed within Kant's cosmopolitanism.

Keywords Hobbes • Rousseau • Locke • Pufendorf • DeVattel

On the one hand, among the great thinkers of the seventeenth and eighteenth centuries, there emerges a contractual and exclusionary idea of State identity and *jus gentium*. On the other hand, it is precisely this vision that promotes and encourages the occupation of new territories. We will analyse this fundamental passage of exclusionary identity through *écarts* between the key philosophers who have addressed the themes of *jus gentium*.

© The Author(s), under exclusive license to Springer Nature Switzerland AG 2026

A. Lazari, *Relational Identity in International, Comparative and European Union Law*,
https://doi.org/10.1007/978-3-031-59482-3_3

3.1 The *Écart* Between Hobbes' *Societas* and Rousseau's *Communitas*

A first fundamental *écart* refers to the very existence of a European *societas* ("*in magna illa humani generis societate*", states Grotius[1]), governed by this fundamentally mercantile dynamic.[2] The European *societas* implies a juxtaposition of commercial interests, unlike the *communitas* internal to the State, which, on the other hand, in this period is being strengthened for reasons of collective security.[3] In Tönnies' work, the opposition between *Gemeinschaft* and *Gesellschaft*[4] is constructed, where the first conception is often translated as 'society' and represents a more contractual, impersonal type of social relationship based on individual interests, in contrast to the *Gemeinschaft* which is based on affective and traditional ties.

As seen previously, Hobbes' *communitas* arises from the *pactum societatis* or social contract that gives rise to civil society. However, Rousseau's philosophy focuses on how this covenant, based on fear and the pursuit of individual self-preservation, sacrifices authentic community.[5] Rousseau argues that an aggregation of individuals united only by one master does not constitute an association or political body. *Communitas* is presented as a more original collective, linked to a shared fault or duty (*munus*), while the modern *societas* is often described as arising from the need for individual protection and based on agreements or contracts.[6] "*El Estado moderno no sólo no elimina el miedo a partir del cual originaria mente se genera, sino que se funda precisamente en él, haciéndolo motor y garantía de*

[1] For example, H. Grotius, "*The Freedom of the Seas, or the Right Which Belongs to the Dutch to take part in the East Indian Trade*", with an introduction by J. Brown Scott, Oxford University Press, New York, 1916, p. 17.

[2] R. Esposito, Communitas. *The Origin and Destiny of Community*, Stanford University Press, Stanford, 2009.

[3] T. Hobbes, *De cive*, Alianza Editorial, Madrid, 2020, p. 127; T. Hobbes, *Leviatán: O la materia, forma y poder de un estado eclesiástico y civil*, Alianza Editorial, Madrid, 2018, p. 163.

This conceptual distinction is also found in H. Arendt, *La vie de l'esprit*, Puf, Paris 2005; Idem, *Condition de l'homme moderne*, Gallimard, Paris 2002. Cf. G. Nieves Loja, *El problema de la comunidad: Arendt, Tönnies y Leroux*, in *Veritas*, 2016, pp. 117–131.

[4] F. Tönnies, *Gemeinschaft und Gesellschaft*, Fues's Verlag, Berlin, 1897, p. 33 regarded soil as the first *res* that "human communities properly possess". About this point see S. Chignola, *Quidquid est in territorio est de territorio. Nota sul rapporto tra comunità etnica e Stato-nazione*, in *Filosofia Politica*, 1993, p. 49–71; also, more generally, E. Balibar e I. Wallerstein, *Race, nation, classe. Les identités ambigües*, Puf, Paris, 1988.

[5] J.J. Rousseau, *Del contrato social*, Libsa, Madrid, 2017, p. 284.

[6] Cf. Q. Skinner, *La Libertà prima del liberalismo*, Einaudi, Torino, 2000.

su propio funcionamiento. Esto significa que una época – la modernidad- que se define a sí misma sobre la base de la ruptura con el origen, lleva por eso dentro de sí una impronta indeleble de conflicto y de violencia".[7]

In this regard, John T. Scott also discusses how Locke linked private property to individual and State sovereignty.[8] According to Locke, property derived from labour justified the acquisition of land, even in colonial contexts, thus legitimising European expansion. Scott has explored how Rousseau criticised the relationship between property and inequality in his "Discourse on the Origin of Inequality." The Rousseauian idea that the first private appropriation marked the beginning of inequality also influences contemporary critiques of sovereignty based on territorial dominion.

3.2 The *Écart* Between Locke and Pufendorf's Theories of Property

Another thinker who addresses the social contract is Locke, who, while maintaining the liberal idea of the *pactum*, places at the heart of his theory the protection of absolute rights to life and property. To support his political conceptions, Locke begins his argument with the famous phrase, "In the Beginning, All the World Was America",[9] equating the New World with the state of nature, where everything is permitted. In relation to this idea, the English philosopher's perception that the lands being appropriated were null due to exploitation and ownership is significant.[10] The assertion that the new lands did not belong to anyone because they had not been properly cultivated was not merely a description of a belief but a redescribing of the experience itself. This redefinition rejected the doctrines of the Conquest, which had required the recognition of the property rights of the conquered. "By predicating property and improvement on monetization, Locke construes the absence of monetization in America as the sign that the continent remains in the state of "natural common"

[7] R. Esposito, idem, cit., p. 60.

[8] J.T. Scott, *The Sovereignless State and Locke's Language of Obligation*, in *American Political Science Review*, 2000, pp. 547–561; J.T. Scott (ed.), *Jean-Jacques Rousseau: Critical Assessments of Leading Political Philosophers*, Routledge Taylor and Francis, London, 2005.

[9] J. Locke, *Two Treatises of Government*, Thomas Tegg; W. Sharpe and Son; G. Offor; G. and J. Robinson, London, 1893.

[10] G. Agamben, *Il potere sovrano e la nuda vita*. Homo sacer, Einaudi, Torino, 2005.

open to nonconsensual appropriation".[11] All this allowed the conquistadors to ignore the demands of the Indigenous peoples and to present themselves as 'settlers', that is, as people occupying land that previously belonged to no one. In carrying out this redefinition, the colonisers also began to use the idea of occupation as part of an argument that had been foreign to De Vitoria's thesis. It was not just a question of Law, but a narrative about a stage of economic and historical development. The theory of stages of history began to be developed in José de Acosta's *Historia de las Américas* at the end of the sixteenth century, and the distinctions made by Acosta regarding societal levels were used by promoters of the English colonies in the early seventeenth century.[12]

The English also used the language of conquest, but they were the ones who fully seized the opportunity to present themselves in North America as occupying lands that had previously been without ownership. Applying the idea of occupation created difficulties for the English colonisers when they began to establish permanent plantations in America in the early seventeenth century. They responded by changing their descriptions of the Native American peoples and using the concept of occupation to describe both a stage in history and a system of Law. Although, initially, the first settlers often commented on the civility of these people and observed signs of their exploitation of nature, they later argued that the native inhabitants resembled wild beasts. This was the only way they could claim that the land had not been occupied by anyone. John Locke incorporated this progressive theory of history into his understanding of property, noting that labour was what made the difference in the value of property.[13] What has been described as a Lockean or agricultural argument became a powerful justification for colonisation in America during the eighteenth century. "By invoking a fictive "universal tacit consent of mankind" as the origin of money, Locke bridges the gap between his liberal theory of private property and the illiberality of extralegal colonial expansion in the

[11] O.U. Ince, *Colonial Capitalism and the Dilemmas of Liberalism*, Oxford University Press, Oxford, 2018, p. 67.

[12] J. Acosta, *Historia Natural y Moral de las Indias*, Sevilla, Atlas, 1994, pp. 189–190.

[13] A. Greer, *Property and dispossession: Natives, empires and land in early modern North America*, Cambridge University Press, Cambridge, 2018; R. Míguez Núñez, *Terra di scontri. Alterazioni e rivendicazioni del diritto alla terra nelle Ande* centrali, Giuffrè, Milano, 2013; A Guevara Gil, *La propiedad agraria en el derecho colonial*, in *Estudios sobre la propiedad,* ed. G. Priori Posada, Fondo Editorial de la Pontificia Universidad Católica del Perú, Lima, 2012, 265.

New World".[14] Some authors who have explored the relationship between property and sovereignty focus on John Locke's "Second Treatise on Civil Government", which treats property as a natural right.[15] The English thinker argues that the work of his body, the products of his hands, we could say, truly belong to him. "This understanding of colonisation, which placed so much emphasis upon land and labour, was a 'peculiarity of the English'".[16]

It was, however, the seventeenth-century Natural Law theorists, particularly Hugo Grotius, Thomas Hobbes, Samuel Pufendorf and John Locke, who made use of the concept of the state of nature to distinguish levels of historical progress. In the process, they refined many of the assumptions that had been employed by the colonial promoters at the beginning of the century. Grotius and Hobbes were trained in the Renaissance Humanist tradition, but they sought to develop a theory of natural rights that avoided (or, for Grotius, extended) the medieval assumptions of sociability, which, during the religious wars, no longer provided a persuasive explanation of human action. Northern Europe thinkers embraced the late Humanist concern for self-preservation, which was more in tune with the violence of the time, and presented it as the foundation of rights, distancing themselves from the Thomistic thought of the School of Salamanca.[17] These seventeenth-century philosophers and historians argued that property was first created in nature through occupation. They argued that the origin of property did not lie in nature itself but in mutual agreements. According to this theory, property came into being because groups of people, seeking self-preservation, agreed upon rules that would define its nature. Therefore, property was created by the consent of a group of people.[18] To protect that property and their lives, these peoples climbed another rung in history by creating civil societies. Civil society created its own rules governing property, but, again with the exception of Hobbes, these authors agreed that one of the rules that all civil societies adopted was occupation: civil society recognised the

[14] O.U. Ince, *Colonial Capitalism and the Dilemmas of Liberalism*, cit., p. 98.

[15] Idem.

[16] C. Tomlins, *Freedom bound: law, labor and civic identity in colonizing English America, 1580–1865*, Cambridge University Press, Cambridge, 2010, p. 133.

[17] Cf. O.U. Ince, *Colonial Capitalism and the Dilemmas of Liberalism*, cit.; R. Nichols, *Theft Is Property! Dispossession and Critical Theory*, Duke University Press, 2020.

[18] A. Fitzmaurice, *Sovereignty, Property and Empire, 1500–2000*, Cambridge University Press, Cambridge, 2014.

importance of occupation for survival. For Locke, in contrast, occupation and property preceded the agreements that, according to Grotius and Pufendorf, led to civil society. Many historians have portrayed Locke's understanding of property and labour as the dominant justification for colonisation in the United States, as well as the basis for the ideology that fuelled the American Revolution.[19] "As much land as a man tills, plants, improves, cultivates, and can use the product of, so much is his property. Whatever is beyond this, is more than his share, and belongs to others."[20]

Indeed, Fitzmaurice argues that up until the period of the Salamanca School, the occupation of territories was framed within a discourse of rights, which defined the boundaries of individual or communal claims over the Church (as charity) and the State (as rights). For example, as for Pufendorf, it can be said that "the origin of property was part of an account of ethical voluntarism and he placed this human power to shape the world, and the ability to create property within, an account of history."[21] Pufendorf also viewed property as an institution derived from Natural Law and consent, but he insisted more on the concept of sovereignty as a guarantor of social order. For him, sovereignty had the role of structuring access to property, ensuring peace and stability.

3.3 The *Écart* Between the Theories of Pufendorf and De Vattel Regarding *Jus Gentium*

From the late eighteenth century onwards, the universalist spirit of the founders of the School of Natural Law was replaced by the understanding of *jus gentium* as a Law of European nations, that is, as a result of the constant development of positivism and the growing awareness of a European identity and power during that period of rapid expansion.[22]

Pufendorf rejected the arguments that Francisco de Vitoria had put forward, as we saw, when he stated that the Indigenous peoples could not prevent the Spanish from travelling and trading peacefully on their lands. In Pufendorf's view, these arguments of De Vitoria were in fact designed

[19] Cf. M. Mazzucato, *The Value of Everything: Making and Taking in the Global Economy*, Allen Lane, London, 2018.

[20] J. Locke, *Second Treatise of Government*, cit., Chapter 5: "Of Property", p. 219.

[21] A. Fitzmaurice, *Sovereignty, Property and Empire, 1500–2000*, Cambridge University Press, Cambridge, 2014, p. 121.

[22] B. Arneil, *John Locke and America: The Defence of English Colonialism*, cit., p. 34.

"to justify their compatriots in their struggle against the Indians."[23] Pufendorf defended the right of each people to decide for themselves, on the basis of their own customs, the *nomoi* of Herodotus, without granting access to arriving foreigners. In presenting this argument, he seems to reject the justifications of Western civilisation. Indeed, Pufendorf cites a passage in which Montaigne, in his Essays, recounts the responses given by the Indigenous people to the Spanish in defence of their lands and religious traditions against the claims of the King of Castile, supported by the Pope. At the same time, Pufendorf acknowledges that the rights of peoples take precedence over the rights that the West claims through conquest. All this emerges clearly when Pufendorf unreservedly rejects what Francisco Bacon in his "Advancement of Learning"[24] offers as "sufficient reason for making War upon the Americans,[25] which is mainly summed up in that "they were to be look'd upon as People proscribed by the Law of Nature, inasmuch as they had a barbarous Custom of sacrificing Men, and feeding upon Man's Flesh".[26] Once again, we return to the episode of Herodotus' *nomos basileus*, or the guardianship of the Indigenous people set forth by De Las Casas, naturally in different contexts.

Samuel Pufendorf denied the existence of a separate Law of Nations as a body of positive legislation agreed upon by all nations. Following Thomas Hobbes, he argued that the norms prevailing between sovereign States were nothing more than the application of the Law of Nature to inter-State relations. However, the *Écart* with Hobbes is evident on the point concerning the principles of sociability. The different methods of Hobbes and Pufendorf for deriving Natural Law are linked to their differing understanding of the nature that this law assumes outside of civil society. In his political theory, Hobbes had maintained that the most

[23] S. Pufendorf, *Of the Law of Nature and Nations: Eight Books*, trans. Basil Kennett, 4th ed., printed for J. Walthoe, R. Wilkin, J. and J. Bonwicke, S. Birt, T. Ward, and T. Osborne, London 1729, lib. III, chap. III, § 9, p. 247 "*titulis, ex quibus Hispani Indos debellare potuerint*".

[24] S. Pufendorf, *Of the Law of Nature and Nations*, cit., bk. VIII, chap. VI, § V, p. 837. Pufendorf refers to Francis Bacon's *De Dignitate & Augmentis Scientiarum* Libri IX, London, 1613.

[25] See F. Bacon, *De Dignitate & Augmentis Scientiarum Libri IX*, in *The Works of Francis Bacon*, in four volumes, vol. 1, A. Millar, London 1740.

[26] S. Pufendorf, *Of the Law of Nature and Nations*, bk. VIII, chap. VI, § V, p. 837. In Latin: "[...] *quod ad bellum Americanis inferendum putat sufficere, quod isti possint intelligi velut per ipsum ius naturae proscripti, ideo quia apud illos sit consuetudo sacrificandi homines, & humanas carnes manducandi.*"

fundamental requirement for preserving one's life was peace, and he had identified several laws of nature that human beings must observe to maintain peace. For Pufendorf, the crucial question lay, rather, in the moral relationship that prevails between them. Hobbes had written that when human beings "are not subject to each other or to any common ruler", they are "enemies [*hostes*] of each other."[27] Pufendorf views this situation through the lens of the moral relations between States. In the chapter on the laws of war, he explains that when someone is my enemy, this means that morally I am permitted to "use force against them to any degree, or to the extent that I deem necessary."[28] In the case of an enemy, one always has the right to carry out a pre-emptive attack. Pufendorf argues significantly and firmly that, although war is, due to human nature, an inescapable element of the human condition, it should always be seen as an aberration of the natural human condition, which is peace. In stating this, he directly connects the situation to the moral duty of defending peace as far as possible. Peace is the state "the creation and preservation of which constitutes one of the principal reasons why the law of nature has been deposited in the hearts of men."[29] The reciprocal duty to cultivate peaceful sociability prevails not only in civil society, but also in the state of nature, imposing a duty to refrain from harming those who cause no harm. This is perhaps a prelude to relational identity.

Pufendorf emphatically states that "all men enjoy a natural freedom to the same extent and degree"[30] and if they consent to a lesser freedom, such consent must be true, whether express or tacit or subject to interpretation. "His argument against Vitoria's and Grotius's justifications for colonialism relied on the idea that Europeans and the inhabitants of colonialized countries share reciprocal duties and rights."[31] Hence Pufendorf's unequivocal rejection of Plato's and then Aristotle's thesis that it was law for the Greeks to rule the barbarians, since "if we were to intend to destroy any nation that differs from us in customs and manners, it would only be to brand them with the reprehensible name of barbarians, and then invade

[27] T. Hobbes, *De cive*, cit., chap. xiv, § 19.

[28] S. Pufendorf, *Of the Law of Nature and Nations*, lib. VIII, chap. VI, § 5, p. 880: "in infinitum, *aut quantum mihi videatur*".

[29] S. Pufendorf, *Of the Law of Nature and Nations*, lib. VIII, chap. VI, § 5, p. 843.

[30] S. Pufendorf, *Of the Law of Nature and Nations*, lib. VIII, chap. VI, § 5, p. 883.

[31] K. Saastamoinen, *Pufendorf on the Law of Sociality and the Law of Nations*, in *The Law of Nations and Natural Law 1625–1800*, S. Zurbuchen (ed.), Oxford University Press, Oxford, 2024, cit., p. 128.

them without further colour or excus*e*".[32] When the Europeans failed to recognise these rights, they violated what Pufendorf described as the most universal and necessary of all duties of natural law: the duty not to harm other human beings. This allowed Pufendorf to argue that humanity was a moral *communitas*, whose members had duties to one another simply because of their shared humanity. "When sovereigns violated these precepts, they did not merely jeopardize the long- term security and welfare of their country. They also did something morally wrong to their fellow human beings".[33]

Unlike Pufendorf, De Vattel declares that it is his intention to write for the sovereigns of the States: "*Si les Conducteurs des Peuples, si tous ceux qui sont employés dans les affaires publiques daignoient faire* ***une étude sérieuse d'une Science,*** *qui devroit être leur Loi & leur boussole, quels fruits ne pourroit-on pas attendre d'un bon* ***Traité du Droit des Gens****?*"[34] [emphasis added]. The task he assigns to his work is to develop scientific criteria for interpreting the relations between States through *jus gentium* and to offer guidance to those who have the responsibility to govern peoples. The key actors in De Vattel's system are sovereign States.[35] In the preface to his "Right of Nations" he argues that by nation he is referring to the sovereign state (*état souverain*), or any politically independent entity. This independence of any supra-state legal order is a matter that De Vattel clearly underlines.[36] The system envisioned by De Vattel thus rests on the complex network of diplomatic relations and interests formed between

[32] S. Pufendorf, *Of the Law of Nature and Nations*, bk. III, chap. II, § VIII, p. 232; emphasis in the original. In Latin: "*Hoc modo in proclivi esset, omnes populos a moribus nostris dissidentes barbarorum convitio notare, & ex solo isthoc praetexto eosdem invadere*"; S. Pufendorf, *De iure naturae et gentium*, cit., lib. III, chap. II, § 8, p. 233.

[33] K. Saastamoinen, *Pufendorf on the Law of Sociality and the Law of Nations*, in *The Law of Nations and Natural Law 1625–1800*, S. Zurbuchen (ed.), cit., p. 129.

[34] E. De Vattel, *Le Droit des Gens, ou Principes de la Loi Naturelle, appliqués à la Conduite et aux Affaires des Nations et des Souverains*, vol. 1, Carnegie Institution of Washington, Washington, D.C., 1916; orig. pub. 1758, *Préface*, p. XXIII.

[35] E. Fiocchi Malaspina, *L'eterno ritorno del Droit des gens di Emer de Vattel (secc. XVIII–XIX) L'impatto sulla cultura giuridica in prospettiva globale*, Max Planck Institute for European Legal History, Frankfurt am Main, 2017, p. 4: "*Diritto costituzionale, diritto interno e internazionale sono tenuti insieme dall'esigenza di scrivere per « la pratica », esclusivamente per i sovrani e per coloro che, come diplomatici e pratici, si trovavano quotidianamente ad affrontare questioni legate al diritto delle genti*".

[36] Cf. M. Koskenniemi, *The Philosophy of International Law*, Oxford University Press, Oxford, 1996, esp. *Vattel: Natural Law and the Law of Nations*, 2010.

sovereign states, referring to any nation that governs itself, in whatever form it may take, without depending on any foreign power.[37] The so-called Westphalian system takes its first steps through an idealised interpretation of the European legal framework, as proposed by Emer de Vattel in the mid-seventeenth century, an interpretation that did not accurately reflect the positive European Law of Nations. This model was presented as a *prius* to all other legal systems. It is a clearly inter-State and static approach. "The development of International Law thus needs to be studied against the background of the complex and shifting legal order within and among the European states, including conflicts connected to imperial expansion".[38]

Indeed, after the description of the world of Western states come the hunters and gatherers, who are peaceful, but whose social organisation could only have made sense in "the first ages of the world, when the earth, without cultivation, produced more than was sufficient to feed its small number of inhabitants. But at present, when the human race, is so greatly multiplied, it could not subsist if all nations were disposed to live in that manner".[39] This is where the presumed superiority of European nations over the "savages" of the primitive world clearly emerges.[40]

Through this lens, De Vattel contrasts "the conquest of the civilised empires of Peru and Mexico" with "the establishment of many colonies on the continent of North America", concluding that while the former was a "notorious usurpation" ("*une usurpation criante*"), the latter was "extremely legitimate" ("*très légitime*"), as the first settlers set out for the new lands "confining themselves within just limits".[41]

The main question after the Peace of Westphalia was how to ensure peaceful coexistence among European states through diplomacy, alliances, arbitration, guarantees and (the threat of) intervention, the latter often linked to the idea of the balance of power. Such legal and political arrangements were theorised within the framework of the Law of Nature and of Nations, although never from a single and unified perspective, as we have seen. On the contrary, the doctrines of the Law of Nations were forged

[37] E. De Vattel, *Le Droit des Gens*, cit., bk. III, chap. III, § 47, p. 496.

[38] S. Zurbuchen, *Introduction*, in *The Law of Nations and Natural Law 1625–1800*, S. Zurbuchen (ed.), Brill, Leiden, 2019, p. 2.

[39] E. De Vattel, *Le Droit des Gens*, cit., bk. I, chap. VII, § 81, p. 129.

[40] Cf. G. Gozzi, *Rights and Civilizations: A History and Philosophy of International Law*, cit., pp. 69–70.

[41] E. De Vattel, *Le Droit des Gens*, cit., bk. I, chap. VII, § 81, p. 121.

and developed in various contexts, where issues of State power and interest were intermingled with attempts to conform to the rules of justice of Natural Law. This *écart* became even more evident during the Napoleonic Wars. These latent identity tensions also permeate Kant's philosophy.

3.4 Kant's Rationalist *Cosmopolis*

Kant's rationalist *cosmopolis* stands in stark contrast to the colonial mindset, as it deviates from the *jus gentium* predicted by De Vattel. On the contrary, Kant regarded Grotius, Pufendorf and De Vattel in harsh terms as "tiresome comforters" (*leidige Tröster*), in the sense that, ultimately, they sought to provide a legal justification for waging wars and, we should add, especially with Grotius and De Vattel, for carrying out the colonial project of the West.[42]

For Kant, public law can be understood with the function of punishing violations of Natural Private Law.[43] Public Law provides the conditions under which to 'implement' the laws of reason that govern the natural condition. In this way, Kant grounds the transition from the "state of nature" to the "legal state" (*der rechtliche Zustand*). This represents the form of civil society within the *Rechtsstaat* (based on the Rule of Law), and although it is not explicitly stated, it is clearly recognisable. "Kant's radical criticism of the Western tradition in the law of peoples goes hand in hand with his criticism of Western colonialism".[44]

It is the violent denial of that right, along with the refusal to fulfil the corresponding duty, that most accurately describes the behaviour of Western nations in their dealings with other peoples and nations of the world. The explanation for this lies in the ethnocentric judgement of non-Western nations as different and inferior, leading to the conclusion that the conquest of such nations is, therefore, legitimate.[45]

[42] I. Kant, *Die Metaphysik der Sitten*, in Wilhelm Weischedel (ed.), *Werke Suhrkamp*, Frankfurt am Main, 1993; orig. pub. 1797, vol. VIII, p. 123.

[43] Cf. R. Tuck, *The Rights of War and Peace. Political Thought and the International Order from Grotius to Kant*, Oxford University Press, New York, 1999.

[44] G. Gozzi, *Rights and Civilizations: A History and Philosophy of International Law*, cit., p. 91.

[45] I. Kant, *Die Metaphysik der Sitten*, in Wilhelm Weischedel (ed.), Werke Suhrkamp, Frankfurt am Main, 1993; orig. pub. 1797, vol. VIII, p. 350. Cf. B. Stråth and P. Wagner (eds.), *European Modernity: A Global Approach*, Cambridge University Press, 2017.

Kant's critiques entails, firstly, exposing the underlying premise behind the unsustainable legitimisation of the conquest of the West undertaken by civilised States (*gesitteten Staaten*): "America, the black countries, the Spice Islands, the Cape, etc., when discovered, were regarded as lands that belonged to no one; because the native inhabitants were regarded as nothing [*die Einwohner rechneten sie für nichts*]".[46] Secondly, Kant demonstrates how the devaluation of the Other translates into a logic of conquest carried out in the name of civilisation.[47] After outlining an idea of how peaceful relations should be under a "cosmopolitan constitution", Kant asks that we consider, by comparison, "the inhospitable behaviour of civilised nations, especially the **commercial** states of our continent" [emphasis added].[48] The injustice they display when visiting foreign lands and races—which, in their eyes, is equivalent to conquest (*Erobern*)—is so profound that it fills us with horror (*Erschrecken*).[49]

Finally, Kant dismisses the idea that violence against foreign nations may be justified on the basis that it has acted "for the benefit of the world, in part because these rudimentary peoples will be civilised" ("*durch Kultur roher Völker*").[50] In fact, he writes, "all these supposed good intentions cannot wash the stain of injustice on the means used for them."[51]

But there is more. In describing these differences, Kant unexpectedly resorts to stereotypes and taxonomic prejudices: the ethnocentric comparative background emerges.

He begins by stating that "there are four races on Earth".[52] Then, following the same generalising classificatory line, he proceeds to outline their characteristics. Firstly, we have the American people, who "do not acquire culture" ("*nimmit keine Bildungen*") and "have no incentives" ("*keine Triebfedern*"), because affection and passion are absent in them.

[46] I. Kant, *Zum ewigen Frieden: Ein philosophischer Entwurf von Immanuel Kant*, in Wilhelm Weischedel (ed.), Werke Suhrkamp, Frankfurt am Main, 1993, 1795, vol. XI, p. 214.

[47] Cf. S. Muthu, *Enlightenment against Empire*, Princeton University Press, Princeton, 2003, p. 23.

[48] I. Kant, *Zum ewigen Frieden: Ein philosophischer Entwurf von Immanuel Kant*, cit., p. 240.

[49] I. Kant, *Zum ewigen Frieden: Ein philosophischer Entwurf von Immanuel Kant*, cit., p. 400.

[50] I. Kant, *Zum ewigen Frieden: Ein philosophischer Entwurf von Immanuel Kant*, p. 477.

[51] Ibid.

[52] I. Kant, *Immanuel Kants Menschenkunde oder philosophische Anthropologie: Nach handschriftlichen Vorlesungen*, ed. Friedrich Christian Starke, Leipzig, 1831. 353.

[...] They hardly speak [...] and, moreover, they do not care about anything, are lazy, and paint their faces in an ugly way. Next we have the "black race", which is the exact opposite of the American. They are full of affection and passion, very lively, talkative and vain. They acquire culture, but only a culture of slaves ("*Knechte*"); that is, they allow themselves to be manipulated. They have many incentives, they are also sensitive [...], and they also do many things for honour. In the third group are the Hindus: "It is true that the Hindus have incentives, but they possess a high degree of composure (*Gelassenheit*), and all seem like philosophers. Nevertheless, they are "very inclined towards anger and love." As a result, they acquire culture to the highest degree, but only in the arts, not in the sciences. This entire description provides the backdrop to situate the "white race", which, by contrast, "contains all the incentives and talents within itself". This so-called white race is further divided into two components: one Western and the other Eastern. In the latter, Kant includes the Turks and the Kalmyks.[53] Thus, the whole discussion is framed from the perspective of the white race's capacity for innovation and progress, and to prove this capacity, Kant places history in service, offering a special interpretation of it.[54] As Wynter argues,[55] the main issue, linked to the Comparative Law theme, lies in the fact that any theory analysed starts from our methodological incipit: there is a conceptual *prius*, and it is the Western subject. The Western identity and the European State itself is nourished by this dynamic of difference, in contrast to previous identities such as Christian. This new definition was consolidated through the exclusion and subjugation of those considered Other, such as Indigenous and African peoples[56].

This secular reinvention of human identity by Renaissance Humanists was carried out on the basis of what Aníbal Quijano identified as the

[53] Cf. E. Chukwudi Eze, *Race and the Enlightenment*, Wiley-Blackwell, London, 1997.

[54] Cf. R. Bernasconi, *Kant as an Unfamiliar Source of Racism*, in J. K. Ward, T. L. Lott (eds.), *Philosophers on Race: Critical Essays*, Blackwell Publishers, Oxford, 2002, pp. 145–166.

[55] S. Wynter, *Unsettling the Coloniality of Being/Power/Truth/Freedom*, in *CR: The New Centennial Review* 3, 2003, pp. 257–337, which speaks of an equation at the basis of all philosophical reasoning: "*one genre, one mode of being*".

[56] S. Wynter, *Unsettling the Coloniality of Being/Power/Truth/Freedom*, cit., p. 262: "*One of the major empirical effects of which would be 'the rise of Europe' and its construction of the 'world civilization' on the one hand, and, on the other, African enslavement, Latin American conquest, and Asian subjugation.*"

"*colonialidad del poder*"[57] and what Walter Mignolo referred to as the "colonial difference".[58] In order for the secular world to abandon its subordination to the Church and its evangelising mission, this new definition of what it means to be human was enabled. However, its practical implementation as the first secular form of being human in history occurred through the creation of a distinction between human and subhuman, as well as between human and nature. The Law of this new Human became the non-supernatural foundation for distinguishing between human groups, replacing earlier distinctions such as mortal/immortal or human/ancestors. The laws of Indigenous peoples in the Americas and enslaved Africans were transformed into the conceptual referents for this 'Other Human', irrational or subrational. Costa recalls the passage from Kant in the *Physische Geographie* of 1802 as a prime example of the paradoxes of the time and Kant's own reflection on human rights.[59]

Viveiros de Castro emphasises the different anthropological vision of the Encounter: "*Nas Antilhas, alguns anos após o descobrimento das Américas, enquanto os espanhóis despachavam comissões de inquérito para saber se os indígenas possuíam alma ou não, estes tratavam de submergir prisioneiros brancos, para verificar, com base numa longa e cuidadosa observação, se os seus cadáveres apodreciam ou não*".[60]

The richness of the anecdote lies precisely in perceiving that, while both Europeans and Indigenous people doubt the humanity of the other, the quality of this doubt is different. For the Spanish, it was important to know whether Indigenous people had souls, as their cosmology was guided by metaphysical and religious assumptions. The Indigenous people, on the other hand, sought to resolve their doubt through physical experience, in order to determine whether those beings presented to them as spirits, those souls, had bodies, were mortal, appearing, in this case, more rational and "scientific" than the Spanish.[61] This story shows both

[57] A. Quijano, *Colonialidad del poder, eurocentrismo y América Latina*, in *Cuestiones y horizontes: de la dependencia histórico-estructural a la colonialidad/descolonialidad del poder*, CLACSO, Buenos Aires, 2014, pp. 777–832.

[58] W. Mignolo, *Local Histories/Global Designs: Coloniality, Subaltern Knowledges and Border Thinking*, Princeton University Press, Princeton, 2000.

[59] S. Costa, *Dois Atlânticos*, Belo Horizonte, Editora UFMG, 2006, p. 41.

[60] E. Viveiros de Costa, *Metafísicas Canibais. Elementos para uma antropologia pós-estrutural*, Cosac Naify, São Paulo, 2015, p. 45.

[61] Cf. *International Law in Early Modern Europe*, R. Lesaffer (ed.), Cambridge University Press, Cambridge, 2025.

the ethnocentric quality of these different perspectives and their symmetry.[62] The Spanish and the Indigenous people were both ethnocentric, much like the Asians and Greeks in Herodotus, but not equally ethnocentric; rather, they were symmetrically ethnocentric. If European ethnocentrism "consisted of doubting that the bodies of others contained a soul formally similar to the one inhabiting their own bodies", Amerindian ethnocentrism, on the other hand, "consisted of doubting that other souls or spirits were endowed with a body substantially similar to Indigenous bodies."[63]

As De Las Casas has taught us, it would be an inconceivable practice outside the singularity of Indigenous perspectivism. Here, then, is Viveiros' vision according to which Indigenous thought should not find a fit in the Western binary perspective of rational versus irrational.[64]

The *écarts* that run through the works of pre-scientific thinkers testify to this gradual shift towards extreme positions, which would be exacerbated in the nineteenth century.[65] Though with all the nuances we have pointed out, this Humanist perspective, while secularising, legitimised the occupation of territories and the subjugation of non-European populations by defining them as inherently inferior to the European human paradigm, ostensibly rational and superior. The comparative legal classification of Indigenous Americans as irrational savages and Africans as sub-rational beings became a constitutive part of this new international order with positivist overtones. The abyssal line deepened in the nineteenth century through the emerging sciences of Comparative Law and International Law would replace previous theological and rational distinctions, in order to maintain, through the sciences of facts, the hierarchy between peoples. Thus, the consolidation of the new definition of Man as the universal

[62] Cf. J. Neuenschwander Magalhães, *La costruzione giuridica della diversità. Per un dialogo tra antropologia e diritto a partire dal prospettivismo multinaturalista*, in M. Meccarelli (ed.), *Diversità e discorso giuridico*, Universidad Carlos III, Madrid, 2016.

[63] E. Viveiros de Costa, *Metafísicas* Canibais. idem, cit., p. 34.

[64] E. Viveiros de Costa, *Metafísicas Canibais. Elementos para uma antropologia pós-estrutural*, cit., p. 69.

[65] R. De Giorgi, *Temi di filosofia del diritto*, Lecce, Pensa Multimedia, 2006, pp. 137–138, on the idea of equality: "*Il principio allora non esclude affatto la disuguaglianza di trattamento, ma la rende possibile condizionandola. Il diritto riassume al suo interno la relazionalità dell'uguaglianza: posizioni giuridiche sono uguali o disuguali ad un tertium comparationis*".

representation of the human was intrinsically dependent on the creation and maintenance of categories of racialised and subjugated Others, whose negative characteristics served to define, by contrast, the superiority of the Western model.[66]

[66] Cf. D. Bonilla Maldonado, *Los bárbaros jurídicos: Identidad, derecho comparado moderno y el Sur global*, Siglo del Hombre Editores, Bogotá, 2020.

CHAPTER 4

The Second Encounter with the Other: The Law of Separation

Abstract In the second encounter with the Other, the analysis shifts to the nineteenth century, specifically within the context of the Congress of Berlin. The theoretical frameworks previously discussed now assume the scientific dimension of International Law and Comparative Law. Although traditionally examined as separate disciplines, both branches of Law share the characteristic of reinforcing an exclusionary European legal *communitas* and conceptualising Law as a tool for exclusion. The foundational sequence supporting Western identity is further highlighted: classification, separation and exclusion. Comparative Law systematically classifies legal systems in exclusionary terms, while International Law formalises these disparities by positioning the Western 'civilized' state at its core.

Keywords Epistemic community • International Law • Comparative Law • The International Congress of Paris in 1900

The theses of Natural Law and modern thinkers lead to an idea of exclusionary Western identity, rooted in Comparative Law classification and International Law separation. There exists a State *communitas* with a strong Hobbesian physiognomy, substantially grounded in fear of the Other, and an international *societas* built around the mercantile interests of

© The Author(s), under exclusive license to Springer Nature Switzerland AG 2026

A. Lazari, *Relational Identity in International, Comparative and European Union Law*,
https://doi.org/10.1007/978-3-031-59482-3_4

European States.[1] All of this has led to the exclusion of the Other's Law and epistemicide through the appropriation of foreign lands, with the consequent imposition of the idea of Western private property.[2]

4.1 The Exclusionary Identity of the European State in the Nineteenth Century

As Polanyi recalls, "what we call land is an element of nature inextricably interwoven with man's institutions. To isolate it and form a market for it was perhaps the weirdest of all the undertakings of our ancestors".[3] Whereas this process lasted centuries on the European continent, colonial powers were able to impose it much more quickly in colonised territories and the areas of the world under their control.[4]

Between approximately 1500 and 1800,[5] in the context of an emerging Law governing the relationships between European states, it would appear that the norms (or more properly, jurisdictions) that governed the encounters between Europeans and non-Europeans were quite varied.[6]

An exclusionary structure is evident in the nineteenth century, at the height of imperial expansion and the period when positivism became established as the most important scientific theory in Law. Unlike naturalism, which holds that all States are subject to a universal higher Law, positivism, in general, asserts that the State is the exclusive creator of Law and cannot be obliged to comply with any norm unless it has explicitly

[1] A. Cassese stated: "[o]n the purely normative level, the international community has moved from the mere existence or mere coexistence of subjects to communal living in a true and genuine sociality. At the level of reality, however, it is still paralyzed in the juxtaposition of entities, sometimes cooperating and sometimes in conflict" (A. Cassese, I diritti umani nel mondo contemporaneo (italic), Laterza, Roma-Bari, 1988.).

[2] M. Graziadei, *On Universalizing 'Nature' and 'Property': the Unravelling of a Master Narrative*, in *Journal of Interdisciplinary History of Ideas*, 2023, p. 29: "*Indeed, in the intellectual history of the West the very notion of property has been associated with the notion of civilisation and the association of these two ideas is still evident in certain contexts*".

[3] K. Polanyi, *The Great Transformation*, Beacon Press, Boston 2001, p. 187.

[4] Cf. L. Benton and L. Ford, *Rage for Order: The British Empire and the Origins of International Law, 1800–1850*, Harvard University Press, Cambridge, MA, 2016.

[5] Cf. M. Graziadei, *On Universalizing 'Nature' and 'Property': the Unravelling of a Master Narrative*, in *Journal of Interdisciplinary History of Ideas*, 2023, pp. 1–26.

[6] A. Jackson and A. Jaffer, *Encounters: The Meeting of Asia and Europe 1500–1800*, Victoria & Albert Museum, London, 2004.

consented to it. This theoretical approach to legal unity impacts the very idea of identity itself.

"Unity relates to identity. Unity confers on an instance of law an identity, and how unity is depicted determines how identity is conceived".[7] If unity is understood as phenomenal unity, created by formal criteria of organisation, identity is understood as formal identity. For legal positivism, unity is the formal unity of phenomenal law. Such unity can only produce a formal identity: identity as selfhood, as Ricouer would say.[8] Legal positivism ignores substantive unity, intertwined in juridical-cultural layers. As a consequence, it also ignores substantive identity, or identity understood as selfhood. The connection between unity and identity highlights the management of diversity and the implicit presence of plurality. As we have seen, identity implies non-identity; the existence of the non-identical, of the Other.

Positivist jurists created a series of formal doctrines that used explicitly racial and cultural criteria to claim that there were some civilised, and thus sovereign, States and other uncivilised, non-sovereign States. Consequently, non-European societies were driven out of the scope of International Law. Lacking legal personality, these societies were unable to develop any legally acceptable objections to oppose their dispossession, and were then reduced to being the object of conquest and exploitation.[9] The line of separation between European Law and other laws, which existed in earlier thinkers, became increasingly profound, eventually becoming abyssal.

From the Eurocentric perspective, those we now consider Asians, for example, were seen as pagans and infidels, but this circumstance did not influence the European perception of all aspects of Asian culture. "Likewise in Asia, Europeans were often seen as inferior and as barbarians, but this did not necessarily detract from an interest in European technology",[10] and when Europeans went to centres of domination, such as the courts of the Mughals, the Ming and Qing (China) or Japan Tokugawa, the encounter took place in Asian terms, and observed the laws of diplomacy and encounter (the jurisdictional forms) that operated in those spaces.

[7] K. Tuori, *The Properties of Law. Modern Law and After*, Cambridge University Press, Cambridge, 2021, p. 206.

[8] P. Ricœur, *Soi-même comme un autre*, Seuil, Paris, 1990.

[9] Cf. E. Jouannet, *The Liberal-Welfarist Law of Nations: A History of International Law*, Cambridge University Press, Cambridge, 2012.

[10] S. Pahuja, *Laws of encounter: a jurisdiction account of International Law*, in *London Review of International Law*, Volume 1, Issue 1, 2013, p. 74.

However, during the nineteenth century, and at the same time as the rise of European imperial power, European International Law began to displace more strongly these other laws of encounter, as well as many others, including in particular the rules of encounter observed by Indigenous peoples in many places. Attention has been drawn to "*la coincidencia de las políticas expansivas de los reinos cristianos, dispuestos a llevar su competencia militar y económica, a cualesquiera espacios ultramarinos, con la decisión del Imperio Chino (1436) de prohibir la construcción de naves para la navegación oceánica, por considerar que solo desde tierra podía ser amenazado*".[11]

For a variety of historical reasons, the legal model used in the West since the eighteenth century was truly partial and did not capture the full legal spectrum concerning the rest of the known world. Therefore, the spread of this legal model across the world from the nineteenth century onwards is of the utmost importance, as it was destined to disrupt other ways of organising societies.[12]

"Closure of the sources of public International Law facilitated not only the construction of states (they became the primary source of the law of their own relations) but the exclusion from the international realm of non-state or 'uncivilized' peoples."[13] This juridical and conceptual apparatus has gradually created States isolated from one another, communicating through minimal legal channels, such as the customary principle of State immunity, and zealously maintaining this compartmentalisation through the principle of recognition of other legal subjects.[14] Such a separative and exclusionary trait of Comparative Law and International Law was

[11] A. Remiro Brotóns, R. Riquelme Cortado, E. Orihuela Catalayud. J. Diez-Hochleitner, L. Pérez-Prat Durbán, *Derecho Internacional. Curso General*, Tirant Lo Blanch, Valencia, 2010, p. 46.

[12] Cf. M. Graziadei, *El trasplante de normas jurídicas: una perspectiva crítica*, in J. Cañabate Perez y M. Hernandez Valles (eds.), *Derecho no oficial: experiencias jurídicas más allá del Imperio de la Ley del Estado*, Dickinson Madrid, 2025; B. Dupret and G. Parolin, *The great divide in legal discourse: towards a global historical ontology of the concept of positive law*, in B. Dupret and J.L. Halperin (eds.), *State law and legal positivism*, The Netherlands: Brill | Nijhoff, Leiden 2021.

[13] H. P. Glenn, *The Cosmopolitan State*, Oxford University Press, Oxford, 2013, p. 239. In another essay, Glenn talks about the logic of separation. Cf. H.P. Glenn, *Com-paring*, in *Comparative Law. A Handbook*, edited by E. Örücü, D. Nelken, Hart Publishing, 2010, p. 93.

[14] Cf. *International Law in Early Modern Europe*, R. Lesaffer (ed.), Cambridge University Press, Cambridge, 2025.

intensified in the nineteenth century with the second encounter with the African Other, assuming a dangerously paroxysmal dimension.

In the late eighteenth century, Robert Ward stressed that "what is commonly called the Law of Peoples, is very far from universality; and that, therefore, the Law is not the Law of all nations, but only of particular classes of them; and therefore there may be a different Law of Nations for different parts of the globe."[15] So, up until the second half of the nineteenth century, there was a plurality of legal systems, and the European model "was only one of numerous historical types of regional units, which existed in variously structured ways around the world."[16] The Polish-British legal historian Alexandrowicz had put forward the view that relations between Europeans and Islamic communities and those of the East Indies up until the nineteenth century had been based on an extensive network of reciprocal treaties. It was not until the nineteenth century, with the rise of positivism, that Europeans began to impose their behavioural norms on others.[17]

The *jus publicum europæum* constituted a set of rules to regulate coexistence and maintain a balance of power between these sovereign entities (*principe d'équilibre*).[18] In this scenario, the prohibition of intervention began to be seen as a corollary of the sovereign equality of States and as a normative shield against the hegemonic ambitions of the great power of the time: the recognition that the government of each country is supreme within its territory implies that no external authority, whether universal or national in character, should interfere with the exercise of its governmental powers in internal affairs, as this would undermine the very basis of its sovereignty.[19] Therefore, intervention in the affairs of other States came to be considered inadmissible not because it was prohibited by a universal

[15] R. Ward, *An Enquiry into the Foundation and History of the Law of Nations in Europe, from the Time of the Greeks and Romans, to the Age of Grotius*, J. Butterworth, London 1795, vol. I, Preface, p. xiv.

[16] An Inquiry of the History of International Law from an Intercivilizational Perspective, in Journal of the History of International Law / Revue d'histoire du droit international, pp. 1–66.

[17] C. H. Alexandrowicz, *Constitutional Developments in India*, Oxford University Press, Bombay, 1957.

[18] M. Roscini, *International Law and the Principle of Non-Intervention: History, Theory, and Interactions with Other Principles*, Oxford University Press, Oxford, 2024, especially *The Development of the Principle of Non-Intervention from the End of the Religious Wars in Europe to the Outbreak of the Second World War*, pp. 9–97.

[19] R. Grote, *Westphalian System*, in *MPEPIL Online*, para 7.

rule, but because it invaded the sovereignty of the State. "In the course of the eighteenth and nineteenth centuries, private law discourse 'subjectivized' states, that is, it recreated the seventeenth-century sovereign subject, as prominently as the distinct yet converging subjectivization process that took place in public (international) law discourse. In this sense, private law complemented constitutional (and international) law in creating the modern liberal state."[20]

Schematically, this transition can be captured by the gradual replacement of De Vattel by Wheaton as the primary authority on matter. The latter said with certainty that "[t]he public law, with slight exceptions, has always been, and still is, limited to the civilized and Christian people of Europe or those of European origins."[21]

The fact that Wheaton's "Elements of International Law" were translated into Chinese in 1864 with great success meant that, gradually, advocates of radically different interpretations of International Law began to use the language of statehood, sovereignty and civilisation to advance their interests in the international arena.

Let us analyse some components of the progressive closure of European identity in the nineteenth century: the exclusionary consciousness of the European legal *communitas* and Law as the exclusionary vector of the exclusionary European *communitas*.

4.1.1 The Exclusionary Consciousness of European Legal Communitas

The fundamentally dualistic conception of International Law prevents its classical internationalist thought from being reduced to strict positivism. In fact, the Law of Nations has always been shaped by two categories in the authors analysed: Theoretical Law, motivated by religious or rationalist reasons, and Positive Law. Both express, albeit in different ways, the legal principles and values of the civilised European States. In the mid-nineteenth century, a paradoxical convergence of rationalist and Natural Law currents with the German Historical School occurred precisely at this

[20] L. Niglia, *The New Transformation of Europe: Arcana Imperii*, in *The American Journal of Comparative Law*, 2020, p. 155; Idem, *The Struggle for European Private Law: A Critique of Codification*, Hart Publishing, Oxford, 2015.

[21] H. Wheaton, *Elements of International Law*, A. C. Boyd ed., 3rd edn, Stevens and Sons Ltd, London, 1889, p. 17.

point. This convergence also bolsters these authors in their shared conviction of the evident necessity and scientific nature of their work in systematising the Law, and it can be explained by the fact that European internationalist thought has not, obviously, fully transformed into a historicism and relativism of complete values. This perspective is further solidified by the deeply optimistic historical view that unfolds regarding the capacities of humankind and peoples to rationalise and perfect themselves (and, therefore, to civilise). "*Ce aspect caractéristique d'une pensée internationaliste exclusiviste et discriminatoire, qui de façon typique va jouer comme un mécanisme d'exclusion de l'autre, s'ancre à une autre grande racine intellectuelle de la pensée européenne qui est l'humanisme juridique, mais tel que il sera profondément remanié et projeté, par anthropomorphisme, aux Etats*".[22]

The legal humanism referred to in Jouannet's quote is based on the aforementioned Cartesian *summa divisio*, according to which man, and not nature or God, is the subject and creator of the Law; hence, he can propose and give himself legal and ethical norms that will govern his existence, using human nature as both the foundation and the ultimate purpose of the Law. When the eighteen-century authors examined based the Law of Nations on the principles of reason, they envisioned a common nature for all, without explicitly offering a very clear opinion on the question of the so-called savage tribes, but at least affirming the original and principled universalism of their Natural Law. "*En revanche quand la nature _ où plutôt la conscience- civilisée va devenir le fondement du droit des gens rationnel, elle ne fait plus référence à cette simple raison commune, à cette* ***identité*** *minimale qui pouvait rassembler les hommes quels que soient leur race ou leur degré d'organisation*" [emphasis added].[23]

Certainly, as demonstrated by Dufour,[24] some representatives of the School of Natural Law had already incorporated history into the field of Natural Law, but it was only with the intellectual movement of Savigny, initiated in 1814, that this historical role was consolidated by internationalist thought in the formation and understanding of the Law of Nations. Indeed, the Historical School stands in contrast to the School of Natural

[22] E. Jouannet, *Colonialisme européen et néo-colonialisme contemporain*, in *Baltik Yearbook of International Law*, 2006, p. 70.

[23] E. Jouannet, *Colonialisme européen et néo-colonialisme contemporain*, in *Baltik Yearbook of International Law*, 2006, p. 70.

[24] A. Dufour, *Droits de l'homme, droit naturel et histoire*, PUF, París, 1991.

Law and Nations, which proposed a static version of *jus gentium* whose fundamental principles were deduced either from human nature alone or from the inherent nature of States. The Historical School, by contrast, introduced the idea of Law as the result of the dynamic and evolving history of peoples. This is a Law that is less a product of reason and more a product of national popular consciousness, a living law, intrinsic to each constituted community. Therefore, it becomes a Law of Nations that is particular to the community formed between civilised nations. "There clearly emerge here the defining traits of International Law in the second half of the nineteenth century: this law was the outgrowth of a common European consciousness formed against the background of a shared European culture".[25] It is clear now that "we can easily appreciate that the nineteenth-century internationalists were at one in proclaiming the superiority of European civilization and its International Law. For they were all in favour of colonial expansion and the domination exercised over noncivilized peoples, however much highlighting different concerns in the positions they stated."[26] It was, therefore, the idea of sovereignty that powerfully identified European International Law, serving as the basis upon which to define relations between Western States, while legitimising their domination over lands gained through colonial expansion. Koskenniemi significantly adds that "the founding conception of late nineteenth-century International Law was not only sovereignty but a collective (European) conscience – understood always as ambivalently either consciousness or conscience, that is, in alternatively rationalistic or ethical ways."[27]

Scientific reason and the emerging classificatory drive of the nineteenth century provided a model for governing the world during this period. International jurists welcomed the emerging science of Ethnology as a raw material they could use to develop normative systems. Lorimer regarded Ethnology, or the "science of races", as the most relevant discipline for International Law of his time, and pointed to Peter Camper, James

[25] G. Gozzi, *Rights and Civilizations: A History and Philosophy of International Law*, cit., p. 110.

[26] G. Gozzi, *Rights and Civilizations: A History and Philosophy of International Law*, cit., p. 115.

[27] M. Koskenniemi, *The Gentle Civilizer*, cit., p. 51. As Koskenniemi clarifies, it was understood that consciousness referred to the general principles of the doctrine, which were resolved in the thesis that Law is organic to society, while consciousness referred to the moral feelings (and prejudices) of European societies.

Prichard, and Johann Blumenbach as pioneers whose work would form the backbone of ethics and Comparative Law.[28] "Comparison and classification were essential methods to bring order to the amalgam of facts about different political communities and, therefore, to come up with legally binding prescriptions about their appropriate place within the 'family of nations."[29]

There are two specific consequences that stemmed from the commitment of Western States to the Otherness of the peoples they colonised. On the one hand, International Law, understood as an embodiment of the science of Western States, was limited to this inter-State system and, consequently, distinguished itself from other systems of Law. On the other hand, the proclaimed superiority of this European International Law, based on the concept of State sovereignty came with the recognition that non-civilised peoples needed to be treated 'humanely', and, therefore, natives were recognised as bearers of the Human Rights.

Thus, the idea of the Human Rights resurfaced throughout the nineteenth and early twentieth centuries, but only as a way to complement the primacy of State sovereignty, and almost as a way to legitimise that primacy. Thus, Pasquale Fiore affirmed that the "savage populations" had their own rights based on a principle of respect for the person.[30] The fact that these rights had been proclaimed meant that International Law – 'charged with studying the complex problem of colonial expansion'—should also address the need to establish the legal principles "*qui devrait régir la manière dont les états civilisés colonizateurs devraient se behaveà l'égard des races indigènes et barbares.*"[31] In summary, it was the role of International Law to identify the principles that would form the foundation for regulating relations between civilised peoples on the one hand (the *prius* discussed in the introductory paragraph), and Indigenous, African or Asian peoples (the "Other") on the other, with the aim of supporting and promoting their 'progress'. Ultimately, these considerations clearly defined the purpose of International Law, which was entrusted not only with establishing the rights of States in their mutual relations but also

[28] J. Lorimer, *The Institutes of the Law of Nations: A Treatise of the Jural Relations of Separate Political Communities*, William Blackwood and Sons, Edinburgh, 1883. pp. 93–94.

[29] N. Tzouvala, *Capitalism as civilisation: a history of International Law*, Cambridge University Press, Cambridge, 2020, p. 23.

[30] P. Fiore, *La science du droit international: Horizons nouveaux*, in *Révue Générale de Droit International Public*, 1909, p. 471.

[31] P. Fiore, *La science du droit international: Horizons nouveaux*, cit., p. 477.

with identifying and formulating legal norms to regulate the interactions of all entities (*êtres*), be they states, individuals or groups, within the international community.[32] Other thinkers emphasised the need to protect so-called uncivilised peoples from colonial powers. In this regard, Robert Adam argued that the morality of nations (*Völkermoral*) consists in "protecting inferior races (*die niedrigen Rassen*) from the violence of superior ones".[33] More specifically, in a study on German colonial Public Law, he argued that relations between civil and non-civil peoples are subject to the principles of Natural Law, that is, to a "set of principles emanating from ethical nature (*aus der sittlichen Natur*) and from man's reason."[34] Specifically, non-civilised peoples had to be recognised as possessing a property right over the lands they occupied.

It is particularly important to examine the relationship between Natural Law and positive International Law, as it is within this relationship that some authors have located the foundation for the claim to universality asserted by Western International Law. For example, it was on this basis that Bluntschli sought to define the relationship between Western civilisation and non-European peoples. This jurist made a distinction between civilised and uncivilised peoples, but he believed that International Law could be extended to all the peoples of the earth,[35] without them needing to abandon their own cultures. Certainly, International Law could be applied to all of humanity, but at the same time, it served as a criterion for distinguishing between civilised and uncivilised peoples, recognising the former within this law, while the latter remained outside of it.[36] However, although European Law was the product of the conscience and consciousness of the Christian nations of Europe, its scope was universal, and therefore non-Christian peoples could also be included within its sphere.

[32] Cf. M. Koskenniemi, *The Gentle Civilizer*, cit., p. 128.

[33] R. Adam, *Völkerrechtliche Okkupation und deutsches Kolonialstaatsrecht*, in *Archiv für Öffentliches Recht*, 1891, p. 234.

[34] Cf. M. Koskenniemi, *The Gentle Civilizer*, cit., p. 128.

[35] See B. Röben, *Johann Caspar Bluntschli, Francis Lieber und das moderne Völkerrecht 1861–1881*, Nomos, Baden-Baden, 2003, pp. 174–175.

[36] In an 1866 work, Bluntschli praised the fact that only in the great continents of Asia, and especially in Africa, where civilisation had not yet penetrated with force (*Macht*), resistance to foreign Law (*Fremdenrechtes*) still persisted, but he argued that this certainly would not last much longer. J.C. Bluntschli, *Die Bedeutung und die Fortschritte des modernen Völkerrechts*, in R. Virchow y F. von Holtzendorff (eds.), *Sammlung gemeinverständlicher wissenschaftlicher Vorträge*, Lüderitz'sche Verlagsbuchhandlung, Berlin, 1866, p. 36.

4.1.2 Law as an Exclusionary Vector of the European Exclusionary Communitas

"*La valorisation du droit est au cœur de cette problématique: le droit des gens civilisé, théorique et positif, rationnel et volontaire, est présenté comme un modèle dont les principes fondamentaux, sinon les règles du droit, doivent être transposables au reste du monde, car il est conçu comme une valeur particulièrement éminente et donc supérieure aux autres systèmes juridiques non européens.*"[37] Formally understood as a set of objective rules applicable to relations between States, International Law is considered a value. In fact, from this formal perspective, it represents a value of organisation, order and stability, which stands in opposition to barbarism, considered rebellious to any Law and any organised society. The distortion, sometimes real, of the degree of organisation between European states and non-European peoples, as well as the complete ignorance at that time of the true meaning of the customs and traditions existing among the tribes or colonised peoples (reduced to the status of barbarians or savages) reinforces this distinction between the Rule of Law and the Lawless State. By doing so, International Law is perceived not only as a symbol but also as a condition for the progress of humanity, simply by virtue of existing and governing a community. International Law is also a value in itself, defined by the fundamental principles that shape and establish it, while simultaneously representing a horizon towards which peoples must aspire. From this perspective, the duality of the Law of Nations (as upheld by these authors) between Theoretical Law and positive Practical Law, comes into play to show, through a Theoretical, Natural or Rational Law of Nations, what positive, contingent and relative Law of Nations should be. From a material standpoint, the Law of the civilised peoples of that time, as presented in various textbooks, is a Law aimed not only at organising the coexistence of State sovereignty but also at enforcing a particular conception of Law. Thus, we see the fundamental values of a legal humanism that is both liberal, because it respects the sovereignty and equality of States, and equitable, because it is based on the principles of sociability, justice and fairness for people living in society. Therefore, it is interesting to observe how the idea of Law, even before the concept of peace, is constantly posited as the ultimate ideal to be achieved by the Law of Nations. That tension we have always noted between *jus gentium* and Natural Law

[37] E. Jouannet, *Colonialisme européen et néo-colonialisme contemporain*, cit., p. 74.

in figures such as De Vitoria, Grotius and Pufendorf now assumes a more secular connotation, associated with 'civilised values'.

Nineteenth-century jurists resolved the difficulty posed by De Vattel by attempting, as we will see, to formulate these principles of justice in an objective and scientific manner. The aspiration to create "a science of facts" is a significant *écart*, as it also marks a notable break from the earlier humanist liberalism.

Although he was an enthusiastic member of the newly established Institute of International Law, Lorimer's references to the early defenders of the Law of Nations, such as Grotius, Wolff, De Vattel, Martens and Wheaton, were few and mostly critical. Certainly, he did not wish to present himself as a continuer of the tradition they represented.[38] The essence of Law is cultural and distinct from legal phenomenology. For Lorimer, as for conservative thinkers in general, Law is (or should be) a reflection of deeper social realities. His writings are filled with critical remarks about the illusory nature of a law that fails in this regard. The fiction of legal equality, for instance, which European states declared between themselves and Turkey at the end of the Crimean War in 1856, was senseless and counterproductive. The provisions of this treaty made Turkey a civilised state. Law, and this agreement in particular, fails because it deviates from a precise understanding of the true nature of the communities that were part of the agreement. At its core, Law is, in fact, only Western Law. Legal science must delve beyond its superficial similarities to bring to light its internal and true value. Lorimer's task, through his 'principle of fact', was to penetrate the surface of nations and, thus, allow for such distinctions.

According to the jurist J. de Hornburg, for example, "*Le civilizateur doit donner l'exemple d'une justice supérieure à la civilisée. Les nations doivent aider les « races inférieures » à entrer dans le système politique des États.*"[39] Similarly, J. Lorimer relied on natural law to demonstrate the inequality between civilised States and barbaric peoples. He developed his famous theory of the three spheres, differentiated according to the degrees of humanity and civilisation among peoples, and to which different sets of rules must be applied: "As a political phenomenon, humanity, in its

[38] M. Koskenniemi *Race, Hierarchy and International Law: Lorimer's Legal Science*, in *European Journal of International Law*, 2016, p. 416: "*Lorimer was not liberal. He was a conservative. He was also an elitist and a racist.*"

[39] J. Hornung, *Civilisés et barbares*, in XVII *Revue de droit international et de législation comparée*, 1904, p. 552.

present condition, is divided into three concentric zones or spheres: that of civilized humanity, that of barbaric humanity, and that of savage humanity. To these [...] three stages of recognition belong to civilized nations: full political recognition, partial political recognition, and natural or merely human recognition."[40] Alphonse Rivier, the famous professor at the Universities of Bern and Brussels, went even further, pointing out in his 1896 work *Principes du droit des gens* that "*Entre nous et les peuples de la race inférieure, un abîme s'ouvre.*"[41]

After all, as Rolin-Jaequemyns pointed out: "[T]his is a science of facts, in the same way as the sciences more particularly called natural. But the facts it is concerned with are of a different order in comparison to the phenomena the observation of which forms the basis of natural sciences properly so called. These are the facts of moral and historical life either of man or of humanity."[42] These two factors contributed powerfully to the epiphany of the modern sciences of International Law and Comparative Law.

4.2 The Epistemic Communities of the Nineteenth-Century "Modern Sciences of Facts"

As Kuhn explains, "science education instills what the scientific community has previously acquired with effort, a strong commitment to a particular way of seeing the world and of exercising science in it."[43] All disciplines are devoted to providing a correct interpretation of their object of study and to establishing the parameters for their theoretical representation. In this context, the concepts of '*episteme*' and 'epistemic community'[44] are useful. I use here the concept of '*episteme*' to refer to the 'knowledge' that is held in a particular field, to the way in which knowledge is apprehended in theory, used in practice and its exercise explained. In other words, I mean the set of collectively shared beliefs and

[40] J. Lorimer, *The Institutes of Law of Nations*, cit., pp. 101–103.

[41] A. Rivier, *Principes du Droit des gens*, Harvard University Press, Cambridge, 1896, p. 8.

[42] G. Rolin-Jaequemyns, '*Les Principes Philosophiques du Droit International*', in *Revue de Droit International et de Législation Comparée*, 1885, p. 521.

[43] H. Kuhn, *The Structure of Scientific Revolutions*, University of Chicago Press, Chicago, 1996, p. 34.

[44] A. Bianchi, '*Epistemic Communities*', in Jean d'Aspremont and Sahib Singh (eds.), *Concepts for International Law Contributions to Disciplinary Thought*, Edward Elgar, London, 2019, p. 251.

assumptions that characterise the field of International Law, understood as a scientific field of intellectual inquiry and as social practice.

The main function of epistemic communities[45] is to establish the terms of the discourse and to shape the way we look at and think about Law.[46] As Michel Foucault argued: "In every society, the production of discourse is at the same time controlled, selected and redistributed by a certain number of procedures."[47] One of the 'procedures for controlling and defining discourse' is the culture of a discipline.[48] Members of the same discipline should speak the same language and share certain values.[49]

The search for a principle of systemic and deeply rooted cohesion, which, according to Foucault, explains the purpose of a 'Law of Coherence' to resolve the contradictions within discourse, is a key feature of many of these doctrinal theories.[50] This rational, fragmented, reified and supposedly objective view of Law is accompanied by specific attitudes. The critical intellectual work done by Koskenniemi in *The Gentle Civilizer of Nations*[51] does not only concern International Law but also addresses a

[45] Stanley Fish uses the concept of 'interpretive communities' in the same sense. Fish uses the notion of 'interpretative communities' not in a normative sense, but in a sociological sense. In other words, it is a concept that, if we were to apply it to Law, would not allow us to know which rules are 'true' and which are not, but it does allow us to see which institutional processes norms are considered as such by the actors of International Law: Stanley Fish, *One More Time*, in G. Olson and L. Worsham (eds.), *Postmodern Sophistry: Stanley Fish and the Critical Enterprise*, State University of New York Press, 2004, pp. 277–279. Fish defines the concept of 'interpretive community' as "a point of view or a way of organizing experience that [shares] individuals, in the sense that their supposed distinctions, categories of understanding, and dispositions of relevance and irrelevance [are] the content of the consciousness of the members of the community, who, therefore, are no longer individuals but, As long as they are immersed in the enterprise of the community, they are part of the property of the community"; also S. Fish, *Doing What Comes Naturally, Change, Rhetoric, and the Practice of Theory in Literary & Legal Studies Change, Rhetoric, and the Practice of Theory*, Duke University Press, 1990, p. 141.

[46] A. Bianchi, *International Law Theories: An Inquiry into Different Ways of Thinking*, Oxford University Press, Oxford, 2017.

[47] M. Foucault, *The Order of Discourse*, in Robert Young (ed), *Untying the Text: A Post-Structuralist Reader*, Routledge & Kegan Paul, 1981, p. 52.

[48] M. Foucault, '*The Order of Discourse*', cit, p. 56, argues that one 'is right' only if one obeys the rules of a discursive 'control' that must be reactivated in each discourse. Discipline is a principle of control over the production of discourse.

[49] É. Balibar, *Le renversement de l'individualisme possessif*, cit., p.

[50] Foucault, M. (1975). Surveiller et punir. Naissance de la prison. París: Éditions Gallimard, p. 230.

[51] M. Koskenniemi, *The Gentle Civilizer*, cit.,

cultural *epistemé*, of which contemporary Comparative Law is also a part. Western identity is reinforced through the combined efforts of classificatory legal science and the branch of law that normatively shapes relations with Others. "To put it slightly differently, when we repeat the familiar aphorism that the 'state is neither fact nor idea, but both fact and idea', we forget that the 'fact' part of that formulation is only 'fact' insofar as a particular juridical frame has already determined what the 'facts' are. It is a juridical 'fact' built on jurisdictional forms which shape life."[52] The conceptual sequence we are reconstructing, which played a decisive role in the development of our current epistemological lens, is simple: classification through the methodology of emerging Comparative Law, separation through the very structure of International Law, and the exclusion of non-civilised peoples from the normative reach of the Law.[53]

One doctrinal element is worth emphasising: both the early internationalists and the initial Comparative Lawyers tended to move away from pure legal positivism: the former invoking moral reasons,[54] while the latter already advanced anti-positivist considerations at the 1900 International Congress in Paris.

4.3 The Influence of Epistemic Communities on the Formation of State Identities: The Science of International Law (1)

The first theoretical movement within the English-speaking world, formulated and explicitly embraced by some proponents of Comparative Law, takes the form of an inductive and positivist approach. This trend seeks to formulate legal categories that are general, as it is based on an analysis of the legal phenomenon that goes beyond the single legal system to which the jurist is subject. The approach can, therefore, be described to some extent as "empirical" or a posteriori, as it aims to start from the facts that constitute the various manifestations of Law, and through induction, attempt to abstract from them a core of common concepts, institutions, mechanisms, reasoning, etc. The gathering and systematisation of these

[52] S. Pahuja, *Laws of encounter: a jurisdictional account of International Law*, in *London Review of International Law*, Volume 1, Issue 1, 2013, p. 72.

[53] M. Koskenniemi, *The Gentle Civilizer*, cit., p. 130.

[54] See for example É. Engelhardt, *Le droit d'intervention et la Turquie*, in *Revue Dr. Internat. Legisl. Comp.*, 1880, p. 365.

elements would then form the general theory of Law. From the perspective of the general theory of Law, this is, quite clearly, the view of John Austin, the founder of analytical jurisprudence.[55] Thus, he writes: "I mean, then, by General Jurisprudence, the science concerned with the exposition of the principles, notions, and distinctions which are common to systems of law [...] Of the principles, notions, and distinctions which are the subjects of general jurisprudence, some may be esteemed necessary. For we cannot imagine coherently a system of law [...], without conceiving them as constituent parts of it."[56] It follows that, according to him, the "key to the science of law" is the concept of order or mandate. It is through this notion, presented as elementary, that he manages to explain a complex network of fundamental legal concepts (obligation, sanction, subjective right, etc.) and political concepts (sovereignty, state, independence, obedience, etc.).

However, the early proponents of International Law, the pragmatic men of 1873, the year the *Institut de Droit International* was established, in their attempt to structure the international order and address the question raised by Austin,[57] began to build a legal system around the Law of civilised societies. At the very moment they recognised their own identity within a legal profession related to the new 'International Law', one of the first projects for the Institute's members was aimed at determining the rules that would allow for the peaceful resolution of the 'partition of Africa'.

By the end of the nineteenth century, a **'science of facts'** emerged, in which the universalisation of European Law and its comparison to Domestic Law within the framework of comparative jurisprudence created scientific identity narratives, which would become the epistemic truths of international legal sciences.

Do some internationalists not consider themselves to be "*l'organe de la conscience juridique civilisée*" of the world[58]? This was the expression used by the members of the Institute of International Law when it was founded in 1873 in Ghent, which included Mancini (Italy), G. Rolin-Jacquemyns

[55] J. Austin, *The Province of Jurisprudence Determined and The Uses of the Study of Jurisprudence*, Intro. Hart, H. L. A., Weidenfeld and Nicholson, London, 1954, pp. 365–366.

[56] Ibid., p. 367.

[57] J. Austin, *The Province of Jurisprudence Determined*, Prometheus, London, 2000, argued that the province of International Law could not be considered law, as it could not be enforced by a legislator comparable to a State parliament.

[58] M. Koskenniemi, *The Gentle Civilizer of Nation*, cit., pp. 42 ss.

(Belgium) and De Parieu (France).[59] This expression is a faithful translation of the prominent view internationalists held of their own work, and it is based on their particular conception of Law and History. The idea of conscience or consciousness, which appears so frequently in their writings, seems to stem directly from the Historical School of Law, which popularised it by making it the source of both Natural and Human Law. It allows for the reconciliation of the human origin of Law and a reaction against the excesses of the rationalist current of the School of Natural Law, as, by doing so, it is considered that Law originates from the consciousness of men (or peoples) and not from abstract and incorporeal reason, as proposed by Natural Law theorists.

The notion of the organ of civilised legal consciousness is indicative of an organicist view of the international *societas*, in which the International Lawyer, seen as the true component and not merely the representative of the community of civilised States, can express the fundamental interests and legal principles of this community of separate subjects. This notion, therefore, suggests—using terms comparable to those found in the French and German theories of State during this period—the complete insertion, or even integration, of the enlightened jurist into this society of States, and how they are necessarily led, as an organic part, to express its collective consciousness.[60]

4.3.1 The Subject-Monad of the New International Law: The Civilised State

The notion of the civilised State in the context of emerging International Law is particularly interesting to explore, as it encapsulates the tension between the particularity of a European community embedded in a supposedly universal Law. Indeed, International Law is defined by all thinkers as a Law between equal States that only functions through the acceptance by the subjects of the synallagmatic logic of mutually shared and accepted obligations. Therefore, the very fact that we speak of a State implies that we imagine political entities sufficiently organised to have a will and a

[59] "*L'institut du droit international … 1° Doit favoriser le progrès du droit international en s'efforçant de devenir l'organe du monde civilisé*", in *Annuaire de l'IDI,* 1877, Session de Gand 1873, p. 18.

[60] On the idea of exclusionary epistemic community see A. Bianchi, '*Epistemic Communities*', in J. d'Aspremont and S. Singh (eds.), *Concepts for International Law Contributions to Disciplinary Thought*, Edward Elgar, London, 2019, p. 251.

consciousness that allows them to follow the precepts of International Law, grounded in this fundamental idea of reciprocity. The French jurist R. Piédelièvre summed up the general opinion of his contemporaries in 1894 by stating that "*le droit international suppose essentiellement la réciprocité c'est-à-dire une conscience suffisamment développée chez les nations dont il gouverne les relations extérieures, ainsi que leur volonté réfléchie et persistante d'appliquer à leurs rapports mutuels les préceptes du droit et de la justice.*"[61] The authors of all these treaties on the Law of Nations will therefore be based on an anthropomorphic figure of the State, built directly on the model of the individual, in which the State is not limited to its constituent elements (territory, population and government), but is characterised by a will and consciousness of man, which animals or human beings and underdeveloped peoples cannot claim. As we will see in the section dedicated to colonial treaties, in terms of transnational phenomena during the eighteenth and nineteenth centuries, the discourse of Private Law contributed significantly to rethinking the sovereign subject of the seventeenth century, just as much as the distinct but convergent process of subjectivation that took place within the discourse of International Law.[62] In this regard, Private Law complemented International Law in the creation of the modern liberal State. Indeed, what was needed at the time was both internal and external identity attribution. It was necessary to define the question of public subjectivity as sovereign power in contrast to non-European populations, that is, the European sovereign public personality, according to the prevailing standard of civilisation. At the same time, what was required (and herein lies the relevance of the tools of Private Law) was a legal system capable of adapting as much as possible to the pursuit of private initiative and trade; in other words, a law free from the legal constraints of the *ancien régime*.

The notion of a legal person here translates this anthropomorphic legal humanism and directly consolidates the colonising process by specifying at the legal level who can be subjects of the Law of Nations, and, at the same time, who are the parties that can stipulate land cession treaties.[63] Thus, European consciousness acts as a natural factor of legal exclusion and

[61] R. Piedelievre, *Précis de droit international public ou droit des gens*, F. Pichon, Paris, 1894, p. 19.

[62] See M. Koskenniemi, *International Law as Political Theology: How to Read the* Nomos der Erde, in *Constellations*, 2004, p. 498.

[63] Cfr. S. Goyard-Fabre, *Sujet de droit et objet de droit: défense del humanisme*, in *Sujet de droit et objet de droit, Cahiers de philosophie politique et juridique*, Caen, 1992, pp. 9–30.

differentiation, as it allows for the exclusion of all non-organised peoples (referred to as savages and barbarians) from the circle of subjects of International Law. Regarded as incapable of creating and applying the norms of International Law, these peoples cannot be assimilated into legal persons. Under these conditions, tribes and colonies, whose territories are occupied by civilised States, are treated, at best, as objects of the Law of Nations, along with the territories they inhabit. More often, they are incorporated into the real property of the colonising State or into its territory, and are then primarily a matter of its internal Public Law, rather than the Law of Nations itself. This explains why their legal status is not addressed in textbooks on European Law, why there was no true international legal system for colonialism at that time, and why some issues related to colonisation are only glimpsed through chapters dedicated to territory or the economic rights of the State that holds exclusive sovereign power over it. The process of reification (the transformation of peoples into objects, their assimilation into the real property of the state, or their identification with a territory rather than a community of individuals) completely excludes and disqualifies them. A true reflection of this dynamic of exclusion is the plundering of the identity-related assets of colonised peoples.

On the other hand, political entities considered to be States and, therefore, legal persons, are entitled to invoke the application of the Law of Nations. However, it is no longer sufficient for them to simply be States; they must also demonstrate an adequate level of civilisation. It is important to note that, through the same anthropomorphic movement derived from the legal humanism underlying all these constructs, the mechanism of replacing the civilised with the strictly rational is also transferred to States. The eventual inclusion of these States into the circle of subjects under Euro-American International Law thus relies on the decisive technique of recognising an acceptable level of civilised consciousness by the members of the community of States.[64] And if they do not appear to have acquired this state of civilisation, then other modalities are considered to govern their relations with fully civilised States. The status of semi-civilised States, the practice of protectorate agreements, spheres of influence, leases, and the use of Special Law are widely discussed legal techniques that confirm the dissociation of status between the civilised State and the others.

[64] J. Lorimer, *Principes de droit international*, cit., p. 104.

This is what Frédéric Mégret defined the "specific statism of International Law", which "participated in a dogma the consequences of which is to delimit the possibilities of imagining judicial forms other than the state".[65] In the end, we are not very far from the abyssal line drawn by De Vitoria concerning the political organisation of the Spanish conquerors in relation to Indigenous peoples, who were always considered *Imago Dei*.

Ernest Nys summed up a widely held conviction among internationalist jurists that the *de jure* and de facto monopolisation of violence was essential for a political community to be considered a civilised state: "The modern State has drawn up a programme which in its main lines is almost everywhere the same. It has claimed the right to make war and has put an end to the barbarous practices of private war".[66] Likewise, Westlake considered the creation of a centralised State as both a legal requirement and a matter of necessity: "[i]f any fanatical admirer of savage life argued that the whites ought to be kept out, he would only be driven to the same conclusion by another route, for a government on the spot would be necessary to keep them out."[67] The structure of the Euro-American State is elevated to the unique *prius* of the civilisation model.[68]

4.3.2 The Exclusionary *Communitas*: The Principle of Recognition of a Civilised Nation

Just like the State, the Western *communitas* opened itself up to the world in its entirety, in order to regulate it *pro domo sua*, but in doing so, it had to be a falsely open community. It was a body of International Law scientifically grounded and closed in relation to the very idea of Law.

Lorimer dedicated long passages to demonstrating the impossibility of a religion like Islam being part of an international legal community. As a religion of revelation, he wrote, it could not accept any possibility of gradual development: there would always be a sharp line drawn between the

[65] F. Mégret, *L'Étatisme Spécifique de Droit International*, in *Revue Québécoise de Droit International*, 2011, pp. 105–129, esp. p. 107.

[66] E. Nys, *The Independent State of the Congo and International Law*, J. Lebègue and comp., Brussels, 1903, p. 3.

[67] J. Westlake, *Equality and Independence of States*, Cambridge University Press, Cambridge, 1894, 143.

[68] É. Balibar, *Le renversement de l'individualisme possessif*, in H. Guineret and A. Milanese, *La propriété: le propre, l'appropriation*, Ellipses, París, 2004, p. 78.

faithful and the infidels. For a non-believer, the only alternatives were "Islam or the Sword".[69] The Turks could never become equal to Christians or, again in Lorimer's fantastical phrase, "[t]o talk of the recognition of Mahometan ... as a question of time is to talk nonsense."[70] For this clearly stated reason, International Law was deeply rooted in the Jural Relations of Separate Political Communities[71]; it was a **Law of Separation**, culminating the sublimation of the modern State, as analysed in the previous paragraph. The principle of recognition, which we saw emerge in the early Renaissance period of *jus gentium*, is now elevated to an abyssal divide, following the same trajectory as the discourse of Comparative Law. The mercantilist *societas* thus becomes an exclusionary *communitas* thanks to the contribution of consciousness in a project specifically conceived at a certain historical moment.

The problem of inter-State order, then, only arose in the context of European sovereign States, and the transformation of this issue into the central theoretical dilemma of the discipline systematically avoided the study of non-European societies.

Thus, for instance, the following question was avoided: how was diversity shaped in this second Encounter? This question, in turn, leads to further inquiries. Instead of adopting the traditional perspective that sovereignty is exclusively a European product that can be extended to a non-sovereign, non-European world by nature, we can see the doctrine of sovereignty partially accommodated by mechanisms of exclusion that expel non-European societies from the realm of sovereignty and power. In the first Encounter, naturally, this conceptual device did not even exist.

In this period, during the second half of the nineteenth century and in certain colonialist circles, the prelude to the great redemptive project of granting sovereignty to the most remote corners of the Earth emerged. In other words, the doctrine of sovereignty expels the non-European world from its space and then proceeds to legitimise the imperialism that results from the incorporation of the non-European world into the system of International Law. The process of transforming the non-European world was completed through decolonisation, which would allow the

[69] J. Lorimer, *La doctrine de la reconnaissance: Fondement du droit international*, in *Revue de droit international et de législation comparée*, 1884, p. 343.

[70] J. Lorimer, *The Institutes of the Law of Nations: A Treatise of the Jural Relations of Separate Political Communities*, cit., p. 78.

[71] J. Lorimer, *The Institutes of the Law of Nations: A Treatise of the Jural Relations of Separate Political Communities*, cit., p. 78.

non-European State to emerge as a sovereign and equal member of the global community.

Gradually, Japan and the Ottoman Empire came to stand as examples, demonstrating that non-European and non-Christian powers were capable of achieving a civilised status and becoming full members of international society.

Indeed, according to this line of reasoning, the Ottoman Empire was admitted, at least partially, into the 'family of civilised nations' in 1856,[72] and in 1899, Japan was fully recognised as sovereign when extraterritoriality was abolished.

Westlake wrote: "we have nothing here to do with the mental or moral characters which distinguish the civilised from the uncivilised, nor even with the domestic or social habits, taking social in a narrow sense, which a traveller may remark".[73] The gap, the abyssal line, is evident and it is based, as previously observed in the works of naturalist and rationalist thinkers, on the idea of Western identity. This concept roots itself even deeper in the Private Law notions of property and contract, as explicitly stated by Carlos Calvo, who particularly emphasised the sanctity of contracts as the cornerstone of civilisation. He warned that, "[t]he state that stops applying this rule is isolated from the general movement of civilisation and would soon return in a fatal slope to the state of barbarity of savage tribes."[74]

Kaneko Kentarō, the Japanese statesman who received an honorary doctorate from Harvard Law School for his role in drafting the first Japanese constitution and shortly thereafter became Minister of Justice, wrote that the only means for Japan to achieve civilised status and thus end the era of extraterritoriality, was "to elaborate a civil code as it happens in Europe and to make a single law, obligatory for strangers and the Japanese".[75]

[72] "The conventional wisdom maintains that an explicit standard of "civilization" dates back to 1856, to the time when the Ottoman Empire is traditionally assumed to have been formally admitted as a "civilized" member of European society"; also G. W. Gong, *The Standard of Civilisation in International Society*, Oxford, Clarendon Press, 1984, p. 31.

[73] J. Westlake, '*Equality and Independence of States*', p. 143.

[74] C. Calvo, *Le Droit International Théorique et Pratique*, vol. 2, p. 213.

[75] K. Kentarō, '*Les Institutions Judiciaires du* Japon', in *Revue de Droit International et de Législation Comparée*, 1893, p. 350.

The elimination of indigenous notions of property and the promotion of particular forms of private land rights,[76] extraterritoriality[77] and international arbitration for harm suffered by foreign citizens[78] were just some of the mechanisms deployed to universalise Western capitalist legal standards. By showing the path to progress, the standard of civilisation became a way to systematise and legitimise a wide range of legal practices that aimed to globalise the protection of property rights, the judicialisation of social relations and the bureaucratic State separate from the economy and society. All of this was justified by a strong sense of moral responsibility, aimed at civilisation.

For Western business enterprises to be able to operate overseas, it was essential that certain guarantees be provided for their security, mainly for their property rights and for the operational nature of the contracts. Approaching this debate from a different angle, Craven makes a similar observation regarding the essential guarantees necessary for colonial trade to function peacefully. Seeking to find a way out of the debate on whether the Berlin Conference focused exclusively on facilitating colonial trade or led to the formalisation of colonialism,[79] Craven points out that, regardless of the conscious plans of the political elites of the time, some degree of formalisation was essential for colonial trade to flourish.[80] The

[76] M. Mamdani, *Citizen and Subject: Contemporary Africa and the Legacy of Late Colonialism*, Princeton University Press, Princeton, 1996; B. Bhandar, *Colonial Lives of Property: Law, Land, and Racial Regimes of Ownership*, Princeton University Press, Princeton, 2018.

[77] On the centrality of legal and institutional reform as preconditions for the abolition of extraterritoriality, see T. Kayaoğlu, *Legal Imperialism: Sovereignty and Extraterritoriality in Japan, the Ottoman Empire, and China*, Cambridge University Press, Cambridge, 2010; N. Tzouvala, '"*And the Laws Are Rude, Crude and Uncertain*": *Extraterritoriality and the Emergence of Territorialised Statehood in Siam*' in D. Margolies, U. Özsu, M. Pal and N. Tzouvala (eds.), *The Extraterritoriality of Law: History, Theory, Politics*, Routledge, Abingdon, 2019), pp. 134–150.

[78] Cf. K. Greenman, *Aliens in Latin America: Intervention, Arbitration and State Responsibility for* Rebels, in *Leiden Journal of International Law*, 2018, pp. 617–39, 636–8.

[79] Treaties like the 1885 Berlin Act formalised the principle that sovereignty (and therefore territorial ownership) belonged to European States that exercised effective colonial administration. Private companies, such as the British East India Company and the Dutch East India Company, operated as hybrid subjects of both sovereignty and property, controlling vast territories with the support of International Law.

[80] M. Craven, '*Between Law and History: The Berlin Conference of 1884–1885 and the Logic of Free Trade*', in *London Review of International Law*, 2015, pp. 31–59, esp. 35.

protection of rights related to commerce was a significant aspect of this trend towards juridification.

One such technique was the legalisation of individual rights as part of the process of achieving 'civilised' status under International Law.

In other words, only those political communities that had been successfully co-opted as modern, bureaucratic and legally separated from society and the economy were considered civilised and thus subjects of full International Law: "these new European states had interpellated, independently and willingly, as subjects of International Law, thereby demonstrating their 'rationality' (on European/Hegelian terms), their 'reciprocating will' and their capacity for 'self-government and mutual recognition.'"[81]

Finally, the abolition of slavery constituted another primary condition for achieving civilisation status.[82] In line with an initiative by Lord Castlereagh, the Congress of Vienna issued a Declaration on the Abolition of the Slave Trade, stating that "public opinion, in all civilised countries, clamours for the prompt suppression of slavery."[83] In his effort to legitimise the European civilising mission in Africa, and in particular in the free state of the Congo as a legal entity nominally dedicated to such a mission, Descamps painted a vivid image of African 'savagery', where "cannibalism, sacrifice, human hunts and slavery" occupied a prominent place.[84] Similarly, Nys identified the suppression of servitude and slavery as an essential precondition for the emergence of the modern, civilised state.[85]

David Dudley Field, a staunch opponent of slavery in his native United States, focused on the abolition of slavery when discussing "the progress of the law of war required by modern civilisation." He also employed 'slavery' as a broader metaphor for intolerable political domination. "To

[81] R. Parfitt, *The Process of International Legal Reproduction: Inequality, Historiography, Resistance*, Cambridge University Press, Cambridge, 2019, p. 146.

[82] For the study of an *écart* between the declaration of the rights of man and the existence of slavery in Santo Domingo: R. Knox, '*Valuing Race? Stretched Marxism and the Logic of Imperialism*', in *London Review of International Law* 2016, pp. 81–126. Also L. Obregón, '*Empire, Racial Capitalism and International Law: The Case of Manumitted Haiti and the Recognition Debt*, in *Leiden Journal of International Law*, 2018, pp. 597–615.

[83] W.G. Grewe, *The Epochs of International Law*, De Gruyter, Berlin, 2001, p. 554.

[84] E. Descamps, *L'Afrique Nouvelle: Essai sur l'État Civilisateur dans les Pays Neufs et sur la Fondation, l'Organisation et le Gouvernement de l'État Indépendant du Congo*, Hachette, Paris, 1903, p. 3.

[85] E. Nys, *The Independent State of the Congo and International Law*, J. Lebègue and c., Brussels, 1903, p. 605.

allow a victorious army to subject the people of a country to a government which they detest, is to allow the conqueror to reduce a conquered people to a modified slavery."[86]

When Japanese international jurists such as Sakuye Takahashi[87] argued for their country's readiness to be admitted as an equal member of the 'family of civilised nations', they juxtaposed Japan's norms and conduct of war with those of neighbouring China. In doing so, they were not merely addressing a strategic issue.[88] Rather, they operated within a general framework of argumentation that relied heavily on comparison, and more specifically on comparison aimed at creating and reproducing graduated international legal hierarchies and personalities.[89] In 1895, Lawrence defined International Law as "the rules which determine the conduct of the general body of civilized states in their mutual relations".[90]

James Lorimer inadvertently summed up the *écart* that permeates civilisation as a way of arguing about the distribution of rights and duties in International Law: "The international question is, whether, in the presence of ethnical difference which for jural purposes we must regard as indelible, we are entitled to confine recognition to these branches of alien races which consent to separate themselves from the rest".[91] In fact, the discourse of civilisation was intrinsically linked to a sensitivity that confined the 'savage' to the realm of humanity and occasionally protested

[86] "And it cannot be doubted that if a belligerent were to attempt reducing to personal slavery captives in war, the courts of the other belligerent, and the courts also of every civilised neutral, would declare the captives free whenever brought within their jurisdiction"; also D.D. Field, '*Amelioration of the Laws of War Required by Modern Civilisation*', in *The Law Magazine and Review* 1888, p. 112.

[87] T. Sakuyé, *1867–1920: Cases on International Law during the Chino-Japanese war*, The University Press, Tokio, 1899.

[88] Cf. J. A. Carrillo Salcedo, *Hacia una nueva interpretación de la noción de «estados civilizados» en derecho internacional contemporáneo*, in *Anales de la Real Academia de Ciencias Morales y Políticas*, 1996, Session of 31 October 1995, p. 658.

[89] On the question of differentiated international legal personality, see: R.S. Parfitt, *Empire des Nègres Blancs: The Hybridity of International Personality and the Abyssinia Crisis of 1935–1936*, in *Leiden Journal of International Law*, 2011, pp. 849–872; N.G. Wheatley, *Spectral Legal Personality in Interwar International Law: On New Ways of Not Being a State*, in *Law and History Review* 2017, pp. 753–787.

[90] T.J. Lawrence, *Principles of International Law*, Macmillan and Co., London, 1895, p. 1.

[91] J. Lorimer, *The Institutes of the Law of Nations: A Treatise of the Jural Relations of Separate Political Communities*, 2 vols 1883, p. 98.

against the atrocity, while articulating legal justifications for the broader imperial project.[92]

4.4 The Influence of Scientific Communities on the Formation of State Identities: The Science of Comparative Law (2)

The new "positive science of facts" in Comparative Law emerged alongside the new nineteenth-century International Law. Although it displays distinct idiosyncratic features, which we will examine below, it shares the same causal vectors as the latter. "*Le 'droit compare', en tant que domaine spécifique du savoir juridique est un produit intellectuel moderne de l'Europe du XIXe siècle. Il est la résultante historique de deux forces majeures: l''etatisation' du droit et sa cristallisation dans des ordres juridiques séparés et autonomes, d'une part; et l'attitude 'scientiste' des théoriciens du droit, d'autre part*".[93] Both legal sciences contribute to the creation of what we have defined from the beginning as a Western legal identity, capable of reconciling nationalism and universalism. In the field of Comparative Law, there emerges—mutatis mutandis—a call to establish a discipline with clear and unquestionable academic legitimacy, rooted in scholarly work and shaped by a specific national identity. The once medieval heritage of a *universitas aeuropea* gradually fragments under the pressure of rising nationalism.[94] Comparative legal study first takes hold in the area of Private Law. In contrast, Public and Constitutional Law remain too closely tied to the project of forging an exclusionary national identity within the national (scientific) context, making them less open to comparative approaches, which might be seen as undermining the perceived purity of that national

[92] J. M. Hornung, *Civilisés et Barbares*, in *Revue de Droit International et de Législation Comparée* 1885, pp. 447–470; C. Salomon, *L'Occupation des Territoires sans Maître. Etude de Droit International*, A. Giard, Paris, 1889. In this sense, the inclusion of Hornung and Salomon in the list of the sceptics of "civilisation" requires a very generous reading of their work. Cf. A. Fitzmaurice, *Scepticism of the Civilizing Mission in International Law*, in M. Koskenniemi, W. Rech and M. Jiménez Fonseca (eds.), *International Law and Empire: Historical Explorations*, Oxford University Press Oxford, 2017, pp. 358–384.

[93] G. Resta, *Les luttes de clocher en droit comparé*, in *McGill Law Journal/Revue de droit de McGill*, 2017, p. 1153.

[94] P. Sirena, *Introduction to Private Law*, Il Mulino, Bologna, 2019, p. 78.

project.[95] Both branches of law—Constitutional and Private—are moving in the same direction: the creation of an exclusionary State identity within the national perimeter, the former within the national context, and the latter within the Comparative Law sphere.[96] In the second half of the nineteenth century, we witness the gradual institutionalisation of the discipline, marked by the establishment of the first specialised journals, followed by the creation of associations and new university chairs. The main drivers of this scientistic effort in Comparative Law remain the doctrinal traditions of France and Germany. Within both contexts, two distinct sensibilities gradually emerge: the first leans more towards the practical needs of Comparative Law, while the second current prioritises the speculative or theoretical dimension of the nascent discipline.[97] The practical thread of Comparative Law, which focuses mainly on the improvement of laws, represents the most conspicuous trend and leads to the initiative of the International Congress of Comparative Law in Paris of 1900.

4.4.1 The Influence of French Doctrine

Comparison originally served a clearly nationalistic purpose and focused on periods when legal codes or constitutions were not being drafted. In France, academic and government institutions worked in tandem to make the most of the country's comparative advantage, proudly asserting their role as pioneers of the new discipline. It is no coincidence that the term "Comparative Law" (droit comparé) appeared first in France, in 1863. A few years later, in 1869, the *Société de Législation Comparée* was founded in Paris, thanks to the efforts of two young lawyers, Paul Jozon and Alexandre Ribot. The motto chosen was *Lex multiplex, Jus Unum*, and its primary purpose was the translation of foreign legislative texts. To appreciate just how ahead of its time the founding of the Société was, we should bear in mind that equivalent associations in England and Germany would not be established until more than twenty years later. The French

[95] Cfr. T. Amico di Meane, *Sulle spalle dei giganti*, Editoriale Scientifica, Napoli, 2022, p. 72.

[96] On this subject, see. M. Reimann, *Comparative Law*, in *The Oxford Handbook of Comparative Law*, (2nd edn), Oxford University Press, 2019, p. 40.

[97] See, among others G. Resta, *Le tassonomie e la precomprensione del comparatista*, in *Diritto pubblico comparato ed europeo*, 2017, p. 1200; M. Ponthoreau, *Le droit comparé en cuestion(s). Entre pragmatisme et outil épistémologique*, in *Revue internationale de droit compare*, 2005, pp. 7–27.

government not only provided generous funding for the *Société*, but in 1876 it also created the *Comité de législation étrangère et de droit international* within the Ministry of Justice, turning it into a permanent body (unlike the earlier Napoleonic-era experiment) dedicated to collecting and cataloguing foreign law. This was the setting in which the *Société de Législation Comparée* found the momentum to propose the idea of the 1900 Paris Congress to the government. At the same time, while the scientific boundaries between the two fields (International Law and Comparative Law) were still being defined, modern comparatists expressed growing enthusiasm to give the discipline a broader international outlook, the early signs of which can already be seen in the second half of the nineteenth century. The opportunity arose, for example, with the creation of the Universal Postal Union, as well as the drafting of numerous international agreements on trademarks and patents, and conferences on international peace, such as the one held in The Hague in 1893.[98] The two disciplines deal with different and separate areas, but they share perspectives that, as we know, are driven by the same nationalist and exclusionary outlook.

Explorations beyond the East in Comparative Law, and to some extent the evolution of the discipline itself, inevitably intertwine with the management of colonial rule. Suffice it to say that prominent scholars of Comparative Law were involved in their respective governments' colonial administrations. From Henry James Sumner Maine to Albert Post, then later Josef Kohler (who also took part in the Paris Congress) and Enrico Cerulli. In this context, Comparative Law took on a different role from simply managing colonial possessions; it became a vast space for encounter and dialogue between cultures, administering diverse legal systems. Here, the United Kingdom not only had to address legal disputes arising in the colonies but also, for example, enact legislation applicable across its own territories around the world. This is the context in which we see the gradual maturing of Comparative Law, which, as Annalise Riles notes, evolves from being driven by involuntary enthusiasts of legal comparison ("amateurs") to becoming a field led by knowledgeable comparatists ("academics"), scholars who consciously choose to dedicate themselves to it with the aim of establishing it as a formal discipline.[99]

[98] K. Zwigert, H. Kötz, *An Introduction to Comparative Law*, cit., p. 59.

[99] A. Riles, *Introduction*, in A. Riles, (dir.) *Rethinking the Masters of Comparative Law*, Hart, Oxford, 2001, pp. 11–12.

4.4.2 *The Influence of the German Historical School of Law*

The first scientific university chairs and societies in the field of comparative legislation were established in France and England, in the mid-nineteenth century.[100] But in terms of theoretical production, it was the German jurists who played a pioneering role in developing two main approaches to comparison[101]: one more pragmatic, focused on the knowledge of foreign rules and especially foreign legislation, and used as a source of inspiration for the reform and interpretation of national legislation; and the other more specific in nature and more directly related to the use of the comparative method by modern sciences.[102] These two approaches, which would leave a lasting impact on the work of the 1900 Paris Congress, share a common stance of opposition to the dominant legal culture, particularly the Historical School of Law, which also had a profound influence on the discipline of International Law.

The relationship between the Historical School and legal comparison was, in fact, deeply ambivalent.[103] 'Historicism', a characteristic attitude of the German culture of the time,[104] led to the examination of Law as a human creation endowed with a historical existence. On the one hand, freed from theology and the timeless abstractions of the School of Natural Law, Law was reduced to its positive, relativised dimension, and thus returned to a dimension open to criticism and understanding by Reason.

[100] In 1869, the Society of Comparative Legislation was founded in Paris and Sir Henry Sumner Maine was appointed "Professor of History and Comparative Jurisprudence at Oxford (see Sir F. Pollock, *The History of Comparative Jurisprudence*, in *J Society Comparative Legislation* 1903, pp. 74–86; B. Fauvarque-Cosson, *Development of Comparative Law in France*, in M. Reimann and R. Zimmermann, dirs., *Oxford Handbook of Comparative Law*, Oxford University Press, 2006, Oxford, pp. 41–42.

[101] Cf. L.J. Constantinesco, *Traité de droit comparé*, t. 1, Librairie générale de droit et de jurisprudence, Paris, 1972, p. 52.

[102] Regarding this twin comparison, see P. Koschaker, *L'histoire du droit et le droit comparé surtout en Allemagne*, in *Introduction à l'étude du droit comparé: recueil d'études en l'honneur d'Edouard Lambert*, Sirey et Librairie générale de droit et de jurisprudence, Paris, 1938, pp. 275–76; M. G. Losano, *Sistema e struttura nel diritto: dalle origini alla scuola storica*, vol. 1, Giuffrè, Milano, 2002, pp. 140–50.

[103] Geist des römischen Rechts auf den verschiedenen Stufen seiner Entwicklung, Breitkopf und Härtel, Leipzig, 1852.

[104] F.C. Beiser, *The German Historicist Tradition,* Oxford University Press, Oxford, 2011, pp. 1–26; A. Dufour, *Le paradigme scientifique dans la pensee juridique moderne*, in P. Amselek (dir.), *Théorie du droit et science,* Presse Universitaires de France, Paris, 1994, pp. 144–167.

On the other hand, the very selective use of history by Friedrich Karl von Savigny and his disciples in the construction of a positive legal system created a serious obstacle to the spread of comparative reasoning. Savigny's historicism is linked to a very deep epistemological background, which led him to limit his interest to certain specific manifestations of the phenomenon and to deny the usefulness of comparison, particularly synchronic and diachronic comparison with legal systems outside the Romanist tradition. It is not only intended to refer to the theory of the "national character of rights",[105] and in particular to the idea of Law understood as an expression of the "spirit of a people"[106]; but also to von Savigny's tendency to view Roman Law, not in its contingent historicity, but rather as the repository of a universal reason, capable of providing the inspiration and material for a true historicity.

This science, as we can read in his *Methodenlehre,*[107] had to correspond to the Kantian paradigm of scientific knowledge. Therefore, it had to be a science focused on the idea of system and the understanding of empirical contingent data through universal forms of knowledge, such as concepts and dogmas.

However, it should not be forgotten that jurists gathered around Heidelberg University (such as Anton Justus Thibaut, Eduard Gans, Carl Joseph Anton Mittermaier and Karl Salomón Zachariae, author of the famous French civil law treatise translated by Charles Aubry and Charles Rau[108]) were all experts in Comparative Law and founders of the first Comparative Law journal, *Kritische Zeitschrift für Rechtswissenschaft und Gesetzgebung des Auslandes*, published between 1829 and 1852 under the editorship of Mittermaier and Zachariae.[109] For these authors, working in

[105] Idem.

[106] Several authors have tried to trace this idea back to the influence of romantic philosophy and, in particular, J.G. Herder. Cf. W. Ewald, *Comparative Jurisprudence (I): What Was It Like to Try a Rat?*, In *Pa. L. Rev.*, 1995, pp. 2016–2017.

[107] Cf. F.K. von Savigny, *Juristische Methodenlehre: nach der Ausarbeitung des Jakob Grimm*, K. F. Koehler Verlag, Stuttgart, 1951.

[108] L.J. Constantinesco, *Traité de droit comparé,* t. 1, Librairie générale de droit et de jurisprudence, Paris, 1972, pp. 79–88.

[109] For the features of this review, see H. Mohnhaupt, *Historische Vergleichung im Bereich von Staat und Recht vom spaten 18. bis zur Mitte des 19. Jahrhunderts: Beobachtungen zue deutschen Bezugnahme auf Italien,* in A. Mazzacane and R. Schulze (eds.), *Die deutsche und die italienische Rechtskultur im Zeitalter der Vergleichung*", Duncket & Humblot, Berlin,1995, pp. 49–52.

a legal context characterised by the presence of elements from French Law, Roman Law and Comparative Law represented both a tool for understanding Positive Law and a source of inspiration for legislative reform. However, this comparison was never accepted by the dominant currents of legal thought, which, fascinated by the idea of nationality, the technical practice of Roman Law, and the notion of the spontaneous evolution of Law, continued the development of a unitary system of Law from an eminently particularistic perspective.

The final stage of convergence between historical and comparative methods was forged thanks to the efforts of jurists such as Kohler,[110] Post[111] and several other contributors to the newly created Review for Comparative Jurisprudence *(Zeitschrift für vergleichende Rechtswissenschaft)*, which opened up the field of research to the rights of so-called primitive peoples of the time.[112] These studies marked the beginning of legal ethnology and were strongly influenced by the political and intellectual conditions of the time, especially colonialism and the mechanistic conception of evolution. At the same time, this current had the objective merit of broadening perspectives and overcoming the lack of interest from the historical school and orthodox legal science in foreign cultures during the Romanist era.[113] Maine himself, while identifying the typical perspective error of ethnocentric comparison and expanding legal knowledge to other legal families, ultimately ended up classifying them according to a Eurocentric historical system.[114] At the Paris Congress, the two idiosyncratic elements discussed above were condensed.[115]

[110] J. Kohler, *Das Recht als Kulturerscheinung: Einleitung in die vergleichende Rechtswissenschaft*, Würzburg, Druck und verlag des stahel'schen, 1885.

[111] A.H. Post, *Der Ursprung des Rechts: Prolegomena zu einer allgemeinen vergleichenden Rechtswissenschaft*, Oldenburg, Schulzesche, 1876.

[112] J. Whitman, *From Philology to Anthropology in Mid-Nineteenth-Century Germany*, in G.W. Stocking (dir.), *Functionalism Historicized: Essays on British Social Anthropology*, University of Wisconsin Press, Madison, 1984, pp. 214–216.

[113] Cf. Constantinesco, *Traité de droit comparé*, cit., pp. 112–113.

[114] "The characteristic error of the direct observer of unfamiliar social or juridical phenomena is to compare them too hastily with familiar phenomena apparently of the same kind. But the best contemporary historians, both of England and of Germany, are evidently striving to increase their resources through the agency of the Comparative Method; and nobody can have been long in the East without perceiving and regretting that a great many conclusions, founded on patient personal study of Oriental usage and idea, are vitiated through the observer's want of acquaintance with some elementary facts of Western legal history"; S. Maine, *Village Communities in the East and West*, 7e ed., Murray, 1895, London, pp. 6–8.

[115] W.F. Menski, "*Comparative Law in a Global Context: The Legal Systems of Asia and Africa*", Cambridge University Press, 2009, p. 58.

4.4.3 *The Paris International Congress of 1900: The Contrasting Epiphany of a New Universal Legal Science*

Between 31 July and 4 August 1900, against the backdrop of the universal exhibition, the *Congrès International de Droit Comparé* was held, which would go down in history as "as a new branch of legal science in its own rights."[116] Naturally, the spirit of Paris, the common ground of the time, which we have already invoked on several occasions, maintains a continuity with the earlier-mentioned fertile ground. A positivist and vigorously nationalist atmosphere emerges, displaying its pragmatic nature, anchored exclusively in Private Law and manifestly Eurocentric. The initiative itself was born with the somewhat undisguised goal of positioning the French system at the forefront of civilised nations, under the auspices of the French Ministry of Commerce and Industry.[117] The nationalist objective was already clearly stated by President Picot within the *Société de Legislation Comparée* in the attempt to restore France to its strength and rank in the world[118]: "helping France regain its pride of place among civilised nations".[119] The Private Law feature is clear from the outset: Saleilles clearly explains that this is not a congress of Public Law.[120] This is primarily because the emerging Constitutional Law is inextricably linked to State matters, preventing the fundamental exercise of what was then Comparative Law: the unification of Law or the awareness that there could be a circulation of legal experiences.

At this point, one must wonder whether this Eurocentrism (that is, Franco-centrism) of the Paris Congress had any impact on the content of the reports presented. There is a widespread impression that the two

[116] I. De la Rasilla, *A Very Short History of Internacional Law (1869–2018)*, in *Europ. Journ. Internat. Law*, 2018, pp. 137–168.

[117] Episode extrapolated by A. Aragoneses, *Un jurista del modernismo: Raymond Saleilles y los orígenes del derecho comparado*, Universidad Carlos III, Madrid, 2008, p. 12.

[118] Société de Législation Comparée, *Bulletin de la Société de Législation Comparée*, 1899, p. 71.

[119] M. Fournier, *Comparative Law Gets Entitled: the 1900 Paris Congress in Contexts*, Fournier, available in: https://ssrn.com/abstract=4973485

[120] R. Saleilles, *Rapport présenté a la Commission d'organisation sur l'utilité, le but et le programme du Congrès, Procès-Verbaux des séances et documents du Congrès international de droit comparé de 1900*, F. Pichon et Durand-Auzias, Paris, 1900. Cf. J. Christophe, *Le vieux rêve de Saleilles et Lambert revisité. A propos du centenaire du Congrès international de droit comparé de Pari*, in *Revue internat. de droit comp.*, 2000, pp. 733–751; A. Aragoneses, *Un jurista del modernismo: Raymond Saleilles y los orígenes del derecho comparado*, Universidad Carlos III, Madrid, 2008.

"branches" of Comparative Law represented in Paris, although operating within very different geographical contexts, show a substantial convergence in the view that Comparative Law should continue to exclude dialogue with legal systems belonging to so-called primitive societies and semi-civilised peoples ('*demi-civilisation*'). The exchange of possible legislative models, which characterises the foundational phase of Comparative Law, was focused on a very specific horizon: certain Western legal systems. The only Law considered valid was Western Law, primarily, but not exclusively European. This Eurocentrism, largely rooted in the Franco-German sphere, clearly emerges in the contributions of two of the leading figures in the emerging field of Comparative Law: Lambert and Kohler. Although he would later smooth the rough edges of his Parisian statements, the French jurist does not show any hostility towards legal cultures different from the Western one, simply because, as they do not have a "*fonds juridique commun*" they cannot be recipients of legal harmonisation.[121] For the German scholar, human progress follows a single path with several evolutionary stages, along which so-called inferior peoples must be guided by a group of *presque surhumains*, ultimately accepting the *civilisation du conquérant*.[122] Until this monumental legal transplant has been fully carried out, the European jurist cannot, in their view, properly study cultures that are "not yet civilised."

In the new scientific discipline of Comparative Law, two souls coexist, which we can identify through *écart*. In the wake of new industrial and scientific transformations, Western legal scholars claim the identity requirement to prove the scientific nature of their knowledge. The response, more diffusely offered by European jurists to these demands, consists of strengthening the characteristics of coherence, logic and completeness in the emerging discipline, similar to what happened within the national frameworks of codifications. It is a scientific strategy that emphasises and recalls the precision and impartiality with which the scientist uses their test

[121] E. Lambert, *Rapport* in *Congrès international de droit comparé, Procès-verbaux des séances et documents*, t. 1, L.G.D.J., 1905, pp. 44–45. Cf. D. López Medina, *El nacimiento del derecho comparado moderno como espacio geográfico y como disciplina*, in *International Law: Revista Colombiana de Derecho International*, 26, 2015, p. 152.

[122] J. Kohler, *De la méthode du Droit Comparé*, in *Congrès international de droit comparé, Procès verbaux et documents*, vol. I, L.G.D.J., Paris, 1905, pp. 230–233.

tubes in the laboratory, a concept Koskenniemi defines as *bricolage*, drawing from the anthropological tools of Levi Strauss.[123]

In both the Austro-German area and the French-speaking zone, indeed, there are voices that, although few, appeal to foreign references to free themselves from the yoke of the historical school, as in the case of Jhering.[124] The testimony of the great German jurist will be taken by French scholars who define themselves as "*juristes inquiets*".[125]

4.5 The *Écart* Between the Two Modern Sciences of Law of the Other

At this point in the work, we define Law of the Other[126] as the convergence of the two emerging nineteenth-century sciences: International Law and Comparative Law. We have demonstrated how this Law, which contemporaneously governs the relationship with other legal cultures, clearly or latently manifests a legal discourse that, starting from specific and identifiable interests in nineteenth-century Europe, seeks to universalise its claims in the name of a superior legal civilisation. However, tensions can be established between these two legal disciplines, which we will examine through *écarts*, that is, without any scientific *prius*.

Naturally, following in the wake of Koskenniemi's excellent research, the two essential pillars of the European epistemic community are the predominantly philosophical German school and the French school, which focuses on the 'sociology' of International Law.[127] In the first doctrine, indeed, according to the teachings of a young Jellinek, ethics had to redeem itself from metaphysical speculations and individualistic obsession, and investigate the emergence of different types of social consciousness, as

[123] M. Koskenniemi, *To the Uttermost Parts of the Earth: Legal Imagination and International Power 1300–1870*, cit., p. 12. Lévi-Strauss presents *bricolage* as a type of mythical thought used in the concrete solution of a problem where the *bricoleur* is "adept at performing a large number of diverse tasks", managing them with "whatever is at hand". Cf. C. Levi Strauss, *The Savage Mind*, University of Chicago Press, Chicago, 1966, pp. 16–22.

[124] Particularly illustrative in this regard is the work of K. Zwiger, K. Siher, *Jhering's Influence on the Development of Comparative Legal Method*, in *Amer. Journ. Compar. Law*, 1971, p. 230.

[125] M. Bellau, *The 'Juristes Inquiets': Legal Classicism and Criticism in Early Twentieth-Century France*, in *Utah Law Review*, 1997, pp. 379–411.

[126] The clear reference is to E. Levinas, *De l'unicité*, Rivages, Paris, 2018.

[127] M. Koskenniemi, *The Gentle Civilizer of Nations. The Rise and Fall of International Law 1870–1960*, Cambridge University Press, Cambridge, 2009, espec. pp. 232 ss.

we will see in the Comparative Law aspect.[128] Responding to the Austinian dilemma about the province of International Law, the German jurist constructs a complex thesis on the *Rechtsstaat* which, on the one hand, grants autonomous status to Public Law and, on the other hand, firmly anchors it to sociology in the understanding of the power of the State. The binding force of International Law, then, resided in the practical validity of *Geltung*, understood as the will of a legal subject.[129] All of this occurs both in the field of International Law, as well as in the sphere of Comparative Law, in which the two souls of the subversion of this new anti-positivist science and the proclamation of national particularism coexist. From an internationalist perspective, the role assumed by the French governments was positioned as supposedly respectful of International Law, even contrary to English aggressiveness and German revanchism. The perfect correspondence with the underlying discourses of the organisation of the Paris Congress of 1900 once again testifies to the coexistence of a cosmopolitan and solidarity-based vision and an exacerbated defence of Gallic nationalism.

Indeed, modern Comparative Law was born (or, as we will see, seeks to be born) as a 'subversive' act in relation to the 'tradition' embodied by legal positivism, which permeates the education of the respective 'founding fathers'.[130]

While nationalisation invites the jurist to limit their attention to the microphenomena of National Law, scientific positivism (reinforced by the colonial encounter with non-European Others) leads the jurist to look beyond territorial borders to achieve a descriptive rationalisation of the differences and similarities between legal institutions and understand their dynamics of development. "*Il s'agit d'une tension, au fond, entre nationalite et internationalite, qui a marqué profondement l'histoire de la*

[128] G. Jellinek, *Die sozialethische Bedeutung von Recht und Strafe*, Olms, Hidelsheim, 1878, espec. p. 41.

[129] G. Jellinek, *Die rechtliche Natur der Staatenverträge. Ein Beitrag zur juristischen Construktion des Völkerrechts*, Hölder, Viena, 1880, p. 4.

[130] G. Fletcher, *Comparative Law as Subversive Discipline*, in *The American Journal of Comparative Law*, 46, 1998, pp. 683–700; H. Muir Watt, *La function subversive du droit comparé*, in *Revue international de droit comparé*, 52, 3, 2000, pp. 503–527.

discipline et qui ne manque pas de projeter ses effets sur l'experience contemporaine".[131]

The minutes of the 1900 International Congress in Paris shed light on how the ethnohistorical approach described earlier was considered an essential component of the discipline by several renowned jurists. "*En particulier, nous rappelle Lambert, cette première conception considérait le droit comparé essentiellement comme une branche de la science sociale, chargée de l'observation et de la découverte des régularités causales dans le développement du droit, et aussi de la classification des types juridiques et des familles de droit selon un procédé similaire à la taxonomie botanique ou zoologique. Cependant, **l'identité** du droit comparé et de l'histoire comparative du droit ne fut pas acceptée par la totalité de la communauté académique naissante*".[132]

This *gap*, as defined by Jullien, this abyssal line as conceived by Sousa Santos, this dynamic of difference as described by Anghie, is normatively embodied in the emerging International Law. "The idea that the non-European world was civilisationally inferior and that the influx of (Western) capital would remedy these shortcomings has been, I argue, constitutive of modern International Law at least since its emergence as a distinct discipline during the last quarter of the nineteenth century".[133]

The 'standard of civilisation' oscillated between two identity logics. On the one hand, as we have already seen, the logic of progress rewarded equal participation in International Law subject to a comprehensive internal reform in accordance with the imperatives of modernity extended to new worlds. Within this framework, the attributes of a civilised State were relatively easy to identify, although not necessarily easy to achieve. The legalisation of social affairs, the adoption of a legal system focused on the notions of individualism, private property and judicial independence, as well as the bureaucratisation and territorialisation of State power, were of the utmost importance.

[131] G. Resta, *Les luttes de clocher en droit comparé*, in *McGill Law Journal/Revue de droit de McGill*, 2017, p. 1154.

[132] G. Resta, *Les luttes de clocher en droit comparé*, in *McGill Law Journal/Revue de droit de McGill*, 2017, pp. 1183–1184.

[133] N. Tzouvala, *Capitalism as civilisation: a history of International Law*, Cambridge University Press, Cambridge MA, 2020, p. 10.

On the other hand, the logic of the gap constantly denied such a possibility, perpetually confining non-Western political communities to an inferior position within the architecture of International Law. In this framework, legal, economic or cultural differences were attributed to immutable characteristics, and the gap between the West and 'the rest' was seen as unbridgeable. I would argue that these two inherently conflicting poles have coexisted in international legal reasoning since the nineteenth century, both in Comparative Law and in International Law.

CHAPTER 5

The Aftermath of the Law of Separation in the Twentieth Century

Abstract Throughout much of the twentieth century, International and Comparative Law further emphasised the divisions between legal systems. Key comparative theories and the structure of International Law both intensified these distinctions, with works like those of René David and functionalist approaches reinforcing Western perspectives on legal comparison. Similarly, early twentieth-century International Law, through debates like monism versus dualism and discussions on sources, contributed to this growing separation.

Keywords Structuralism • Sacchian formants • Functionalism • Monist and dualist theories • Sources of International Law

Comparative Law, like International Law, has for decades shared an exclusionary form of universalist ambition, but within both disciplines there have also been tensions pushing towards the inclusion of the Law of the Other. Throughout the twentieth century, International Law has shown a tendency towards a humanisation of Law,[1] leading to a fragile but significant trend towards a supranational legal system governed by rules

[1] A very insightful contribution in this regard is made by A. Mangas Martín, *Humanización, democracia y Estado de derecho en el ordenamiento internacional,* speech of admission as an

© The Author(s), under exclusive license to Springer Nature Switzerland AG 2026

A. Lazari, *Relational Identity in International, Comparative and European Union Law*,
https://doi.org/10.1007/978-3-031-59482-3_5

independent of the will of sovereign States, such as the concept of *jus cogens*. In Comparative Law, this effort is carried out through the tendency to demystify Western Positive Law, and in International Law, through its deconstruction and provincialisation.

The disciplines of International and Comparative Law, which emerged around the 1870s with a strongly exclusionary shared epistemic background, initially interacted, as we have seen, but then followed separate paths, though occasionally maintaining some dialogue. Scientific cooperation was never systematic. On the contrary, as the epistemic community tightened with the creation of centres for Comparative and International Law and specialised journals,[2] signs of systematic interaction grew weaker and eventually faded away.

As Rasilla[3] points out, several factors explain the gradual decline of liberal reformist internationalism based on Comparative Law. Among these are the progressive consolidation of the two branches of Comparative Law as distinct fields of legal study, which coincided (not by chance) with the rising nationalist instrumentalisation of these studies and their national practice in the early twentieth century.

Moments of 'reunion' have been sporadic and almost always developed in the sphere of Common Law. Only in the last ten years has the academic initiative of Comparative International Law, led by Roberts and strongly supported by Koskenniemi, sought to provincialise the foundations of the international legal structure. This operation had only been partially carried out years earlier by the interwar generation of British International Lawyers, led by A.D. McNair and H. Lauterpacht in their edition of the *Digest of Public International Law*,[4] who spearheaded what A. Carty called the "practitioners' approach"[5] to International Law in interwar England.[6]

academic member, session held on 8 April 2014, Madrid, Real Academia de Ciencias Morales y Políticas, p. 7.

[2] Cfr. I. De la Rasilla, *A Very Short History of Internacional Law (1869–2018)*, in *Europ. Journ. Internat. Law*, 2018, pp. 137–168.

[3] I. De la Rasilla, *A Very Short History of International Law (1869–2018)*, in *Europ. Journ. Internat. Law*, 2018, p. 5.

[4] H. Lauterpacht, *Annual Digest of Public International Law Cases: 1919–1922*, 1932, p. l.

[5] A. Carty, *Why Theory? The Implications for International Law Teaching*, in P. Allott et al. (eds) *Theory and International Law: An Introduction*, 1991, p. 77.

[6] Cf. H. Lauterpacht, '*The so-called Anglo-American and Continental Schools of Thought in International Law*', in *British Yearbook of International Law*, 1931, p. 32.

The general approach of the English jurist deserves to be further explored from our identity-community perspective.

The universalism shaped by the spread of the Western human rights creed distanced the possibility of a relational approach to Law, one focused on the inclusive study of the legal cultures that form part of International Law.

5.1 Comparative Law on Separation in the First Part of the Twentieth Century

However, it is no surprise that nationalist logic and a hierarchy of exclusion played a decisive role in shaping the methods and functions of Comparative Law.[7] At the start of the twentieth century, the identification of Law with territory reached its peak, alongside the very idea of the homeland itself.[8] The construction of theoretical models, which supported the work of comparatists, could not easily break free from these constraints. The same can be said of other widely held preconceptions, such as equating Law solely with legislation, and the dichotomy between Private Law (seen as comparable and open to legislative harmonisation) and Public Law (regarded as immeasurable and beyond supranational approaches).

In the early decades of the twentieth century, the functionalist method was a genuine methodological innovation, but it cannot be seen as subversive.[9] For example, Rabel's perspective does not question several assumptions of the dominant legal culture that would become part of the new functionalist orthodoxy. Although he advocated a comparative science free from (French) nationalism, he still identified Law with the State legal system and maintained the distinction between Private and Public Law.[10] The lack of interest in Public Law within comparative studies, and the scientistic view of Law, whether national or foreign, was shaped as an entity

[7] P.G. Monateri, *Methods in Comparative Law: An Intellectual Overview*, in P.G. Monateri, *Methods of Comparative Law*, Edward Elgar, Cheltenham, 2012, p. 13; Idem, *Elements de comparaison des etudes comparatives*, in P. Legrand (eds.), *Comparer les droits, résolument,* Presses Universitaires de France, 2009, Paris, pp. 92–93.

[8] Again, P.G. Monateri, *Geopolitica del diritto: genesi, governo e dissoluzione dei corpi politici,* Laterza, Roma-Bari, 2013, pp. 11–25.

[9] E. Rabel, *Aufgabe und Notwendigkeit der Rechtsvergleichung*, in E. Rabel, *Gesammelte Aufsätze,* JCB Mohr, Tubingen, 1967, p. 6.

[10] Cf. A. Somma, Introduzione al diritto comparato, 3ª ed., Torino, Giappichelli, 2025.

ontologically capable of being described and compared in a detached, neutral and objective way. The implicit premise of the functionalist perspective (that legal problems are the same everywhere) also suggests that this is true "at least if one limits attention to the closed circle of Western legal systems."[11]

It can be said that Comparative Law, from its beginnings, has only partly sought to counteract particularism (narrow-mindedness elevated to the status of a universal system) as well as the methodological reductionism of the dominant legal culture. Only in the second half of the twentieth century, and with many nuances, did many of the century's anti-formalist movements identify with, or at least have deep connections to, the intellectual environment of Comparative Law.[12] This is true of Rabel's functionalism and his school,[13] as well as Rodolfo Sacco's structuralist approach.[14] From this perspective, both its role as a tool in forging a critical understanding of Law[15] and the more subtle assertion of Western law as the only legitimate form of Law have coexisted at the heart of Comparative Law and in varying balances.

In this regard, it is worth noting that orthodox Comparative Law has indeed played a role of resistance, but always in a limited and necessarily selective way. On the one hand, as has been noted, it helped to erode the particularism and methodological unilateralism of national legal science. On the other hand, however, it rarely managed to overcome the epistemological limitations stemming from the context of its origins, restrictions

[11] R. Hyland, *Gifts: A Study in Comparative Law*, Oxford University Press, Oxford, 2009, pp. 65–66; T. Ruskola, Legal Orientalism: China, the United States, and Modern Law, Cambridge, MA, Harvard University Press, 2013; G. Frankenberg, *Comparative Law as Critique,* Edward Elgar, Cheltenham, 2016, p. 58.

[12] A. Riles, *Introduction* in A. Riles (dir.), *Rethinking the Masters of Comparative Law,* Hart, Oxford, 2001, pp. 9–10.

[13] For a review on the subject, see Duncan Kennedy, *Political Ideology and Comparative Law*, in M. Bussani and U. Mattei (eds.), *The Cambridge Companion to Comparative Law,* Cambridge University Press, 2012, Cambridge, p. 13; A. Somma, *Introducción crítica al Derecho comparado*, Ediciones Jurídicas Olejnik, 2017.

[14] Cf. U. Mattei, *The Comparative Jurisprudence of Schlesinger and Sacco: A Study in Legal Influence*, in A. Riles, *Rethinking the Masters*, cit., p. 251; P.G. Monateri, *Critique et difference: le droit compare en Italie*, in *Rev. Int. Droit Comp.*, 1999, pp. 292–293.

[15] See G. Ajani, Sistemi giuridici comparati. Lezioni e materiali, 2ª ed., Turín, Giappichelli, 2006.

that often operate beneath the surface, like 'cryptotypes'.[16] What we are referring to here are the assumptions inherent in the model of State Positivism: the idea that the legal order of the State is tied exclusively to a specific territory; the notion that formal rules issued by the State are the sole sources of legal normativity; and the 'scientificist' attitude, the belief that it is possible to arrive at a purely descriptive rationalisation of legal phenomena based on scientific criteria.[17] Hence the well-known weaknesses of 'traditional' Comparative Law: the dominance of taxonomic projects,[18] directly or indirectly shaped by Eurocentrism; the concealment of the political dimension inherent in any act of classification or comparison[19]; the focus on State Law to the exclusion (especially at the level of micro-comparisons) of religious and customary laws[20]; and the reduction of the object of comparison to formal rules,[21] among other limitations.

5.2 Comparative Law on Separation in the Second Half of the Twentieth Century

In the 1960s and 1970s, René David argued that one of the missions of Comparative Law was to promote a better understanding of peoples within the field of International Law. In practice, however, both David and Zweigert-Kötz perhaps unconsciously conceived of Comparative Law in an ancillary role in relation to other legal sciences, and in any case, their approach remained strongly marked by Eurocentric undertones, as Bonilla Maldonado has shown.[22] International Law, for its part, continued to present itself in a universalist key, promoting Western canons grounded in

[16] R. Sacco, *Legal Formants: A Dynamic Approach to Comparative Law (Instalment II of II)*, in *Am J Comp. L.* 1991, p. 385.

[17] For a synthesis of the traditional positivist, see M.W. Hesselink, *The New European Private Law: Essays on the Future of Private Law in Europe*, Kluwer Law International, The Hague, 2002, p. 11–36.

[18] M. Pargendler, *The Rise and Decline of Legal Families*, in *Am. J. Comp. L.*, 2012, p. 1043.

[19] Cf. J. Basedow, *Comparative Law and Its Clients*, in *Am J Comp L* 2014, p. 837.

[20] R. Michaels, *Global Legal Pluralism*, in *Annual Rev L & Social* Science, 2009, pp. 247–248; W. Menski, *Comparative Law in a Global Context: The Legal Systems of Asia and Africa,* 2e ed., Cambridge University Press, Cambridge, 2006, p. 29.

[21] Cf. H. P. Glenn, *The Aims of Comparative Law*, in J. M Smits (eds.), *Elgar Encyclopedia of Comparative Law,* 2e ed., Edward Elgar, Cheltenham, 2012, p.141.

[22] D. Bonilla Maldonado, *Los bárbaros jurídicos: Identidad, derecho comparado moderno y el Sur global*, Siglo del Hombre Editores, 2020.

the principles of sovereignty, jurisdictional immunity, sovereign equality and subjectivity, under the conviction that this internationalist universalism should be respected in every corner of the world. Aside from sporadic exchanges promoted by certain authors such as Lauterpacht, the two epistemic communities of Law, particularly within the realm of Civil Law, only engage in dialogue under the renewed belief in the existence of a single Euro-Western Universal Law.[23]

Throughout much of the twentieth century, there has been a long history of using Comparative Law techniques to harmonise and unify International Law. David and Brierley, for example, strongly advocated the standardisation of International Public Law to restrict the ongoing plurality of rules, which they described as anarchy, and explicitly criticised those who opposed legal unification as being rooted in nineteenth-century thinking,[24] arguing that there can be "no true science of law unless it is universal in scope and in spirit".[25] Linked to their ideas on the progress of Law, this modernist statement sits uneasily with genuine recognition of legal diversity. As we have seen historically, this push for uniformity traces back at least to the first period, marked by a strong belief in human rationality and progress, or even further back to De Vitoria's ecumenical civilising mission.

The same authors suggested that Comparative Law first emerged after the disintegration of the concept of *jus commune*, or universally applicable Law, as a result of nationalism and the ensuing focus on statist positivism. However, positivism quickly created its own claims of universality and 'good practices', especially in post-Napoleonic France, which left no room for Comparative Law.[26] Secondly, the objective of improving National Law through comparative legal study led to a unifying approach in "comparative legislation" during the nineteenth century, the creation of cultured societies and "in a very concrete way, a true concordance of legislative developments and not merely a generally similar tendency."[27]

Thirdly, the claim made by Comparative Law that it can foster an understanding of foreign peoples made it particularly appealing to internationalist jurists.

[23] Cf. idem.

[24] R. David and J. E.C. Brierley, *Major Legal Systems In The World Today*, Stevens and Sons, London, 1978, p. 10.

[25] R. David and J. E.C. Brierley, *Major Legal Systems in the World Today*, cit., p. 16.

[26] R. David and J. E.C. Brierley, *Major Legal Systems in the World Today*, cit., pp. 6–7.

[27] R. David and J. E.C. Brierley, *Major Legal Systems in the World Today*, cit., p. 3.

Closely tied to these debates, which ultimately revolve around Western values in relation to Law, many scholars have pointed out the renewed prominence of Natural Law approaches in the twentieth century. Jurisprudence in the field of human rights has become a "human rights industry",[28] largely based on unifying assumptions, often stubbornly denying the possibility of protecting human rights by reconstructing indigenous norms locally, rather than imposing uniform norms and legal systems on a global scale.

While "the model of rights is today hegemonic, and imbued with an emancipatory aura",[29] Cotterrell observes how one consequence of globalisation is that "[c]omparative law is powerfully driven now, as through much of its history, by the urge to unify or harmonize law. Recognizing difference does not, in these contexts, lead to its celebration, but to devising means of removing it".[30] However, he also argues that in the field of human rights, "appreciation of difference alongside a search for uniformity seems widely recognized as a continuing necessity" and explains why there is a continuing struggle. "[T]he universalization of human rights is a matter of the export, reception or transplanting of fundamental values or beliefs [...] in legal form. These values can be variously interpreted, or confronted by opposing values, in certain settings. Hence the drive for universalism, seeking similarity in human rights jurisdictions, is challenged by so-called cultural relativism that demands the appreciation of difference. Nonetheless, the drive for uniformity is very strong given that the universality of the values to be represented in human rights law is powerfully championed".[31] Comparative Law scholars have long been fascinated by the prospects of building a global legal system and have often contributed to this design. In this context, intense debates arise about the balance

[28] Cf. among others W. Twining, *General Jurisprudence: Understanding Law from a Global Perspective*, Cambridge University Press, Cambridge, 2009.

[29] *Culture and Rights*, J.K Cowan., M.B. Dembour, A.R. Wilson, (eds.), Cambridge University Press, Cambridge, 2010, p. 1.

[30] R. Cotterrell, *Is it so Bad to be Different? Comparative Law and the Appreciation of Diversity*, in *Comparative Law. A Handbook*, E. Örücü and D. Nelken (eds.), Hart publishing, Oxford, 2007, p. 136.

[31] R. Cotterrell, *Is it so Bad to be Different? Comparative Law and the Appreciation of Diversity*, cit., p. 139.

to be struck between the pursuit of similarity and the appreciation of difference.[32]

Since the mid-twentieth century, the modernist phase of the discipline has coincided with the rise of functionalism, which combines structural analyses with factual narratives. Leading comparatists aimed to identify the optimal legal system by producing or providing better (if not the best possible) legal solutions to problems arising from conflicts in organised societies. It goes without saying, once again, that what was considered a "problem" or a "better solution" was defined from a Western perspective, interpreted through Anglo-European Civil Law and Common Law frameworks.

5.2.1 Structuralism and Sacco's Theory of Formants

We have seen how legal comparison asserts itself as a critical science against the dogmas nurtured by legal positivism, and particularly against the principle of the unity of the legal rule. In Italy, this was largely achieved by relying on the theory of formants, developed by Rodolfo Sacco based on linguistic structuralism.[33]

The term 'formant' comes from acoustic phonetics, the study of the physical consistency of vocal sounds and their diffusion through a medium such as air. In this context, formant indicates the frequency of resonance of the sounds that take place in the oral cavity and that characterise its timbre. It allows these sounds to be broken down and, above all, their different components to be highlighted and identified.

Similarly, among Comparative Law scholars, the 'formant' indicates, as we have seen so far in an occasional and unsystematic manner, the components of Law, which may potentially be incoherent since they do not refer to a system free from gaps and contradictions, hence the talk of their dissociation. In this regard, among others, a legal formant is identified, referring to the rules produced by the legislator; a doctrinal formant, composed of the precepts formulated by scholars; and a jurisprudential formant, which coincides with the guidance coming from the courts.[34] When the

[32] R. Cotterrell, *Is it so Bad to be Different? Comparative Law and the Appreciation of Diversity*, cit., p. 140.

[33] R. Sacco, *Introduzione al diritto comparato*, Utet, Turín, Torino, 1995, pp. 44 ss.

[34] See, for example, R. Scarciglia, *Introduzione al diritto pubblico comparato*, Il Mulino, Bolonia, Bologna, 2006, pp. 56 ss.

comparatist acts as a systemologist, they must classify by reconstructing, for each legal system, the degree of dissociation between formants, measure the real distances between them, and verify their coherence. If, on the other hand, they are comparing specific legal constructions, they must first identify the content of the corresponding formants in order to later use them as a point of reference in their analyses.

The break introduced by the theory of formants in relation to the ideal foundation of legal positivism is evident. Legal positivism takes into account only the formal sources of Law and does not consider jurisprudence or doctrine, unless it is necessary to analyse a Common Law system or Religious Law, respectively. The attitude of those who do not tolerate inconsistency in interpreting the words of formal legal sources is also characteristically positivist, attributing such inconsistency to an error of interpretation: this reflects the principle of the unity of legal rule.[35]

Therefore, it is not only the devaluation of context that makes the structuralist method problematic. It is also the scientism it implies, exemplified by the belief that, by identifying the structures of legal systems and thus confirming their impermeability to context, the scholar can provide precise indications about the state of the objects in question regarding a particular property: they can "measure" without relying on data from a political science, ethics or any other science external to the study of linguistic data.[36]

Scientism is also implicit in the reference to the possibility of faithfully reconstructing the content of the various formants, which leads to viewing structuralism as a way to multiply (rather than overcome) the flaws of positivism. Structuralists do not believe in the uniqueness of legal rule, but they believe they can identify the plurality of rules indicated by the dissociation between formants, whose internal coherence they verify. By consistently basing structural decomposition on the same patterns, structuralists tend to apply their Western assumptions to organisational systems where the Law is neither reducible to nor assessable by these patterns. In this way, the risk of pushing structuralist theory to its extreme consequences is a covert return to Kelsenian formalism.[37] This is the outcome of the

[35] Cf. A. E. Platsas, *The Functional and the Dysfunctional in the Comparative Method of Law: Some Critical Remarks*, in *Electronic Journal of Comparative Law*, vol. 12.3, December 2008, pp. 1–15.

[36] R. Sacco, in P. Legrand, *Questions à Rodolfo Sacco*, in *Revue international de droit comparé*, 1995, pp. 949, 959.

[37] H. Kelsen, Pure Theory of Law, University of California Press,, Los Angeles, 1967.

assertion that "we, after having broken down any legal system and reduced it to a series of distinct formants, can establish the degree of dissociation between the formants and, above all, to what extent the formal sources of a country, the law applied there, and the knowledge that jurists have of their systems are in agreement."[38]

Those who practice dissociation between formants aim to demonstrate the fallacy of the unity of the legal system. They seek to reconstruct the organisation of a certain disciplinary area in a descriptive way, that is, setting aside the prescriptive viewpoint typically embraced by those who follow legal positivism. On the one hand, the demonstration that norms codified in legal texts inevitably circulate in their operational version (as seen in the original example of contracts requiring unilateral formation[39]) refutes the systemic separation proclaimed by theorists and legislators, constituting a starting point for a relational view of Law. Cryptotypes themselves, systemic inconsistencies and trans-systemic interactions between formants anticipate a dynamic understanding of legal circulation.[40] However, the context in which legal constructions operate is often sidelined to an epistemological backwater or even dismissed outright, resulting frequently in comparisons that serve to unify rather than differentiate.[41]

5.2.2 *Functionalism and the Method of the Purpose of the Norm*

While in the Italian context Comparative Law has drawn on structuralism to deconstruct the traditional approach to legal study, in other contexts this role has been assumed by the functional method. Specifically, this has been the case in the German and American spheres: in the latter, largely due to the influence of Ernst Rabel, who was forced to leave Nazi Germany because of his Jewish heritage.[42]

As a scholar of International Private Law, Rabel addressed, among other issues, the question of characterisation, that is, the interpretation of

[38] R. Sacco, *Introduzione al diritto comparato*, cit., p. 12. 17 *Ivi*, p. 49.

[39] R. Sacco, *Introduzione al diritto comparato*, Utet, Torino, 1995, pp. 78–93.

[40] Cfr. M. Graziadei, *a compasso allargato. La comparazione giuridica nel mondo attuale e le questioni di metodo*, in *Diritto pubblico comparato ed europeo*, 2024, p. 39.

[41] A. Somma, *Introducción crítica al Derecho comparado*, Ediciones Jurídicas Olejnik, 2017, p. 158.

[42] E. Rabel, *The Conflict of Laws*, vol. 1, University of Michigan Press, Ann Arbor, 1945, pp. 49 s.

the concepts within conflict-of-law rules that identify the substantive scope of application and determine the applicable Law in cases involving elements of internationality. If international courts were to interpret these concepts according to the typical standards of the legal system in which they operate, they would reach incorrect conclusions from the perspective of the foreign legal system to which the conflict rule refers. Therefore, according to Rabel, characterisation should not follow the conceptualism typical of a national legal system, but rather the meaning to which the factual situation referred to by the conflict rule points.

Rabel's theory has not been widely accepted; instead, the prevailing view is that characterisation must be carried out according to the standards of the legal system to which the conflict rule belongs. Nonetheless, his theory played a significant role in the development of the functional method, whose most influential formulation is attributed to Konrad Zweigert and Hein Kötz.

These two German comparatists observe that, although all societies turn to Law to resolve similar problems, the technical-legal solutions adopted are often divergent. Therefore, the comparatist should begin their research with questions framed in factual, rather than conceptual, terms. For example, if they come from a legal system where the premature conclusion of a contract is governed by formal requirements, they should not compare their system with a foreign one by looking for its regulation of contract form. Instead, they should focus on identifying the technical-legal solutions adopted to protect the contracting parties, which may differ from those found in the "typical conceptual system of their own legal order." Zweigert and Kötz warn that, in this way, the comparison could include solutions that, from the perspective of the comparatist's home legal system, are not technical-legal solutions. The comparatist must direct their attention to the "same sources used by the jurist of the foreign legal system and assign them the same value and weight as the foreign jurist does."[43]

The most evident vice of the functional method is the observation that, although they present "differences in historical development, in their systematic-theoretical structure and in the style of practical applications", different legal systems adopt "identical or very similar solutions, right down to the smallest details". To the extent that the comparatist, despite

[43] K. Zweigert- H. Kötz, Einführung in die Rechtsvergleichung auf dem Gebiete des Privatrechts, 3.ª ed., Mohr Siebeck, Tübingen, 1996, cit., pp. 37 ss.

noting significant differences at the technical-legal level, may begin with a "presumption of similarities in practical solutions", which holds true at least in all areas not "influenced by value judgements or moral imperatives."[44] From this, it is concluded that, outside the realms of family, personal and succession law, there is an 'apolitical Private Law' which essentially corresponds to Property or Commercial Law.[45]

Another critical aspect of the method emerges when considering the limits that Zweigert and Kötz place on the comparatist's task: to compare "only those things that serve the same purpose, with the same function."[46] It is precisely this limitation that enables the two German authors to achieve what effectively appears predetermined as a self-evident, elemental and indisputable truth: although national legal systems differ, the concrete solutions (or their functions) are comparable.[47] In essence, this approach sidesteps the usual problems arising from measuring the states of the objects compared with respect to a specific property.

The functional method is designed to produce a unifying comparison and to dismiss as outside the scope of the comparatist's work anything that might contradict the image of an apolitical (and, as such, Universal) Law. Above all, this applies to research in areas of the legal system considered to be held hostage by cultural or ideological choices. The underlying hypothesis of the functionalist method is *praesumptio similitudinis*, that is, "despite differences in their historical development, all societies essentially face the same problems."[48]

In any case, what has been said about the dissociation between formants applies equally to the functional method. Although it pertains to specific cultural orientations and is therefore flawed from the perspective of alternative viewpoints, it can nonetheless prove highly useful in supporting comparative research aimed at promoting certain outcomes, such as the examination of the connections between the norm and the socio-political system in which it is embedded.

[44] K. Zweigert, *Des solutions identiques par des voies différentes*, in *Revue internationale de droit comparé*, 18, 1966, pp. 5 ss.

[45] K. Zweigert, *Des solutions identiques par des voies différentes*, in *Revue internationale de droit comparé*, cit., p. 10.

[46] M. Graziadei, *The Functionalist Heritage*, AA.VV., *Comparative Legal Studies: Traditions and Transitions*, edited by P. Legrand, R. Munday, Cambridge University Press, Cambridge, 2003, p. 102.

[47] Zweigert, Kötz, *Introducción al Derecho Comparado* cit., p. 37.

[48] Zweigert, Kötz, *Introducción al Derecho Comparado* cit., p. 23.

5.2.3 The Evolution of Postmodern Comparative Law Theories

Comparative Law was deeply involved as a willing servant in the processes of legal unification ("*Comparative Law as a harmonising handmaiden*" is the title of a chapter in the formidable work of Menski[49]). We have noted that the first objective outlined by David and Brierley is the contribution to other branches of knowledge, such as philosophy, history and sociology, as if comparative science did not pursue its own independent functions and goals.

Secondly, the fundamental creed of traditional Comparative Law, clearly expressed by the two authors as "there is no true science of law unless it is universal in scope and spirit",[50] reflects an evident disregard for global diversity, tolerating it only as a provisional measure. Postmodern comparative legal theory now turns to linguistics and aesthetics to understand the nature of comparison as "the clarification of similarities and the clarification of differences."[51] Even the structuralist and functionalist theories themselves, immersed in their harmonising-universalist reality and taken to their extreme conclusions, tended to favour a commitment to unification.

In this sense, the synergy (albeit unintentional) between Comparative Law and International Law permeates the very idea of legal transplants. Through reference to a particular article, Maldonado Bonilla exposes the deeply ethnocentric ideology of David concerning the supposed imperative of legal transplantation in the Ethiopian context.[52] The criterion of the "implicit concept of Law" is combined with that of "culture as a source of Law" to create a hierarchy among the world's legal systems. In this narrative, "European culture and law are thus presented as autopoietic." [...] The taxonomies constructed by twentieth century Comparative Law, therefore, are built upon an implicit concept of law.[53]

[49] W. Menski, *Comparative Law in a Global context. The Legal Systems of Asia and Africa*, cit., p. 20.

[50] R. David, J. E. C. Brierley, *Major legal systems in the world today*, cit., p. 16.

[51] AA.VV., *Rethinking the masters of Comparative Law*, edited by A. Riles, Hart, Oxford and Portland, 2001, p. 17.

[52] D. Bonilla Maldonado, *Los bárbaros jurídicos: Identidad, derecho comparado moderno y el Sur global*, cit., p. 104: "*El proyecto de Código Civil para Etiopía es, para David, un ejercicio de derecho comparado. El punto de partida del proyecto es un análisis funcionalista de Etiopía y Europa*".

[53] D. Bonilla Maldonado, *Los bárbaros jurídicos: Identidad, derecho comparado moderno y el Sur global*, cit., p. 110.

On the other hand, the idea of an implicit, coherent legal system has played a crucial role in establishing the previously discussed "standard of civilisation." Oppenheim, for example, asserted that "there is no civilised State whose municipal law is not codified to a greater or lesser extent."[54] In his textbook on International Law, Oppenheim referred to Japan as a "non-Christian member of the 'Family of Nations'", stating that "through marvellous efforts, Japan has become not only a modern State, but also an influential Power.[55] Part of the "marvellous efforts" that led to Japan being recognised as part of the 'Family of Nations' was the introduction of a Civil Code in 1898, largely inspired by the first draft of the German Civil Code. This kind of thinking is still evident in academic statements that demand a legal tradition be sufficiently coherent to be considered as a 'legal system' in order to be taken into account when identifying the general principles of International Law.

In the field of Comparative Law, not only is the phase of distilling uniform norms (general principles of Common Law) relevant, but also the subsequent transplantation into the receiving legal systems. The "donors" of the transplant argued that legal rules can be successfully borrowed, even if the socioeconomic, geographic and political circumstances of the recipient differ significantly from those of the donor. The theory of legal transplants was championed by Watson (originally in 1974, and later in 1993[56]), under whose banner the "donors" of legal transplants gathered, disregarding his warnings against blind faith in total unification. After cautioning that even the possibility and desirability of a uniform legal system for the Western world was questionable, Watson clearly stated that "a complete legal union is neither possible nor desirable",[57] thus he cannot be simplistically included as a supporter of the vision of global unification. Watson was fully aware that differences would arise due to many non-legal factors, including a fair amount of chance, and he reassessed the scope and desirability of legal transplants.[58]

In fact, the issue is central to comparative studies and had already been clearly highlighted in the work on transplants, diffusion and the

[54] L. Oppenheim, *International Law. A Treatise*, I, Longsman Green and Co., New York and Bombay, 1905, p. 34.

[55] L. Oppenheim, *International Law. A Treatise*, cit., p. 35.

[56] A. Watson, *Legal transplants: An approach to Comparative Law*, 2 ed., University of Georgia Press, Athens, GA, 1993.

[57] A. Watson, *Legal transplants: An approach to Comparative Law*, cit., p. 100.

[58] A. Watson, *Legal transplants: An approach to Comparative Law*, cit., p. 81.

circulation of legal formants. Rodolfo Sacco's position on legal circulation is more nuanced, insofar as it shows certain points of contact with that of Watson (for example, the rejection of contamination by sociological or economic perspectives), but also elements from which it diverges, such as a greater appreciation for contextual diversity and a strong interest in legal anthropology, alongside the consideration of the variety of formants, their dissociation and the role of cryptotypes.[59] The recovery of legal and cultural contexts is notably central to Pierre Legrand's comparative approach and to his provocative claim regarding the impossibility of legal transplants, a thesis that does not deny the factual occurrence of receptions, but rather rejects the notion that a linguistic and legal object retains the same meaning in the recipient context as it had in the context of origin, in light of the interpretative frameworks and cultural conditioning of each legal culture.[60] The merit of Legrand's theory lies in its emphasis on the unavoidable challenge of managing Otherness.

Conscious jurisprudence of plurality demands a great deal from jurists for whom the Law has remained restricted to State Law. "Comparative Law today, perceived as trendy, is taken up by inadequately qualified researchers who lack the necessary skills and erudition to effectively engage in the comparative study of foreign laws. Comparative research and analysis is often undertaken with a myopic view limited to the juxta position of the regulations of one legal system with those of another, with little or no critical analysis".[61] Legrand, on the other hand, argues that such comparatists "do not compare, they contrast",[62] avoiding the intrinsic complexities of genuinely comparative study and remaining at a flat, merely descriptive level. Once again, Western, particularly State-centred legal identity emerges through opposition to legal systems that, in most cases, are not even recognised as being in accordance with the Law.

The second point, of an epistemological nature and closely linked to the approach formulated by Legrand, concerns the nature of comparative legal study in Europe and North America, and the methodological

[59] R. Sacco, *Circolazione e mutazione dei modelli*, in *Digesto delle discipline privatistiche—Sezione civile*, vol. 2, Torino, 1988, p. 365 ss.; Idem, *Antropologia giuridica. Contributo a una macrostoria del diritto*, Il Mulino, Bologna, 2007.

[60] P. Legrand, *The Impossibility of 'Legal Transplant'*, in *Maastricht Journal of European and Comparative Law*, 1997, p. 111 ss.

[61] W. Menski, *Comparative Law in a Global context. The Legal Systems of Asia and Africa*, cit., p. 34.

[62] P. Legrand, *How to compare now*, in *Legal Studies*, 1996, Vol. 16, No. 2, pp. 232–242.

shortcomings in identifying similarities and relationships between concepts from different legal systems. The almost irresistible tendency of comparative jurists has been to translate roughly equivalent concepts (or those that appear to be so) from two or more legal systems and then contrast them, rather than analyse their respective socio-legal contexts. In line with Carol Harlow,[63] who speaks of 'deep structure', comparatists who have engaged more profoundly with the cultural-legal terrain do not merely translate concepts; rather, they seek to explore the substantive differences between terms and concepts that may initially appear similar.

The third key challenge faced by Comparative Law scholars in Europe and North America when researching Asian and African legal systems lies in the accurate understanding, interpretation and comparison of the normative systems recognised by the cultures and societies that the comparatist seeks to study. This is a core issue not only within the field of Comparative Law, as discussed in the introductory phase of this work, but one that touches the very heart of legal identity. It demands thorough and hands-on research into those legal systems, setting aside certain pre-established conceptions. One cannot truly understand Common Law, except in a superficial and therefore ultimately meaningless way, unless one grasps the *mentalité* of the system analysed; a mindset that necessarily requires a socially, historically, culturally and epistemologically complex study.

From a postmodern legal perspective, while the harmonisation of national legal systems may remain a practically desirable endeavour, any push for uniformity that seeks to fully assimilate the Other appears unrealistic, as it fails to account for the inherent plurality of all Law. Recent studies show that the theoretical aspirations to globalise legal uniformity are little more than questionable attempts to privilege one type of law over all others. "Positivist law-making at the international level ultimately seeks to supersede nation states, which themselves have unsuccessfully sought to override and legislate away various local forms of law-making. In reality, local and global elements of law are always involved in visible and invisible dynamic interaction, leading to pluralistic glocalisation rather than uniformising globalisation. New secular natural law ideologies, seeking to place themselves above all other forms of law, even the laws of Gods, merely insist in familiar legocentric (and hence myopic and unrealistic)

[63] C. Harlow, *Voices of Difference in a Plural Community*, in *The American Journal of Comparative Law*, Vol. 50, No. 2 (Spring, 2002), pp. 339–367.

fashion on the superiority of their own values, which evidently the whole world does not share".[64]

International legal norms (an expression of an active and fertile international community, rooted primarily in a renewed notion of *jus cogens*) would often become intertwined with national rules, the former drawing nourishment from the socio-cultural contextualisation of local legal realities, while the latter find in supranational regulation the scope and legal force that transcend the limitations of national or collective jurisdictions. The aim is to make International Law a genuinely pluralistic system, open to all its constituent realities. To achieve this, it is necessary to engage with the Law of the Other, not merely as the Law of the Other, but in a way that is not already framed by an initial *prius*: Ours. "Western hubris and so-called rational superiority attempt to dictate to all 'others' how they should develop their laws, with predictable reactions of opposition or simple silence, which remains a powerful strategy to avoid plurality-conscious negotiation with a participant unwilling to take account of the basic facts of legal pluralism worldwide".[65]

5.3 The International Law of Separation in the First Part of the Twentieth Century

"*La forma en la que los supuestos teóricos moldean nuestra comprensión de las estructuras y sistemas de autoridad que conocemos como derecho internacional está lejos de ser neutral. La idea, aún hoy sostenida por muchos en la profesión, de que el derecho internacional es una lengua franca a través de la cual nos comunicamos y hacemos cosas juntos en el plano internacional es incorrecta y hasta un poco inocente.*"[66] We have uncovered the epistemological mechanisms that link the disciplines of International Law and Comparative Law at their inception, examining how the emergence of Western identity has always rested on systems of inclusion and exclusion with respect to Others. Though originating from a specific Western

[64] W. Menski, *Comparative Law in a Global context. The Legal Systems of Asia and Africa*, cit., p. 78.

[65] W. Menski, *Comparative Law in a Global context. The Legal Systems of Asia and Africa*, cit., p. 89.

[66] A. Bianchi, *International Law Theories: An Inquiry into Different Ways of Thinking*, Oxford University Press, Oxford, 2017. For a critical version in the field of Comparative Law, see. A. Somma, *Introducción crítica al Derecho Comparado*, Universidad Carlos III Madrid, 2015.

national territory, rooted in the great colonial empires, by universalising themselves, these disciplines have helped build the tools through which we perceive the contemporary world. The scientific identities of these two fields of knowledge have, in synergy and during historically coeval moments, powerfully shaped and distorted our understanding of reality, particularly with regard to who we are: our national identity. Both disciplines emerge with a significant and powerful nationalist connotation.

The idea that the validity and identity of Law must be determined according to the parameters existing within the Law itself is a conviction of all traditional approaches to Comparative Law and International Law. Incidentally, the posture of self-assertion and the claims to knowledge inherent in the affirmation of disciplinary autonomy are comparable to the exercise of power mechanisms that operate to the benefit of those who control the discursive politics of the discipline.

It is argued that "International Law assumes the natural existence of a Being of the State and that this ontology of statehood constitutes the ontology of International Law" y que "the ontology of statehood having been transformed into an epistemology ultimately leads to the violent suppression of alterity".[67] The ontology of the State—the natural law idea that States existed naturally as beings in the world—is an integral part of the fundamental structure of the international legal system, shaping its own identity. In nineteenth-century theories, the State is conceived first as a *prius*, a pre-existing entity, and only secondarily as a legal subject. As such, it is International Law that becomes subject to the doctrine of statehood and the principle of separation between monads.[68]

5.3.1 *Monist and Dualist Theories: The Conceptual Separation*

In the International Law of separation (understood as a legal discourse aligned with Glennian closure), the progressive affirmation of the principle of State sovereignty celebrated the desire to armour-plate each emerging national entity.[69] International Law was thus conceived as a normative

[67] S. Jodoin, *International Law and Alterity: The State and the Other*, A. Orford (ed.), Cambridge University Press, Cambridge, 2006, pp. 87–107.

[68] Cf. J.E., Nijman, *Paul Ricoeur and International Law: Beyond 'The End of the Subject'. Towards a Reconceptualization of International Legal Personality*, in *Leiden Journal of International Law*, 20, 2007, pp. 25–64.

[69] Cf. H. Baron, *The Crisis of The Early Italian Renaissance: Civic Humanism and Republican Liberty In An Age of Classicism and Tyranny*, New Jersey University Press,

toolkit for designing an institutional framework governing non-armed relations between nations. These relations would remain non-armed only insofar as they respected legal norms forged through inter-State will[13]. The modern State was to concentrate both the monopoly on normative authority and the monopoly on the use of force. Likewise, it was expected to use both to protect the lives and property of all citizens and to resolve disputes arising between them. International Law, for its part, functioned as a law of juxtaposition, since its institutions were configured to preserve a power vacuum in international relations, one that could be filled effortlessly through agreements based on the Private Law principle of *pacta sunt servanda*[14].To what extent, however, could this independence be sustained? Would there be any limits? It is precisely in this context (and in line with the dual purpose of preserving the void while managing it) that the theoretical binary of monism and dualism sought to guide the interaction between International Law and Domestic Law. These two theories translate, at the theoretical level, the defining line of separation characteristic of the period straddling the nineteenth and twentieth centuries.

Dualism presents the idea that there is no conflict between the two legal systems, since they are different legal systems that do not overlap. International Law deals with inter-State relations, focusing on the multilateral will of States, while Domestic Law addresses intra-State matters, driven by the unilateral will of States. Monism holds that International Law and Domestic Law form a single legal order, which can give rise to potential conflicts or contradictions between their rules. For some scholars, monism required that the international legal order should prevail over Domestic Law. "The search for a single and stable solution for such a problem in International Law derives from the influence of the modern discourse. Indeed, this particular narrative is characterized by always looking for a fixed a priori hierarchy to solve social and scientific conflicts".[70] Thus, the search for a single and stable hierarchical approach to dealing in a predictable manner with the interaction between International Law and Domestic Law characterises the modern status of International Law. Monistic or dualistic approaches are expressions of a modern impulse that

Princeton, 1966; J. A. Carrillo-Salcedo, *El Derecho Internacional en un Mundo en Cambio*, Tecnos, Madrid, 1984; Idem, *Permanencia y cambios en Derecho internacional*, Admission Speech as a Full Member of the Real Academia de Ciencias Morales y Políticas, Madrid, 2005.

[70] A.R. Capella Giannattasio, *The Interaction between International and Domestic Legal Orders: Framing the Debate according to the Post-Modern Condition of International Law*, in *German Law Journal*, 2019, p. 7.

pursues precise and certain limits for or against this freedom of Domestic Law with respect to International Law.

In the wake of the First World War, Hans Kelsen addressed the problem of State sovereignty and laid the foundations for a monistic theory of International Law focused on the primacy of International Law over the Domestic Law of States.

Kelsen argues that sovereignty is an attribute of the State understood as a legal order, and this means that the principle on which the validity of the legal order rests lies in a basic rule that functions as the basis of the Positive Law system. But most importantly, he points out, "what we want to know is not whether the state in general or any given state 'is' sovereign, but whether the theory of the state can or must recognize [...] the sovereignty of the state's legal order or, on the contrary, only the sovereignty of the international legal order".[71]

A set of norms constitutes a system when those norms derive from a basic norm, and thus two systems can only be distinguished from one another if they are based on different basic norms. However, as Kelsen points out, reasoning from the postulate of the unity of knowledge, only one system can be valid: it is not possible for two different normative systems to be recognised simultaneously as binding.

By rejecting the dualism between International and Domestic Law, Kelsen opposes the principal proponent of this view, Heinrich Triepel.[72] As Kelsen explains, Triepel's dualism assumes the primacy of Domestic Law, as it reflects the nineteenth-century conception of the supremacy of the Nation-State, thereby denying the very possibility of an international legal system. Kelsen observes that, in Triepel's dualist conception, the distinction between the national and international systems ultimately derives from the distinction between their respective sources of normativity.

The dualist and monist theories of International Law portray a divisive and exclusionary worldview: the underlying logic is that of *Aut Aut*.[73] The former continues to ground its reasoning in the notion of State sovereignty,

[71] H. Kelsen, *Das Problem der Souveränität und die Theorie des Völkerrechts: Beitrag zu einer reinen Rechtslehre*, J.C.B. Mohr (Paul Siebeck), Tübingen, 1920, p. 45.

[72] H. Triepel, *Völkerrecht und Landesrecht*, Scientia Antiquariat, Aalen, 1958; orig. pub. 1899.

[73] On this subject, see *New Perspectives on the Divide Between National and International Law* edited by Janne E. Nijman, André Nollkaemper, Oxford University Press, Oxford, 2007; M. A. Waters, *Creeping Monism: The Judicial Trend toward Interpretive Incorporation of Human Rights Treaties*, in *Colum. L. Rev.* 2007, p. 628.

positing the existence of two distinct legal systems and assigning to Domestic Law the authority to determine the conditions under which international norms are transposed. In more technical terms, a system is dualist when it only recognises the validity of a norm of International Law on the express condition that it has been incorporated into the national legal order. From this perspective, International Law becomes national law through the mechanism of State transposition, or else it does not exist at all. This position is reflected, for instance, in the Constitution of the United States.[74] The opposing conception was championed not only by Hans Kelsen,[75] but also by Georges Scelle. The monist theory envisions a single unified system, merging International and Domestic Law into one. Both theories, however, represent two sides of the same coin, minted within the exclusionary framework of an identity-based legal paradigm.

Both visions take for granted the existence of a *prius*, either the national system or the international system: they do not really interact, or they should not.

"The divide between national and International Law is based on a territorial conception of the law".[76] To a large extent, this is a truism. States, which have been the main organisational units at least since the eighteenth century, are territorially defined entities. Legally, this has been translated into the precept that "every State enjoyed exclusive competence for developments within its territory",[77] as expressed by the 'Lotus' principle: "International Law governs relations between independent States. The rules of law binding upon States therefore emanate from their own free will as expressed in conventions or by usages generally accepted as expressing principles of law and established in order to regulate the relations between these co-existing independent communities or with a view to the achievement of common aims".[78] Either way, both approaches relate to a

[74] Art. VI, Clause 2 of the United States Constitution (emphasis added): "[A]ll Treaties made, or which shall be made, under the Authority of the United States, shall be the supreme. Law of the Land; and the Judges in every State shall be bound thereby, any Thing in the Constitution or Laws of any State to the Contrary notwithstanding."

[75] H. Kelsen, *The Pure Theory of Law* [Reine Rechtslehre], M. Knight trans., 1978, p. 215.

[76] C. Brölmann, *Deterritorialization in International Law: Moving Away from the Divide Between National and International Law*, in *New Perspectives On The Divide Between National And International Law* 84 *et seq.*, Janne Nijman & André Nollkaemper eds., 2007, pp. 84–105.

[77] C. Tomuschat, *Obligations for States*, in *Recueil des Cours de l'Académie de droit international*, 1993, p. 210.

[78] Case of the SS 'Lotus' (France v Turkey), PCIJ Series A, No. 10 (1927) p. 18.

legal universe that recognises territorial subdivisions of authority, i.e., territorially limited jurisdictions. Such a classification is, in any case, grounded in the idea of territorially bounded legal spheres which are, therefore, distinguishable. Moreover, it derives from legal domains that are mutually recognised and formally separated.

Thus, the European Union, in collaboration with the World Health Organization, the Food and Agriculture Organization of the United Nations and the World Organisation for Animal Health monitors and regulates avian influenza alongside the States, for whom animal health, food safety and economic resilience constitute elements of a comprehensive policy of authority within a defined territory[79].

"Deconstructive post-modern International Law perceives the international legal order as relying in the autonomous and spontaneous customary normative process of each society. The plural and unstable definition in time, space, and subject of what will hold the opinio juris sive necessitatis aura should be regarded as the touchstone of International Law and as the guide to define which order should prevail in case of conflict. In other words, custom and its uncontrollable outcomes should be the basis of an International Law framework".[80] Regimes that involve 'deterritorialisation' are, in practical terms, regimes that constitute a normative authority independent of that of the State. "[s]ystems of rule need not be territorial

[79] N. Luhmann, *Das Recht der Gesellschaft*, Suhrkamp, Frankfurt am Main, 1995, 571–590.; IDEM, *Die Gesellschaft der Gesellschaft*, Suhrkamp, Frankfurt am Main, 1997, Vol 1, 158–160.

Cf. A. Paulus, *From Territoriality to Functionality? Towards a Legal Methodology of Globalization,* in I.F. Dekker and W.G. Werner (eds), *Governance and International Legal Theory*, Martinus Nijhoff, Leiden/Boston, 2004, pp. 59–95 A. Fischer-Lescano and G. Teubner, '*Regime-Collisions: The Vain Search for Legal Unity in the Fragmentation of Global Law*, in *Michigan Journal of International Law* 2004, pp. 999–1000; S. Sassen, *Losing Control? Sovereignty in an Age of Globalization*, Columbia University Press, New York, 1997, p. 61; *Fragmentation Of International Law: Difficulties Arising From The Diversification And Expansion Of International Law*, Report of the Study Group of the International Law Commission directed by M. Koskenniemi (UN Doc. A/CN.4/L.682; 13 April 2006), with explicit reference to the transfer of territory to the function, in para 133, n 138. See also M. Koskenniemi y P. Leino, *Fragmentation of International Law. Postmodern Anxieties?*, in *Leiden Journal of International Law*, 2002, p. 553.

[80] A.R. Capella Giannattasio, *The Interaction between International and Domestic Legal Orders: Framing the Debate according to the Post-Modern Condition of International Law*, in *German Law Journal*, 2019, p. 16.

[...] or, while territorially fixed, they need not be **exclusive**" [emphasis added].[81]

5.4 Sources of International Law of Separation

Moving from doctrinal sources and their theories, we now turn to the analysis of their manifestation in the key areas of International Law (which I define as those of separation), in the order established by Article 38 of the Statute of the International Court of Justice.

5.4.1 International Custom

Various forms of custom are often the result of social interactions and relationships between individuals within a given society, which in turn give rise to legal obligations. A prominent characteristic of these societies, regardless of geographical location or ethnicity, is that custom develops through recurring practices which regulate or influence behaviour.[82] It is the Greek *nomos* of Herodotus. These developed practices tend to be rooted in cultural, religious and other historical experiences developed collectively within a given community. "In these circumstances, wide acceptance and application are expected based on the representation of collective interests within that society. Human relationships and interactions are known to transcend immediate borders in areas of different cultures, religions, and historical experiences, and especially in the field of trade".[83] In such situations, the principles and applications of custom acquire international dimensions of a hegemonic nature.[84] "The encounter between Europeans and Africans during colonialism was characterised by the use of force, intimidation, deceit and conquest in order to institute

[81] J.G. Ruggie, *Territoriality and Beyond: Problematizing Modernity in International Relations,* in *International Organization*, 1993, p. 149.

[82] J. Chinwe Okubuir, *Application of Hegemony to Customary International Law: An African Perspective*, in *Global Journal of Comparative Law*, 2018, pp. 232–271.

[83] J. Chinwe Okubuir, *Application of Hegemony to Customary International Law: An African Perspective*, cit., p. 240.

[84] U.D. Acharya, *Globalization and Hegemony Shift: Are States Merely Agents of Corporate Capitalism?*, in *Boston College Law Review*, 2013, p. 937; R.W. Cox, '*Gramsci, Hegemony and International Relations: An Essay in Method*', in L. Amoore (ed.), *The Global Resistance Reader*, Routledge, London and New York, 2005, p. 35.

and maintain 'particular binding principles' derived from Europe".[85] Customary International Law, as one of the main sources of International Law, is defined by this European form of International Law.[86]

An example of the relevance of Customary International Law is found in the areas of State immunity discussed previously, where broad multilateral treaties have yet to be negotiated.[87] It also serves as a tool to fill gaps within treaties and to clarify the meaning of ambiguous or undefined terms in a text.

Customary International Law is based on the traditional notion of sovereignty, which considers States as the sole entities enjoying full legal personality under International Law.[88] This position places the creation of Customary International Law within the State system. As previously mentioned, historically, the State (particularly the European State) was regarded as the central element around which all International Law revolved.[89] Despite the involvement of non-European societies (Africa, for example) in the development of Customary International Law, only Eurocentric origins have been adopted, to the exclusion of others. Because of this European bias, the first definition of Customary International Law, as it is known today, dates back to 1920 and to the Advisory Committee of Jurists to the Permanent Court of International Justice.[90] The initial draft of the treaty defined international custom as "*une pratique commune des nations acceptée par elles comme loi*".[91] In the final draft, some changes were made and the paragraph read "*La preuve d'une pratique générale acceptée comme norme juridique*". This definition was reproduced in

[85] A. Anghie, '*Finding the Peripheries: Sovereignty and Colonialism in Nineteenth Century International Law*' in *Harv. Int'l L. J.*, 1999, p. 1.

[86] J. Chinwe Okubuir, *Application of Hegemony to Customary International Law: An African Perspective*, cit., p. 239.

[87] Cf. P. Andrés de Saénz Santamaría, *Las dinámicas del Derecho internacional en el siglo XXI: acordes y desacordes*", in *Estados y organizaciones internacionales ante las nuevas crisis globales*, Asociación Española de Profesores de Derecho Internacional y Relaciones Internacionales, Iustel and Universidad de La Rioja, 2010, p. 83.

[88] Cf. J. L. Brier, *The Basis of Obligation in International Law*, Clarendon Press, Oxford, 1958.

[89] See *North Sea Continental Shelf (Federal Republic of Germany/Netherlands; Federal Republic of Germany/Denmark)* 1969 ICJ Reports p. 3, p. 43.

[90] A. Pellet, *Article 38*, in A. Zimmermann et al. (eds.), *The Statute of the International Court of Justice: A Commentary*, Oxford University Press, Oxford, 2006, p. 750.

[91] Procès-Verbaux of the Proceedings of the Advisory Committee of Jurists (1920), Annexe No. 3, p. 306.

Article 38(1)(b) of the Statute of the International Court of Justice.[92] In light of this, Customary International Law is conceived and constructed by and for sovereign States. This article argues that Customary International Law is not only hegemonic in its form (in the sense that it tends to favour centralised power structures, modelled on the Westphalian state), but also in its substance (in the sense that major powers are more likely to influence the creation of customary norms).[93]

5.4.2 *The Principle of Extraterritoriality*

Perhaps the most illustrative and debated institution of international custom in this period was extraterritoriality, which might ultimately be seen as a clear exercise in exclusionary Comparative Law.

As we shall see below, Twiss pointed out that the unequal treaties that granted Western governments extraterritorial jurisdiction over their nationals in 'semi-civilised' states were "to the highest extent exceptional" but nevertheless necessary.[94] One of the reasons for this extraordinary situation was that Islamic and Indian law did not grant the same rights to foreigners, and their legal systems were fundamentally different from Western ones, without distinguishing between Law and morality. Likewise, Westlake observed that laws, habits, family structures, literature and the arts in Europe and the Americas were similar enough that "no one who has had a liberal education feels himself a stranger in the houses, schools, law courts, theatres, scarcely even in the churches, of another country".[95] This was because he shared a common civilisation that was, however, absent from Asia. Therefore, Europeans and Americans residing there would not feel safe under the local administration of justice which, even when they accepted its integrity, they felt could not have the necessary structure to give adequate protection to unknown interests arising from a

[92] Draft Plan for the Establishment of the Permanent Court of International Justice referred to in Article 14 of the Covenant of the League of Nations submitted to the Council of the Society by the Advisory Committee of Jurists, Official Journal, Special Supplement No. 2, Article 35, September 1920; Article 38, paragraph 1 (b), of the Statute of the Permanent Court of Justice.

[93] J. Chinwe Okubuir, *Application of Hegemony to Customary International Law: An African Perspective*, cit., p. 239.

[94] T. Twiss, *The Law of Nations Considered as Independent Political Communities*, Oxford University Press, Oxford, 1861, p. 224.

[95] J. Westlake, *Equality and Independence of States*, cit., p. 102.

foreign civilisation. The U.S. Supreme Court also intervened on the issue: "The circuit court might have found an additional ground for not calling in question the legislation of Congress in the uniform practice of civilized governments for centuries to provide consular tribunals in other than Christian countries [...] down to the time of the formation of our government, of the fact that the establishment of such tribunals was among the most important subjects for treaty stipulations".[96]

Such was his blind confidence in the standard of civilisation that Martens considered extraterritoriality not merely a right, but a duty, a part of the civilising mission or, as Ruskola puts it, "a kind of white lawyer's burden."[97] Decades later, when a French and a Turkish ship collided on the high seas a few miles from Turkey, the latter insisted that it had jurisdiction to try the French captain for manslaughter for the deaths of eight Turkish crew members. The French challenge to this claim struck a raw nerve in the young republic, which had only recently succeeded in abolishing extraterritoriality.

In the previously mentioned Lotus case, the principle was established that jurisdiction is territorial in nature.[98] The ruling affirms that a State exercising jurisdiction beyond its own territory must be authorised to do so by an international treaty or a rule of Customary International Law. Extraterritoriality was explicitly, consistently and repeatedly justified and contested by reference to the notion of a civilisational difference. Moreover, the fierce opposition and resistance from jurists, politicians and mass movements outside the West compelled clarification of the specific criteria required for a political system to be deemed 'sufficiently civilised' to warrant the abolition of extraterritoriality.

The principle of territorial jurisdiction beyond a State's own borders served to legitimise colonial domination through treaties concluded between colonial powers and African leaders. For instance, Britain signed treaties with several African chiefs through which sovereignty over Nigeria was transferred to the British Crown.[99] It is worth noting that, although Turkey did not achieve the same hegemonic position as other major

[96] In Re Ross, 140 U.S. 453 (1891) ('In Re Ross').

[97] T. Ruskola, *Legal Orientalism: China, the United States, and Modern Law*, Harvard University Press Cambridge, MA/London 2013, p. 151.

[98] *SS Lotus Case: France v. Turkey (1927)* PCIJ Rep Ser. A No. 10, 18.

[99] One illustrative example is the treaty between King Dosumu of Lagos and Great Britain.

Western European powers, it was nonetheless engaged in a global power struggle during the 1920s.[100]

The codification and consistent application of civil, commercial, bankruptcy and patent laws were, for example, highlighted in 1926 by the Commission on Extraterritoriality in China as necessary prerequisites for the abolition of the practice.[101] The logic of progress was at the heart of scientific arguments and State practice regarding extraterritoriality.

The underlying idea behind the application of extraterritoriality was that this principle constituted an anomalous and temporary arrangement, which would be lifted as soon as these countries became 'fully civilised' by reforming their legal, judicial and administrative systems to align with the imperatives of capitalist modernity. Kayaoğlu has argued that this required comprehensive reforms along three main axes: legal codification, centralisation of the judiciary and the consolidation of State law throughout the national territory.[102] Indeed, the aforementioned Commission on Extraterritoriality in China offered a detailed account of both the formal legal systems in place and the perceived everyday functioning of this legal framework, which was allegedly undermined by State weakness, civil conflict, warlordism and inadequate infrastructure, particularly the lack of prisons and mental health institutions.[103] Furthermore, in a confidential note from 1889 recommending the continuation of extraterritoriality in Japan, the UK Foreign Office highlighted the lack of concrete guarantees that all Japanese laws would conform to Western standards, as well as the lack of clarity regarding the reorganisation of the police and the role of the courts.[104] As early as 1891, the United States Supreme Court referred to the abolition of the practice of extraterritoriality as a matter of time, reaffirming Japan's progress: "It is true that the occasion for consular tribunals in Japan may hereafter be less than at present, as every year that country progresses in civilization and in the assimilation of its system of

[100] Cf. T.F. Nas, *Tracing the Economic Transformation of Turkey from the 1920 to EU Accession*, Martinus Njihoff Publishers, Leiden-Boston, 2008.

[101] United States Department of State, 'Report of the Commission on Extraterritoriality in China, Peking, September 16, 1926' (Washington: Government Printing Press 1926), p. 107.

[102] T. Kayaoğlu, *Legal Imperialism: Sovereignty and Extraterritoriality in Japan, the Ottoman Empire, and China*, Cambridge University Press, Cambridge, 2010, p. 47.

[103] 'Report of the Commission', pp. 89–104.

[104] 'Japanese Treaty Revision: Provisions for Abolition of Consular Jurisdiction', 19 June 1889, FO 410/1310.

judicial procedure to that of Christian countries, as well as in the improvement of its penal statutes".[105]

Writing from within this logic, semi-peripheral jurists reversed legal reform and codification, and the adoption of central institutions of capitalist modernity, with legal significance. Therefore, it is not surprising that invocations of the doctrine *rebus* sic *stantibus*, which allows for the unilateral termination of treaties in the event of a fundamental change in circumstances, became a common argumentative movement. When writing about the abolition of extraterritoriality in 1931, the Chinese jurist Tseng Yu-Hao dedicated an extensive chapter to the doctrine. Examining the writings of Western, Japanese and Chinese scholars, as well as in practice, he advocated the legal validity of the doctrine, as well as its applicability in the case of China's unequal treaties.[106] The argument was that China's reform process had been so deep and successful that the conditions that made extraterritoriality necessary or at least tolerable had ceased to exist. The gap had finally been filled.

But there is more. This hegemonic mechanism was applied by Japan in its war against China in 1894. The language of civilisation acted as a rhetorical device that justified both violent and non-violent imperialist practices, including extraterritoriality. The First Sino-Japanese War of 1894 was legitimised both nationally and internationally as a clash between 'civilisation and barbarism', among other reasons because Japan emphasised that it would conduct hostilities in accordance with International Law, in other words, that it would wage war as a civilised nation.[107]

Therefore, it cannot be inferred that Customary International Law solely represents the spontaneous interaction between the traditional subjects of International Law at the time. "The logic of International Law is that the power to make International Law lies in the domain of the state [...] many colonised countries were said to lack this distinct 'statelike' structure, resembling that of the Europeans. Therefore, any practice

[105] In Re Ross, p. 45.

[106] Yu-Hao Tseng, *The Termination of Unequal Treaties in International Law: Studies in Comparative Jurisprudence and Conventional Law of Nations*, The Commercial Press, Shanghai, 1931, pp. 51–80.

[107] In fact, Japan enlisted both Westlake and Holland to vouch for its civilised status, as evidenced by its compliance with International Law during the 1894 conflict. P. R. Anand, '*Family of "Civilized" States and Japan: A Story of Humiliation, Assimilation, Defiance and Confrontation*', in Journal of the History of International Law 2003, pp. 1–76.

arising from, for example, African societies did not amount or contribute to customary International Law".[108]

5.4.3 International (Colonial) Treaties

From the perspective of International Law, this period was characterised by conquest and cession based on 'unequal treaties' concluded by European and non-European States. In view of the above, the criteria for being accepted into the 'family of nations' emphasised the European perception of sovereignty (often aligned with adherence to the Christian faith) and civilisation. Later, the European standard became the universally accepted standard, as it defined the rules of International Law.[109] These criteria were aimed at granting legal personality in order to qualify for participation in the development of international standards through processes in which non-European States were supposed to be placed 'on an equal footing'.[110] The dilemma, therefore, regarding the negotiation of treaties with representatives of Indigenous populations boils down to the legitimacy of the sovereignty of these populations. Stanley for Belgium, Brazza on behalf of France, and Nachtigal representing Germany signed international treaties ceding African lands to the European states. "*Il n'y a pas un seul voyageur moderne qui ne joue pas le rôle d'agent diplomatique et qui n'apporte avec lui,* ***au-delà des collections****, un traité relatif aux cessions territoriales*" [emphasis added].[111] This issue arises from the new colonial powers' need to break away from a previous practice, described earlier, which was based on the evangelisation of Indigenous peoples, conquest, or Locke's theories on the optimal organisation for land exploitation. However, the legitimacy of a cession treaty lay in the fact that "*un traité de cession ne peut être conclu qu'entre des États qui reconnaissent le droit*

[108] J. Chinwe Okubuir, *Application of Hegemony to Customary International Law: An African Perspective*, cit., p. 258.

[109] A. Angie, *Identifying Regions in the History of International Law*, in B. Fassbender y A. Peters (eds.), *The Oxford Handbook of the History of International Law*, Oxford University Press, Oxford, 2012, p. 1058.

[110] R. J. Vincent, *Racial Inequality*, in H. Bull and A. Watson (eds.), *The Expansion of International Society* Oxford University Press, Oxford, 1984.

[111] C. Salomon, *L'occupation des territoires sans maître. Étude de droit international*, Giard, Paris, 1889, p. 218.

international".[112] The postulates of the sovereign equality of States stem from the normative organisation of relations arising from the treaties that enshrined the Peace of Westphalia of 1648. The sovereign equality of States is perhaps the most fundamental principle among those that form the core of International Law. So much so that some authors even consider the sovereign equality of States as the fundamental norm of International Law.[113] Nor could one speak of consent freely granted by the rulers of such populations. Although the Berlin Conference did not accept the US proposal for the legitimisation of these treaties, this idea was incorporated as a recommendation.[114] In the end, the doctrinal proposals could be summarised as a paternalistic attitude: the Indigenous people were not in a position to appreciate their own interests. "Being universalist and yet recognizing the difference between cultures was possible, as well as common: the synthesis was operated by arranging the differences within a single hierarchical and evolutionary scheme".[115] But there is something deeper regarding the very structure of domination through Private Law, of which colonial treaties are a clear expression.[116] Niglia calls it 'Jurisdomination'.[117] As a transnational phenomenon, during the eighteen and nineteenth centuries, the discourse of Private Law 'subjectivised' States (that is, it reconceptualised the sovereign subject of the seventeenth century) just as prominently as the distinct yet convergent process of

[112] *Annuaire de l'Institute de Droit international*, IX, 1887–1888, p. 247. On this matter, see the Case concerning the S.S. Wimbledon, Permanent Court of International Justice, Series A, no. 1, 1923.

[113] C. Tomuschat, *International Law: Ensuring The Survival Of Mankind On The Eve Of A New Century. General Course On Public International Law*, in *Recueil des Cours de la Académie de Droit International*, vol. 281, 2001, pp. 13 et seq., on p. 161 uses the Kelsenian word '*grundnorm*' to refer to sovereign equality.

[114] H. Bonfils, *Manuel de droit international public*, P. Fauchille (ed.), Rouseeau, Paris, 1898, accepts the validity of these treaties, while J. Westlake, *International Law*, Cambridge University Press, Cambridge, 1910, I, pp. 123–124 considers them only as a factual indication of the factual situation.

[115] M. Koskenniemi, *The Gentle Civilizer of Nations. The Rise and Fall of International Law 1870–1960*, cit., p.177.

[116] A. Quijano, *Colonialidad del poder, eurocentrismo y América Latina*, in *Cuestiones y horizontes: de la dependencia histórico-estructural a la colonialidad/descolonialidad del poder*, CLACSO, Buenos Aires, 2014, pp. 777–832; W. Mignolo, *Local Histories/Global Designs: Coloniality, Subaltern Knowledges and Border Thinking*, Princeton University Press, Princeton, 2000.

[117] L. Niglia, *The New Transformation of Europe: Arcana Imperii*, in *The American Journal of Comparative Law*, 2020, pp. 151–185.

subjectivisation that occurred within the discourse of (Public) International Law.[118]

What was also required (and herein lies the relevance of Private Law) was a legal system capable of adapting as much as possible to the pursuit of private initiative and trade; in other words, a Law free from the legal constraints of the *ancien régime*. This enfranchisement occurred within and among non-European States as European powers imposed 'market economic' relations (colonialised), for example, by ending the non-transferable status of lands owned by religious entities, or *waqf*, in North African colonies, as was the case under Islamic law prior to the colonisation of Algeria in 1830.[119] This State-building strategy was culturally and ideologically made possible by the vocabulary of Private Law centred on individualism (absolute property rights, absolute contractual freedom, fault-based liability), paradigmatically shaped around the dogmas of property (Article 544 of the *Code Napoleon*) and the will of the parties (Articles 1134, 1108 of the same code).[120] The European cultural consciousness, referenced above, prevailed in the nineteenth century in its drive to defeudalise and, consequently, liberate the bourgeoisie from obstacles to commerce and land ownership. Private Law became a tool of domination to justify the diplomatic strategies of sovereign States. The liberal European market economy was an essential requirement to be able to join the club of civilised nations.

5.4.4 General Principles of Law Recognised by Civilised Nations

When Koskenniemi analyses the "myth of civilisation" in terms of a logic of exclusion/inclusion by reconstructing the doctrinal formant of international legal science of the time, drawing on the contributions of Westlake, Fiore, Heilborn, it becomes absolutely evident that, beyond individual

[118] See M. Koskenniemi, *International Law as Political Theology: How to Read the* Nomos der Erde, in *Constellations*, 2004, p. 498.

[119] F. Wieacker, *Aufstieg, Blüte und Krisis der Kodifikationsidee*, in *Festschrift für Gustav Boehmer*, 1954, Geburtstag, p. 34.

[120] Cfr. B. Bhandar, *Colonial Lives of Property Law, Land, and Racial Regimes of Ownership*, Duke University, 2018. Bhandar argues that the modern concept of private property developed in close connection with European colonial expansion. Through exclusionary law, property was used to legitimise the appropriation of Indigenous lands and to structure racially hierarchical societies.

theoretical distinctions, there lay an underlying idea of a hierarchical legal order, shaped by different levels of development. This is analogous to the theory of Maine, which has been reinterpreted critically by Daniel Bonilla.[121] Therefore, both branches of Law encompassed a positivist worldview which, while recognising a plurality of civilisations, ultimately ranked them as civilised, barbaric or savage, following Lorimer's tripartite classification.[122] Koskenniemi and Glenn both affirm the Eurocentric identity of twentieth-century law.[123]

This hermeneutical osmosis clearly culminates in the general principles of civilised nations as enshrined in Article 38 of the Permanent Court, reproduced verbatim in the current Article 38 of the Statute of the International Court of Justice. It was a thoroughly logical consequence of the worldviews held by Comparative and International Law, which ultimately served to consolidate the exclusionary identity of the Western world. The enterprise of juxtaposing sovereign States was preceded by a comparative legal construction of an identitarian order and turned into a war of attrition centred on State sovereignty declared against Others and all that is different. This operation transforms populations into foreigners and renders them irritating, alarming: the lines of demarcation must always be clearly visible and sharply defined.[124]

The observations of internationalists such as Koskenniemi on one hand[125] and comparatists such as Bonilla[126] on the other each coincide within their respective scope in this direction. "In the process the concept of 'civilization' was used as a form of the exclusion of non-Western values, of non-Western identity and even of legal personality. This process can be

[121] D. Bonilla Maldonado, *Los bárbaros jurídicos: Identidad, derecho comparado moderno y el Sur globa*, cit., pp. 89 ss.

[122] J. Lorimer, *The Institutes of the Law of the Nations. A Treatise of the Jural Relations od Separate Political Communities*, Blackwood, Edinburgh-London, 1883, vol. I, pp. 93–100.

[123] H.P. Glenn, *Comparative Law: Problems and Prospects*, in *American University International Law Review*, 26 no. 4, 2011, p. 958. Cf. H.P. Glenn, *Comparative Legal Families and Comparative Legal Traditions*, in *The Oxford Handbook of Comparative Law*, M. Reimann, R. Zimmermann (ed.), 2006, pp. 421–439.

[124] Z. Bauman, *Modernidad líquida*, Fondo de Cultura Económica, Buenos Aires, 2004, pp. 57 and 67.

[125] M. Koskenniemi, *The Gentle Civilizer of Nations. The Rise and Fall of International Law 1870–1960,* Cambridge, Cambridge University Press, 2001; trans.

[126] D. Bonilla Maldonado, *Los bárbaros jurídicos: Identidad, derecho comparado moderno y el Sur global,* cit., pp. 175–231.

traced through writers such as Westlake just as much as through statesmen such as Bismarck or events such as the Maori wars".[127]

From an early standpoint, the figure of Descamps is particularly noteworthy. A professor of International Law at the University of Louvain, he was a committed proponent of international arbitration and served as a member of the Belgian delegation at the 1899 Hague Conference. As part of the *Comité des juristes*, he drafted the Statute of the Permanent Court of International Justice and successfully proposed the inclusion of "the general principles of law recognised by civilised nations." In 1899, as Koskenniemi notes,[128] we find him writing a colonialist pamphlet titled *L'Afrique nouvelle*,[129] in which he speculates on the advantages that smaller countries, such as Belgium, might have gained from colonisation. He argued that every effort had been made to fulfil the so-called civilising mission. For Descamps, the colonisation of Africa was not merely justified, it was imposed by the dual law of preservation and progress, which is the law of humanity.[130] Given that the expression "general principles of law recognised by civilised nations" is reproduced with the same numerical placement in the Statute of the International Court of Justice, adopted on 26 June 1945, one can observe a significant continuity in this civilising identity. The involvement of international legal scholars in their respective colonial projects has already been extensively demonstrated by Koskenniemi.[131]

This is not, of course, a process of delimitation driven solely by a specifically European logic of exclusion. On the other side of the Atlantic, in the United States, Henry Wheaton identified these "civilised nations" in his influential treatise *Elements of International Law*, as "the Christian people of Europe or those of European origin".[132]

[127] J. Crawford, *Foreword*, A. Anghie, *Imperialism, Sovereignty and the Making of International Law*, Cambridge University Press, Cambridge, 2005, p. 6.

[128] M. Koskenniemi, *The Gentle Civilizer of Nations. The Rise and Fall of International Law 1870–1960*, cit., p. 221.

[129] E. Descamps, *L'Afrique Nouvelle*, Paris, Hachette, 1903.

[130] E. Descamps, *L'Afrique Nouvelle*, cit., p. 123.

[131] M. Koskenniemi, *The Gentle Civilizer of Nations. The Rise and Fall of International Law 1870–1960,* Cambridge University Press, Cambridge, 2001; Idem, *El discreto civilizador de las naciones. El auge y la caída del derecho internacional 1870–1960,* Editorial Ciudad Argentina, 2005, pp. 160–220.

[132] H. Wheaton, *Elements of International Law*, George Grafton Wilson (ed.), Carnegie Endowment for International Peace / Clarendon Press / Oxford University Press / Washington DC, 1936, p. 5.

Subparagraph (c) of paragraph 1 of Article 38 emerged as a compromise between the Common Law and Civil Law members of the Committee of Jurists of the League of Nations. However, some members adopted positions that diverged from the principles of their own legal systems. Notably, it was members of the Committee who belonged to the Civil Law tradition (where the judge's role is generally confined to applying codified law) who sought to grant international judges broad discretion in identifying principles inherent in the "legal conscience of civilised nations", as expressed by Descamps,[133] or "in accordance with law, justice, and equity", in the view of France's Lapradelle.[134] Their primary concern was to avoid the risk of *non liquet*, whereby a judge might be forced to refrain from deciding a dispute due to the absence of an applicable treaty or Customary Law. A type of rule was needed that would allow judges to 'complete' or 'fill gaps' in the Law as necessary. Meanwhile, members from the Common Law tradition (where judges play an active role in the normative process through precedent creation) sought to restrict the discretionary power of international judges by adopting a positivist stance grounded in the primacy of State consent. Phillimore (United Kingdom) and Root (United States) advocated 'subjective conceptions of principles of justice', arguing that the open-ended nature of the provision might discourage States strongly committed to voluntarism from submitting to the Court's Statute. In their opinion, such States would not be "willing to accept the compulsory jurisdiction of a Court that would apply principles, understood differently in different countries" or that "he would administer not only the law", but also "what he considers to be the conscience of civilized people".[135] To encourage more States to submit to the Court, they deemed it necessary to limit judicial discretion and strictly confine the sources of Law.

[133] League of Nations, Permanent Court of International Justice, Advisory Committee of Jurists, Minutes of the meetings of the Committee from 16 June to 24 July, 1920, 1920, p. 306.

[134] Ibíd., 295.

[135] Lord Phillimore, for example, referred to "serious differences of opinion [that] arose from the continental idea of justice". Initially, strict limitations were imposed on judges out of fear of overly restricting them, granting them full freedom within those boundaries. The English system differs: judges take an oath "to do justice in accordance with the law." It was added that the main issue was to limit the role of the international judge to the application of the Law and to deny them the power to participate in lawmaking. League of Nations, Permanent Court of International Justice, Advisory Committee of Jurists, Minutes of the meetings of the Committee from 16 June to 24 July, 1920, 1920, p. 309.

A compromise solution was proposed, which envisaged general principles but limited them to certain 'legal maxims' or principles derived from the general principles of Domestic Law, those principles accepted by all nations within their own legal systems.

The use of the adjective 'civilised' again warrants comment. It seems that some of the drafters considered it superfluous and wanted to discard it. According to Lapradelle, significantly "***qui dit droit dit civilisation***".[136] It is the idea advocated by the conceptual framework of Comparative Law.

5.4.5 *The System of Mandates*

The trauma of the First World War brought about significant changes in International Law and international relations. More importantly, the imperial nature of the discipline was acknowledged and criticised by scholars and statesmen during the interwar period, who condemned nineteenth-century International Law for legitimising colonial exploitation. The League of Nations sought to formulate a new approach towards the colonies, which were now defined in terms of 'backward territories'. Whereas in the nineteenth century the division between Europe and an uncivilised non-Europe was mainly articulated through racial and cultural categories, the League characterised the differences between civilised and uncivilised peoples in economic terms of 'advanced' and 'backward'.

The creation of the mandate system within the League of Nations ushered in an institutional regime of legal and administrative control aimed at producing outcomes essentially designed by the new Western powers of Europe and the United States. The introduction of what Michel Foucault referred to as *governmentality* (the exercise of a complex form of power over populations through techniques of measurement, upon whose supposed neutrality and rational objectivity institutions and systems of governance could be constructed) further reinforced the mechanisms of control and management over non-Western societies. Paradoxically, the emergence of self-government and the statehood later acquired within the framework of the United Nations were themselves the product of managerial and control techniques developed in the West.

[136] League of Nations, Permanent Court of International Justice, Advisory Committee of Jurists, Minutes of the meetings of the Committee from 16 June to 24 July, 1920, (1920), p. 335.

It is important to note that supposedly 'uncivilised' peoples were also portrayed as lacking sufficient responsibility, and therefore undeserving of the 'gift' of sovereignty. Writing about the 'typical African', Lugard asserted: "He lacks the power of organisation, and is conspicuously deficient in the management and control alike of men or business. He loves the display of power, but fails to realise its responsibility".[137] The Mandate System crucially inherited and transformed the 'standard of civilisation'. In doing so, it paved the way for the rhetorical marginalisation of 'civilisation' as an explicit legal standard and its transmutation into a subterranean current of international legal argumentation. This underlying logic continued to manifest itself in various ways across different institutions and legal fields.

The basic framework of the Mandate System was established in Article 22 of the Covenant of the League of Nations, while the specific provisions for each Mandate were set out in the individual mandate treaties signed between the Principal Allied and Associated Powers, the mandatory power and the League, represented by its Council.

The wording of Article 22 revealed the provisional and transitional nature of the arrangement, reintroducing a narrative of progress and improvement. The Mandate System was not intended as a permanent institution, but rather as an intermediate stage deemed necessary for particular peoples who were not yet considered capable of governing themselves.

The Covenant specified that the system applied to "those colonies and territories which as a consequence of the late war have ceased to be under the sovereignty of the States which formerly governed them and which are inhabited by peoples not yet able to stand by themselves under the strenuous conditions of the modern world [...]."

In fact, when the Council of the major powers faced the issue of Iraqi independence, its vice president, Van Rees, pointed out that "the principle – which has been accepted by almost all writers and by the mandatory powers themselves – that the mandates system implies only a temporary charge'.[138] "The hierarchical logic of the 'standard of civilisation', and

[137] Lord Lugard, *The Dual Mandate in British Tropical Africa*, Frank Cass, London, 1965, pp. 69–70.

[138] Note from *M. van Rees: General Conditions that must be fulfilled before the mandate regime can be brought to an end in respect of a country placed under that regime*, 1931, in *Permanent Mandates Commission Minutes*, annex 3, p. 19.

especially of its pole that emphasised immutable differences between different political communities, was at the core of the Mandate System".[139] Article 22 incorporated the tension between the two poles of the 'standard of civilisation': the logic of exclusion and the assertion of equality between States in continuous tension.[140]

5.4.6 *The Concept of Humanitarian Intervention*

In the previous sections, what repeatedly comes through is the seemingly benevolent (or gentle, as Koskenniemi puts it) nature of including Indigenous peoples within the framework of European rationality. However, this inclusion was in fact a form of violent control, aimed at transforming Indigenous peoples and making them behave and see themselves like the rest of the so-called civilised world.[141] "The use of International Law as a tool with which to define legal relations among colonial powers also became the basis on which to legitimize 'humanitarian' intervention aimed at peoples regarded as noncivilized".[142] International Law became the benchmark for assessing a people's level of civilisation, and any form or degree of civility that fell short of its standard was not only grounds for exclusion, but also served as justification for a Western power to exercise its so-called benevolent sovereignty and intervene.

But the concept of humanitarian intervention also proved useful to justify the intentions with which Western powers sought to expand their spheres of influence. Thus, for example, the power to intervene on humanitarian grounds was included in the Treaty of London of 1827 and the Treaty of Berlin of 1878[143]: under the former, France, the United Kingdom and Russia secured the right to intervene in Greece; under the latter, the signatory powers acquired the right to intervene in response to any

[139] N. Tzouvala, *Capitalism as civilisation: a history of International Law*, Cambridge University Press, 2020, p. 97.

[140] Cf. R. Wilde, *International Territorial Administration: How Trusteeship and the Civilizing Mission Never Went Away*, Oxford University Press, Oxford 2008.

[141] A. Bianchi, *International Law Theories: An Inquiry into Different Ways of Thinking*, Oxford University Press, Oxford, 2017. Tirant Lo Blanch, Valencia, 2023, p. 231.

[142] G. Gozzi, *Rights and Civilizations: A History and Philosophy of International Law*, Cambridge University Press, Cambridge, 2019, p. 120.

[143] Y. Ben Achour, *Le rôle des civilisations dans le système international*, Bruylant, Brussels, 2003, pp. 127–150.

violation of the rights of populations within European Turkey.[144] In this way, a systematic framework of International Law was established, one that defined relations between Western powers in such a manner as to prevent hostilities within the territories of Western civilisation itself, while at the same time legitimising their right to carry out 'humanitarian' interventions in territories within their spheres of influence.

[144] Cf. P. Fiore, *La science du droit international*, cit., pp. XC and CXXII.

CHAPTER 6

Comparative Law and International Law in the Twenty-First Century

Abstract The current landscape of Comparative and International Law demonstrates a focus on examining inclusive and complex identities from multiple perspectives. In Comparative Law, examples include the Comparative International Law movement and the TWAILs' Decolonising School. Similar considerations pertaining to constitutional law are present in emerging schools of International Law, which aim to influence the global order through concepts such as *ius cogens*. As a result, there is an identified need to develop new concepts of Law that address the construction of relational subjectivity. Additionally, the development of this relational identity is regarded as being closely connected to Esposito's concept of *communitas*.

Keywords Comparative International Law • TWAIL School • Jus cogens • *Communitas* and *Immunitas*

"Comparative Law thus shared many features with contemporaneous International Law, both public and private, which similarly projected a view of the world according to the aspirations of European colonial powers. However, while the latter dealt with an international legal order composed of sovereign states, subordinating the private sphere, comparatism concentrated on the study of the private laws thus enclosed within the

© The Author(s), under exclusive license to Springer Nature Switzerland AG 2026

A. Lazari, *Relational Identity in International, Comparative and European Union Law*,
https://doi.org/10.1007/978-3-031-59482-3_6

state, perceived in accordance with the epistemological tradition of the great civilian codes as sheltered from the intrusions of politics and thus amenable to scientific study as a system and ultimately to unification".[1] In this compartmentalised conception of Law, comparative and internationalist legal sciences could collaborate in the ***reductio ad unum*** and in the ***exclusio maioris multitudinis*** of the general principles recognised by civilised nations. However, precisely because of its inherently divisive nature, no true epistemological synergy exists between them. "Comparatists are focused on national systems and have by and large ignored international law as an object of study. That sounds plausible in theory, but comparative law is so rarely employed in practice here that it plays no significant role. [...] Still, on the whole, the use of comparative law in traditional public international law remains very limited".[2] The tables have recently turned.

At the American Association of Comparative Law Conference, in a notable article published in a special issue of the *American University International Law Review*, President George Bermann argued that "It can be said without exaggerating that Comparative Law has contributed importantly, alongside other sources, to the creation of public International Law. Conversely, I believe that public International Law has contributed importantly to Comparative Law's sense of mission. Helping develop public International Law is by no means Comparative Law's only mission, far from it. But it is among them. In sum, I discern in the relationship between comparative and International Law a healthy symbiosis whose continuation we have no reason to doubt".[3] This is echoed by Kim Lane Scheppele: "I very much agree with George Bermann that one of the key challenges for our field is the increasing role and increasing penetration of International Law into Domestic Law: **we should no longer think of Domestic Law as particularly self-contained"** [emphasis added].[4] Glenn closed the

[1] H. Muir Watt, *Globalization and Comparative Law*, in AA.VV., *The Oxford Handbook of Comparative Law*, edited by M. Reimann–R. Zimmermann, Hart, Oxford, 2006, p. 230.

[2] M. Reimann, *Comparative Law and neighbouring disciplines,* in AA.VV., *The Cambridge Companion to Comparative Law (Cambridge Companions to Law)*, edited by M. Bussani–U. Mattei, Cambridge University Press, 2012, p. 50.

[3] Bermann's intervention in G. Bermann–P. Glenn–K. Lane Scheppele–A. Shalakany–D. V. Snyder–E. Zoller, *Comparative Law: Problems and Prospects*, in *American University International Law Review* 26 No. 4, 2011, p. 938.

[4] Lane Scheppele's intervention in G. Bermann–P. Glenn–K. Lane Scheppele–A. Shalakany–D. V. Snyder–E. Zoller, *Comparative Law: Problems and Prospects*, in *American University International Law Review* 26 No. 4, 2011, p. 950.

conference, adding that, in line with what had already been said about his theory earlier, the function of Comparative Law lies in fostering coexistence among peoples, drawing on a specific period in Spanish history as an example. "So com-paring can be seen as a process of existing with an equal, or that which is taken to be an equal, in spite of evident differences. It is a process of what was once referred to in Spain as convivencia, the process of living together in a nonconflictual manner in spite of profound differences or beliefs. I think it is today the main task of Comparative Lawyers to develop multiple means of convivencia, as a way of enabling the world to live in a non-violent manner".[5]

6.1 The Emergence of New Scientific Perspectives

In short, in recent times, the ultra-national dimension of the legal experience has come to dominate scholars' understanding of law and has finally been recognised as perhaps its most distinctive feature.

It is now rare for any part of the legal system to be regulated without taking into account sources originating internationally, produced within the many intergovernmental organisations operating on a global scale. Lastly, consider the impact of Transnational Law: the body of rules adopted outside national borders at the initiative of private lawmakers, as we have already noted in the emergence of private corporations.[6]

Given these circumstances, those who study Comparative Law should be experiencing their most fortunate moment, the peak of their popularity. "From Cinderella complex to queen of the legal sciences!" has been exclaimed. The study of foreign laws, their comparison and interaction with international, supranational and transnational law, is indeed the daily bread of Comparative Law scholars. The discipline should therefore serve as a necessary reference point for legal discourse as such; it ought to represent the nexus where knowledge and practices intersect, deriving their legitimacy from the law. International Lawyers, whether consciously or not, use comparative methods. And yet, this does not seem to be the case. Or rather: legal comparison is now employed across all areas of law simply because it is impossible to ignore what happens beyond the national level.

[5] Patrick Glenn's intervention in G. Bermann–P. Glenn–K. Lane Scheppele–A. Shalakany–D. V. Snyder–E. Zoller, *Comparative Law: Problems and Prospects*, in *American University International Law Review* 26 No. 4, 2011, p. 944.

[6] G. Frankenberg, *Comparative Law as Critique*, Edgar, London, 2014, p. 6.

But this happens without any significant involvement from Comparative Law scholars, or at least, not to the extent warranted by the importance of the knowledge at the heart of their discipline.

One of the most influential voices in the American legal school, Professor Glendon, enthusiastically states that "there is a tendency on the part of many public international lawyers, human rights specialists, and international business law experts to be impatient with, or even dismissive of, national differences. I would like to think, however, that those obstacles can be surmounted, and that the future of international legal studies will be marked by fruitful collaboration and interaction among comparatists, public international lawyers, international business law specialists, and all who labor on behalf of human rights".[7] There is one key element that has emerged throughout this work: the comparatist's perspective on Law comes from an external, and therefore critical, vantage point. It is the viewpoint of someone who observes Law not only in its structure but also in its function; who considers it both as a set of rules and as institutions that enforce those rules to imperatively distribute goods and values. It is the gaze of one who, more than focusing on Law itself, examines the legal experience, both in its empirical dimension and in its essence as a discursive practice. This was a subversive aim that surfaced with the early anti-positivist comparatists. This perspective helps us understand the two primary functions of Comparative Law: its cognitive capacity and its critical stance.

To understand our relational view of Law, which we will explore further in the *pars construens*, let us first compare three theories that have sought to connect International Law with comparative studies.

6.1.1 *The Studies of Comparative International Law*

The first approach to systemic studies of International Law and Comparative Law that we will examine is *Comparative International Law*,[8] whose clear objective is to reveal the universal sublimation of International Law through the tools of the comparative method. "A serious comparative study of international law would contribute to that same shift – to think-

[7] A.M. Glendon, *Comparative Law in the Age of Globalization*, in *Duquesne Law Review* Vol. 52, 2014, pp. 1–24.

[8] AA.VV., *Comparative International Law*, A. Roberts, P. B. Stephan, P.-Hugues Verdier and M. Versteeg (eds.), Oxford University Press, Oxford, 2017.

ing of the world no longer in terms of what Hegel used to call abstract universals but seeing all players as both universal and particular at the same time, speaking a shared language but doing that from their own, localizable standpoint".[9]

The complexity surrounding the issue of unity raises a series of specific difficulties related, for example, to the determination and acceptance of secondary norms by judges, the 'invisibility' of the college of international jurists (*The Divisible College of International Lawyers*, as defined by Anthea Roberts[10]), or the study of the interaction between different orders of value. The first point is that there are many ways in which International Law can be 'one'. The second is that, depending on the perspective taken, unity will mean different things in different contexts. The objects, criteria and dynamics of unity vary from one level of analysis to another. Ultimately, unity presents itself as a complex set of forces and dynamics that may either complement or contradict each other. The notion of *Unitas multiplex* captures this complex and plural reality of Law.[11] It is interesting to observe how this vision has been shaped across various national schools. Koskenniemi already emphasised how state doctrines have strongly influenced the very structure of International Law itself.[12] Here we are exploring the reasons why "I found myself having a comparative international law experience in that classroom where I did not realize how national the international law we sometimes teach is (in both materials and assumptions) until I found myself in another national setting. Dislocation was the key. By dislocating myself from my normal environment, I was able to experience international law from a different location. In doing so, I became conscious not only of the located way in which my students were approaching international law, but also the (differently) located way in which I had been approaching my field".[13] A first contribution of this strand of International Law lies in the awareness that there are multiple versions of this discipline. If International Law aims to 'rebuild' itself, it

[9] M. Koskenniemi, *The Case for Comparative International Law*, in *Finnish Yearbook of International Law*, 2011, p. 4.

[10] A. Roberts, *Is International Law International?* Oxford University Press, Oxford, 2017, pp. 4–20.

[11] M. Prost, *The Concept of Unity in Public International Law*, Hart, Oxford, 2012, p. 123.

[12] M. Koskenniemi, *The Gentle Civilizer of Nations. The Rise and Fall of International Law 1870–1960,* Cambridge University Press, Cambridge, 2001.

[13] A. Roberts, *Is International Law International?* Oxford University Press, Oxford, 2017, p. 10.

must keep in mind not only diversity but also the importance of interactions between various systems. A second contribution unfolds on the practical level.

"Public international law and comparative law have so far been regarded as largely distinct fields, with little to no overlap between them. Multiculturalism, which lies at the heart of the concept of "comparative international law" and conveys the idea that international law could be approached differently depending on the culture of each country, society, or peoples, is not a neutral approach".[14] In the field of International Law, comparisons between national practices are particularly important for the identification and formation of international customary norms, which largely depend on the evaluation of existing State practice and *opinio juris*.

It would, to put it somewhat grandly, contribute to the ideological critique of International Law and the institutions upheld by that professional vocabulary. The idea that there is a single, universal International Law, with a homogeneous history and a political-institutional project, stems from a deeply Eurocentric worldview.[15] Thus, the very act of recognising diversity in how International Law is viewed and even taught once again reveals the knowledge and measurement of the Other.[16]

The question remains how to identify and compare indigenous ways of understanding intercommunity relations that are not necessarily subsumable under European legal categories, but rather stand on their own, and, in doing so, provide a broader comparative perspective from which European categories themselves can be examined as being just as 'provincial' as any others.[17]

We have seen this perspective, at least in part, in the protection of indigenous cultural heritage, where we have had to set aside our notions of

[14] M. Forteau, *Comparative International Law. Within, not against, International Law: lessons from the International Law Commission*, in *American Journ. Intern. Law*, Vol. 109, 2015, p. 498.

[15] M. Koskenniemi, *The Case for Comparative International Law*, in *Finnish Yearbook Int'l L.* 1, 3–4, 2009, p. 4.

[16] M. Koskenniemi, *The Case for Comparative International Law*, cit., p. 5.

[17] A. Becker Lorca, *Universal International Law: Nineteenth-Century Histories of Imposition and Appropriation*', in *Harvard International Law Journal*, 2010, pp. 475–552; L. Obrégon, *Completing Civilization: Creole Consciousness and International Law in Nineteenth-Century Latin America*, in AA.VV., *International Law and its Others,* Cambridge University Press, 2006, pp. 247–264; O. Yasuaki, *When was the Law of International Society Born? An Inquiry of the History of International Law from an Intercivilizational perspective*', in *Journal of the History of International Law,* 2000, pp. 1–64.

private property and contracts to embrace an indigenous understanding of the same asset. In fact, this paradigm shift in the concept of property has challenged our initial ideas. This is precisely why Koskenniemi encourages the use of comparative studies applied to International Law. "International Law has always consisted of a heterogonous aggregate of units that pretended to be 'sovereign' in theory and acted often precisely in the solipsistic and imperial".[18] This monological mindset cannot be taught in Law schools.

Comparative studies examine how different national communities of International Lawyers construct their interpretations of International Law in ways that challenge the field's claim to universality and perpetuate certain forms of difference and dominance. In doing so, this approach encourages them to be more reflective about the particularities of their own frameworks and perspectives, and more attentive to how these relate to the broader scientific field.[19] Provincialising International Law (an essential task in legal deconstruction) is only the first step in the new configuration of Law, which must be founded on a new relational scientific identity; that is, on a new, distinct theoretical framework that is different from, but not disconnected from, the current one. This school of thought only partially captures the legal hybridisations and interactions at play.[20] Moreover, it runs the subtle risk that any desired reform of International Law might simply amount to further harmonisation, unless it is grounded in and supported by a genuinely new theoretical framework.[21]

[18] M. Koskenniemi, *The Case for Comparative International Law*, cit., p. 9.

[19] A. Roberts, *Is International Law International?* Oxford University Press, Oxford, 2017, p. 1.

[20] "Comparative International Law, by contrast, focuses on comparative assessments of national court decisions only (unlike transjudicial dialogue) as a means of identifying and interpreting International Law only (unlike comparative constitutional law)"; also A. Roberts, *Comparative International Law? The Role Of National Courts In Creating And Enforcing International Law*, in *Intern. Comparat. Law Quarter.*, 2011, p. 78.

[21] Roberts adopts, in fact, a functionalist view of Comparative Law, with the inevitable tendency towards uniformity that such an approach entails. "Comparative law, by contrast, encourages us to examine how various legal systems approach similar issues or functional needs in different ways. Instead of seeing national court decisions through the prism of whether they enforce or breach international law, the comparative international law lens focuses our attention on the way in which domestic courts nationalize substantive International Law in diverse ways"; A. Roberts, *Comparative International Law? The Role Of National Courts In Creating And Enforcing International Law*, cit., p. 74.

6.1.2 The TWAIL's Decolonising School[22]

Scholars affiliated with the Third World Approaches to International Law (TWAIL) movement and postcolonial studies[23] of Law critically examine both the conceptual opposition between the "rights-bearing subject" and the "legal barbarian", and the ways in which this dichotomy shapes their central object of inquiry: the relationship between Law and the processes of colonialism, neo-colonialism and post-colonialism, or International Law.[24] We share the view that the distinctions articulated by the dominant narrative of modern Comparative Law between these two kinds of subject are not neutral descriptions of a world existing independently of the observing subject. Rather, they are classificatory schemes, taxonomies and ideal types which, in constructing the Law of the "Other" in opposition to Modern Law, inevitably subordinate it. The critical legal scholar, often drawing on the tradition of Critical Legal Studies,[25] seeks to challenge the hegemonic status of the narrative that underpins the theory and practice of modern law. The epistemological aims of the Western subject who constructs this counter-narrative are closely tied to the critique and renewal of the discipline itself. Western Law, along with its traditions and outputs, is often portrayed in dominant narratives as the product of reason or civilisation. Critical legal scholars interrogate this framing and seek to expose its underlying tensions, yet in doing so, they often evoke a counterposing effect that risks reproducing a dichotomy. Indeed, in many of the most influential works within this intellectual tradition, there is a tendency to present two fundamentally opposed worlds that appear not to interact, but rather to remain locked in perpetual antagonism.

[22] Recently, I. Zirion Landaluze, *Una invitación a repensar la disciplina desde las aproximaciones del tercer mundo al derecho internacional*, in *Rev. Esp. Der. Inter.*, 2023, pp. 161–187.

[23] A. Bianchi identifies two distinct phases within the TWAIL movement. I am referring here to his invaluable contribution in *International Law Theories: An Inquiry into Different Ways of Thinking*, Oxford University Press, Oxford, 2017, pp. 134–159.

[24] Idem.

[25] Including, among other many others, M. Mutua, *What Is TWAIL?* in the *Proceedings of the ASIL Ann. Meeting*, 2000, p. 31; E. Darian-Smith, *Postcolonial Theories of Law*, in *Law and Social Theory*, R. Banakar and M. Travers (eds.), Hart Publishing, Oxford, 2017, pp. 247–264; B.S. Chimni, *International Law and World Order: A Critique of Contemporary Approaches*, Cambridge University Press, Cambridge, 2017; J. Thuo Gathii, *Economic Integration and the Question of the Third World*, Cambridge University Press, Cambridge, 2015.

It has two chief merits. On the epistemological front, every scholar aligned with this doctrine exposes the political commitments of International or Comparative Law academics who present themselves as neutral. They employ the conceptual tools of deconstruction to unpack the structures of thought underpinning the disciplines of International and Comparative Law. Secondly, TWAIL scholars challenge the very lenses through which traditional academics often uncritically observe, describe or assess the legal discourses and practices of the Other. This school of thought, which has gained significant visibility within international legal scholarship, has also stimulated critical reflection on the legal heterogeneity that exists (and has historically existed) across the globe, not only within legal systems but across broader cultural and normative frameworks. Today, few International Law faculties regard these studies as either irrelevant or marginal. On the contrary, they have proliferated, particularly within Anglo-American and South American academic contexts.

The dissection of identities can be constructed through various discursive and practical mechanisms, many of which often remain implicit. TWAIL's deconstructive thinking is grounded in a series of sharp oppositions; while it aims to critique these divisions, it often ends up mirroring them in reverse. The critical legal scholar, in examining the dynamics of difference within International Law through oppositional frameworks, ultimately ends up reproducing, from different angles, a contrastive and identity-bound vision of the world.[26]

6.2 *Epistemological Intertwining and the Question of* Jus Cogens

Highlighting the fruitful aspects of the two approaches analysed so far, and underscoring the lack of attention paid to legal hybridisations, we now turn our attention to other attempts at a multifaceted and synergistic analysis of the comparative method (often emerging from constitutionalist thought) applied to International Law from a dual perspective: both constitutionalist and internationalist. The aim of both theoretical frameworks is to move beyond the solipsism of isolated epistemic communities. The theses put forward below ultimately converge on the axiological plane of the emerging concept of *jus cogens*.

[26] Cf. J. Farr, *Locke, Natural Law and New World Slavery*, in *Political Theory*, 2008, pp. 495–522.

6.2.1 *From the Constitutional Perspective: Weiler's 'Three Waves'*

The third doctrinal movement chosen focuses on the role of judges' in judicial control through the norms of International Law, similar to what we have seen in Lauterpacht's perspective.[27]

The discourse advanced by Weiler and other authors closely resembles Elster's *Ulysses Unbound*, particularly regarding the two binding cords that restrain the otherwise exclusionary and violent state.[28] The two waves of judicial review mirror these binding cords on state legislators[29]: one is constitutional, internal to the State itself through constitutional review mechanisms; the other is internationalist, involving the review of national norms for their compatibility with the international legal system. This body of research focuses on how domestic courts apply internationalist norms to scrutinise and potentially constrain national legislative actions.[30] By contrast, a third wave features a reassertion of the national legal system by domestic judges, who may invoke constitutional identity to declare supranational provisions invalid.

The value of this analysis lies in its explanation of how the culture of judicial review (so closely intertwined with the culture of rights) becomes an essential component, and at times even a target, of contemporary discourse. This discourse laments the breakdown of communitarianism, collective responsibility and human solidarity, which have become increasingly localised and pronounced, particularly during periods of economic crisis and intensifying social and national divisions. It is therefore unsurprising that judicial review becomes, in part, the object of political narratives that foreground identity.[31] What deserves scholarly attention is the focus placed on the Voice of the Other, which must be understood in dialogical terms; not solely as opposition or rejection, but also as engagement and correc-

[27] D. Lustig and J. H. H. Weiler, *Judicial review in the contemporary world—Retrospective and prospective*, in *International journal of constitutional law*, 2018, pp. 315–372.

[28] J. Elster, *Ulysses Unbound: Studies in Rationality, Precommitment, and Constraints*, Cambridge University Press, Cambridge, 2000.

[29] I am referring to A. Lazari, *Modelli e paradigmi della responsabilità dello Stato*, Giappichelli, Torino, 2005.

[30] M. Cappelletti, *Judicial Review in Comparative Perspective*, in *California Law Review*, 1970, pp. 1017–1053; M. Cappelletti, J. Weiler, M. Soccombe, *Integration Through Law: Europe and the American Federal Experience. A General Introduction*, De Gruyter, 1986.

[31] D. Lustig and J. H. H. Weiler, *Judicial review in the contemporary world—Retrospective and prospective*, cit., p. 330.

tion. However, this Voice may also tend towards withdrawal: retreating from the benefits of multilateralism and transnational governance, both of which are essential to addressing problems that transcend national solutions; stepping back from genuine commitments to individual human rights, often under the guise of collective goods; and shifting away from legitimate concerns for identity and patriotism as disciplines of solidarity towards an ethos and ethics marked by xenophobia and tribalism.[32]

Another significant merit of this work lies in its identification of the fact that one dimension of the third wave must be understood as a national judicial response to the two earlier, interconnected phenomena. Within a monist framework, International Law asserts itself as a higher legal order within domestic jurisdiction while, at the same time, lacking robust democratic credentials. This issue has become more acute with the intensification of the second wave of judicial review, coupled with the exponential growth of international and transnational norms claiming such primacy. Secondly, if judicial review, as part of its very essence and justification, consists in asserting control over legislators in the name of a 'Higher Law', one must ask: what is the Higher Law of International Law itself, and who is to serve as its enforcer? This problem and the corresponding need for a 'Higher Law' (that is, metaphorically, above International Law itself) was acknowledged within International Law through the enthusiastic introduction of the concept of *jus cogens* in the 1960s. However, the initial fervour gradually faded as it became clear that "it marks a step forward into poorly charted territory [...]". Ultimately, the recognition of peremptory norms was reached through consensus, a process bearing the unmistakable scent of oligarchy, often at the expense of medium and small states, which found themselves marginalised. For the time being, the structure of international society simply offers no further reach.[33]

Two decisions have been analysed in greater depth from this threefold perspective.

The Kadi jurisprudence of the Court of Justice of the European Union[34] embodied the logic of the second wave of judicial review. In the view of

[32] D. Lustig and J. H. H. Weiler, *Judicial review in the contemporary world—Retrospective and prospective*, cit., p. 330.

[33] A. Remiro Brotóns–R. Riquelme Cortado- E. Orihuela Catalayud. J. Diez-Hochleitner–L. Pérez-Prat Durbán, *Derecho Internacional. Curso General*, Tirant Lo Blanch, Valencia, 2010, p. 233.

[34] CJEU, 3 September 2008, joined cases C-402/05 P and C-415/05 P, Yassin Abdullah Kadi and Al Barakaat International Foundation v. Council and Commission, ECR 2008, p. I-6351.

the two authors, however, the decision also has a darker side. In a way, it privileged the specific constitutional assets of the European Union as the correct criterion for review, rather than, perhaps more appropriately, attempting to address the Rule of Law deficit at the international level through criteria reflecting the customs of the international community as a whole. From this standpoint, the approach of the General Court (as it was then) might be considered more fitting. In practice, the outcome could be the same, but the assertion of one's own values above those of the international community in whose name the sanctions were adopted could be seen precisely as the Voice sliding towards the Exit.

The following section presents two national decisions that challenge rulings of the International Court of Justice, effectively acting so to speak as appellate instances before a court which, as has often been noted, serves as both court of first and final instance.[35] On 3 February 2012, the International Court of Justice required Italian courts to extend jurisdictional immunity to Germany, even in respect of actions constituting war crimes and crimes against humanity that violated inviolable human rights. Following the ICJ's judgement, the Italian legislature adopted provisions aimed at implementing the Court's decision. However, in its Ruling No. 238/2014, the Italian Constitutional Court explicitly refrained from questioning the ICJ's interpretation of the principle of State immunity. Nevertheless, the Constitutional Court's decision subjected International Customary Law to constitutional review. The Italian Constitutional Court sought to exercise internal constitutional review over the central international judicial body and to express its opposition to a rule of International Law that undermines the protection of fundamental human rights. Although much of the ruling appears to delineate between the ICJ's supremacy in interpreting International Law and the constitutional courts' supremacy in safeguarding fundamental rights within the constitutional legal order, it also touches upon the potential role of its constitutional intervention should other national courts join it, thus forming, collectively, an oppositional stance that could give rise to a new interpretation of International Law. While the Italian Constitutional Court refrained from directly reviewing the ICJ's decision, it nonetheless put forward an alternative interpretation of International Law governing State immunity, one that excludes acts classified as war crimes and crimes against humanity,

[35] Cf. M. P. Hanna, *The Substantive/Procedural Distinction: Law's Solution to the Problem of Jus Cogens in a World of Sovereign States*, in *G e r m. La w J ou r n.*, 2022, pp. 21–22.

insofar as they violate inviolable human rights. To present such an alternative and to declare the custom, as interpreted by the Court, unconstitutional (and even to call upon other courts to do the same) is an attempt to express opposition to the authority of the International Court and to offer a framework aimed at limiting and constraining its exercise of judicial power.

It is questionable whether such a measure is productive for the administration of justice, but it is a clear example of the dialectical relationship between third-wave jurisprudence and its predecessors.

The Italian legal philosopher Palombella, in his work on interlegality (also referencing the two landmark decisions, Kadi from the CJEU and Germany v. Italy from the ICJ) has provided what is currently one of the most sophisticated attempts to explain and systematise this type of judicial decision not as an act of judicial rebellion, but as a reflection of jurisprudence in a far more complex world, where linear hierarchies enjoy diminishing acceptance; in fact, this is a hallmark of third-wave judicial review.[36] His thesis is articulated around the pragmatic idea of in-between solutions (which we allow ourselves to translate using Jullien's concept of *écart*), without advancing any a priori systemic approaches. From a Relational Law perspective, which we shall outline below, we fully endorse the position regarding the absence of a comparative *prius* in Palombella's thesis,[37] and we appreciate the value attributed to constitutional identity in terms of the Voice of the State.

This thesis represents a rejection of the binary systemic framework of monism and dualism.

When legality is conceived 'in the plural', attention shifts to the space 'in between', as Palombella[38] describes it. This is the realm of inter-legality, which in the comparative methodology we propose takes the form of Jullien's *écart*, a continual tension between two distinct poles.[39] If both (or more) legal systems are sources of legal effect, if both embody legal

[36] J. Klabbers - noy "y" G. Palombella, *The Challenge of Inter-Legality*, Cambridge University Press, Cambridge, 2019.

[37] A view expressed more fully in A. Lazari, *Las redes y el écart: reflexiones a en torno a "El Estado de derecho y la Unión Europea"*, in *Peace & Security-Paix et Sécurité Internationales (EuroMediterranean Journal of International Law and International Relations)*, 2020, pp. 497–549.

[38] G. Palombella, *Theory, Realities, and Promises of Inter-Legality. A Manifesto*, in *The Challenge of Inter-Legality*, cit., p. 378.

[39] F. Jullien, *Il n'y a pas d'identité culturelle*, Éditions de l'Herne, Paris, 2016, p. 15: It cannot be a matter of 'differences' that isolate cultures, but of écarts that place them face to face and in tension, promoting what is common between them.

value rather than serving merely as criteria to evaluate one another, then Law is what emerges from the interconnection of these various legalities. Law is, by necessity, composite and multi-versed. This is where the specific theoretical utility of the inter-legality perspective lies. From this perspective in the 'in-between', there is no legal vacuum that needs to be filled by political dialogue strategies; rather, there is Law. In particular, there is an interface between concurrent rights in the specific case.

What escapes Weiler's vision is the ontological presence of terms that are in tension, not in contradictory terms. On the contrary, one (national identity under Article 4.2 TEU) could not exist without a dialogical relationship with the other (Article 2 TEU), since it forms part of a *communitas*, and vice versa, simply because the Union's values arise as common and draw nourishment from the shared constitutional heritage. While emphasising the importance of this national jurisprudential line (since it in some way separates the protection of human rights from its classical liberal anchors—individual versus State/nation/public authority)—the Weilerian approach regards this tension as merely "complicated and not easily resolvable."[40] From the perspective of the 'in-between', there are no belligerent legal conflicts, nor a legal void to be filled by political dialogue strategies; rather, there is Law, in particular the interface between concurrent rights in the concrete case. This is Law that results from the interconnections between legal systems; it is not the monopoly of any single system.

On the contrary, the supranational axiological heritage requires the Other, in other words, the relational contribution of European Constitutional Law. This fact underscores the relevance and necessity of developing relational mechanisms for intersystemic communication that transcend the dichotomy of monism/dualism and international/national.

6.2.2 From the Internationalist Perspective: 'International Constitutionalism'

In his 1970 General Course on Public International Law at The Hague Academy, Tomuschat clearly outlined how international society evolved into an international community. Addressing the complexity of the international legal order, he identified several key stages: the first was a Law of

[40] See also J. Ríos-Figueroa, *Judicial review and democratic resilience. Afterword to the Foreword by Doreen Lustig and J. H. H. Weiler* in *International journal of constitutional law*, 2019, pp. 17–23.

Coexistence, marking the origins of the international legal order; the second phase was one of cooperation. Alongside these references to the international community, the Court, in analysing the fundamental principles of International Law, has also referred, for example, to the significance of the principles governing diplomatic and consular relations for the international community as a whole.[41] However, the most salient case with regard to the concept of the international community is arguably the ruling on *Reparations*. In that 1949 decision, the Court held that fifty States represented "the great majority of the members of the international community".[42] Previously, in the famous and widely cited Lotus case, the Permanent Court of International Justice (PCIJ) had referred to the "community of States" when interpreting the expression "principles of International Law" contained in Article 15 of the Lausanne Convention.[43]

A third stage was that in which social law came to the fore. Finally, Tomuschat concluded with reflections and questions regarding the present-day existence of an international community.[44] An important example in this context is Article 53 of the Vienna Convention on the Law of Treaties, as well as the Barcelona Traction ruling of the International Court of Justice.[45]

It should be emphasised, in any case, that the Court refers to this concept when analysing the principles and values of International Law (*jus cogens* and *erga omnes*), which are regarded as the shared principles or norms that propel international society towards the condition of an international community. For decades, it has been argued that a State's acceptance of International Law is itself a manifestation of sovereignty, as established in the well-known Wimbledon case,[46] in the sense that States are also free to limit their own competences in favour of Supranational

[41] ICJ, *United States Diplomatic and Consular Staff in Tehran* (United States of America v. Iran), Judgment of 24 May 1980: I.C.J. Reports 1980, para. 92.

[42] ICJ, *Reparation for injuries suffered in the service of the United Nations*, Advisory Opinion of 11 April 1949: I.C. J. Reports 1949, p. 185.

[43] PCIJ, *The Case of S.S. Lotus* (France. v. Turkey.), Judgement, 1927 P.C.I.J. Series A-No. 10, p. 16.

[44] C. Tomuschat, *Obligations arising for states without or against their will*, cit., p. 45.

[45] ICJ, Barcelona Traction, Light, and Power Company, Ltd [1970] ICJ 1.

[46] "No doubt any convention creating an obligation of this kind places a restriction upon the exercise of the sovereign rights of the State, in the sense that it requires them to be exercised in a certain way. But the right of entering into international engagements is an attribute of State sovereignty". PCIJ, Case of S.S. Wimbledon (United Kingdom and ors. v. Germany), Judgement, 1923 P.C.I.J. Series A-No. 01, p. 25.

Law. This latter point was succinctly expressed by Combacau and Sur, who remarked that sovereignty '*suggère la possibilité pour un État d'aliéner aussi largement qu'il le juge opportun sa liberté future, pourvu qu'il le fasse en usant de sa liberté actuelle*'.[47]

But the *vexata quaestio* is always the same. What International Law are we speaking of? Is it the Law of the "international community of civilised nations"? Or is it the supposed extension of that community, which still marginalises powerless populations and communities? And what values nourish today's international community? We wholeheartedly agree on the urgent need for an international community governed by Law. However, to escape the persistent uncertainties that cloud virtually every contemporary study of International Law, regardless of geographical context, we must embrace an *écart*, a deliberate, unconsulted shift; a reframing that starts with identifying the blind spots of International Law.[48] Otherwise, we risk descending once again into a frenetic, yet ultimately fruitless, struggle over the meaning and authority of Law. In short, what we have been questioning are the underlying reasons behind the structural shortcomings of International Law. Here, we find invaluable assistance in the work of the Critical Legal Studies and TWAIL scholars, who point out the obvious (what might be called Moscarda's nose), yet at the same time fall into the very perspectival error they critique: observing Western reality through monocular, compact, distorted lenses. It is the State, along with its hegemonic forces, that has constructed the edifice of the various International Laws in an inter-State, compartmentalised manner, supported by the epistemic communities that have reinforced its foundations: this forms the basis of an exclusionary identity. If we are to study another kind of International Law, we must change our viewing lenses and observe identity interactions, in order to then discuss a truly International Law, an international custom understood in the sense of a Herodotean *nomos* rather than a Platonic one;[49] one that is concerned with the reality

[47] J. Comacau - S. Sur, *Droit International public*, 13 ed., LGDJ, Paris, 2019, p. 216.

[48] David W. Kennedy, *The Disciplines of International Law and Policy*, in *Leiden J. Int'l L. 9*, 1999, p. 12; Idem, *The Dark Side of Virtue: Reassessing International Humanitarism*, Princeton University Press, Princeton, 2004.

[49] M. Vogliotti, *La fine del "grande stile" e la ricerca di una nuova identità per la scienza giuridica*, in *L'identità delle scienze giuridiche in ordinamenti multilivello*, edited by V. Barsotti, Maggioli, 2014, p. 104, discusses the second social dimension of Contemporary Law that should be observed "*come la novella incarnazione degli agraphoi nomoi di Antigone, della seconda dimensione del diritto, quella che viene non dall'alto del potere politico (la Costituzione come lex superior), ma dal basso*".

of legal circulation or legal transfer rather than the university of the Hyperuranion place of legal Ideas (translated into the general principles of civilised nations).[50] This way, custom will be queen (*nomos basileus*), and our legal systems will open themselves up to conceptual interactions, as already occurs in the field of cultural and environmental protection, where such cross-fertilisation of concepts has already taken place. This is an identity-related issue: understanding which legal dynamics are already under way and what kind of Law can truly be shaped by an (ideally) inclusive international community.

The universalisation of International Law (alongside the contemporaneous phenomenon of the unification of Comparative Law, as discussed above) appears to be an irreversible process. This is due to the mechanisms of decolonisation, the affirmation of the principle of self-determination and the consolidation of a society in the process of institutionalisation, both universal and regional, general and sectoral. The global affirmation of the sovereign State, through the universalisation of International Law, also raises the possibility of the existence of an international community as a whole.

With the 1970 Declaration on Principles of International Law,[51] the unanimous will of the member States aimed to lay the legal foundations for the values of such a community. This significant document brings together both the founding principles of an inter-State community and the early seeds of a *communitas* governed by values independent of the aggregate interests of (powerful) States. When reasoning in terms of values and identity, Jullien offers us a particularly useful warning:[52] "*Los valores pueden hacernos recaer en la identificación cultural excluyente, [...] e incluso excluyente entre sí: si adhiero a los valores cristianos, me sería difícil adherir a los valores ateos.*"[53] This axiological definition by opposition can also be dangerous in practice. Difference, when associated with exclusive identity, as we have analysed so far, isolates and essentialises legal cultures. When we speak of the common (in terms of values and principles, as referenced in Articles 2 and 6 TEU), we must open *écarts* and generate

[50] The *topus uranus* is a Platonic concept referring to the world of perfect ideas, and, later in the Middle Ages, to the realm inhabited by God beyond the heavens.

[51] Declaration concerning the principles of International Law concerning friendly relations and cooperation among States in accordance with the Charter of the United Nations (res. 2625-XXV, 1970, of the United Nations General Assembly)

[52] F. Jullien, *Il n'y a pas d'identité culturelle*, Éditions de l'Herne, Paris, 2016, p. 75.

[53] F. Jullien, idem, cit., pp. 75–76.

shared resources: "*lo común no está hecho de clonaje y repetición; tampoco es banal, condición que lo haría perder su fecundidad.*"[54]At this stage, the possibility re-emerges of shaping a legal order based on a *communitas*, understood in the terms we now employ, rather than a legal order resulting merely from the juxtaposition of States. The objective would be to construct a *communitas* grounded in shared values and principles, thereby fracturing the structure of the Law of Separation that we have thus far reconstructed. "In its black-box model, Legal Positivism treats national legal orders as mutually closed normative entities, isolated in their respective compartments".[55]

As observed previously, the dialectical tension between the universal and the particular has characterised the international legal order from its very inception. Vitoria had already referred to this dynamic, and in the early seventeenth century Francisco Suárez spoke of the *jus praeceptivum*. Vattel, for his part, also drew attention to the existence of a Law of immutable nature, whose obligations are necessary and indispensable.[56] International jurisprudence has, on rare occasions, referred to a category of norms that are independent of the will of States, such as the ICJ did in the Corfu Channel case,[57] the Legality of the threat or use of nuclear weapons[58] and in the ruling on Armed activities in the territory of the Congo.[59] International legal doctrine regarding *jus cogens* has often described this category as an 'empty box',[60] a vehicle that 'rarely leaves the garage',[61] or as an 'insubstantial image of a norm—lacking flesh and bone'.[62]

[54] Again, F. Jullien, idem, cit., p. 89.

[55] K. Tuori, *European Constitutionalism,* Cambridge University Press, Cambridge, 2015, p. 206.

[56] E. Vattel, *The Law of Nations or Principles of the Law of Nature Applied to the Conduct and Affair of the Nations and Sovereigns*, AMS Press, New York, 1982.

[57] ICJ, Corfu Channel case, Judgment of 9 April 1949, ICJ Reports, 1949.

[58] ICJ, Legality of the Use of Nuclear Weapons, Advisory Opinion of 9 July 1996, ICJ Reports 1996, p. 66.

[59] ICJ, Armed Activities on the Territory of the Congo, Judgment of 3 February 2006, ICJ Reports, 2005, p. 168.

[60] Cf. G. Abi-Saab, *The Third World and the Future of the International Legal Order*, in *Revue Egyptienne Droit International*, 1973, p. 53.

[61] Cf. I. Brownlie, *Discussion*, in *Change And Stability In International Law-Making* 108, 110 (Cassese A.- Weiler J.H.H. (eds.), 1988, Walter de Gruyteer, Berlín /Nueva York, pp. 98–128).

[62] Cf. A. D'Amato, *It's a Bird, It's a Plane, It's Jus Cogens, Conn. J. Int'l L. 1*, 1990, p. 6.

The very existence of *jus cogens*, even if not practised daily or specifically defined, draws attention to an axiological moment, or, as some International Law scholars would put it, a constitutional one.[63] While on the one hand, the axiological elevation of fundamental rights to norms of the global constitution is evoked,[64] on the other, a distinction is drawn between substantive constitutional norms (*erga omnes* applicable to all subjects of International Law) and constitution in institutional terms, concerning the separation of powers and the democratic functioning of institutions.[65]

In the constitutionalisation of International Law, the systematisation carried out by Tomuschat[66] and the theses of Erika De Wet on the International Community stand out.[67] The hierarchy of norms in International Law is mentioned, with *jus cogens* and *erga omnes* obligations as emerging values. The proposal of a stratified global constitutional order includes norms of *jus cogens*, international customary law, and emerging *erga omnes* norms. The intertwining of the threads of contemporary International Law and Constitutional Law, more attuned to international dynamics, is absolutely necessary. Equally unavoidable is the correlative question of the international *communitas*. Habermas has powerfully contributed to the debate by emphasising the transition towards a post-national constellation of a global society, as the current international community "is indeed in transition towards the postnational constellation

[63] B. Simma, *The Contribution of Alfred Verdross to the Theory of International Law*, in *Europ. Journ. Intern. Law*, vol. 6, 1995, pp. 33 ss.; J. Klabber, *Constitutionalism Lite*, in *IOLR*, vol. 1, 2004, pp. 31–58; R. McDonald, D.M. Johnston, *Towards World Constitutionalism: Issues in the Legal Ordering of the World Community*, Martinus Nijhoff, The Hague, 2005.

[64] A. Peters, *Compensatory Constitutionalism: The Functions and Potential of Fundamental International Norms and Structures*, in *Leiden Journal of International Law*, 2006, pp. 579–610.

[65] For example, P.M. Dupuy, *The Constitutional Dimension of the Charter of the United Nations Revisited*, in *Max-Planck Yearbook of International Law*, vol. I, 1997, pp. 1–33.

[66] C. Tomuschat–J.M. Thouvenin, *The Fundamental Rules of the International Legal Order: Jus Cogens and Obligation Erga Omnes*, Martinus Nihjoff, Leiden, 2006; C. Tomuschat, *International Law: Ensuring the Survival of Mankind on the eve of a New Century*, in *RCADI*, vol. 281, 199, pp. 10 ss, Idem, *Obligations Arising for the States without or against Their Will*, in *Recueil des Cours de l'Académie de Droit International de la Haye*, vol, 241, 1993, pp. 195 ss.

[67] E. de Wet, *The International Constitutional Order*, in *Intern. Compar. Law Quart.*, vol. 55, 2006, pp. 51–76; Idem, *The emergence of International and Regional Value System as a Manifestation of the Emerging International Constitutional Order*, in *Leiden Journal of International Law*, vol. 19, 2006, n.3, pp. 611–632.

of a global society".[68] Habermas' intervention highlights the importance of participatory and democratic values within a communicative International Society.

The text *The Constitutionalization of International Law* by Klabbers, Peters and Ulfstein explores the verticalisation of International Law and the distinction between international and national constitutionalism.[69] Klabbers argues that international pluralism leads to the elevation of *jus cogens* norms to the status of a *Grundnorm* within a material form of constitutionalism. But he also states that "besides, international constituzionalization must necessary differ from national constitutionalism, and it is therefore not possible to copy one or a few constitutions. The idea is not to create a global, centralized government, but to constitutionalize global (polyarchic and multilevel) governance. This project must indeed take more fully into account the needs and interests of developing countries and their populations."[70] Therefore, the phenomenon of global constitutionalism must be understood through epistemological guidelines different from our traditional State-centric conception. The constitutionalisation of International Law continues to be processed according to national patterns, "as an attempt to explain developments in International Law in terms borrowed from domestic constitutionalism, with the aim of furthering a normative agenda of internationalism, integration and legal control of politics".[71]

Only among a few jurists and sociologists can we begin to glimpse an epistemological shift that moves beyond already ossified frameworks. From the outset, Luhmann's approach is rooted in the project of replacing the theory of closed systems with that of open systems: a system exists only in relation to its own environment, from which it draws the stimuli necessary for an ongoing process of increasing complexity, reproducing itself in ever more articulated forms. This is a challenge that we aim to take up and explore further in the second part of this work.[72]

[68] J. Habermas, *The Divided West*, Polity Press, Cambridge, 2006, p. 115.

[69] J. Klabbers–A. Peters–G. Ulfstein, *The Constitutionalization of International Law*, Oxford University Press, Oxford, 2009.

[70] J. Klabbers–A. Peters–G. Ulfstein, *The Constitutionalization of International Law*, cit., 346.

[71] W. Werner, *The Never-ending Closure: Constitutionalism and International Law*, in AA.VV., *Transnational Constitutionalism: International and European Perspective*, edited by N. Tsagourias (ed.), Cambridge University Press, Cambridge, 2007, p. 330.

[72] N. Luhmann, *Soziale Systeme. Grundriss einer allgerneinen Theorie*, Suhrkamp, Francfort, 1984.

6.3 From a Law of 'Classification, Separation and Exclusion' to a (Possible) Relational Law of Inclusion: The Need for the Law of the Other

The Westphalian State may have succeeded in its project of legal centralisation and in suppressing the legal plurality of the medieval period, along with spontaneous Customary Law. Yet, in their colonial and imperial enterprises, the leading European powers soon found themselves confronted with new Encounters and a new form of legal pluralism, grounded in Indigenous customary practices. The International Law of Separation is structured around hermetically sealed compartments: sovereign, autonomous States that coexist (at times!), but do not truly live together within a shared community.[73] The black box model presupposes that national legal systems mutually acknowledge each other's universal and exclusive claims to authority within their respective State territories: they treat each other as black boxes. Moreover, the model presupposes agreement on the precise demarcation of the boundary line that delineates the compartments of national legal systems. Border disputes concerning the exact extent of overlapping claims to authority arise only sporadically and are typically resolved through conflict-of-law mechanisms within the framework of International Private Law. Yet, through various Encounters, we have seen that Non State Law does not define its jurisdictional claims territorially. Rather, it does so substantively (as in the case of Transnational Law) or personally (as in the case of Indigenous or Religious Law). In the context of post-national plurality, fundamental conflicts of authority (in which the very autonomy or identity of at least one of the parties is at stake) are not merely possible, but likely. A salient example is the ongoing debate between the Court of Justice of the European Union and the German Constitutional Court over the protection of Member States' constitutional identity in the face of (perceived) encroachments by EU law. The black box model of separation is binary and lacks the conceptual tools to articulate fundamental conflicts of authority. This Western identity-based model can accommodate International Law only as a variant of State Law. International Law is thus understood as being confined to its own domain, limited to regulating the external relations of sovereign States. As such, it does not disturb the self-contained nature or the territorially

[73] K. Tuori, *The Properties of Law. Modern Law and After*, Cambridge University Press, Cambridge, 2021, p. 25.

bound, universal and exclusive authority of national legal systems within a model of mere coexistential juxtaposition.[74]

In the identity-based model of separation, plurality is subordinated to the pursuit of unity. What matters for positivist legal theory is to reconstruct and explain the (self-)contained unity of a national legal order. The very structure of the International Law of Separation gives rise to such coherence and unity. This is a form of legal plurality marked by solipsism or legal plurality of separation. Each State legal system is governed solely by its own national legal order and does not interfere with the territorially bounded, exclusive, and universal jurisdiction of other State legal systems. National legal orders can only preserve their autonomy if normative autonomy is complemented by the legislative and judicial sovereignty of the respective State. Both unity conceived in formal Kelsenian terms and the solipsistic view of plurality as mere diversity rest on the premise that the normative legal order exists only as Phenomenal Law or as a declaration of principles, as Sacco suggests in his notion of the cryptotype and in the second thesis of Trento.[75] Indeed, it would be difficult to sustain the internationalist model of separation if one were to acknowledge the multifaceted nature of Law and the porosity of State legal orders at the legal-cultural level, as is evident in the transnational circulation of legal formants.[76] Law is not merely surface: it possesses a social and practical dimension.

At this stage of our research, it is clear that the still occasional examples of cross-fertilisation in the field of International Law and the cross-fertilisation of European Union Law (for example, through the channel of common constitutional traditions or shared values)[77] have brought about

[74] K. Tuori, *The Properties of Law. Modern Law and After*, Cambridge University Press, Cambridge, 2021, p. 54.

[75] "Comparison focuses on the various legal phenomena that have existed concretely, whether in the past or present, according to a criterion that treats as real both what has actually taken place and what is said to have occurred. In this sense, comparison shares the same standard of validation as the historical sciences." On this subject, see G. Ajani, *Sistemi giuridici comparati. Lezioni e materiali*, 2ª ed., Torino, Giappichelli, 2006, p. 22.

[76] On this subject, see A. Di Martino, *Circolazione delle soluzioni giuridiche e delle idee costituzionali. Questioni di metodo comparativo e prassi tra culture costituzionali e spazi globali*, in *DPCE online*, 2021.

[77] As Tuori rightly highlights, these examples are evidence of a new, Non-State Law, though there remains a clear difference in how each asserts its own identity. "In contestations involving indigenous or religious law, a common cultural understanding on which dialogue could rely is more difficult to attain. Neither do indigenous or religious law possess much

a necessary epistemological shift. Sousa Santos argues that we are living "in a time of porous legality or of legal porosity, multiple networks of legal orders forcing us to constant transitions and trespassing and that our legal life is constituted by an intersection of different legal orders, that is, by interlegality."[78] The conceptual positions still anchored to exclusionary sovereign paradigms, resulting in the pre-eminence of the procedural factor of jurisdictional immunity regarding violations of *jus cogens*, have prevented, in the first case, the infusion of common constitutional values into the principles of a supposed international *communitas*. What is understood as 'common' in this sense becomes merely the expression of an exclusive typology of identity. The axiologisation of Union Law through common values and traditions points towards extra-legal terms, which in turn reflect a social dimension of the *nomos*, rather than its merely positivist legal transposition.[79]

At the State level, the development of the category of 'supreme constitutional principles' led to the recovery of a space (the perimeter of a society's fundamental values) that the modern paradigm had ultimately excluded from Law and, consequently, from the scope of legal scholarship.

"On the side of law's normativity, 'legal institution' is a conceptual counterpart to 'sociolegal practice' on the side of sociality. Both concepts adopt a **relational** view on law where normativity and sociality are seen as interlinked."[80] [emphasis added]. This dynamic as a whole also refers naturally to the culture of Living Law and constitutional identity.[81]

latitude for negotiation when autonomy or identity is at stake. As a counterweight, though, national or transnational law does not usually interpret the conflicts as a menace to autonomy or constitutional identity. This should allow for concessions and compromises, provided that human rights considerations as new repugnancy rules are not seen to raise obstacles"; also in K. Tuori, *The Properties of Law. Modern Law and After*, Cambridge University Press, Cambridge, 2021, p. 67.

[78] B. Sousa Santos, *Toward a New Legal Commonsense: Law, Globalization and Emancipation*, Butterworths, Toronto 2002, p. 56.

[79] Exclusionary identity, as observed here, is based on the positivist reductionism dealt with by K. Tuori in *The Properties of Law. Modern Law and After*, Cambridge University Press, Cambridge, 2021, p. 23: "Legal positivism makes three reductive moves. It reduces law to the normative dimension; it reduces legal normative to its surface; and it reduces all law to state law".

[80] Again, K. Tuori, *The Properties of Law. Modern Law and After*, Cambridge University Press, Cambridge, 2021, p. 86.

[81] A. Di Martino, *Comparare le identità costituzionali: circolazione degli argomenti giuridici e contesti storico-politici*, in *Esperienze giuridiche in dialogo. IL ruolo della comparazione*, Graziadei M. - Somma A. (eds.), Sapienza Università Editrice, Rome, 2024, p. 199.

From the European perspective, the reclamation of the second dimension of Law is owed to the Court of Justice, which, in its daily empirical practice, has effectively compelled European Law to respect fundamental rights as a consequence of the shared values and constitutional traditions of the Member States.[82]

How is this axiological-identitarian process articulated? First and foremost, by moving beyond the dichotomies traditionally posed in Comparative and International Law, namely, uniformity versus differentiation and universalisation versus nationalism. In recent decades, jurists across disciplines have increasingly identified this dynamic, particularly within the mechanisms of balancing. That is, in how the Voice (the legal system of the Other, their identity, values) enters into and contributes to the European legal system. Refined constitutional techniques of balancing and proportionality are gradually being developed, especially as they relate to the market/values dynamic and to the modulation of national and European identities.

Even the very notion of a limit in International Law, if it is to exist and operate meaningfully, must be constructed through the interweaving of Wittgensteinian threads and (Constitutional) National Law. This, indeed, is the essence of the relational and scientific identity of Law. If not, we will once again (unsuccessfully) find ourselves grappling with the *vexata quaestio* of the effectiveness of International Law, and with Weiler's notion of selective exit.[83]

Marta Cartabia briefly deals with this subject in her interesting Editorial,[84] mentioning the same rulings of the International Court of Justice (Germany v. Italy in the matter of jurisdictional immunities[85]) and the Court of Justice of the European Union (CJUE Kadi[86]), which are chosen as examples of the third wave by Lustig and Weiler, on the one

[82] P. Grossi, *Un impegno per il giurista di oggi: ripensare le fonti del diritto*, Istituto Universitario Suor Orsola Benincasa, Napoli, 2009, referred to in *Paolo Grossi*, G. Alpa (ed.), Laterza, Roma-Bari, 2011, p. 31.

[83] J.H.H. Weiler, *The Transformation of Europe*, in *Yale Law Journal*, 1991, p. 2412 understands selective exit to be "the practice of the Member States of retaining membership but seeking to avoid their obligations under the Treaty, be it by omission or commission".

[84] M. Cartabia, *Editorial. Courts' Relations*, in *Intern. Rev. Const. Law*, 2020, p. 7.

[85] ICJ, *Jurisdictional Immunities of the State (Germany v. Italy: Greece intervening)*, Judgment, I.C.J. Reports 2012, p. 99.

[86] See, for example, the CJEU, 3 September 2008, joined cases C-402/05 P and C-415/05 P, Yassin Abdullah Kadi and Al Barakaat International Foundation v. Council and Commission, ECR 2008, p. I-6351.

hand, and Palombella, on the other. Rather than as a contrast between different and conflicting judicial attitudes, albeit interactive,[87] the Italian jurist argues in terms of relational identity.

In the European context, the Luxembourg court, in its Taricco II ruling,[88] for example, has been able to engage in dialogue with the constitutional courts. In the internationalist scenario, the aforementioned constitutionalisation of International Law has not been effective in safeguarding *jus cogens* through national axiological constitutional experiences, due to a reason conceptually tied to the defence of national sovereignty. This will be observed through the lens of the concepts of *communitas* and *immunitas* in Roberto Esposito's theory.

6.3.1 The Écart Between Communitas and Immunitas

It is evident that whenever a judge seeks to try a foreign legal subject with immunity, whenever reference is made to the values of the international community to demand State responsibility, it injures the body of national sovereignty. The presence of international responsibility arising from a violation of *jus cogens* would constitute an initial breach in the core of the immunity-based Law of Separation, in favour of a norm that could be defined as a 'Common Law'. If community is the only axiological and legal context that gives relevance to immunity, how is its relationship defined? From a monist/dualist binary perspective or with a constitutionalist or internationalist pre-eminence? Is it a simple opposition or a complex dialectic where one term implies the other as its necessary presupposition?

Roberto Esposito and etymology provide us with an initial answer: '*Inmunitas*' derives from the Latin '*munus*', which means function or obligation. Thus, '*immunis*' refers to someone who has no duties towards anyone, either due to original autonomy or by dispensation from a previous debt, being exempt from the obligation of '*munus*'. The true opposite of '*immunitas*' could be '*communitas*', which involves participation in

[87] For a comparison of the judicial attitudes of the two international courts in the context of judicial dialogue, allow me to refer to A. Lazari, *Dialogo judicial y resolución de controversias internacionales*, in E.M. Vázquez Gómez, M.D. Adam Muñoz, N. Cornago Prieto (coord.) *El arreglo pacífico de las controversias internacionales*, XXIV Jornadas de la Asociación Española de Profesores de Derecho internacional y Relaciones internacionales (AEPDIRI), Córdoba, 20–22 October, Tirant lo Blanch, 2013, pp. 169–184.

[88] CJUE, C-42/17, MAS and MB, 5 December EU:C:2017:936.

common commitments. In this sense, immunity is particular and belongs to a specific individual, marking a fundamental difference with community.

This dialectic is crucial in Law, understood as an immune device of the social system, manifesting in all its complexity in certain rulings, such as the aforementioned Germany v. Italy case before the International Court of Justice. Sovereignty itself, in its modern logic, can be seen as an attempt to immunise power from the political community. The points of rupture between two conceptions of Law (not only international) are evident. "*En las violaciones graves y sistemáticas a derechos humanos es cuando se plantea la falta de coherencia en las estructuras normativas internacionales; hay una divergencia abismal entre inmunidades del Estado y el bloque normativo de derecho imperativo que son los derechos humanos*".[89]

Since the eighteenth century, according to Niklas Luhmann, Law has become a function of the immune system, evolving into a Law of 'immunities' rather than one of *communitas.* Simone Weil describes it as inherently private and exclusive, always belonging to someone and never to all. In legal modernity, only the claim to what is one's own is common The *societas* of International Law, and the aforementioned case of Germany v. Italy regarding jurisdictional immunity, clearly supports this: it is a system of *immunitates* rather than a *communitas.* However, two novel elements have recently emerged from a perspective far removed from the exclusionary legal identity: a shift in the Western proprietary paradigm and a new idea of community.

From the first point of observation, in the latest rulings of the Inter-American Court of Human Rights, the two moments have been reversed.[90] The phenomena of hybridisation in the field of cultural restitution lie within a much deeper mechanism of epistemological cross-fertilisation,[91] which signals a *quid pluris* conceptually, both with respect to the often

[89] A. Mangas Martín, *Humanización, democracia y Estado de derecho en el ordenamiento internacional,* speech of admission as an academic member, session held on 8 April 2014, Madrid, Real Academia de Ciencias Morales y Políticas, p. 87.

[90] Moiwana Village v. Suriname, Ruling of 15 June 2005, IACHR, (Ser. C) No. 145 (2005); YakeAxa vs. Paraguay, 17 June 2005. Series C No. 125, paras. 124, 131. Cf. J.M. Pasqualucci, *La evolución de los derechos internacionales indígenas en el sistema interamericano de derechos humanos*, in *Human Rights Law Review*, 2006, 281 ss.

[91] M. Lupoi and M. Graziadei, *The Historical Context of Saunders v Vautier* in *Edinburgh Law Review*, volume 29, number, 2025, pp. 1–27.

hegemonic mechanism of legal transplantation[92] and with respect to the transfer or circulation of models, because it involves a relational view of the Other, articulated around the necessary existence of the Law of the Other.[93]

From the second perspective, as P. Ricœur has reminded us, today's humanity is conceived in its dual form of unity (the human) and plurality (the diversity of systems and cultures).[94] This humanism does not signify the strict individualism defended by certain Anglo-Saxon neoliberal counterparts, but rather is based on a community that is necessarily intersubjective.[95] The envisaged perspective does not involve discarding any consideration of moral values by International Law, but rather rethinking how these values can be codified into Law. However, the legal and collective process of discussion allows for the production of norms that are deliberated intersubjectively among subjects and international actors, incorporating the most essential moral values of a plural international community, grounded in diversity.

The legitimacy of International Law also depends on its ability to represent various legal traditions. As Georges Abi-Saab observes: "If we really want International Law to take hold and be taken seriously by all, it has to be, both in its creation and in its interpretation and application, the product of the community as a whole, reflecting, by synthesis or symbiosis, the legal visions, needs and aspirations of all the components of this community".[96] It is all about understanding that "no entity can ever keep at bay that analytical antithesis on whose ontological isolation its identity depends. Or, to put it slightly less abstractly, every Self carries within it an ineradicable trace of its external Other, which is to say that the Other is

[92] M. Graziadei, *El trasplante de normas jurídicas: una perspectiva crítica*, in J. Cañabate Perez and M. Hernandez Valles (eds.), *Derecho no oficial: experiencias jurídicas más allá del Imperio de la Ley del Estado*, Dykinson, Madrid, 2025, p. 121.

[93] On this subject, see H. Muir Watt, *Alterity in the Conflict of Laws: An Ontology of the In-Between,* in *Rabels Zeitschrift für Auslandisches und Internationales Privatrecht*, 2023, pp. 7–8; A. Bianchi, idem, cit., p. 232.

[94] P. Ricœur, *Cultures, du deuil à la traduction*, in *Le Monde*, 25 mai 2004, p. 1.

[95] E. Jouannet, *La Communauté Internationale Vue Par Les Juristes*, in *Annuaire français des relations internationales*, 2005, Vol. VI, p. 24.

[96] G. Abi-Saab, *The Portrait of the Jurist as an international Judge*, in C. Peck and R.S. Lee (eds), *Increasing the Effectiveness of the International Court of Justice: Proceedings of the ICJ/UNITAR Colloquium to Celebrate the 50th Anniversary of the Court*, 1997, p. 171.

never really external and, moreover, never really an Other".[97] Herodotus' *nomos*, understood as Customary Law intertwined with various identities, takes on an essential value in social coexistence, not only considering the number of legal systems in the legal world that adopt *consuetudo*, but also in the qualitative comparison with Non-State Law systems.[98] We cannot ignore or minimise these data that are in contrast to the blackboxistic structuring of classical International Law. Not only is there a need to redefine international custom in a more inclusive way,[99] but also to reconsider the core values traditionally associated with International Law and the methods for achieving them. It has been argued that "democracy can be conceived as a process of participation rather than representation and presents a conception of 'compound custom' which combines the elements of custom as a source of law, as a mode of rights, and as a foundation of interaction".[100]

Is it possible to have a different legal framework, one that is no longer serving the interests of the great powers that 'use' it in a makeshift way, as a form of *bricolage*, to find a conceptual fit to their benefits?[101] I believe that another form of State and supranational relational identity is possible,

[97] A. Rasulov, *International Law and the Poststructuralist Challenge*, in *Leiden Journal of International Law*, 2006, p. 801.

[98] One essential reference in this regard is K. Tuori, *The Properties of Law. Modern Law and After*, Cambridge University Press, Cambridge, 2021, pp. 215–214 ("*Non-state law*").

[99] On a conception of international custom that is more attentive to real practice and democracy, see M. Hakimi, *Making Sense of Customary International Law*, 2019. In general, see Jean d'Aspremont, *Formalism and the Sources of International Law*; 2011; B.D. Lepard, *Customary International Law: A New Theory with Practical Applications*, Cambridge University Press, Cambridge, 2010; M. Mutua, *Savages, Victims, and Saviors: The Metaphor of Human Rights*, 2001; B. S. Chimni, *The TWAIL Perspective on International Law and Globalisation*, 2000.

[100] N. Roughan, *Democratic Custom V. International Customary Law*, in *Vict. Univ. Wellin. Law Rev*, 2007, p. 403. From a relational point of view, these reflections on page 410 are particularly enlightening: "Democracy in this light is a matter of participation and interaction among all groups – including those who are ultimately overruled by countervailing interests, and those whose interests are ultimately satisfied. For International Law, this notion that participation is foundational and crucial to any overlaid structure of representation implies that law making processes may start at a more basic and societal level than orthodox theories have explained".

[101] M. Koskenniemi, *To the Uttermost Parts of the Earth: Legal Imagination and International Power 1300–1870*, cit., p. 12.

always challenging and questioning traditional International Law.[102] It is a way of interpreting the Law, starting from the opposite premise to the one previously analysed: not through exclusion, but through the necessary presence of the Other.[103] An identity that is progressively forged not through classifications and Huntingtonian separations,[104] but through the incessant and necessary interactions with the Other. Thus, if we promote a communality that is not reduced to uniformity and hegemony, the common aspect (for example, Articles 2 and 6 TFEU) of this *communitas* will truly be active and will not lead to assimilation.

More than separation or stratification, the new legal world is characterised by the intersection of levels (particularly in the realm of general principles), the interaction and interdependence of legal systems, their porosity and '*sconfinatezza*',[105] their 'lateral openness',[106] the partial overlaps of general and sectoral systems, and the cooperation of their respective actors, especially the courts, which build communicative bridges performing an essential function of 'de-fragmentation' of 'systems born separate'.[107] With the revival of the method of the practical sciences (which can be traced back to the 1950s in the form of a theory of argumentation inspired by the

[102] We are referring to the intellectual tools, among many others, of J. Habermas, *The Theory of Communicative Action. Volume 1: Reason and the Rationalization of Society*, Beacon, London, 1985. Habermas is fundamental in contemporary social and political theory, with his focus on identity as a result of communication and recognition processes. The identity of individuals and social groups is shaped through linguistic interaction and participation in public space. This approach has been influential in the study of political and social identities, including State identity.

C. Taylor, *Sources of the Self: The Making of the Modern Identity*, cit. Taylor focuses on how individual and collective identities are shaped by a historical narrative and interactions with others. In terms of State identity, his work has been used to understand how national identities are constructed in relation to collective narratives and interactions with other groups.

[103] See, for example, P. Fitzpatrick, *Modernism and the Grounds of Law*, Cambridge University Press, Cambridge, 2001.

[104] Admirable for its visionary observations is the passage by A. Remiro Brotóns–R. Riquelme Cortado–E. Orihuela Catalayud. J. Diez-Hochleitner–L. Pérez-Prat Durbán, *Derecho Internacional. Curso General*, Tirant lo Blanch, Valencia, 2010, p. 60, where it is argued that "*de aplicarse al paradigma huntingtoniano todo Occidente acabaría aplicando políticas de limpieza étnica bajo regímenes legitimados por la voluntad popular. Los valores consagrados por la Constitución, aquí y allá, serán puesto a prueba.*"

[105] M.R. Ferrarese, *Diritto sconfinato. Inventiva giuridica e spazi nel mondo globale*, Laterza, Roma-Bari, 2006.

[106] S. Cassese, *Il diritto globale*, Einaudi, Torino, 2009, p. 24.

[107] S. Cassese, *I tribunali di Babele. I giudici alla ricerca di un nuovo ordine globale*, Roma, 2009, p. 99.

topical-dialectical method of the Anglo-Saxon pragmatics of Lauterpacht, and later by Sacco's operational hermeneutics), continental legal science rediscovered, after a long modern hiatus, the relational character of the Being of Law. Law thus comes to be conceived anew as a relationship between normative actors and the changing contexts of application: a physiological and virtuous tension. The language of the jurist who has crossed the boundaries of modernity to construct a new paradigm, and therefore a new identity for legal science, no longer concerns itself with the substance of 'Positive Law', but rather with actions, judgements and intersystemic tensions.[108]

Perhaps the time has come to change our legal glasses in order to read it, starting precisely in the territory where it was created: Europe.[109] "*L'Europa potrebbe essere il cantiere nel quale sperimentare non tanto ciò che ci unisce, ne ciò che ci divide, ma una politica del* tra, *e da questo di vista potrebbe essere il luogo dove sperimentare, non solo per l'Europa, una modalità non più imperiale della politica non più fondata sulla dicotomia tra amico e nemico*".[110]

Perhaps the time has come to define identity not by opposition, as was arduously attempted in the preamble of the "Treaty establishing a Constitution for Europe." Is Europe only Christian in opposition to 'immigration invasion'? Or is it merely secular, invoking the powerful Enlightenment creation of Kant's rationalism? Both epistemes have caused irreparable harm, as we have seen. What constitutes Europe is the *écart*, being both Christian and secular, among many other identity qualities. Being in between, where 'between' which does not mean agreement, nor concession, but tension between both terms, which enliven each other.[111]

And finally, perhaps the time has come to highlight a dual indispensability: the relevance of Law as a limit in opposition to unbridled Power,

[108] Cf. G. Zaccaria, *Sul concetto di positività del diritto*, in Idem (ed.), *Diritto positivo e positività del diritto*, Einaudi, Torino, 1991, p. 358.

[109] On the importance of regional identity in a cosmopolitan world, see A. Remiro Brotóns–R. Riquelme Cortado–E. Orihuela Catalayud. J. Diez-Hochleitner–L. Pérez-Prat Durbán, *Derecho Internacional. Curso General*, cit., p. 63: "*la región defiende su identidad e intereses comunes en un medio universal cuyo cosmopolitismo refuerza. Al igual que el particularismo, el regionalismo puede ser beneficioso para el multilateralismo si responde a actitudes cooperativas; pero no lo será si se concibe como una alternativa animada por el espíritu autárquico o de confrontación*".

[110] R. Masiero, *Prefazione* a F. Jullien, *Contro la comparazione. Lo 'scarto' e il 'tra'. Un altro accesso all'alterità*, Mimesis, Milano, 2014, p. 20.

[111] Idem, p. 61.

and the importance of a type of Relational Law.[112] It is now inevitable to redefine the very idea of Law within this possible *communitas*, no longer imbued with the archaic flavour of exclusionary norms inherited from hegemonic and violent periods, but open to communication and diversity, and enacted in a social and practical version.[113] *Inde datae leges, ne firmior omnia posset*. Is this possible?

[112] The thesis by K. Tuori is essential reading for a clearly relational vision: *The Properties of Law. Modern Law and After*, Cambridge University Press, Cambridge, 2021, p. 269: "In my own portrayal of modern state law, arrived at through criticism of Legal Positivism, I emphasise the importance of a **relational** approach" [emphasis added]. G. Palombella also makes an interesting contribution on the subject in *Il* rule of law. *Argomenti di una teoria (giuridica) istituzionale*, in *Sociologia del diritto*, 2009, pp. 46–47.

[113] According to new civic virtues argued by J.H.H. Weiler, *The Political and Legal Culture of European Integration: An Exploratory Essay*, in *Int'l J. Const. L.*, 2011, p. 678.

PART II

Pars Construens: Encounters with the Other in Europe

CHAPTER 7

The Relational Identity of Inclusion

Abstract This chapter examines the concept of relational identity of inclusion within the context of plural International Law. It analyses the European Union's proposal of a new identity paradigm grounded in respect for the Other, as opposed to one based on assimilation. This methodology stands in contrast to exclusionary notions of State sovereignty and encourages a conflictual yet integrative dialogue. The chapter traces the development of constitutional identity in Europe, emphasising the interaction between national and European legal systems. It further considers the ongoing tension between the rise of populism and the imperative for a community identity rooted in shared values. The discussion of relational identity is specifically confined to the legal sphere, focusing on the dialogue between the European Union court and national judiciaries.

Keywords Judicial dialogue • European Union • Relational identity

In the previous chapter, we discussed the importance of regional experiences within a framework of plural International Law. Europe, and the European Union in particular, proposes a new approach to managing diversity. Respecting diversity can only be achieved by moving beyond an identity paradigm based on internal unification of the State and separation from Others (other States). This second part does not aim to glorify a new,

© The Author(s), under exclusive license to Springer Nature Switzerland AG 2026

A. Lazari, *Relational Identity in International, Comparative and European Union Law*,
https://doi.org/10.1007/978-3-031-59482-3_7

shining legal future but rather to examine a new identity paradigm that is created and consolidated through the foundational recognition of the Law of the Other. This paradigm remains fragile and in its early stages. Its distinctiveness lies in its full respect for the Other, rather than assimilating it into pre-existing legal frameworks in Comparative Law. Studying this paradigm means recognising relational inclusion as part of the general values and principles of (EU) Law, the voice of the Other. The Secretary General of the Council of Europe, Thorbjørn Jagland, describes populist parties and movements within the Council of Europe as "political forces that appeal to widespread public grievances while trying to exclude other voices".[1]

Regarding this exclusive and exclusionary voice, a closer examination suggests that counter-limits could help restore an intrinsic dialogue within the relational logic. This logic is inevitably conflictual but always aimed at *integrating* rather than *disintegrating* the plurality of interacting systems. Such a dialogue would give a *voice* to constitutional courts,[2] which might otherwise risk being marginalised in the process of defining and protecting national constitutional identity.[3]

7.1 Prodromos: Ancient and New Identity Scenarios

After the tragedy of the Second World War, the exclusionary nature of State identity entered a profound crisis. The dividing line between internal and external gradually faded, and Western Law began to open up, at least formally, to the international community. At the same time, this community was slowly developing new values and principles, which had traditionally originated within the State framework.

From the outset, modern constitutions not only reflect the values of their national communities, nor do they seek to impose these values externally as universal. On the contrary, they open themselves to the world: recognising the existence of a proto-international community and Law

[1] T. Jagland, *State of democracy, human rights and the rule of law. Populism: How strong are Europe's checks and balances? Report of the Secretary-General of the Council of Europe 2017*, April 2017, p. 8.

[2] M. Cartabia, *Principi fondamentali e integrazione europea*, Giuffrè, Milan, 1995, p. 260.

[3] Cfr. S. Cassese, *Fine della solitudine delle corti costituzionali, ovvero il dilemma del porcospino*, in *Atti Sc. Mor.*, 2015, pp. 15–25.

beyond the State; engaging in a dialectical relationship with these systems and the values they represent. The highest expression of this openness lies precisely in the willingness to relinquish sovereign prerogatives in order to build an external order that guarantees the universal values of peace and justice.[4]

Outside the State, a vision of international organisation has developed primarily based on the United Nations system. Within this system, to ensure peace, the San Francisco Charter prohibits States from using force except in self-defence. Furthermore, monopoly over the use of force is granted to a centralised international body: the Security Council, precisely "created to maintain peace and not to change the world".[5]

Although the United Nations has taken from States the main right linked to sovereign identity, that is, the use of force, this loss has quickly been offset by the dominant role played by States, or more precisely, certain States, within the United Nations itself. In short, it seems that the Charter of the United Nations aims to counter a hegemonic form of sovereign identity through the will of (some) States. As a result, their sovereign equality, which is only formal, has become a different kind of balance that ultimately reflects the power relations between States. This creates, *mutandis mutandis*, a prolonged oligarchic situation that is not very different from the earlier hierarchical model of identity. Less powerful States are, in fact, protected by the prohibition on the use of force, provided they do not seriously interfere with the plans of the major powers. "*Se si dovesse definire in una formula lo stato della sovranità dopo l'istituzione delle Nazioni Unite che vada oltre l'orpello della sovrana eguaglianza fra gli Stati, non sarebbe forse inappropriato parlare di feudalesimo della sovranità.*"[6] The Other approaches the club of First World nations, but still remains on the threshold of recognition, even though it is part of the roster of United Nations Member States.[7]

Unlike the exclusionary conception of Law, the European experiment has gradually created a conceptual tension between different ideas of constitutional and national identities within the State itself and beyond it, in continuous interaction with international and European legal systems. In

[4] E. Cannizzaro, *La sovranità oltre lo Stato*, Il Mulino, Bologna, 2020, p. 61.

[5] Advisory Opinion of 21 June 1971, Legal Consequences for States of the Continued Presence of South Africa in Namibia, dissenting opinion of Sir Gerald Fitzmaurice, par. 115.

[6] E. Cannizzaro, *La sovranità oltre lo Stato*, cit., p. 85.

[7] Cfr. E. Oliete-E. Aldea, *The Porosity of Identity Boundaries*, in *Hybrid Heritage on Screen*, Palgrave Macmillan, London, 2015.

contrast to the foundational design of the United Nations, the European integration process has had to advance without undermining State sovereignty while at the same time progressively eroding its content and preparing the ground for other, more demanding forms of integration. The early European Communities were not intended to compete with the State in systematically controlling and regulating the life of the territorial community. In short, they were established to integrate the economies of the different States in anticipation of future forms of integration; the perspective and strategy adopted are functional. This political philosophy is based on an antithetical conception of sovereignty. It is not based on the eschatological idea of a supreme and feudal power but rather on a vision of shared competences aimed at integrating the various social communities from the ground up. In contrast to the conceptual and Manichean mechanism of sovereignty, the dynamics of European integration are instead focused on an incremental approach to political power, subtly and profoundly fostering a perceived community of individuals. However, the underlying identity of closure does not disappear; rather, it re-emerges disguised as the sovereign *arcana imperii*.[8] Can limited sovereignty exist? "Sovereignty cannot be conceived as an absolutist 'Lotus-like' concept; it confers rights but also duties on the State. The current resurgence of sovereignty in the political discourse challenges the balance between the two."[9] The very conception of sovereignty is shaped in a completely different way. Instead of being the foundation of the State's powers, which finds in its sovereignty an attribute that gives it 'the right to enter into international commitments', it is becoming (or becoming once again) an instrument for challenging existing legal norms. And when it is wrongly invoked, it aims to flatter the populist and sovereign instincts of the people, while at the same time it is largely devoid of any real conceptual use. "That the Westphalian international society was built on a defensive and absolute conception of sovereignty (non-intervention, immunities ...) is not in doubt. However, not without jolts, the balance has shifted in favour of a vision that is better adapted to the needs of a society of equals, in which the sovereignty of each State is limited by the equal sovereignty of all the others. And this movement has become more pronounced as the

[8] L. Niglia, *The New Transformation of Europe: Arcana Imperii*, in *The American Journal of Comparative Law*, 2020, p. 155.

[9] A. Pellet, *Guest Editorial—The Proper Use of Sovereignty*, in https://esil-sedi.eu/esil-newsletter-autumn2021/#guest_editorial

awareness of the solidarity imposed by the 'force of things' has increased: pollution, climate change, epidemics, terrorism, etc. know no borders and imply decided and coordinated action by all countries."[10]

The Hobbesian exclusionary attitude has reappeared with renewed vigour in recent years. It is clearly evident not only in the rise of populism but also in the corresponding tendency to withdraw from international treaties, particularly those of a multilateral nature. "It demonstrates that, in their rhetoric, populist governments promote an understanding of international law as a mere law of coordination."[11] The return to an exclusionary idea of Law emerges in the Joint Declaration on the Promotion of International Law, issued by the Russian Federation and China on 25 June 2016[12]: "the fact is that there was a plan that those present at the creation of the post-1945 world order shared to a degree, that was supplemented by subsequent common action, that was interrupted but not destroyed by Cold War rivalry, and that constituted a sort of genetic program for that order which was largely completed following the gradual end of the Cold War."[13] The declaration, which emphasises in particular the sovereign equality of all States, the principle of non-intervention and the consent of States as the foundation of International Law, may also be understood as an attempt by these two States to interpret International Law as a system of coordination norms.[14]

This exclusionary policy is evident in the different episodes of withdrawal from multilateral agreements, threatened (as in the case of South Africa from the Rome Statute[15]) or real (not only in the case of the famous

[10] A. Pellet, *Guest Editorial—The Proper Use of Sovereignty*, in https://esil-sedi.eu/esil-newsletter-autumn2021/#guest_editorial

[11] H. Krieger, *Populist Governments and International Law*, in *Europ. Journ. Intern. Law*, 2019, Vol. 30 No. 3, p. 996.

[12] Declaration of the Russian Federation and the People's Republic of China on the promotion of International Law, signed in Beijing on 25 June 2016 at http://www.mid.ru/en/foreign_policy/news/-/asset_publisher/cKNonkJE02Bw/content/id/2331698.

[13] J. Crawford, *The Current Political Discourse Concerning International Law*, in *Common Mar. Law Rev.*, 2018, p. 4.

[14] Cf. D.F. Wajner, *Populism in power and regional (dis-)integration: charting paths of populist regionalism in Europe and Latin America*, in *Journal Europ. Integr.*, 2025, pp. 1–24.

[15] High Court of South Africa *Democratic Alliance* v *Minister of International Relations and Cooperation and Others* Ruling of 22 February 2017, Case No 83145/2016, (Guateng Division) (*Democratic Alliance*).

Brexit[16] but also the United States from the Paris Agreement[17]). "Over time, this may precipitate a broader retreat into nativism and unilateralism. We should be ready to defend the communitarian values of international law against this possibility."[18]

To preserve their identity-based policies, populist governments often rely on the more traditional elements of International Law, on those ideas of separation in Law. Their ideal tends to promote international norms that protect State sovereignty and the ***domaine réservé***: "Us in opposition to Others."

The two speeches President Trump gave before the UN General Assembly in 2017[19] and 2018[20] show that the former US administration outlined a vision of the international legal order that resembled a rule of coordination rather than a rule of cooperation. His discourse is a clear affirmation of a foreign policy driven by exclusionary national interest. It focuses on separation, on the autonomy of political communities, and on "closed statehood": a perspective underlined with an explicit reference to the Monroe Doctrine in his 2018 speech. Recent speeches and actions on the international stage testify to a renewed idea of exclusionary identity in contrast to the fragile relational identity that has been developing in Europe through Law.

The notion of sovereignty is not only exaggerated, benefiting the rights it involves and harming the duties that come with it, but it is also distorted, risking the loss of all its specific meaning. The explicit and implicit appeal to the defence of State sovereignty has reappeared strongly in recent years, also within the scope of the European Union.

The real problem is the use of the term 'Sovereignty' for the European Union. It challenges the classic definition of sovereignty as an exclusive attribute of the State. By invoking 'European sovereignty' at every turn,

[16] Cfr. UKSC. (on the application of Miller and another) (Respondents) v Secretary of State for Exiting the European Union (Appellant) [2017] UKSC 5.

[17] Cfr. White House Press Secretary, 'Statement by President Trump on the Paris Climate Accord', 1 June 2017 at https://www.whitehouse.gov/the-press-office/2017/06/01/statementpresident-trump-paris-climate-accord

[18] Again, J. Crawford, *The Current Political Discourse Concerning International Law*, cit., p., p. 22.

[19] AGNU, Speech by Mr. Donald Trump, President of the United States of America (President Trump's 2017 Speech), UN Doc. A/72/PV.3, 19th September 2017.

[20] AGNU, Speech by Mr. Donald Trump, President of the United States of America (President Trump's 2018 Speech), UN Doc. A/73/PV.6, 25 September 2018.

many committed Europeans (starting with French President Emmanuel Macron) are inadvertently doing a disservice to the European integration project they believe they are promoting. Paradoxically, speaking of limiting sovereignty reflects an absolutist and mistaken conception of sovereignty that has been shaped over centuries: sovereignty cannot be limited, divided or 'fragmented'. It is the defining criterion of the State and the source of its competencies at the international level; if an entity holds sovereignty, it is a State and, as such, possesses all the powers that International Law grants to States; if it is not sovereign, it is not a State[21] Along similar lines, Schiemann adopts a general and basic understanding of sovereignty focused on its internal manifestation. The author states that sovereignty "includes an alleged right of a state to organize affairs within its borders as it pleases, and an alleged right to be free from interference by other states".[22]

But terms like economic, food, cultural or cyber sovereignty are misleading expressions; they are used to refer to the State's competencies in the specific areas they name. However, qualifying sovereignty in this way overlooks its irreducible nature which, properly understood, includes both a prohibitive and a permissive dimension. But, "the more international order grows the less room is for independent decisions".[23] Furthermore, institutionalisation helps to constitutionalise the international community.[24] It is undeniable, then, that the proliferation and even the so-called constitutionalisation of International Law place at the centre of many doctrinal analyses the relevance of an international community from which not only inter-State norms are segregated.[25] "The proliferation and law-making, or even legislative, functions of many international organizations made us aware of the existence of—perhaps not the emergence of a world government—but at least of global governance 'beyond the state' in what

[21] Island of Palmas case, (Netherlands, USA), 4 April 1928, Reports of International Arbitral Awards, Vol. II, p. 838.

[22] K. Schiemann, *Europe and the loss of sovereignty*, in *Int Comp Law Q* 56(3):475, 2007, p. 475.

[23] C. Tomuschat, *Obligations arising for states without or against their will*, in *Recueil des Cours. Collected courses of the Hague Academy of International Law*, vol 241, 1993, p.184.

[24] Carrillo Salcedo refers to the constitutionalisation of international society. J.A. Carrillo Salcedo, *Droit international et souveraineté des états: cours général de droit international public*. In*: Recueil des Cours, Collected courses of the Hague Academy of International Law*, vol 257, 1996, pp.125–126.

[25] Cfr. G. Fernández Arribas, *Contemporary Challenges to the Fundamental Principles of International Law and EU Interaction*, Springer, 2024.

is sometimes normatively framed in familiar 'communitarian' terms: a 'world community'."[26]

Communitas, as we have been considering it, conflicts with the idea of sovereignty. Claims of an idiosyncratic uniqueness under Article 4.2 of the Treaty on European Union, and claims of having a Voice in a community, should not turn into a sovereignist view of identity. When constitutional identity becomes an exclusionary sovereignist factor, it is incompatible with a community of values.

Claims of the 'We' in the international arena can follow two identity paths. The first is exclusionary, preserving the purity of traditions and the integrity of State geographical territories. The second argues that national identity exists only insofar as the 'We' is part of a *communitas*.

From the first perspective, exclusionary nationalism and nativism, identity politics, criticism of globalisation and internationalism, and calls for democratic re-empowerment of the *demos* have politically come together in a new form of inflated territorial sovereignty. This demands "taking back control" in the name of a radically redefined community, with a defensive re-territorialisation of power along the existing fault lines of national statism. Once again, the key problem lies in the strongest form of the exclusionary paradigm: sovereignty as the absolute right to decide alone. "Sovereignty is at the very heart of this challenge; it is its primary justification, diagnosis, and roadmap of radical change for the future. 'Taking back control' is the standard rallying cry on behalf of a radically re-defined community ('we')."[27]

The new porous and relational identity of the European Union is shaped as a shared space, formed by a web of interconnections and strongly supported by a relational and value-based vision of Law, in which identity must be seen as a source of richness. Faced with the threatening return of various forms of exclusionary and hegemonic identities, based either on the rejection of Law or on its blatant subordination to the interests of certain States, can we truly speak of a Union identity based on a 'community of values'? What features must it possess?

The dialogue between constitutional courts and the Court of Justice of the European Union will be the main focus of this second part, which

[26] R.A. Wessel, *Studying International and European Law: confronting perspectives and combining interests*, in Grotius Centre Working Paper Series, No. 2018/071-PIL2018.

[27] A. Kallis, *Populism, Sovereigntism, and the Unlikely Re-Emergence of the Territorial Nation-State*, in *Fudan J. Hum. Soc. Sci.*, 2018, 11, pp. 285–302.

begins with a study of the mechanisms of inclusion, in order to examine the origins of the process through which the voice of the Other has been integrated into a European *communitas*. The progressive interweaving of the internationalist and constitutionalist strands of EU Law will then be analysed, in order to outline the contours of a relational mechanism of cross-fertilisation. This will be explored in its axiological dimension through values, common constitutional traditions and the general principles of the European Union. My doctrinal proposal and conclusions will, in turn, be structured into their *pars construens* and *destruens*. In this second part, before delving into the analysis of the EU's relational identity, two preliminary caveats must first be made.

7.2 Caveat: Delimitation of the Analysis to the Legal Field

Delving into the study of constitutional identity, we should note that it is an ontologically fluid concept, as we have already seen in the Introduction of the first part, which escapes predefined frameworks. Perhaps, as a preliminary step, we could try to outline some more precise defining features.

Firstly, it is, at one and the same time, a historical-sociological, legal and political concept. Identity is a historical-sociological concept because it refers, at least in part (not entirely coinciding with 'national' identity), to a past that has shaped the culture, ways of life and economy of a country and its people.[28] Constitutional identity is nourished by ipseity, which is associated with the reflective awareness of the self. Subject to its temporary condition, this consciousness does not imply any substrate of permanence but rather alludes to the "maintenance of the self", modelled on the promise towards the Other. It has a great deal to do with the tension towards the Other. It is an attitude that shapes identity through the relationship with other individuals.[29] Constitutional identity is also a political concept, as it constrains the actions of political forces, which in turn cannot deny it without subverting the order that must be able to determine convergence within identitarian values without ideological degeneration, transforming national identity into nationalism and democratic action into populist

[28] The work of G.J. Jacobsohn is absolutely fundamental, *Constitutional Identity*, Harvard University Press, Harvard, 2010.

[29] P. Ricouer, *Soi-même comme un autre*, Éditions du seuil, Paris, 1990.

behaviour: in other words, they must channel the generating force of the *demos* within the forms and limits of the Constitution.

Finally, it is a legal concept because a more relevant part of these values has been transferred to constitutional principles that are fundamental precisely because they establish the foundations (the fundamentals, in fact) for the particular type of society to develop following the values that originally composed it as a unit; in this legal sense, identity loses any connotation of rigidity that may derive from being rooted in the past.[30]

For a member country of the European Union, its three declinations of constitutional identity acquire peculiar characteristics. In fact, from a historical-sociological perspective, national history is inseparably linked to the process of creation and integration, first of the Communities and then of the European Union, as well as to the history of the other Member States. From a political point of view as well, the State can no longer ignore the objectives of the European Union and must contribute to achieving them. At the same time, however, the EU cannot disregard national policies and must step in whenever a State is struggling, particularly when it is unable to manage transnational phenomena that directly affect the planning, implementation and direction of domestic policies. The first step in the process of European integration is always political: it involves, in other words, the decision to enter into a *communitas*. Finally, at the legal level, constitutional principles (including, it should be remembered once again, the European clause that allows limitations on sovereignty in favour of a supranational order) must also be reconciled with the values on which the EU is founded, as interpreted by the Court of Justice. These principles should help to make those values a reality and, in turn, be applied by them.

All these analytical layers cannot be separated. The science of International Law and Comparative Law would not understand society if it were limited to studying a strictly positivist dimension, as has been done and continues to be done in some academic circles. This is not an epistemic proposal; it is the complex reality today.

In some very recent conclusions presented, the Advocate General asserts: "156. One can imagine different societies: autocracies not based

[30] *Constitutionalism Identity, Difference and Legitimacy* (M. Rosenfeld ed.), Duke University Press, Durham, 2004; M. Rosenfeld, *The Identity of the Constitutional Subject: Selfhood, Culture, and Community*, Routledge, London, 2010; G. Jacobsohn, *Constitutional Identity*, cit.

on the separation of powers; societies in which the elected majority is not limited by the requirement to respect human rights; societies that are ruled by men and not by law; societies that do not treat minorities equally and reserve human dignity only for the majority; or societies that do not recognize that women are equal to men. Such societies do indeed exist and are emerging throughout the world. 157. The vision of what ***a good society*** is in the EU Constitution is different. This vision is expressed in Article 2 TEU. The values enumerated in that provision: respect for human dignity, freedom, democracy, equality, the rule of law and respect for human rights, including the rights of persons belonging to minorities, read together, paint a picture of a ***constitutional democracy that respects human rights***" [original emphasis].[31]

A reassessment of European identities is necessary for three reasons. The first reason concerns the management of diversity. By its nature, constitutional identity is a form of individual expression which, as we have seen, can be assimilated or even erased. Even without being eliminated, constitutional identities can overlap or be mutually exclusive, yet they always reflect the individuality of a Member State. The resulting diversity must be viewed and understood through a different lens so that the phenomenon of constitutional identity becomes more than just an abstract notion. The second reason is closely linked to the first and concerns the interpretation of Article 4(2) of the Treaty on European Union. The European Union can only respect the constitutional identity of its Member States if these identities are clearly expressed by the national constitutional bodies responsible for interpreting their fundamental principles. The EU must have reliable constitutional resources that it can use and draw upon in applying Article 4, paragraph 2, of the Treaty on European Union. The third reason is that there is great potential in the circulation of values, even before legal norms, from the national level to the community reservoir. This movement is not easy to understand through the simple binary lenses of epistemic exclusion. Even the inherent conflict in the expression of a Member State's constitutional identity, which seeks to qualify or reject the primacy of EU Law, must be addressed through a dialogical approach with the framework of Articles 2 TEU and 6 TEU. Situations where Member States express and wish to protect their constitutional identities require

[31] Advocate General Ćapeta's conclusions in Case C-769/22, *Commission/Hungary*, presented on 5 June 2025.

careful study to understand their possible effects on the primacy of EU Law and the future of Law in the European Union.

From this perspective, perhaps the constitutional identity of Member States should, by definition, become a dialogical identity, one that is built gradually and through dialogue with the institutions of the European Union, primarily the Court of Justice of the European Union. This should be done with the awareness that "*l'identità non è un dato fisso, acquisito una volta per tutte, ma un punto di riferimento mobile e relativamente fluido, soggetto a continui controlli e cambiamenti indotti dall'esterno*".[32] We will not directly address political forms of State identities, but it is important to note some considerations.

Political counter-limits are implemented through instruments of direct democracy, which tend to be more specific than those mentioned earlier because they often occur after the institutions of the European Union have taken certain actions that, in practice, are seen as harmful to the national system. However, these instruments are also more vulnerable to populist and anti-European changes in sentiment. We are referring, in particular, to the Greek referendum of 5 July 2015 and the UK referendum of 23 June 2016.

What is most interesting here is that, in the Greek case, the referendum was used to defend a particular aspect of Greek national and constitutional identity, namely a certain welfare model that was at risk of being dismantled by austerity measures, especially those imposed by the Troika on States from the so-called Democratic Party that signed the Memorandum of Understanding. Indeed, these measures, precisely because of their excessive rigidity (perhaps even unreasonableness), raised concerns about their compatibility with the provisions of the Treaties (see, in particular, the so-called non-regression clause under Article 9 of the Treaty on the Functioning of the European Union) and, above all, the Charter of Nice. However, as is well known, the EU courts, in various rulings—which scholars have not hesitated to describe as "pilate-esque"—refused to examine the substance of the national austerity measures and, in any case, did not use the Charter of Nice as a standard to assess their validity.

This situation could lead us to view the Greek referendum from a particular perspective: not only as a (national) response to the well-known democratic deficit that still affects the institutions of the European Union—as shown by the lack of parliamentary involvement in the Greek

[32] F. Ferrarotti, *Identità dialogica*, ETS, Pisa, 2007, p. 8.

crisis[33]—but also as a "protest" against a more general lack of safeguards within the European Union's highest levels.[34]

In other words, it seems that Greek constitutional identity was affirmed 'from the ground-up' but not in opposition to European Union policy and therefore without anti-European features. Instead, it was affirmed in a subsidiary way in relation to the EU, precisely because the EU was the legal and political instrument Greece used to reject the strict austerity measures. This emphasised the incompatibility of those measures with social rights protected by the national social welfare system and, at the same time, also indirectly with the values enshrined in the Treaties and the Charter of Nice, where the EU's safeguarding bodies, especially the Court of Justice, have not intervened.

On the other hand, populist and anti-European traits appear to be evident in the result of the British referendum on Brexit, not only because of the clear patterns shown by the analysis of the vote such as the number and type of voters who took part but also in light of the troubled history of European integration that characterises the United Kingdom. In this context, the referendum revealed the 'tragic choice' faced by countries that prefer differentiated integration, not to create a Europe of multiple speeds, which is possible within certain limits, but to choose a 'Europe à la carte', which is a prelude to its disintegration. In fact, the United Kingdom made extensive use of the opting-out mechanism. However, in light of the

[33] B. Caravita, *"Parlamentarizzare" la crisi greca*, and Aravantinou LeonidI, *La sfida di Atene all'Europa dell'austerità: il referendum del 5 luglio 2015*, both in *Federalismi.it*, 14/2015; Yannakourou, *Desafiar las medidas de austeridad que afectan los derechos laborales a nivel nacional e internacional. El caso de Grecia*, en AA.VV., *Los derechos sociales en tiempos de crisis en la eurozona: el papel de los desafíos de los derechos fundamentales*, Kilpatrick, C.-De Witte B. (eds.), Fiesole, 2014, 19 ss.

[34] Here is the bitter reflection of S. Rodotà, *Il pensiero debole dell'Europa che s'accontenta*, in *MicroMega*, 10 January 2014 (and in *La Repubblica*, 9 January 2014), who wrote: "*Quel che sta accadendo nell'Unione europea è appunto [...] una decostituzionalizzazione. Il suo sistema è stato amputato della Carta dei diritti fondamentali, del suo Bill of Rights, che pure, com'è scritto nell'articolo 6 del Trattato di Lisbona, "ha lo stesso valore giuridico dei trattati". [...] Oggi l'orizzonte è mutato, l'Unione agisce come se la Carta non vi fosse, nega ai cittadini il valore aggiunto ad essa affidato proprio per acquisire legittimità attraverso la loro adesione, e muta i cittadini da attori del processo europeo in puri spettatori, impotenti e sfiduciati di fronte all'arrivo da Bruxelles di imposizione di sacrifici e non di garanzie dei diritti. V'è in tutto questo una contraddizione, un abbandono della logica che volle il passaggio dell'espressione "Mercato unico" a "Unione europea", che avrebbe dovuto avvicinare istituzioni e cittadini, e questi tra loro. E vi è pure un abbandono di quanto è scritto nel Preambolo della Carta, dove si afferma l'Unione "pone la persona al centro della sua azione*".

outcome of Brexit, it seems fair to say that these clauses were used not so much to protect its national-constitutional identity beforehand but rather to jealously preserve parts of its political sovereignty that it did not want to share with the Union. This was within a framework of common limitation of national sovereignty by all Member States, but it ultimately degenerated into a return to Eurosceptic nationalism, more precisely anti-European nationalism, which finally led to the UK's withdrawal from the Union. These situations have highlighted a different political approach to contributing to a common identity. In the first, Greek, case, national identity converged with and reinforced an aspect of *communitas*. In contrast, in the British case, the appeal to sovereignty once again led to withdrawal and isolation from the Union.

The dialogical dynamic between identities clearly also takes shape in the political sphere, producing effects specific to that domain. Judicial controls applicable, for obvious reasons, a posteriori, in other words, only once harm to national constitutional identity has occurred or there is a concrete threat of such harm caused by a derived act of the EU. For this reason, part of the academic literature has proposed giving renewed attention to controls that could be described as 'political' or 'non-judicial'. These would fall under the scope of political negotiation practices and aim to protect, in advance, the core constitutional principles that could be affected by external sources.[35]

In summary, the instruments through which these controls operate can be divided into two categories, depending on whether they are triggered by an individual State or necessarily by a group of States. In the first category, we can include mechanisms such as the requirement for unanimity in decision-making in certain areas, as provided for in the Treaties, and differentiated integration negotiated through opting-out clauses. In the second category, which involves political controls that must be triggered by multiple Member States, we find the procedures laid out in the Protocol on the Principle of Subsidiarity. These involve the participation of national

[35] Cfr., in particular, P. Faraguna, *Taking Constitutional Identity away from the Courts,* in *Brooklyn Journal of International Law*, n. 41/2016, spec. 501 et seq.; Idem, *Alla ricerca dell'identità costituzionale. Tra conflitti giurisdizionali e negoziazione politica*, in *Costituzionalismo.it*, n. 3/2016, p. 197.

parliaments in what is known as the early warning[36] mechanism and in the exercise of substantial veto powers.[37]

Although these are political decisions taken *ex ante*, that is, before the secondary act of the Union produces its effects, political controls may only appear to offer more complete protection of constitutional identity than judicial controls can provide.[38] In reality, they carry a genuine risk of excessively fragmenting European identity. Moreover, because these controls are exercised *ex ante*, it cannot be said with certainty that the EU legislation in question would, in practice, violate the fundamental principles of National Law. That assessment can only be made by a court (particularly a constitutional court) on a case-by-case basis. In short, identity-based political controls could lead to an absolutist interpretation of national constitutional identity. Yet this identity should instead be seen as a relational concept, built with reference to European values and aimed at fostering the mutual integration of identity. Political control clearly operates within the sphere of representative democracy and political negotiation, without necessarily taking into account the required contextual balancing. Furthermore, the legal systems of the Member States are consistently recognised as sources of EU Law. This is reiterated in Article 41(3) of the Charter of Fundamental Rights and again in Article 52 of the same

[36] This is a request for review (so-called early warning), expressed through reasoned opinions by a third of the national Parliaments, in relation to each piece of draft legislation (*quorum* which is reduced to one quarter with regard to matters falling within the area of freedom, security and justice). National Parliaments are also empowered to bring cases before the Court of Justice through their governments to assert, under Article 263 of the Treaty on the Functioning of the European Union, a breach of the principle of subsidiarity.

[37] This represents a substantial veto power over legislative initiatives, particularly concerning legislative proposals that follow the co-decision procedure, when a majority of national parliaments, combined with a majority of votes in the European Parliament, considers that the legislative proposal is not compatible with the principle of subsidiarity. Despite the cumbersome procedures and the necessary expression of such cases, in which a form of 'majority *controlimiti*' would apply, it cannot be ruled out that safeguarding the principle of subsidiarity might also protect the axiological and constitutional identities of the Member States, which ultimately do not always and necessarily coincide with the so-called common constitutional traditions.

[38] Cfr., in particular, P. Faraguna, *Ai confini della Costituzione*, cit., 115 et seq.; ID., *Taking Constitutional Identity away from the Courts*, in *Brooklyn Journal of International Law*, n. 41/2016, spec. 501 et seq.; and in ostensibly more subdued tones, ID., *Alla ricerca dell'identità costituzionale. Tra conflitti giurisdizionali e negoziazione politica*, in *Costituzionalismo.it*, n. 3/2016, 197 et seq. Cfr., inoltre, M. Luciani, *Il brusco risveglio. I controlimiti e la fine mancata della storia costituzionale*, in *Rivista Aic*, n. 2/2016, spec. 9

Charter, although with slightly different wording. The former refers first to 'principles' and the latter to 'traditions'.

We will focus on the legal arena of constitutional identity and, within this context, we will examine the judicial trajectory.

The requirement for joint decision-making also applies to the legislative process, since the protection of constitutional identity should not be solely an *ex post* concern left to the courts. As already explained, in some Member States, the right to define constitutional identity (also) lies with the legislative bodies. Therefore, such considerations should also be incorporated into the European dimension of the debate. This would also give EU legislative institutions the opportunity to shape EU legislation in ways that take into account, in advance, potential conflicts with the constitutional identity of the Member States. On the other hand, the need to involve legislative bodies to a greater extent than is currently advocated also stems from the observation that the invocation of constitutional identity, used to justify limiting the application of EU Law, is unfortunately often misused by Member States as a way to express general dissatisfaction with European decisions.

As a result, political bodies, by virtue of their greater democratic legitimacy, should play a more prominent role in the debate on the 'protection of constitutional identity'. This applies both to the Member States and to the institutions of the European Union. In short, the chapter dedicated to Article 4(2) TEU has outlined in detail the existing mechanisms for interpreting secondary EU legislation and has proposed the implementation of an identity claim procedure by national parliaments. Another idea could be to characterise Article 4(2) TEU as an exception to Article 16(3) TEU, thereby making the application of the unanimity principle mandatory in matters relating to the constitutional identity of the Member States. This idea may seem persuasive from the Member States' perspective, as it offers a straightforward and absolute safeguard of their constitutional identity.

However, only joint decision-making makes it possible to take into account the mutual interdependence between different legal systems and, therefore, to produce outcomes that equally respect both the protection of Member States' constitutional identities and the principles of EU Law. The interpretation proposed here of the EU legal system as a *Verbund* and the consequences drawn from this approach represent a way to engage constructively with the pluralist framework established by the Member States and the EU's own legal self-conception. This enables both legal unity and effective problem-solving within the pluralistic European legal space. Ernst Hirsch Ballin rightly points out that in order to survive, the EU needs "the willingness to accept the particularities of others without forgetting that we are all sailing in the same boat".[39]

7.3 The Mechanisms of Inclusion in the European Union

Beyond these initial political examples, shared normativity can be found at all legal levels. It is a complex mechanism. Within the shared legal space between the EU and the Member States, legal unity is determined neither solely by the provisions and principles of EU Law nor by National (Constitutional) Law. As a result, the legal order of the EU is a complementary structure, interwoven by both EU Law and National (Constitutional) Law.

For this reason, it is worth anticipating that the new European relational identity is not confined to the notion of constitutional identity as set out in Article 4(2) TEU. Rather, it constitutes a mutual paradigm of exchange between legal systems. "The codification of constitutional counter-limits in Article 4(2) TEU is intrinsic to the genetic code of European constitutional Law."[40]

Among the most significant examples of this interweaving is the EU directive, which must be implemented by the Member States. However, particular attention should be paid to the analysis of other, more complex sources. As we will see, the EU's values (Article 2 TEU), the common constitutional traditions and the general principles (Article 6 TEU) provide strong confirmation of the entangled nature of legal orders, as they are derived from the comparison and selection of national constitutional elements. It is particularly interesting to observe the relationship some scholars have highlighted between counter-limits and those common constitutional traditions. These are connected through fundamental principles drawn from national legal systems and used by the CJEU as sources of EU Law.

[39] E. H. Ballin, *Constitutional identity in the Netherlands: Sailing with others*, in *Constitutional identity in a Europe of multilevel constitutionalism*, cit., pp. 222–242.

[40] L. Burgorgue-Larsen, *Sobre un acercamiento dialógico al Derecho Constitucional Europeo*, in *Sobre un acercamiento dialógico al Derecho Constitucional Europeo, in Revista de Derecho Constitucional Europeo*, 2016, pp. 13–38.

What emerges, then, is a new paradigm, one that transcends the elements of exclusive identity outlined in the first part of this study. "Closure of the sources of public international law facilitated not only the construction of states (they became the primary source of the law of their own relations) but the exclusion from the international realm of non-state or 'uncivilized' peoples."[41] Logic, however, does not allow for a single or simple definition. The most well-known definition comes from Aristotle, who originally formulated what is now known as the rule of the excluded middle. This has sometimes been (slightly) reformulated as the Law of Non-Contradiction, which therefore requires consistency. The most obvious form of social reification is found in the modern State system.[42] Contemporary States have claimed to be the sole sources of Law within their territories. The same method of reification has been used by the American political scientist Samuel Huntington when talking about a clash of civilisations, in which civilisations are defined as 'monadic entities', making comparison impossible and the only possible relationships being of a conflictive nature. "We know we are only when we know we are not and often only when we know whom are against."[43] A logic of diversity necessarily involves moving away from binary conceptions of the Law.[44] "The reification process has thus manifested itself in term of systems, cultures, civilisations and further even in terms of 'mentalities'. These have all been boundary-tracing endeavours with both homogenise (within) and differentiate (without), in a way incompatible with comparing or Convivencia."[45]

This logic of 'both and' (A and not/A) is therefore inherent to institutional relationality. This "allows the different legal orders to adjust to the claims of the others and so prevents conflict between these claims."[46] Nicolas Barber has explicitly stated that the principle of non-contradiction

[41] Cf. H.P. Glenn, *The Cosmopolitan State*, OUP, Oxford, 2013, p. 239.

[42] H.P. Glenn, *Com-paring*, in *Comparative Law. A Handbook*, E. Örücü and D. Nelken (eds.), Hart Publishing, Oxford, 2010, p. 93.

[43] S.P. Huntington, *The Clash of Civilizations and the Remaking of World Order*, Simon & Schuster, New York: 1996, p. 43: "*We know who we are only when we know who we are not and often only when we know whom we are against.*"

[44] N. Krish, *Beyond Constitutionalism: the Pluralist Structure of Postnational Law*, 2010, p. 305.

[45] H.P. Glenn, *The Cosmopolitan State*, OUP, Oxford, 2013, p. 240.

[46] M. Poiares Maduro, *Contrapunctual Law: Europe's constitutional pluralism in action*, in N. Walker (ed.), *Sovereignty in transition (Essays in European Law)*, Hart Publishing, Oxford, 2003, p. 524.

is inapplicable in the legal relationships of the EU, where one encounters an 'inconsistent' rule of recognition and there is no higher constitutional body to resolve the dispute through adjudication.[47] The divisive dichotomy between monism and dualism also becomes blurred. Glenn individualises this new logic through the Solange jurisprudence. "The best example is in the Solange jurisprudence, by virtue of which the German Constitutional Court acts on a presumption of the validity of EU legislation in German constitutional law, while reserving its ultimate power of appreciation. The law in question are non-monotonic, subject to intervening invalidation. Both sides may claim victory; neither side must admit defeat, and 'inconsistent' laws need not demand inconsistent action."[48]

The Kadi I (and similarly Kadi II) case exemplifies this epistemological mechanism in a paradigmatic way. This ruling has been criticised for its potential to generate systemic tensions and for being perceived as 'blind' from a diplomatic perspective. However, these tensions should not be classified as insurmountable conflicts but as tools that enable a dynamic and osmotic system, capable of opening doors to a critical comparison of identities. This approach, which integrates the principles of the Kadi I and II cases and counter-limits, breaks away from the exclusionary *forma mentis* mindset, focused on sovereignty, written norms, territoriality, hierarchy and borders.

Martinico, arguably the scholar who has best unpacked the complexity of the European system, also contributes to this analysis. "While constitutional conflicts have frequently been depicted as elements of disturbance along the path towards legal coherence, they are physiological and might even be functional to the development of the European legal order, which should not be understood in a deterministic manner. The secret of the European Constitution can be identified in a vertical fusion connecting national and supranational legal orders, a fusion that makes the EU an 'interlaced' (i.e. complex) legal system."[49]

The European Union, and to some extent the early European Communities, conceived as a *communitas*, not only preserves but also promotes and enriches the common values that underpin its structure

[47] N. Barber, *Legal pluralism and the EU*, *European Law Journal*, 12, 2006, pp. 306 ss.

[48] H.P. Glenn, *Com-paring*, in *Comparative Law. A Handbook*, E. Örücü and D. Nelken (eds.), Hart Publishing, Oxford, 2010, p. 93.

[49] G. Martinico, *The Tangled Complexity of the EU Constitutional Process. The Frustrating Knot of Europe*, Routledge, Second Edition, 2023, p. 5.

while dignifying the diversity of cultures and traditions specific to the peoples of Europe. Likewise, it deeply respects the national identities of the Member States and the organisation of their public powers at national, regional and local levels. This dialectical interaction between national values and the supranational framework not only reinforces those values but also amplifies them through a pan-European dimension.

It is worth noting that the values that define the very essence of the European Union would struggle to persist and evolve within strictly national boundaries. Hence, the EU's identity should be conceived as a circular and mutually enriching entity, where plurality becomes a source of cultural and spiritual wealth rather than an obstacle to shared progress. "This 'tension' is highlighted in the main works dedicated to European integration that find a common core (putting to one side their different starting perspectives) in the acceptance of this phenomenon as *novum*."[50] This continuous and existential tension of the EU is defined as *écart*. This idea closely resembles the synallagmatic complexity put forward by Martinico. "Constitutional synallagma is the whole of the principles, practices and rules that circulate uninterruptedly from one level to another in two directions (from top to bottom and vice versa). Constitutional synallagma conforms to the definition of a new kind of law that is not reducible to the legal provisions of the Treaties or of the national legislations."[51]

These interactions create a type of additional information that is not visible to an outside observer. New properties that cannot be explained from the properties of the individual elements emerge through interactions between levels or poles. These characteristics are generally referred to as emergent properties, and they correspond to those constitutional principles that cannot be fully reduced to either the national or supranational level alone. In this sense, a complex system should not be understood as the mere sum of its parts but rather as something marked by added value, a product of all the interactions between those parts. The idea of common properties relates to entities that 'emerge' from more fundamental ones and yet remain 'novel' or 'irreducible' in relation to them. The emergence of such properties is often linked to evolutionary dynamics that shape and reshape the natural order arising from the various

[50] G. Martinico, *The Tangled Complexity of the EU Constitutional Process. The Frustrating Knot of Europe*, Routledge, Second Edition, 2023, p. 34.

[51] G. Martinico, *The Tangled Complexity of the EU Constitutional Process. The Frustrating Knot of Europe*, Routledge, Second Edition, 2023, p. 121.

types of interactions possible among the actors operating across different levels or poles.

> The creation of interdependencies in all policy areas, the policy of intertwining, which makes Europeanisation permanent, is by no means a one-off cooperation, which in the end leaves the cooperating nation-states untouched. On the other hand, Europeanisation profoundly undermines and modifies state power and the state sovereignty it implies. [...] Europeanisation therefore implies that Member States develop strategies of reflexive self-limitation in their own national interest.[52]

Beck outlines a vision of identity that replaces the logic of 'either/or' with the logic of 'both/and'. He freely uses the modular structure of global identities and shapes self-image as one of progressive inclusion. We are faced with the proud assertion of a mixed and colourful identity.[53] Beck also argues that it would be a serious mistake to think that cosmopolitan empathy replaces national empathy. Rather, they interpenetrate, integrate, modify and influence each other. This does not mean, however, that the territorial theory of identity is anything but a fatal error, what we might call the prison error of identity. And he emphasises that "the national gaze is also an essentialist gaze, because it separates culturally and politically what was historically intertwined".[54]

Relationality is a challenge because it calls us to a different way of thinking. "Law is plural. In all but the simplest situations multiple laws overlap—national laws, subnational laws, supranational laws, non-national laws. Our jurisprudential accounts of law have mostly not taken this in. When we speak of law, we use the singular. The plurality of laws is, at best an afterthought. This is a mistake. Plurality is built into the very reality of law."[55] State identity and the legal system remain singular nouns for the modern legal tradition. As we have seen, the defining feature of legal mandate is its exclusivity. Positivist dogma asserts that the norm is accepted as the sole and exclusive regulator of practical activity.

[52] U. Beck, *The Cosmopolitan Vision,* Polity Press, Cambridge, 2006, p. 224.

[53] U. Beck, p. 15.

[54] U. Beck, p. 43.

[55] R. Michaels, *Law and Recognition—Towards a Relational Concept of Law*, in *In Pursuit of Pluralist Jurisprudence*, N. Roughan & A. Halpin (eds.), Cambridge University Press, Cambridge, 2017, p. 90.

But beware: if these values, constitutional traditions and shared general principles do not become an inclusive *nomos*, a truly lived dimension, they are nothing more than empty words. This is not a glorification of the European messianic ideal[56] but a simple observation. If the Union intends to be a truly *sui generis* legal order, it must abandon a solipsistic view of identity and continue to pursue a relational one. It was born for and with this purpose. If it fails to do so, it will return to the spectres of the *arcana imperii* that we described in the first part.

Indeed, using the language of Niklas Luhmann, Law, like any specialised system, emerges through the definition of boundaries that allow it to select from an environment of infinite possibilities the modes of action that characterise the individual system. At the core of Law lies an asymmetry between the (legal) system and its context.[57] This separation acts as *actio finium regundorum*, or what Glenn describes as the obsession with closure, which we have previously mentioned. In the modern era, there is naturally a plurality of legal systems, but compatibility between the exclusivity of the legal criterion and this plurality is established through the relativity of the distinction between legal value and fact. Other legal systems exist for the legal order taken as the point of view of the starting legal system, but they do not exist as legal values. They exist merely as facts or as part of the environment surrounding that legal order. This distinction is both relative and reciprocal, in the sense that any legal order can become a fact or part of the environment for another legal order. These are the foundations of International Law, both public and private. What matters is that the distinction between a legal value and a fact, or between a system and its environment, must never disappear, on pain of undermining the legal condition as the exclusive criterion of evaluation. "We no longer need a concept of law. We need a concept of laws."[58]

[56] J.H.H. Weiler, '*Federalism without Constitutionalism: Europe's Sonderweg*', in K. Nicolaidis & R. Howse (eds), *The Federal* Vision, Oxford University Press, 2001, esp. pp. 54–68.

[57] N. Luhmann, *Das Recht der Gesellschaft*, Suhrkamp, Frankfurt am Main, 1995, 571–590.; Idem, *Die Gesellschaft der Gesellschaft*, Suhrkamp, Frankfurt am Main, 1997, Vol 1, pp. 158–160. Recently, N. Luhmann, *La constitución como logro evolutivo*, Tecnos, Madrid, 2024.

[58] R. Michaels, *Law and Recognition—Towards a Relational Concept of Law*, in *In Pursuit of Pluralist Jurisprudence*, N. Roughan & A. Halpin (eds.), Cambridge University Press, Cambridge, 2017, p. 90.

Relationality presupposes the end of this legal world. Systemic interrelation necessarily becomes a plural noun.[59] There is no cognitive *prius* from which one might leap into the recognition of another legal system. The underlying identity scenario is a world in which the plurality of legal orders forms an interfacial mechanism; it is the ongoing tension of the *écart* and also the epistemic foundation of a new Comparative Law. This new approach transcends both the assimilative, unifying tendencies that defined much of the twentieth century and the notion of incomparable *mentalités* found in the culturalist comparative model *à la* Legrand.

When identity is relational or complex, the Law that matters is Jullien's *écart* or Palombella's *in-between*.[60] It is inter-legal Law, one that does not assimilate the Other's Law into a predetermined *prius*, as we saw in the first part. If both or more legal systems produce legal effects, if both embody indispensable axiological and legal value for each other rather than serving as criteria to evaluate one another, then Law is what emerges from the interconnection between legal systems. Law is necessarily composite and multiverse. Such is the Law of the European Union, and this is how it should be taught. In this view, the specific theoretical advantage of the cross-fertilisation perspective comes to the fore, as a legal mechanism that expresses relationality.

The condition of relational legality excludes the presence of a legal dimension, so to speak, that is superior to the rest of the legal systems. There is no 'Common Law of Humanity' that imposes itself abstractly and universally over other legal systems, precisely because the standard for evaluating Law is not singular. A gap identified by Jullien or a blind spot highlighted by David Kennedy comes to light when different systems confront each other at the level of their fundamental norm.[61] Several recent cases, including the aforementioned Taricco case,[62] bear witness to this openness at the apex of identity and the absence of a Law that resolves fundamental disputes through a single system. When the constitutional court and the Strasbourg Court rule differently on the Law arising from

[59] E. Scoditti, *Legalità al plurale*, in *Quaderni costituzionali*, 2013, p. 307.

[60] G. Palombella, *Theory, Realities, and Promises of Inter-Legality. A* Manifesto, in J. Klabber, G. Palombella (eds.), *The Challenge of Inter-Legality*, cit., p. 378.

[61] In the opinion of N. Krisch, *Beyond Constitutionalism. The pluralist Structure of Postnational Law*, Oxford, 2010, p. 152 when legal systems are plural and concurrent, the system is open at its apex.

[62] CJEU judgement, C-42/17, MAS and MB, 5 December 2017.

the articulation of the Constitution and the Treaty, which Law should be respected?

Relational legality excludes the notion of a superior legal dimension that imposes its hegemony over other legal systems. There is no 'Common Law of Humanity' that can serve as an absolute benchmark in a context of normative plurality. The relationship between different legal systems inevitably confronts fundamental discrepancies, exemplified by emblematic cases such as Taricco, which challenge any monist or hierarchical approach to legal interpretation.

In the absence of a predefined normative framework like the preliminary ruling procedure before the Court of Justice in Luxembourg, judicial dialogue becomes a relational dynamic that transcends the rigid structures of traditional Law. This space of interaction provides fertile ground for cross-fertilisation, where the concept of the *écart* fosters a productive distance that encourages comparison and integration between legal systems without asserting the supremacy of one over the other.[63] In this context, Counterpoint Law emerges as the theoretical expression of these interconnections between legal systems, highlighting the need for a plural and relational understanding of Law. This perspective allows for the essence of national systems to be preserved in dialogical interaction with the Union while the Union itself finds support in the national rights that nourish it. Far from being a mechanism of altruism, inter-legality becomes the epistemological foundation of a normative coexistence that gives voice to each implicated legal order, ensuring that all contribute to the resolution of controversies in equitable and enriching terms.

Likewise, this dynamic of legal interrelation demands that constitutional traditions, general principles of Law and community values be interpreted from a multiversal perspective. In the new community and regional configuration of International Law, Comparative Law stands as an unavoidable imperative. Historically, it has served as a tool to consolidate principles of exclusion, such as those underpinning the foundations of the Common Law of the more 'civilised' nations. However, its current role must transform into a vehicle for inclusion. Where it once reaffirmed hegemonies through an exclusionary conception of identity, leading to legal unification, it must now advocate establishing a common space for dialogue in which differences are recognised and respected.

[63] F. Jullien, *Il n'y a pas d'identité culturelle, Éditions de l'Herne*, Paris, 2016.

Comparative Law must play a fundamental role in the construction of an inclusive legal framework, documenting even the most subtle or unnoticed movements of judicial circulation. From this perspective, it becomes a means to foster a common identity that, based on the European values enshrined in Article 2 of the TEU, respects diversity within the context of shared constitutional traditions. This approach, to which Jullien refers as the inclusive *écart*, requires the assimilation of a collective constitutional heritage.

However, this epistemological synergy and the development of general principles that transcend traditional territorial levels will only be possible if Eurocentric or ethnocentric perspectives are overcome. This means that International Law practitioners must come to understand the dynamics inherent to constitutionalism, while Constitutional Law practitioners must move beyond their nationalist confines. Ultimately, the construction of a common legal space in Europe requires an epistemological convergence, as aptly noted by thinkers such as Weiler and Von Bogdandy.

The preservation of normative plurality allows each legal system, when faced with a specific case, to acknowledge the reasoning of the other. This process strengthens the legitimacy of a composite and relational legal order, which is essential for the survival of both national systems and the European Union itself.

7.4 The (New) Principle of Recognition

We have previously seen the crucial role the principle of recognition plays in identity theory. Historically, it has served as the doctrinal foundation for restricting the admission of new States into the ranks of the so-called civilised or first world nations.

Hart acknowledges that "[t]he legal system of a modern state is characterized by a certain kind of supremacy within its territory and independence of other systems."[64] Kelsen speaks of the relations between 'systems of norms' as if the only connections were those of independence or subordination.[65] Joseph Raz explains that "[a]ll legal systems are potentially incompatible at least to a certain extent. Since all legal systems claim to be supreme with respect to their subject-community, none can acknowledge any claims to supremacy over the same community that may be made by

[64] H.L.A. Hart, *The Concept of Law*, 2nd ed., Clarendon Press, Oxford, 1994, p. 24.
[65] H. Kelsen, *Pure Theory of Law*, University of California Press, Berkeley, 1967, p. 330.

another legal system."[66] This would not imply, however, that legal systems can be considered hermetically closed. On the contrary, it is possible to conceive of them as open systems, insofar as they incorporate provisions that give validity and effectiveness to norms that are not an intrinsic part of their own structure. This invites a deeper reflection on how the interactions between State legal systems are perceived. It is worth noting that Private International Law, also known as 'Conflict of Laws', has developed an entire body of legal science and terminology centred on the expansion of the State and the conceptualisation of legal systems. This leads to a fundamental question: why are discrepancies between legal norms conceptualised as inherent conflicts? Glenn responds: "because the co-existence of sharply defined, mutually exclusive, sovereign entities will inevitably be perceived as a conflictual situation."[67] The risk posed by acknowledging the existence of a variety of other legal systems is clear: their assimilation into the dominant Western conception of Law. The notion of non-Law presupposes the existence of (Western) Law. This is the identity dynamic that runs throughout our investigation. Yet there is a Comparative Law alternative. "One brings together and if there are tendencies to drift apart one continues to bring together. The process of comparison would thus in no way imply resulting uniformity. Indeed, if anything it implies the reverse, that differences remain which must be somehow brought together, such that coexistence of difference is possible. [...] It implies rejection of a millennium of teaching as a ius unum, whether the ius unum is the ius commune on the law of the state."[68]

It is true that legal doctrine itself has long grappled with what could be called an asymmetrical plurality of normative orders. Once a galaxy of normative systems is acknowledged, the question arises concerning the relationship between official (State) Law and Customary Law, with various proposed solutions. Hart and Kelsen regard Customary Law as an imperfect and more primitive version of State Law. Eugen Ehrlich and Lon Fuller, by contrast, suggest that Customary Law—or what they respectively term the "Living Law" (Ehrlich) and "Implicit Law"

[66] J. Raz, *The Authority of Law: Essays on Law and Morality*, Clarendon Press, Oxford, 1979, p. 119.

[67] H.P. Glenn, *Doin' the Transsystemic: Legal Systems and Legal Traditions*, in *McGill L.J.*, 2005, p. 863.

[68] P. Glenn, *Aims of Comparative Law*, in *Elgar Encyclopedia of Comparative Law*, J.M. Smits (ed.), 2015, p. 63.

(Fuller)—is, in fact, more real than State Law.[69] More recently, scholars such as Rodolfo Sacco, who theorised the existence of three *formanti* to disaggregate the unity of the legal system (clearly derived from the Western legal experience), have had to reconsider this conception when confronted with African legal systems. Hence, his remarkable study of Mute Law.[70] However, all these debates concern the asymmetrical relationship between so-called normal Law (State Law) and other normative orders. It is ultimately a question of identity, which revisits the classificatory sequence we have analysed thus far.

The Law of the Other is not a mere fact or a contextual element for the legal order taken as a point of reference; it is a legal value or a legal order in its own right. The legal order of the European Union is complex and contrapuntal: it does not exist without the national systems, and there is no prior hierarchy. These national systems, as long as they are part of a *communitas*, cannot disregard the EU legal order. As such, the constitution of any State is not validated by that of any other, nor is it validated by EU Law. For each State, the internal validity of Community Law, in the sense required by the doctrine of 'supremacy', stems from the modification of constitutional and sub-constitutional Law by the State to the extent necessary to give direct effect and applicability to Community Law. On the other hand, the legal order of the EU is not subject to the validity of any one State's constitution nor to the sum of conditions that States may impose, as that would no longer constitute a true Community. "It would amount to no more than a bundle of overlapping laws to the extent that each state chose to acknowledge 'Community' laws and obligations. So relations between states inter se and between states and the Community are **interactive** rather than hierarchical [emphasis added].[71] Nico Krisch has referred to rules such as the external recognition rule as 'interface norms'.[72] The concept of linkage rules is an indispensable component of any descriptive theory that is more than a mere interpretation of one

[69] Respectively E. Ehrlich, *Fundamental Principles of the Sociology of Law*, 1936; L. Fuller, *Anatomy of the Law*, 1968, pp. 67–89. Cf. G.J. Postema, *Implicit Law*, in *Law & Philosophy*, 1994, p. 361.

[70] R. Sacco, *Il diritto muto. Neuroscienze, conoscenza tacita, valori condivisi*, Il Mulino Bologna, 2015.

[71] N. MacCormick, *Beyond the Sovereign State*, in *Modern Law Review*, 1993, pp. 117–118.

[72] N. Krisch, *Beyond Constitutionalism: The Pluralist Structure of Postnational Law*, 2010, pp. 285–296. Cf. P. Schiff Berman, *Global Legal Pluralism: A Jurisprudence of Law Beyond Borders*, 2012, pp. 152–170.

particular practice and has overcome Kelsen's epistemological limits [of monism]."[73]

How is this new identity reflected in general theory of Law and in the principle of recognition?

7.5 The Relational Recognition

Firstly, the current framework of International Law on the recognition of States is based on the criteria for defining a State established by the Montevideo Convention, which includes territory, population, government and the capacity to maintain international relations.[74] However, there is debate over whether recognition is necessary for the constitution of a State.[75] Lassa Oppenheim summarised the clearest version of the constitutive theory: "A State is, and becomes an International Person through recognition only and exclusively."[76] However, this theory has practical and normative shortcomings. In practice, it could lead to what might be called a "limping statehood": a community could be considered a State by some States, that is, those that have recognised it, but not by others, who do not. From a normative standpoint, it subordinates emerging new States to the recognition of established old States, which, as we have seen before, constitutes the issue of international subjectivity in a hegemonic order. These are some of the reasons why declaratory theory is now preferred. According to this theory, already expressed in Article 3 of the Montevideo Convention, States are entities independent from recognition when they meet substantive criteria. However, this approach has its own problems. Firstly, recognition may be necessary as the best available proof that the criteria have been met. Secondly, indeed, a State will not be able to adequately exercise its rights unless it is recognised.

Finally, Lauterpacht's combined theory suggests that recognition is both declaratory and constitutive. This theory allows a State to meet the

[73] D. von Daniels, *The Concept of Law from a Transnational Perspective*, Ashgate Publishing (actualmente bajo el sello Routledge), Farnham / Burlington, 2010, p. 161.

[74] Convention on the Rights and Duties of States, Seventh International American Conference, Montevideo, 1933.

[75] I. Brownlie, *Recognition in Theory and Practice*, in *British Yearbook of International Law*, 1982, pp. 197–211.

[76] L. Oppenheim, *International Law*, H. Lauterpacht (ed.), 8th ed., Longmans, Green and Co., London/New York, 1955, §§ 71, p. 125.

substantive criteria independently of recognition but requires recognition in order to fully exercise its rights.[77]

These different approaches to recognition in International Law reflect well on the question of what constitutes Law. The declaratory theory in International Law suggests that we must first decide what Law is before exploring its relationship with other systems. Whether one legal order recognises another is irrelevant to the definition of Law. In this context, Lauterpacht's combined theory of State recognition is particularly appealing to legal theory. For Lauterpacht, recognition is both "declaratory of facts and constitutive of rights."[78] Under this approach, the substantive criteria for Statehood are met regardless of recognition. However, in order for a State to effectively exercise the rights that stem from being a State, recognition is required. This line of reasoning translates into the distinction between internal recognition and an external rule of recognition. Internal recognition is one of several ways to establish the factual conditions necessary for the existence of a legal system. The definition of Law as a fact would remain independent of whether recognition is granted by other States. Moreover, recognition would give rise to an egalitarian system: it would not imply any form of subordination. Yet this response remains only partial: without recognition by other legal systems, that legal order would have no effective status beyond its own borders.

Two conclusions can be drawn. Firstly, there is an understanding that substantive criteria and recognition are neither necessarily independent nor strictly sequential. According to constitutive theory, recognition by other States is a constitutive act, and even under declarative theory, recognition plays an essential role. An entity is not a complete State until it is recognised by other States. Secondly, and perhaps most importantly, the status of a State is not necessarily universal. It is universal if an entity is recognised by all States. By contrast, it is a "relative State" if the entity is recognised only by some, but not all, States.

[77] H. Lauterpacht, *Recognition in International Law*, Cambridge University Press, Cambridge, 2012, p. 55: "[T]he full international personality of rising communities [...] cannot be automatic [...] [A]s as its ascertainment requires the prior determination of difficult circumstances of fact and law, so there must be someone to perform that task. In the absence of a preferable solution, such as the setting up of an impartial international organ to perform that function, the latter must be fulfilled by States already existing. The valid objection is not against the fact of their discharging it, but against their carrying it out as a matter of arbitrary policy as distinguished from legal duty."

[78] H. Lauterpacht, *Recognition*, cit., p. 75.

The conclusion is that the traditional image of Law, as derived from Western legal theory, requires significant revision. As we have already seen, this elitist view once made sense in a framework largely based on the Law of Separation and filtering governed by Western States, which overlooked both the rights of sovereign States and those of colonies. It worked for a world in which customary norms in the colonies could be considered as not Law, requiring their elevation to the status of Law through recognition and by the Law of the coloniser.

At this point, von Daniels' proposal that rules of engagement are Janus-faced deserves attention. Recall that von Daniels suggested that rules of engagement are interfacial: they pertain both to how a legal system treats a foreign norm and how that foreign norm treats the legal system. However, currently, there is no objective International Law norm that transcends relations between systems and provides the source for such rules of engagement, although Nicole Roughan proposes an idea of shared authority.[79] External recognition does not describe the situation where legal systems negotiate which of them governs which section of the legal sphere, even though this may be possible. External recognition describes the previous situation in which different legal systems mutually recognise each other as systems in order to make shared authority possible.

Since such rules operate only between legal systems, they lead to a relational concept of Law. The nature of Law is no longer determined in absolute terms but rather in relation to other legal orders. This relationality and relativity of the concept of Law is the necessary consequence of global legal pluralism. There is no longer a *prius* from which we can definitively determine whether something is or is not Law. If we accept that the definition of Law is itself the result of the relational operation between legal systems, then we must seek these rules within Law itself. And if legal systems are interrelated, we should not only search for these rules within each individual system but also look within other legal systems.

The suggested introduction of tertiary rules by Michaels, the contrapunctual systems of Maduro and Kirsch's interface law, all grounded in the idea of mutual systemic contingency, allow us to conceptualise legal orders not as fully separate entities but as mutually constitutive. This allows us to find a concept of Law that is not confined within the boundaries of the State and does not depend solely on the self-definition of legal personality.

[79] N. Roughan, *Authorities. Conflicts, Cooperation, and Transnational Legal Theory*, Oxford University Press, Oxford, 2013.

"It enables us to think of law as one and plural at the same time."[80] The Ancient idea of unity and uniqueness of Law in the context of the European Union is diminishing.

Within the European Union, two distinct and distant systems already coexist in juxtaposition. The principles that regulate the relationship between these two systems—effectiveness, primacy and responsibility—which are at once autonomous and necessarily interrelated, form an identity paradigm that has recently begun to permeate the EU's existential dimension: its values. The Law of the Other is no longer a mere factual occurrence. The legal mechanisms that define this juxtaposition are no longer built upon separation. The question is, above all, one of identity and concerns the principle of constitutive legal recognition of the Other.

In the relationship between systems, Luhmann's theory of asymmetry between system and environment no longer applies: each legal order is valid in the presence of the Other as a system, not merely as an external environment.

In the world of relationality, the axioms of legality in the singular no longer hold. First, the principle of exclusive identity falls away, and then the evaluation criterion also loses value. Both the axiological dimension and the purely legal dimension are intertwined and must be shared among several legal systems. Pluralism is an effective criterion in the sense that they are legal systems with constant legal effects: this effectiveness does not cease once the viewpoint of a legal system is assumed. Even though they are different, they are always in tension, without one prevailing over the other.

Secondly, the principle of validity of Law falls away. Valid law excludes the validity of other laws and presupposes a criterion for determining when the Law is valid, whether it is a norm presupposed in a logical-transcendental sense *à la* Kelsen or a social practice of recognition of valid rights *à la* Hart. The validity of one Law does not exclude the validity of another Law governed by a different norm of recognition: therefore, validity is no longer a criterion for identifying the Law. On the contrary, the validity of one mutually interferes with the other system. We should accept not one but two rules of recognition within the concept of Law. The first is well known: the rule of *internal recognition*, developed by

[80] R. Michaels, *Law and Recognition—Towards a Relational Concept of Law*, in *In Pursuit of Pluralist Jurisprudence*, N. Roughan & A. Halpin (eds.), Cambridge University Press, Cambridge, 2017, p. 112.

H. L. A. Hart. This refers to the idea that a developed legal system requires recognition as Law by its own subjects. The second, often overlooked but equally important, is the rule of *external recognition*, which holds that something qualifies as Law to the extent that it is recognised by other legal systems. The rule of internal recognition is an example of a secondary rule. The rule of external recognition, however, is of a different kind; it is a tertiary rule. Hart argued that a legal system is not complete unless, in addition to primary rules, it also includes secondary ones. In the same way, a legal order is not fully constituted without such tertiary rules.

In addition, the well-known distinction introduced by Herbert Hart between the internal point of view (that of the participant who adopts the rule as a standard of conduct) and the external point of view (that of the observer who sees the system as a social fact) begins to fade. In a world characterised by legal pluralism, the separation between internal and external perspectives no longer applies in the same way.[81] However, paradoxically, the seed of constitutional identity has begun to assert itself in the name of that dualistic approach never fully abandoned by the judges of national laws, in clear contrast to the monist thesis always upheld by the Luxembourg judge.[82] But let us take it step by step. Firstly, let us examine the initial stage of the Encounter with the Other: the political moment.

[81] L. Antoniolli, "*L'identità delle scienze giuridiche in ordinamenti multilivello: il diritto comparato*", in *L'identità delle scienze giuridiche in ordinamenti multilivello*, V. Barsotti (ed.), Maggioli, 2014, p. 27.

[82] F. Salmoni, *Unità nella diversità o diversità nell'unità? I concetti di identità nazionale e identità costituzionale e il dialogo simulato tra Corte di giustizia e Corte costituzionale*, in Rivista AIC, 2019, 531 ss., 542.

CHAPTER 8

The First Encounter with the Other: The Origin of the First European Communities

Abstract This chapter explores the evolving complex identity of the European Union, tracing its origins to the principle of relational recognition and the early European Communities. It highlights how limits and openness shape integration, with national constitutions embracing 'mutual embedded openness' towards European Law. The same openness towards the Other is found in the Schuman Declaration. The limits are represented by respect for the Law against any delirium of dictatorial omnipotence. The EU's legal order develops through dialogue and tension between national and supranational identities, favouring constitutional tolerance and cross-fertilisation over absolute supremacy. After the CJEU's early landmark judgments in Van Gend en Loos and Costa v. ENEL, and a significant period of silence, case law, such as the Solange and *controlimiti* doctrines, established porous boundaries and fostered dialogical engagement between the Court of Justice of the European Union and national courts.

Keywords Openness • Limits • European Communities • *Controlimiti* • Schuman Declaration

According to a principle of relational recognition, the very constitutional identity of the European Union can be understood as a reservoir, one that

© The Author(s), under exclusive license to Springer Nature Switzerland AG 2026

A. Lazari, *Relational Identity in International, Comparative and European Union Law*,
https://doi.org/10.1007/978-3-031-59482-3_8

is constantly in motion. If it were ever to reach a point of perfect equilibrium, it would cease to exist.[1] Hence, "*depurato da qualsivoglia forma di degenerazione (populistica e antieuropeistica), il richiamo al rispetto dell'identità costituzionale degli Stati membri potrebbe fungere addirittura da stimolo nei confronti dell'Unione, per realizzare compiutamente gli obiettivi previsti nei Trattati, nel rispetto delle peculiarità dei singoli ordinamenti, ma sempre in una logica solidaristica, che ne rafforzi parimenti l'Unione.*"[2] With the theory of relational recognition, the very idea of a limit as a barrier of separation is transformed into a limit to the possible abuses of the unleashed State that we referred to at the end of the first part. The first European Communities are born under the sign of Elster's limit[3] and openness towards the Other.

8.1 The Raison d'Être of European Communities: Limits and Openness

From the first perspective, a limit means the capacity to contain the potential delusions of omnipotence of an unbound Ulysses (and we witness this tension daily in our own time).[4] It forms the conceptual foundation of the European Rule of Law and the process of integration through Law, which we will explore shortly. On the other hand, the depth of this integration process no longer depends solely on limitation, as seen in the first part, but rather on the opening up of national constitutions to new international organisations, and vice versa.

Many national constitutional orders commit themselves to a general openness to European Law and consider that the normative constitutional vision of European integration is compatible with their own national constitutional legitimacy frameworks. In many cases, the need to engage with the EU constitutional order is already deeply embedded within national constitutions themselves. The EU and the national constitutional systems are based on what Daniel Halberstam defines as "mutual embedded openness", with both being "each deeply embedded in the

[1] Cfr. J. Derrida, *Points de suspension. Entretiens*, Galilée, Paris, 1992.

[2] S. Polimeni, *L'identità costituzionale come controlimite*, in *Ianus*, 2017, p. 62.

[3] J. Elster, *Ulysses Unbound: Studies in Rationality, Precommitment, and Constraints*, Cambridge University Press, Cambridge, 2000.

[4] For a very similar view, see J.H.H. Weiler, *The Constitution of Europe*, cit., p. 67, in the part referring to fundamental limits.

constitutional operating system of the other".[5] Most State constitutions are explicitly committed to constitutional openness, ceding and sharing authority with supranational institutions that pursue similar objectives. To cite a few examples, Article 23(1) of the German *Grundgesetz* expressly commits Germany to the European integration process and establishes that sovereign rights may be transferred to international organisations for this purpose. The Swedish Constitution explicitly requires Sweden's membership of the European Union. Article 7, paragraph 6, of the Portuguese Constitution states that "Portugal may agree to the joint exercise, in cooperation or through the institutions of the Union, of the powers necessary for the construction and deepening of the Union". In contrast, European treaties recognise the authority of national constitutions and require respect for their core principles and their "fundamental political structures" through the "identity clause" of Article 4, paragraph 2, of the Treaty on European Union (TEU).

The concept of diversity is not confirmed by the mere coexistence of entities or the simple juxtaposition of clearly defined, static identities with precise boundaries, but rather by coexistence based on complex processes that arise, evolve and fade through a dynamic of contacts, mutual integrations and various forms of contamination. It is the play of complexity, rather than simplification, that overcomes the reduction of meaning and allows for a deeper understanding of differences. For this reason, it can be said that through the creation of supranational rules of coexistence—unlike the previous mere juxtaposition—the emerging European identity, expressed *in nuce* in the Schuman Declaration, is founded on the inclusion of the Other, extending even beyond Europe, and is significantly intertwined with the philosophy opposing hegemonic State identities, as articulated in the *Manifesto di Ventotene*.[6] The first European Communities introduce an existential factor that coincides with the structural transformation of the State, where *communitas*, in its etymological sense composed of cum and *munus*, binds members through a reciprocal commitment (a *munus*, precisely), as explicitly provided for in Article 4.3 of the Treaty on European Union.

[5] D. Halberstam, *Systems Pluralism and Institutional Pluralism in Constitutional Law: National, Supranational, and Global Governance*, in *Univ. of Michigan Public Law Working Paper* No. 229, 2011.

[6] G. Zagrebelsky, *L'identità europea, in Religione e spazio pubblico in Europa*, Donzelli Editore, Roma, 2007, pp. 3–14.

We have already discussed the difference between conceptions of boundaries as an impenetrable wall and as a porous frontier (see "1.1 The modality of exclusion mechanisms: the boundary as a breach"). The intertwining of the internal and external constraining ropes of the State creates a new legal identity within the European Union. This idea of the boundary remains very vivid today. In the conclusions of Advocate General Ćapeta from June 2025, a fundamental knot of the EU's community of values is made explicit. In paragraph 224, the Advocate General argues that "violations of the rights in the Charter could be part of the Union's constitutional dialogue, and not of the denial of values". The EU's legal system develops through this dialogue. This means that there can be different views on how common values should be implemented. This is the implementation of the *grundnorm* of diversity. Discrepancies are not conflicts; rather, they form part of the constitutional dialogue within the EU legal order, which allows for different interpretations of rights. However, such disagreements do not negate the fundamental values themselves.[7] When they do, however, that is when some States cross the red lines, undermining the existential foundations of the European Union. The Advocate General repeats seven times that the community of values would be greatly harmed, not by discrepancies but by the absolute denial of its values, as these are its identity. The European Communities and the current Union exist for this very reason: to restrain, through the ties of Law, the madness caused by the siren song of nationalism. "However, national constitutional choices cannot go beyond this common framework. In this respect, as I have previously suggested, Article 2 of the TEU could be understood as imposing 'red lines' which, if crossed, require a response to defend the Union's constitutional model." But to reach this crucial point, we must start from the beginning: the encounter between two enemies, the French and German States after the Second World War.

[7] Once the balance has been struck at the EU level, or the EU legislator has clarified the content of a right more precisely, Member States can no longer maintain different solutions within the areas covered by EU Law. For example, see the ruling of 26 February 2013, Melloni (C-399/11, EU:C:2013:107).

8.2 *The Schuman Declaration: The Need for a New* Communitas

"In this way, there will be realised simply and speedily that fusion of interest which is indispensable to the establishment of a common economic system; it may be the leaven from which may grow a **wider and deeper community** between countries long opposed to one another by sanguinary divisions. [...] With increased resources Europe will be able to pursue the achievement of one of its essential tasks, namely, the development of the African continent." This is an excerpt from the Schuman Declaration. How do we interpret it? In terms of neo-colonialism or as a method for managing diversity both within and beyond Europe? Is it about assimilating and/or subordinating the Other, or taking responsibility for the Other?

In political 'messianism', the justification for using mobilising force does not come from the process, as in classical democracy, nor from the results or success, but from the ideal pursued, the goal to be reached, the 'Promised Land' waiting at the end of the tunnel. In fact, in messianic visions, the end always justifies the means.[8] The aim was to call for unity and somehow connect the two pillars of European civilisation: the Christian tradition in Europe and the rationalism of the Enlightenment,[9] which we have already identified as dominant epistemologies in the early Encounters with the Other.

Rather than focusing on legitimising political messianism, which we will revisit at the end of our analysis, we will pause on another seed sown by the Schuman Declaration, the Ventotene Manifesto and the proceedings of the Congress of Europe held in The Hague: the opening towards the Other as a means to achieve peace, or more precisely, a stable and peaceful configuration in Europe. Peace through the creation of a Community.

The messianic model offers only a partial explanation for why the early European Communities were able to operate for so long without a genuine commitment to the principles required of candidate countries:

[8] J.H.H. Weiler, Deciphering the Political and Legal DNA of European Integration: An Exploratory Essay, in Philosophical Foundations of European Union Law, J. Dickson & P. Eleftheriadis (eds.), Oxford University Press, Oxford, 2012, pp. 137–158.

[9] Cf. J. Habermas & J. Derrida, *February 15, or, What Binds Europeans Together: Plea for a Common Foreign Policy Beginning in Core Europe*, in D. Levy et alia, *Old Europe, New Europe, Core Europe: Transatlantic Relations after the Iraq War*, Verso, London, 2005, pp. 5–12.

democracy and human rights. Candidate countries must adhere to the European Convention on Human Rights, whereas the European Union itself is not obliged to do so. Additionally, candidates must demonstrate democratic credentials, a requirement that does not apply to the European Union. It is worth noting that messianic traits are reflected not only in the flowery rhetoric. In its original and unpublished version, the declaration is quite accomplished. However, the words democracy and human rights do not appear. Of course, it is possible, as has been argued, that this silence concealed the intention of the Founding Fathers to leave it to the Member States, through their constitutional courts and judicial systems, to ensure the safeguarding of fundamental rights, including in relation to the Community institutions.[10]

What does emerge strongly in the actions following the political moment of accession to the European Communities is a predominant legal vector.

The Treaty of Paris, with its explicit reference to supranationality, represents an unprecedented exercise in the juridification of a transnational organisation, significantly surpassing the innovation already present in the European Convention on Human Rights. Its institutions of self-governance, transnational administration, adjudication and enforcement are fundamental.[11] The political project of European integration was to be realised through an economic programme—the European Coal and Steel Community and the European Economic Community—grounded in the Rule of Law. Over time, we see the central role granted to Law and, in particular, to a judicial body: the Court of Justice of the European Union, which has been decisive in driving European integration. A legal regime that is not validated through democratic practice and does not respect human rights cannot be considered a legitimate expression of the new legal order.[12]

[10] M. Cartabia, *L'ora dei diritti fondamentali in Europa*, in M. Cartabia (ed.), *I diritti in azione*, Il Mulino, Bologna, 2007, p. 16. Cf. also F. Rubio Llorente, *Derechos fundamentales, principios estructurales y respeto por la identidad nacional de los Estados Miembros de la Unión Europea*, in *AFDUAM*, 2013, p. 515.

[11] Cf. P. Craig, *The Nature of the Community: Integration, Democracy and Legitimacy*, in P. Craig & G. De Búrca (eds.), *The Evolution of EU Law*, Oxford University Press, Oxford, 1999, p. 25.

[12] J. Habermas, *Between Facts and Norms: contributions to a discourse theory of law and democracy*, MIT Press, Cambridge, 1998; Idem, *Postnational Constellation*, MIT Press, Cambridge 2001.

With the early rulings from the 1960s, the mission the Court of Justice had taken on from the start became clear: to safeguard the uniform application of Community Law within the Member States.

It also seems no coincidence that this period of European resistance to the internal constitutional factor, from the perspective of inter-systemic restrictions, corresponds to the phase in the history of European integration when the Luxembourg Court was most inclined to make specific and precise references—something it would no longer do in the future—to the legal experiences of the Member States. Take, for example, the reasoning in the 1957 Algera ruling,[13] which, after a preamble regarding the possibility of revoking unlawful administrative acts, clarifies that this is a well-known problem in the case law and doctrine of all Community countries, but for which the Treaty contains no legal rule to provide a solution. The Community judge concluded that the Court of Justice, in order not to deny justice, is obliged to resolve this problem by informing itself of the legislation, doctrine and jurisprudence of the Member States.

"Integration through law"[14] essentially means the predominance of Law in the integration process. Was it a Law naturally similar to the International Law of separation? On the one hand, at first glance and with reference to the case law of the Court of Justice of the Communities, the answer is affirmative. Although the political *communitas* proclaimed the advent of a new identity, and despite the innovation of the landmark Vand Gend & Loos and Costa Enel rulings, the result was a declaration of independence from the Member States, in line with the Schuman Plan, rather than an interconnection with them. These two decisions were revolutionary in terms of breaking the umbilical cord with the Law of the States, but they did not sow the seed of interaction with them.

Once the constitutional revolution was carried out through the introduction of direct effect, citizens took advantage of the new supranational legality as a powerful instrument to compel the Member States to comply with their obligations under the Treaty. However, this also inevitably involved formalism and self-legitimation.[15] The question that arises is: 'why should I obey?' Even more so, in the direct confrontation between

[13] Ruling of the Court of Justice of 12 July 1957, Dinecke Algera and others v European Parliament, Joined Cases C-7/56 and C-3/57 to C-7/57, ECLI:EU:C:1957:7.

[14] M. Cappelletti, J. Weiler, M. Soccombe, *Integration Through Law: Europe and the American Federal Experience. A General Introduction*, De Gruyter, Brussels, 1986.

[15] Cf. T. Hartley, *The Foundations of European Union* Law, Oxford University Press, Oxford, 2010.

the Italian Constitutional Court and the Court of Justice in the Costa case, why did the latter prevail? Messianic political projects, by their very nature, go hand in hand with a formalist and self-referential concept of the Rule of Law.[16]

The Court of Justice sought to implement and give effect to the political project of the High Contracting Parties as enshrined in their respective Treaties. Quite simply, the messianic project was not initially concerned with issues related to democracy or, at first, with human rights. Its legitimacy was grounded in the strength and nobility of Law, yet detached from the democratic and human rights triad.[17] This initial stance—better described as a starting condition than an 'original sin'—has ultimately cast a long shadow over the very identity of the European Communities. These institutions have remained more focused on safeguarding individual legal situations than on the human dimension or the notion of community, particularly in a political sense.

By drawing an *écart* from the two Costa judgements, we can discern the full significance of this point.

In the early 1960s, however, the need for an ever-closer union between States seemed to dissipate under the weight of entrenched Realpolitik. Nevertheless, the institutional framework of the founding treaties of the European Communities, along with the underlying anthropological and political conception, led the Court of Justice in Luxembourg to recover the idea of a *sui generis* international organisation. This organisation was autonomous and in(ter)dependent from the Member States and was doubly tethered to the regulatory principles governing its relationship with those very States. Therein lies *in nuce* the heart of the new European paradigm, understood in the univocal terms of the concept of independence between legal systems. However, in the Costa v ENEL judgement (Case C-6/64, 15 July 1964), the Court of Justice cloaked this novel principle of supremacy in epistemological garments not so different from those of the previous exclusionary paradigm, likely in reaction to the national theories advanced in the pleadings themselves.[18]

In the *écart* between the aforementioned decision and the earlier ruling of the Italian *Corte Costituzionale*, we find elements of great significance.

[16] Idem.

[17] Cf. P. Pescatore, *The Doctrine of Direct Effects: An Infant Disease of Community Law*, in *European Law Review*, vol. 8, 1984, p. 155.

[18] Costa vs ENEL, C-6/64, 15 July 1964, ECLI:EU:C:1964:66.

Paradoxically, although from different perspectives and reaching different conclusions, both courts employ similar legal terminology and reasoning. On the national side, it is argued that "*nessun dubbio che lo Stato debba fare onore agli impegni assunti e nessun dubbio che il trattato spieghi l'efficacia ad esso conferita dalla legge di esecuzione. Ma poiché deve rimanere saldo l'impero delle leggi posteriori a quest'ultima, secondo i principi della successione delle leggi nel tempo, ne consegue che ogni ipotesi di conflitto fra l'una e le altre non può dar luogo a questioni di costituzionalità*".[19] From the Community point of view, the Costa v. Enel ruling states that Community Law rules will take precedence over any rules of Domestic Law. There is no hint of communication or cross-fertilisation.

The dialogue between conceptual paradigms—a cornerstone of the Community paradigm—remains silent, relegated to a few isolated legislative provisions such as Article 215 EEC (now Article 288 TFEU), which refers to a model of liability common to national legal systems.[20] The (virtually non-existent) use of comparative methods, on the one hand, and the persistent distinction between Public and Private Law, on the other, bear witness to the fact that the Community paradigm has yet to take off in a genuinely collaborative sense, in spite of the principled declarations in the Van Gend & Loos and Costa v. Enel rulings.

Despite the fact that the substance of the new legal system revealed, in retrospect, a new epistemological approach aimed at the interactive coexistence of two autonomous and independent systems, its form remained grandiose and absolute in nature. The primacy of Community Law was asserted regardless of its rank over any source of Law from the Member States: "the law stemming from the treaty, an independent source of law, could not, because of its special and original nature, be overridden by domestic legal provisions, however framed, without being deprived of its character as Community law and without the legal basis of the Community itself being called into question."

[19] Italian Constitutional Court, Judgment No. 14 of 7 March 1964, Costa v. ENEL, IT:COST:1964:14.

[20] In the doctrine, the conclusions surrounding the comparative method put forward by A. Trabucchi are particularly enlightening: *Per una visione sistematica del diritto comunitario*, in *Quaderni del Centro di documentazione e studi sulle Comunità europee*, Università degli Studi di Ferrara, Milan, 1967, 3 ss.

This primacy, in its Community dimension, prevailed even over the constitutional texts of the Member States, as was explicitly confirmed in the *Internationale Handelsgesellschaft*[21] case.

The Community king's first robe is lavish, and the posture of the Court of Justice, in asserting its autonomy through the principles of primacy and direct effect, appears somewhat aloof from its privileged interlocutors, the national courts. Yet the success of the Court's case law is closely tied to the early sketch of a dialogical conversation with national ordinary judges.[22] The strict dichotomy between the public and private spheres, although softened by repeated references to the role of citizens *in primis* in the Van Gend & Loos and Costa v ENEL rulings, remains intact in the Court's jurisprudence.[23] The citizen in those two landmark decisions is not a person in the full and universal sense of the term, as described in the 1948 Universal Declaration of Human Rights. The Court's own refusal to address matters related to the protection of individuals sets a clear limit to the reach of the claims made in Van Gend & Loos and Costa.[24]

Recently, the need to reconsider the case law doctrine of the absolute supremacy of Community Law has been perceived by the most discerning jurists, revealing a variety of valuable argumentative nuances. By intertwining the underlying *querelle* over this principle with the deeper constitutional question about the limited legitimacy of the community legal system, Weiler ends up asserting that "the supremacy cannot but be a contingent and limited concept subject to Member-State control". Donning the imperial attire of the European court, the professor at New York University asks: "would I want to give effect to a principle that rendered the Community's undemocratic laws supreme over the very

[21] Ruling of the Court of Justice, 17 December 1970, C-11/70 Cf. J.P., Puissochet, *La primacía del Derecho comunitario*, in *Estudios de derecho judicial*, 2006, 95, 30.

[22] J.H.H. Weiler, *Rewriting Van Gend & Loos*, in AA.VV., *Judicial Discretion in European Perspective*, edited by Ola Wiklund, 2003, p. 160: "The paradox is thus that the legitimacy challenge to the Court's constitutional jurisprudence does not rest as has been assumed in its hermeneutics – a good outcome based on a questionable interpretation. But quite the opposite: an unassailable interpretation but an outcome which underpins, supports and legitimates a highly problematic decisional process."

[23] Only very limited mention is made of Private Law in certain rulings such as C-56/64 and C-58/64, *Consten and Grundig v Commission* [1966] ECR 429.

[24] CJUE, 4 February 1959, *Friedrich Storck & Co. v High Authority of the European Coal and Steel Community*, Case 1/58, ECLI:EU:C:1959:1; CJUE, 5 July 1960, *Präsidenten der Ruhrkohlen-Verkaufsgesellschaft mbH and Others v High Authority of the European Coal and Steel Community*, Joined Cases 36, 37, 38/59 and 40/59, ECLI:EU:C:1960:36.

constitutional values of the Member-State?" The legitimacy of the dualistic formulation found in the Van Gend & Loos and later Costa rulings is thus called into question. In the face of widespread violations of the nascent Community law, the firm stance of the European Court translated into a values-based framework that was, in essence, hierarchically superior to the legal systems of the then six founding States. What appears less open to criticism is the Court's interpretive reasoning; rather, it is the extreme nature of its outcomes that raises concern. The success of the Court's constitutional-style jurisprudence, particularly in terms of its growing acceptance by national judges, lies primarily in its interpretive strength. This hermeneutic ability proved more decisive than the rulings themselves, which were initially met with resistance by national counterparts. "However, it is precisely in this context that we can see the problematic nature of the dark side of this moon. The situation implicated in preliminary references always posits an individual vindicating a personal, private interest against the public good. Paradoxically, European rights, in some interesting way, become anti-community rights."[25]

The argument about new Community Law is that formalist Kelsenian positivist models no longer offer a normatively meaningful or acceptable representation of the Rule of Law unless they meet two fundamental conditions: that lawmaking is embedded within a democratic process, and that it respects human rights. The evidence lies in the deafening silence of national constitutional courts which, until only a few decades ago, refrained from referring any preliminary questions to the Court of Justice of the European Union. Instead, they issued judgements of containment or even rulings that directly contradicted EU Case Law. Comparative Law must learn to interpret these silences and these phenomena of silent resistance.[26] Studying cross-fertilisation requires an understanding of cryptotypes, the implicit, often cultural, elements embedded within and shared between legal systems. "*Within the context of the European legal space, a more defined and restricted area has to be taken into account, which is named 'inner core', where legal comparison has become more likely and possibly more successful.*"[27]

[25] Idem.

[26] A.M. Burley and W. Mattli *Europe before the Court: A Political Theory of Legal Integration*, in *International Organization*, 1993, pp. 41–76, highlight the immediate application of the principles of direct effect by ordinary national courts and the silent frontal opposition of constitutional courts.

[27] S. Ragone, *European Comparative Law: Reasons for «Enhanced Comparison» and Role of the CJEU*, en *Revista de Derecho Político*, 2021, p. 297.

The European Court of Justice embraced the second of these conditions through an activist line of Case Law that began in 1969. It asserted that Community norms that failed to respect the common constitutional traditions of the Member States and the principles enshrined in the European Convention on Human Rights would not be acceptable. The Court even recognised that democracies themselves could lead to a tyranny of the majority. However, it is precisely in this context that we begin to glimpse the problematic nature of the Rule of Law's darker side. The situation implicated in preliminary references always posits an individual vindicating a personal, private interest against the public good. Once again, and mutatis mutandis, we witness—if only in the background—a reinforcement of Esposito's concept of *immunitas*, this time tied to the self-centred subject rather than a genuine *communitas*.

The argument concerning Law is that the formalist, Kelsenian positivist models—detached from any social or practical dimension, as we glimpsed in the previous chapter—no longer offer a normatively meaningful or acceptable vision of Law unless they are interwoven with the other poles of the triad: a truly democratic process and respect for human rights. These two values, not being part of any original political project, were never subject to a formal transfer of competences to the Communities.

As a result, the European Court of Justice embraced the second of these conditions through an activist line of Case Law that began in 1969. It asserted that Community norms that failed to respect the common constitutional traditions of the Member States and the principles enshrined in the European Convention on Human Rights would not be acceptable. The Court recognised that even democracies can give rise to a tyranny of the majority and that any integration of human rights into the original mission could only occur through the comparative lens of shared constitutional traditions. But this intertwining of constitutional and international strands, both fine and coarse, comes after an operation of separation from the Other, which in this case occurs by distancing itself from the dynamics of classic International Law and national rights. It is a true *actio finium regundorum*, which, as already mentioned, is established more as a declaration of independence than of interdependence, which will come later in the 1970s.

The *actio finium regundorum* has not marked the overcoming of an identity based on separation. The very existence of political resistance (dramatised by the 'empty chair' crisis and the establishment of summits of heads of state outside the Community institutions, both initiatives promoted by Charles De Gaulle) attests to the arduous path of 'Integration through Law'. The process of conversion[28] into an identity and a *communitas* has only partially taken its first steps—only with regard to the delimitation of a new legal territory, not its structuring.

On the contrary, while the rulings on primacy have been enthusiastically celebrated, they in fact represent a reproduction of the monist views upheld by the Court of Justice of the European Union and the dualist perspectives advocated by national constitutional courts in the early years of European integration. As noted earlier, the two constraining ropes do not intertwine. For this reason, despite asserting its *sui generis* character, the Court of Justice failed to fully grasp either its need to engage horizontally with the differentiating institution of the Parliamentary Assembly or the necessity of entering into genuine dialogue with its key interlocutors: the constitutional courts.

The two constraining ropes of the absolute and exclusive State are different and distant. And Comparative Law has a very limited role in this first Encounter.

8.3 The Inclusion of the Other: The Origin of Intertwined Ropes

In the European experience, the first appearance of matters related to national identity has demonstrated a versatile, flexible and, under certain political circumstances, effective means of mitigating federal or centripetal centralisation, as recently defined by the Advocate General.[29] It could be said to have played a role in the self-understanding of the European constitutional project as a process informed by a certain set of values. Undoubtedly, it has also enriched the constitutional and political project

[28] T. Kuhn, *The Structure of Scientific Revolutions*, University of Chicago Press, Chicago, 1962, argues in terms of the transfer of trust from one paradigm to another as an experience of conversion that cannot be imposed by force.

[29] Conclusions of the Advocate General, Mr. Spielmann, 11 March 2025, Case C-448/23, European Commission v. Republic of Poland, "The present case clearly highlights the interaction between two principles which, from the point of view of the national court, may appear to be opposed: on the one hand, the primacy of EU Law, a principle intended to be 'centripetal', which is the very foundation of supranational integration and, on the other hand, respect for the national identities of the Member States, a concept with a 'centrifugal' effect, laid down in Article 4(2) TEU, which relates to 'what differentiates one State from another, what enables it to be recognised and distinguished from others" (para. 35).

of European coexistence, which from the very outset manifested itself "as one that undermines categories of thought which have been settled for centuries, overturns deeply-rooted political ideologies and strikes at powerfully organized interests."[30]

The doctrines of autonomy and primacy referred to in the Case Law of the Luxembourg Court form the unitary foundations of EU Law. Primacy constitutes an "existential requirement" of EU Law, according to the famous expression coined by Pierre Pescatore.[31]

Autonomy in its first absolute version implies that courts cannot link the effect of European rules within their jurisdiction to domestic rules, including rules of constitutional status, which determine the domestic effect of international legal rules. And once the decision to centralise is interpreted as deriving from the Treaty itself, which is a source of Law independent of the decisions of its signatories or its legal system, "the autonomy of the European legal order becomes immunized and secure".[32] We are returning to an immunised and secure concept of identity, but one that is a far cry from the emerging identity relationship of the European Communities' genetic code.

The national challenge to the supremacy of European Law and the primacy of its rules over those originating in domestic legal systems takes the form of a theoretical explanation of dual or reciprocal supremacy. The essence of this view is that under the EU's limited constitutional and institutional capacities, only cooperation or acceptance of national constitutional guardians can give EU legislation an aspect of legal reality.

Karen Alter sums up this view as follows: "the ECJ can say whatever it wants, the real question is why anyone should heed it."[33] Therefore, whatever internal tension the claim for supremacy in national legal systems may have, its explanation cannot be reduced to the CJEU pronouncements we have analysed so far. The sources of such traction must be sought, rather, in the continuous reaction of national legal systems. European Union Law, and specifically its guardian in Luxembourg, relies fundamentally on its relationship with national legal systems and their respective institutions;

[30] P. Pescatore, *The Law of Integration*, Sijthoff, Leiden, 1974, p. 4.

[31] P. Pescatore, *L'ordre juridique des Communautés européennes: étude des sources du droit communautaire*, Presses universitaires de Liège, Liège, 1973, p. 227.

[32] V. Perju, *Identity Federalism in Europe and the United States*, in *Vanderbilt Journal of Transnational Law*, 2020, p. 300.

[33] K. Alter, *The European Court's Political Power: the Emergence of an Authoritative International Court in the European Union*, in *West Eur. Pol.*, 1996, p. 459.

it cannot function independently of them. It is a Law defined by tension, and for this reason, it is ontologically relational. And, from that national perspective, European primacy, not Kelsenian positivist supremacy, has a peculiar dimension, "which is decisive for determining whether the Court's doctrines have an impact on legal reality: the attitude of national courts and other institutions".[34]

Therefore, the reception of European Union Law "depends on its incorporation into the constitutional orders of the Member States and its affirmation by their supreme courts".[35] While both the CJEU and the supreme national courts claim ultimate authority, neither claim by and in itself captures the nature of constitutional authority within the European Union; only both perspectives, together, do so. According to this view, the reception of the CJEU doctrine of supremacy in National Law is not external to the doctrine itself; rather, it becomes a constitutive part of it. It is ontologically intertwined: one identity nourishes and reflects the other through a principle of mutual recognition. The primacy of the European Union is **necessarily** two-dimensional[36] in the sense that it is co-constituted by two perspectives, each of which originates within legal systems that are initially considered to be mutually incompatible. According to this account, the CJEU's positions of primacy are not placed higher or lower but in tension with it. At this point we see the biggest difference, the *écart* with the first part of this work. Comparison is not the operation dismissed by Jullien and Derrida: it does not serve to reinforce exclusionary identities. The principle of *primauté* is placed on an equal footing with the doctrines of national courts which incorporate—or not—supranational doctrine into the constitutional systems of the various Member States. And this is how it should be taught in Law Schools. It is the clearest manifestation of the principle of constitutional tolerance, enshrined, for example, in Article 4.3 TEU. The following account is one of integration as an inclusive relationship, not as fusion or assimilation. **It does not establish any hegemonic *prius*, at least, not if it is to function effectively.** Indeed, the expression of this foundational identity within the framework of the current first eight articles of the Treaty on European

[34] B. de Witte, *Direct Effect, Primacy and the Nature of the European Legal Order*, in *The Evolution of Eu Law*, G. de Búrca & P.P. Craig (eds.), p. 346.

[35] J.H.H. Weiler, *The Community System: the Dual Character of Supranationalism*, in *Y.B. EUR. L.*, 1982, pp. 275–276.

[36] J.H.H. Weiler, *The Community System*, cit., p. 275.

Union constitutes an explicit recognition of the communitarian ideas of Schuman, Monnet and Spinelli. The image of a continuous, incessant dialectical process (towards Others) can be seen in reference to the creation of an ever-closer union between the peoples of Europe (Article 1 TEU) and in the enshrining of values common to the Member States (Article 2 TEU), in respect of the richness of their cultural diversity (Article 3.3 TEU), as in the principle of conferring competence, constitutional identity and loyal cooperation (Articles 4.1, 4.2, 4.3 TEU), on fundamental rights arising from constitutional traditions common to the Member States (Article 6.3 TEU).

From the outset, for a Member State of the European Union, the different dimensions of constitutional identity assume special features; they are weighted in an environment. In fact, historically and sociologically speaking, national history is inexorably linked to the process of creation and integration, first of the Communities and now of the European Union, as well as to the history of the other Member States. The characteristics of the European identity of relatedness and complexity[37] therefore imply a conceptual operation of "**fundamental weighting**".[38] As we will see in more detail below, national identity is not constitutional identity, since it must be weighted within the framework of the Constitution.[39] Thus, constitutional identity contributes to shaping the European Union's identity by balancing national constitutional identities within the repository of common constitutional traditions and, consequently, the values enshrined in Article 2 TEU.

This ongoing axiological and legal cross-pollination has taken place within the realm of Primary Law, occasionally invoking the particularities of national identities, as seen, for example, in Protocol No. 35 concerning Article 40.3.3 of the Irish Constitution, or the Joint Declaration annexed

[37] Von Bogdandy, A., Grabenwarter, C., y Huber, P. M., "Constitutional Science in the European Legal Space", en A. von Bogdandy, P. M. Huber y P. Cassese (eds.), The Max Planck Handbooks in European Public Law, Volume I: The Analysis of Public Law, Oxford University Press, Oxford, 2017, pp. 581–609.

[38] As defined by J.H.H. Weiler, *The Constitution of Europe. 'Do the New Clothes Have an Emperor?' and Other Essays on European Integration*, Harvard University, Massachusetts, 1999, espec. 181 ss.

[39] Cf. Bon, P., «L'identité nationale ou constitutionnelle, une nouvelle notion juridique», in Mélanges en l'honneur du Professeur Jean-Arnaud Mazères, Éditions l'Épitoge, Toulouse, 2013; L. Diez Picazo, *Observaciones sobre la cláusula de identidad nacional, en Constitución europea y constituciones nacionales*, edited by Cartabia M., De Witte B., Pérez Tremps P., Tirant lo Blanch, Valencia, 2005, pp. 437–448.

to Greece's Act of Accession to the European Communities on 28 May 1979.[40] Here, spiritual and religious reasons are invoked, reasons the Community will take into account, particularly in matters of taxation and customs. The special status of Mount Athos expressly prohibits the entry of women, regardless of nationality, thereby contravening the Community principle of equality between men and women.[41]

The dialogical dynamic between identities clearly also takes shape in the political sphere, producing effects specific to that domain. Judicial controls are applicable, for obvious reason, a posteriori, in other words, only once harm to national constitutional identity has occurred or there is a concrete threat of such harm caused by a derived act of the Union. For this reason, part of the academic literature has proposed giving renewed attention to controls that could be described as 'political' or 'non-judicial'. These would fall under the scope of political negotiation practices and aim to protect, *ex ante*, the core constitutional principles that could be affected by external sources.[42]

8.4 The First Jurisprudential Approaches of the 1970s: The Solange Method

For this reason, over time, the situation of exclusive autonomy was overcome and the constitutional courts began to talk about two systems that would be "autonomous and separate, although coordinated".[43] At the same time, the CJEU has shown its appreciation for the efforts of these national actors by sometimes assuming a benign and tolerant attitude: some scholars have defined such a situation of partial convergence using

[40] V. Constantinesco, *La confrontation entre identité constitutionnelle européenne et identités constitutionnelles nationales: Convergences ou contradictions? contrepoint ou hiérarchie?*, in *Mélanges en l'honneur de Philippe Manin*, LGDJ, Paris, 2010, p. 79.

[41] Cf. J. Bonet Navarro, "*El estatuto especial del monte Athos ante la tradición religiosa. el derecho eclesiástico griego y el derecho comunitario europeo*", in *Boletín de la Facultad de Derecho*, de la UNED, issue 27, 2005, pp. 93 ss.

[42] See, in particular, P. Faraguna, *Taking Constitutional Identity away from the Courts*, in *Brooklyn Journal of InterNational Law*, n. 41/2016, spec. 501 et seq.; ID., *Alla ricerca dell'identità costituzionale. Tra conflitti giurisdizionali e negoziazione politica*, in *Costituzionalismo.it*, n. 3/2016, p. 197.

[43] For example, the Italian Constitutional Court, Judgment No. 170 of 8 June 1984, S.p.a. Fragd v. Amministrazione delle finanze dello Stato (Granital), IT:COST:1984:170.

the concept of "(limited) flexibility of supremacy".[44] The Kuhnian paradigm shift emerges precisely in the context of presumed conflicts, which have played a crucial role in fostering this convergence: it is best understood in terms comparable to the concept of *écarts*.

An analysis of the internal structure of the so-called pillar of integration, as represented, for instance, by the core provisions of the former Treaty of Rome, brings to light the pairing of Articles 28 and 30 of the EEC Treaty. Article 28 functions as the prohibitive instrument underpinning the establishment of the internal market from a material perspective, essential for the realisation of open markets. This provision seeks to maximise efficiency and minimise inefficiency, aiming towards increased production and wealth creation. Within this conception and setting aside Article 2 of the EEC Treaty (where the internal market is framed as an instrument in the service of welfare), there is no room for human rights values.

On a different level and purely as an exception, Article 30 of the now outdated Treaty of the European Community stands out, referring to public morality, public order, environmental matters, health and safety, among others. Certain elements emerge as particularly significant within this framework, which is applied across all factors of production, the freedom to provide services, the free movement of workers and so on.

The European Economic Community and its freedoms embody the principles of the free market while certain minimal national values are pushed into the background; they must be proven and justified. As these are exceptional measures, the set of national value-based regulations must be interpreted strictly and narrowly. The two coercive ropes that bind Ulysses—the thread of the supranational market and the line of national values—do not intertwine. At the legislative level, there has been a deliberate effort to keep these two spheres of competence clearly separate and distant: market/supranational and human rights/national. The relationship established between the two ropes is structured as a quasi-hierarchical one: the rule/primacy of Union Law versus the exception/national values.

[44] V. Ferreres Comella, *La Constitución española ante la clausola de primacia del Derecho de la Unión europea. Un comentario a la Declaración 1/2004 del Tribunal Constitucional 1/2004*, in A. Lopez Castillo, A. Saiz Arnaiz & V. Ferreres Comella, *Constitución española y constitución europea*, Centro de Estudios Políticos y Constitucionales, Madrid 2005, pp. 77–90.

For these reasons, up until the 1970s, the Court of Justice's approach to rights had been limited to the economic rights enshrined in the Treaty of Rome. This naturally gave rise to scepticism and concern on the part of national constitutional courts. From 1969 onwards, however, a series of cases began to frame the protection of fundamental rights within the scope of Community Law. In the second of these judgements, the CJEU explicitly stated that "the validity of a Community act or its effects in a Member State cannot be affected by allegations that it is contrary to certain fundamental rights as formulated by the constitution of that State or by the principles of its constitutional structure".[45] By aligning European Union Law and its existential primacy with the respect for human rights—a value absent from any originally political project—the European Court has continued to follow the path set out in the Costa v. ENEL judgement of 1964.

The Italian Constitutional Court, in its Frontini judgement of 1973,[46] began to develop its *controlimiti* doctrine. The Court argued that Italy's participation in European integration entailed certain limitations on Italian sovereignty. However, these limitations must themselves be constrained by the fundamental principles of the Italian Constitution. The transfer of sovereignty to the European Communities, the Court maintained, was subject to constitutional limits. In the words of the Italian Court: "It must be ruled out that such limitations of sovereignty, as established concretely in the Treaty of Rome — signed by countries whose systems are based on the rule of Law and which guarantee the essential freedoms of their citizens—could nonetheless grant the EEC institutions an unacceptable power to violate the fundamental principles of our constitutional order or the inalienable rights of the individual. And it is clear that [...] in such a case, the guarantee would always be upheld that this Court would ensure the continuing compatibility of the Treaty with the aforementioned fundamental principles." The Italian Court, then, although it does not use the term "constitutional identity" explicitly in its judgement, clearly places the concept at the heart of its doctrine. It establishes a boundary that is difficult to overcome, marking a firm constitutional limit to the primacy of European Law.

Another early trace of constitutional identity can be found in the *Solange* Case Law of the German Constitutional Court.

[45] 17 December 1970, Internationale Handelsgesellschaft mbH v Einfuhr- und Vorratsstelle für Getreide und Futtermittel, Case 11/70, ECLI:EU:C:1970:114.

[46] Italian Constitutional Court, 27 December 1973, *Frontini Pozzani*.

In *Solange I*,[47] the *Bundesverfassungsgericht* (BVerfG) declared itself competent to review Community measures in terms of their respect for fundamental rights "as long as the process of integration has not progressed to the point where Community Law includes a catalogue of fundamental rights". The German Constitutional Court argued that this was necessary because the section of German Basic Law concerning fundamental rights formed "an inalienable and essential part of the Constitution's fundamental structure". Although the German Constitution commits Germany to European integration (a move towards openness), its provision on regional integration "does not pave the way for altering the basic structure (*Grundgefüge*) of the Constitution, on which its identity rests" (a limit to openness). This position was later reaffirmed on several occasions. Even when the Federal Constitutional Court, in its subsequent *Solange II* judgement, withdrew its claim to review specific provisions of European Union Law (acknowledging that a sufficient level of fundamental rights protection had been developed at the European level), it nonetheless reaffirmed constitutional identity as a limit to European integration. It stated once again that "the transfer of sovereign rights to international institutions does not permit the abandonment of the constitutional order's identity through interference with its basic structure".[48]

In these early encounters, the scholarship that has examined these rulings has been predominantly constitutionalist in nature. As Burgorgue-Larsen[49] argues, this marks a shift from the initial period of judgements in the 1960s, which was heavily shaped by the focus of International Law scholars. Legal scholarship also remains divided into epistemic communities, much like State identities themselves.

This scholarship points to the opposition of the supreme and constitutional courts through a series of seminal judgements: Semoules,[50]

[47] Bundesverfassungsgericht [BVerfG] [Federal Constitutional Court] 29 May, 1974, 37 Entscheidungen Des Bundesverfassungsgerichts [BVerfGE] 271, 285 [hereinafter referred to as Solange I].

[48] *Solange II,* Judgement of the Second Senate BVerfGE 89, 155, 12 October 1993, para 106.

[49] L. Burgorgue-Larsen, *Pour une approche dialogique du Droit constitutionnel européen*, in Annuaire de droit européen 2012, vol. X, Bruylant, Brussels, 2014, pp. 29–53; L. Burgorgue-Larsen (ed.), *L'identité constitutionnelle saisie par les juges*, Pedone, Paris, 2011.

[50] Conseil d'Etat, Syndicat général de fabricants de semoules de France, C.M.L.R. 395 (1970).

Solange,[51] Cohn-Bendit,[52] *controlimiti*,[53] among others. It is also important to note that when Member States recognised the primacy of EU Law, they did so, with few exceptions, using their national constitutions rather than EU doctrine as the basis for that limited recognition. It was an opposing resistance with national concepts and terminology, following in the wake of the aforementioned Enel judgement of the Italian *Corte Costituzionale*.

Whether it be Article 11 of the Italian Constitution, the doctrine of parliamentary sovereignty in the United Kingdom, Article 24(1) of German Basic Law, Article 55 of the French Constitution or Article 93 of the Spanish Constitution, the acceptance of EU primacy rarely, if ever, rested on the Costa judgement of the Court of Justice itself. Even after some of these original constitutional anchors were transformed into provisions referring explicitly to EU membership, national courts continued to reject absolute and unconditional supremacy, opting instead for a relative and conditional acceptance. There is no relationality and there is no cross-fertilisation. From the perspective of EU doctrine, the use of InterNational Law to frame the national reception of the European legal order was, in itself, contrary to the interpretation of the CJEU that the Treaty is an autonomous and original source of Law through which the EU forms an autonomous legal order of International Law. Hence, basing the authority of EU Law on the national constitutional text, and not on the Founding Treaty, means rejecting the claim of the Costa v. ENEL judgement of an unconditional and absolute primacy of supranational rules. What we are witnessing is the continuation of exclusionary identity-based reasoning.

But there is more. The *Solange* decision and the Italian doctrine of *controlimiti* paved the way for ongoing engagement between the CJEU and national constitutional courts. They established a channel of dialogue concerning the development of the principle of primacy and emerging (proto-)constitutional identities. This body of Case Law initiates a dialogue that, although initially marked by clear disagreements, has been essential to the relational identity paradigm. Otherwise, I repeat, the ideas

[51] Bundesverfassungsgericht [BVerfG] [Federal Constitutional Court] 29 May 1974, 37 Entscheidungen Des Bundesverfassungsgerichts [BVerfGE] 271, 285 [hereinafter referred to as Solange I].

[52] French Council of State, Judgment of 22 December 1978, Minister of the Interior v. Cohn-Bendit, [1980] 1 C.M.L.R. 543.

[53] Italian Constitutional Court, Judgment of 17 December 1973, Frontini v. Ministero delle Finanze, [1974] 2 C.M.L.R. 372.

put forward by Advocate General Ćapeta in June 2025 concerning the necessity of disagreement for the construction of a European Union identity could not be properly interpreted. "In this interpretation, European Law differs from the 'global' approach to international Law as well, remaining linked to national laws in a way that is possible exclusively in the European legal space. European law is based on an interconnection between the systems involved that goes beyond any other experience of supranational/international governance, creating a unique example of legal space where the use of comparison becomes more useful and even necessary."[54]

As noted previously, the initial idea of the *controlimiti* has been conceived as a retaining wall rather than a porous border. "This belief is difficult to achieve in its absoluteness because the incorporation-postulate into the legal systems of the Member States isn't free from contradictions when taking into account older and more recent decisions on the concept of autonomy, i.e. the independence of Union Law vis-à-vis National Law and international Law alike. If the jurisprudence boils down to an outwardly dualistic, inwardly monistic approach the ECJ doesn't do much different than national constitutional courts in federal states."[55] But they have spurred ongoing responses from the CJEU, opening up a space for a new type of critical thinking. Indeed, the concept of primacy in the *Internationale Handelsgesellschaft* ruling differs from the Omega and Kadi rulings, since in these latter judgements, the CJEU shows a clear openness to the constitutional identity of the Member States through common constitutional traditions.[56] But there is an *écart* that must be recognised.

In the Stauder ruling of 1969,[57] and in particular in the *ratio decidendi* of the *Internationale Handelsgesellschaft* ruling of 1970,[58] the Court of Justice recognises that although the application of the principle of primacy

[54] S. Ragone, *European Comparative Law: Reasons for «Enhanced Comparison» and Role of the CJEU*, in *Revista de Derecho Político*, 2021, p. 299.

[55] F. Weber, *The Identity of Union Law in Primacy: Piercing Through Euro Box Promotion and Others*, in *European Papers* www.europeanpapers.eu ISSN 2499–8249, Vol. 7, 2022, No 2, p. 761.

[56] Cf. B. Davies, *Integrity or Openness? Reassessing the History of the CJEU's Human Rights Jurisprudence*, in *American Journal of Comparative Law*, 2016, pp. 801–834.

[57] Judgment of the Court of Justice of 12 November 1969, Erich Stauder v City of Ulm - Sozialamt, Case 29-69, ECLI:EU:C:1969:52.

[58] Judgment of the Court of 17 December 1970, Internationale Handelsgesellschaft mbH v Einfuhr- und Vorratsstelle für Getreide und Futtermittel, Case 11-70, ECLI:EU:C:1970:114.

of Community Law is indifferent to possible national constitutional consequences, the "protection of fundamental rights constitutes an integral part of the general legal principles whose observance the Court of Justice ensures", and "the safeguarding of these rights, informed by the constitutional traditions common to the Member States, must be guaranteed within the framework and objectives of the Community". In the *Internationale Handelsgesellschaft* ruling, the Court of Justice therefore uses the central (albeit uncertain at the time) notion of "common constitutional traditions of the Member States" to determine the material content of the general principles of Community Law, recognising, for the first time, that the reworking of these traditions will take into account the structure and purpose of the Treaties.[59] With the subsequent Nold ruling of 1974,[60] the same body would supplement the use of common constitutional traditions by incorporating instruments for the protection of human rights and fundamental freedoms, to which the Member States contribute or have acceded.

This is a significant point which, despite separatist opposition, will bear fruit in the subsequent Case Law of the Court of Justice.

Moreover, with regard to the identity-related dimension of the integration process, the strengthening of the Rule of Law no longer depends solely on the affirmation of the principle of independence; it must also be sustained by extra-legal factors, as previously noted above. "Western legal tradition is normative; it speaks to questions which legal systems, as purported facts, are unable to speak to. This is why Article 6 of the Treaty of the European Union speaks of Europe's 'common constitutional traditions', since it is necessary to resort to such underlying common tradition as a means of critiquing, com-paring, and going beyond, the national systems of Europe."[61]

In the construction of these extra-legal elements drawn from common constitutional traditions, the nature of the 'filter' applied by the Court of Justice plays a key role, which depends on the attitude expected of national

[59] Cf. B. Davies, *The Internationale Handelsgesellschaft Case: The Source of the European Court of Justice's Human Rights Jurisprudence*, in *EU Law Stories: Contextual and Critical Histories of European Jurisprudence*, Nicola, F. - Davies, B. (eds.), Cambridge University Press, Cambridge, 2017, pp. 153–178.

[60] Judgment of the Court of 14 May 1974, J. Nold, Kohlen- und Baustoffgroßhandlung v Commission of the European Communities, Case 4/73, ECLI:EU:C:1974:51.

[61] H.P. Glenn, *Com-paring*, in *Comparative Law. A Handbook*, E. Örücü, D. Nelken (eds.), Hart Publishing, Oxford, 2010, p. 93.

courts and on the specific needs of the case at hand. As a result, the Court's Case Law on constitutional traditions calls for the involvement of national interlocutors in the name of the Member States' 'constitutional tolerance'.[62] In subsequent judgements handed down by national courts and the Luxembourg Court, we see the emergence of an *écart*, a productive space in which one judgement cannot be fully understood without the other, and vice versa. When examined in retrospect, this decision (significantly marked by extensive references both to the provisions of the European Convention and to the German Constitution) reveals the strategy pursued by the Community Court. The hermeneutic 'zipper' connecting the protection of fundamental rights between the Treaties and national constitutional rules will continue to be the Court of Justice. It will not, therefore, relinquish its unconditional defence of its role as guardian of the specificity and primacy of Community Law, through the exclusive reinterpretation of constitutional traditions internally and of ECHR rules externally.[63]

This also invites reflection on how, within this context of paradigmatic shift, a thorough comparative analysis of the constitutional experiences of the Member States was no longer fully aligned with the evolving interpretative needs of the Court of Justice. It is no coincidence, then, that the latter gradually pushed the Cartesian reasoning typical of early cases such

[62] It is clear that reference is made to the concept of 'constitutional tolerance' which Weiler considers to be the peculiar feature of the Community legal system. See J.H.H. Weiler, *Federalism and Constitutionalism, Europe's sonderweg*, in K. Nicolaidis, R. Howse (eds.), *The Federal Version: Legitimacy and Levels of Governance in the US and the EU*, Oxford University Press, Oxford, 2001, 54 ss., 69. In accordance with this reconstruction, the constitutional subjects of the Member States accept the European constitutional framework "not because as a matter of legal doctrine, as in the case in the federal state, they are subordinate to a higher sovereignty and authority attaching to norms validated by the federal peoples, the constitutional demos. They accept it as an autonomous voluntary act endlessly renewed by each instance of subordination [...] The Quebecois are told in the name of the people of Canada, you are obliged to obey. The French or the Italians or the Germans are told: in the name of peoples of Europe, you are invited to obey [...]. When acceptance and subordination is voluntary, it constitutes an act of true liberty and emancipation from collective self-arrogance and constitutional fetishism: a high expression of Constitutional Tolerance."

[63] This is explained from his perspective as Court Judge by S. Rodin, *Constitutional Relevance of Foreign Court Decisions*, in *Am J Comp Law* (2016), 827: "While the rights under the Convention are fully incorporated, the Convention itself is exogenous and foreign to the European Union. Since the adoption of the Charter, the CJEU normally does not cite articles of the Convention, but regularly refers to the Charter itself. What at first glance seems to be a paradox represents the defense line of constitutional identity of the European Union."

as Algera to the margins. In this context, the connection between the principle of primacy of Community Law and the Court's responsiveness to common constitutional traditions proves particularly significant. Though often overlooked, this development is key to understanding the interpretative dynamics behind this evolution and the filtering method adopted by the Luxembourg Court.[64]

These are, ultimately, judicial contortions—driven by comparative instruments with a clear aspiration to protect fundamental rights—in an area where the Court did not yet hold full competence and which wavers *ab imis* between the doctrine of *primauté* and the attempt to reconcile it with common constitutional traditions and with the European Convention on Human Rights and Fundamental Freedoms. "Unity, the principle of primacy, in diversity, common constitutional traditions."

During this period, there is little room to reconcile the primacy of Community Law with national constitutional supremacy, and precisely for this reason, the comparative method finds limited application. In the Hauer[65] decision, the Court of Justice reaffirmed that potential issues concerning violations of fundamental rights could indeed be assessed within the framework of Community Law. Referring to special assessment criteria derived from national laws or constitutions, the Court warned, would undermine the unity of the common market. The hermeneutic guardian of this dual dimension is—and will remain—the CJEU. The paradigm used to defend the autonomy and primacy of Community Law closely mirrors the approach taken by national constitutional courts: it is the *Aut Aut*—an either/or logic; it is inherently exclusive. Here too, when viewed in retrospect, we can discern the same logic previously outlined in relation to Articles 28 and 30 of the EEC Treaty: there is a rule of *primauté*, accompanied by exceptions or niches carved out by national constitutional provisions or by the European Convention on the Protection of Human Rights and Fundamental Freedoms, which may serve to inform or inspire the content of Community Law. For judicial decisions to be legitimate, they must be justified. Where sufficient justification cannot be found within EU Law itself, the CJEU turns to the Law of the Member States.

[64] O. Pollicino, *Corte di giustizia e giudici nazionali: il moto "ascendente", ovverosia l'incidenza delle "tradizioni costituzionali comuni" nella tutela apprestata ai diritti dalla Corte dell'Unione*, in A. Ruggeri and others (coord.), *Crisi dello stato nazionale, dialogo intergiurispudenziale, tutela dei diritti fondamentali*, Giappichelli, Torino, 2015, p. 47.

[65] Ruling of the Court of Justice, 13 December 1979, Hauer, Case C-44/79, CLI:EU:C:1979:290.

Joseph Weiler coined the expression "comparative distillation" to describe such references to common constitutional traditions, beginning with the Nold ruling.[66] In this decision, one highly relevant point appears in paragraph 20 of the Hauser judgement: "It is therefore also necessary, in answering this question, to take into account the guidance provided by the constitutional norms and **practices** of the nine Member States" [emphasis added]. This is the nomos of Herodotus—the lived dimension of Law. Here we find, still in an embryonic stage, the essence of the *écart*. Weiler draws on a biblical vision to describe a legally anti-Kelsenian circumstance. "The Community is its Member States and their citizens. The Community is also an autonomous identity. If one cannot grasp this pluralistic aspect, think of the two thousand years of intense theological reflection that Christianity has made on the Holy Trinity."[67] This constitutional *ethos* does not yet emerge, or only to a small extent, in this first period. In my view, separatist differences remain intact, reflecting fundamental social choices and constituting an important part of the heterogeneous ways of being of societies and systems. They are often part of that social identity to which citizens are especially attached.

From a purely legal perspective, the hermeneutic operation that defines the identification of the common constitutional matrix seems to be resolved in an analysis that involves the combination of three different interpretative methods: comparative, teleological and systematic. Firstly, the use of Comparative Law is, if examined in more detail, a method for interpreting the Law proposed by the Court of Justice. Secondly, the *telos* of this interpretation, already embryonic in *Internationale Handelsgesellschaft*, becomes clear in the previously cited passage from Hauer: to achieve the objectives of the Community legal order in the best possible way. Moreover, it is no coincidence that the clearest epiphany of this process of functionalisation emerges from reasoning in Hauer, a case in which the Court of Justice, having taken into account the constitutional provisions of nine Member States (a circumstance more remarkable than rare) then effectively decided, albeit without explicitly stating so and with a certain degree of assertiveness, that "the best Law", the constitutional

[66] J.H.H. Weiler, *Fundamental Rights and Fundamental Boundaries: on Standards and Values in the Protection of Human Rights*, in N.A. Neuwahl & A. Rosas (eds.), *The European Union and human rights*, The Hague, 1995, and J.H.H. Weiler, *The Constitution of Europe*, cit..

[67] J.H.H. Weiler, *The Constitution of Europe*, cit., p. 211.

tradition most capable of realising the interests and objectives of the Community, was, in that instance, the German principle of proportionality.

The discourse on common constitutional traditions appears to resolve into a rhetorical screen with a strong symbolic dimension, in which the Court of Justice seeks (in the often more fictional than real connection between the proposed solution in a given case and the constitutional experiences of the Member States) an argumentative legitimacy that allows it to continue doing what, in the early period, it alone was able to do unchallenged.[68] The only case approaching Hauer (although without mentioning specific constitutions) is a 2000 judgement,[69] which is a rare, if not unique, 'negative' case: in fact, in § 17 the Court states that a certain principle cannot be "deduced from the constitutional traditions common to the Member States". In virtually all other cases, the CJEU merely asserts that a given principle derives from the common constitutional traditions, almost as if it were a matter of fact. Hauer belongs to the early line of cases, so if there is an exception, it is a rather distant one and certainly not indicative of any recent shift towards more in-depth analysis. Such a hypothesis is, therefore, refuted.

While the foundations for a potential dialogue are laid, the comparative legal method remains superficial. The Court undertakes no real act of comparison. This is a serious constraint on the incipient relational channel.

Nevertheless, among the various possible approaches to resolving 'constitutional' questions, through this argumentative technique, the Court of Justice in Luxembourg tends to favour the one that appears to be most widely shared across national legal systems, precisely because it has a common constitutional foundation and is therefore likely to command the greatest degree of consensus among the majority of Member States. It is clear that the role of common constitutional traditions facilitates intersystemic constitutional dialogue.

Since then, the Court has developed the now well-established method of incorporating those traditions through the recognition of general principles of Law "whose observance the Court ensures", drawing inspiration from the common constitutional traditions of the Member States.

[68] E. Stein, *Lawyers, Judges and the Making of a Transnational Constitution*, in *Am. J. Int'l Law*, 1981, 1.

[69] CJEU, 11 January 2000, Netherlands and Gerard van der Wal v Commission, C-174-189/98 P, EU:C:2000:1.

However, the first logical limit encountered by the comparative method of harmonisation arises from the tension between the functions a rule performs within national systems and within the Community legal order. This is the issue of legal functionalism in Comparative Law, as introduced by Zweigert and Kötz.

As the Comparative Law scholar Jaakko Husa points out, the fundamental question is: "What socio-legal function does the rule perform within its own social context?" "Is it possible to transplant the rule and its underlying social function into the Community context?" However, in the Case Law of the CJEU, the comparative method is not employed to find functional equivalents but rather to identify Member State legislation relevant to an area of EU regulatory competence.

It should be noted that national and European rules may, and often do, serve different functions. The process of European integration, as one of the EU's principal ontological identities, does not seek to replicate the functions of national legal norms at the European level but to formulate new ones. It is clear that national rules, along with their corresponding functions, cannot simply be projected *tout court* onto the supranational level. In response to this challenge, the CJEU has developed two lines of reaction. First, it has consistently held that in exercising their competences, Member States must comply with EU Law, in particular the provisions relating to the principle of non-discrimination. Second, the CJEU developed the doctrine of procedural autonomy (framed by the principles of equivalence and effectiveness) beginning with the Rewe judgement.[70] This gave rise to a further outline of judicial dialogue, operating within the two parameters established and monitored by the Court itself. For now, it is important to recognise that each court will act as a spokesperson for its own principles and identities within its margin of discretion and competence. We will examine this mechanism of cross-fertilisation in detail below.

[70] Judgment of the Court of Justice of 20 February 1979, Rewe-Zentral AG v Bundesmonopolverwaltung für Branntwein, C-120/78, ECLI:EU:C:1979:42.

CHAPTER 9

Second Encounter: Tempering Exclusive Identities Through Ponderation—The *fin de siècle* Ponderation of Interests

Abstract This chapter explores the evolution of EU Law's approach to balancing Community primacy with the protection of national identities and fundamental rights. It discusses the gradual shift from an absolutist conception of primacy towards a system of critical balancing, allowing for exceptions when higher national standards exist, particularly in environmental or consumer protection. Key judgements such as Wachauf, Solange II and Bosphorus are highlighted, illustrating the emergence of 'equivalent protection' and the relational interplay between national and EU legal orders. The chapter also examines the Maastricht Treaty's provisions on constitutional identity, including the Grogan Protocol, reflecting ongoing pluralism and the dynamic redefinition of national identity within the EU's legal and political framework.

From the perspective of economic integration and beginning in the mid-1970s notably with the Rewe judgement, EC Case Law reached a minimal level of dialogue with national systems protecting substantive rights (Judgment of the Court of Justice of 20 February 1979, C-120/78). This dialogue would later assume a primary normative dimension under the revised Article 100a of the EEC Treaty on the harmonisation of legislation, subsequently renumbered as Article 95 of the EC Treaty. The initial rule of reason established by the Rewe judgement gradually extended, albeit slowly, to matters concerning human rights.

© The Author(s), under exclusive license to Springer Nature Switzerland AG 2026

A. Lazari, *Relational Identity in International, Comparative and European Union Law*,
https://doi.org/10.1007/978-3-031-59482-3_9

Keywords Constitutional identity • Maastricht Treaty • European values

What we intend to emphasise here is the progressive tempering of the absolutist primauté and the weighted inclusion of the voice of the Member States.

This dialectical system makes it possible to derogate from the principle of Community primauté, where there are higher standards of protection for certain environmental or consumer rights. Such derogations represent an in melius exception to the standard imposed by the Community measure of positive integration. Although only partial and limited, the point of legal balance is shifting from a static 'rule-exceptions' mechanism to a critical composition of national and Community interests or, in any case, to an area of greater relational exchange.

Indeed, the progressive introduction of a certain degree of pluralism into Community Law corresponded to the equally timid and progressive statement that "the European Economic Community is a community based on the Rule of Law, in the sense that neither the Member States nor their institutions are exempt from control over the conformity of their

---

In the early cited constitutional decisions, the reference to fundamental rights centred on a then rudimentary comparative tool involving common constitutional traditions and the Case Law of the European Court of Human Rights. In the economic sphere of legislative approximation for the achievement of the internal market, the pursuit of greater legislative harmonisation is made conditional upon a dialectical system of critical balancing between national interests and the aforementioned fundamental European freedoms. This operation is carried out by the European Commission and is provided for in paragraphs 3, 4 and 5 of the then Article 95 of the EC Treaty.
This still embryonic dialectical system allows for derogations from the principle of Community primauté where higher standards of protection exist in areas such as the environment or consumer protection. Such derogations represent an in melius exception to the standard imposed by the Community measure of positive integration. Although only partially and limited, the point of legal balance is shifting from a static 'rule-exceptions' mechanism to a critical composition of national and Community interests or, in any case, to an area of greater national dialogue.

acts with the Fundamental Constitutional Charter constituted by the Treaty".[1]

On the eve of the Maastricht Treaty, the *1989 Wachauf ruling* comprehensively systematised the concerns previously raised by the Italian and German courts, affirming definitively that "fundamental rights form part of the general principles of Law whose observance is ensured by the Court of Justice. In safeguarding such rights, the Court of Justice is required to draw inspiration from the common constitutional traditions of the Member States, such that measures incompatible with the fundamental rights recognised by those States' constitutions cannot be accepted within the Community. International instruments concerning the protection of human rights, to which the Member States have contributed or to which they have acceded, may also offer guidance that should be taken into account within the framework of Community Law."[2] With the subsequent German responses in the Eurocontrol case (1981) and Solange II (1986), a period of constitutional peace was established, along with an implicit demarcation line. This ushered in a form of moderated primacy of Community Law, setting a minimum threshold for fundamental rights protection. This is the doctrine of 'equivalent protection', definitively affirmed by the German Federal Constitutional Court in its 2000 decision on the "Bananas Market" case,[3] and by the French Constitutional Council in the 2004 Bioethics case.[4] But there is more: this new comparative approach is not limited to assessing and defining the EU model; it also extends to the hermeneutic activity itself. That is to say, even when dealing nominally with the same principle, such as equality, the CJEU intervenes to impose a form of interpretative primacy, as seen in the *Cordero Alonso* ruling of 2006.[5]

On the *ad extra* side, this approach was later confirmed in the Bosphorus case of 2005,[6] where the European Court of Human Rights adopted a

[1] 23 April 1986, Parti écologiste "Les Verts" v European Parliament, Case 294/83, ECLI:EU:C:1986:166.

[2] Judgment of the CJUE (Third Chamber) of 13 July 1989, Hubert Wachauf v Bundesamt für Ernährung und Forstwirtschaft, C- 5/88, ECLI:EU:C:1989:321.

[3] Judgment of the German Federal Constitutional Court of 7 June 2000, BVerfGE 102.

[4] French Constitutional Council, Decision No. 2004-496 DC of 10 June 2004, Act to confidence in the digital economy, FR:CC:2004:2004.496.DC.

[5] 7 de septiembre de 2006, Mariano Cordero Alonso contra Fondo de Garantía Salarial (Fogasa), C-81/05, ECLI:EU:C:2006:529.

[6] European Court of Human Rights (Grand Chamber) of 30 June 2005, Bosphorus Hava Yolları Turizm ve Ticaret Anonim Şirketi v. Ireland, Application no. 45036/98, ECLI:CE:ECHR:2005:0630JUD00450369.

formula similar to that used earlier by the German Federal Constitutional Court in its *Solange II* judgement. The Strasbourg Court granted a presumption of conformity between EU Law and the ECHR, a presumption that may be rebutted if it is shown that EU Law does not provide protection equivalent to that offered by the Convention. Such was the case in the ECHR's Michaud v. France judgement of 2012.[7]

In this regard, it has been argued that judgements such as Bosphorus[8] may be compared to the landmark Solange case.[9] As we know, the *Solange* method involves recognising a form of 'reserve jurisdiction' (a limiting boundary for national courts) and granting EU Law a kind of conditional primacy: such primacy is accepted only insofar as it does not infringe upon the fundamental constitutional principles of the Member State. In the Bosphorus case, the ECHR declined to review a European Community regulation implementing a United Nations Security Council resolution, despite the fact that the measure in question restricted the right to property. The conclusion reached by the Strasbourg Court was grounded in the comparability between the fundamental rights protection system at EU level and that established by the ECHR. Thus, in the Bosphorus case, the ECHR employed the same formula ('provided that') used by the German Constitutional Court in the *Solange* judgement to introduce a form of presumption of equivalence, thereby avoiding a conflict between jurisdictions.

However, Article 95 of the Maastricht Treaty, now Article 114 TFEU, in the context of legislative harmonisation, and the Wachauf[10] Case Law also envisaged a preventive mechanism aimed at both the co-legislators and the Community Court on both fronts: the Community provision concerning the approximation of legislation in the fields of health, safety, environmental protection and consumer protection must be based on a high level of protection. This underpins the renewed role of the comparative methodology, which is not limited to establishing a minimum

[7] Judgment of the European Court of Human Rights (Fifth Section) of 6 December 2012, Michaud v. France, Application no. 12323/11, ECLI:CE:ECHR:2012:1206JUD001232311.

[8] Judgment of the European Court of Human Rights (Grand Chamber) of 30 June 2005, Bosphorus Hava Yolları Turizm ve Ticaret Anonim Şirketi v. Ireland, Application no. 45036/98, ECLI:CE:ECHR:2005:0630JUD004503698.

[9] German Federal Constitutional Court, 29 May 1974, *Solange I*, 37 BVerfGE 271.

[10] Judgment of the CJUE (Third Chamber) of 13 July 1989, Hubert Wachauf v Bundesamt für Ernährung und Forstwirtschaft, C- 5/88, ECLI:EU:C:1989:321.

common denominator (as is often the case within the protection system organised by the ECHR) but rather measures the distances between the different national systems and selects the most appropriate solution for the "key ontological identities".[11]

The process of integration through Law is increasingly marked by relational dimensions, as it opens itself up to the consideration of the voice of the Other. In some cases, this takes the form of a straightforward reference to judgements external to the Union's legal system (*ad extra*). In others, *ad intra*, the voice of the Other is already incorporated and becomes part of the Community system itself. Once again, this confirms the significance of judicial interactions within these dynamics, as well as the circulation of models (interpretative techniques, approaches and styles) among judges.

9.1 The Identity Écart in the Maastricht Treaty: The Article on Constitutional Identity

Article F(1) of the Treaty on European Union (commonly known as the Maastricht Treaty) stipulates that "the Union shall respect the national identities of its Member States, whose systems of government are founded on the principles of democracy". This initial formulation, which juxtaposes respect for 'national' identity with the definition of the democratic character inherent in that identity, underwent a significant formal evolution with the amendments introduced by the Amsterdam Treaty. Article F(1) was transformed into the more concise Article 6(3), which states simply: "The Union shall respect the national identity of its Member States." At the same time, a new provision—Article 6(1)—was introduced, stating: "The Union is founded on the values of respect for human dignity, freedom, democracy, equality, the rule of law [...] These values are common to the Member States." In the ongoing process of reworking the EU's legal and institutional framework, this wording was further developed by the Lisbon Treaty. The revised version of the Treaty on European Union introduces an even more pronounced *écart*, dividing the concepts into two physically separate articles whose language is marked by notable complexity and density.

The weak link in the triad of 'democracy, the Rule of Law and respect for human rights' (namely the democratic element) served to highlight

[11] S. Rodin, *Constitutional Relevance of Foreign Court Decisions*, in *Am. J. Comp. Law* (2016), p. 816.

the importance of liberal principles as the fundamental pillars upon which the governmental structures of the Member States rest. In my view, this addition carries a clear interpretative significance: the 'national identity' referred to in what is now Article 6 TEU is primarily framed in political and State-related terms. Above all, the addition evidently aims to impose a minimum level of political and constitutional homogeneity, namely the requirement that Member States' systems of government be unequivocally founded on democratic principles.[12]

Thus, it is evident that the notion of 'national identity', since its incorporation into the community framework, has been subject to constant reinterpretation and adjustment, reflecting the dynamics and plurality of the political, legal and cultural traditions that make up the framework of European Union. This development calls for a deeper analysis of its interaction with the other fundamental categories that structure the Union and to consider its role within the democratic and pluralist fabric of Europe.

It can be said immediately that it is not this aspect of Article 4.2 TEU (guaranteeing democratic identity) which raises a problem. This aspect is closely linked to Article 2 of the current Treaty on European Union. According to Cruz Villalón, "the issue arises with the notion of 'singularity', which remains present in that provision today. While its earlier formulations could be understood in terms of a purely 'State identity' (as an abstract category implying equal treatment), the subsequent formulations (in the Constitutional Treaty and the Treaty of Lisbon) now lead us—or at least have come to be understood as leading us—towards the notion of singularity."[13] In parallel, this conception of constitutional identity as national, individual and idiosyncratic aligns closely with the dominant understanding in pluralist theories of EU Law, which we will explore further below. Both the *controlimiti* doctrine and pluralist theory present a distinctly 'interfacial' view of the relationship between EU Law and National Law. However, in the view of national constitutional courts and of 'radical' pluralists, the most accurate way to describe this relationship is to characterise both as autonomous legal orders, each with a 'juxtaposed' scope of application.

[12] P. Cruz Villalón, *La identidad constitucional de los Estados miembros: dos relatos europeos*, in *AFDUAM*, 2013, p. 502.

[13] P. Cruz Villalón, *La identidad constitucional de los Estados miembros: dos relatos europeos*, in *AFDUAM*, 2013, p. 502.

Here, however, it is a question of addressing a more profound issue that we have been dealing with until now: the management of diversity. States are not only general political entities but also possess unique characteristics that distinguish them. This uniqueness lies mainly in the fundamental structures of their constitutions, which reflect a particular identity. Thus, each State's constitution incorporates elements that render it unique within the context of its political framework, setting it apart from other features of State entities which, by contrast, tend to converge around shared values, constitutional traditions and general principles. These latter elements will not necessarily coincide over time, nor should they, in a pluralist context. There will be varying degrees of convergence and divergence, and one of the aims of Comparative Law is precisely to measure these distances. A distinct identity does not imply absolute or unrepeatable singularity, but it does exclude any form of uniformity. For instance, Article 4(2) TEU explicitly mentions that a Member State's federal or politically decentralised structure, while not unique in itself, clearly reflects an aspect of singularity and the legitimate choices made by that State. This example highlights that respect for the fundamental constitutional structures of each Member State lies at the core of the guarantee of its constitutional identity. The process of integration involves, structurally, the projection of national constitutions to the supranational level. Integration is a 'means' through which the constitutional project of the Member States is effectively realised.[14] It also signifies that this respect for diversity is embedded in the genetic code of the Union, in continuous tension with Article 2 TEU (both as it was initially formulated and, in my view, how it should be interpreted).[15] For this reason, rather than resistance according to a juxtaposed *Aut Aut* model (characteristic of earlier Encounters), this should always be understood as operating in tension with Article 2 TEU.[16] The initial dualistic rhetoric of both the Court of Justice of the European Union and the national constitutional courts represents, at this point, a

[14] A. J. Menéndez Menéndez expresses this in terms of resistance in *Una concepción alternativa de la identidad constitucional en el derecho comunitario: de las excepciones idiosincráticas a la resistencia constitucional colectiva*, in *AFDUAM* 17 2013, p. 563.

[15] A. J. Menéndez Menéndez, *Una concepción alternativa de la identidad constitucional en el derecho comunitario: de las excepciones idiosincráticas a la resistencia constitucional colectiva*, in *AFDUAM* 17 2013, p. 562.

[16] A. J. Menéndez Menéndez expresses this in terms of resistance in *Una concepción alternativa de la identidad constitucional en el derecho comunitario: de las excepciones idiosincráticas a la resistencia constitucional colectiva*, in *AFDUAM* 17 2013, p. 562.

reproduction of an outdated, exclusionary identity, which makes a profound understanding of the relationship between the two legal orders impossible. "The relationship between a transnational judge and a national judge; therefore a relationship of collaboration in which the sense of one's own identity focuses not so much on one being a national body and the other a transnational one but rather on the common belonging to the judiciary, so as to avoid sterile conflicts and instead strengthen the respective capacity to enforce the law. It is therefore not a zero-sum game but a positive-sum one, in which both parties are benefited."[17] Respect for 'national identity' is not merely a generalisation or codification of Member States' public interests, as in the previously discussed black-box mentality, but rather the expression of the Union's *grundnorm* of identity, which is of axiological and normative importance, even overriding economic freedoms. Respect for constitutional identity means that not on account of the idiosyncrasies of the Republic of Austria but by virtue of the value the Union places on internal diversity, the choice of a Member State's form of government becomes a matter for the *communitas* itself. Accordingly, all decisions flowing from that choice (such as the prohibition on the use of noble titles in personal names) must equally be regarded as such. This entails upholding a principle of relational *primauté*, whereby the constitutional arrangements of Member States must be respected insofar as they can be meaningfully related to the axiological framework set out in Article 2 TEU. The demand that Union Law refrain from interfering with the essential singularity of the State is not so much out of external respect for a peculiar national constitutional identity but rather out of respect for the European constitutional identity itself, which is enriched by such diversity. Seen in this light, the tension between the content of Article 4(2) TEU and Article 2 TEU opens up an *écart* from which both benefit: it is, I would say (as we have already seen) what Jullien calls a means. It is hard to disagree with Menéndez Menéndez's idea that the protection of national identity is a principle of the Union, a manifestation of the Union's pluralistic and complex identity.[18] This complex situation requires ever-closer cooperation between judicial orders, especially among supreme or constitutional courts, which increasingly confront each other with references to

[17] J.H.H. Weiler, *The Constitution of Europe*, cit., p. 123.

[18] A. J. Menéndez Menéndez, *Una concepción alternativa de la identidad constitucional en el derecho comunitario: de las excepciones idiosincráticas a la resistencia constitucional colectiva*, in *AFDUAM* 17 2013, p. 563.

each other's Case Law while also multiplying encounters and contacts. Moreover, it requires a paradigmatic shift in the understanding of these relationships, where one element (the supranational) cannot exist without the other (the State), and the latter, if it belongs to a *communitas*, exists only in relation to its context, unless it wishes to 'live alone' once again. The consequent influences, the interconnections established, the reciprocal legitimacy, the reference to comparison as a method of interpretation have led scholars to talk about a relational identity. Just two decades ago, jurist Louis Favoreu wrote: "*Le corti costituzionali sono l'ultimo baluardo della sovranità degli Stati*" and that "*non possono essere controllate dall'esterno*".[19] Now, however, constitutional courts no longer have the final word; rather, they are part of a broader dialogue that involves both lower and higher courts.[20] The choral nature of the review of compliance with rights enshrined in both national and supranational charters transforms the role of constitutional court rulings, as it reinforces one particular element: the scrutiny of reasonableness and proportionality. Constitutional courts are increasingly required to compare and balance institutions, rules and their application at both national and supranational levels. "*Ora, in presenza di doppie tutele, si accentua il compito di comparare, ponderare, valutare la proporzionalità e la ragionevolezza delle diverse opzioni interpretative. Solo in questo modo, infatti, si possono tenere sotto controllo i controllori ed evitare loro scelte arbitrarie.*"[21] They also have initial competence to define the constitutional identity which will then be transmitted by a review pursuant to Article 2 TEU to the CJEU.

Decades ago, Louis Favoreu posed the pessimistic question: "*si, dans quelques années, nous serons en mesure de donner un sens à l'**enchevêtrement** des compétences dans le domaine de la protection des droits fondamentaux en Europe*" [emphasis added].[22] Maria Rosaria Ferrarese has observed that the proliferation of judicial and 'quasi-judicial' bodies creates a paradox: a "*riduzione del* [...] *'ruolo' delle Corti costituzionali e, al tempo stesso, il loro*

[19] L. Favoreu, Cours constitutionnelles nationales et Cour européenne des droits de l'homme, en Revue universelle des droits de l'homme (RUDH), vol. 15, n.° 1-2, 2003, pp. 1–6.

[20] S. Cassese, *Fine della solitudine delle corti costituzionali, ovvero il dilemma del porcospino, in Atti Sc. Mor.*, 2015, pp. 15–25.

[21] S. Cassese, *Fine della solitudine delle corti costituzionali, ovvero il dilemma del porcospino, in Atti Sc. Mor.*, 2015, p. 25.

[22] L. Favoreu, *Avertissement - article n. 2*, in *Revue internationale de droit comparé*, 1981, pp. 251–253.

'trionfo'".[23] The increase in institutions authorised to deliver the final ruling shows that it is not so much who has the last word that matters but who takes part in the dialogue and how they do so.[24]

9.2 The Identity Écart in the Maastricht Treaty: The 'Grogan Protocol'

The progressive axiologisation of both EU and national legal orders is evident not only in Article F(1) of the Treaty on European Union but also in the defence of national identities found even within the Protocols to the Maastricht Treaty.

This collection of protocols and declarations was described by Curtin as an attempt to 'hijack' the *acquis communautaire*, and within this dense landscape of hard and soft law sources, the Grogan case deserves particular attention, especially in light of its subsequent developments. The Grogan Protocol (No. 17) stipulates that nothing in the Treaty on European Union, the Treaties establishing the European Communities, or in any Treaties or acts amending or supplementing them shall affect the application in Ireland of Article 40.3.3 of the Irish Constitution. This Protocol is rooted in the famous Grogan judgement, delivered in a preliminary ruling procedure, in which the CJEU declared that "the medical termination of pregnancy, performed in accordance with the legislation of the State in which it is carried out, constitutes a service within the meaning of Article 60 of the Treaty".

This judicial saga led Ireland to insist on the introduction of Protocol No. 17. Curtin rightly highlighted the danger of such a protocol as it potentially offered all Member States the possibility of obtaining a similar document, demanding respect for a specific provision of their national constitution. This spectre of a Pandora's box being opened is, of course, deeply destabilising and strikes at the very core of the singularity of Community Law, as well as at the carefully cultivated image (since the early 1970s) that the Community takes the protection of human rights seriously. However, this concern has faded over time since notably the

[23] M.R. Ferrarese, *Dal "verbo" legislativo a chi dice l' ultima parola": Le Corti costituzionale e la rete giudiziaria*, in *Annuario di diritto comparato e di studi legislativi*, 2011, pp. 63–87.

[24] M. Wendel, *Lisbon before the courts. Comparative perspectives*, in J. M. Beneyto & I. Pernice (eds.), *Europe's constitutional challenges in the light of the recent case law of national constitutional courts*, Nomos, Baden-Baden, 2011, p. 65–104.

relational dimension of constitutional identity in the Eighth Amendment of the Irish Constitution did not arise from judicial tension but rather as an expression of popular sovereignty, as we have already seen in the Greek popular referendum. This time, however, the particular expression of popular sovereignty was not directed towards the Union's legal order but rather towards a previous manifestation of identity at a certain historical moment (see below the caveat on Tacitus in the Introduction), which was not set in stone but could be altered by the people through a subsequent constitutional amendment.

Accordingly, in May 2018, a referendum was held that approved the replacement of Article 40.3.3, gaining a 66% majority. Far from being a spontaneous whim or political convenience, the amendment should be understood as the final step in a long process culminating in a modification of an aspect of Ireland's constitutional identity.

CHAPTER 10

Second Encounter: Tempering Exclusive Identities Through Ponderation—The Mechanisms of Relational Identity in the Twenty-First Century

Abstract This chapter examines the role of cross-fertilisation in shaping general principles of EU Law and common constitutional traditions, highlighting the importance of judicial dialogue and comparative methodology. These are juridical elements that significantly go beyond the positivistic sphere of which we have spoken in the *pars destruens*. Rather than imposing harmonisation or assimilation, the EU paradigm encourages a dynamic, circular exchange of legal ideas, allowing national identities and constitutional traditions to inform and enrich the Union's legal order. This part argues that conflicts and divergences are not pathological but essential for integration and that the legitimacy of constitutional identity claims depends on their presentation within a pluralistic framework of overlapping authorities.

Keywords Cross-fertilisation • Openness *ad intra* and *ad extra* • CJEU

All this legislative and jurisprudential material leads us to emphasise the mechanisms of dialogical accommodation, whereby the voices of the Member States are integrated into the interpretative activity of the Court of Justice of the European Union (CJEU). These include the set of

© The Author(s), under exclusive license to Springer Nature Switzerland AG 2026

A. Lazari, *Relational Identity in International, Comparative and European Union Law*,
https://doi.org/10.1007/978-3-031-59482-3_10

Protocols and Declarations introduced by the Maastricht Treaty, Article 34 of the Treaty on European Union (TEU), all provisions concerning national laws and practices contained in the Charter of Fundamental Rights of the European Union (CFREU), the Charter's explanations and, finally, Article 4 TEU following the enactment of the Lisbon Treaty. It is worth reiterating that these are not merely occasional mechanisms; they represent manifestations of relational identity. What is therefore required is a contextual reading that reveals the existential openness of EU Law and the need for national/supranational boundaries to be nurtured within the EU framework, not in terms of closure (of identity) but of openness. The main difference compared to the First Part lies precisely in this cluster of mechanisms, which are not limited to the general principles governing relations between Member States and the Community legal order but extend to the Union's identity itself. The first articles of the current Treaty on European Union (TEU) make this clear. Article 1 TEU talks of Unity in Diversity, understood in a relational sense; Article 2 TEU sets out the values of the Union, common to all Member States. Article 3 TEU enshrines the following Union objectives: "It shall respect its rich cultural and linguistic diversity." Article 4 TEU significantly regulates, within the same provision, competence, respect for national identity and the duty of loyal cooperation. Article 5 TEU specifies the division of competences as well as the principles of Subsidiarity and Proportionality, which can only be properly understood when read together. Finally, in Article 6 TEU, the importance of common constitutional traditions emerges as general principles of the community order. The relational apparatus extends to the entire body of EU Law and in particular to Articles 52(4) and 53 of the Charter of Fundamental Rights of the European Union.

But as we have been seeing since the beginning of this Second Part, it lies within the very identity of the Union to provide mechanisms for the coordination of the supranational paradigm with national models, of which the very structure of the EU directive is yet another example.

Such interference may seem pathological in a properly functioning inter-order system, but in reality it is possible to find analogies in many other constitutional cases. The European Union is unique in this, and these interactions between the judiciary and politics confirm the non-mechanical nature of the interpretative dynamics (the judge is not the *bouche de la loi*) and the 'collective' nature of interpretation understood as an enterprise involving all actors operating in a constitutional system. This creates disagreements, responses and even 'conflicts', but it would be wrong to conceive of these conflicts as pathological, as Advocate General Ćapeta recalls in her oft-quoted conclusions.[1] On the contrary, conflicts are natural and fundamental in the constitutional dynamics of any political entity, and the European Union does not deviate from this trend. The main difference from the experience of the United States is probably the vertical/federal path of conflict.

Finally, this set of relational embedding clauses will not necessarily usher in a more cooperative era; on the contrary, divergences remain crucial to the development of European Union Law. Whether the framework will succeed in its aims remains to be seen, but in any case, much will depend on the interaction with other courts operating at both national and international levels (namely national Supreme/Constitutional Courts and the European Court of Human Rights), particularly in relation to the application of the clauses included in the Charter of Fundamental Rights of the European Union. In this respect, once again, the European Union will continue to suffer from its democratic deficit, as the vagueness of provisions supposedly central to the system (see Article 52 of the Charter) ultimately seems to confirm the significant role of the judiciary in the multilevel framework. What will not change, therefore, are the so-called conflicts. What should change is how to interpret them from the perspective of Comparative Law.

10.1 The Critical Comparative Methodology in the CJEU

At the end of the 1990s, the CJEU clearly experienced a new comparative methodology, typical of Common Law systems, but difficult to comprehend for practitioners of Civil Law. The conclusions drawn by some Advocates General explain this new approach: in particular, those presented by Advocate General Trstenjak in the Audiolux case and by Maduro in the FIAMM case. The first opinion is particularly relevant and is quoted verbatim: "According to one definition put forward in legal literature, the general principles include the fundamental provisions of unwritten primary Community Law which are inherent to the legal order of the European Communities itself or are common to the legal orders of the Member States. In principle, a distinction can be drawn between general principles of Community Law in the narrow sense, namely those which are

[1] In Advocate General Ćapeta's Conclusions, 5 June 2025, Commission v. Hungary, C-769/22. ECLI:EU:C:2025:408.

developed exclusively from the spirit and system of the EC Treaty and relate to specific points of Community Law, and those general principles which are common to the legal and constitutional orders of the Member States. Whereas the first category of general principles can be derived directly from primary Community Law, the Court essentially uses a critical legal comparison in order to determine the second category, which does not, however, amount to using the lowest common denominator method" [emphasis added].[2]

The second conclusions formulated by Poiares Maduro refer, instead, to the other nerve point of community construction: the community model of responsibility.

"Although the Court of Justice must certainly be guided by the most characteristic provisions of the systems of domestic law, it must above all ensure that it adopts a solution appropriate to the needs and specific features of the Community legal system. In other words, the Court has the task of drawing on the legal traditions of the Member States in order to find an answer to similar legal questions arising under Community law that both respects those traditions and is appropriate to the context of the Community legal order. From that point of view, even a solution adopted by a minority may be preferred if it best meets the requirements of the Community system. To be persuaded that this is so, one need only recall the example of the ... '*Vertrauensschutzprinzip*' which was enshrined in Community law even though it occurred only in German law. Hence, the fact that only Spanish and French law provide for the public authorities to incur liability by reason of a lawful legislative act cannot prevent such liability being recognised in Community law. The decisive question is whether such a solution would best meet the specific needs of the Community legal system. That does not mean that the principle of public authorities' liability for a lawful legislative act should be enshrined in the Community legal order inasmuch as it would appear to be the best legal solution, and as such must be adopted in the Community legal order. Its enshrinement in Community law can only be the result of a comparison of the mechanisms adopted in this respect by the different national legal

[2] Conclusions of Advocate General Verica Trstenjak submitted 30 June 2009, Case C-101/08 Audiolux et al., ECLI:EU:C:2009:410. ECLI:EU:C:2011:559, endorsed in the successive Opinions of Advocate General Verica Trstenjak, 8 September 2011, Case C-282/10, Maribel Domínguez v. Centre informatique du Centre ouest Atlantique v. Préfet de la région Centre.

systems in order to identify the solution best suited to the particular requirements of the Community legal order."[3] The conclusions put forward by Advocate General Kokott in the Akzo (2010) case shed further light on this issue.[4] In her view, although the principle is recognised only in a minority of Member States, it may nonetheless constitute a general principle of EU Law insofar as it reflects a mission entrusted to the EU by the Treaties' authors or aligns with a broader trend in the protection of fundamental rights. Such was the case with the principle of non-discrimination on the grounds of age: as indicated by Article 19 TFEU, the fight against age-based discrimination has, since the Treaty of Amsterdam, been one of the objectives pursued by the authors of the Treaties.

"The comparative law method is not tantamount to finding the 'lowest common denominator [...] This shows that the comparative law method and teleological interpretation are deeply intertwined. With a view to ascertaining the different interpretative options available in national legal systems, the ECJ will first have recourse to the comparative law method in order to identify them. Next, it will choose the option which is best suited to the attainment of the objectives pursued by EU law," argues Lenaert, the current president of the Luxembourg Court.[5]

In considering a particular case, the CJEU will want to avoid 'going too far' and therefore can opt for a solution that is not necessarily the most ambitious, considered from the exclusive angle of EU Law, but which has the advantage of being compatible with the traditions of the Member States and not prejudicing special sensitivities in some Member States. Similarly, when assessing the compatibility of a national measure with EU Law, the Court of Justice will gauge the 'temperature' of the legal systems of the Member States in order to determine the credibility and 'acceptability' of its decision across the entire EU. From this it follows that in the absence of legislative harmonisation measures, a lack of consensus favours choosing a normative solution that does not risk facing misunderstanding or resistance in some Member States, resistance that

[3] Conclusions of Advocate General M. Poiares Maduro presented on 20 February 2008, Joined Cases C-120/06 P and C-121/06 P, ECLI:EU:C:2008:98.

[4] Conclusions of Advocate General Juliane Kokott in Case C-550/07, *Akzo Nobel Chemicals Ltd and Akcros Chemicals Ltd v European Commission*, paragraph 95.

[5] K. Lenaerts, *The constitutional traditions common to the Member States: the comparative law method*, in *EUnited in diversity: between common constitutional traditions and national identities*, Riga, Latvia—2–3 September 2021, Conference proceedings, p. 23.

could undermine the effectiveness and uniform application of EU Law. This comparative process took place in the context of State liability, with the transition from the Spanish objective model adopted in the *Francovich* decision to the French system of *faute administrative*, developed through the sufficiently serious breach criterion in the *Brasserie de Pêcheur/ Factortame III* judgement of March 1996. To achieve this, the Court of Justice held that "since the Treaty contains no provision expressly and specifically governing the consequences of breaches of Community Law by Member States, it is for the Court, in fulfilment of the task conferred upon it by Article 164 of the Treaty [...], to rule on such matters [...] in accordance with the fundamental principles of the Community legal order and, where appropriate, the general principles common to the legal systems of the Member States."[6] Therefore, according to the CJEU, Article 164 concerns legal comparison. "The judgment will 'tend to be the result of "cross" contributions of different legal systems'" or, in other words, the comparative method in its thoughtful version serves the crucial cause in the process of Community integration of the tension between Unity and Diversity. "That approach produces cross-fertilization and mutual influence between the EU and national legal orders, thereby creating a 'common legal space' and giving concrete meaning to the motto 'United in diversity'."[7]

This new 'critical comparative approach' follows the Case Law of the Court of Justice in relation to the pairing Market Freedoms-Protection of the Person. At first, Comparative Law serves to underpin through fundamental rights the weighting of economic freedoms with fundamental rights. The initial totemic vision (rule [Article 28 EC]—exception [Article 30 EC]) mediated solely by the proportionality principle is no longer upheld. However, this theoretical and jurisprudential construction only captures part of a much more complex reality.

[6] Conclusions of Advocate General Giuseppe Tesauro, presented on 28 November 1995, Joined Cases C-46/93 And C-48/93. ECLI:EU:C:1995:412.

[7] K. Lenaerts, *The constitutional traditions common to the Member States: the comparative law method*, in *EUnited in diversity: between common constitutional traditions and national identities*, Riga, Latvia—2–3 September 2021, Conference proceedings, *EUnited in diversity: between common constitutional traditions and national identities*, p. 30.

10.2 The Mechanism of Cross-Fertilisation and the Relational Dynamic *Ad Intra* and *Ad Extra*

The only way for the national/Community/international circulation system to function (even while rendering these boundaries porous) is to maintain its openness both towards national constitutional courts and international tribunals, through a relational conception of autonomy. Otherwise, we risk returning to the topic of rights protected by the European Union as hegemonic vectors. The exclusionary nature of certain claims of constitutional identities hidden behind the shield of the democratic factor cannot be countered by the Court of Justice if it is later reproduced *ad extra* towards accession to the European Convention on Human Rights, and the consequent role played by the European Court of Human Rights,[8] or the resolutions of the United Nations Security Council. The mechanism of cross-fertilisation is ontologically a system of opening and closing gates to the legal circulation that can work by transposing rules, general principles, constitutional traditions and even values from the inside out and vice versa. It will be repeated many times over the following sections that cross-fertilisation is circular and two-directional. We will see that the principles of general and common constitutional traditions are fuelled by national legal heritage and, once developed within the EU's identity by the CJEU, return to national contexts. This means that, as argued by Scholtes,[9] constitutional identity is not a binary switch: it is a *sliding scale* with respect to a continuum of relative authority. The same mechanism applies to Article 2 TEU, the axiological reservoir of the European Union, with a twofold caveat: first, that the absolute principles of autonomy and primacy must be understood in a relational and open manner; and second, that conversely, anything that asserts a *prius* without passing through the filter of the *communitas* of Article 2 TEU (in the case of values) or of

[8] In this respect, the ECHR's contribution to the integration process is crucial. B. De Witte makes a relevant contribution in *The role of the ECHR in the evolution of EU law*, in *Maastricht Journal of European and Comparative Law*, 2025, pp. 111–119, setting out three fundamental contributions *ad extra* of the court in Strasbourg: "the ECHR became a 'semi-binding' source of fundamental rights within the EU legal order, both before and after the Lisbon Treaty; the ECHR acts as a reference point in EU legislation; the ECHR acts as a normative standard in the EU's external and enlargement policy; and the ECHR is a source of law for national authorities and courts when applying EU law."

[9] J. Scholtes, *The Abuse of Constitutional Identity in the European Union*, Oxford University Press, 2023, p. 211.

Article 6 TEU (in the case of constitutional traditions, general principles, and the Union's openness to the European Convention on Human Rights) constitutes a return to hegemony. This short circuiting of both State and community origin would prevent judicial cross-fertilisation and constitute a *vulnus* to the Union's core principle of diversity.

10.3 Epistemic Requirements

The term cross-fertilisation refers not so much to the assertion of one specific rule (in this case, State liability) over others but rather to the cultural circulation process that leads to the affirmation of that particular rule at national level. Of course, this movement is not only top-down (from the Court of Justice to national courts) but also bottom-up. Both directions influence one another: the first sets the paradigm to be combined with national nerve endings. And in creating such a paradigm, the model chosen is not necessarily the most 'advanced' but rather the *paradeigma* most amenable to integration with the majority of national systems. In this case, the *prius* is not intended to impose (to classify, separate or exclude) but rather to be accepted. The construction of the initial *prius* depends on the holder of competence or power (in matters of State liability, the Court of Justice; in constitutional identity, the constitutional courts). And if it does not work, if it does not conjugate well with national inflections, it will be updated, refined and modified. Comparative legal scholarship must interpret these *écarts* and read them as discrepancies. We just need to read certain passages from the Court's rulings to understand how indispensable comparison is for assessing the presence of principles common to the Member States and to grasp how the comparative method is used by the judges themselves, correctly and with awareness.[10] It is worth anticipating that this mechanism has been judicially applied in the context of the Union's general principles, only to a limited extent with regard to common constitutional traditions, and is still in the process of being developed in relation to the Union's values.

[10] D. Chalmers, *Judicial Preferences and the Community Legal Order*, in *Modern Law Review* 60 (2), 1997, 191: «*The logic is not consociational, but one of control. It entails the construction by the Court of Justice of positive legal institutions in a more detailed and extensive manner than previously, with a corresponding loss of autonomy for national courts whose role would be reduced to that of fact-finding agencies and administrators of the Court's judgments.*»

The phenomenon of cross-fertilisation is, in fact, distinct from the operation of legal transplantation (which we analysed in the First Part), because "it implies that an external stimulus promotes an evolution within the receiving legal system", meaning that domestic development is a different yet organic outcome of an external stimulus.[11] This circulation involves two elements: the external one (the EU paradigm of Member State liability) and the national discipline of State liability. Unity in diversity, we might say.

The cross-fertilisation of the community paradigm of responsibility bears witness to the circulation of models of State responsibility but also to the cultural tensions found in the community conceptual paradigm.[12] In cultural cross-fertilisation, not only are the 'successes' of applying the *Brasserie* framework analysed but also the resistances and tensions between conceptual paradigms: the State and the community. However, it is not limited solely to the analysis of Case Law where aspects of EU Law appear; it is also possible to glimpse the extent to which the EU paradigm is accepted beyond these cases by comparatively analysing State-level acceptance or resistance.

However, this is not about studying a phenomenon of legal transplantation; on the contrary, it involves analysing some hidden or lesser-known aspects of European cultural convergence.[13] Cross-fertilisation is not a legal phenomenon comparable to the harmonisation of national legislations, as provided for in Articles 94 and 95 of the EC Treaty; rather, it is a more complex cultural phenomenon that operates beneath the legal surface.

From the perspective of comparatists attentive to cultural circulation, the main objection to EU Law, particularly to the system of State liability, lies in a deep conceptual layer, namely the idea that the EU paradigm would deny or limit certain "habits, customs and practices" that remain impermeable to any external interference.[14] However, the equally pro-

[11] J. Bell, *Mechanism for Cross-fertilisation of Administrative Law in Europe*, in *New Directions in European Public Law*, cit., p. 147.

[12] C. Lyons, *Perspective on Convergence Within European Integration*, in AA.VV., *Convergencia y Divergence in European Public Law*, edited by P. Beaumont, C. Lyons, N. Walker, Hart Publishing, 2002, p. 88.

[13] C. Lyons, *Perspective on Convergence Within European Integration*, in AA.VV., *Convergence and Divergence in European Public Law*, cit., p. 95: «*The process of convergence is just as amorphous in its many manifestations as national legal cultures can be.*»

[14] C. Harlow, *Voices of Difference in a Plural Community*, cit., 6.

found phenomenon of cross-fertilisation does not in itself exclude the notion of Legrand's *mentalité*[15] or Sacco's cryptotype,[16] since, indeed, it reveals precisely what Sacco suggests. The diachronic and synchronic analysis of national systems shows that each system is characterised by specific historical and constitutional connotations, but at the same time, no system is entirely set in stone and isolated. The new EU paradigm, along with porous national identities, promotes not only the construction of a new way of interpreting the legal world[17] but also a substantial change in the exchange and circulation of legal models.[18]

The artificially self-sufficient world of Separation Law and nineteenth-century codes (where the circulation of national models was actually more complicated) has been succeeded by a legal system in continuous tension with other national models.

"In looking at some of the instances of convergence here I see a system of constitutional interactions and relationships operative both beneath and above the more formal and overt ones which are well recognised."[19] *Cultural analysis of the Law does not therefore flow only towards the defence (exclusionary even) of national identities.*[20] Cross-fertilisation is a virtuous circulation mechanism, but the other side of the cross-fertilisation coin is undeniable: it is slow; it depends on the absorption of community impulse, and it is often a source of disparity and uncertainty. These are the relational discrepancies of *écarts.*

[15] "*Specifically, rules and concepts do little to disclose that legal systems are but the surface manifestation of legal cultures and, indeed, of culture 'tout court'*"; so says Legrand, P., *European Legal Systems Are Not Converging*, in *International and Comparative Law Quarterly*, 1996, 56.

[16] "*Esiste dunque un diritto non prodotto dallo Stato, non autoritativo, non previsto da nessuna costituzione. […] Questo diritto entra spesso nel bagaglio dell'interprete in modo inavvertito. Si parla al riguardo di crittotipi. Si può parlare, al proposito, di diritto muto*"; R. Sacco, L'interpretazione: dato oggettivo e spirito dell'interprete», en Derrida, J. - Vattimo, G. (eds.), Diritto, giustizia e interpretazione, Laterza, Bari, 1998, 125.

[17] Cf. S. Cassese, *L'arena pubblica. Nuovi paradigmi per lo Stato*, in *Riv. trim. dir. pubbl.*, 2001, 645: «*al centro non c'è più lo Stato, ma l'Unione, che opera, però, secondo il modello della* indirect rule, *del 'governo, attraverso altri 'governi'.*»

[18] See La struttura istituzionale del nuovo diritto comune europeo: competizione e circolazione dei modelli giuridici, Università degli Studi di Trento, Trento, 1996.

[19] Cft. among many others, R. Caranta, *Learning from the Neighbours: Public Law Remedies and Homogenization from Bottom Up*, in *Maastricht Journ. Europ. Comp. Law*, 1997, 220 ss.

[20] Sempre C. Lyons, *Perspective on Convergence Within European Integration*, in AA.VV., *Convergence and Divergence in European Public Law*, cit., 88.

On the other hand, there is an ongoing debate about the impermeability of the deep cultural structure to perceive EU impulses. This is a conceptual operation that is not formally imposed—unlike, for example, Directives No. 1999/34 and 85/374/252 on faulty goods. It relates to cultural traditions, social customs, conceptions of the State and, ultimately, relational identity. To fully understand the underlying dialectic in the system of State liability, the contribution of Comparative Law is essential. Only through a dynamic analysis can we avoid the dangerous temptation to enclose national identity or to describe the circulation of models in terms of cross-infection.[21] This is the new task for comparative and EU legal scholarship. Therefore, rather than speaking of a 'system', a term more properly applicable to established national disciplines, it is preferable to talk of an EU paradigm or *paradeigma*.[22] With regard to traditional systems at the national level, this term designates a main matrix that gives shape to the successive and necessary national operation.[23]

This theoretical construction fits well with Roughan's argument, which understands relationality as linked to the very construction of authority. Here, we are not really dealing with multiple irreconcilable claims to *ultimate* authority. In these views, there is always a *prius*—a prior point of reference to look to ultimately. For this reason, the multiple claims to ultimate authority are seen as 'epistemically incommensurable' and do not allow for comparative analyses of the constitutive interactions. Any attempt to understand authority in this way is, in that understanding, bound to be disrupted by constitutional actors invoking their claims to ultimate authority. These interactions are disruptions. Rather than seeing authority itself as relative, they acknowledge a pragmatic need for coordination and mutual accommodation between different seats of authority. Within the Union, authority is limited and constituted through Others: it is relative from the moment a State joins the Union. "The construction of authority, even within domestic constitutional sites, then, indeed no longer seems

[21] Again C. Harlow, *Francovich and the Problem of the Disobedient State*, in European Law Journal, 1996, pp. 199–225.

[22] The Greek word directly calls for the "verbal etymus" (*paradeiknumi*), which is an action of comparison or confrontation, which, as will be seen, is also essential in the functioning of the Community system of State responsibility.

[23] A. Lazari, *Paradeigma e Logos: la responsabilità del legislatore ed i destini dell'Europa*, in *Rivista Diritto Civile*, 2002, pp. 109–168; A. Lazari, *La cross-fertilisation y la formación del paradigma comunitario de responsabilidad del Estado: «el esquema de la crisis»*, in *Revista de Derecho Comunitario Europeo*, 2005, pp. 177–225.

purely monadic, but increasingly relational, and the balance of authority can swing from one constitutional site to another under changed circumstances."[24]

The conclusion to be drawn from such a conception of relative authority is that the legitimacy of constitutional identity claims is tied to the manner in which these claims are presented. Given their situation within a pluralistic configuration of overlapping authorities, constitutional identity claims should not be viewed as peremptory assertions of national constitutional supremacy but rather as arguments aimed at enhancing relative authority. The key point is that we are no longer dealing with a legal system in which each component expresses itself in absolute and mutually exclusive terms. Instead, we have an open and complex system, where the rule arises from interactions between components. National courts cannot simply assert their constitutional identity as a means to put an end to the discussion, just as the CJEU cannot avoid dialogue with its national counterparts regarding its doctrine of primacy. Both are distinct legal orders with different elements of legitimacy affecting their relative authority. This is the epistemic basis for understanding the functioning of cross-fertilisation, which we will apply to the three sections of one of the general principles of Law, to common constitutional traditions and to values.

10.4 The Cross-Fertilisation Mechanism in the General Principles of EU Law

Coinciding with the historic date of the Maastricht Treaty negotiations, the Court of Justice issued the *Francovich* ruling,[25] which set out the requirements for State liability arising from the failure to transpose a directive. These are, first, that the outcome prescribed by the Directive entails the conferment of rights in favour of individuals; second, that the content of these rights can be identified based on the provisions of the Directive; and third, that there is a causal link between the State's failure to comply with its obligation and the damage suffered by the affected persons. These three conditions represent the *paradeigma* that must be reconciled within

[24] N. Roughan, *Authorities. Conflicts, Cooperation, and Transnational Legal Theory*, Oxford University Press, Oxford, 2013, p. 89.

[25] CJEU, 19 November 1991, C-6 and C-9/90, *Francovich* et al. v *Italian Republic*, ECLI:EU:C:1991:428.

the national systems of administrative liability, always within the framework established by the principles of equivalence and effectiveness.[26]

The foundations were laid for the emergence of the new paradigm of State liability, which was consummated with the *Factortame* ruling of 1996.[27] Its requirements apply when the breached rule of Community law aims to confer rights, the violation is sufficiently established and there is a direct causal link between this violation and the harm suffered by individuals. This jurisprudence of the Community judge is limited to elevating to the status of a general principle a specific situation set out in the 1991 Decision. The focus is on national judges, who, after 4 years of golden silence, begin to properly receive the Community's message. However, the assimilation process reveals a profound rethinking of the national legal disciplines themselves: judges do not simply apply the basic framework of Community Case Law but adapt this framework to national coordinates. The analysis of national decisions, the most sensible doctrinal proposals and State reforms clearly indicates a very deep general phenomenon that goes beyond the mere application of a Community principle at the national level.

The emergence of a beneficial circulation of legal models, directly or indirectly fostered by Community Law, does not instantly erase the mindset underlying the normative structure of the various national legal systems. However, the historical trajectory ultimately leads to the discovery of elements of strong convergence among the national legal orders: "traditional attitudes affect cross-fertilisation profoundly."[28] Thanks to the new Community paradigm, the European landscape (marked by the patchwork of national reactions to the European impetus) is interpreted anew. The deepening of these suggestive cultural factors does not move towards a bitter defence of national mindset or the democratic conception of the State; on the contrary, the terms proposed in Harlow's citation will be reversed ("familiar words like fault, with apparently similar or even identical meanings when translated, may be differently understood and

[26] Cf. A. Lazari, *Paradeigma e logos: la responsabilità dello Stato legislatore e i destini dell'Europa*, in *Riv. dir. civ.*, 2002, pp. 109–136.

[27] Judgment of the Court of Justice of 5 March 1996, Brasserie du Pêcheur SA v. Bundesrepublik Deutschland and The Queen v. Secretary of State for Transport, ex parte: Factortame Ltd et al., C-46/93 and C-48/93, ECLI:EU:C:1996:79.

[28] J.W.F. Allison, *Transplantation and Cross-fertilisation in European Public Law*, in *New Directions in European Public Law*, *Law*, J. Beatson & T. Tridimas (eds), Hart Publishing, Oxford, 1998, p. 174.

applied in different legal cultures"[29]). Although it is established that the term fault acquires different, sometimes contradictory, meanings within national legal systems, it is equally true that by studying the phenomenon of cultural cross-fertilisation, we see that consolidated jurisprudential arrangements or doctrinal proposals which at first glance appear different reveal a substantial commonality of views. Unveiling the underlying substantial affinity is a more difficult task than asserting the formal differences in regulation.[30] In the systems analysed, national elements undertake a slow and challenging revision of the foundations of the institution of State liability under the banner of the Community paradigm. This phenomenon of cultural circulation of the Community paradigm is not, nor can it be, significantly imposed from above.[31] It is the result of complex judicial dialogue between the European Court and the national courts, united in an *écart*. Without the second stage of national implementation, the great potential of the formal proclamation of the principle in question is deactivated. Even in the analysis of the State liability paradigm, the comparative methodology plays an absolutely fundamental role. It is precisely here that the problem of tensions regarding the national pole arises.[32]

We have already noted that the community paradigm is at times independent of and even in contrast with national interests; however, it cannot disregard experiences, cultures and State traditions. "The European Union can be considered as emblematic of that new liberal effort that seeks to protect the Eros intrinsic to what is 'national', keeping its demonic sides within civil limits, and to ensure in the Union a legitimacy that recognizes

[29] C. Harlow, *Voices of Differences in a Plural Community*, in *Convergence and Divergence in European Public Law*, cura di P. Beaumont, C. Lyons, N. Walker, Hart Publishing, Oxford, 2002, p. 211.

[30] Sacco himself demonstrates that theoretically and formally different solutions are hidden behind similar or closely related operational rules. R. Sacco, *Introduzione al diritto comparato*, Utet, Torino, 1992, 54.

[31] Cf. G. Benacchio, *L'Unione Europea e il diritto provato. Fenomenologia di un'evoluzione*, Cedam, Milano, 2024.

[32] J. Tallberg, *European Governance and Supranational Institutions: Making States Comply (Routledge Advances in European Politics)*, Routledge, London, 2003, 89 ss.; L. Conant, *Justice Contained: Law and Politics in the European Union*, Cornell University Press, Ithaca/ Londres, 2002; D. Caruso, *The Missing View of the Cathedral: The Private Law Paradigm of European Legal Integration*, in *European Law Journal*, 1997, pp. 3–32.

the constituent elements of democracy and the demos without compromising the non-state telos of the Community."[33]

The institution of State accountability through judicial cross-fertilisation reflects the relational dialectic in a nuanced way, understood as a paradigm. It is not based on legislative substitution via the technique of repealing national liability rules in favour of EU rules; this was the legislative option promoted in the first point of the European Commission's proposal.[34] Instead, it reveals the institutional tension between centralisation and decentralisation of enforcement mechanisms in cases of EU Law infringement: between "police-patrol enforcement" and "fire-alarm enforcement,"[35] and between fundamental limits and individual rights.[36] In the United States, it is about the need to exclude "sensitive polycentric issues from the ambit of judicial inquiry".[37] Legislative harmonisation techniques are clear and evident: the primary or secondary rules of Community Law derived from the legislative harmonisation provided for in Articles 94 and 95 of the EC Treaty. The Court, on the other hand, follows a certainly more complex and delicate harmonisation technique, often silent and covert: the *communautarisation* of national sanctions. We have seen how, since the 1960s, the Court has pursued a strategy based on its judgements but also on the capacity of national courts to assimilate these principles within the domestic sphere. The first phase of proclaiming Community principles is often conditioned by the pursuit of a dialogue aimed at the second phase of national application. From this perspective, the Court of Justice recovers, from the standpoint of judicial sensitivity, what it cannot impose on national courts from a hierarchical viewpoint. The legitimacy of any Community legislative or judicial measure will depend on its tension with the national provisions of 'metabolisation', just as the legitimisation of certain identity instances will pass through the normative framework of Articles 2, 4(1), 4(3) and 6(3) TEU, among oth-

[33] J.H.H. Weiler, *Bread and Circus: the State of European Union*, in *Columbia Journal of European Law*, 4, 1998, 248.

[34] European Commission, *Initial Contributions by the Commission to the Intergovernmental Conference on Political Union: Composite Working Paper*, SEC (91) 500. 15 May 1991, 130.

[35] J. Tallberg, *European Governance and Supranational Institutions: Making States Comply (Routledge Advances in European Politics)*, Routledge, 2003.

[36] J.H.H. Weiler, *The Constitution of Europe*, cit., p. 75.

[37] M. Andenas -D. Fairgrieve, *Sufficiently Serious? Judicial Restraint in Tortious Liability for Public Authorities and the European Influence*, in M. Andenas (ed.), *English Public Law and the Common Law of Europe*, London, Key Haven Publications, 1998.

ers. If this mechanism of cross-fertilisation is to function, it must operate in tension between both identities, principles or traditions. If it aims to classify, separate and exclude, we would be dealing with a different identity and normative typology. Moreover, this mechanism requires much greater attention from the doctrines of Comparative Law, International Law and Constitutional Law, which must move beyond their initial epistemic boundaries or risk failing to properly interpret this circulation.

The first step envisaged by the Court of Justice provided for an objective model of State liability for the failure to transpose a Community directive.[38] What did this provoke? A cryptotype similar to the regulatory silence following the 1954 Law of Forced Expropriation in Spain.[39] It did not become a lived *nomos*. This jurisprudential system was expected to be poorly suited to assimilation at the national level, to internalisation within national disciplines. In other words, it was not conducive to the proliferation of judicial cross-fertilisation. Only one national system has an objective model of liability (administrative liability in Spain); therefore, imposing a general objective criterion would have meant imposing Community legislation *tout court*, replacing national rules on State liability. The necessary national background for the success of the cross-fertilisation process would have been lacking. "Adapting or evolving a distinct legal system in response to an external impetus may involve legal doctrines, prevailing theories and judicial institutions and procedures."[40] The Community model cannot be resolved, as we have seen happen in the past, through a mere process of *legal transplantation*: the normative framework forged in the halls of Luxembourg must be applied to different national realities, occasionally acquiring different nuances. It represents "a model for potential cross-fertilisation",[41] not a risky and undesirable operation of *legal transplantation*.[42]

[38] R. Alonso García, *La responsabilidad de los Estados miembros por infracción del Derecho Comunitario*, Civitas, Madrid, 1997.

[39] A. Lazari, *Modelli e paradigmi della responsabilità dello Stato*, Giappichelli, Torino, 2005, pp. 134–205.

[40] J.W.F. Allison, *Transplantation and Cross-fertilisation in European Public Law*, cit., p. 175.

[41] J. Beatson & T. Tridimas, *Introduction*, in AA.VV., *New Directions in European Public Law*, cit., p. 10.

[42] I am referring to the aforementioned dialectical dispute between O. Kahn-Freund, *On Uses and Misuses of Comparative Law*, in *Mark. Law Rev.*, 1974, 1 ss. and A. Watson, *Legal Transplants: an Approach to Comparative Law*, Edinburgh, 1974; Idem, *Aspects of Reception of Law*, in *Americ. Journ. Compar. Law*, 1996, pp. 335–340.

The *Brasserie de Pechêur-Factortame III*[43] case not only implies a modification of the necessary conditions to assert claims for damages but rather a modified scope for the principle of liability.

The latter applies not only to instances of failure to transpose a Directive into National Law, where a profile of liability *in re ipsa* arises, but also to any breach of EU Law. Consequently, this modification presupposes the establishment of the requirement of a sufficiently serious breach. But what is a sufficiently serious breach? Is it a grave breach, as some EU Law manuals state? No, it is a fault that adapts to the degree of discretion enjoyed by the national authority.

With the *Brasserie du Pêcheur* judgement, the flexibility of the Community model becomes even more evident, and thus the methodological proximity, mutatis mutandis, to the French system also becomes more explicit,[44] since the range of unlawful hypotheses is not limited solely to purely objective cases but also extends to the introduction of subjective elements.

One might indeed query: "*l'appel à la notion de 'violation suffisamment caracterisée' n'a-t-il pas pour conséquence d'introduire dans le régime de la responsabilité de l'État pour violation du droit communautaire une dimension subjective?*"[45] The rigidity of the objective system is followed by the flexibility of a general framework that, moreover, offers a greater margin of interpretation to national judges and which also conceptually approaches the established model of liability of Community institutions, as well as that of the various national systems. In the EU paradigm, as in the French model, illegality does not always entail the right to compensation.[46] However, without understanding the 4 years of golden silence following the *Francovich* decision, or the national models, the meaning of a sufficiently serious breach is not comprehensible.

[43] Judgment of the Court of Justice of 5 March 1996, Brasserie du Pêcheur SA v Bundesrepublik Deutschland and The Queen v Secretary of State for Transport, ex parte Factortame Ltd et al., C-46/93 and C-48/93, ECLI:EU:C:1996:79.

[44] The expression "sufficiently serious breach" or the French term *infringement suffisamment caractérisée* more accurately reflect the Community judge's intention to design a general evaluative parameter, in which not only can serious breaches be subsumed but also breaches *in re ipsa*. The concept of serious fault is nothing more than a subset of the sufficiently serious breach.

[45] S. Aboudrar-Ravanel, *Responsabilité et primauté, ou la question de l'efficiencie de l'outil*, in *Revue de l'Union européenne*, 1999, p. 548.

[46] P. Eeckhout, *The European Court of Justice and the Legislature*, in *Yearbook of European Law*, Vol. 18, 1998, p. 10.

The increasingly subjective approach to evaluating the conduct of State authorities signals the intention to consolidate the institution of State liability through an empirical attitude, akin to the evolutionary method of the *Conseil d'État*.[47] This technique is made explicit in the *Dillenkofer* case,[48] where the Court of Justice stated that the assessment of a breach of EU Law must be carried out in light of the specific circumstances of each case. For instance, the failure to transpose a Directive has been the subject of different evaluations by the Court: in the *Wagner Miret* case,[49] the mere failure to transpose a Directive resulted in a condemnation of the Member State. In contrast, the *British Telecom*[50] and *Dillenkofer*[51] judgements suggest that once a Directive has been transposed, factors such as good faith come into play.

In other words, the Case Law of the Court of Justice increasingly reveals an effort to reconcile, within an objectivised framework, the dual imperatives of safeguarding national interests and upholding the rights of injured parties. This reflects a relational dynamic seen previously, now refined even further in this context. It remains open to debate whether the Court's approach is the most effective means of consolidating the doctrine of State liability under EU Law; nonetheless, it cannot be considered either unfounded or inappropriate. Moreover, the Court's departure from a purely subjective standard is driven by the aim of preventing the fragmentation of the EU model, given the wide divergence in national understandings of *faute, fault* or *culpa*.[52]

[47] 103 S. Aboudrar-Ravanel, *Responsabilité et primauté, ou la question de l'efficiencie de l'outil*, cit., 554: «*La jurisprudence de la jurisdiction française administrative suprême ayant même, semblet-il, inspiré la solution retenue par le juge communautaire*».

[48] CJEU, C-104 C-178, 179 and 188–190/94, *Dillenkofer e altri*, in [1996] 3 *C.M.L.R.* 469.

[49] CJEU, C-334/92 *Wagner Miret* v. *Fondo de Garantía Salarial*, in [1993] *ECR*-I-6911.

[50] CJEU, C-392/93, *R.* v. *HM Treasury, ex parte British Telecom*, in [1996] 2 *C.M.L.R.* 217.

[51] CJEU, C-178, 179 e 188–190/94, *Dillenkofer e altri*, in [1996] 3 *C.M.L.R.* 469.

[52] The Court of Justice is also aware of the national heterogeneity in the notion of fault. Indeed, in paragraph 76 of the *Brasserie du Pêcheur* judgement, it avoids including the requirement of fault among the three essential conditions because "*la nozione di colpa non ha lo stesso contenuto nei differenti sistemi Giuridici*". For further confirmation, see P. Craig, *The Domestic Liability of Public Authorities in Damages: Lessons from the European Community?*, in AA.VV., *New Directions in European Public Law*, cit., 78: «*[F]ault is a word which is given different meanings in different legal systems*». Cfr. also N. Dantonel-Cor, *La violation de la norme communautaire et la responsabilité extracontractuelle de l'Etat*, in *Rev. Trim. Dr. Eur.*, 1998, p. 90.

By adopting the "normally (or reasonably) diligent authority under the circumstances"[53] test, the Court draws on the English subjective model, with the added consequence that the cultural foundations underpinning the determination of State fault differ significantly across Member States.

On the other hand, it would be excessive to expect the Court of Justice to adopt a fully objective model.[54] Even the framework of a strictly objective model, such as the Spanish one, presents troubling ambiguities which, if transposed into the EU context, would take on even more concerning dimensions. Concerns about phenomena such as overcompensation constitute essential coordinates in the construction of a system of State liability. It is undeniable that there has been a decisive shift from a purely objective model of liability towards a more subjective conception, in which the sanctioning function has re-emerged.[55]

The EU liability regime appears closely aligned with the French *responsabilité administrative*: it includes cases of "objectivised liability" for breaches of EU Law, as well as liability adjusted according to the level of discretion exercised.[56] This helps to strengthen the principle of EU legality, which is essential to building a Rule of Law within the EU.[57] Therefore, it spans *faute anonyme* up to *faute lourde*, "by distinguishing between (i) breaches of a clear *'obligation de résultat'[…]*; and *(ii)* breaches of an *'obligation de moyen'*".[58]

[53] Così W. Van Gerven, *Taking Article 215 EC Treaty Seriously*, in AA.VV., *New Directions in European Public Law*, cit., p. 44.

[54] S. Aboudrar-Ravanel, *Responsabilité et primauté, ou la question de l'efficiencie de l'outil*, cit., 549, who adds that « *si la consécration jurisprudentielle d'un principe de responsabilité de l'État pour violation du droit communautaire avait eu pour seule visée la protection des droits des particuliers, la Cour de justice aurait dû s'en tenir à une conception strictement objective de la responsabilité* ».

[55] S. Aboudrar-Ravanel, *Responsabilité et primauté, ou la question de l'efficiencie de l'outil*, in *Rev. Marc. Com.*, 1999, 550.

[56] On this point, see F. Fines, *Quelle obligation de réparer pour la violation du droit communautaire. Nouveaux développements jurisprudentiels sur la responsabilité de l''Etat normateur'*, in *Revue de l'Union européenne*, 1997, p. 94: «*ceci fait penser à la distinction faute simple/faute lourde ou inexcusable, que l'on recontre notamment en France*». The tendency to approach the French "functionalist" model is also critically acknowledged by C. Harlow, *European Administrative Law and the Global Challenge*, European University Institute, Working Paper CSR n. 98/23.

[57] Cf. D. Simon, *La responsabilité de l'État saisi par le droit communautaire*, cit., 489.

[58] W. Van Gerven, *Taking Article 215 EC Treaty Seriously*, cit., p. 43. The same summary framework had been outlined by W. Van Gerven, *Bridging the unbridgeable: Community and national tort laws after Francovich and Brasserie*, in *Int. Comp. Law Quart.*, 1996, p. 518.

Therefore, behind extreme terms such as *faute pour violation de la legalité communautaire* and *faute suffisamment caracterisée* are the French equivalent concepts of *faute simple* and *faute lourde*: "*l'exigence communautaire peut recevoir une traduction nationale en termes exprès de faute*".[59]

From an institutional perspective, the Court of Justice has sought to reinvigorate judicial dialogue through the mechanism of cross-fertilisation,[60] by introducing the requirement of a sufficiently serious breach and leaving national courts the necessary legal space to internalise this standard within their respective legal frameworks. This meta-legal shift corresponds to a structural turn towards a semi-objective liability regime, centred on the concept of a sufficiently serious breach. Objective liability is thus confined to specific instances of *in re ipsa* infringement, such as the failure to transpose a Directive. The deterrent function of State administrative liability is accordingly tempered or attenuated, except where national authorities enjoy only minimal discretion. But does this represent a step back in achieving the goal of maximising the effectiveness of EU Law? The answer is no. Firstly, the model of objective liability (limited to the specific case of a failure to transpose a Directive into Domestic Law), though generous in terms of compensation, had produced no tangible results in national courts, as ironically highlighted by Harlow's expression "the four years of golden silence".[61]

Secondly, once liability was elevated to the status of a general principle of the legal order, thereby extending its scope to all breaches of EU Law, a reversion to a semi-objective system *à la française* appeared inevitable.[62]

[59] F. Fines, *Quelle obligation de réparer pour la violation du droit communautaire. Nouveaux Développements jurisprudentiels sur la responsabilité de l''Etat normateur'*, cit., 69, who, confirming the eclecticism of the current EU system, has previously spoken of '*Une approche objective de la violation de la norme comunautaire*'.

[60] Cf. F.G. Jacobs, *El diálogo judicial y la fertilización cruzada de los sistemas jurídicos: la Tribunal de Justicia, Judicial Dialogue and the Cross-Fertilization of Legal Systems: The European Court of Justice*, in *Texas International Law Journal*, 2003, pp. 547–556.

[61] This expression is taken from C. Harlow, *Francovich and the Problem of the Disobedient State*, cit., 202.

[62] The reasons underlying the reactivation of the judicial virtuous circle are explained by Advocate General Léger in Case C-224/01, Gerhard Köbler. In paragraph 53 of his Opinion, he states: "Established by law, the European Communities have been developed and consolidated essentially through law. Since the national courts have the function of applying the law, including Community law, they inevitably constitute an essential cog in the Community legal order. [...] We can also detect the progressive development of a real Community judicial ethic."

Indeed, the first cautious and tentative positive responses from national courts to the common paradigm only began to emerge following the 'downgrading' of the evaluative standard. "There is no mellowing down, but consolidation and studied deference."[63] The Court of Justice is not in a hierarchical relationship with national jurisdictional bodies; the prestige of the Community institution and the result of its jurisprudence inevitably depend on the relational capacity of cultural persuasion and the legal responsiveness of the Luxembourg Court.

From this perspective, it becomes easier to understand why the principle of State liability has come to extend beyond EU-specific cases, emerging instead as a broader cultural paradigm. It is equally unclear why various national reform initiatives regarding State liability appear to gravitate towards the *Brasserie* model. If the entire dynamic between the European and national courts were to be reduced to a matter of political confrontation, it would be difficult to explain why certain national supreme courts would voluntarily seek to revise their own domestic doctrines in the direction of the EU's liability framework. Nor would it be possible to account for the fact that resistance to *Francovich* manifests in a fragmented, 'leopard-spot' pattern. If national courts were merely instruments of the State's political will, it would be hard to see why some (such as the UK Supreme Court, the Spanish *Tribunal Supremo* or the Italian *Corte di Cassazione*) would embrace the *Brasserie* approach while others (like the French *Conseil d'État*) would reject it. Moreover, even within the highest national courts, opposing currents coexist, as is evident in the House of Lords, the Supreme Court and the Court of Cassation.

These institutions reflect and are shaped by the diverse national legal cultures from which they emerge. While they may share certain interests, they do not constitute a unified or compact judicial body. It is for this reason that negative or resistant reactions must be understood through the lens of European cultural diversity. The inherent tension in the EU's attempt to align the *Factortame III* paradigm with national legal outcomes is, in this sense, entirely logical. Within this area of inquiry, the works of Legrand and Harlow become particularly relevant. It is therefore essential to interpret the responses of national legal systems (and especially of national courts) to the rulings of the Court of Justice of the European Union, given that they often find themselves in a situation of *écart* or

[63] T. Tridimas, *Liability for Breach of Community Law: Growing up and Mellowing down?*, in *C.M.L. Rev.*, 2001, 332.

divergence from it. "Legal integration is not simply the issuing of legal decisions which create new doctrine, but more importantly the acceptance of this jurisprudence within national legal systems and by national politicians."[64] Community Law cannot and must not dispense with this tension of comparative techniques, which interpret, for example, what the sufficiently serious breach really consists of and how it is reconciled at the national level.[65]

10.5 The Cross-Fertilisation Mechanism in Common Constitutional Traditions

The permanent centre of gravity in this new conceptual architecture is the judge, no longer a mere *bouche de la loi* in the Napoleonic sense, but a critical agent responsible for the interweaving of legal paradigms. Neither an absolutist judge-king nor Dworkin's Hercules,[66] this figure is instead a judicial weaver, equipped with new epistemological tools within the context of two integrated legal orders.[67] The task is no longer to interpret the legal universe solely through the lens of the national system, reducing every external legal manifestation to a mere factual occurrence. "This introduces a certain degree of pluralism in the jurisprudence of the Court, and in its dialogue with the national Courts. This pluralism is now guaranteed by the notion of 'constitutional identity of the Member States, which was first introduced in the Treaty on European Union, in then-Article F para. 2, to acknowledge that the Union was based on the Member States (9). Art. 4(2) of the Lisbon Treaty articulates this idea adding new

[64] K. Alter, *Explaining National Court Acceptance of European Court Jurisprudence: A Critical Evaluation of Theories of Legal Integration*, in *The European Courts and National Courts: Doctrine and Jurisprudence*, A.M. Slaughter, A. Stone Sweet, J.H.H. Weiler (eds.), Hart Publishing, Oxford, 1999, p. 227.

[65] D. Chalmers, *Judicial Preferences and the Community Legal Order*, in *Modern Law Review* 60 (2), 1997, p. 191: «*The logic is not consociational, but one of control. It entails the construction by the Court of Justice of positive legal institutions in a more detailed and extensive manner than previously, with a corresponding loss of autonomy for national courts whose role would be reduced to that of fact-finding agencies and administrators of the Court's judgments.*»

[66] R. Dworkin, *El imperio de la justicia*, Editorial Gedisa, Barcelona, 1988.

[67] Cf. R. Alonso García, *El Juez nacional como juez europeo a la luz del Tratado Constitucional*, in *Constitución europea y constituciones nacionales*, I. Gómez Fernández-M. Cartabia – B. de Witte – P. Pérez Tremps (eds.), 2005, p. 682.

dimensions to it."[68] In other words, the reference to constitutional traditions common to the Member States is part of a dialectical relationship with the notion of constitutional identity.[69] "It may well be that the view articulated by the *BVerfG* in its own *Gauweiler* ruling (17) is misconceived, at least from the point of view of the adherence of the German State to the ECHR and to other international instruments, for example. All too often identities, like traditions, are conceived in a monolithic way, while they are not, as a comparative approach to their study shows."[70]

Common constitutional traditions represent a kind of 'Phoenician tale', that is a creative lie: a false narrative of the origin of the order of things that favours an awareness of the state of things and, in so doing, also provides a justification. As a result, we have moved from attempts to seek a true community of constitutional traditions, to consider as common those traditions present in most of the constitutions of the Member States or in a number of constitutions, or even to consider as common a particularly relevant constitutional tradition present in just one Member State. The principle of 'inviolable human dignity' is an example of this, found only in the German constitutional tradition.[71]

Therefore, if it is ultimately acknowledged that common constitutional traditions are, in themselves, a 'source of inspiration' for EU Law, one can once again grasp the underlying significance of the 'Phoenician tale': these common constitutional traditions are more than just European

[68] M. Graziadei & R. Decaria, *The "Constitutional Traditions Common to the Member States" in the Case-law of the European Court of Justice: Judicial Dialogue at its Finest*, in *Rivista Trimestrale di Diritto Pubblico*, 2017, p. 950.

[69] See V. Constantinesco, *La Conciliation Entre la Primauté du Droit de l'Union Européenne et l'Identité Nationale des Etats Membres: Mission Impossible ou Espoir Raisonné?*, in *Common European Legal Thinking. Essays in Honour of Albrecht Weber*, H.-J. Blanke, P. Cruz Villalón, T. Klein, J. Ziller (eds.), Springer, Berlin, 2015, 104: «*Si la primauté, telle qu'initialement conçue par la Cour de justice, revêt un caractère absolu (tout le droit de l'Union l'emporte sur tout le droit interne contraire), le fait que la réalisation concrète de la primauté dépende aujourd'hui d'une multiplicité d'instances vient incontestablement la relativiser. Témoin de cette évolution, la notion d'identité nationale que lon peut considérer comme un infléchissement à la primauté du droit de l'Union*». See also O. Pollicino, *Della sopravvivenza delle tradizioni costituzionali comuni alla Carta di Nizza: ovvero del mancato avverarsi di una (cronaca di una) morte annunciata*, in *Dir. Ue*, 2016, p. 253.

[70] See S. Cassese, *Fine della solitudine delle corti costituzionali, ovvero il dilemma del porcospino*, in *Ars Interpretandi*, 2015, pp. 21–49; M. Graziadei, *Comparative Law, Legal History and the Holistic Approach to Legal Cultures*, in *ZeUP*, 1999, p. 531.

[71] J. Jones, *'Common Constitutional Traditions': Can the Meaning of Human Dignity under German Law Guide the European Court of Justice?*, in *Public Law* 2004, pp. 167–187.

traditions.[72] They have been developed by the Court of Justice of the European Union through an undeniably complex hermeneutic process, in which national constitutional traditions have influenced[73] the outcome, either directly or indirectly, at the outset or at the conclusion of the process and in varying ways at different times. However, this comparative process is not made explicitly transparent. We have already seen how in the realm of fundamental rights, a comparative and axiological operation of special interest has been completed, which very much resembles the idea of tradition developed by Patrick Glenn. "In computer language the expression LAN has been used, indicating a Local Area Network of computer information. In the same way adherents to a tradition, or a group within a tradition, constitute a local area network of information, or private cloud."[74] In the legal sphere, the interweaving of threads or ropes (national and supranational constitutional) that bind the State-Ulysses occurs silently in the implicit and non-verbalised rules of common constitutional traditions.[75] The robustness of these ropes or threads according to Wittgenstein is due to the ability to intertwine their fibres: "[i]n weaving a thread we weave fiber with fiber. And the robustness of the yarn is not due to the fact that a fiber runs throughout its length, but from the overlap of many fibers, to one another."[76] We have also seen how the initial phase of Integration through Law is accompanied by the successive era of Integration through Constitutional Law through the progressive use of common constitutional traditions.

One might argue that common constitutional traditions are a powerful counterpart to the notion of 'constitutional identity'. However, in my

[72] A. Ruggeri, *Tradizioni costituzionali comuni" e "controlimiti", tra teoria delle fonti e teoria dell'interpretazione*, in *Diritto pubblico comparato ed europeo*, 2003, p. 115.

[73] See M. Cartabia, *"Unità nella diversità": il rapporto tra la Costituzione europea e le costituzioni nazionali*, in *Sul trattato che istituisce una costituzione per l'Unione Europea*, in *Giornata di studio in ricordo di A. Predieri*, Florence, 2005 available at http://www.giustamm.it/new_2005/Cartabia.pdf18

[74] H.P. Glenn, *Legal Traditions of the World*, Oxford University Press, Oxford, 2014, p. 21.

[75] Cf. R. Scarciglia, *The Silent Language: From Chthonic Law To Global Legal Pluralism, Normative Pluralism and Religion Diversity: Challenges and Methodological Approaches*", in R. Scarciglia & W. Menski (eds.), Kluwer, London, 2018, p. 129: "*The forms with which the law manifests itself – or shows itself silent or mute – tend to intertwine over time as the threads of a rope.*"

[76] L. Wittgenstein, *Philosophische Untersuchungen*, cit., p. 45.

view, they represent something more. They are intimately bound together in an *écart*. These traditions may even constitute a flexible, meta-legal phase of the Union's identity,[77] one that does not rise to the level of a formal EU value but nonetheless forms an indispensable meta-legal sphere for the European Union. Precisely for this reason, they would deserve greater attention in the reasoning of the CJEU. Whereas constitutional identities tend to serve the purpose of safeguarding and reaffirming a certain pluralism, which in some cases may be tinged with a more pronounced sense of national sovereignty (albeit within the framework of loyal cooperation, mutual assistance and institutional respect as set out in Article 4(3) TEU), references to common traditions mostly move in the opposite direction, acting as a centripetal force. Therefore, framing a preliminary reference by choosing to highlight one or the other is a weighty decision. A deeper exploration of this dynamic would require a more in-depth analysis of the role of national traditions in the formation of the Court's Case Law and of its use of comparative arguments, which would pose a formidable challenge.[78]

From this perspective, it is probably no coincidence that common constitutional traditions often feature in landmark cases or in cases where much is at stake. Bosman, Omega, Berlusconi et al., Mangold, Unibet, Intertanko, Kadi, the Internationale Handelsgesellschaft itself and, more recently, Achbita, all illustrate this point. Advocate General Cruz Villalón raises this in one of his Opinions.

We may therefore borrow some of his words from the historic case concerning the legality of the ECB's OMT programme (Gauweiler): "61. [...] I think it useful to recall that the Court of Justice has long worked with the category of 'constitutional traditions common' to the Member States when seeking guidelines on which to construct the system of values on which the Union is based. Specifically, the Court of Justice has given preference to those constitutional traditions when establishing a particular culture of rights, namely that of the Union. The Union has thus acquired

[77] G. Martinico, *The tangled complexity of the EU constitutional process. The frustrating knot of Europe*, cit., p. 76.

[78] For two enlightening contributions on this matter, see: F. Nicola, *National Legal Traditions at Work in the Jurisprudence of the Court of Justice of the European Union*, in *Am. J. Comp. Law*, 2016, p. 865; K. Lenaerts & K. Gutman, *The Comparative Law Method and the European Court of Justice: Echoes Across the Atlantic*, ibid., p. 841.

the character not just of a community governed by the Rule of Law, but also of a **'community imbued with a constitutional culture**.' That common constitutional culture can be seen as part of the common identity of the Union, with the important consequence, to my mind, that the constitutional identity of each Member State, which of course is specific to the extent necessary, cannot be regarded, to state matters cautiously, as light years away from that common constitutional culture.[79] Rather, a clearly understood, open attitude to EU Law should in the medium and long term give rise, as a principle, to basic convergence between the constitutional identity of the Union and that of each of the Member States" [emphasis added].[80] My interpretation of these reflections moves in a relational direction: when, culturally, these common constitutional traditions (CCT) tend to converge within the Union's identity framework, there is a harmonising vision of EU Law. But the Union itself must, by its very nature, enshrine relational diversity when the difference of constitutional identity is a Derridean *différance*—that is an expression of the singularity of its own existential motivation.

On the other hand, common constitutional traditions and national identity under Article 4(2) TEU are not necessarily opposing concepts. As we have seen, from the outset, CCT were born with the aim of establishing a dialectical relationship, insofar as the primacy of EU Law depends on the tension between, on the one hand, reinforcing its dialogical construction in relation to State Law, including constitutional identities, and, on the other, asserting the autonomy of EU Law. Viewed from the perspective of a socio-legal approach, constitutional identity could become a key normative ideology, a strategy of legitimation and a structuring tool for a relational EU Law, insofar as it is considered part of the Union's own relational identity. It is the *Grundnorm* of relational tolerance. Once again, identities can become a source of tension between national legal orders, depending on what is (or is not) common among these constitutions, and between them and European Law, which could transcend them. Identities are national, but they are not necessarily exclusionary as they may reflect

[79] S. Ragone, Constitutional identities and traditions: a conundrum for comparative lawyers, in *Revista de Direito Administrativo & Constitucional*, 2022, n. 89, p. 11–36.

[80] Conclusions of the Advocate General Cruz Villalón of 14 January 2015, Gauweiler, C-62/14, EU:C:2015:7.

multiple legal orders. To the extent that they engage in dialogue, they tend to pursue shared objectives and, ultimately, help define the identity of the EU, becoming an essential factor in the current framework, in which new challenges have emerged, the foremost being the need to achieve a common understanding of the Rule of Law as part of the EU's identity through the comparative national prism. A circular understanding of the relationship between these components (EU values, national identities and conditional monetary transfers) provides a fruitful environment. Within the circularity of cross-fertilisation, it is assumed that the identities of Member States are consistent with Article 2 TEU and that national courts manage constitutional identities as conceptualisations capable of contributing to the development of CCT by the CJEU, the content of which can, in turn, inform Article 2 in a virtuous circle.

Thus positioned differently, CCT and constitutional identities represent varying degrees of coexistence within the same *communitas*. Again, comparison need not necessarily aim for harmonisation, common constitutional traditions or a single Union identity. State identities may converge towards the functionalist and constructivist direction of harmonisation, but they may also retain their singularity, their *différance*, always naturally within the framework of a *communitas*. Otherwise, mimetic claims (those that invoke the same terms of value, identity or tradition in the exclusionary sense described in Part One) fall outside the Union's framework.

Promisingly, the notion of constitutional identity applies here to the Union itself. Therefore, at least potentially, CCT remain an excellent candidate to help bridge the gap between the constitutional identity of the Union and the evolving constitutional identities of the Member State. Therefore, as President Lenarts stated extrajudicially, "that openness, on the part of the CJEU, to the views of national courts and the ECtHR, not only makes possible cross-fertilization of ideas between those judicial actors, but also serves to prevent normative conflicts from arising" [emphasis added].[81] This is only partly true. Congenital openness to the new relational identity of the European Union facilitates cross-fertilisation, but it does not necessarily have to avoid conflicts: discrepancies, as we have seen, are essential in the consolidation of the European paradigm.

[81] K. Lenaerts & K. Gutman, *The Comparative Law Method and the European Court of Justice: Echoes Across the Atlantic*, ibid., p. 840.

The further peculiarity of common constitutional traditions lies in the continuity that this process establishes between the future and the past. The 'general principles' that should govern future cases stem from what is common to past national regulations. Therefore, the future is formed on the basis of the past. History becomes part of the normative procedure. This procedure includes a temporary dimension (as in the case of an 'ever closer union' or the identity clauses of national constitutions). Furthermore, it is absolutely fundamental that "general principles do not derive from national legislation but must be part of a tradition, and this tradition must be shared by several countries. The concept of a common constitutional tradition is therefore basically an anti-positivistic one,"[82] putting the comparative study of *praxis* on the normative table. Another peculiarity of common constitutional traditions is that this way of combining National Law and supranational law does not apply to all matters, only to fundamental rights. This means that those responsible for drafting the European 'constitution' believed that, in this area, history was particularly relevant and, therefore, new European rules should be bound to pre-existing legal traditions. "The concepts of 'common constitutional heritage' and Constitutional Common Traditions are to be confronted [...] with those, for example, of pluralism and complexity."[83]

On the other hand, the conception rightly put forward by some judges weaving general principles of Law,[84] not conceived to build an exclusionary identity of International Law as enshrined in Article 38 of the Statute of the International Court of Justice but as an occasion for inclusion. The general principles of EU Law are built on common constitutional traditions, as clearly emerged from the dictation of Article 6.2 TEU. The porous identity we speak of involves a gradual conceptual and institutional convergence, not unlike the Schopenhauerian metaphor of the porcupine

[82] S. Cassese, *The European Common Constitutional Traditions*, in *Liber Amicorum Luigi Moccia*, E. Calzolaio, R. Torino, L. Vagni, Roma tre, Roma, 2021, p. 29.

[83] L. Lacché, *Crossing boundaries. Comparative constitutional history as a space of communication*, in *Glossae: European Journal of Legal History*, 15, 2018, p. 132.

[84] A. Lazari, *Últimas tendencias en la jurisprudencia del Tribunal de Justicia de la Unión Europea*, 2008–2011, J. Díez-Hochleitner Rodríguez, C. Martínez Capdevila, I. Blázquez Navarro, J. Frutos Miranda (eds.), 2012, pp. 209–236; Idem, "*La aplicación judicial del Derecho de la Unión Europea en España: el diálogo entre jueces tejedores*", in *Tratado de derecho y políticas de la Unión Europea*, J. Maillo González-Orús, B. Becerril Atienza (ed.); José María Beneyto Pérez (dir.), Vol. 4, 2011 (Las fuentes y principios del derecho de la Unión Europea), pp. 665–748.

coined for this purpose by Pedro Cruz Villalón[85] and cited by Sabino Cassese[86] regarding the solitary identity of judges: the dilemma of this animal, which during the winter tries to combat the cold by drawing close to its peers but also risks injuring itself on their quills.

[85] P. Cruz Villalón, *Rights in Europe: The Crowded House, King's College London, Centre of European Law*, in *Working Papers in European Law*, n. 01/2012; Idem, "*La identidad constitucional de los Estados miembros: dos relatos europeos*", in *Anuario de la Facultad de Derecho de la Universidad Autónoma de Madrid*, n. 17, 2013, pp. 501–514.

[86] S. Cassese, *Fine della solitudine delle corti costituzionali, ovvero il dilemma del porcospino*", *Ars interpretandi*, 2015, pp. 1–14.

CHAPTER 11

Second Encounter: Tempering Exclusive Identities Through Ponderation—The *écart* Between Common Constitutional Traditions, Constitutional Identity and Values of the European Union

Abstract In this chapter we examine the dynamic interplay between common constitutional traditions, national constitutional identity and the core values of the European Union. Analysing landmark rulings by the Italian, German, Polish and Hungarian constitutional courts, it highlights contrasting approaches—ranging from relational and inclusive to exclusionary and sovereigntist—towards integrating national identity within the framework of EU Law. The text explores the risks of invoking constitutional identity for exclusionary purposes, especially in the context of political reforms and judicial resistance to EU primacy. Ultimately, it argues for a relational and dialogical conception of constitutional identity, fostering cross-fertilisation between national and European legal orders, and ensuring the protection of shared values and fundamental rights within a pluralistic and cooperative Union.

Keywords Italian *Corte Costituzionale* • German *BVerfG* • Polish constitutional court • Hungarian constitutional court • Opinion 2/13

© The Author(s), under exclusive license to Springer Nature Switzerland AG 2026

A. Lazari, *Relational Identity in International, Comparative and European Union Law*,
https://doi.org/10.1007/978-3-031-59482-3_11

The Italian Constitutional Court, in the ruling on the preliminary reference "*Taricco II*",[1] decisively assumes jurisdiction to describe and defend national constitutional identity. It does so not in an atomised and self-referential manner (an approach that seems, by contrast, to characterise the German BVerfG) but rather by seeking to situate Italian constitutional identity within the broader spectrum of European identity and to interpret the values and principles of its Constitutional Charter 'systematically' in 'harmony' with the corresponding provisions of European Law, particularly the Charter of Nice.

Far from substituting the Court of Justice in interpreting EU Law, the Italian Constitutional Court appears to invite the Luxembourg judges to engage in a two-way integration of judicial protections, using constitutional traditions (here evidently also understood as 'part' of Italian constitutional identity) as elements to apply principles already present within the European system, thereby broadening their scope and thus strengthening the related protection.[2]

11.1 The First Pole on the Sliding Scale Spectrum: The Italian Corte Costituzionale and the German BVerfG

The *Corte Costituzionale* acknowledges the importance of the primacy of EU Law and seeks to encourage the CJEU to review its earlier ruling based on the fact that the principle of legal certainty is "a requirement common to the constitutional traditions of the Member States, is present in the protection system of the ECHR and, as such, enshrines a general principle of EU Law". Accordingly, while the Italian court leaves open the possibility of invoking the counter-limits doctrine against future CJEU rulings, it does not adopt a confrontational stance grounded in the idea of exclusionary constitutional identity.

[1] Judgment of the Court of Justice (Grand Chamber), 5 December 2017, Case C-42/17, M.A.S., M.B., ECLI:EU:C:2017:936.

[2] «*Questa Corte tiene a sottolineare che l'interpretazione appena delineata, se da un lato serve a preservare l'identità costituzionale della Repubblica italiana, dall'altro non compromette le esigenze di uniforme applicazione del diritto dell'Unione e si propone pertanto come soluzione conforme al principio di leale cooperazione e di proporzionalità*» (Italian Constitutional Court, Order No. [Número]/[Año], [Nombre de las partes si aplica], ECLI, points 8–9).

Defending its constitutional heritage once again, as it did, for example, in the case of the Italian Republic v. Germany,[3] before the International Court of Justice, the Italian Supreme Court seems to propose an alternative discourse regarding the protection of the untouchable core of the constitutional order, compared with the identity-based language used by the German Constitutional Court in Gauweiler, for instance.[4] It is a relational approach, stemming from an open conception of its own constitutional identity, convergent with the European system of fundamental rights. A common terminology is used, invoking the principle of critical primacy, which allows for degrees of diversity. Once again, there is comparative tension between the approach pioneered by the Italian Court and the different, more exclusionary stance consolidated not only in the German Constitutional Court but also in the Hungarian, Polish and Danish courts.

It is not just a formal, linguistic difference but a substantial one. Constitutional tradition is by definition pluralistic in nature while the exclusionary reference to constitutional identity, in its current majority interpretation, is not. As pointed out, the *Corte Costituzionale*'s reasoning moves from the national constitutional tradition to the European one, trying to encourage the CJEU to reconsider its previous ruling in the light of values that are part of the European constitutional heritage.

More specifically, Article 6(3) TEU could be the solid reference applied as a possible limit to the implementation of *Taricco I*, on the basis of the constitutional traditions of Member States. This provision classifies fundamental rights as a result of the constitutional traditions common to Member States, among the general principles of EU Law.

Unlike constitutional identity, then, constitutional traditions are intended to include and preserve fundamental rights. The option to invoke Article 6(3) for a partial *reactivatio* of the CJEU, enriching the content of the principle of legality, is consistent with the approach of the Italian

[3] International Court of Justice, Jurisdictional Immunities of the State (Germany v. Italy: Greece intervening), 3 February 2012.

[4] "The request of a preliminary ruling in Gauweiler, far to be an expression of cooperative constitutionalism, represented the apex of polemic constitutional patriotism in which the language of constitutional identity played an absolute protagonist role. A language which was not constrained by any set of essentials that are themselves compliant in general outline with the basic values of Article 2 TEU"; also O. Pollicino, Common Constitutional Traditions in the Age of the European Bill(s) of Rights: Chronicle of a (somewhat prematurely) death foretold, in *Italian Journal of Public Law*, vol. 2, n° 1, 2010, p. 69.

Court, which emphasised the importance of a pluralistic vision of constitutional traditions rather than seeking an explicit and forceful defence of constitutional identity. It is true that Article 6(3) refers to constitutional traditions common to the Member States; however, this reference should not prevent a certain degree of pluralism from being injected into the concept of constitutional tradition, as the Italian Court has suggested. This allows for reconciling a higher level of protection rooted in the national Constitution and in the primacy of Union law, thereby reinforcing the harmonising function of Article 4(3) TEU, seeking an explicit and vigorous defence of constitutional identity.

The Italian judge's ruling states: "According to Article 4(3) of the Treaty on European Union, relations between the Union and the Member States are defined by the principle of loyal cooperation, which implies mutual respect and assistance. This means that the parties are united in diversity. **There would be no respect if the reasons for unity demanded the annulment of the core values on which the Member State is founded. Nor would there be respect if the defence of diversity's reasons exceeded that core, obstructing the construction of a future of peace based on common values, as referenced in the preamble to the Charter of Nice.** The primacy of EU Law does not merely express a technical articulation of the system of national and supranational sources. Rather, it reflects the conviction that the goal of unity, within a system guaranteeing peace and justice among Nations, justifies a renunciation of sovereign spaces, even if defined by constitutional norms. At the same time, the legitimacy (derived from Article 11 of the Italian Constitution) and the strength of unity within an order characterised by pluralism (Article 2 TEU) arise from its capacity to include a minimum but necessary degree of diversity to preserve the national identity inherent to the fundamental structure of the Member State (paragraph 2 of Article 4 TEU). Otherwise, the European treaties would contradictorily aim to dissolve the very constitutional foundation from which they originated by the will of the Member States" [emphasis added].[5]

By placing in tension the principle of democracy as formulated by the Italian *Corte Costituzionale* and the jurisprudence of the German *BVerfG*, a significant judicial *écart* emerges concerning the principle of democracy, which in the former case is associated with the exercise of the judicial

[5] Italian Constitutional Court, Order No. 24/2017, 26 January 2017, ECLI:IT:COST:2017:24.

function, while in the latter is strongly linked to its representative parliamentary version. "*Un contenuto pregnante dell'identità costituzionale italiana è rinvenibile (nel principio di separazione dei poteri, ma soprattutto) nel ruolo della magistratura, per cui la Corte costituzionale, in quanto "giudice dei controlimiti", si erge a difensore del corretto svolgimento della funzione giurisdizionale, accentuando il legame tra art. 1 e art. 101, II co., della Costituzione e coinvolgendo così la magistratura nella concretizzazione dei princìpi costituzionali, che definiscono l'identità costituzionale nazionale.*"[6] According to the Italian Constitutional Court, the defence of constitutional identity primarily involves ensuring the proper application of the supreme principles of the legal system, chiefly established by the judiciary, rather than through the political decision-making process, which guarantees the proper exercise of the instruments of representative democracy, as is the case in Germany. The nationalist conception of values embodied by some constitutional court rulings, especially those of the German Constitutional Court, revolves around the idea that democracy can only be rooted within the nation-state. The logical and institutional *prius* resides in the national parliaments. Specifically, the democratic legitimacy of the powers exercised by the Union on behalf of the German people would be realised within the relationship of trust established between the German Parliament and the government member authorised to contribute their vote to decisions in the European Council and the Council of the European Union.[7] "*La sentenza sul Trattato di Maastricht appare solo come la più elaborata espressione di un orientamento teso a riaffermare l'esclusività dell'ordinamento politico di uno Stato, concepito come la forma politica e giuridica di una comunità autosufficiente e autodeterminata.*"[8] Once again we are facing a demand for exclusion based on the concept of sovereignty: "the constitutional identity doctrine developed by certain domestic courts is essentially premised on an assertion of State sovereignty."[9]

[6] S. Polimeni, *L'identità costituzionale come controlimite*, cit., p. 65.

[7] BVerfG, Judgment of the Second Senate of 05 May 2020 - 2 BvR 859/15, 2 BvR 980/15, 2 BvR 2006/15, 2 BvR 1651/15, ECLI:DE:BVerfG:2020:rs20200505.2bvr085915.

[8] E. Cannizzaro, *La sovranità oltre lo Stato*, cit., p. 64. See an important judgement of the BVerfG, Order of the Second Senate of 15 April 2021 - 2 BvR 547/21, ECLI:DE:BVerfG:2021:rs20210415.2bvr054721.

[9] Cloots, E. "*National Identity, Constitutional Identity, and Sovereignty in the EU*", *Netherlands Journal of Legal Philosophy* 2016 (45), p. 8.

11.2 The Second Pole of the Sliding Scale Spectrum: The Polish and Hungarian Constitutional Courts

In this singular regard is the reconstruction of constitutional identity recently carried out by the Hungarian Constitutional Court, in Decision No. 22/2016.[10]

Let us take the example of identity and the interpretation of Article 4.2 of the Treaty on European Union, proposed by the Polish and Hungarian governments. More recently, the Hungarian Constitutional Court has attempted to use the tendency to interpret the national identity of the Member States to establish problematic 'deviations' from EU Law.[11] In this passage, the Hungarian Constitutional Court initially takes Article 4.2 TEU as its starting point. However, later on, it ends up using the concept of 'constitutional identity' alongside the need to preserve national sovereignty (a term not used in the literal wording of Article 4 TEU). Finally, the Hungarian Constitutional Court offers an interpretation of constitutional identity in light of Article R3 of the Hungarian Constitution, thus providing an alternative reading of the same category. In doing so, the Hungarian judge deliberately ignores that respect for national identity must necessarily be read together with Article 4.3 TEU, which governs the principle of loyal cooperation and fits within the combined framework of Articles 2 and 6 TEU. In other words, the alternative interpretation of national identity offered by the Hungarian Constitutional Court is clearly at odds with the Treaty provision cited by the judges themselves in the ruling. This confirms the selective and instrumental use of relevant supranational regulatory provisions by populists.[12] After the ruling, in 2018, a constitutional reform was adopted, which introduced the "constitutional

[10] Constitutional Court of Hungary (Alkotmánybíróság), Decision 22/2016 (XII.5.) AB on the Interpretation of Article E(2) of the Fundamental Law, 30 November 2016, ECLI:HU:CC:2016:22. For a commentary, see H. Kelemen, *The Hungarian Constitutional Court enters the dialog on national constitutional identity*, *Diritti comparati*, 30 March 2017; and DRINÓCZI, J., "The Hungarian Constitutional Court on the Limits of EU Law in the Hungarian Legal System", *Int'l J. Const. L. Blog*, Dec. 29, 2016.

[11] Hungarian Constitutional Court, Judgment no. 22/2016 (XII.5.) AB, https://hunconcourt.hu/letoltesek/en_22_2016.pdf.

[12] Cf. Z. Kortvelyesi, – B. Majtényi, *Game of Values: The Threat of Exclusive Constitutional Identity, the EU and Hungary*, in *German Law Journal* 18(7), December 2017, pp. 1721–1744.

identity" formula in the Hungarian text, Article R. 4: "The protection of the constitutional identity and Christian culture of Hungary shall be an obligation of every organ of the State."[13] It is, once again, a solipsistic and exclusionary conception of national identity, detached from its axiological and legal framework. This passage brings us back to the dichotomous approach of populism, which tends to set up 'the people' in opposition to 'Others', following an exclusionary and anti-pluralist dynamic. As Abromeit has pointed out, populism appeals to a "mythical *Volksgemeinschaft*" and tries to build "imagined communities",[14] seeking the political enemy, according to an anti-pluralist approach.

Both in the Case Law of the two constitutional courts[15] and in the related governmental documents, there are references to foreign rulings that have employed the concept of constitutional identity, especially the decisions of the *Bundesverfassungsgericht*, including the one of 5 May 2020 on ultra vires acts, as well as the doctrine on constitutional pluralism.[16] The question concerns what type of constitutional tolerance is compatible with a critical primacy and what kind of Comparative Law is being used in these decisions and documents: clearly, the red line marking the limit from which the European *communitas* was born has been crossed, and this is evidently an exclusionary[17] and mimetic[18] comparative methodology. This national Case Law uses terms born in the context of Western liberal democracy only to distort them and return, under a different guise, to a period of separation of Law within a *communitas*, which, on the contrary, emerged with the opposite aim.

But these references were introspective, meaning they had the purpose (albeit not openly stated) of legitimising the controversial reforms and

[13] Art. Q.4 of the Hungarian Constitution, https://www.kormany.hu/download/f/3e/61000/TheFundamentalLawofHungary_20180629_FIN.pdf

[14] J. Abromeit, *A Critical Review of Recent Literature on Populism*, in *Politics and Governance*, 2017, p.177.

[15] See mainly Constitutional Court of Hungary, Decision 32/2021 (XII. 20.) AB of 7 December 2021, ECLI:HU:CC:2021:32, para. 70; Constitutional Tribunal of Poland, Judgment of 7 October 2021, Case K 3/21, ECLI:PL:TK:2021:K.3.21, paras. III. 1.3, 4.1, 4.2, 4.4, 4.5.

[16] J. Scholtes, *Abusing Constitutional Identity*, cit., p. 552 s.

[17] A. Di Martino, *Comparare le identità costituzionali: circolazione degli argomenti giuridici e contesti storico-politici*, in *Esperienze giuridiche in dialogo*or *Il ruolo della comparazione*, (eds.) M. Graziadei & A. Somma, Sapienza Università Editrice, Rome, 2024, p. 225.

[18] Cf. G. Martinico, *Between Mimetism and Parasitism: Italian Populism in a Comparative Perspective*, in *European Public Law*, 2020, p. 26–29.

political choices of the governing majorities. They had little to do with even minimal dialogue; they represented a full stop, expecting no response or tension with the CJEU. Moreover, a paradox can be discerned in this jurisprudential orientation: the concept of constitutional identity, which normally carries *longue durée* characteristics, is used to cement and shield constitutional changes that have occurred within a very short period. Such innovations, sometimes even formal, through constitutional revisions as in Hungary, arise from the aim of solidifying a fluid and complex reality.[19] I would like to briefly recall the areas in which these transformations have concentrated, carried out by the governments of the Fidesz party led by Viktor Orbán in Hungary and the PiS party in Poland: interventions in the composition of the constitutional court and the ordinary and administrative judiciary, as well as in the governing body of judges and the disciplinary commission, making them dependent on the executive and the parliamentary majority; the reduction of autonomy and independence of bodies controlling the media and the electoral process; the restriction of political freedoms and scientific autonomy, and of the rights of migrants, women and minorities. In short, these measures clearly relate to the courts, whose objective is to protect the rights of the Other and to the Other directly.

The concept of constitutional identity has played a central role in at least two decisions of the Hungarian Constitutional Court, both related to the migration crisis. The issue directly affected one of the pillars on which the illiberal regime has built greater consensus: that of an ethnically homogeneous nation, impermeable to external contamination. In the first ruling, in 2016,[20] the Court of First Instance identified in abstract terms certain aspects in which the European Council decision on relocation, approved the previous year as an embryonic form of solidarity among States in response to the massive wave of refugees from Syria, could have

[19] Cf. R.D. Kelemen & L. Pech, *The Uses and Abuses of Constitutional Pluralism: Assessing the 'Arguments of Resistance' of the Polish and Hungarian Constitutional Courts*, in *Common Market Law Review*, 2019, 69 et seq. Another doctrine that is "abused" is that of *political constitutionalism*, which is invoked without regard to its assumptions (political pluralism, competition between parties, effective guarantees of freedom of expression, political freedoms and minority rights): cf. R. Dixon & D. Landau, *Abusive Constitutional Borrowing*, in *Oxford Journal of Legal Studies*, 2017, pp. 158 et seq.

[20] Constitutional Court of Hungary (Alkotmánybíróság), Decision 22/2016 (XII. 5.) AB on the Interpretation of Article E(2) of the Fundamental Law, 30 November 2016, ECLI:HU:CC:2016:22.

been unconstitutional.[21] One of the arguments developed by the Court pertains to constitutional identity, understood as self-identity referring to the living conditions of Hungarians and their responsibility in decision-making, as well as the historical constitution: a datum that pre-existed the formal constitution and cannot be overridden by an international treaty. The assertion of the Hungarian community through the claim of its own immutable identity means, among other things, a rejection of the European *communitas*, governed by the *munus* of solidarity and attention to the Other. The bond forged by this type of identity cannot fail to be sovereigntist and exclusionary. "*L'identità costituzionale è vista anche come il profilo contenutistico della sovranità e della statualità: la prima cade se vengono meno le seconde.*"[22] The Court's decision served to bolster the political line against migration, following a popular referendum, which, although largely in favour of the government, had failed to reach the necessary quorum. In turn, it helped trigger the 2018 constitutional review, which introduced the concept of constitutional identity, specifying that this identity is rooted in the "historical Constitution" (Preamble) and that "the protection of Hungary's constitutional identity and Christian culture is an obligation of all State organs" (Art. MR 4). The reference to the religious dimension is explicit, in line with the government-backed idea that an aspect of the national tradition represented by Hungary acts as a barrier to the advance of Islamic peoples into Europe. Formally, it would appear that the Court seeks to join the dialogue on constitutional identity, as many other courts have done. The ruling draws heavily on German Case Law on constitutional identity, including the distinction between ultra vires review and identity review, and makes extensive reference to Comparative Case Law. Is it true Comparative Law? What is it for? Naturally, the aim leans far more towards the exclusionary identity discussed in the First Part of our work than the latter. The notion of dialogue becomes little more than anecdotal when one considers the legal-argumentative reality. It is true that, on several occasions, the Court of Justice refers to "constitutional dialogue" (e.g. in the context of Comparative Law), viewing the use of Comparative Case Law as an expression of the

[21] Decision 2015/1601 of the European Council, on which see the work of M.I. Papa, *Crisi dei rifugiati, Principle di solidarietà ed equa ripartizione delle responsabilità tra gli Stati membri dell'Unione europea*, in *Costituzionalismo.it*, 3/2016.

[22] A. Di Martino, *Comparare le identità costituzionali: circolazione degli argomenti giuridici e contesti storico-politici*, in *Esperienze giuridiche in dialog*or *Il ruolo della comparazione*, (eds.) M. Graziadei & A. Somma, Sapienza Università Editrice, Roma, 2024, p. 226.

importance it attaches to "constitutional dialogue within the Union".[23] Another reference to "constitutional dialogue" arises in the context of the EU's respect for national constitutional identity.[24] However, unlike the Case Law cited by the judgement, the text of the ruling makes no mention of the principle of loyal cooperation, let alone the obligation to use the preliminary reference procedure.

The closest it comes to any form of collaboration with EU Law is the assertion that the protection of constitutional identity will take place "within the framework of informal cooperation with the [Court of Justice] based on the principles of equality and collegiality".[25] Rather than offering a framework for judicial dialogue on constitutional identity and rather than addressing its interlocutor in Luxembourg (even terminologically), the ruling seemed to form part of an internal conversation about how to harness constitutional authority in support of political resistance to the implementation of EU Law. The dynamic triggered by the decision has more to do with internal roots than with any outward-facing dialogical projection. Neither openness (to dialogue) nor limits (relations to the State-Ulysses): the Hungarian court once again expresses itself in defence of an exclusionary identity.

The second judgement, handed down on appeal by the Minister of Justice, was issued in 2021[26] and provides for the unconstitutionality of the ruling of the Luxembourg Court which had convicted Hungary of violating European directives on the status of international protection, reception and repatriation. In particular, European judges found that the Hungarian administration's practice of restricting access to transit zones where applications for international protection could be lodged, as well as its systems of detention, repatriation and expulsion, violated EU Law due to their failure to comply with appropriate procedures and safeguards. Migrants were also prevented from remaining in the territory while awaiting the outcome of their application or potential appeal.[27] Once again (this time with the support of the new constitutional text), the Hungarian

[23] Constitutional Court of Hungary (Alkotmánybíróság), Decision 22/2016 (XII. 5.) AB on the Interpretation of Article E(2) of the Fundamental Law, 30 November 2016, ECLI:HU:CC:2016:22.

[24] Idem.

[25] TCH, Dec. 22/16 (XII.5), par. 63.

[26] TCH, Dec. 32/ 2021(XII. 20) AB.

[27] Judgment of the Court (Grand Chamber) of 17 December 2020, European Commission v Hungary, Case C-808/18, ECR I-000, ECLI:EU:C:2020:1029.

Constitutional Court invoked the concept of constitutional identity to reinforce a compact and homogeneous vision of the nation's identity. This identity was defined as the object of the "most fundamental and inalienable right of the State and the political community that constitutes it"; while framed by the Constitution, it is also rooted beyond the text itself. It was emphasised that national identity carries a strong Christian connotation, and Hungary's self-perception as a defender of Europe (i.e. against foreign peoples and values) was reasserted. As such, constitutional identity has been understood as an amalgam of sovereignty, population, traditions and historical constitution. Although this was already hinted at in the 2016 judgement, by 2021 the instrumental interpretation had extended to the principle of dignity, broadly construed as the foundation of both individual and collective self-determination. Since this self-determination is not exercised in the abstract but within concrete contexts, the Hungarian judges went so far as to argue that the presence of people from other parts of the world alters the social environment (its ethnic, linguistic, cultural and religious components, which together form a network of 'natural bonds'). According to the Court, this transformation profoundly modifies the substrate of constitutional identity, thereby endangering the community's ability to exercise its own self-determination.[28] It is the clearest manifestation of the exclusionary and sovereigntist identity paradigm, also present in some decisions of the Polish Constitutional Court issued between 2021 and 2022.[29] They thus represent a short-circuit in the mechanism of cross-fertilisation. In these rulings, no sliding scale emerges, as Scholtes asserts, nor is the CJEU spurred to address new issues: there is only a denial of dialogue and

[28] Constitutional Court of Hungary, Decision 32/2021 (XII. 20.) AB on the interpretation of Article E(2) of the Fundamental Law, 7 December 2021, ECLI:HU:CC:2021:32, paras. 32 et seq., 94 et seq. The 2018 review had also affirmed Hungary's "inalienable right to determine its territorial integrity, population, political system and form of government" (Art. 2). Regarding this decision, see also V. Salese, *The EU Integration through the Lenses of Domestic Constitutional/ Supreme Courts: the Material Scope of Constitutional Clashes*, in *Rivista di Diritti comparati*, 3/2022, p. 896 sq.

[29] The dates refer to the publication of the device, but for certain reasons in some cases they had to wait a long time. Constitutional Tribunal of Poland, Judgment of 14 July 2021, Case P 7/20, ECLI:PL:TK:2021:P.7.20, paras. 109, 116 et seq., 204, 230; Constitutional Tribunal of Poland, Judgment of 24 November 2021, Case K6/21, ECLI:PL:TK:2021:K.6.21, paras. 68; Constitutional Tribunal of Poland, Judgment of 10 March 2022, Case K 7/21, ECLI:PL:TK:2022:K.7.21, paras. 157, 312, 373, 393.111.

exclusion of the Other, as argued by Advocate General Ćapeta.[30] However, national constitutional choices cannot go beyond this common framework. In this respect, as I have previously suggested, Article 2 of the TEU could be understood as imposing 'red lines' which, if crossed, require a response to defend the Union's constitutional model. These rulings have denied the application of certain decisions by European courts,[31] decisions which had highlighted deficiencies regarding the independence, autonomy and impartiality of Polish judges, constitutional and otherwise. The concept of constitutional identity appears in some passages of judgement K 6/21, which declared Article 6(1) of the ECHR unconstitutional in the interpretation given by the Strasbourg Court, where the latter had extended the scope of the provision to constitutional courts. Its use is more frequent in Decision K 7/21, where Article 6 of the ECHR was again declared unconstitutional insofar as, according to the Polish Court, Strasbourg Case Law had extracted from it a subjective right of judges not to be dismissed from their functions and had violated the legal reserve regarding judicial organisation. Previously, constitutional identity had been invoked in judgement P 7/20, which declared ultra vires a precautionary measure by the Luxembourg Court.[32]

[30] In Advocate General Cápeta's Conclusions, 5 June 2025, Commission v. Hungary, C-769/22.

[31] The case law of the Court of Justice of the European Union has been particularly dense in recent years, having compensated for the paralysis of the political sanctioning procedure provided for in Article 7 TEU. See, inter alia, the CJEU Order of 8 April 2020, C-791/19, *European Commission v. Republic of Poland*; Judgment of 2 March 2021, C-824/18, *A.B.*; Judgment of 15.7.2021, C-719/19, *European Commission v. Republic of Poland*; 14 July 2021 Order, C-204/21 R, *European Commission v. Republic of Poland*. For an overview of this Case Law of the Court of Justice and the relations with the Polish Constitutional Court, see J. Sawicki, *La Unión Europea como barrera a la erosión del Estado de Derecho constitucional. Al margen de una comparación compleja, y tal vez un poco ingrata*, in *Costituzionalismo.it* 3/2020; Id., La *colisión irremediable entre el derecho primario europeo y el derecho constitucional interno como producto de la manipulación hermenéutica de este último*, in *DPCE en línea* 4/2021, 3601 et seq. To the Court of Strasbourg v. ECHR, sent. 7 May 2021, *Xero Flor* v Polonia, n.° 4907/18; judgment of 8 November 2021, *Dolinska-Ficek y Ozimek v Poland*, n.° 49868/19; judgment of 29 September 2021, *Broda & Bojara v Poland*, n.° 26691/18; judgment of 22 July 2022, *Reczowicz v Poland*, n.° 43447/109. In this regard, see, among many others, M. Szwed, *La crisis del Tribunal Constitucional polaco desde la perspectiva del Convenio Europeo de Derechos Humanos*, in *Revista Europea de Derecho Constitucional*, 2022, pp. 133 et seq.; Id., *¿Cientos de jueces nombrados en violación del CEDH?* in *verfassungsblog.de* (29 July 2021).

[32] Constitutional Tribunal of Poland, Judgment of 24 November 2021, Case K 6/21, ECLI:PL:TK:2021:K.6.21, paras. 68, 111.

Along the same lines, but in even harsher terms, was the K 3/2021 ruling (whose reasoning was published more than a year after the operative part): this is the decision that openly and broadly challenged the principle of the primacy of EU Law, invoking instead the supremacy of the Polish Constitution, which formally remains that of the 1990s, but which, in substance, has been thoroughly transformed by the reform laws of the PiS and the interpretations of judges loyal to the government. The ruling did not concern specific provisions of secondary EU Law, nor a particular judgement of the Court of Justice, even though the jurisprudential context was the one previously mentioned: namely the increasingly assertive decisions of the Luxembourg judges, which influenced Polish judicial reforms through a joint reading and expansive interpretation of Articles 2 TEU, 19 TEU, and 47 of the Charter of Fundamental Rights of the European Union. It is no coincidence that among the treaty provisions censured by the Polish Constitutional Court (alongside some with a very broad scope, such as Articles 1, 4(3), and 2 TEU), Article 19 TEU also appears, which pertains to the structure of the European judicial system. These provisions were deemed ultra vires on the basis of a highly generic assessment as they were found to conflict with the principle of constitutional supremacy and the democratic principle, as well as with a series of constitutional rules concerning the organisation of the judiciary, understood in the illiberal configuration imposed by the government. Here, the concept of constitutional identity is used as a synonym for sovereignty and separation, and is intertwined with ultra vires review: the Union is accused of having acted beyond its competences by intervening in the organisation of the judiciary, which is considered a competence reserved for the Member States. "*Un'identità costituzionale, dunque, dai tratti fortemente omogeneizzanti ed escludenti, che ha interiorizzato una concezione autoritaria del potere e la negazione dei relativi limiti.*"[33] The judicial reforms (particularly the Polish government's changes to the National Council of the Judiciary and the Supreme Court) have prompted significant criticism regarding judicial independence and have had wide-reaching repercussions throughout the European legal order. One of the most significant responses to these reforms was the Court of Justice of the European

[33] A. Di Martino, *Comparare le identità costituzionali: circolazione degli argomenti giuridici e contesti storico-politici*, in *Esperienze giuridiche in dialogo*r *Il ruolo della comparazione*, (eds.) M. Graziadei and A. Somma, Sapienza Università Editrice, Rome, 2024, p. 232.

Union's ruling in AK and Others.[34] The EU's response to the so-called gag law thus carries a dual significance, rooted in the substantive interconnection of European Law. Polish legislation represents not only an act that further undermines judicial independence and the Rule of Law in itself but also a repudiation of Europe's genetic pluralism. Glenn's Closure resurfaces here, as State Law delineates a legal space through limits/walls, within which European rules are to be considered entirely alien to judicial reasoning.

The K 3/21 case, in which the Polish Constitutional Court declared the CJEU's Case Law on judicial independence incompatible with the Polish Constitution, was likewise decided at the request of the Polish Prime Minister, Mateusz Morawiecki, who appealed to the Court following the CJEU's ruling in the AB case. In his submission, Morawiecki reproduced arguments concerning constitutional pluralism and Comparative Case Law from the constitutional courts of various EU Member States (including Germany, the Czech Republic, Denmark and Italy), which have, in certain instances, declined to apply European Union Law. He concluded that non-compliance with CJEU rulings on the grounds of conflict with national constitutions forms "part and parcel of the long-standing constitutional acquis of the Member States, indeed, a certain constitutional tradition".[35] Just like in the Hungarian ruling, Comparative Law is used as a typical tool of exclusion, a "retreat into oneself": it confirms a certain outdated idea of Comparative Law. It is not the terms themselves that make the difference but how they are used. Alongside the word Identity, terms like Tradition, Democracy and Values are frequently employed in the exclusionary rhetoric of figures such as Orbán, Trump and Putin.

However, the fact that in Poland and Hungary the constitutional courts have abused the concept of constitutional identity does not mean it should be cast aside, as has been suggested,[36] because its removal from the

[34] CJEU, AK and others, 19 November 2019, C-585/18, C-624/18 and C-625/18, ECLI:EU:C:2019:982.

[35] K. Lane Scheppele, D. Vladimirovich Kochenov, B. Grabowska-Moroz, *EU Values Are Law, after All: Enforcing EU Values through Systemic Infringement Actions by the European Commission and the Member States of the European Union*, in *Yearbook of European Law*, 2020, p. 98.

[36] R.D. Kelemen & L. Pech, *The Uses and Abuses of Constitutional Pluralism*, cit.; F. Fabbrini & A. Sajó, *The Dangers of Constitutional Identity*, in *European Law Journal*, 2019, p. 457. ss. Also G. Martinico-O. Pollicino, O., "The National Judicial Resistance

European lexicon will not solve the problem (which in fact has political, historical, economic and cultural roots) of illiberal democracies. Rather, it is appropriate to redirect the concept of constitutional identity to a semantic domain in which its original link to constitutionalism is clear (and therefore to the ideas of *limiting* and organising power, on the one hand, and democratic legitimacy and participation, on the other[37]). The effectiveness of a relational grammar of constitutional identity is also evident from the Court of Justice's ruling on the conditionality mechanism, in particular, the requirement to uphold the Rule of Law as a precondition for protecting the Union's budget. This ruling can be seen as a symptom of the successful cross-fertilisation of this judicial argument: it is now the European Court that turns this notion against Hungary and Poland, reaffirming that legal limits on power and the independence of the judiciary, as expressions of the principle/value of the Rule of Law (Article 2 TEU), are part of a shared constitutional identity.[38] The constitutional State identity is ontologically linked to the incipient identity of the Union: it cannot and must not be eliminated. "*Ancora, affinché possa parlarsi, in maniera piena di senso, di identità costituzionale, questa dovrebbe avere un sufficiente radicamento sociale, all'interno di una comunità politica che abbia un orizzonte simbolico condiviso.*"[39] Constitutional identity must not be understood in an essentialist way and is therefore open to possible changes, but as we have seen in the preceding paragraphs, for example in the aforementioned Irish Grogan case, it has firm roots in the republican, democratic and social constitutionalism of the second post-war period. In the current European context, interaction with the supranational level is inevitable,

Against the European Court of Justice and the EU Charter of Fundamental Rights: Use and Abuse of a Promising Concept", en F. Fontanelli, G. Martinico y P. Carrozza (eds.), Shaping Rule of Law Through Dialogue: International and National Courts, Groningen, Europa Law Publishing, 2010, pp. 243–270.

[37] J. Scholtes, *Abusing Constitutional Identity*, cit., p. 551–570. Regarding the link between particular constitutional identity and general constitutional identity, see also B. Tripković, The Metaethics of Constitutional Adjudication, Oxford, Oxford University Press, 2017, p. 46 sq.

[38] CJEU, ruling 16.2.2022, C-156/21, *Hungary v Parliament and Council*, pt. 127, 232; sent. 16 February 2022, C-157/22, *Poland v. Parliament and Council*, pt. 145, 264; specifically on the aspect of constitutional identity, see P. Faraguna & T. Drinóczi, *Constitutional Identity in and on EU Terms*, in *verfassungsblog.de* (21 febbraio 2022).

[39] A. Di Martino, *Comparare le identità costituzionali: circolazione degli argomenti giuridici e contesti storico-politici*, in *Esperienze giuridiche in dialogo*r *Il ruolo della comparazione*, (eds.) M. Graziadei & A. Somma, Sapienza Università Editrice, Rome, 2024, p. 233.

and constitutional identity is an important concept for articulating conflicts and negotiating the assignation of authority between the different levels of government. Judgements situated outside the framework of judicial dialogue often cite this. So, once again the question is not terminological but conceptual.

As I argued at the beginning of this chapter, the only way to reconcile the openness of European constitutional democracy with a supranational landscape characterised by the same, or analogous, values is through some form of relationality that relativises the claim to absolute and ultimate authority, belonging to times long past, and therefore allows for compromise with peer constitutional centres within the same community. The impulse to defend one's own constitutional order against external intrusion cannot give way to the petrification of that order through the internal absolutisation of conceptions of constitutional identity. The real denial of dialogue and of the Union's identity, as previously argued, automatically places the State interlocutor outside the *communitas*. And this closed-mindedness must also be avoided within the State's own precincts. The tendency towards this denial of relationality bursts forth, or is even the cause, within the State itself. The conception of constitutional identity forged in the wake of Hungary's constitutional revolution is not the constitutional identity of an open society under constitutional democracy: it is the identity of the Law of Separation and exclusion of the Other (whether migrant or member of the LGBTQ+ collective). There is a virtuous cross-fertilisation and a vicious one. Denying social pluralism and avoiding the procedural openness of democracy under the guise of an artificially fabricated social homogeneity implies placing oneself outside the *communitas*. Its historicisation through the idea of the 'historical constitution' similarly suggests a form of constitutional identity deprived of dynamic properties, kept locked away in the vaults of its national past.

A historicised constitutional identity, inflexible to instability from within, will be similarly, if not more, insensitive to compromise with internal and external constitutional perspectives. "The Constitutional Court establishes that the constitutional self-identity of Hungary is a fundamental value not created by the Fundamental Law – it is merely acknowledged by the Fundamental Law. Consequently, constitutional identity cannot be waived by way of an international treaty – Hungary can only be deprived of its constitutional identity through the final termination of its sovereignty, its independent statehood. Therefore the protection of constitutional identity shall remain the duty of the Constitutional Court as long as Hungary is a sovereign State. Accordingly, sovereignty and constitutional identity have several common points, thus their control should be performed with due regard to each other in specific cases."[40]

Therefore, apparently basing constitutional identity on grounds that do not need to be tied to the constitutional text as such, the decision effectively judicialised the political claims of an exclusionary ethno-cultural constitutional identity, according to which the settlement of "culturally foreign" refugees would be unacceptable.[41] Halmai thus criticises the decision as an "abuse of constitutional identity" and a form of "national constitutional provincialism, an attempt to abandon the European constitutional context".[42] In a White Paper published by the government in English, the government's arguments are set out. The government declares: "*169. The legal system of the European Union is based on constitutional pluralism of the member states. […] Each country has specific constitutional solutions that are rooted in its history and legal traditions and these differences are protected by the treaty law* of the European Union. Article 4 of the Treaty on European Union quoted above shows that the Union respects national identity which is inherent in the fundamental political and constitutional structures of the member states. 170. Constitutional identity, a core value of each national community, determines not only the most fundamental values and resulting tasks for state authorities, **but also sets the limit for regulatory intervention of the European Union**. 176. The right to introduce its own **sovereign** institutional solutions concerning the judiciary is a pillar of each national constitutional system in Europe. […] 177. As has already been mentioned before, the new Polish regulations cannot be an exact copy of the legislation of other EU member states. It is obvious that there are differences in legal systems within the EU, this follows from separate constitutional identities of individual states, and this diversity is protected by the Treaty on European Union" [emphasis added].[43] It is the sovereign paradigm, not based on cross-fertilisation,[44]

[40] J. Scholtes, *The Abuse of Constitutional Identity*, cit., p. 133.

[41] K. Kovács, The Rise of an Ethnocultural Constitutional Identity in the Jurisprudence of the East Central European Courts, in German Law Journal, vol. 18, n° 7, 2017, pp. 1703–1720.

[42] G. Halmai, *Abuse of Constitutional Identity: The Hungarian Constitutional Court on Interpretation of Article E) (2) of the Fundamental Law*, in *Review of Central and East European Law*, 2018, pp. 23–42.

[43] The Chancellery of the Prime Minister, White Paper on the Reform of the Polish Judiciary (2018) <www.prem ier.gov.pl/ files/ files/ whit e_ pa per_ en_ f ull.pdf>.

[44] The essay by K. Lenaerts is particularly illuminating in this regard: K. Lenaerts, *Interlocking Legal Orders in the European Union and Comparative Law*, in *International and Comparative Law Quarterly*, vol. 52, n° 4, octubre 2003, pp. 873–906.

on constitutional and then European contextualisation but on a compartmentalised set of sovereign and solipsistic systems.

Constitutional identity is a fundamental principle of the Union, alongside Articles 2 and 19 TEU, requiring commitment to a constitution not as a means to an end that exists outside it but as an end in itself, providing a framework for public life within which a political organisation can politically negotiate its purpose and direction.

Among other changes, a provision was introduced in the Basic Law stating that "no foreign population shall settle in Hungary". Moreover, the amendment added a phrase to Article R, establishing that "the protection of the constitutional identity and Christian culture of Hungary shall be an obligation of all State organs". The Ninth Amendment, on the other hand, is much clearer in linking political issues with constitutional identity. Much of the amendment focuses on issues related to the importance of the family and traditional gender roles. The Ninth Amendment constitutionally enshrines a series of views on gender and the family. In its amended form, Article L) now states: "Hungary will protect the institution of marriage as the union of a man and a woman established by voluntary decision, and the family as the basis for the survival of the nation. Family ties will be based on marriage or the relationship between parents and children. The mother will be a woman, the father will be a man." Additionally, Article XVI has been amended to establish that "Hungary will protect the right of children to an identity corresponding to their sex at birth, and *will guarantee education in accordance with values based on the constitutional identity and the Christian culture of our country*". The solution to this dilemma lies in changing the concept of constitutional identity from something inherent to *the constitution* to something inherent to the *people* and therefore placed *beyond* the constitution.

But there is more. Some countries in the Union have invoked Article 4.2 of the Treaty on European Union (TEU) to justify reservations about EU Law, arguing that their national identities (marked by rejection of migration and multiculturalism) deserve to be respected and exempted from certain common obligations, such as the relocation of refugees.[45]

[45] The CJEU rejected this claim, requiring the primacy of EU Law and held that these countries had failed to fulfil their obligations to the EU. CJEU (Grand Chamber), 2 April 2020, European Commission v Republic of Poland, Hungary and Czech Republic, Joined Cases C-715/17, C-718/17 and C-719/17, ECLI:EU:C:2020:25. See also CJEU, (Grand Chamber), 6 September 2017, Slovak Republic and Hungary v Council of the European Union, Joined Cases C-643/15 and C-647/15, ECLI:EU:C:2017:631. The Hungarian,

Along a similar line of reasoning, the States that make up the Visegrád Group (the so-called V4: Czech Republic, Hungary, Poland and Slovakia) maintain that the preservation of the 'traditional family' constitutes an essential value, protected as part of their national identity within the European legal framework. On this basis, these countries argue that the European Union should recognise the legitimacy of maintaining a divergent position regarding the recognition of same-sex marriage.

What is particularly revealing is that this stance converges, in certain respects, with positions adopted by governments such as the Russian Federation or the United States under the Trump administration. Gender identity, within the framework of exclusionary identity, led the European Commission to bring a case before the Court of Justice regarding the persecution of certain groups based on gender in the already extensively mentioned case, currently pending resolution.

The adoption of the Treaty of Lisbon has proven to be a turning point. The concept of constitutional or national identity appeared in the Case Law of the constitutional courts in the context of the Visegrád Group (V4) countries' membership in the European Union. Since the Treaty of Lisbon entered into force in 2009, the courts of the V4, following the example of the German Federal Constitutional Court (FCC), have drawn on identity discourse and have tended to protect the distinctive identities of their nations. The Hungarian Constitutional Court (HCC) and the Polish Constitutional Court (*Trybunał Konstytucyjny*) have even provided ethno-cultural justifications for the legal concept of identity.

In defining the meaning of identity, they have relied on selective historical narratives and events from the "glorious" past of their respective countries to serve as a foundation for future constitutional interpretation. In alignment with their governments, they often portray their nations as victims of 'foreign aggression', possessing the necessary greatness to overcome repression, an element that becomes essential to their national identity, in a manner not unlike that of the Russian Constitutional Court. In 2010, the President of the Russian Constitutional Court introduced the concept of identity as a tool to preserve the traditional values of Russian society. Since then, the Court has deployed this concept in opposition to the tradition of human rights, portraying them as alien to Russian

Polish and Slovak governments submitted written observations on this matter in Case C-490/20, *VMA v. Stolichna obshtina, "Pancharevo" district* (Municipality of Sofia, Pancharevo district, Bulgaria).

civilisation.[46] Moreover, these constitutional courts have invoked identity in areas beyond the traditional scope of constitutionalism, namely in political matters such as migration or Family Law.

11.3 The Structuring of the European Union: Cross-Fertilisation *Ad Intra* and *Ad Extra*

The comparative method is intrinsically associated with the action of the European Court, as Mauro Cappelletti stated back in 1986, "unlike the American Supreme Court and the European Constitutional Courts, the Court of Justice has almost no powers that are not ultimately derived from its own prestige, intellectual and moral force of its opinions".[47] The comparative method in our study signifies respect for otherness, both within and beyond the European territory: *ad intra* and *ad extra*. Relationality is always two-way; otherwise, it becomes a regression into hegemony. This defining feature of the European Union's identity has been present since its inception, as evidenced by the reference to Africa in the Schuman Declaration. There, we questioned whether it represented a reproduction of the hegemonic identity described in the First Part or whether it constituted a *quid novum*; this *écart* remains throughout the Second Part, despite the reconstruction of a new typology of identity. The legal structuring of the European Union's identity takes place through the circulation of principles, constitutional traditions and identities, filtered through the *Kadi* doctrine, and through the reconfiguration of the internal/external divide as a separative dynamic. The connotation of the 'in-between' is expressed via Habermasian communicative discourse, both between the national (constitutional) system and the EU legal order, and between the latter and the international legal system. The idea of autonomy and the primacy of a given identity and its legal order applies mutatis mutandis

[46] A. Zoteeva & M. Kragh, *From constitutional identity to the identity of the Constitution*, in *Communist and Post-Communist Studies*, 2021, pp. 176–195. The jurisprudence of the Russian Constitutional Court on the prohibition of "propaganda of non-traditional sexual relations" and the prohibition of "books containing misrepresentations" might well be guiding some Hungarian and Polish judges. Ibid., 185–88. Indeed, this is an identitarian issue that also emerges in the Hungarian case, dealt by the CJUEC-769/22 (cf. next Chapter).

[47] M. Cappelletti, y D. Golay, *The Judicial Branch in the Federal and Transnational Union: Its Impact on Integration*, in AA.VV., *Integration Through Law*, Volume 1, *Methods, Tools and Institutions, Book 2: Political Organs, Integration Techniques and Judicial Process*, De Gruyter, 1986, 277.

both to the relationships between constitutional courts and the CJEU, and between the CJEU and the international legal order. Naturally, this mechanism of cross-fertilisation inevitably enhances the role of the CJEU as a zipper-figure, defending both the identity and the legal order of the Union, *ad intra* and *ad extra*. However, it also imposes a responsibility on both the EU legal order and the Court itself. For this system to function effectively, it must avoid the mistake of separating itself from (and excluding) the Other, this time understood in an international sense. Such an error would be adolescent in nature and would risk undermining the very functioning of the relational mechanism, just as much as social rejection of the Other in its various forms (migrants, LGBTQ+ communities, etc.) threatens internal cohesion.

Ultimately, the relationship between the Court of Justice and national constitutional courts is based on the exercise of the principle of constitutional tolerance, as defined by Weiler. In the present work, this principle is nourished by a comparative epistemology. That the comparative method has helped shape the EU legal category of general principles and common constitutional traditions is only one part of the legal narrative.

The full scope of the substantial difference between the delimitation of identity and its structural articulation lies entirely in the *écart* between the *Costa v. ENEL* judgement of 1964 and the *Kadi II* ruling of 2008. The former reflects an exclusionary identity paradigm; the latter gives way to an inclusionary identity paradigm, marked by the significant presence of common constitutional traditions. Seen *à rebours*, the history of national judgements concerning the defence of constitutional identity is evidence of the fruitful dialectic of the national Voice expressed within the broader context of the integration process. That voice may disappear altogether through the right of withdrawal under Article 50 TEU, but once it becomes embedded within the legal order, the constitutional and European threads become inextricably intertwined. There is no Article 2 TEU without the study of the decisions of the Italian and German Constitutional Courts: it is the evolution of the Voice or the judicial voice. The measure of this assertion is given by comparing the combination of the *Enel* judgement by the Italian Constitutional Court and the Court of Justice, on the one hand, with the recent decisions on constitutional identity issued by both judicial bodies. "The identification of the constitutional identity of a state implies a comparison with other states, and their common traditions are identified by surveying the multiplicity of traditions that exist in the states concerned. If we abandon a comparative constitutional perspective when considering European law, we run the risk of favouring a monistic approach at the risk of losing the advantages offered by the pluralist approach."[48]

"EU law is characterised by the fact that it stems from an independent source of law, namely the Treaties, by its primacy over the laws of the Member States, and by the direct effect of a whole series of provisions which are applicable to their nationals and to the Member States themselves. Those characteristics have given rise to a **structured network of principles, rules and mutually interdependent legal relations** binding the European Union and its Member States reciprocally as well as binding its Member States to each other" [emphasis added].[49] The Court clarifies that this network-like construction is composed of States that have freely and voluntarily adhered to these values so that "EU law is thus based on the fundamental premiss that each Member State shares with all the other Member States, and recognises that they share with it, a set of common values on which the EU is founded" [emphasis added].[50] When expressed through a constitutional register, the Luxembourg Court must take into account a dialectical vision of identity, what Ricoeur would call an identity in terms of ipseity. It advocates a systematic interpretation of Article 4(2) TEU in light of the provisions of Articles 4(3) and 6(1) TEU. This is precisely what it did in the *Kadi I*,[51] *Digital Rights*,[52] *Google Spain*[53] and

[48] S. Bartole, *Comparative Constitutional Law—an Indispensable Tool for the Creation of Transnational Law*, in *European Constitutional Law Review*, 2017, pp. 601–610. Cf. M. Maduro, *Three claims of constitutional pluralism*, in M. Avbely & J. Komarek (eds.), *Constitutional Pluralism in the European Union and* Beyond, Hart, Oxford, 2012, p. 67.

[49] Judgment of the Court of Justice (Grand Chamber) of 6 March, 2018, Slowakische Republik v. Achmea BV, Case C-284/16, ECLI:EU:C:2018:234, p. 456.

[50] Judgment of the Court (plenary) of 10 December 2018, Andy Wightman and Others v. *Secretary of State for Exiting the European Union, Case C-621/18,* ECLI:EU:C:2018:999, p. 167–168.

[51] Judgment of the Court of Justice (Grand Chamber) of 3 September 2008, Yassin Abdullah Kadi and Al Barakaat International Foundation v. Council of the European Union and Joined Cases C-402/05 P and C-415/05 P, Case Law 2008 I-06351, ECLI:EU:C:2008:461.

[52] Judgment of the Court of Justice (Grand Chamber) of 8 April 2014, Digital Rights Ireland Ltd. v. Minister for Communications, Marine and Natural Resources and Others and Kärntner Landesregierung and Others, Joined Cases C-293/12 and C-594/12, ECLI:EU:C:2014:238.

[53] Judgment of the Court of Justice (Grand Chamber) of 13 May 2014, Google Spain, S.L. and Google Inc. v. Agencia Española de Protección de Datos (AEPD) and Mario Costeja González, Case C-131/12, ECLI:EU:C:2014:317.

Schrems I and II[54] judgements, among many others. The principle of subsidiarity, enshrined in Article 5(3) TEU, can be considered a constitutional commitment of the Union to the spirit of cooperation. Like the principle of subsidiarity, the principle of respect for the national identities of the Member States fits perfectly with the model of cooperative federalism. The identity clause requires the drafting and interpretation of European rules to be sensitive to the nation, and it publicly acknowledges the necessary multinational composition of the Union.[55]

In each of the decisions cited above, the reference to common constitutional traditions takes on a new dimension of constitutional significance and openness.[56] In dialogue with the constitutional courts, the Court of Luxembourg is acquiring the aforementioned technique of "fundamental weighting",[57] which is absent from the Case Law of its first 30 years. At the same time, as Schütze explains, a new model of political organisation, which he calls cooperative federalism, is progressively developing.[58] The structural defect in these relevant *arrêts* is the lack of clarity in comparative operations. The more transparent the operation of cross-fertilisation (both in the conclusions of the Advocates General, who in many cases now produce genuine essays in Comparative Law, and above all in the Court's judgements), the more involved constitutional judges will feel in the construction of general principles, constitutional traditions and supranational identity. It is, as we have already argued, the 'Mangold syndrome'. A greater use of common constitutional traditions by the CJEU must be accompanied by a stronger participatory responsibility towards constitutional courts, lest the elaborations from Luxembourg fail to take root as Living Law at the national level.

[54] Judgment of the Court of Justice of the European Union, Data Protection Commissioner v Maximillian Schrems and Facebook Ireland, Case C-311/18,, 16 July 2020, ECLI:EU:C:2020:559.

[55] E. Cloots, *National Identity, Constitutional Identity, and Sovereignty in the EU*, in *Netherlands Journal of Legal Philosophy* 2016 (45), p. 2.

[56] Cf. A. Ruggieri, *Struttura e dinamica delle tradizioni costituzionali nella prospettiva dell'integrazione europea*, in *Anuario Iberoamericano de Justicia Constitucional*, n. 7, 2003, pp. 373–339.

[57] As defined by J.H.H. Weiler, *The Constitution of Europe*, cit., p. 123.

[58] R. Schütze, *From Dual to Cooperative Federalism. The Changing Structure of European* Law, Oxford University Press, Oxford, 2009, pp. 76–77.

11.4 Failed Structuring Cross-Fertilisation System: The Opinion 2/13

Akin to what was set out in the *Kadi* I case, the CJEU carefully delineated the pillars that constitute its autonomy, considering them the essential and inviolable core of its legal order. This recognition underscores the uniqueness and particularity of that normative system, through an operation similar to the claims made by national constitutional courts. This is evidenced in paragraphs 159 and following of the Opinion, where, after listing the conditions for accession, the CJEU reaffirmed the *sui generis* nature of EU Law, highlighting the "specific characteristics stemming from the very nature of EU law" (para. 165). Does this assertion of autonomy imply separation and exclusion, or rather a tendency towards relationality with the international legal order?

The Court's reasoning stems from the fundamental principle of the autonomy of its legal corpus, transforming it into the argumentative foundation on which its narrative is built, and then proceeds to define a set of irreducible principles that must be shielded from any infringement. Once again, this seems like a *déjà vu* of the vast majority of constitutional court rulings. In this context, as the Court has repeatedly emphasised, European Union Law is distinguished by deriving from an independent source (the Treaties) and by the primacy it holds over the national laws of the Member States.

These essential attributes have given rise to an intricate web of principles, rules and interdependent legal relationships, which bind not only the Union and the Member States but also the Member States to one another. This structure, as stated in the second paragraph of Article 1 of the Treaty on European Union (TEU), is framed within "a process of creating an ever closer union among the peoples of Europe". Founded on the cardinal premise that each Member State shares with, and recognises in, the others a set of common values enshrined in Article 2 TEU, this legal architecture stands as an unequivocal testament to the collective commitment to those values.

Furthermore, the protection of fundamental rights marks a point of divergence between *Opinion 2/13* and the *Kadi* judgement in terms of outcome. While *Kadi* ultimately made the safeguarding of fundamental rights a core element of its concept of autonomy, here (between autonomy and the potential enhancement of fundamental rights protection), the CJEU appears to regard the former as the prevailing interest (even though, in its reasoning, the protection of fundamental rights is included in the untouchable core identified in paragraph 169 of the Opinion).

"It is impossible not to agree with those lines and not to recognise that, in Opinion 2, the logic 'thou shalt have no other courts before me'169 has prevailed, unless one does not want to conceive of this Opinion as a sort of blackmail to oblige Member States to reinforce the protection of fundamental rights by giving more jurisdiction to the Luxembourg Court."[59] This time, the dynamics of limits (whether as walls or porous borders) are projected onto the international stage.[60] This means that without entering into the debate over the similarities (and differences) between *Kadi* and *Solange*, the first attempts at intertwining the legal threads in the 1970s stand as a perfect example of the importance of relational identities that, 30 years later, the Court of Justice in Luxembourg would promote at the international level. What many interpreted at the time as a potential crisis in the European integration process in fact served as a highly positive turning point in the jurisprudential relationship between the CJEU and national constitutional courts. This cross-fertilisation, inherent to the open or closed nature of primacy and autonomy, can indeed be replicated at the international level, provided that the outward momentum driven by the European Court is met with a corresponding receptiveness by constitutional courts within the European territory. Otherwise, we would revert to a time of separation and exclusionary identity, as glimpsed in Opinion 2/13. "This belief is difficult to achieve in its absoluteness because the incorporation-postulate into the legal systems of the Member States isn't free from contradictions when taking into account older and more recent decisions on the concept of autonomy, i.e. the independence of Union law vis-à-vis national law and international law alike. If the jurisprudence boils down to an outwardly dualistic, inwardly monistic approach the ECJ doesn't do much different than national constitutional courts in federal states."[61]

Perhaps the *Kadi* saga paves the way for a new season of constraint and, hopefully, for stronger protection of fundamental rights at the

[59] G. Martinico, *The Tangled Complexity of the EU Constitutional Process. The Frustrating Knot of Europe*, Routledge, Second Edition, 2023, p. 67.

[60] A. von Bogdandy & S. W. Schill, "*Overcoming Absolute Primacy; Respect for National Identity under the Lisbon Treaty*, in *Common Market Law Review*, 2011, pp. 1417–1453.

[61] F. Weber, *The Identity of Union Law in Primacy: Piercing Through Euro Box Promotion and Others*, in *European Papers* www.europeanpapers.eu ISSN 2499–8249, Vol. 7, 2022, No 2, p. 761.

international level. The *Schrems* case shares the same spirit (and indeed *Kadi* was mentioned in the judgement, 176). On that occasion, the CJEU declared Decision 2000/520 invalid, as it violated, among other things, "the essence of the fundamental right to respect for private life, as guaranteed by Article 7 of the Charter" (paragraph 94). As mentioned, *Kadi* appears in paragraph 60, recalling the Court's consistent Case Law according to which the European Union is a Union based on the Rule of Law, in which all acts of its institutions are subject to judicial review of their compatibility, in particular, with the Treaties, the general principles of Law and fundamental rights. As Sarmiento pointed out, *Schrems* tells us that "privacy is a super-fundamental right that reigns above all other rights",[62] and along with other decisions, it conveys the impression of a Court that is highly committed to the protection of fundamental rights and to actively using the Charter of Fundamental Rights.

Porous identity not only implies preserving one's specificity but also opening up to the Other outside (as occurred in *Kadi*, with its principle of *primauté* applied critically to International Law), while Opinion 2/13 marks a return to closure and to an exclusionary identity.

The CJEU focused on the idea of autonomy, creating uncertainty about the 'place' of fundamental rights within the identity of the EU as a constitutional entity. Moreover, in a statement delivered at the plenary session of the FIDE conference, the then President of the Court of Justice declared that "the Court is not a human rights court: it is the Supreme Court of the Union". These are the words of a Court of Justice that is not aligned with its own Charter of Rights, with the Charter of Fundamental Rights of the EU, whose scope remains unclear following judgements such as *Fransson* and *Siragusa*. This factor is by no means secondary; on the contrary, it is highly revealing of the recent challenges encountered by the CJEU. In this sense, the Opinion may be seen as part of a broader crisis of values that casts doubt on the application of Article 6 TEU. Furthermore, these conclusions can be read in conjunction with a series of judgements from many national courts that oppose the activism of the ECHR. In this regard, I agree with colleagues who argued that the word autonomy in Opinion 2/13 should be understood as equivalent to

[62] D. Sarmiento, *What Schrems, Delvigne and Celaj Tell us about the State of Fundamental Rights in the EU*, 2015, http://verfassungsblog.de/author/daniel-sarmiento/

sovereignty.[63] "Without any doubt, this Opinion is the product of a Court that does not know how to handle the axiological part of its constitution (the Charter of Fundamental Rights) and understands the ECHR as a source of problems rather than an added value This has a clear consequence on what we could call the case law of the EU constitutional identity, with an approach that could appear schizophrenic but is tremendously coherent if seen from the perspective of a court that has always been interested in protecting the autonomy of its own legal system."

This tendency to understand autonomy and primacy in a solipsistic or adolescent way contrasts with the preamble to the Charter of Fundamental Rights, which states that the exercise of the rights contained therein "generates responsibilities and duties towards others, as well as towards the human community and future generations. Thus, the responsibilities, 'duties' and action of the Community are outside the limitation of space, since explicit reference is made to 'Others', to the 'human **community**' as a whole, the 'external' relevance of its action, and also to the limitation of time, since responsibility is also directed to 'future generations'". "*Il destino della Carta, e con esso quello dell'Unione, non è affidato a una qualche identità che ne congeli gli spiriti, la chiuda in una logica oppositiva nei confronti degli altri, proprio quegli 'altri' che, invece, il Preambolo indica come riferimenti necessari, inseparabili dal mondo che l'Unione vuole contribuire a edificare, proiettandosi al di là dei suoi stessi egoismi.*"[64] But it is not just about considering the community order as a compound but recognising the essential nature of interactions and drawing fluid boundaries in national identities. "We may be observing a transition from the fragmentary experience of the various national legal orders to a global legal space constructed from the raw materials of national experiences - as we see happening today in Europe. Therefore, a comparative methodological approach is still important and productive, and not only for the sake of

[63] "Structurally, the ECJ seems to understand autonomy in a similar way as national constitutional courts conceive of sovereignty: EU law should reign supreme in its jurisdiction and any encroachment by another authority must be put under the ECJ's check. This comes in the form of various instruments safeguarding the ECJ a place, which is quite unparalleled to that of any constitutional court of the parties to the Convention. It shall be remembered that the ECJ asked for these safeguards in a "discussion paper", by which it became involved in the drafting process of the Accession Agreement in a way unthinkable in any European constitutional system," J. Komárek, '*It's a Stupid Autonomy*, 2014, http://verfassungsblog.de/its-a-stupid-autonomy-2/

[64] S. Rodotà, *Il diritto di avere diritti*, Laterza, Bari, 2012, p. 31.

scientific research and knowledge. The comparative methodological approach might even prove more immediately practical and operationally useful than in the past, as demonstrated by the European experience."[65] Only in this way will we perceive the porosity of borders and analyse the complexity of reality, which is shaped by the tension between Eros, positing attachment to land as a form of identity, and civilisation, understood here as legal culture, as Herbert Marcuse reminds us.[66]

Regarding the institutions, bodies and agencies of the EU as addressees of this provision, Article 4.2 of the TEU not only serves as a tool for the judicial protection of the Member State's position but also, as a core principle of diversity, must be taken into account at every stage of the decision-making processes within the Union.[67]

It is clear that the values enshrined in Article 2 TEU form part of the political and/or constitutional structures and, therefore, of the national identity of each and every Member State of the European Union. This follows from the system laid down in Articles 2, 7 and 49 TEU. All Member States wishing to join the European Union must respect the values of Article 2 TEU (Article 49 TEU).[68] Therefore, accession, in most cases, initiates a process of convergence of the political and constitutional structures of the acceding State in order to meet this requirement (part of the so-called Copenhagen criteria). Once admitted, permanent compliance with these values is ensured through the penalties provided for in Article 7 TEU. "Common" values can find a "specific" form in the Member State considered individually.[69] Once admitted, permanent compliance with these values is ensured through the penalties provided for in Article 7 TEU. In contrast to these values that unite the Member States, the essential elements of the structures of the Member States are largely

[65] S. Bartole, *Comparative Constitutional Law—an Indispensable Tool for the Creation of Transnational Law*, in *European Constitutional Law Review*, 2017, pp. 601–610. Cf. M. Maduro, *'Three claims of constitutional pluralism'*, in M. Avbely & J. Komarek (eds.), *Constitutional Pluralism in the European Union and* Beyond, Hart, Oxford, 2012, p. 68.

[66] Marcuse, H., Eros and Civilization: A Philosophical Inquiry into Freud, Boston, Beacon Press, 1955.

[67] I. Pernice, *Der Schutz nationaler Identität in der Europäischen Union*, in *Archiv des öffentlichen Rechts*, 2011, pp. 185–221.

[68] H.J. Blanke, *Article 4 [The Relations Between the EU and the Member States]*, in *The Treaty on European Union (TEU). A Commentary*, H.-J. Blanke & S. Mangiameli (eds.), Springer, 2010, Berlin, Heidelberg, pp. 185–253.

[69] E. Di Salvatore, *L'identità costituzionale dell'Unione europea e degli Stati membri*, Giappichelli, Torino, 2008.

found in historically developed internal peculiarities that the Treaty explicitly highlights in the form of "fundamental structures, political and constitutional, of regional and inclusive local self-government". From these considerations, we can extrapolate two important corollaries: the duty to respect the values deriving from the moment of the free choice to join the Union (the constitutive moment) and the duty to defend these values (the proactive moment). This is a highly significant consideration, already present in the aforementioned ruling of the Italian Constitutional Court in the so-called *Taricco* case. The first moment is constitutive of the identity coexistence, safeguarding constitutional identity within the community framework. The second moment is proactive because it implies an attitude of every Member State to act and defend the community identity.

11.4.1 The Third Encounter with the Other: The European Union as a 'Community of Values'

We have reached the European Union's final encounter with the Other, going back over our work. Whereas in the previous sections of this Second Part, the issue of identity remained relevant but largely implicit, in the last 10 years it has become unmistakably visible. In Part One, we asked whether it is possible to structure the European Union by means of integration through values; in short, whether it is possible to construct a European Union identity. "The values enshrined in Article 2 of the Treaty on European Union have been identified and are shared by the Member States. They define the very identity of the European Union as a common legal order. Therefore, the Union must be able to defend these values, within the limits of its powers established by the Treaties."[70]

[70]Twin judgements CJEU, 22 February 2022, C-156/21, Hungary v European Parliament and Council of the European Union; ECLI:EU:C:2022:97, para. 127; CJEU, 22 February 2022, C-157/21, Poland v European Parliament and Council of the European Union, ECLI:EU:C:2022:98, para. 145.

CHAPTER 12

The Third Encounter with the Other: The European Union as a 'Community of Values'—Article 2 TEU as a Limit, Standard of Conduct and System of Values

Abstract This chapter explores the European Union's identity framework, emphasising Article 2 TEU as a triple foundational element. Article 2 TEU serves as the EU's foundational standard, embodying shared values and forming a dynamic, interconnected system. It underpins both the Union's and Member States' identities, mediates constitutional pluralism,

We have reached the European Union's final encounter with the Other, going back over our work. Whereas in the previous sections of this Second Part, the issue of identity remained relevant but largely implicit, in the last ten years it has become unmistakably visible. In Part One, we asked whether it is possible to structure the European Union by means of integration through values; in short, whether it is possible to construct a European Union identity. "The values enshrined in Article 2 of the Treaty on European Union have been identified and are shared by the Member States. They define the very identity of the European Union as a common legal order. Therefore, the Union must be able to defend these values, within the limits of its powers established by the Treaties." (Twin judgements CJEU, 22 February 2022, C-156/21, Hungary v European Parliament and Council of the European Union; ECLI:EU:C:2022:97, para. 127; CJEU, 22 February 2022, C-157/21, Poland v European Parliament and Council of the European Union, ECLI:EU:C:2022:98, para. 145.)

© The Author(s), under exclusive license to Springer Nature Switzerland AG 2026

A. Lazari, *Relational Identity in International, Comparative and European Union Law*,
https://doi.org/10.1007/978-3-031-59482-3_12

and sets limits for membership and national divergence. Article 2 TEU obliges Member States to respect and promote common values proactively, ensuring no backsliding, with ongoing obligations beyond accession, maintaining EU membership as a mutual commitment. Article 2 TEU establishes a system of interrelated values and principles forming the EU's constitutional identity, balancing national and European identities. The principle of diversity is the basis of the European system, always within the framework of a Popperian open society.

Keywords Article 2 TEU • European values and principles • Constitutional identity

The general identity framework of the European Union does not consist solely of Article 2 TEU but is derived from an analysis of the wording of the identity clause and its relationship with other provisions and principles of the Treaty, in particular those laid down in Articles 4, sections 1, 2 and 3 TEU, Article 3(3) TEU, Article 167 of the Treaty on the Functioning of the European Union (TFEU), the fundamental rights protected by the Charter of Fundamental Rights of the EU, and the various provisions that protect elements of regional and local autonomy. This does not mean that Article 2 TEU, like the principle of primacy of EU Law, is not autonomous. It is, as argued capably by the General Advocate Ćapeta.[1] However, the primacy of EU Law and the Union's values should not imply separation; on the contrary, they are built upon a porous and inclusive identity, in contrast to the approach analysed in Part One. This entire framework should resemble a web in relation to national identity constructs. Until now, this comparison has often been framed as a gap, a source of tension and conflict viewed primarily through an adversarial lens. "The identity clause, understood as a *Verbundnorm*, only opens the EU legal order for the recognition of the normative content of national legal orders and does not transform such into autonomous content of EU Law. The conflict between EU Law and Member States' constitutional identity is still fundamentally a conflict between two different legal orders and their respective

[1] In the conclusions of Advocate General Ćapeta, presented on 5 June 2025, Commission v. Hungary, C-769/22; the legal profiles of violations of Article 2 TEU are analysed in paragraphs 164–175.

content. In light of the identity clause, the conflict merely presents itself as a conflict within the frame of the EU legal order."[2]

This is where the idea of relational identity comes into play. While constitutionalisation creates a system of fertilisation and mutual stabilisation in which European Constitutional Law and national Constitutional Law influence each other and develop mutual compatibility, the primacy of EU Law, in contrast, requires national Constitutional Law to conform to European requirements of homogeneity. As such, national Constitutional Law may have to accept a considerable degree of relativisation. At the same time, National Constitutional Law (conveyed through the general principles of Law) remains the most important reservoir for the reception of European Constitutional Law.[3] Consequently, in this composite and interwoven legal system, unity is achieved through balancing, that is, through the *écart* between different interests, with the aim of ensuring the effective resolution of issues within the shared legal space. This shared normativity can be found at all levels of the legal system. Within the shared legal space between the EU and the Member States, legal unity is determined neither solely by the provisions and principles of European Law nor by National (Constitutional) Law.

If viewed through this lens, Article 4.2 TEU can be regarded, in the first place, simply as the expression of a principle that existed from the beginning of the integration process, albeit *in nuce*. As confirmed by Advocate General Poiares Maduro in *Spain v. Eurojust* and then in the *Michaniki* case before the introduction of Article 4(2) TEU: "The European Union is obliged to respect the constitutional identity of the Member States. That obligation has existed from the outset. It indeed forms part of the very essence of the European project initiated at the beginning of the 1950s, which consists of following the path of integration whilst maintaining the political existence of the States."[4] Apart from its specific legislation in a specific case, the national identity clause of Article 4(2) TEU is therefore also a political signal that the EU is not and will not become a federation: instead, it is open fertile ground for the

[2] A. Schnettger, *Article 4(2) TEU as a Vehicle for National Constitutional Identity in the Shared European Legal System*, in *Identity In A Europe of Multilevel Constitutionalism*, C. Calliess & G. van der Schyff (eds.), Cambridge University Press, Cambridge, 2020, p. 78.

[3] An example of this is Article 6(3) TEU on fundamental rights or Article 340 TFEU on the responsibility of the Union.

[4] Opinion of Advocate General Poiares Maduro in Case C-160/03 Spain v. Eurojust ECLI:EU: C:2005:168, para. 31.

écart. "At the same time, the Court should also make clear once and for all, that national identity claims, as is the opinion of almost all commentators, cannot go against the founding values of Article 2 TEU. 'Exclusive' or 'absolute' constitutional identities are not welcomed in the EU legal space."[5]

These cultural and social frictions, however, must not be interpreted negatively: once again, they attest to growing maturity within the very idea of European pluralist identity. To ensure that a political community is truly inclusive so that all its citizens feel "at home and live well together", citizens must feel that their identity, including their national identity, is respected. Consequently, although it may sound paradoxical, a multinational political subject such as the European Union will have to pay attention to the loyalties that its citizens feel towards their own national groups if it wishes to gain the loyalty of its citizens and ensure its viability. "Many national constitutional courts have understood this, and have developed a theoretical basis for their claim that EU Law must comply with the identity of their constitution."[6]

The politics of constitutional identity, like any procedural mechanism in cross-fertilisation, do not end once a claim has been made. The need to engage with competing constitutional sites means that any claim must be placed in an appropriate relationship with the claims and legitimacy resources of these dialoguing authorities. The incorporation of Supranational Law into the legal systems of the Member States implies that the integrity and maintenance of those other legal systems are also an integral concern for national legal systems. As a result, the legitimacy of a claim to constitutional identity also depends on the ways in which it is used to relate to overlapping legal regimes. The authority of one order is only legitimate if it does not fundamentally affect the authority of the other order.

From these considerations, we can extrapolate two important corollaries: the duty to respect values stemming from the moment the choice is made freely to join the Union (the constitutive moment) and the duty to defend these values (the proactive moment). This is a highly significant

[5] M. Bonelli, *National Identity and European Integration Beyond 'Limited Fields'*, in *European Public Law* 27, no. 3, 2021, p. 558. Cfr. also Z. Körtvélyesi & B. Majtényi, *Game of Values: The Threat of Exclusive Constitutional Identity, the EU and Hungary*, in *Germ. Law Jour.*, 2017, p. 564.

[6] E. Cloots, *National Identity, Constitutional Identity, and Sovereignty in the EU*, in *Netherlands Journal of Legal Philosophy*, 2016, p. 2.

consideration, already present in the aforementioned ruling of the Italian Constitutional Court in the so-called *Taricco* case. The first moment is constitutive of identity coexistence, safeguarding constitutional identity within the community framework. The second moment is proactive because it implies an attitude of every Member State to act and defend the community identity.

It will be argued that constitutional claims of identity should not be seen as peremptory claims of absolute authority but as arguments within a broader framework of relative authority. This makes it incumbent on national authorities to present arguments of constitutional identity in a manner that respects other constitutional areas. Instead of ending a dialogue with an introspective stance, constitutional identity claims initiate one: they cannot, in themselves, provide a reason to disengage from dialogue with competing constitutional sites. The cross-fertilisation mechanism puts into practice the very idea of supranational pluralism. "As a result of this pluralism, the nation- state is no longer unrivalled in its claim to constitutional authority but finds itself increasingly interacting with competing or overlapping sites of authority."[7]

In this regard, Scholtes' appeal to Richard Rorty's theory of ironism is very suggestive. As we have already seen in the preliminary phase of this Second Part, recognition of the Other is a fundamental principle in an inclusive understanding of identity. We must then add to this an attitude that is not *tranchant* or absolutist in its approach to the Other. This is the ironism of dialogical actors.[8] Rorty defines "ironism" as an attitude of sceptical detachment towards one's own way of understanding the world, derived, we might say, from the idea that there is no initial *prius* in the observation of reality. The ironist harbours radical and continuous doubts about the final vocabulary they currently use, because they have been impressed by other vocabularies taken as definitive by people or books they have encountered, and they realise that their own vocabulary can neither resolve nor dissolve these doubts, since it is no closer to reality than others (or) in contact with a power that is not itself. "The confrontation with rival constitutional sites highlights the contingency, and thus the

[7] J. Scholtes, *The Abuse of Constitutional Identity in the European Union*, Oxford University Press, Oxford, 2023, p. 211.

[8] R. Rorty, *Contingency, Irony, and Solidarity,* Cambridge University Press, Cambridge, 1989.

capacity for change, of one's own constitutional identity."[9] This is the attitude with which the mechanism of cross-fertilisation works, and it has a great deal to do with the idea of tolerance advocated by Weiler.[10]

We have already seen how constitutional identity is not affirmed in isolation from the EU level, but by making use of the avenues available for coordination and cooperation, most importantly, the pre-judicial referral procedure, but also more 'hidden' dialogue mechanisms,[11] as well as political avenues. Treating separate constitutional demands as immeasurable and therefore equally legitimate does not provide actors with a licence for "constitutional solipsism".[12] It merely underlines, as Kaarlo Tuori points out, the perspective of constitutional orders: the fact that beneath the multiple claims of authority by different legal systems are different interpretations of Law, rooted in national legal cultures and in the "concepts, principles and theories" of these cultures.

As Miguel Maduro points out, in an open society, agreements are never final; they never conclusively capture the true constitutional identity of a political organisation and always allow for the possibility of change. This should affect the confidence and determination with which "constitutional identity" is defended.[13] Likewise, recognising the dynamism of democratic politics internally must translate into a willingness to commit and have one's perspective of one influenced by external constitutional sites. Otherwise, in their quest to defend constitutional identity against external influence, a political organisation might petrify within a momentary image of itself and inadvertently undermine the openness of democratic decision-making.[14]

[9] R. Rorty, *Contingency, Irony, and Solidarity,* Cambridge University Press, Cambridge, 1989.

[10] In this sense, this notion is closely related to Weiler's famous postulate of "constitutional tolerance". See J.H.H. Weiler, 'In Defence of the Status Quo: Europe's Constitutional Sonderweg' in Marlene Wind and Joseph HH Weiler (eds), *European Constitutionalism beyond the State,* Cambridge University Press, Cambridge, 2003.

[11] G. Martinico, *Judging in the Multilevel Legal Order: Exploring the Techniques of 'Hidden Dialogue'*, in *King's Law Journal*, 2010, p. 257.

[12] K. Tuori, *European Constitutionalism,* Cambridge University Press, Cambridge, 2015, p. 102.

[13] M. Poiares Maduro, *Three Claims of Constitutional Pluralism,* in M. Avbelj & J. Komárek (eds), *Constitutional Pluralism in the European Union and Beyond*, Bloomsbury Publishing, London, 2012, p. 78.

[14] H. Lindahl, *The Purposiveness of Law: Two Concepts of Representation in the European Union*, in Law *and Philosophy*, 1998, p. 481.

Relational dynamics express the identity of the European Union through Article 2 of the TEU. It is the choice of a good society, an open society based on constitutional democracy that respects human rights. This is the reflection put forward by Advocate General Ćapeta, who, because of its axiological depth, deserves to be quoted verbatim:

> 155. Article 2 TEU expresses the *choice* of the founders of the European Union as to the type of society that the Member States have pledged to create together within the framework of the European Union.
> 156. One can imagine different societies: autocracies not based on the separation of powers; societies in which the elected majority is not limited by the requirement to respect human rights; societies which are ruled by men, and not by law; societies that do not treat minorities equally and reserve human dignity only for the majority; or societies that do not recognise that women are equal to men. Such societies do indeed exist, and are emerging, throughout the world.
> 157. The vision of what a *good society* is in the EU constitution is different. That vision is expressed in Article 2 TEU. The values enumerated in that provision: respect for human dignity, freedom, democracy, equality, the rule of law and respect for human rights, including the rights of persons belonging to minorities, read together, paint a picture of a *constitutional democracy that respects human rights.*
> 158. That choice is expressed in the opening provision of the Treaties, and, therefore, as explained by the Court, represents the *very identity* of the European Union. In short, without those values, the European Union would cease to be the Union as envisaged by the Treaties.

For these reasons, Article 2 of the Treaty on European Union can be understood as a freely chosen commitment (both by the Union and by the Member States), as active behaviour and as a system of interconnected values and principles.

12.1 The Configuration of Article 2 TEU as the EU'S Freely Contracted Existential Limit[15]

We have seen how the 'European clauses' (implicit or express) enshrined in contemporary European constitutions offer clear proof of the movement of openness[16]: they imply that membership of the European Union, sharing values on which it is based and the pursuit of the objectives that it seeks to achieve, are an integral part of the national constitutional identity itself. The latter can, and must, establish the porous boundary of singularity, diversity, clearly inserted in a *communitas.* It is worth recalling that the opening and closing of boundaries, the theme of greater inclusivity, and, simultaneously, the survival clauses of the Popperian open society form the core of our work. This implies a fluid system which, as Koskenniemi masterfully emphasises in the conclusion of *The Gentle Civilizer of Nations*,[17] cannot be definitively fixed in legal content once and for all, binding it to certain normative institutional structures. Rather, it is a formal ideal, advocating the construction of communality through the awareness that every community is founded on exclusion and that, consequently, the way a community self-defines must also foresee that such exclusion is constantly renegotiated with a view to broadening the communal horizon.

It is the first political step: Ulysses freely limits himself, placing constraints on his freedom of action. If this existential assumption is accepted, then we can say that the defence of national identity could never be considered as a form of anti-Europeanism, to the extent that anti-European State decisions would go against it, resulting in its degeneration, as they would produce the negation of a necessary constitutive element for the correct configuration of constitutional identity (at least as long as the country is a member of the Union).[18] This view is found in the arguments of the *Taricco* judgement handed down by the Italian[19] *Corte Costituzional*

[15] L. S. Rossi,, '*Concretised', 'Flanked', or 'Standalone'? Some Reflections on the Application of Article 2 TEU*, in *European Papers—A Journal on Law and Integration* Vol. 10, No. 1, 2025, pp. 1–24.

[16] M. Claes, *Le "clausole europee" nelle costituzioni nazionali*, in *Quad. cost.*, n. 2/2005, 283 et seq.

[17] M. Koskenniemi, *The Gentle Civilizer of Nations*, cit., p. 634.

[18] This is the vision emphasised in the Italian context by F. Fabbrini and O. Pollicino, *Constitutional Identity in Italy. Institutional Disagreements at a Time of Political Change*, in *Constitutional Identity in a Europe of Multilevel Constitutionalism*, cit., pp. 201–221.

[19] Italian Constitutional Court ruling, No. 24 of 2017.

and the *Achmea* ruling, where the Court of Justice held that EU Law is based "on the fundamental premise that each Member State shares with all other Member States and recognises that they share with it a set of common values on which the EU is based, as laid down in Article 2 TEU".[20] Respect for the values and principles of Article 2 TEU is an essential requirement of EU members, as it results from a combined reading of Articles 2 TEU and 49 TEU.[11] The inherent connection between Article 2 TEU and EU membership emerged for the first time in *Wightman*,[21] referring to the values of freedom and democracy. The Court noted that "as stated in Article 49 TEU, which provides for the possibility for any European State to apply for membership of the Union [...] the Union is made up of States that have freely and voluntarily committed themselves to those values, so EU Law is based on the fundamental premise that each Member State shares with all other Member States, and recognises that those Member States share those same values with it".[22] Article 2 TUE here is understood as the existential red line of the Union, the denial of which implies the reaction of the Popperian immune system.

12.2 The Configuration of Article 2 TEU as Proactive Behaviour of Member States

In *Repubblika*,[23] the Court took a step forward.[24] Firstly, it pointed out that the Union is composed of States which, in accordance with Article 49, have freely and voluntarily committed to respect the common values referred to in Article 2 TEU and to "undertake to promote them".[25] The Court of Justice added that "respect by a Member State for the values enshrined in Article 2 TEU constitutes a requirement for all the rights

[20] Case C-284/16, *Slovak Republic v Achmea BV* (EU:C:2018:158), paragraph 34 and case-law cited.

[21] Case C-621/18, *Andy Wightman and Others v Secretary of State for Exiting the European Union*, ECLI:EU:C:2018:999.

[22] Ibid., p. 63.

[23] 20 April 2021, *Repubblika v Il-Prim Ministru*, C-896/19, ECLI:EU:C:2021:311, paras 63 and 64.

[24] As pointed out by A von Bogdandy and L.D. Spieker, *Transformative Constitutionalism in Luxembourg: How the Court Can Support Democratic Transitions*, in *Columbia Journal of European Law* 2023, p. 74, the Court of Justice in this judgment, while combining Article 2 with Article 19 TEU, placed the former at the centre of its reasoning.

[25] *Repubblika*, cit., paragraphs 61 and 62.

derived from the application of the Treaties to that Member State".[26] On this basis, the Court affirmed the so-called principle of non-regression. "The Court has, moreover, held that a Member State cannot amend its legislation so as to reduce the protection of the rule of law. [...] in this way, The Member States are thus required to ensure that, in the light of that value, any regression of their laws on the organisation of justice is prevented, by refraining from adopting rules which would undermine the independence of the judiciary."[27]

On the one hand, respect for these values is not limited to the moment of accession, since, according to Article 49 TEU, the Member State must not only respect the values set out in Article 2 TEU at the time of accession but also be 'committed to promoting' those values. This general commitment refers to the post-accession periods and reflects the parallel obligation imposed on the Union by Article 3(1) TEU to promote its values, "which are embodied in principles which entail legally binding obligations for the Member States".[28]

Respect for the values of Article 2 TEU is therefore not only the condition for becoming a 'member of the Club' but also for 'remaining fully in the Club'. This is confirmed by the procedures laid down in Article 7 TEU and, more recently, by the adoption of the Regulation on conditionality, which links solidarity with respect for the values set out in Article 2 TEU. EU membership could also be seen as an 'inclusive package', in which the costs in terms of sovereignty and the benefits of being part of a common system go hand in hand.

As the Court of Justice has pointed out, the values contained in Article 2 TEU have been identified by the Member States.[29] There is no doubt that the duty to respect the values of Article 2 TEU has not been imposed on the Member States against their will, since, by ratifying the Treaty of Lisbon (or successive accession treaties), they accepted Articles 2 and 49, thus freely and voluntarily committing themselves to respect and promote those values. Consequently, similar to the concept of common constitutional traditions, once these values have been identified and accepted by

[26] *Repubblika*, cit., paragraphs 61 and 62.

[27] *Repubblika*, cit., paragraphs 63 and 64.

[28] CJEU, 19 November 2024, C-808/21, European Commission v. Czech Republic, ECLI:EU:C:2024:962.

[29] 16 February 2022, Hungary v Parliament and Council, C-156/21, ECLI:EU:C:2022:97, para. 127.

Member States, they become 'common' so that they cannot be unilaterally altered by a single State.

12.3 Article 2 TEU as a System of Interconnected Values and Principles

According to Koen Lenaerts, the values set out in Article 2 of the TEU "are embedded in the very DNA of the European integration project. These values are the soul of the EU that allows Member States to grow together while preserving their national identity."[30] They are part of the European 'constitutional framework' to which the Court expressly referred in Opinion 1/17.[31] As the Court of Justice has stated in the twin judgements on conditionality, Article 2 TEU enshrines the fundamental values and principles that "define the very identity of the Union as a common legal order", an identity that the Union "must be able to defend". According to the CJEU, "article 2 TEU is not a mere declaration of guidelines or intentions, but contains values [...] which are embodied in principles containing legally binding obligations on the Member States".[32] Moreover, Article 2 TEU is not just a list of unconnected values and principles, but as the Court of Justice pointed out in its Opinion *2/13*, "it is a set of common values on which the Union is founded".[33]

Article 2 TEU is a reservoir[34] where national constitutions cannot be unified. Article 2 does not define demarcations: it underlines the essential features of European identity 'as a common legal system'. At the same time, the essence of EU membership, as noted above, cannot accept any unilateral derogation from this model.

In the *RS* case, the Court outlined the delicate balance between the opening and closing gates of national identity and European identity, in relation to Articles 2 and 19 TEU.[35] On the one hand, "neither Article 2

[30] K. Lenaerts, *On Checks and Balances: The Rule of Law within the EU*, in *Columbia Journal of European Law*, 2023, p. 63.

[31] Opinion 1/17 on the CETA EU-Canada (EU:C:2019:341), paragraph 110.

[32] CJEU, *Judgment Hungary v European Parliament and Council*, cit., paragraph 232.

[33] See Opinion 2/13 on EU accession to the ECHR (EU:C:2014:2454), paragraph 167.

[34] According to Lenaerts, *On Checks and Balances: The Rule of Law within the EU*, cit., 53: "Article 2 TEU requires an 'alignment', but not a 'constitutional modelling', which would be contrary to the respect of national identity by the Union prescribed by Article 4 (2) TEU."

[35] CJEU, 22 February 2022, RS (Effect of the decisions of a constitutional court), C-430/21, ECLI:EU:C:2022:99.

TEU, nor the second subparagraph of Article 19(1) TEU, nor any other provision of EU Law obliges Member States to adopt a particular constitutional model governing relations and **interactions** between the different powers of the State, in particular as regards the definition and delimitation of their powers. In fact, under Article 4(2) TEU, the European Union must respect the national identities of the Member States, which are inherent in their fundamental political and constitutional structures."[36]

Furthermore, the same judgement states that when choosing their respective constitutional model, Member States are obliged, *inter alia*, to comply with the requirement for the independence of the courts arising from the provisions of European Union Law mentioned above. While Article 4(2) TEU recognises that the Union shall respect the national identity of Member States, the same Article also affirms the principle of equality of Member States before the Treaties. The formula "United in diversity" summarises the balance between national constitutional identities and a European identity based on the essential requirements inherent in accession, which, as stated in the *Repubblika*, are based on Articles 2 and 49 TEU. According to the cross-fertilisation mechanism, *paradeigma* is the value of judicial independence within the framework of the Rule of Law, whose combinations may be hybridised with respect to national constitutional identities. Any hybridisation that respects Article 2 TEU shall be recognised in accordance with Article 4.2 TEU in respect of constitutional tolerance. State discrepancies are always welcome as long as they are not *contra valorem*, which would deny the Union's very purpose. Since Article 2 TEU is a system of interdependent values,[37] it is important to take into account the interconnections between the different parts of this Article and the connections between the latter and other provisions of Primary Law. "Being part of the same model, all the values and principles of Article 2 TEU are interconnected and operate in synergy."[38]

[36] Ibid., 43.

[37] See, in this regard, K. Lenaerts and J.A. Gutiérrez-Fons, *High Hopes: Autonomy and the Identity of the EU*, in *European Papers* 2021, p. 1500.

[38] L. S. Rossi, *Concretised', 'Flanked', or 'Standalone'? Some Reflections on the Application of Article 2 TEU*, in *European Papers*, 2025, p. 12.

12.3.1 Definition of Constitutional Identity Through Interactions Within Article 4 TEU

With the Treaty of Lisbon, the EU's system for the protection of rights has become much more structured. Article 6 TEU, with its reference that gives full effect to the Charter of Fundamental Rights, to common constitutional traditions *ad intra* and to the Case Law of the ECHR *ad extra*, gains new depth and becomes, together with Article 2 TEU, the core of the European Union's identity in terms of values. Above all, however, the Charter of Fundamental Rights (alongside the accompanying Explanations) constitutes the primary reference instrument for rights within the Union. It sets out an extensive range of value-based limitations on EU action, thereby also indirectly protecting the fundamental rights enshrined in national constitutions. The connection with the latter is key to understanding the relational nexus. National constitutional charters are mentioned in particular in article 52, para 4, and 53 of the Charter. The first provision requires that the Charter be interpreted in harmony (but not, as with the ECHR, in conformity) with the common constitutional traditions of the Member States, while the second is understood without prejudice to the rights and freedoms set out in Member States' constitutions within the scope of those constitutions. All of these are rules of connection, of reconciliation.

Moreover, the reference to fundamental rights in Article 2 TEU elevates them to the status of essential values of the legal order as a whole. Consequently, in the relationship between legal systems, some jurists describe fundamental rights, thanks to the Charter of Fundamental Rights, as "shared counter-limits". More precisely, one might speak of formulating the *grundnorm* of the principle of diversity and its practical relational linkage. In theory, this should make it less necessary for States to invoke national counter-limits in matters of fundamental rights. On the contrary, the very definition of Article 2 TEU will always exist in constitutive tension with Articles 6(3) and 4(2) TEU. Constitutional identity is not an external limit to Article 2 TEU; it is part of it.

However, experience shows that comparisons between the Court of Justice and constitutional courts can arise when the European and national standards of protection diverge. This can happen, first of all, when national constitutions provide for more favourable treatment to European rules. In such cases, the Court of Justice does not accept that the EU legal order should automatically yield to the limits of national constitutions. The core of the cross-fertilisation mechanism is rooted in the principle of autonomy (understood as the ability to adapt to the specific features of national systems) and must be balanced by the Court of Justice with the principle of the primacy of European Union Law, which ensures the consolidation of a common *paradeigma*. Fundamental rights are general principles of this legal order, and although inspired by the constitutional traditions of the Member States, they belong to the EU legal order itself. Accordingly, it is the Court of Justice that undertakes to balance the various values at stake, on a case-by-case basis. Therefore, the application of the relational system is casuistic.[39] "*In conclusione, anche se i diritti fondamentali pongono sicuramente un limite ed un parametro di legittimità con riferimento all'azione dell'Unione europea, limite rafforzato dal richiamo effettuato dall'art. 2 TUE, si tratta di un limite riferito ad una nozione "comune" di diritti fondamentali, in cui l'incorporazione di valori di uno o più Stati membri è sottoposta al vaglio della Corte di giustizia. Essi potrebbero costituire il nocciolo del concetto di identità costituzionale europea, evocato dai Preamboli del Tue e della Carta, cui la Corte di giustizia ha talvolta fatto riferimento, proprio in relazione ai diritti fondamentali.*"[40] It is the two-way system of *cross-fertilisation*.[41]

Therefore, it ends up conceiving the "idea of the EU and Member States being in a shared legal system characterized by mutual connectivity and interdependence" and the Union itself as an "entity whose sovereignty, territory, and citizens are shared between the European and national levels".[42] A central element of relational identity is the concept of "shared normativity", which, in turn, requires that the normative content of a legal provision be the result of a continuous interaction between EU Law and National Law. Article 4.2 TEU, in particular, is to be interpreted

[39] See, for example, the judgements of the Court of Justice of 14 October 2004, C-36/02, Omega, and earlier still, the Court of Justice of 28 November 1989, C-379/87, Groener. On this point, see also M. Safjan, *Between Mangold and Omega: Fundamental rights* versus *constitutional identity*, in *Dir. Un. eur.*, 2012, p. 437–461.

[40] L. S. Rossi, '*2, 4, 6 (TUE)... l'interpretazione dell'"Identity Clause" alla luce dei valori fondamentali dell'UE, en Liber Amicorum in Onore Di Antonio Tizzano: De la CECA à la Cour de l'Union: Le Long Parcours de la Justice Européenne,* R. Adam, et al. (eds.), Giappichelli, Torino, 2018, p. 45.

[41] Once again, CJEU, 3 September 2008, C-402/05 P and C-415/05 P, Yassin Abdullah Kadi and Al Barakaat International Foundation v. Council and Commission.

[42] C. Callies, A. Schnetter, *Comparative Constitutional Identity and Multilevel Constitutionalism*, in *Constitutional Identity in a Europe of Multilevel Constitutionalism*, cit., p. 353.

as a piece of a mosaic, i.e. "a provision building on the connectivity between the legal orders and by its permeable structure establishing and ensuring the functioning of the common legal system as a whole."[43]

Therefore, the first paragraph of Article 4 TEU in itself serves to limit the temptations of unilateral use of the reference to national identity. This confirms the need to analyse this provision within the system of the principles of attribution and competence. This appears to confirm the origin of Article 4(2) TEU as a provision (also) concerning competence, a conclusion also supported by the explicit reference to Member State competences, insofar as it is demonstrated that, in particular, national security remains the exclusive competence of each Member State.

In addition to the limit of competence, the principle of cooperation set out in paragraph 3 must also be added. Moreover, some Advocates General have pointed to the link between respect for national identity and the principle of cooperation. It should be noted that the reference to respect for national identity renders the principle of loyal cooperation bilateral, not to be understood solely in reference to the duty to apply EU Law but also as an obligation to respect the Constitutional structure of national legal systems.

The second paragraph of Article 4 TEU establishes not only respect for the national identity of the Member States but also the principle of equality of the Member States before the Treaties.[44] The principle of equality prohibits Member States from seeking favourable situations at the expense of others. The *Commission v Italy* judgement, in particular, noted that "for a State unilaterally to break, according to its own conception of national interest, the equilibrium between advantages and obligations flowing from its adherence to the Community brings into question the equality of Member States before Community Law and creates discrimination at the expense of their nationals [...] This failure in the duty of solidarity accepted by Member States by the fact of their adherence to the Community strikes at the fundamental basis of the Community legal order."[45] In this judgement, a link emerges between the principle of equality between the Member States and the principles of loyal cooperation and

[43] C. Callies, A. Schnetter, *Comparative Constitutional Identity and Multilevel Constitutionalism*, in *Constitutional Identity in a Europe of Multilevel Constitutionalism*, cit., p. 360.

[44] F.X. Millet, '*Successfully Articulating National Constitutional Identity Claims: Strait Is the Gate and Narrow Is the Way*', in *European Public Law* 27, no. 3, 2021, pp. 571–596.

[45] CJEU, 7 February 1973, C-39/72, *Commission v. Italy*, *EU: C: 1973: 13*.

solidarity, which are now clearly reflected in the general wording of Article 4 TEU.[46] The relationship between Article 2 TEU and the principle of loyal cooperation was emphasised in the *Achmea* judgement.[47]

Along with this conceptual web of Article 4 TEU, the identity dimension of the Member States in the area of fundamental rights is integrated into a complex and relational system, composed of Article 6 TEU, the Charter of Fundamental Rights, the ECHR and the common constitutional traditions of the Member States. In this system, on the one hand, the fundamental rights affirmed by the constitutions of the Member States are taken into account by the Union, not through the different "national identities" in the sense of Article 4(2) TEU but in the light of a "system of rules" consisting of Article 2 TEU, Article 6(3) TEU and the Charter.[48] From this framework it follows that the Common Constitutional Traditions of the Member States are, like the ECHR, sources of general principles of Law (Article 6(3) TEU); that the Charter must be interpreted in accordance with the level of protection provided by those traditions (Article 52(4) of the Charter); and that the standards of protection established in the Constitutions of the Member States may not be undermined by the Charter (Article 53).[49]

The interpretation of the concept of constitutional identity does not correspond exclusively to the constitutional courts of the Member States, even though they are the ones who will trigger the cross-fertilisation mechanism. The Court of Justice is the only judge that can clarify when a constitutional tradition takes on the role of 'common' in the legal order of the Union, raising it to the level of a general principle of that system and verifying on a case-by-case basis its potential capacity to constitute a tempering in the application of EU Law. The national identity to which this rule refers is structural identity and, therefore, does not coincide with that

[46] L. S. Rossi, *Il valore giuridico dei valori. L'Articolo 2 TUE: relazioni con altre disposizioni del diritto primario dell'UE e rimedi giurisdizionali*, in *Federalismi*, 19/2020, p. 34.

[47] Ruling of 6 March 2018 C—284/16 *Slowakische Republik v. Achmea* BV EU: C: 2018: 158 p. 34.

[48] See also Article 67(1) TFEU, which, in the context of the Area of Freedom, Security and Justice, provides for "respect for fundamental rights and for the different legal systems and traditions of the Member States".

[49] These are mentioned in particular in Articles 52(4) and 53 of the Charter. The first provision sets out an interpretation of the Charter "in harmony" (but not, as with the ECHR, in conformity) with the common constitutional traditions of the Member States, while the second safeguards the rights and freedoms set out in Member States' constitutions within the scope of those constitutions.

broader and more encompassing concept of "*identité constitutionnelle*",[50] which was initially developed by the French Constitutional Council. Since then, this notion has become a shorthand—taken up by the Case Law of several other constitutional courts, including the German,[51] Polish,[52] Czech,[53] Portuguese[54] and Danish courts—to denote the various forms of national constitutional review exercised by Member States, varying in scope and intensity depending on each legal system. When it is not a relationship and when it is interpreted in *absolutus* terms, constitutional identity languishes without the lifeblood of fundamental rights. As Anna Sledzinska-Simon argues, "the question of whether constitutional identity in a nation-state in Europe can dismantle the European identity [...] is unfounded, since the two are not exclusory, but complementary notions".[55]

On the other hand, due to its necessary complementarity with the other principles affirmed in the remaining paragraphs of that article (namely the equality of Member States and the principle of loyal cooperation, which, as previously mentioned, limit its scope and effects), Article 4(2) cannot be regarded as an 'open door' for *controlimiti* beyond the realm of fundamental rights.

A systematic reading leads to the exclusion of any overlap between Article 4(2) and Article 6(3) TEU, which also encompasses the fundamental rights provided for in the Constitutional Law systems of the Member States.[56] On the basis of this interpretation, Article 4(2) could

[50] Cf. L. Burgorgue-Larsen (dir.), L'identité constitutionnelle saisie par les juges en Europe, Paris, Editions Pedone, 2011.

[51] Cf. C. Tomuschat, *The Defence of National Identity by the German Constitutional Court*, in A. Saiz Arnaiz y C. Alcoberro Llivina (eds), *National Constitutional Identity and European Integration, Intersentia*, Antwerp, 2013, pp. 205–220.

[52] Polish Constitutional Tribunal, Judgment of 24 November 2010, Case K 32/09 (Treaty of Lisbon). http://www.trybunal.gov.pl/eng/summaries/documents/-K_32_09_EN.pdf

Cf. J. Rideau, *The Case-law of the Polish, Hungarian and Czech Constitutional Courts on national Identity and the 'German Model'*, in *National Constitutional Identity and European Integration*, cit., pp. 243–263.

[53] Czech Constitutional Court, Judgment of 31 January 2012, Pl. ÚS 5/12 (Slovak Pensions XVII / Landtová).

[54] Portuguese Constitutional Court, Judgment (Acórdão) No. 187/2013, 5 April 2013.

[55] A. Śledzińska-Simon, *Constitutional Identity in 3D: A Model of Individual, Relational, and Collective Self and Its Application in Poland*, in *Int'l J. Const. L.*, 2015, p. 124.

[56] Where fundamental rights are at stake, it seems more appropriate to refer to Article 6.3 TEU instead of Article 4.2 TEU. On this point, see L. S. Rossi, 'How to resolve the "Taricco question" ... without relying on Art. 4, para. 2 TEU', SIDIBlog, 17 May 2017, http://www.sidiblog.org.

only justify national "counter-limits" linked to what we might call structural identity and competences, an issue that, in reality, could also underpin the need for EU institutions to respect the scope of application of the Charter. However, none of these principles has been invoked to protect individual rights; indeed, in certain cases, the principle was cited by Member States specifically to justify a suspension of such rights on their part.[57] Article 4(2) TEU makes no reference to values, unlike those envisaged in Article 6(3) TEU or Article 2 TEU. By invoking their constitutional reservations, Member States find in the fundamental values of the Union (as set out in Articles 2, 4 and 6 TEU) a firmer foundation for matters concerning fundamental rights than in their structural principles, since the former appear, in contrast to the latter, to lend themselves more readily to the concept of "European identity" implicitly underpinning Article 2 TEU.

Actually, on more than a few occasions, national identity has been invoked precisely when the European standard establishes a higher level of protection for a right than guaranteed at the national level, but it comes into conflict with other principles considered fundamental by the State system involved. Obviously, in this case, not only does Article 4, para. 2 not overlap with Article 6 TEU, it actually tends to oppose it. Here too, a conflict between the courts may arise, as demonstrated by the reactions of the German and Danish courts to the *Mangold* judgement.[58] However, in light of a systematic interpretation, Article 4, para. 2 (and therefore also the identity clause) takes on a new, much-reduced configuration compared to the expectations that its inclusion in the Treaty of Lisbon had raised.

Ultimately, it could be argued that Article 4(2) TEU refers solely to the facet of constitutional identity which, by differentiating between the various Member States, becomes a value (precisely: Diversity) that must be

[57] See CJEU, 2 June 2016, Nabiel Peter Bogendorff von Wolffersdorff and Standesamt der Stadt Karlsruhe, Case C-438/14, ECLI:EU:C:2016:40; CJEU, 22 December 2010, Sayn-Wittgenstein, C-208/09, ECLI:EU:C:2010:80.

[58] In relation to the Court of Justice judgement of 22 November 2005, C-144/04, *Mangold*, although with different outcomes, the ultra vires question has been raised by the BVG (Honeywell, 2 BvR 2661/06) before (https://www.bundesverfassungsgericht.de/SharedDocs/Entscheidungen/EN/2010/07/rs20100706_2x2bvr266106en.html) and the Danish Supreme Court (http://www.supremecourt.dk/supremecourt/Nyheder/pressemeddelelser/Pages/TherelationshipbetweenEUlawand/Danish lawinacase concerning asalariedemployee.aspx).

preserved for and within the Union itself, representing that part of National Sovereignty which has not been limited in the European integration process (competences and the principle of attribution set out in Article 4(1) TEU itself), but which will gradually diminish the more one begins (if and when this occurs), through an initial political decision and then a legal one, moving towards the establishment of an ever-closer Europe.[59]

In this regard, the principles of Subsidiarity and Proportionality also apply to situations involving potential infringements by EU Law of the essential Political and Constitutional Structures of the Member States. The reason for this includes the fact that both the guarantee of Identity and the principle of Subsidiarity relate, at least as far as the Identity control of Derived EU Law is concerned, to the exercise of competences by the Union, but do not, however, address the prior question of the delimitation of competences between the Union and the Member States. An infringement of this core indicates that a Union measure is unlawful, as it is manifestly unsuited to achieving the objective pursued by the competent institution. In general, the principles of Subsidiarity and Proportionality, in their function as limits on the exercise of Union competences, are neither excluded nor weakened, so a parallel and independent identity test is not necessary. Rather, the obligation to respect the national identities of the Member States is a normative reference point in individual cases to determine the constituent elements of Subsidiarity and Proportionality. However, the principle of Subsidiarity applies only to the exercise of non-exclusive Union competences, as occurred in the *Melloni* case.[60] Therefore, in light of the indissoluble link between the guarantee of identity and the principle of subsidiarity, the exercise of its exclusive powers cannot be examined in the light of Article 4.2 TEU by the CJEU. This is logical, since a violation of the core of national identity can only be presumed for the exercise of the non-exclusive powers of the Union.[61]

The dynamics of cross-fertilisation enshrined at the axiological level in *Articles 2 and 6 TEU strengthens rather than weakens the identity of the*

[59] Cf. G. Di Federico, *L'identità nazionale degli stati membri nel diritto dell'Unione europea. Natura e portata dell'art.*4, Par.2, TUE, Napoli, 2017.

[60] CJUE, 26 February 2013, case C-399/11, Stefano Melloni and Ministerio Fiscal, ECLI:EU:C:2013:107.

[61] H.J. Blanke, *Article 4 [The Relations Between the EU and the Member States]*, in *The Treaty on European Union (TEU). A Commentary*, H.-J. Blanke & S. Mangiameli (eds.), Springer, 2010, Berlin, Heidelberg, pp. 185–253.

Member States. Rather than arising from the European Union's federal "ambitions" (which have been set aside for the foreseeable future), challenges to the common principles of European constitutional democracies are currently emerging much more *ad intra* from the political discourse of the Member States, some of which support the contradictory idea of an illiberal democracy. However, the constitutional values "common to the Member States" (Article 2 TEU) and the "constitutional traditions common to the Member States" (Article 6, para. 3, TEU) should not be regarded as a threat but rather as a reinforcement of the constitutional identity of a Member State. Perhaps we could say that this is currently the only way to preserve, at the supranational level, the historically consolidated values within the States. "This approach may provide a message for our times, with constitutional identity becoming liberated from its backward-looking bias and seen as a way to connect past and future in current constitutional law making. In this message, and unless it is exposed to nationalistic exploitation, constitutional identity should not be viewed, in a separating sense, as 'national' and in opposition to other nationalities, but instead as a distinctive articulation of meta-national ideas."[62]

[62] E.H. Ballin, *Constitutional Identity in the Netherlands Sailing with Others*, cit., p. 230. Cf. P. Blokker and C. Thornhill, *Sociological Constitutionalism*, Cambridge University Press, 2017, p. 192.

CHAPTER 13

Epilogue. The Relational Identity: Openness and Limits

Abstract This final chapter analyses the European Union's relational identity, emphasising openness, diversity and constitutional limits. The relational identity of the Union takes on various meanings both in its relationship with respect to State peculiarities and with respect to the very way of living together. This means that relational identity does not exist without a *communitas* behind it that ontologically nerves it. And this community must be based on the *munus*, understood as a denial of the mere synallagmatic mercantilist relationship. This idea of *communitas* is naturally refracted both in a new way of understanding politics and in an innovative epistemology of International Law as a community of values, where the contribution of Comparative Law (cum-*paro*) is absolutely necessary. Attention: defending values shloud not be about intransigence, but openness yo other realities. An exclusionary defense is destined either to fail or to hegemonic reconquest.

Keywords Relational identity • Legal ways of living together • International and Comparative Law • *Communitas*

As we saw in the first section of this Second Part, the Union was born with the aim of harmonising States (a function already present in the universalism of International Law and Comparative Law) but also of respecting the

© The Author(s), under exclusive license to Springer Nature Switzerland AG 2026

A. Lazari, *Relational Identity in International, Comparative and European Union Law*,
https://doi.org/10.1007/978-3-031-59482-3_13

diversity, discrepancies and pluralism of Article 2 TEU, a critical function of Legrand's cultural comparatism. This tension is existential and has been variously configured in the ruling of the Italian *Corte Costituzionale* in *Taricco II*, as well as in the conclusions of Advocate General Ćapeta. Without this tension, the European Union would be a different international organisation. Naturally, this is only so if these discrepancies do not represent an attack on the very existence of the European Union. In such cases, as Advocate General Ćapeta specifies in the extensively cited conclusions of 5 July 2025, porous and relational boundaries turn into red lines,[1] into the immune antibodies of Esposito's *communitas* or into the paradox of tolerance of Karl Popper's open society.[2] An open community, as we have seen the current European Union to be *ab urbe condita*, should tolerate any discrepancy. But should this include manifestations that deny the very *communitas* itself? This is the dilemma that haunts Attorney General Ćapeta.[3]

The Union's identity is truly defined by its inclusive openness and its defence of diversity, constitutionally recognised in Article 4 of the TEU. In short, the intrinsic complexity of the Community paradigm suggests that the internal, national element be metabolised in the creation of European Law and vice versa. In the words of Ćapeta: "The EU legal order is a composite order, consisting of rules enacted at EU and at Member State level. The EU-level rules are dependent on the national-level rules and on the proper functioning of the Member States' legal orders. For such a composite legal order to exist, it is indispensable that common values are respected at both EU and national levels".[4] Hence, the—"weighted"—

[1] However, national constitutional choices cannot go beyond this common framework. In this respect, as I have previously suggested, Article 2 of the TEU could be understood as imposing 'red lines' which, if crossed, require a response to defend the Union's constitutional model.

[2] As is well known, K. Popper's main work, *The Open Society and Its Enemies*, Princeton University Press, Princeton, 2013, defends a democratic and liberal society, criticising totalitarian philosophies and their roots in thinkers such as Plato, Hegel and Marx. Popper argues that these philosophies promote closed societies, opposed to the open society which values individual freedom, critical discussion and tolerance. This work also introduces the paradox of tolerance: an open society must be tolerant, but it cannot tolerate intolerance without risking its own existence. Popper argues that a tolerant society must be able to defend itself from those who seek to destroy it.

[3] These points are reflected in Advocate General Ćapeta's conclusions, presented on 5 June 2025, Commission v Hungary, C-769/22.

[4] In Advocate General Ćapeta's Conclusions, 5 June 2025, Commission v. Hungary, C-769/22, paragraph 160.

inclusion of the Other discussed by Habermas.[5] "In the context of transnational legal integration, constitutional identity acquires relational and collective dimensions that supplement the individual dimension of identity as national particularity."[6] The opening of this common European space "requires studying and rebuilding them in light of the new broader context".[7] Hence also the importance of a new Comparative Law.

This identity inclusion leads to the "European constitutional heritage"[8] and materialises in the creation of communality by comparing, for example, common constitutional traditions or in the relational construction of Article 2 TUE. The rule of legal systems does not really represent the Other. It is not a mere fact foreign to the supranational legal system: it is a common deposit from which to draw, as Boniolo argues regarding the *identità plurime*.[9] Exclusionary claims regarding constitutional identity advocate an *epistemology of provenance* that associates the protection of an identity with a *claim to an exclusive domain of knowledge*.[10] And identity conflicts themselves form part of a process of dialogic inclusion, as Martinique says, referring to Mouffe's political theory,[11] provided that they remain within the axiological perimeter laid down by Article 2 TUE.

The interactions generated by constitutional traditions and their embodiment in the value terms of Article 2 TUE are the subject of Comparative Law studies, which in turn draw fully on the national constitutional heritage and the science of International Law.[12]

The importance of silence in the idea of tradition must be emphasised: it is an unwritten source that delves into the values expressed by society. It is the *basileus nomos* of Herodotus, which is not far from the latest research

[5] J. Habermas,The Inclusion of the Other: Studies in Political Theory, Polity Press, Cambridge, 1998.

[6] J. Scholtes, *Abusing Constitutional Identity*, in *German Law Journal*, 2021, p. 550.

[7] von Bogdandy, A., The Transformation of European Law: The Reformed Concept and its Quest for Comparison , in European Law Journal , 2016, pp. 519–538.

[8] A. Pizzorusso, *Il patrimonio costituzionale europeo*, Il Mulino, Bologna, 2002.

[9] Boniolo, G. *Molti. Discorso sulle identità plurime*, cit., p. 20.

[10] Kruks, S., "Identity Politics and Dialectical Reason: Beyond an Epistemology of Provenance", *Hypatia* 1, 1995, p. 10.

[11] Martinico, G., "Conflictos constitucionales y pluralismo agónico: ¿Qué podemos aprender de la teoría política?", in *Diálogos judiciales en el sistema europeo de protección de derechos: Una mirada interdisciplinar*, G. Fernández Arribas, M. Hermosín Álvarez, A. Lazari (ed.), 2018, pp. 21–40. Cf. Mouffe, C., *En torno a lo político*, Fondo de Cultura Económica, Buenos Aires, 2007.

[12] Idem.

on Sacco's mute law.[13] "In the legal field, the adjective 'silent' may have different meanings and sometimes linked to the concept of 'mute.' [...] we can assume as a preliminary hypothesis that the implicit, and not verbalised, rules can produce legal effects. The forms with which the law manifests itself – or shows itself silent or mute – tend to intertwine over time as the threads of a rope."[14] The new Comparative and International Law must be much less dependent on divisive formalism.

There is, therefore, a way to relate and communicate with different traditions and values. This perspective would suggest that States should not impose a unilateral vision of their own identity (Closure) but that there should be open spaces where different traditions can come together, engage in dialogue and reconcile. "The feature of these spaces should be the porosity. About the porosity of relationships between traditions, Glenn remarks that this tendency is essentially reversed."[15] National identities can converge in common constitutional traditions as they are part of the same group of States that share the values enshrined in Article 2 TEU, and these may also have non-convergent identities but always compatible with the *Grundnorm* of Article 2 TEU.

The latest reflections woven by Koskenniemi in *The Gentle Civilizer of Nations* are highly illuminating, addressing the new challenges facing International Law, no longer rooted in cosmopolitan reason, yet still animated by a legal vision and project. The energy and hope of International Law reside in its ability to express the tensions towards transformation, already present within it, in the language of rights and duties, giving voice to those who would otherwise be regularly excluded. It is a formal ideal, advocating the construction of what is common through the awareness that every community is founded on exclusion and that, consequently, the way a community self-defines must also foresee that such exclusion is constantly renegotiated with a view to broadening the communal horizon. A

[13] As Sacco points out, the 'unwritten rule' is biologically and culturally related to man. This phenomenon has not disappeared; on the contrary, it is particularly vital. In all legal systems, together with visible norms, there are quasi-invisible or latent norms, such as interpretative means, scientific concepts, general principles, values and cryptotypes; as stated by R. Sacco in *Il Diritto Muto*, Einaudi, Torino, 2015, p. 149.

[14] R. Scarciglia, *The Silent Language: From Chthonic Law To Global Legal Pluralism*, in *Normative Pluralism and Religion Diversity: Challenges and Methodological Approaches'*, R. Scarciglia & W. Menski (ed.), Kluwer, 2018, p. 34.

[15] R. Scarciglia, *The Silent Language: From Chthonic Law To Global Legal Pluralism*, cit., p. 38.

different matter is that some Member States, both politically and in judicial determinations, place themselves outside this common European area by virtue of a supposed exclusionary constitutional identity.[16] The *communitas*, as its Latin etymology suggests, indicates a set of duties, in this case associated with the values of Article 2 TUE. The European Union does not contemplate a procedure for excluding members that are recalcitrant in fulfilling their obligations; it is the States that place themselves beyond the territory of the *communitas*.

On the comparatist side, P. Glenn, associating himself with the words of his colleague at McGill University, argued that "*Latin word 'comparo.'* [...] *is a composite word, composed of the word com (or cum), in English 'with,' and par, in English 'peer' or 'equal.' So com-paring can be* seen as a process of existing with an equal, or that which is taken to be an equal, in spite of evident differences. It is a process of what was once referred to in Spain as *convivencia*, the process of living together in a non-conflictual manner in spite of profound differences or beliefs."[17] We have seen that Comparative Law contributes to the study of the relational aspect of Law, studying webs rather than building the walls of taxonomies, often the result of hegemonic views. "A missing element in the very rich scholarship on constitutional courts, judicial review, and constitutional adjudication is an analysis that puts the courts' relations at the center. A comprehensive comparative investigation of courts' relations is still missing."[18] Governments and national judges who do not understand the significance of this set of *écarts* place themselves beyond the community territory; they isolate themselves once again, pursuing an insular and hypostatic identity, outside of space and time. But there is more.

"The Holy Trinity of values provides the conditions for action—individual and collective—but not its content."[19] Values and virtues have a complicated relationship. The two do not necessarily correspond. A value is a moral or ethical proposition: an abstraction, an ideal in which we can

[16] The reference is the recent ruling handed down by the Polish Constitutional Court, 8 October 2021.

[17] H.P. Glenn, *Comparative Law: Problems and Prospects*, in *American University International Law Review* 26 no. 4, 2011, p. 950.

[18] J. Nedelsky, *Law's relations: A Relational Theory of Self, Autonomy, and Law*, Oxford, Oxford University Press, 2011. Cf. F. Fabbrini & A. Sajó, *The danger of constitutional identity*, in *European LawJournal*, 2019, pp. 1 et seq.

[19] J.H.H. Weiler, *The European Circumstance and the Politics of Meaning: Not on Bread Alone Doth Man Liveth (Deut. 8:3; Mat 4:4)*, in *German Law Journal*, 2020, 21, p. 96.

believe. Virtues are related to personal traits, an "operative habit" in the language of Thomas Aquinas, a "disposition to act" in the language of Aristotle, the *basileus nomos* of Herodotus.[20] The rigid nature of the Constitution, although very important, has not in itself been able to protect the Law from new collective delusions of omnipotence. To achieve this result, it was necessary to abandon the one-dimensional and divisive conception of Law, characteristic of legal positivism (i.e. the reduction of the entire legal phenomenon as a manifestation of *auctoritas,* the 'collapse of law into legalism')[21] and to see the Constitution as something profoundly different from a mere *superior lex*, capable of creating and interpreting social customs.[22] It refers to the construction of the category of "supreme principles" of identity,[23] removed from the power of the constitutional legislator and, through the doctrine of the *controlimiti* already mentioned, also under the protection of a possible attack from European Supranational Law. This operation materialises with a formal act, reiterated by subsequent Case Law and supported by the constitutionalist culture that, in the meantime, had also 'discovered', together with the rest of the legal communities, the novelty of the living Constitution. This trajectory led to the recovery of a conceptual space (rather than a strictly legal one) defined by the perimeter of society's fundamental values, which the modern paradigm had ultimately excluded from Law and, by extension, from the scope of legal scholarship. The transposition of these national identity values into the common constitutional traditions of the Member States provides vital sustenance to European constitutionalism, through an unwritten yet judicially recognised source. In doing so, it brings to a close, in some respects, the long legacy of modern legal[24] absolutism and is part of a longer—yet to be completed—itinerary of redefining the

[20] Cf. K. Sikkink, *The Hidden Face of the Right: towards a Politics of Responsibility*, Yale University Press, 2020.

[21] G. Zagrebelsky, *La virtù del dubbio. Intervista su etica e diritto*, Roma-Bari, Laterza, 2007, p. 67 ss.

[22] G. Capograssi, *Il diritto dopo la catastrofe*, cit., p. 180.

[23] The first pronouncement of the Italian *Costituzionale Court* in which the category of the 'supreme principles' appears is the Judgment of 24 February 1971, n. 30. Two years later, in its landmark Judgment No. 183 of 27 December 1973, the Court developed the concept of 'counter-limits' (*controlimiti*). Cf. M. Cartabia, *Principi inviolabili e integrazione europea*, Giuffré, Milan, 1995.

[24] P. Grossi, *Assolutismo giuridico e diritto privato*, Giuffré, Milano, 1998.

identity of legal science, just as in literature, the multiple identities of Pirandello's Moscarda.[25]

As Paolo Grossi noted, "*il nuovo ordine giuridico europeo, che assume giustamente l'individuazione e il rispetto dei diritti fondamentali dell'uomo al cuore del suo programma, ha il proprio basamento non in una norma progettata e scritta nei palazzi alti del potere, ma nella stessa storia dei popoli, nelle tradizioni che i popoli hanno accumulato nella loro vicenda storica, nelle radici solidissime di principi non scritti.*"[26]

Even on a global scale, we can perceive the first signs of a process of constitutionalisation of the Law, albeit in an embryonic form and with different protection measures depending on the region and the sector in question. In the more traditional province of International Law, the reconquest of the second dimension of Law, and therefore the imposition of limits on the action of States, took place, according to internationalist doctrine, through the category of *ius cogens*, enshrined in 1969 by the Vienna Convention on the Law of Treaties.[27]

As an expression not of *auctoritas* but of the axiological heritage of society in its historical development, rights are not a closed and fossilised catalogue in the texts of one Charter or the other but the ever-evolving product of the maturing legal culture and transformations in the spirit of society. Here, primacy does not go to the source (to the written text, which is only the epiphenomenon of a much deeper reality) but to the interpretation that allows Charters to preserve a living connection with the dimension of Law to which they constitutively belong and with the other dimensions of other legal orders with which they share a certain identity.

[25] M. Vogliotti, *Les nouveaux chemins de la légalité Au-delà de la modernité juridique*, Presses de l'Université Saint-Louis Année, 2020, p. 28–29: "*La crise de la légalité ressemble à celle qui saisit le protagoniste du roman de Pirandello[..]. Vitangelo Moscarda, c'est le nom de ce personnage, finit par remettre en cause l'image positive qu'il avait toujours eue de lui-même après que sa femme lui ait fait remarquer, un jour qu'il s'observait au miroir, un défaut de son nez et, à partir de là, bien d'autres défauts encore. Or, si nous aussi observons la réalité sans les vieilles lunettes du « paradigme juridique moderne», nous ne verrons plus le visage de la légalité que la science juridique était habituée à contempler d'un regard complaisant.*"

[26] P. Grossi, *Un impegno per il giurista di oggi: ripensare le fonti del diritto*, Istituto Universitario Suor Orsola Benincasa, Naples, 2009, edited by G. Alpa, Laterza, Roma-Bari, 2011, p. 31.

[27] On the genesis and content of *ius cogens*, see A. Cassese, *Diritto internazionale*, vol. I, *I lineamenti*, Bologna, 2003, pp. 234 ss.

The theme that constantly surfaces in this work, and in contemporary reflection, is therefore twofold. On the one hand, the perceived flow of ideas, institutions and cultural traits, which continuously crosses geographical spaces bordered by increasingly porous and artificial boundaries, and incessantly produces processes of redefining identities, aggregation in unstable and precarious forms, hybridisations and antagonisms.

On the other hand, the emphasis on the reorganisation of identities induced by globalisation processes is linked to the awareness that the purely European (or at least Western) matrix[28] of the traditional theoretical tool can be an objective limit to a comparative thought that seeks to acquire a broader scope in order to interpret the evolution of society in all its dimensions.[29] This gives rise to a heightened attention to the Other. "Equal respect for *each person* does not encompass the similar, but rather embraces the person of the other or others in their otherness. And this shared responsibility for the other as *one of us* refers to the flexible 'we' of a community that opposes anything substantial and continuously expands its porous boundaries. This community, conceived constructively, is not a collective that compels uniform members to affirm their own way of being. Here, inclusion does not mean incorporation of what is one's own and exclusion of what is alien."[30]

In conclusion, we will see below how the idea of relational identity is reflected in the different conceptual knots analysed in this work, intertwining each other and creating concentric circles that range from the legal factor to the social and political domains.

[28] T.W. Bennett, *Comparative Law And African Customary Law*, in *The Oxford Handbook Of Comparative Law*, edited by M. Reimann—R. Zimmermann, Oxford University Press, 2006, p. 321: "*The history of comparative law has, in fact, been markedly eurocentric. It was only in the fifteenth and sixteenth centuries that lawyers in Europe started looking to the wider world.*"

[29] G. Resta, "*L'albero e l'onda: il discorso della comparazione al crocevia delle discipline*, in *Comparare. Una riflessione tra le discipline*, in V. Zeno-Zencovich y R. Onesti (eds.), Comparare. Una riflessione tra le discipline, Roma, RomaTrE-Press, 2011, p. 65.

[30] Idem.

13.1 Relational Identity and Constitutional Identity

"*Questo processo è stato sviluppato secondo una logica bottom-up, attraverso la valorizzazione di elementi comuni agli Stati membri: per questo motivo in questo contributo si parla di "europeizzazione delle identità nazionali degli Stati membri.*"[31] The Europeanisation of national identities also implies the development of a top-down process, capable of (re)defining the participation of States in the Union. Lenaerts speaks of "constitutional alignment",[32] which he defends with the sword of absolute primacy to guarantee the autonomy of the Union.

But the link between the national identities of the Member States and the supranational identity of the Union is not only manifested in the need for the former to conform to the latter. Furthermore, in the twin judgements on conditionality issued in 2022, the plenary also clarified that the adherence of Member States to the common values referred to in Article 2 TEU derives from the sharing of these values as common to their own constitutional traditions.

The clarification (which can already be partly inferred from the fact that Article 2 of the TEU states that the Union's values "shall be common to the Member States") is far from being secondary. It gives content to the thesis according to which the enshrinement of the fundamental values on which the Union is based is, above all, the result of an upward process, substantially equivalent to that which led to the affirmation of the protection of fundamental rights in the supranational legal order through the constitutional traditions common to the Member States by means of cross-fertilisation. Furthermore, respect for fundamental rights is one of the fundamental values of the EU system. This reconstruction seems to

[31] F. Casolari, *Il processo di europeizzazione delle identità nazionali degli Stati membri*, in *Quaderni AISDUE - Rivista quadrimestrale*, 2024, p. 34.

[32] K. Lenaerts, *Celebrating 20 Years Together, Opening Speech of the Conference "20 Years since the Accession of 10 States to the European Union: A New Constitutional Moment for Europe", Court of Justice of the European Union*, Luxembourg, 3 May 2024, p. 16, www.curia.europa.eu. Previously, it had also been emphasised that actions by Member States which violate the foundational values of the Union must be regarded as falling outside the scope of the identity clause. In such cases, invocation of that clause by the Member States themselves is therefore ineffective. (K. Lenaerts, *National Identity, The Equality of Member States before the Treaties and the Primacy of EU Law*, in B. Carotti (ed.), *Identità nazionale degli Stati membri, primato del diritto dell'Unione europea, Stato di diritto e indipendenza dei giudici nazionali, Giornata di studio*, Rome, 2022, p. 1 ss., p. 12).

suggest the existence of a structural link between the supranational identity and the national identities of the Member States. As Lenaerts and Gutíerrez-Fons emphasise, “the identity of the Union is based on the constitutional traditions common to the Member States, which are founded on national identities”. Therefore, it is not surprising that following the two twin judgements, the Grand Chamber of the Court of Justice, in its judgement of 5 June 2023 in the infringement proceedings against Poland regarding the reform of the judicial system of December 2019, asserted that “it cannot validly be argued that the requirements arising from respect for the [Union’s] values [...] can affect the national identity of a Member State”.[33] In other words, the national identities of the Member States would end up being reflected (through their common constitutional traditions) in the values of the European Union so that the conduct of the Union’s actors motivated by the need to respect the Union’s values would be essentially functional to the protection of the States’ identities.[34] Neither the identity of the Union nor the correlated primacy nor its own autonomy are understood in a sense of separation, if they are to function.

With the new community, regional identity in the spectrum of International Law, Comparative Law becomes necessary. If it has previously contributed to forging the right of exclusion, for example, in the general principles of the law common to the most civilised nations, it should now be a vector of the right of inclusion. If before it served to reaffirm hegemony through the same exclusionary notion of identity, unifying civil law, seeking and finding the common law of humanity, now Comparative Law must serve the construction of a common space for dialogue, registering, for example the (also silent) movements of judicial circulation. Comparative Law must be used in the perspective of an identity that by means of centripetal force is respectful of difference within the framework of the European values referred to in Article 2 TEU (otherwise, one does not enter the EU or remains there with the sanctions provided for in Article 7 TEU) of common constitutional traditions. As has already been said repeatedly, it is the legal manifestation of Jullien’s inclusive écart. It is the common resource with which Jullien defines the *écart*:

[33] Court of Justice of 5 June 2023, C-204/21, *Commission v Poland*, paragraph 72.

[34] K. Lenaerts, J. A. Gutíerrez-Fons, *op. cit.*, p. 1506: “The identity of the EU and national identities are in a mutually reinforcing relationship when it comes to protecting and promoting European values [...] the identity of the Union prevents the Member States from deviating from th[eir constitutional] traditions, thereby protecting national identities from incorporating authoritarian elements.”

it constitutes a common constitutional patrimony. But this synergy, this tangle of strings, these new general principles that include different levels, instead of circumscribing territories, as in the Westphalian vision, are only possible if the epistemological perspective is also changed. We cannot demand the construction of a common European space without creating epistemological synergies. "*The comparison is no longer the static one of the physical sciences, or of 19th century comparative law, of simple determination or constatation of similarities and differences, but comparison in the sense of the original meaning of the word compare. 'Com' is from the Latin 'cum' or 'with' and 'pare' is the Latin for 'equal' or 'peer', so to compare is to exist with another who, though different, is to be treated as an equal (in German also Vergleichung). Comparison is thus a process of peaceful coexistence of those who are taken as equals, in spite of even major difference in belief, circumstance or tradition. Comparative lawyers are those who contribute to this process.*"[35]

In summary, Article 4(2) TEU refers exclusively to that aspect of constitutional identity which, by distinguishing one Member State from another, becomes a value in itself (namely diversity) that the Union seeks to preserve. It also reflects that portion of national sovereignty which has not been limited in the process of European integration, in accordance with the principles of conferral and competences set out in Article 4(1) TEU. This distinctiveness may gradually diminish as integration advances (if indeed it does) through a process that is initially political and subsequently legal, ultimately moving towards the formation of a federal Europe. This would entail not merely a federal constitution but a progressive and spontaneous alignment, as Advocate General Pedro Cruz Villalón suggested in his Opinion in the Gauweiler case.

Conversely, if Article 4(2) TEU is interpreted as an "open clause" that national constitutional courts may define without constraint, it risks becoming a kind of "Trojan horse" within which wide margins of national sovereignty might be shielded. Such a development would excessively fragment the EU legal order, to the detriment of the integration process *tout court*. Instead, the kind of *unity* to which the EU should aspire lies in convergence around its foundational values, as set out in Article 2 TEU. These values should guide both the Court of Justice and national constitutional courts towards a progressive rapprochement in their

[35] H.P. Glenn, *The National Tradition*, vol. 11.3 *Electronic Journal Of Comparative Law*, (December 2007), <http://www.ejcl.org/113/article113-1.pdf>

respective *fundamental assessments*, without undermining the internal diversity of the Member States' legal systems.

Both international and national courts respond to illegality (real or perceived) on behalf of individual victims. This, as Weiler might say, is the key to understanding the Union's identity: its DNA. However, within this 'alliance' between the EU institutions and the individual, and in the new public space that has emerged in Europe, the courts have placed the individual (more than ever before in history) at the centre of their judicial activity. This has given rise to a powerfully individualised identity, in which values no longer take the form of republican virtue or collective mobilisation. It is an identity which, while it has legally distanced itself from the exclusionary typology of internationalism and Comparative Law of the last century, nonetheless suffers from a form of immunisation, in the sense described by Roberto Esposito. The philosophical analyses offered by Esposito and Weiler are not so far apart. Unlike those legal cultures that have been annihilated or marginalised (such as Indigenous traditions), "a world in which … the individual placed in the center increasingly becomes a self-centered individual to the detriment of the social".[36]

The two defining features of the principle of relationality, as opposed to that of separation, are encapsulated in two terms that could just as easily be used within the framework of an exclusionary identity: openness and limit.

As we saw in the various Encounters in Part I, the appearance of the Other disrupts, in strictly terminological terms, the essentialist conception of identity. Openness to the Other (grounded in the registers of *Imago Dei* or the rational human being) has often gone hand in hand with incompleteness and exclusion. The conceptual tools of Comparative Law have historically contributed to processes of classification and exclusion. International Law has institutionalised such differences, treating them as gaps or as abyssal lines.

In Part II, however, difference becomes the essence of a new legal paradigm. We should reiterate that this is not a matter of idealism or naïve optimism. Legal scholarship should seek to understand and articulate, in academic terms, that difference nourishes the reservoir of the Union, starting with general principles and extending to Article 2 TEU. The notion of discrepancy put forward by Advocate General Ćapeta,

[36] D. Lustig & J. H. H. Weiler, *Judicial review in the contemporary world—Retrospective and prospective*, in *International journal of constitutional law*, 2018, p. 372.

understood as a space of productive tension, is synonymous with the opening up of resources. And thanks to this new conception of mutual openness, through which one identity is placed before another without a *prius* and *ergo* without incompleteness, a new idea of limit emerges, one that differs from the concept analysed in Part I. The limit serves to 'drain' legal circulation, to filter and exclude only those concepts which, by referring to the exclusionary legal identity discussed in Part I, position themselves outside the perimeter of the Union's identity. These are the red lines repeatedly invoked by Advocate General Ćapeta. They represent, therefore, a negation rather than an abuse.[37] In this way, what was once ontologically impossible (or at least extremely difficult), namely the possibility that the values of the international *communitas* could be nourished by national experiences, is now an emerging reality within the European *communitas* through cross-fertilisation, which nevertheless operates within identifiable limits.

For these reasons, I argue that only through the Union's relational identity and the epistemic identity of legal scholarship is it possible to believe in the values of the Union. It is also only under the condition that these values do not relapse into the *arcana imperii* of twentieth-century Law that the idea of Law as a limit, nourished by democratic factors and respect for fundamental rights, can be upheld. The very idea of the liberal order, which in itself is no panacea and bears significant direct and indirect responsibility for the current authoritarian upheaval at the international level, can only survive if it is rethought in relational terms. The consolidation of values that are genuinely lived in both internal and external praxis may forge this new identity of the Union.

As Nicole Roughan[38] argues, when State orders and claims to authority overlap, the legitimacy of authority becomes a matter of the appropriate relationship between those orders. Meanwhile, the constitutional authority of each respective order, from an internal perspective, may be perceived as absolute; legitimate authority becomes a relational matter. This is where constitutional identity comes into play. When the acts of another constitutional order affect aspects of a given order's identity, the normative situation of the latter changes. This may therefore justify a different mode

[37] In this respect I disagree with J. Scholtes, *The abuse of constitutional identity*, cit., pp. 120–149.

[38] N. Roughan, *Authorities: Conflicts, Cooperation, and Transnational Legal Theory*, Oxford, University Press, Oxford, 2018.

of engagement, for example, moving from general acceptance of the primacy of rules from the other order to the imposition of conditions for such acceptance, requesting adjustments or adaptations by the officials of the other order, or, as an ultima ratio, tolerating an open conflict of incompatible rules. As Cormac Mac Amhlaigh[39] argues, from an internal perspective, 'constitutional identity' refers to the set of constitutional rules and principles that mark the boundary between a legal system's openness to the rules of other legal systems, on the one hand, and the assertion of the supremacy of its own legal order, on the other. When constitutional identity is infringed, the balance between openness to external rules and the supremacy of internal rules (what we might describe as a system of legal sluice gates) may tilt in favour of the latter. This shift can then justify a different mode of engagement with the other legal order. Within this relational recalibration, a twofold question arises: is the contribution of national constitutional lifeblood necessary? And, subsequently, is the filtering function (the sluice gate that opens and closes) of the CJEU also required?

From the first point of observation, Fabbrini and Sajó argue that "the concept of national constitutional identity as applied by a growing number of constitutional courts and governments represents a real and present danger to the process of European integration, as the doctrine is drenched with neo-sovereigntist features and is contrary to the rule of law."[40] Indeed, Fabbrini and Sajó argue that the use of arguments of constitutional identity in the judicial discourse "will contribute to European disintegration".[41] Renáta Uitz similarly expressed concern that "it may well be that what we are witnessing is a moment of calm before stronger than ever national constitutional identity claims take the European constitutional project by a storm to shatter its very foundations".[42]

[39] C. Mac Amhlaigh, 'Taking Identity Seriously: On the Politics of the Individuation of Legal Systems', in Oxford Journal of Legal Studies, Vol. 42, No. 2, 2022, pp. 543–544; C. Mac Amhlaigh, *New Constitutional Horizons: Towards a Pluralist Constitutional Theory,* Oxford University Press, Oxford, 2022, pp. 113–114.

[40] F. Fabbrini, A. Sajó, *The dangers of constitutional identity*, in *European Law Journal*, 2019, p. 470.

[41] F. Fabbrini, A. Sajó, *The dangers of constitutional identity*, cit., p. 463.

[42] R. Uitz, *National Constitutional Identity in the European Constitutional Project: A Recipe for Exposing Cover Ups and Masquerades*, in *VerfBlog*, 2016/11/11, https://verfassungsblog.de/national-constitutional-identity-in-the-european-constitutional-project-a-recipe-for-exposing-cover-ups-and-masquerades/

While critics note very worrying developments, "getting rid" of constitutional identity arguments (and the underlying constitutional pluralism) will do little to resolve the issues at hand. Rather, it raises broader normative questions about the balance between legitimacy and authority within the European legal order, questions that are, nonetheless, often overlooked by critics. This is particularly true of criticisms of constitutional identity that advocate the unconditional supremacy of EU Law, thereby sidelining any consideration of national constitutional identity. Moreover, conceptual critiques of constitutional identity (such as its alleged indeterminacy and vulnerability) are likely overstated.

Oreste Pollicino, for instance, proposes abandoning the framework of constitutional identity in favour of grounding judicial dialogue in the concept of common constitutional traditions.[43] Fichera and Pollicino express hope that the language of CCT may facilitate judicial conversations in Europe and foster a much more cooperative constitutionalism as an alternative to the conflict-driven language of constitutional identity.[44] Our proposal, by contrast, asserts the absolute necessity (understood in the terms already analysed) of constitutional identity. It is the lifeblood required for the functioning of cross-fertilisation, which in turn enables the articulation of common principles of EU Law, common constitutional traditions and shared values.

Secondly, assertions that a mere semantic shift could help contain excesses in the use of shared constitutional discourse in Europe deserve rigorous scepticism. Spieker suggests that since Member States lack the prerogative to unilaterally define the common values of the Union, Article 2 TEU is less vulnerable to self-serving manipulation.

However, there is no real obstacle preventing national constitutional courts from distorting the meaning and content of those common values through twisted interpretations guided by ulterior motives. It is evident that Article 2 TEU encompasses concepts of an open texture and, to a considerable extent, are "essentially contested", which makes it easy to imagine multiple paths of misrepresentation in favour of authoritarian or populist projects. Just as the interpretative monopoly of the Court of

[43] O. Pollicino, *Common Constitutional Traditions in the Age of the European Bill(s) of Rights: Chronicle of a (somewhat prematurely) death foretold*, cit., p. 69.

[44] M. Fichera – O. Pollicino, *The Dialectics Between Constitutional Identity and Common Constitutional Traditions. Which Language for Cooperative Constitutionalism in Europe?*, in *German Law Journal*, 2019, pp. 1097–1118.

Justice of the European Union regarding the scope of Article 4(2) TEU cannot completely eradicate abuses related to constitutional identity, neither do its interpretative powers over the values enshrined in Article 2 fully shield those notions from challenge, distortion or deliberate disregard.

Similarly, with sufficient effort, even common constitutional traditions can be fragmented, disputed and reinterpreted, especially given the richness of non-democratic constitutional traditions throughout Europe, both past and present. Nothing prevents constitutional courts from interpreting a particularistic understanding of the common European constitutional traditions that is not tied to contemporary European constitutionalism.

Blaming concepts rather than the actors involved is destined to lead us into a game of 'conceptual whack-a-mole', where cracking down on one concept causes a similar concept to spring up elsewhere in disguise. At the root of the destructive potential of constitutional identity is not the concept itself but rather the emerging reality of illiberal constitutionalism throughout Europe. The increasing abuse of constitutional identity is less indicative that constitutional identity is inherently a bad framework for constitutional disagreements. Rather, it illustrates the simple reality that authoritarians and illiberals across Europe are increasingly seeking legitimacy by using and integrating into existing constitutional discourse, that is by denying it.

These '*demodé*' conceptions surface in the rejection of LGBTQ+ minorities in the pending *Commission v Hungary* case.[45] Through Law LXXIX of 2021, which introduces stricter measures against paedophile offenders and amends certain laws to protect minors, Hungary enacted several modifications in different national legislative acts. Several of these changes, which Hungary claims were adopted to protect minors, effectively prohibit or restrict access to content that represents or promotes "gender identities that do not correspond to the sex assigned at birth, sex change, or homosexuality" ("LGBTQ+ content"). In this matter, the Advocate General considers that the fact that LGBTQ+ persons deserve equal respect in Member States cannot be questioned through dialogue. This case embodies and showcases the core of our work. It is the confrontation between two distinct types of identities. The marginalisation of a group in an exclusionary society represents the 'red lines' imposed by the

[45] Commission v. Hungary, C-769/22; conclusions presented by Advocate General Ćapeta on June 5, 2025.

values of equality, human dignity and respect for human rights. Here, by questioning the equality of LGBTQ+ persons, the Hungarian government does not articulate disagreement or divergence regarding the content of the Union's values. This would be the cornerstone of relational identity. In this case, we are facing a clash between two ways of understanding who we are, which even transcends the European perimeter.

Instead of practising the EU's communal relational identity, this Member State has denied several of these fundamental values, thereby considerably departing from the model of constitutional democracy reflected in Article 2 TEU. The Union's *communitas* cannot, nor should it, be homogeneous and exclusionary. The clash is direct, with the contours of a *communitas* united only by rejection of the Other. "In its focus on fending off the external 'enemy' a polity becomes closed, essentialized, unable to redefine itself through internal processes but only through its relation to what it considers its 'enemy'. The closure of Hungarian society on the one hand— the marginalization of opposing or diverging world views, the erosion of checks and balances— and the fending off of refugees on the other are thus two sides of the same coin, both intent on ensuring the 'homogeneity' of Hungarian."[46] Here the very raison d'être of the Union is at stake, and the Advocate General knows this all too well.

From the perspective of Hungarian constitutional identity, refugees considered "culturally alien" are configured as "the Other", an existential threat to the preservation of indigenous identity and culture. From this standpoint, the dignity owed to them as human beings is relegated to a secondary level. Placing ethnic homogeneity as a *prius* above the dignity of those seeking protection constitutes a flagrant transgression of one of the cardinal foundations of European constitutionalism. The same applies to the LGBTQ+ community: they are Others with respect to Orbán's pre-constitutional national identity.

European multicultural society is not culturally homogeneous but pluralistic. Although this type of society is conflictual by nature, it can be defined as peaceful to the extent that political, social and cultural conflicts are managed through the channels provided by democratic political institutions and the legal order of each country. One of the conditions that make this "peaceful and conflictual coexistence" possible is the mutual respect that members of society show towards each other and their diverse

[46] J. Scholtes, *The Abuse of Constitutional Identity in the European Union*, Oxford University Press, 2023, p. 211.

cultures. In a multicultural society, we must be willing to bear the cost of learning the aforementioned form of tolerance: this is our common and symbiotic ***munus***, that is the price we must pay to live together.

In other words, in a pluralistic society, (constitutional) principles provide a framework and are understood as a "reflective" right,[47] sensitive and, therefore, susceptible—to put it in Weberian terms—to "comprehensive" application, with the aim of negotiation (or compromise): I would even dare to say that they are susceptible to an application oriented towards the principle of reasonableness. It is therefore unquestionable that the values enshrined in Article 2 TEU refer to an idea of 'good society', as Advocate General Cápeta expresses in her quoted Opinion.[48]

13.2 Relational Identity and Legal Ways of Living Together

In a context marked by crises of representation, cultural interactions and illiberal regimes, rethinking the notion of identity has become an urgent task. Against essentialist or closed identity models, in which the individual or collective defines itself by exclusive opposition to an outside, rejecting any form of communication or dialogue, various philosophical and political traditions have developed a relational conception of identity, where the self is not formed in isolation but in tension with the Other. As we saw at the beginning of our monograph, it all starts with an *écart*—an unforeseen movement. The Other is not an object to be appropriated but a point of misalignment that displaces. And that displacement is constitutive.

Let us return to the Opinion of the Advocate General Ćapeta:

> One can imagine different societies: autocracies not based on the separation of powers; societies in which the elected majority is not limited by the requirement to respect human rights; societies which are ruled by men, and not by law; societies that do not treat minorities equally and reserve human dignity only for the majority; or societies that do not recognise that women are equal to men. Such societies do indeed exist, and are emerging, throughout the world. The vision of what a good society is in the EU constitution is different. That vision is expressed in Article 2 TEU. The values enumerated in that provision: respect for human dignity, freedom, democracy,

[47] G. Teubner, *Reflexive Recht*, in *ARSP* 1982, pp. 13–59.

[48] Advocate General Ćapeta's conclusions in Case C-769/22, *Commission/Hungary*, presented on 5 June 2025.

equality, the rule of law and respect for human rights, including the rights of persons belonging to minorities, read together, paint a picture of a constitutional democracy that respects human rights.[49]

The more its integrating hand deepens in the national constitutional terrain, the more Union law comes to regulate matters directly related to "living together", to the (discipline of) social coexistence. "The law plays a significant role in shaping human identity by specifying what constitutes the common good in a given society and which identity features are deemed (un)acceptable."[50] In the jurisprudence of the European Court of Human Rights, the *écart* here is represented by the continuous reference to the concept of national identity with respect to minorities. Identity is personal, while simultaneously it is constituted and shaped by general mechanisms of power. From Derrida's idea of *différance*, identities do not have a fixed essence and depend on excesses, "others", to assume their meaning. In the case law of the Strasbourg Court concerning paternity, the Court of Justice seems to have a specific view of what is presented as an unquestionable part of identity.[51] This ostensibly individual notion of identity becomes untenable in cases where the nature of an identity trait,[52] such as the "headscarf",[53] or a minority that has adopted a national identity that conflicts with the majority national identity,[54] is disputed. In the SAS case, a "*Français conception du vivre ensemble*" emerges that closely reclaims the very idea of *identité constitutionnelle* already analysed *below*. Levinas' alterity has been denied twice: in the rejection of the radical heterogeneity of the other and in the means, i.e. the criminalisation of alterity

[49] Advocate General Ćapeta's conclusions in Case C-769/22, *Commission/Hungary*, presented on 5 June 2025, pars. 156 and 157.

[50] Y. Al Tamimi, *Human Rights and the Excess of Identity: A Legal and Theoretical Inquiry into the Notion of Identity in Strasbourg Case Law*, in *Social & Legal Studies*, 2018, p. 287.

[51] E. Patrignani, *Alterity according to Emmanuel Levinas and Comparison of Laws*, in *Philosophy*, 2016, p. 40.

[52] ECHR (GC) 18 March 2011, no. 30814/06 (Lautsi and Others v. Italy).

[53] ECHR (GC) 1 July 2014, no. 43835/11 (S.A.S. v. France). On the comparison with the corresponding cases addressed by the Court of Justice, cf., A. Lazari, *El diálogo entre jueces como paradigma comparativo europeo*, in *Diálogos judiciales en el sistema europeo de protección de derechos: una perspectiva interdisciplinaria*, Tirant Lo Blanch, Valencia, 2018, pp. 41–71.

[54] ECHR (GC) 30 January 1998, no. 19392/92 (The United Communist Party of Turkey and Others v. Turkey).

or the imposition through criminal law of a certain understanding of freedom and equality.[55]

Something similar is happening at the corresponding headquarters in Luxembourg. It is sufficient to explore the recent jurisprudence of the CJEU in areas closely related to national identity, such as religion and family. In these areas, the EU is not endowed with harmonising competences, and, in different ways, the Treaties recognise the different sensitivity of these crucial issues. In this way, the Treaties limit the scope of the Union's intervention and, more generally, point to the existence of strong national concerns. Better still, they calibrate, weigh (as Weiler would say), joint normative intervention. Therein lies the communitarian paradigm: in the reciprocal and varied need to regulate a supranational community.

In other words, Article 4(2) TEU does not prevent these 'sensitive' areas from falling within the scope of the CJEU and from being influenced by EU Law. This is simply unavoidable unless the CJEU fundamentally changes its views on the functioning of the European legal order and, in particular, the doctrines of primacy and effectiveness of EU Law.

However, Community legislation, such as judicial interpretation, must not necessarily lead to negative consequences from the perspective of a Member State, in terms of loss of domestic autonomy and prevailing uniformity over diversity. Conversely, the national identity clause may influence the practical interpretation and application of EU Law in a particular case. In recent times, the CJEU has been called upon to decide on a wide range of religious issues, such as ritual slaughter,[56] the use of headscarves in the workplace,[57] taxation, church regimes,[58] the selection and dismissal of employees on religious grounds[59] and religious[60] holidays. Very often, rather than freedom of movement, questions relating to the principle of non-discrimination are raised before the Court of Justice. Apart from its

[55] E. Patrignani, *Alterity according to Emmanuel Levinas and Comparison of Laws*, cit., p. 51.

[56] CJEU, C-426/16, Liga van Moskeeën en Islamitische Organisaties Provincie Antwerpen v. Vlaams Gewest, ECLI:EU:C:2018:335 and C-336/19 Centraal Israëlitisch Consistorie van België and Others, ECLI:EU: C:2020:1031.

[57] CJEU, C-157/15, Achbita v. G4S SecureSolutions, ECLI:EU:C:2017:203 and C-188/15, Bougnaoui v. Micropole, ECLI:EU:C:2017:204.

[58] CJEU, C-74/16, Congregation of Pious Schools Bethany Province v. Getafe City Council, ECLI:EU: C:2017:496.

[59] CJEU, C-414/16 Egenberger, ECLI:EU:C:2018:257; and C-68/17, IR v. JQ, ECLI:EU:C:2018:696.

[60] CJEU, C-193/17 Cresco Investigation GmbH v. Markus Achatzi, ECLI:EU:C:2019:43.

specific legislation in a specific case, the national identity clause in Article 4(2) TEU will therefore also be a political signal that the EU is not, and will not become, a federation. "At the same time, the Court should also make clear once and for all, that national identity claims, as is the opinion of almost all commentators, cannot go against the founding values of Article 2 TEU. 'Exclusive' or 'absolute' constitutional identities are not welcomed in the EU legal space."[61]

Once again, national identity is translated in axiological terms: "The headscarf is taken here as a 'mirror of identity' that forces Western societies 'to see who they are and to rethink the kind of societies and public institutions they want to have'."[62] These cultural and social frictions, however, must not be interpreted negatively: once again, they testify to a growing maturity in the very idea of European pluralist identity. To ensure that a political community is truly inclusive so that all its citizens feel 'at home', citizens must feel that their identity, including their national identity, is respected. Consequently, and although it may sound paradoxical, a multinational political subject such as the Union will have to pay attention to the loyalties that its citizens feel towards their own national groups if it itself wishes to become the object of its citizens' loyalty in order to ensure its viability. "Many national constitutional courts have understood this, and have developed a theoretical basis for their claim that EU law must comply with the identity of their constitution."[63]

Unlike the exclusionary identity examined in Part I, the community does not exist not prior to its relations but is constituted in and through them. This identity is neither fixed nor closed (as recently portrayed in the narratives of the Hungarian government, the highest courts of the Visegrád Group, or Russia), nor does it represent a standard to aspire to, but rather an open process, shaped through interaction with the Other.[64] Exposure to otherness is not optional: it is constitutive. It forms part of the very beginning of *communitas*. The Other destabilises, challenges and calls the

[61] M. Bonelli, *Has the Court of Justice embraced the language of constitutional identity?*, in *Diritti Comparati* 2022, available in <https://www.diritticomparati.it/has-the-court-of-justice-embraced-the-language-of-constitutional-identity/>

[62] A. Joppke, *Review Symposium: Is religion the problem?*, in *Ethnicities*, 2009, p. 566.

[63] E. Cloots, *National Identity, Constitutional Identity, and Sovereignty in the EU,* in *Netherlands Journal of Legal Philosophy*, p. 46.

[64] Cf. among others E. Levinas, *Totalité et Infini Essai sur l'extériorité*, cit., p. 201; J. Butler, *Precarious Life: The Powers of Mourning and Violence*, Verso, London, 2004, p. 22; J.L. Nancy, *Être singulier pluriel*, Éditions Galilée, Paris, 1996, p. 37.

subject to an ethical,[65] political[66] or legal response.[67] Since its origins, the process of European Union integration has been an unprecedented political, legal and cultural endeavour that has tested traditional models of State sovereignty and national identity. Far from being founded on ethnic, religious or linguistic homogeneity, or following the patterns of American federalism or Swiss confederalism, the European Union has built its unity on the coexistence of differences, within a complex institutional framework based on the Rule of Law, fundamental rights and democratic cooperation among diverse peoples.

These mechanisms for reconciling paradigms, balancing interests, the very existence of margins of discretion and critical primacy form part of a conceptual toolkit typical of Union law, where there is no *prius*, neither solely constitutional, international, national nor community law. Competences exist. This new identity differs substantially, for example, from the 'identity federalism' of the American federalisation process, where the balance clearly favours competences and the federal system, including its judiciary.[68] It is by no means comparable to Article 3 of the Swiss Constitution: "*Les cantons sont souverains en tant que leur souveraineté n'est pas limitée par la Constitution fédérale et exercent tous les droits qui ne sont pas délégués à la Confédération*," where the balance clearly shifts towards the sovereign States.

In fact, from the American doctrinal perspective, the dynamics associated with constitutional identity, although "the most interesting developments in federalism are happening in Europe", end up being considered a 'legal nuisance', since "as an eminently vague concept identity leaves too much room for judicial discretion and leads to unsolvable conflicts among courts as well as between courts and other branches. Like the old sovereignty-based approaches, identity encourages judges to draw bright lines, resurrects jurisdictional conflicts, and discourages cooperation and compromise. In the age of populism, identity federalism draws courts into new and particularly concerning forms of polarization."[69]

[65] E. Levinas, Totalité et Infini: Essai sur l'extériorité, La Haya, Martinus Nijhoff, 1961.

[66] É. Balibar, *Le renversement de l'individualisme possessif*, in H. Guineret and A. Milanese, *La propriété: le propre, l'appropriation*, Ellipses, París, 2004.

[67] H. Muir Watt, *Alterity in the Conflict of Laws: An Ontology of the In-Between*, in *Rabels Zeitschrift für Auslandisches und Internationales Privatrecht*, 2023, pp. 7–8.

[68] V. Perju, *Identity Federalism in Europe and the United States*, in *Vanderbilt Journal of Transnational Law*, 2020, p. 67.

[69] V. Perju, *Identity Federalism in Europe and the United States*, cit., p. 207.

While each state of the Federation has much in common with the rest, they still differ in relevant aspects. When a system of government surpasses a certain threshold of cultural, social and political homogeneity, it means that those distinctive elements are already diminishing. Edward Rubin's perspectives capture this dynamic well in the context of the United States. Writing in 2001, he argued that "[a]t present, the United States is a socially homogenized and politically centralized nation [...] With the minor exceptions of Utah and Hawaii, there is no American state with a truly distinctive social profile [...] Our political culture is more uniform still. Most important, the primary political loyalty of the vast majority of Americans is to the nation."[70] Note here the impact of uniformity, homogenisation and centralisation on distinctive State identities. As Mark Tushnet has argued, "federalism has its attractions as a principle of government almost entirely because it provides an almost unassailable base for value-pluralism".[71] But from the US doctrine, European Community progress is still understood in terms of exclusion: *Aut Aut*. "The dual structure of European constitutionalism informs an account of reciprocal supremacy."[72]

In the European integration process, openness does not occur without a limit: the encounter with the Other takes place on that edge where difference is affirmed, but exclusion or absorption is avoided.[73] It is the basis of coexistence. The limit itself is not conceived here as an excluding border but as a space of contact. It does not define the difference between oneself and the Other, as in sovereigntist visions, because it is configured as a space in which this difference opens up new resources. The limit, in this sense, is not closure but a condition of possibility for recognition and otherness. Regional International Law benefits from a new methodology that, instead of separating, studies mutual interactions, tangles as Remotti would say.

However, although openness to the Other has been conceived in its first steps, it has not been immediately realised. A relational model involves being willing to be affected, transformed and even destabilised by the

[70] E. Rubin, *Puppy Federalism and the Blessings of America*, in *Annals Am. Acad. Pol. & Soc. Sci.*, 2001, p. 43.

[71] M. Tushnet, *Comment, What Then Is the American?*, in *Ariz. L. Rev.* 1996, p. 876.

[72] V. Perju, *Identity Federalism in Europe and the United States*, in *Vanderbilt Journal of Transnational Law*, 2020, p. 310.

[73] G. Martinico, *Constitutions, openness and comparative law*, in *Estudios de Deusto: Revista de Derecho Público*, 2019, pp. 111–124.

presence and voice of the Other. At the beginning of the integration process, the autonomy of the legal order of the European Communities signified a separation between the supranational and national systems. A new supranational legal system was born, once again by way of opposition.

Over time, starting in the 1970s and particularly during the 1980s, the pluralist and relational character of the European project began to emerge. This dimension was highlighted by scholars such as Joseph Weiler, who proposed a theory of constitutional tolerance as a condition of possibility for the Union.[74] "The genius of the Union lies in the fact that it allows a pluralism of identities within a single legal order."[75] Weiler stresses that the Member States have agreed that in certain areas EU Law takes precedence over their constitutions, not out of subordination but as a voluntary act of self-limitation. The first ethical political step is the free will to limit oneself: "*La relation éthique est une relation asymétrique, qui m'oblige au-delà de ma volonté.*"[76] Weiler argues that this tolerance is not indifference: it is a normative act, a form of reciprocal constitutional subjection, which allows States with different values to coexist under a common legal framework.

In this model of coexistence, Glenn's Comparative Law helps coexistence in the *communitas* of Esposito. But it depends precisely on the initial moment of self-limitation towards a cum-*munus*: EU Law is based on an identity, which has always been traversed by tensions. These *écarts* can culminate in the current situation, which is marked by a continuous *vulnus* to the Other. The return of nationalism, migration crises and legal sovereigntism all reveal the structural limits of the existing model and call for a rethinking of the categories used to understand the identity of the European Union.

In response, we propose an interpretation of European integration based on a relational identity that is open yet self-limiting. This perspective is illuminated by the concepts of openness to the Other,[77] of limit and

[74] J.H.H. Weiler, *The Constitution of Europe*, Cambridge University Press, Cambridge, 1999, p. 287.

[75] J.H.H. Weiler, *The Constitution of Europe*, cit., p. 343.

[76] E. Levinas, *Totalité et Infini Essai sur l'extériorité*, cit., p. 201. Here the limit is not territorial or substantial, but instead the ethical and ontological boundary where the Self meets the Other and constitutes itself as a subject.

[77] E. Levinas, *Totalité et Infini Essai sur l'extériorité*, cit.; J. Butler, *Precarious Life: The Powers of Mourning and Violence*, Verso, London, 2004.

self-restraint,[78] and of *écart* as productive difference.[79] This approach clearly echoes Jon Elster's metaphor of Ulysses and the Sirens. States bind themselves *ad intra* through constitutional constraints, such as the supremacy of the Constitution and the control exercised by its guardian, the constitutional court. They also bind themselves *ad extra* through mechanisms like the primacy of EU Law or the jurisdiction of the Court of Justice of the EU. These bindings serve to prevent States from yielding to nationalist impulses that could endanger the process of integration. "The capacity to commit oneself beforehand is a way of preserving autonomy in the face of future temptations that could destroy it."[80]

13.3 Relational Identity and Epistemology: The New Frontiers of International and Comparative Law

All disciplines aim to providing a correct interpretation of their object of study and to establishing the parameters for its theoretical representation. In this context, it is useful to resort to the concepts of *episteme* and "epistemic community".[81] I use the concept of '*episteme*' here to refer to the 'knowledge' that one has in a particular field, to the way in which knowledge is apprehended in theory, used in practice and its exercise is explained. The main function of epistemic communities[82] is to set the terms of discourse and shape the way we look at and think about International Law. As Michel Foucault argued, "in every society the production of discourse is at the same time controlled, selected and redistributed by a certain number of procedures".[83] One of the "procedures for controlling and delimiting discourse" is the culture of a discipline. "One is 'right' only if one

[78] J. Elster, *Ulysses Unbound: Studies in Rationality, Precommitment, and Constraints*, Cambridge University Press, 2000.

[79] F. Jullien, *L'écart et l'entre. Leçon inaugurale de la Chaire sur l'altérité*, Galilée, Paris, 2012.

[80] J. Elster, *Ulysses Unbound: Studies in Rationality, Precommitment, and Constraints*, cit., p. 36.

[81] A. Bianchi, 'Epistemic Communities', in J. d'Aspremont and S. Singh (eds.), *Concepts for International Law Contributions to Disciplinary Thought*, Edward Elgar, London, 2019, p. 251.

[82] S. Fish, *Doing What Comes Naturally*, cit., p. 141.

[83] M. Foucault, *The Order of Discourse*, in R. Young (ed.), *Untying the Text: A Post-Structuralist Reader*, Routledge & Kegan Paul, London, 1981, p. 52.

obeys the rules of a discursive 'control' that must be reactivated in each of the discourses. Discipline is a principle of control over the production of discourse." Members of the same discipline should speak the same language and share certain values.[84] Theories, our narratives, are "ways of making worlds", to take inspiration from Nelson Goodman's famous book.[85] The worlds they build are products of their own creation. They do not offer subjective explanations of a reality that has a discrete and objective existence but constitute the very reality that they claim to describe on the basis of their own principles and theoretical presuppositions.[86] Hence, the attempt advanced by Koskienniemi and other authors of the International Comparative Law is to "provincialize" the universal vision of International Law. It is important to make the effort to understand these diverse worlds from their own internal perspective: from the premises from which they start and in the context of their fundamental principles.[87] This is not an easy task, as we are all in a 'position': we all look at International Law from our own point of view, which is the product of our intellectual upbringing, the set of presuppositions and beliefs to which we adhere, as well as our personal history, which makes us more sensitive to some issues than others.[88]

I disagree with Koskenniemi, on the contrary, regarding the solution of hegemonic power behind International Law. For me, the weight of open values, understood as the common space of convivence, is fundamental to structuring a new form of International Law. Recently, the same words has used with opposite meanings in the discourse of Putin and Trump, on one hand, and the European Union institutions, on the other. In this metaphorical mirror play between the construction of the identity of the Western world and the affirmation of the identity of the discipline of International Law, also at the temporal level, "*it is hardly a coincidence*

[84] J. Chevallier, *Les interprètes du droit*, in P. Amselek (ed.), *Interprétation et droit*, Bruylant, Bruselles, 1995, p. 20.

[85] N. Goodman, *Ways of Worldmaking*, Hackett Publishing Company, London, 1978.

[86] Cf. N. Petersen, *International Law, Cultural Diversity, and Democratic Rule: Beyond the Divide Between Universalism and Relativism*, in *Asian Journ. Intern. Law.*, 2011, pp. 149–163.

[87] An essential piece of this effort is M. Koskienniemi, *The Gentle Civilizer of Nations. The Rise and Fall of International Law 1870–1960*, Cambridge University Press, Cambridge, 2001.

[88] Outi Korhonen has demonstrated in his work a similar sensitivity to issues related to 'situationality': O. Korhonen, *International. Law Situated: An Analysis of the Lawyer's Stance towards Culture, History and Community*, Kluwer, 2000.

that both international law and comparative law became professionalized in their modern form in the late nineteenth century, at the height of Western imperialism".[89] Recently, and even more so in the common law legal family, the barrier of epistemic separation between scholars of International and Comparative Law is blurring. Knowledge of this large number of theories and methodologies should generate a greater degree of tolerance and relationality towards those who do not share our beliefs. Here it is also a matter of managing difference, in this case disciplinary/scientific. The legitimacy of International Law also depends, to a large extent, on its ability to represent diverse legal traditions. As Georges Abi-Saab observed, "*if we really want international law to take hold and be taken seriously by all, it has to be, both in its creation and in its interpretation and application, the product of the community as a whole, reflecting, by synthesis or symbiosis, the legal visions, needs and aspirations of all the components of this community*".[90]

Justice Weeramantry refused to accept "*shallow cosmopolitanism which so often presents itself as embodying 'the universal'*"[91] and sought to ground a universal International Law on the teachings of a wide range of civilisations, cultures and traditions. For him, the Statute of the Court "expressly opened a door to the entry of such principles into modern international law" through Articles 9 and 38, paragraph 1 (d) of the Statute. In particular, Article 9 mandates the Court to: "*search in all these traditions and legal systems for principles and approaches that enrich the law it administers*".[92]

This relational perspective has been developed methodologically under the lens of global history and, in particular, of what Richard Drayton and David Mota call the connective approach, which seeks to elucidate "how history is made through the interactions of geographically (or temporally) separated historical communities".[93] However, a fruitful extension of this connective approach may well rely on other non-Eurocentric periodisations of International Law history to transcend the exclusionary

[89] T. Ruskola, *China in the Age of the World Picture*, in *Oxford Handbook of the Theory of International Law*, Florian Hoffmann A. Orford (eds.), 2016, pp. 138–155.

[90] G. Abi-Saab, *The Portrait of the Jurist as an international Judge*, in C. Peck & R.S. Lee (eds.), *Increasing the Effectiveness of the International Court of Justice: Proceedings of the ICJ/UNITAR Colloquium to Celebrate the 50th Anniversary of the Court*, 1997, p. 171.

[91] A. Anghie, *C. G. Weeramantry at the International Court of Justice*, in *LJIL*, 2001, p. 846.

[92] ICJ, *Gabčikovo-Nagymaros Project (Hungary/Slovakia)*, ICJ Reports 1997 p 7, 97 (Judge Weeramantry, 109).

[93] R. Drayton and D. Motadel, *Discussion: the futures of global history*, in *Journal of Global History*, 2018, pp. 1–21.

Eurocentrism that remains the gravitational core of most new narratives of historical encounters with Western International Law. Ideally, these non-Eurocentric periodisations would be able to fruitfully combine the current temporal and spatial expansion of the scope of International Law history research to investigate interactions among non-Western peoples over time. These developments could further contribute to the achievement of the goals that, according to Thomas Duve, world legal history should set for itself.[94] These, according to Duve, include "a critical, sometimes even deconstructive, function" because a fundamental aspect of historical research involves the dissemination, examination and, when necessary, revision of explicit and implicit interpretations and conceptions of the past. A further development of historiographical consciousness in the most inherently relational of all legal fields is therefore an integral part of the realisation of such a global legal-methodological promise, the relevance of which increases the more one looks at the timeline of the history of International Law beyond the historical hiatus of Western formal imperialism.[95] "The Euro-centric perspective that privileged the state (legocentrism) and territoriality (nationalist concern) is not only quite parochial, but an idiom based on lost memory which does not lead towards a globally acceptable method of understanding law and its many pluralities, mixed manifestations, and commonalities."[96]

As we have already said, "an important vector of diversity in the future of international law will be that of regional diversity".[97] For these reasons, when we approached the European continent in *the pars construens*, we referred to the *ratio decidendi* of the Kadi judgement[98] seen as an interfacial knot between International Law and European law through cross-fertilisation mechanism. "*There is reason to hope that the best aspects of these regional developments will begin to permeate and influence general*

[94] T. Duve, *History of Global Law: A Methodological Approach*, in *Max Planck Institute for the History of European Law, Research Paper Series*, No. 2016-04, available at: ssrn.com/abstract=2781104

[95] On the variety of these arrangements, see L. Benton, *Law and Colonial Culture: Legal Regimes in World History 1400–1900*, Cambridge University Press, 2002.

[96] W.F. Menski, *Comparative Law in a Global Context: The Legal Systems of Asia and Africa*, Cambridge University Press, 2009, p. 198.

[97] A. Yusuf, *Diversity of Legal Traditions And International Law: Keynote Address*, in *Cambridge Journal of International Comparative Law*, 2013, p. 689.

[98] See, for example, CJEU, 3 September 2008, Joined Cases C-402/05 P and C-415/05 P Yassin Abdullah Kadi and Al Barakaat International Foundation v. Council and Commission.

international law and gradually become global norms."[99] This is the positive aspect of the so-called Brussel effect.[100]

But, as Bradford[101] and Cartabia[102] rightly point out, this relational approach can only be completed if there is no conceptual or political *prius*. "A more interesting and productive approach is to consider what impact and positive contribution legal traditions have made to international law by applying a value-added test."[103] The importance of this approach lies in the fact that International Law will only be truly universal if it can, in the words of Robert Jennings, "comprehend within itself the rich diversity of cultures, civilizations and legal traditions".[104] Therefore, we must study how different cultures and traditions have contributed to creating new legal precepts by interacting with old concepts and changing them mutually: this is an inverse cross-fertilisation, not a legal transplant.

"In addition to domestic legal traditions, we note the growing importance of regional traditions as the role of regional organizations in international law-making keeps acquiring more importance. These regional traditions are likely to provide fresh impetus to the development and evolution of universal international law as some of their innovative legal rules, principles and practices are gradually transferred to the universal level, and as international judicial bodies find inspiration in those rules and practices in resolving international disputes."[105]

For Laurence Helfer, therefore, the "cross-fertilisation of legal norms is one of the interpretative tools that are commonplace in the case law of regional and sub-regional [*human rights*] courts".[106] Joost Pauwelyn

[99] A. Yusuf, *Diversity of Legal Traditions And International Law: Keynote Address*, cit., p. 702.

[100] A. Bradford, *The Brussels Effect – How the European Union rules the world*, Oxford University Press, Oxford, 2020.

[101] A. Bradford, *The Brussels Effect – How the European Union rules the world*, cit., spec. p. 56.

[102] M. Cartabia, *Europe and Rights: Taking Dialogue Seriously*, in *European Constitutional Law Review*, 2009, pp. 5–31.

[103] A. Yusuf, *Diversity of Legal Traditions And International Law: Keynote Address*, cit., p. 702.

[104] R. Y. Jennings, *The Internal Judicial Practice of the International Court of Justice*, in *BYIL*, 1988, p. 44.

[105] A. Yusuf, *Diversity of Legal Traditions and International Law: Keynote Address*, cit., p. 708.

[106] L. Helfer, *The Successes and Challenges for the European Court, Seen from the Outside*, 14 May 2014, <http://www.ejiltalk.org/the-successes-and-challenges-for-the-european-court-seen-from-the-outside>, visited 1 de february 2026.

describes the relationship between law and non-law as one of the following characteristics: "cross-fertilisation" grounding this usage on the idea "that non-law may have a whole range of possible effects on what is law and how it should be interpreted and communicated".[107]

The concept of cross-fertilisation is key in the discussion taken up by Anne-Marie Slaughter on the role of national and international judiciaries in "an emerging global legal system".[108] As Philippe Sands suggests, cross-fertilisation is a means of addressing challenges to International Law: "if a legal agent wishes to understand the meaning or significance of a legal utterance (U1), his understanding may profit by bringing the analysis of U1 to bear on its relationship with other legal utterances (U2, U3, U4, and so on). To talk about cross-fertilisation in international law implies confirmation of this observation."[109]

In this context Comparative Law is not only a technique for classifying legal systems but also a space for reflecting on legal otherness. Traditionally, Comparative Law was based on closed typologies (legal families, codified systems, models of constitutionalism), which implied an essentialist and identitarian conception of legal systems: Roman-Germanic law, Common Law, Islamic law, etc. These categories, while useful, led to an epistemological closure, excluding anything that did not fit into the model. Huntington's 'Clash of Civilizations' is the clearest proof of this Comparative Law typology.

Authors such as Pierre Legrand or Günter Frankenberg have criticised this view for its universalising pretensions and have instead advocated a hermeneutic, critical and situated reading of Comparative Law. "*Comparer, c'est traduire, c'est accepter que l'Autre juridique résiste à l'assimilation.*"[110] But the new scientific identity approach should not fall into the error of the incommensurability of legrandian *mentalités.*

The relational approach proposes that Law be understood 'in relation' and that the legal identity of one system is not given once and for all but

[107] J. Pauwelyn, *Is it International Law or Not, and Does It Even Matter?*, in J. Pauwelyn et al.(eds.), *Informal International Lawmaking*, OUP, Oxford, 2012, p. 153.

[108] A. Slaugther, *Judicial Globalization*, in *Virginia Journal of International Law*, 2000, p. 1103.

[109] P. Sands, *Sustainable Development: Treaty, Custom, and the Cross-Fertilization of International Law*', in A. Boyle and D. Freestone (eds.), *International Law and Sustainable Development: Past Achievements and Future Challenges*, Oxford University Press, New York, 1999.

[110] P. Legrand, *Le droit comparé*, PUF, Paris, 1999, p. 17.

constitutes contact, conflict and translation of the Other. When we compare, we not only study the Other but also move away from our own normativity. It is the critical function of Comparative Law. This productive displacement is precisely what François Jullien calls *écart*: a departure from the starting point that does not break with it but allows us to think through active difference. "*Comparer, ce n'est pas juxtaposer mais écarter — c'est mettre en écart pour penser autrement.*"[111]

In this sense, Comparative Law operates as a form of epistemic self-limitation or ironism according to Rorty: I recognise that my system does not exhaust the Law, and I open a space to see from the Other, without absorbing it. In this way, we can study the tangle of similarities that connect us to the Other or the reciprocal influences that make the Other not truly foreign to me, as in the narrative framework of Herodotus' Histories.

From this perspective, Comparative Law allows us to think of legal systems as normative *communitates*, in the sense explained by Esposito: not because of what they have in common (a legal essence) but because of what they owe each other: mutual recognition and interactions. This legal *communitas* is not harmonious or total: it is marked by the *écart*, by the difference between legal forms, by their mutual exposure to institutional otherness. Comparative Law thus becomes a practice that inhabits the limit, not to erase it but to sustain it as a condition of communality.

This vision has significant limitations. The concept of constitutional identity is not a substitute for sovereignty, used by V4 countries as a form of exclusion in the European *communitas*, this time against the Other (migrant, LGBTQ+ collective). This short-circuits cross-fertilisation. This form of identity, as criticised by Remotti and Jullien, neither enriches nor is enriched. It only separates and excludes with respect to a *prius*, which is ethnicity, the metaphysical people. Or it tends to interrupt a dialogue as in the Polish case due to a project of isolationism. Let us reason again as we did in Part I. It is the existential risk currently faced by the European Union. Comparative Law serves to classify and separate, as in the example of the judgements handed down by the Polish, Bulgarian and Hungarian courts.

Constitutional identity can feed into and be fed by supranational identity, according to a top-down and bottom-up circular phenomenon. Comparative Law records these movements, neither 'encouraging' in favour of Legrandian resistance nor in favour of functionalist unification.

[111] F. Jullien, *L'écart et l'entre*, Gallimard, Paris, 2012, p. 57.

13.4 Relational Identity and the *Communitas*

Throughout our research we have often talked about the relationship between identity and community. Our vision makes it possible to articulate the constitutive tension between unity and difference, between bond and margin, as an essential feature of the European project. The values at the heart of the Union's relational identity compel us to envision a new idea of community, without which this axiological entity would lack coherence. If the European Union aspires today to embody a new form of a good society, it must be grounded in a renewed ideal of community.

Communitas, in the sense developed by authors such as Roberto Esposito or Jean-Luc Nancy, is not a homogeneous collective but a mutual exposure to the Other.[112] It is a way of being together not founded on the identity of belonging but on the fragile bond of communality, what is given and risked in the Encounter. *Communitas* does not erase difference; it inhabits it and recognises it as the very condition of communality. Community is not the place of belonging but the place of dispossession. *Communitas* arises from the experience of limits and the rupture of ethnocentric self-sufficiency. Nancy articulates a radically relational ontology: *there is no identity prior* to the bond, and the *porous boundary is the very condition of plurality*. The cords of self-limitation woven by modern constitutionalism and supranationalism are becoming ever more intertwined, even reaching the status of common constitutional traditions and shared values.

"Being is with. There is not first an 'I' that then enters into a relationship. Existence has always been coexistence."[113] Here there is no evangelising *prius*, nor rationalist, nor does a consequent incompleteness of the Other emerge. It is not a question of imposing a priori the principle of *primauté* or the principle of constitutional supremacy. "*S'ouvrir à l'Autre, ce n'est pas y adhérer ou l'absorber. C'est maintenir un écart qui préserve sa différence et permet une transformation mutuelle.*"[114]

In this way, we can understand the European Union not as a superstate with a homogeneous identity (whether Kelsenian or Schmittian) but as an

[112] J.L. Nancy, *Être singulier pluriel*, Éditions Galilée, Paris, 1996, p. 40.
[113] J.L. Nancy, *Être singulier pluriel*, cit., p. 37.
[114] J.L. Nancy, *Être singulier pluriel*, Éditions Galilée, Paris, 1996, p. 103.

exposed *communitas*,[115] built through reciprocity among singular subjects (the Member States) who do not forgo their individuality. What is common is not an essence (such as a Christian Europe or an Enlightenment Europe) but a *between*, a shared space of values, traditions and principles that enable contact without absorption. "*La pensée se produit entre les deux. Non pas dans l'identité, ni dans la confrontation, mais dans cet espace qui n'appartient à personne, mais qui nous relie.*"[116] The difference between Member States must not be uncritically denied or uncritically celebrated: it must be activated as a driving force for European political and legal thought. A Europe of the *écart* would be one that does not seek to homogenise but productively stretches the distance between its parts, thus generating a community without closure.

The European integration project can be rethought, within this theoretical framework, as a relational identity structured through difference: open to the Other without seeking absorption, yet also equipped with rational mechanisms of self-limitation (Weiler, Elster) that make normative coexistence possible. The concept of *écart* allows us to understand difference not as an obstacle but as the very condition of shared thought.

From this perspective, the EU does not fail because of its pluralism, but rather when it abandons the institutional and symbolic labour of the *in-between*: when it ceases to uphold the space of connection and limitation that makes an open *communitas* possible. It falters when it retreats to the *arcana imperii* of separation and exclusion, as seen in certain rulings of some constitutional courts. "*La limite n'est pas la fin, mais le début: le début d'une relation infinie avec l'Autre.*"[117] The apodictic affirmations of the 'exclusionary' sentences about constitutional identity once again draw an abyssal line of the sovereigntist separation paradigm: they simply indicate an end. Relational constitutional identity, in its very relationality, marks the beginning of cross-fertilisation, whereby each judicial body exercises its own competence: national constitutional courts in establishing constitutional identity and the Court of Justice in identifying a common principle, tradition or shared identity. The porous boundary between identities is essential to the Union's own identity. It is not erased; indeed,

[115] J. Butler, *Precarious Life: The Powers of Mourning and Violence*, Verso, London, 2004, p. 22: "The ego is always in process, constituted by relations that precede it. We are relational, dependent, affected. That exposure is our condition."

[116] F. Jullien, *L'écart et l'entre. Le troisième est ce qui compte*, Gallimard, Paris, 2012, p. 114.

[117] E. Levinas, Autrement qu'être ou au-delà de l'essence, Martinus Nijhoff, La Haye, 1974, p. 128.

it is what enables and promotes plurality. To reiterate: the constitutional identity enshrined in Article 4(2) TEU is an essential principle of the Union legal order, on an equal footing with Articles 2, 6 and 19 TEU.[118]

Such a statement might at first seem to contradict the primacy of the European Union's values over the national identities of the Member States. This primacy, as noted earlier, has been explicitly affirmed by the Luxembourg judges. In reality, however, the statement draws attention to the shared roots of the identity elements referenced in the various provisions of primary EU Law. In this way, it strengthens the idea that a process of "Europeanisation of the national identities of the Member States" has indeed taken place.

The *écart* between judicial decisions is not a clash of identities nor a blending of them. Rather, it allows for the emergence of new thinking, a resource generated in the relationship between terms that differ without excluding one another. For this reason, we might understand the comparison between judgements as a space, as something in-between. Not what separates as an obstacle but what maintains a creative tension. In the terminology recently used by Advocate General Ćapeta, this is what she describes as discrepancy. Relational identity challenges the Western identitarian logic which sees Being as something identical to itself. Without an *écart*, identity risks become rigid or even lifeless. Critical thinking begins precisely at the point where something breaks away from the familiar.

This open conception of identity allows us to see limits not as impenetrable borders or abyssal lines but as spaces that activate critical thinking. Elster's image of Ulysses and his act of self-limitation can thus be reinterpreted in terms of *écart*, understood in two directions. The first meaning is that "to think is to trace an *écart* that allows us neither to succumb nor to merge. The *écart* is also what protects, even as it opens."[119] The second implies that through an infinite series of jurisprudential *écarts*, the self-limitation of the State is actually achieved. When certain democratically elected forces put the very life and functioning of the State in crisis, undermining the Rule of Law and respect for fundamental rights, common values, traditions and principles emerge. Here, the subject does not tie himself up to block himself but to resist the delirium of nationalism's omnipotence, which now sees community ties as a nuisance to supposed sovereign freedom.

[118] Court of Justice of 5 June 2023, C-204/21, *Commission v Poland*, paragraph 72.
[119] F. Jullien, *L'écart et l'entre*, Gallimard, 2012, p. 77.

For these reasons the new identity of the European Union is a very fragile creature. It can be made highly vulnerable by returning to the hegemonic discourse of separation when it tries to alienate the Other, whether migrant and belonging to a vulnerable group. Or simply because adolescent positions are taken regarding autonomy, always understood from a perspective of separation from the Other (e.g. in the case of adherence to the European Convention on Human Rights). If one does not open up to the Other, relational identity simply becomes sclerotic and is destined to fail. It is destined to fail if it is not translated into a proactive and active attitude.

The economic crisis of 2006 has led to an austerity policy that has sparked much criticism, undermining the sense of responsibility towards the Other within the *communitas*. "It has made evident the limits of an – unfortunately still weak – inter-state solidarity that also exploded in the migration crisis."[120] It confirmed the existence of a different British political agenda, which did not agree to sign the Fiscal Pact. This difference in perspective (among other things) famously led to Brexit later on. All events are in contrary to the relational identity that was being forged. It favoured the emergence of sovereigntist populisms that have ended up challenging the values of the Union enshrined in Article 2 of the TEU.

Within the new European economic governance, the asymmetric dimension of the EU has been amplified by two main factors: firstly, due to the instruments used since some of the recently introduced measures have been adopted outside the EU legal framework, namely through the conclusion of international agreements. This factor has enabled the creation of a set of rules shared by a group of EU Member States in the form of a public International Law treaty. As Bruno de Witte has pointed out, this "turn towards international treaties" is not new, as this path has even been followed in other cases.[121] It is quite significant of a shift in direction towards a return to the Law of Separation and disintegration rather than

[120] '*Editorial Comments: From Eurocrisis to Asylum and Migration Crisis: Some Legal and Insti-tutional Considerations About the EU's Current Struggles*', in *Common Market Law Review*, 2015, pp. 1437–1441.

[121] "And yet, what happened then, and what happened later when the ESM Treaty and the Fiscal Compact were concluded by groups of Member States, seems less shocking when seen within a broader evolutionary perspective of European law," also B. de Witte, *Using International Law in the Euro Crisis Causes and Consequences*, in *ARENA Working Paper*, No. 4/2013, 2013, www.sv.uio.no/arena/english/research/publications/arena-publications/workingpapers/working-papers2013/wp4-13.pdf

the affirmation of a *communitas*. "The TSCG is peculiar for many reasons, the most evident being the fact that it intervenes in a situation already dominated by asymmetry, adding another pattern of differentiation."[122] For example, in addition to the existing asymmetry between euro and non-euro members, this second group will now be differentiated between those who signed the new Treaty and those who did not. Brexit, rejection of immigrants and the economic crisis itself are the clearest evidence of the need for a European relational identity. According to Scicluna, the European crisis would have triggered the "EU's identity crisis".[123]

Unfortunately, we often do not consider intergenerational balance as part of the concept of solidarity, and usually when we refer to solidarity, we do so in a synchronous sense and not a diachronic one. This (rightly) leads us to a negative conclusion: the austerity policy and other failures, such as the inability to overcome the Dublin system,[124] with regard to asylum seekers and refugees, seem to lean towards the absence of true supranational solidarity, but if we look closely at these issues, it is difficult to distinguish the responsibility of the EU from that of its Member States.

13.5 Relational Identity and the Need for a New Community Attitude

But are these really the only terms of the identity question? Is trading values to secure Hungary's vote on sanctions against Russia truly giving them an axiological and non-negotiable dimension? What difference is there between merely paying lip service to the equality of human dignity if the outcome is the same? The humanitarian situation in Lampedusa and on the islands of Samos has demonstrated a failure to uphold human dignity, just as much as Hungarian policy towards refugees. In this case, there is something more. The situation of refugees in Greece and the inaction of

See, for instance, the contributions included in B. de Witte, A. Heritier & A. Trechsel (eds.), *The Euro Crisis and the State of European Democracy: Contributions From the 2012 EUDO Dissemi-nation Conference*, Florence: European University Institute, 2013.

[122] G. Martinico, *The asymmetric turn of the new European economic governance: some remarks on the treaty on stability, coordination and governance in the economic and monetary Union*, in *Revista catalana de dret public*, 2013, p. 134.

[123] N. Scicluna, *European Union Constitutionalism in Crisis*, Routledge, London, 2015.

[124] A. Binetti Armstrong, *You Shall Not Pass! How the Dublin System Fueled Fortress Europe*, in *Chicago Journal of International Law*, 2020, pp. 332 et seq.

the Member States in addressing it reveal the impossibility of legislating on the matter and the collective failure of a *communitas* that claims to protect human dignity in the face of Hungary's action.

Here, tolerance takes on the negative value of acquiescence to a disease that could infect the very fabric of the European *communitas*. In this case, if the *communitas*[125] intends to be such, it must intervene by inoculating itself against the spread of this disease, as clearly set out in the conclusions of Advocate General Ćapeta. In this case, there can be no contagiously vicious cross-fertilisation. As we have emphasised until now, this is not a political choice or a legal determination: the very relational identity of the European Union is at stake.[126] "The values contained in Article 2 TEU have been identified and are shared by the Member States. They define the very identity of the European Union as a common legal order. Thus, the European Union must be able to defend those values, within the limits of its powers as laid down by the Treaties."[127]

The situation in Hungary, on the other hand, reflects the functioning of a system that, as an inherent part of its deeply rooted normative logic, does not grant human dignity to refugees. This system operates according to its own expectations, and its maintenance finds constitutional legitimacy, if not explicit prescription. The same cannot be said of the collapse of the Common European Asylum System, whose inefficacy calls into question the foundational values of the European Union, as well as the essence of its constitutional identity and that of most of its Member States. When Hungary refuses to relocate 1294 refugees to its territory for reasons linked to its constitutional identity, it is not merely a denial of European solidarity in a crisis context. It constitutes an affirmation, as a constitutive element of its constitutional identity, of a normative logic

[125] In contrast to a previous more cautious attitude, such as in the judgement of the CJEU (Grand Chamber) of 5 June 2018, C-673/16, Adrian Coman, Robert Clabourn Hamilton, Asociaţia Accept v Inspectoratul General pentru Imigrări, Ministerul Afacerilor Interne, ECLI:EU:C:2018:385.

[126] This is what the CJEU itself asserts in some seminal judgements already cited—Kadi, and CJEU, 20 April 2021, Case C-896/19, Reppublika, ECLI:EU:C:2021:311, para. 63; CJEU, 18 May 2021, Cases C-83/19, C-127/19, C-195/19, C-291/19, C-355/19, C-397/19, Asociaţia 'Forumul Judecătorilor din România', ECLI:EU:C:2021:393, para 162.

[127] Twin judgements CJEU, 22 February 2022, C-156/21, Hungary v European Parliament and Council of the European Union; ECLI:EU:C:2022:97, para. 127; CJEU, 22 February 2022, C-157/21, Poland v European Parliament and Council of the European Union, ECLI:EU:C:2022:98, para. 145.

deeply at odds with the Union's very identity and *raison d'être*. For this reason, ultimately, we would stress that constitutional identity cannot just be a jurisprudential concept.

13.5.1 *Involving Politics*

The relational feature must ultimately involve other bodies of the Member States and of the Union. Constitutional identity is an inherently political ideal that requires the contribution of diverse political actors and must not be limited solely to judicial actions. Constitutional identity constitutes a deeply political ideal that demands the active involvement of a plurality of political actors, transcending the limitations inherent in exclusively judicial interpretations. The judicialisation of this concept can be seen as a process of confinement, whereby an intrinsically political principle is reduced to the judicial sphere, a practice lacking justification both in normative terms and in relation to the historical foundations of the notion itself. Furthermore, it is suggested that the discursive appropriation of constitutional identity by judicial bodies may be regarded as an additional manifestation of the democratic deficit affecting the European framework. In this context, opening identity claims up to national parliamentary bodies would not only deepen the protection of the principle of subsidiarity but also help to partially remedy this democratic deficit. This process would be especially effective if judicial decisions related to constitutional identity were subject to broad and substantive public debate.[128]

It is possible to make the identity voice of one or more States heard through legal techniques previously outlined: the protection of identity via an annulment action against EU Law, the introduction of a procedure similar to the Early Warning Mechanism and through voluntary opt-outs by Member States.

13.5.2 *Involving the Community*

"*In questi anni si è articolata un'identità legittimante da e per l'Unione Europea, un'identità che si è sviluppata insieme al processo di integrazione e si relaziona in modo dialogico con le identità costituzionali che legittimano*

[128] N. de Boer, *Judging European Democracy. The Role and Legitimacy of National Constitutional Courts in the EU*, Oxford University Press, Oxford, 2023.

gli Stati membri (in processo e in evoluzione)."[129] The very constitutional framework of the European Union, despite lacking a formal Constitution, has ultimately allowed for the shaping of at least one identity, through which it seeks to legitimise the Union's action and authority before its citizens. Another issue concerns the greater or lesser capacity of this European identity to foster integrative cohesion, due to its emotional weakness when faced with other identities (particularly State identities, which initially developed in a collective and homogeneous manner) as well as nationalist identities. This process must be understood from the perspective of the historical development of a shared identity relationship between the European Union and the Member States, based on comparison and integration, as if the States express limits to integration due to their own specificities and identities, and due to the different degrees of constitutional density achieved between their respective systems and the European one. The latter, in turn, embraces this diversity and is enriched by this varied relationship with Others.

This identity clause, however, following Zagrebelsky,[130] reflects more a shared past than a genuinely innovative and inspiring project that aspires to the allegiance of citizens who feel European. It is not only about understanding the Union's destiny and *communitas* as a mere Hobbesian necessity and a simple consequence (present in the face of globalisation and market forces, and past in regard to nationalism) but about actively fostering the future of integration as a genuine shared endeavour. In short, it is about taking action.

For this reason, it is necessary to strengthen solidarity, which truly is the genetic code of the Union, not as a naïve or idealistic vision but as a powerful tool to shape communal relations and the resulting collective identity (particularly by promoting reciprocal collaboration and mutual assistance). In this way, the aim is to enhance society's capacity for adaptation and resilience in especially adverse situations, enabling recovery from circumstances such as those experienced by most Member States during the recent economic crisis or the migration crisis. In this way, close bonds are forged between people, as projections of ourselves and as a universal expression of human dignity, regardless of differences, beginning with the

[129] J.F. Sánchez Barrilao, *Tra identità: il futuro dell'integrazione europea nel contesto globale*, in *Nomos*, 2019, p. 5.

[130] G. Zagrebelsky, *La virtù del dubbio. Intervista su etica e diritto*, Roma-Bari, Laterza, 2007, p. 67.

needs of others.[131] If tolerance is respect for the other,[132] solidarity is a reciprocal duty towards the Other, from which a deeper sense of shared identity emerges. Its essence lies in otherness and dignity: when one breaks, the other breaks. In other words, the failure of solidarity towards others leads, or will eventually lead, to a failure of solidarity towards and among ourselves.[133] Therefore, it becomes possible to understand the profoundly negative impact that the migration and refugee crises have had on European collective identity and the process of European integration.

These crises have not only exposed a lack of otherness towards those outside the EU but also a failure of mutual reception among the Member States themselves, leading to nationalist and even xenophobic responses (reactionary identities that nonetheless carry a legitimising dimension) towards the Other. As stated in the Second Part of Article 2.2 TEU and as we have said before, relational identity requires an active attitude, which does not mean closure in its values.[134] Are we able to promote our common identity?

This is not about political messianism: the values of the EU will only take flight if they are translated into *Nomos*, into lived custom or law. The axiological transference of Case Law carried out by the CJEU will only truly succeed if the identity of Laws is accompanied by a *communitas* rooted in collective solidarity and gift. If, in the coming years, the CJEU continues to defend and promote the Union's identity, even as a justiciable norm, will this lead us towards Integration through values? I do not believe so, as long as the Union fails to assume responsibility towards the Other. As I have reiterated throughout this work, if it does not, we will witness a renewed imposition of hegemonic values under the guise of

[131] Cf. A. Schillaci, *Le storie degli altri. Strumenti giuridici del riconoscimento e diritti civili in Europa e negli Stati Uniti*, Jovene Editore, Napoli, 2018.

[132] Cf. J.H.H. Weiler, *Federalism without Constitutionalism: Europe's Sonderweg*', in K. Nicolaidis & R. Howse (eds), *The Federal Vision*, Oxford University Press, Oxford, 2001, p. 68: "They accept it as an autonomous voluntary act, endlessly renewed on each occasion, of subordination, in the discrete areas governed by Europe to a norm which is the aggregate expression of other wills, other political identities, other political communities. [...] When acceptance and subordination is voluntary, and repeatedly so, it constitutes an act of true liberty and emancipation from collective self-arrogance and constitutional fetishism: a high expression of Constitutional Tolerance."

[133] D. Innerarity, *¿Quiénes somos 'nosotros'? Preliminares para una política de la identidad*, in *Doxa*, 2005, pp. 33–54.

[134] About this issue, see F. Jullien, *Il n'y a pas d'identité culturelle*, Éditions de l'Herne, Paris, 2016, p. 46.

Union principles. If this system of legal "sluice gates" fails to filter both *ad extra* and *ad intra*, and if we do not make progress in terms of our perception of the *communitas*, then the European Union and its legal order are fated to fail. Should it betray its genetic code of responsibility towards the Other, it will no longer be a European Union. It will be a poor imitation of other identities. The hallmark of our time might well be difference, standing in opposition to essentialist identity; and the answer might be coexistence, standing against populist solipsism. I do not view the Community microcosm as inherently harmful nor as an ideological Eden: rather, it is a laboratory of ideas, a privileged observatory of a dynamic politico-legal reality that is clearly open to improvement. "A genuine achievement of the EU – the bringing together of the peoples of Europe in ways that promotes cooperation without abolishing their differences."[135] In *A gramática do tempo*, Boaventura de Sousa Santos[136] points to translation as the only viable alternative for cultivating a pedagogy of coexistence. The Brazilian philosopher theorises a new common sense of Law, rooted in an inter-legal hermeneutic dimension.[137] This, ultimately, seems to be the core of the matter. For centuries, Europe has been a space where many languages and cultures have come into contact, sustaining a tradition of continuous dialogue.[138] On another level, many transformations have also taken place in social customs. This *malaise* is perceptively captured by Weiler: "Europe, in large part, has become a post-Christian society, and the profound commitment to the individual and his or her rights, relentlessly (and, in many respects, laudably) placing the individual at the center of political attention, has contributed to the emergence of

[135] R. Bellamy, *The European Constitution is Dead, Long Live European Constitutionalism*, in *Constellations Volume* 13, No 2, 2006, 187.

[136] Boaventura De Sousa, *A Gramática do tempo: para unha nova cultura política*, Porto, Edições Afrontamento, 2006.

[137] Boaventura De Sousa, *Towards a New Legal Common Sense: Law, Globalization and Emancipation*, 2nd edition, Butterworths, London, 2002. See also H. Collins, *Governance implications of the changing character of private law*, in AA. VV., *The Making of European Private Law. Governance Design*, edited by F. Cafaggi – H. Miur-Watt, Edgar Elgar Publishing, Massachusetts, 2008, 279.

[138] On the connatural complexity of the current legal epistemology, see P. Grossi, *La formazione del giurista e l'esigenza di un odierno ripensamento metodologico*, in *Quaderni fiorentini*, vol.32, Milan, 2003, 33: "*La società al contrario di quella creatura semplicissima che è lo Stato moderno è strutturalmente plurale e complessa, il diritto che le è speculare non potrà non registrare queste qualità, non potrà che proporsi plurale e complesso.*" See, again, P. Grossi, *Mitologie giuridiche della modernità*, Milan, 2001, 43 sq.

self-centered individuals."[139] What is lacking is the very sense of *communitas* whose contours we have gradually attempted to trace thus far.

The reason for the constant moral references to identity can be readily understood from our epistemological perspective. This web of Derridean traces, which forges and keeps identities dynamically alive, is nourished by the lifeblood of solidarity: these are the rules of social coexistence.[140] The paradigm of the European Union is rooted in its communitarian solidarity, and it fails to function when it operates according to the synallagmatic contracts of International Law.

Ultimately, this is why the issue of identity spans multiple levels of interpretation and is essential for communal coexistence: it is not merely a philosophical *querelle*, nor a sociological theory, nor can it be reduced to a political proposition. Rather, it challenges and can even facilitate human coexistence itself.[141] "Through their identity, the Other has something to contribute [...] What matters is to generate encounters, processes that build a nation capable of embracing difference. [...] A cultural pact requires us to abandon monolithic understandings of identity."[142] It is precisely the emphasis on a common (non-existent) will that allows populists to simplify and even trivialise. If there is only one popular will, whose epiphany is an exclusive constitutional identity, then there are no nuances, no need to engage with the intricate web of complexity.[143] This is a reassuring, anxiety-soothing vision: there is only one correct, linear answer to the problems of our time; there is no need to think critically, no need to commit. A political community revolves around what it shares: histories, values and symbols (more or less inclusive). In EU Law, this takes shape through common constitutional traditions, which do not demand uniformity of visions. The distinction between uniformity and communality allows us to conceive of democracy as an agora, where divergent

[139] J.H.H.,Weiler, *Deciphering the Political and Legal DNA of European Integration: An Exploratory Essay*, in *Philosophical Foundations of European Union Law*, J. Dickson & P. Eleftheriadis (eds.), Oxford University Press, Oxford, 2012, p. 38.

[140] Changeons de voie: Les leçons du coronavirus, Éditions Denoël, Paris, 2020.

[141] M. Ceruti, – F. Bellusci, *Abitare la complessità*, Mimesis, Milan – Udine, 2020, p. 19: "*Ecco perché raccogliere la sfida della complessità è una necessità del pensiero e soprattutto un imperativo etico, un imperativo di sopravvivenza. O vinciamo insieme, o perdiamo insieme. Tutto è connesso. Tutto è in relazione. Siamo tutti sulla stessa barca.*"

[142] Carta enciclica, *Fratelli tutti. Sobre la fraternidad y la amistad social*, Palabra, 2020, pp. 147 and 149.

[143] Cf. U. Eco, *Il fascismo eterno*, Milan, La nave di Teseo, 2018, p. 46.

perspectives are confronted, rather than as a monolithic space governed by a single truth or a single 'popular will'. More than compatible, the concept of community is coherent with the idea of pluralism. The lexicon of solidarity, equality and tolerance revolves around it. The community is the place of duties towards the collective, overflowing from the simple reciprocal relationship of contract-driven International Law. Here we enter a realm of gratuitous solidarity, of *munus*, opposed to the *arcana imperii* of contractualist International Law.

The epistemological web must become not only a way of interpreting complex reality but a way of being, an Aristotelian virtue. "What will happen in the future will depend on how we exercise our freedom, whether from an inclusive 'we' or from a fragmentation of individuals."[144] The relational identity is not a panacea: it a fragile equilibruum of tension poles. If a community of values takes form of rigidity, it is destined to fail. If it serves as an exclusionary pretext, it will be yet another ethnocentric project. Jullien warns us that values become a vehicle fro closure if they are understood through the exclusionary comparative method. In the face of the rise of ethnocentric ideas that appropriate the same language of identity, freedom of expression, etc, the only genuine fault line lies in the construction of a Arendtian space of common coexistence. It is not about explaining the access of Western culture to Others but its involvement in a truly common world,[145] whose norms of coexistence can be shaped, thanks to the verb 'com-pare'.[146]

[144] A. Cortina, *Ética cosmopolita. Una apuesta por la cordura en tiempos de pandemia*, Paidós, Madrid, 2021, p. 1.

[145] On radical anthropological conceptual change, see D. Graeber & D. Wengrow, *The Dawn of Everything: A New History of Humanity*, Allen Lane, 2021.

[146] M. Merleau-Ponty, *Le visible et l'invisible*, Les Éditions Gallimard, Paris, 1964, p. 67. Cf. M. Garcés, *La filosofía inacabada*, cit., pp. 164–176, para. 173: "la de Merleau-Ponty es una ontología del *entre*, de la no coincidencia. [..] A la verdad se llega solo con los otros."

Correction to: Relational Identity in International, Comparative and European Union Law

Correction to: A. Lazari, *Relational Identity in International, Comparative and European Union Law*, https://doi.org/10.1007/978-3-031-59482-3

The original version of the book was inadvertently published without the funding information included in the book frontmatter. This has been updated.

The updated version of this book can be found at
https://doi.org/10.1007/978-3-031-59482-3

© The Author(s), under exclusive license to Springer Nature Switzerland AG 2026

A. Lazari, *Relational Identity in International, Comparative and European Union Law*,
https://doi.org/10.1007/978-3-031-59482-3_14

Bibliography

Chapter 1: Prologue

Aime, M., *Classificare, separare, escludere. Razzismi e identità*, Einaudi, 2020

Bianchi, A., *International Law Theories: An Inquiry into Different Ways of Thinking*, Oxford University Press, Oxford, 2017

Bonilla Maldonado, D., *Los bárbaros jurídicos: Identidad, derecho comparado moderno y el Sur global* (Filosofía política y del derecho, Siglo del Hombre Editores 2020)

Burgorgue-Larsen, L., *Pour une approche dialogique du Droit constitutionnel européen*, in *Annuaire de droit européen 2012*, vol. X, Bruylant, Brussels, 2014, pp. 29–53

Cartabia, M., *Editorial. Courts' Relations*, en *Intern. Rev. Const. Law*, 2020, pp. 1–4

Derrida, J., *'Force of Law': The "Mystical Foundation of Authority"*, in *Cardozo Law Review*, 1990, pp. 919–1045.

Drayton-D. Motadel, R., *Discussion: the futures of global history*, in *Journal of Global History*, 2018, pp. 1–21

Esposito, R., *Communitas. The Origin and Destiny of Community*, Stanford University Press, Stanford, 2009

Fabbrini–O. Pollicino, F., *Constitutional Identity in Italy. Institutional Disagreements at a Time of Political Change*, en *Constitutional Identity in a Europe of Multilevel Constitutionalism*, Calliess C. - van der Schyff G. (eds.), Cambridge University Press, 2019, pp. 201–221

Faraguna, P., *Taking Constitutional Identities Away from the Courts*, en *Brook. J. Int'l L.*, 2016, pp. 41–68

© The Editor(s) (if applicable) and The Author(s), under exclusive license to Springer Nature Switzerland AG 2026

A. Lazari, *Relational Identity in International, Comparative and European Union Law*,
https://doi.org/10.1007/978-3-031-59482-3

Faraguna, P., *The Constitutional Identity of the EU as a Counterbalance for Unconstitutional Constitutional Identities of the Member States*, in *European Yearbook Of Constitutional Law*, 2023, pp. 342–351

Faraguna, P., *Unconstitutional Constitutional Identities in the European Union*, en R. Hirschl-Y. Roznai (eds), *Deciphering the Genome of Constitutionalism. The Foundations and Future of Constitutional Identity*, Cambridge University Press, 2024

Fukuyama, F., *Identity. Contemporary Identity Politics and the Struggle for Recognition*, Profile Book, London, 2018

Martinico, G., *The Tangled Complexity of the EU Constitutional Process. The Frustrating Knot of Europe*, Routledge, Second Edition, 2023

Graziadei, M., *Obviously European?*, en *Persona e Mercato*, 2021, pp. 243–272

Graziadei, M., *The Anthropology of European Law*, en MC Foblets (ed.), *The Oxford Handbook of Law and Anthropology*, Oxford University Press, Oxford, 2020, pp. 273–294.

Graziadei, M., *What Does Globalisation Mean for the Comparative Study of Law?*, in *The Journal Of Comparative Law*, 2021, pp. 573–599.

Graziadei, M., *The European Court of Justice at Work: Comparative Law on Stage and Behind the Scenes*, in *J. Civ. L. Stud.*, 2020, pp. 2–32

Habermas, J., *The Inclusion of the Other: Studies in Political Theory*, Polity Press, Cambridge, 1998

Scholtes, J., *The Abuse of Constitutional Identity in the European Union*, Oxford University Press, Oxford, 2023

Jullien, F., *L'écart et l'entre*, Galilée, Paris, 2012

Jullien, F., *Il n'y a pas d'identité culturelle*, Éditions de l'Herne, Paris, 2016

Koskenniemi, M., *Histories of International Law: Dealing with Eurocentrism,* in *Rechtsgeschichte - Legal History* 2011, pp. 152–176

Koskenniemi, M., *The Gentle Civilizer of Nations: The Rise and Fall of International Law 1870–1960*, Cambridge University Press, Cambridge, 2001.

Lecourt, R., *Quel eût été le droit des Communautés sans les arrêts de 1963 et 1964?*, en *L'Europe et le droit. Mélanges en hommage a Jean Boulouis*, Dalloz, Paris, 1991, p. 359

Legrand, P., *Jameses at Play: A Traction on the Comparison of Laws*, in *Am. J. Comp. L. (Special Issue)*, 2017, p. 19, disponible en http://www.pierre-legrand.com/jameses-at-play.pdf

Legrand, P., *The impossibility of 'Legal Transplants'*, in *Maastricht Journal of European and Comparative Law*, 1997, pp. 111–124.

Maalouf, A., *La labyrinthe des égarés: L'Occident et ses adversaires* (Grasset & Fasquelle 2023)

Manzano Moreno, E., *España diversa*, Crítica, Barcelona, 2024

Martinico, G., *Contro l'uso populista dell'identità nazionale. Per una lettura "contestualizzata" dell'art. 4.2 TEU*, in 3 *DPCE online* 2020

Martinico, G., *Lo spirito polemico del diritto europeo Studio sulle ambizioni costituzionali dell'Unione*, Aracne, Roma, 2011
Michaels, R., *Law and Recognition: Towards a Relational Concept of Law*, en *In Pursuit of Pluralist Jurisprudence*, N. Roughan – A. Halpin (eds.), Cambridge University Press, Cambridge, 2019, pp. 107–128.
Muir Watt, H., *Alterity in the Conflict of Laws: An Ontology of the In-Between*, in *Rabels Zeitschrift für Auslandisches und Internationales Privatrecht*, 2023, pp. 2–32
Muir Watt, H., *Globalization and Comparative Law*, en M. Reimann y R. Zimmermann (eds.), *The Oxford Handbook of Comparative Law*, 2ª ed., Oxford University Press, Oxford, 2019, pp. 499–538.
Niglia, L., *The New Transformation of Europe: Arcana Imperii*, in *The American Journal of Comparative Law* 2020, pp. 151–185
Pépin, C., *La rencontre, une philosophie*, Allary Editions, Paris, 2021
Rajagopal, B., *International Law from Below: Development, Social Movements and Third World Resistance*, Cambridge University Press, Cambridge, 2003
Remotti, F., *Contro l'identità*, Laterza, Bari, 2001
Remotti, F., *L'ossessione identitaria*, Laterza, Bari, 2010
Remotti, F., *Somiglianze. Una via per la convivenza*, Laterza 2019
Ricoeur, P., *Soi-même comme un autre*, Éditions du Seuil, París, 1990
Riles, A., *Representing In-between: Law, Anthropology and the Rhetoric of Interdisciplinarity*, in *University of Illinois Law Review*, 1994, pp. 597–611
Sen, A., *Identity and Violence: The Illusion of Destiny*, Penguin Books, London, 2007
Skrydstrup, M., *Righting Wrongs? Three Rationales of Repatriation and What Anthropology Might Have to Say About Them*, in G. Mille-J. Dahl (eds), *Utimut. Past Heritage: Future Partnership. Discussions on Repatriation in the 21st Century.* Greenland National Museum and Archives & International Work Group for Indigenous Affairs, 2008, pp. 56–63
Spano, R., *The rule of law as the lodestar of the European Convention on Human Rights: The Strasbourg Court and the independence of the judiciary*, en *European Law Journal*, 2021, pp. 17–35.
Stahn, C., *Confronting Colonial Objects: Histories, Legalities, and Access to Culture*, Oxford University Press, Oxford, 2023
von Bogdandy, A., *The Transformation of European Law: The Reformed Concept and its Quest for Comparison*, in *European Law Journal*, 2016, pp. 519–538
Weiler, J.H.H., *Federalism without Constitutionalism: Europe's Sonderweg'*, in K. Nicolaidis and R Howse (eds), *The Federal* Vision, Oxford University Press, 2001, esp. pp. 54–68
Wittgenstein, L., *Philosophische Untersuchungen*, Blackwell, Oxford, 1968
Ziller, J., *Comparison within Multi-Level Polities and Governance Regimes*, en *The Oxford Handbook of Comparative Administrative Law*, P. Cane, H. C. H. Hofmann, E. C. Ip y P.L. Lindseth (eds.), Oxford University Press, Oxford, 2018, esp. pp. 4–10

Chapter 2: The Genealogy of Mechanisms for Excluding and Including the Other

Agamben, G., *Il potere sovrano e la nuda vita. Homo sacer*, Einaudi, Torino, 2005

Anghie, A., *Imperialism, Sovereignty and the Making of International Law*, Cambridge University Press, Cambridge, 2005

Anghie, A., La evolución del derecho internacional: realidades coloniales y poscoloniales, in Anghie, A., Koskenniemi, M. - Orford, A. (eds), *Imperialismo y Derecho internacional*, Biblioteca universitaria, Universidad de los Andes, Bogotá, 2016

Baccelli, L., *Bartolomé de Las Casas. La conquista senza fondamento* (Feltrinelli Editore, Milano, 2016)

Bhandar, B., *Colonial Lives of Property: Law, Land, and Racial Regimes of Ownership* Duke University Press, Durham, 2018

Brunstetter, D. R., *Sepúlveda, Las Casas, and the Other: Exploring the Tension Between Moral Universalism and Alterity*, in *The Review of Politics* 2010, pp. 409–435

Carrillo Salcedo, J. A., *Soberanía del Estado y Derecho Internacional*, Tecnos, Madrid 1976

Carrillo Salcedo, J. A., *Soberanía de los Estados y Derechos humanos en Derecho Internacional contemporáneo*, Tecnos, Madrid, 2001

Cavallar, G., *The rights of strangers: Theories of international hospitality, the global community and political justice since Vitoria*, Routledge, London, 2002

Chaparro Amaya, A., *Pensar caníbal. Una perspectiva amerindia de la guerra, lo sagrado y la colonialidad*, Katz, Buenos Aires, 2013

Clayton, L. A., *Bartolomé de las Casas. A Biography*, Cambridge University Press, Cambridge, 2012

Dardot, P., Laval, C., *Dominium: Essai sur la souveraineté de l'État en Occident*, La Découverte, Paris, 2020.

Desautels-Stein, J., *The Right to Exclude: A Critical Race Approach to Sovereignty, Borders, and International Law*, Oxford University Press, Oxford, 2023

Douzinas, E., *Fim dos Direitos Humanos*, Unisinos, São Leopoldo, 2009

Fitzmaurice, A., *Sovereignty, Property and Empire*, Cambridge University Press, Cambridge, 2014

Foucault, M., *Histoire de la sexualité, tome I: La volonté de savoir*, Gallimard, Paris, 1976

Gozzi, G., *Rights and Civilizations: A History and Philosophy of International Law*, Cambridge University Press, Cambridge, 2019

Graziadei, M., *On Universalizing "Nature" and "Property": the Unravelling of a Master Narrative*, en *Journal of Interdisciplinary History of Ideas*, 2023, pp. 27–50

Grocio, H., *De jure praedae commentarius*, Martinum Nijhoff, Hague, 1868

Gutiérrez, G., *En busca de los pobres de Jesucristo. El pensamiento de Bartolomé de Las Casas* (Instituto Bartolomé de Las Casas / CEO, Lima 1992)

Iglesias Ortega, L., *Bartolomé de Las Casas: Cuarenta y cuatro años infinitos*, Fundación José Manuel Lara, Sevilla, 2007

Koskenniemi, M., *To the Uttermost Parts of the Earth: Legal Imagination and International Power, 1300–1870*, Cambridge University Press, Cambridge, 2021.

Jouannet, E., *Universalism and Imperialism: The True-False Paradox of International Law?*, in *European Journal of International Law*, 2007, pp. 379–407

Las Casas, B. de, *Brevísima relación sobre la destrucción de las Indias*, Verbum, Madrid, 2006.

Las Casas, B. de, *Obras completas*, Fundación "Instituto Bartolomé de Las Casas" de los Dominicos de Andalucía, Alianza Editorial, Madrid, 1989–1999

Mora Rodríguez, L., *Bartolomé de Las Casas. Conquête, domination, souveraineté* (Presses Universitaires de France, París 2012)

Nichols, R., *Theft Is Property! Dispossession and Critical Theory*, Duke University Press, Durham 2020

Okubuir, J. C., *Application of Hegemony to Customary International Law: An African Perspective*, in *Global Journal of Comparative Law* 2018, pp. 58–80

Palombella, G., *Filosofia del Diritto*, Cedam, Padova, 1996

Pahuja, S., *Laws of encounter: a jurisdiction account of International Law*, in *London Review of International Law*, 2013, pp. 63–98

Pizza, I., *Antropologia e fondazione dello Stato nel De Jure praedae di Ugo Grozio*, () 3 *Storia del pensiero politico, Rivista quadrimestrale* 2020, pp. 447–465

Porras, I. M., *Constructing International Law in the East Indian Seas: Property, Sovereignty, Commerce and War in Hugo Grotius' De Iure Praedae—The Law of Prize and Booty, or "On How to Distinguish Merchants from Pirates"*, en *Brooklyn Journal of International Law* 2006, pp. 861–885

Schmitt, C., *The Nomos of the Earth in the International Law of the Jus Publicum Europæum*, Telos Press Publishing, New York, 2003

Somma, A., *Introducción crítica al Derecho comparado*, Ediciones Jurídicas Olejnik, Santiago de Chile, 2017

Sousa Santos, B. de (ed.), *Reconhecer para Libertar. Os Caminhos do Cosmopolitismo Multicultural*, Civilização Brasileira, Río de Janeiro, 2003

Taylor, C., *Sources of the Self: The Making of the Modern Identity*, Harvard University Press, Cambridge, 1989

Todorov, T., *La conquête de l'Amérique: La question de l'autre*, Seuil, Paris, 1982

van Ittersum, M. J., *Hugo Grotius in Context: Van Heemskerck's Capture of the Santa Catarina and its Justification in De Iure Praedae (1604–1606)*, in *Asian Journal of Social Science*, 2003, pp. 500–529

Vitoria, F. de, *Relectio de indis o libertad de los indios*, Consejo Superior de Investigaciones Científicas, Madrid, 1967

Vizenor, G., Lee, R. A., *Postindian Conversations*, University of Nebraska Press, Lincoln, 1999

Wiessner, S., *Indigenous sovereignty: A reassessment in light of the UN declaration on the rights of indigenous peoples*, in *Vanderbilt Journal of Transnational Law*, 2008, p. 1141

Chapter 3: The Consolidation of State *Communitas* and International Exclusionary *Societas*

Bernasconi R., *Kant as an Unfamiliar Source of Racism*, in J. K. Ward, T. L. Lott (eds.), *Philosophers on Race: Critical Essays*, Blackwell Publishers, Oxford, 2002, pp. 145–166.

Chukwudi Eze E., *Race and the Enlightenment*, Wiley-Blackwell, London, 199

De Giorgi R., *Temi di filosofia del diritto*, Lecce, Pensa Multimedia, 2006

De Vattel E., *Le Droit des Gens, ou Principes de la Loi Naturelle, appliqués à la Conduiteet aux Affaires des Nations et des Souverains*, vol. 1, Carnegie Institution of Washington, European Legal History, Washington, D.C., 1916; orig. pub. 1758

Fiocchi Malaspina E., *L'eterno ritorno del Droit des gens di Emer de Vattel (secc. XVIII–XXI)*, in *European Legal History*, Frankfurt am Main, 2017, pp. 4–31.

Greer A., *Property and dispossession: Natives, empires and land in early modern North America*, Cambridge University Press, Cambridge, 2018

Grotius H., *The Freedom of the Seas, or the Right Which Belongs to the Dutch to take part in the East Indian Trade*, Oxford University Press, Oxford, 1916

Ince O.U., *Colonial Capitalism and the Dilemmas of Liberalism*, Oxford University Press, Oxford, 2018

Kant I., *Die Metaphysik der Sitten*, in Wilhelm Weischedel (ed.), Werke Suhrkamp, Frankfurt am Main, 1993; orig. pub. 1797, vol. VIII, p. 350.

Kant I., *Immanuel Kants Menschenkunde oder philosophische Anthropologie: Nach handschriftlichen Vorlesungen*, ed. Friedrich Christian Starke, Leipzig, 1831

Kant I., *Zum ewigen Frieden: Ein philosophischer Entwurf von Immanuel Kant*, in Wilhelm Weischedel (ed.), Werke Suhrkamp, Frankfurt am Main, 1993, 1795

Koskenniemi M., *The Philosophy of International Law*, Oxford University Press, Oxford, 1996

Lesaffer R. (ed.), *International Law in Early Modern Europe*, Cambridge University

Locke J., *Two Treatises of Government*, Thomas Tegg; W. Sharpe and Son; G. Offor; G. and J. Robinson, London, 1893.

Mazzucato M., *The Value of Everything: Making and Taking in the Global Economy*, Allen Lane, London, 2018

Mignolo W., *Local Histories/Global Designs: Coloniality, Subaltern Knowledges and Border Thinking*, Princeton University Press, Princeton, 2000

Míguez Núñez R., *Terra di scontri. Alterazioni e rivendicazioni del diritto alla terra nelle Ande* centrali, Giuffrè, Milano, 2013

Muthu S., *Enlightenment against Empire*, Princeton University Press, Princeton, 2003

Pufendorf S., *Of the Law of Nature and Nations: Eight Books*, trans. Basil Kennett, 4th ed., printed for J. Walthoe, R. Wilkin, J. and J. Bonwicke, S. Birt, T. Ward, and T. Osborne, London, 1729

Pufendorf S., *Of the Law of Nature and Nations: Eight Books*, trans. Basil Kennett, 4th

Saastamoinen K., *Pufendorf on the Law of Sociality and the Law of Nations*, in *The Law of Nations and Natural Law 1625–1800*, S. Zurbuchen (ed.), Oxford University Press, Oxford, 2024

Scott J.T. (ed.), *Jean-Jacques Rousseau: Critical Assessments of Leading Political Philosophers*, Routledge Taylor and Francis, London, 2005

Scott J.T., *The Sovereignless State and Locke's Language of Obligation*, in *American Political Science Review*, 2000, pp. 547–561

Skinner Q., *Liberty Before Liberalism*, Cambridge University Press, Cambridge, 2012

Stråth B. and Wagner P. (eds.), *European Modernity: A Global Approach*, Cambridge University Press, Cambridge, 2017

Tomlins C., *Freedom bound: law, labor and civic identity in colonizing English America, 1580–1865*, Cambridge University Press, Cambridge, 2010

Tuck R., *The Rights of War and Peace. Political Thought and the International Order from Grotius to Kant*, Oxford University Press, New York, 1999

Viveiros de Costa E., *Metafísicas Canibais. Elementos para uma antropologia pós-estrutural*, Cosac Naify, São Paulo, 2015

Wynter S., *Unsettling the Coloniality of Being/Power/Truth/Freedom*, in *CR: The New Centennial Review* 3, 2003, pp. 257–337

Zurbuchen S., *Introduction*, in *The Law of Nations and Natural Law 1625–1800*, S. Zurbuchen (ed.), Brill, Leiden, 2019

Chapter 4: The Second Encounter with the Other: The Law of Separation

Amico di Meane, T., *Sulle spalle dei giganti*, Editoriale Scientifica, Napoli, 2022

Aragoneses, A., *Un jurista del modernismo: Raymond Saleilles y los orígenes del derecho comparado*, Universidad Carlos III, Madrid, 2008

Austin, J., *The Province of Jurisprudence Determined and The Uses of the Study of Jurisprudence*, Weidenfeld and Nicholson, London, 1954

Balibar, É., *Le renversement de l'individualisme possessif*, in H. Guineret and A. Milanese, *La propriété: le propre, l'appropriation*, Ellipses, París, 2004

Beiser, F.C., *The German Historicist Tradition,* Oxford University Press, Oxford, 2011

Bellau, M., *The 'Juristes Inquiets': Legal Classicism and Criticism in Early Twentieth-Century France*, in *Utah Law Review*, 1997, pp. 379–411

Bhandar, B., *Colonial Lives of Property: Law, Land, and Racial Regimes of Ownership*, Princeton University Press, Princeton, 2018

Bianchi, A., *International Law Theories: An Inquiry into Different Ways of Thinking*, Oxford University Press, Oxford, 2017

Bianchi, A., '*Epistemic Communities*', in Jean d'Aspremont and Sahib Singh (eds.), *Concepts for International Law Contributions to Disciplinary Thought*, Edward Elgar, London, 2019, pp. 251–266

Bluntschli, J.C., *Die Bedeutung und die Fortschritte des modernen Völkerrechts*, in R. Virchow - F. von Holtzendorff (eds.), *Sammlung gemeinverständlicher wissenschaftlicher Vorträge*, Lüderitz'sche Verlagsbuchhandlung, Berlin, 1866

Carrillo Salcedo, J. A., *Hacia una nueva interpretación de la noción de «estados civilizados» en derecho internacional contemporáneo*, in *Anales de la Real Academia de Ciencias Morales y Políticas*, 1996, Session of 31 October 1995, pp. 651–660.

Cassese, A., *I diritti umani nel mondo contemporaneo*, Laterza, Roma-Bari, 1988.

M. Craven, '*Between Law and History: The Berlin Conference of 1884–1885 and the Logic of Free Trade*', in *London Review of International Law*, 2015, pp. 31–59

I. De la Rasilla, *A Very Short History of Internacional Law (1869–2018)*, in *Europ. Journ. Internat. Law*, 2018, pp. 137–168

Descamps, E. *L'Afrique Nouvelle: Essai sur l'État Civilisateur dans les Pays Neufs et sur la Fondation, l'Organisation et le Gouvernement de l'État Indépendant du Congo*, Hachette, Paris, 1903

Dufour, A., *Droits de l'homme, droit naturel et histoire*, PUF, París, 1991

Fauvarque-Cosson, B., *Development of Comparative Law in France*, in M. Reimann and R. Zimmermann (eds.), *Oxford Handbook of Comparative Law,* Oxford University Press, Oxford, 2006, pp. 35–71

Fiore, P., *La science du droit international: Horizons nouveaux*, in *Révue Générale de Droit International Public*, 1909, pp. 472–492

Fitzmaurice, A., *Scepticism of the Civilizing Mission in International Law*, in M. Koskenniemi, W. Rech and M. Jiménez Fonseca (eds.), *International Law and Empire: Historical Explorations*, Oxford University Press, Oxford, 2017, pp. 358–384

Foucault, M., *Surveiller et punir. Naissance de la prison*, Gallimard, París, 1975

Fournier, M., *Comparative Law Gets Entitled: the 1900 Paris Congress in Contexts*, available in: https://ssrn.com/abstract=4973485

Graziadei, M., *On Universalizing 'Nature' and 'Property': the Unravelling of a Master Narrative*, in *Journal of Interdisciplinary History of Ideas*, 2023, pp. 27–50

J. Hornung, *Civilisés et barbares*, in *Revue de droit international et de législation comparée,* 1904, pp. 447–470

Jackson, A. - Jaffer, A, *Encounters: The Meeting of Asia and Europe 1500–1800*, Victoria & Albert Museum, London, 2004

Jouannet, E., *The Liberal-Welfarist Law of Nations: A History of International Law*, Cambridge University Press, Cambridge, 2012

Jouannet, E., *Colonialisme européen et néo-colonialisme contemporain*, in *Baltik Yearbook of International Law*, 2006, pp. 49–77

Kentarō, K., *Les Institutions Judiciaires du* Japon, in *Revue de Droit International et de Législation Comparée*, 1893, pp. 338–356

Knox, R., '*Valuing Race? Stretched Marxism and the Logic of Imperialism*', in *London Review of International Law* 2016, pp. 81–126

Kohler, J., *Das Recht als Kulturerscheinung: Einleitung in die vergleichende Rechtswissenschaft*, Würzburg, Druck und verlag des stahel'schen, 1885

J. Kohler, *De la méthode du Droit Comparé*, in *Congrès international de droit comparé, Procès verbaux et documents*, vol. I, L.G.D.J., Paris, 1905, pp. 230–233

Koschaker, P., *L'histoire du droit et le droit comparé surtout en Allemagne*, in *Introduction à l'étude du droit comparé: recueil d'études en l'honneur d'Edouard Lambert*, Sirey et Librairie générale de droit et de jurisprudence, Paris, 1938, pp. 274–299

Koskenniemi, M., *Race, Hierarchy and International Law: Lorimer's Legal Science*, in *European Journal of International Law*, 2016, pp. 415–429

Koskenniemi, M., *International Law as Political Theology: How to Read the* Nomos der Erde, in *Constellations*, 2004, pp. 492–511

Jellinek, G., *Die sozialethische Bedeutung von Recht und Strafe*, Olms, Hidelsheim, 1878

Lambert, E., *Rapport* in *Congrès international de droit comparé, Procès verbaux des séances et documents*, t. 1, L.G.D.J., 1905, pp. 44–45

Lorimer, J., *The Institutes of the Law of Nations: A Treatise of the Jural Relations of Separate Political Communities*, William Blackwood and Sons, Edinburgh, 1883

Maine, S., *Village-Communities, Village-Communities in the East and West*, 7e ed., Murray, 1895, London

Mamdani, M., *Citizen and Subject: Contemporary Africa and the Legacy of Late Colonialism*, Princeton University Press, Princeton, 1996

Mégret, F., *L'Étatisme Spécifique de Droit International*, in *Revue Québécoise de Droit International*, 2011, pp. 105–129

Nys, E., *The Independent State of the Congo and International Law*, J. Lebègue and comp., Brussels, 1903

Obregón, L. *Empire, Racial Capitalism and International Law: The Case of Manumitted Haiti and the Recognition Debt*, in *Leiden Journal of International Law*, 2018, pp. 597–615.

Onuma, Y., *An Inquiry of the History of International Law from an Intercivilizational Perspective*, in *Journal of the History of International Law / Revue d'histoire du droit international*, pp. 1–66

Pahuja, S., *Laws of encounter: a jurisdiction account of International Law*, in *London Review of International Law*, 2013, pp. 63–98

Parfitt, R., *The Process of International Legal Reproduction: Inequality, Historiography, Resistance*, Cambridge University Press, Cambridge, 2019

Piedelievre, R., *Précis de droit international public ou droit des gens*, F. Pichon, Paris, 1894

Polanyi, K., *The Great Transformation*, Beacon Press, Boston, 2001

Pollock, F., *The History of Comparative Jurisprudence*, in *J Society Comparative* Legislation, 1903, pp. 74–86

Ponthoreau, M., *Le droit comparé en cuestion(s). Entre pragmatisme et outil épistémologique*, in *Revue internationale de droit compare*, 2005, pp. 7–27

Post, A.H., *Der Ursprung des Rechts: Prolegomena zu einer allgemeinen vergleichenden Rechtswissenschaft*, Oldenburg, Schulzesche, 1876

Resta, G. *Les luttes de clocher en droit comparé*, in *McGill Law Journal/Revue de droit de McGill*, 2017, pp. 1153–1199

Resta, G. *Le tassonomie e la precomprensione del comparatista*, in *Diritto pubblico comparato ed europeo*, 2017, pp. 1119–1136

Riles, A., *Introduction*, in A. Riles, (dir.) *Rethinking the Masters of Comparative Law*, Hart, Oxford, 2001, pp. 11–12

Rivier, A., *Principes du Droit des gens*, Harvard University Press, Cambridge, 1896

Röben, B., *Johann Caspar Bluntschli, Francis Lieber und das moderne Völkerrecht 1861–1881*, Nomos, Baden-Baden, 2003

Rolin-Jaequemyns, G., *Les Principes Philosophiques du Droit International*, in *Revue de Droit International et de Législation Comparée*, 1885, pp. 545–562

Saleilles, R., *Rapport présenté a la Commission d'organisation sur l'utilité, le but et le programme du Congrès*, *Procès-Verbaux des séances et documents du Congrès international de droit comparé de 1900*, F. Pichon et Durand-Auzias, Paris, 1900

Salomon, C., *L'Occupation des Territoires sans Maître. Etude de Droit International*, A. Giard, Paris, 1889

Société de Législation Comparée, *Bulletin de la Société de Législation Comparée*, 1899

Tuori, K., *The Properties of Law Modern Law and After*, Cambridge University Press, Cambridge, 2021

Tzouvala, N., *Capitalism as civilisation: a history of International Law*, Cambridge University Press, Cambridge, 2020

von Jhering, R., *Geist des römischen Rechts auf den verschiedenen Stufen seiner Entwicklung*, Breitkopf und Härtel, Leipzig, 1852

von Savigny, F. K., *Juristische Methodenlehre: nach der Ausarbeitung des Jakob Grimm*, K. F. Koehler Verlag, Stuttgart, 1951

Westlake, J., *Equality and Independence of States*, Cambridge University Press, Cambridge, 1894
Wheaton, H., *Elements of International Law*, A. C. Boyd ed., 3rd edn, Stevens and Sons Ltd, London, 1889

Chapter 5: The Aftermath of the Law of Separation in the Twentieth Century

Ajani, G., *Sistemi giuridici comparati. Lezioni e materiali*, 2ª ed., Torino, Giappichelli, 2006
Anand, P. R., *Family of "Civilized" States and Japan: A Story of Humiliation, Assimilation, Defiance and Confrontation*, in *Journal of the History of International Law*, 2003, pp. 1–76
Andrés de Saénz Santamaría, P., *Las dinámicas del Derecho internacional en el siglo XXI: acordes y desacordes*", in *Estados y organizaciones internacionales ante las nuevas crisis globales*, Asociación Española de Profesores de Derecho Internacional y Relaciones Internacionales, Iustel and Universidad de La Rioja, 2010, pp. 81–102
Angie, A., *Identifying Regions in the History of International Law*, in Fassbender, B.-Peters, A. (eds.), *The Oxford Handbook of the History of International Law*, Oxford University Press, Oxford, 2012, pp. 1058–1078
Ben Achour, Y., *Le rôle des civilisations dans le système international*, Bruylant, Brussels, 2003
Bhandar, B., *Colonial Lives of Property Law, Land, and Racial Regimes of Ownership*, Duke University, Durham, 2018
Bonfils, H., *Manuel de droit international public*, P. Fauchille (ed.), Rouseeau, Paris, 1898
Brier, J. L. *The Basis of Obligation in International Law*, Clarendon Press, Oxford, 1958
Capella Giannattasio, A.R., *The Interaction between International and Domestic Legal Orders: Framing the Debate according to the Post-Modern Condition of International Law*, in *German Law Journal*, 2019, p. 5–30
Carty, A., *Why Theory? The Implications for International Law Teaching*, in P. Allott et al. (eds) *Theory and International Law: An Introduction*, 1991, pp. 73–99
Cotterrell, R., *Is it so Bad to be Different? Comparative Law and the Appreciation of Diversity*, in *Comparative Law. A Handbook*, E. Örücü - D. Nelken (eds.), Hart publishing, Oxford, 2007, pp. 133–154
Crawford, J., *Foreword*, A. Anghie, *Imperialism, Sovereignty and the Making of International Law*, Cambridge University Press, Cambridge, 2005, ix–xi
David R.- Brierley, J. E.C., *Major Legal Systems in the World Today*, Stevens and Sons, London, 1978

De la Rasilla, I., *A Very Short History of Internacional Law (1869–2018)*, in *Europ. Journ. Internat. Law*, 2018, pp. 137–168

Descamps, E., *L'Afrique Nouvelle. Essai sur l'État Civilisateur dans les Pays Neufs et sur la Fondation, l'Organisation et le Gouvernement de l'État Indépendant du Congo*, Paris, Hachette, 1903

Fiore, P., *La science du droit international. Horizons nouveaux*, in *Révue Générale de Droit International Public*, 1909, pp. 472–492

Frankenberg, G., *Comparative Law as Critique*, Edward Elgar, Cheltenham, 2016

Glenn, H.P., *The Aims of Comparative Law*, in J. M. Smits (eds.), *Elgar Encyclopedia of Comparative Law*, 2 ed., Edward Elgar, Cheltenham, 2012, pp. 57–65

Glenn, H.P., *Comparative Legal Families and Comparative Legal Traditions*, in *The Oxford Handbook of Comparative Law*, Reimann, M.–Zimmermann, R. (eds.), 2006, pp. 421–439

Gozzi, G., *Rights and Civilizations: A History and Philosophy of International Law*, Cambridge University Press, Cambridge, 2019

Graziadei, M., *Un compasso allargato. La comparazione giuridica nel mondo attuale e le questioni di metodo*, in *Diritto pubblico comparato ed europeo*, 2024, pp. 431–456

Graziadei, M., *The Functionalist Heritage*, in AA.VV., *Comparative Legal Studies: Traditions and Transitions*, P. Legrand, R. Munday (eds.), Cambridge University Press, Cambridge, 2003, pp. 102–124

Harlow, C., *Voices of Difference in a Plural Community*, in *The American Journal of Comparative Law*, 2002, pp. 339–367

Jodoin, S., *International Law and Alterity: The State and the Other*, in *International Law and its Others*, A. Orford (ed.), Cambridge University Press, Cambridge, 2006, pp. 87–107

Kayaoğlu, T., *Legal Imperialism: Sovereignty and Extraterritoriality in Japan, the Ottoman Empire, and China*, Cambridge University Press, Cambridge, 2010

Kelsen, H., *Das Problem der Souveränität und die Theorie des Völkerrechts: Beitrag zu einer reinen Rechtslehre*, J.C.B. Mohr (Paul Siebeck), Tübingen, 1920

Kelsen, H., *The Pure Theory of Law* [Reine Rechtslehre], M. Knight trans., 1978

M. Koskenniemi, *International Law as Political Theology: How to Read the* Nomos der Erde, in *Constellations*, 2004, pp. 492–511

Lauterpacht, H., '*The so-called Anglo-American and Continental Schools of Thought in International Law*', in *British Yearbook of International Law*, 1931, pp. 31–62

Lauterpacht, H., *Annual Digest of Public International Law Cases: 1919–1922*, 1932, pp. 1–32

Legrand, P., *The Impossibility of 'Legal Transplant'*, in *Maastricht Journal of European and Comparative Law*, 1997, pp. 111–134

Legrand, P., *How to compare now*, in *Legal Studies*, 1996, pp. 232–242

Lorimer, J., *The Institutes of the Law of the Nations. A Treatise of the Jural Relations of Separate Political Communities*, Blackwood, Edinburgh-London, 1883

Lord Lugard, *The Dual Mandate in British Tropical Africa*, Frank Cass, London, 1965

Mangas Martín, A., *Humanización, democracia y Estado de derecho en el ordenamiento internacional,* speech of admission as an academic member, session held on 8 April 2014, Madrid, Real Academia de Ciencias Morales y Políticas

Menski, W., *Comparative Law in a Global Context: The Legal Systems of Asia and Africa*, 2 ed., Cambridge University Press, Cambridge, 2006

Mignolo, W. *Local Histories/Global Designs: Coloniality, Subaltern Knowledges and Border Thinking*, Princeton University Press, Princeton, 2000

Monateri, P.G., *Methods of Comparative Law*, Edward Elgar, Cheltenham, 2012

Monateri, P.G., *Geopolitica del diritto: genesi, governo e dissoluzione dei corpi politici,* Laterza, Roma-Bari, 2013

Monateri, P.G., *Critique et difference: le droit compare en Italie*, in *Rev. Int. Droit Comp.*, 1999, pp. 292–293

Nas, T.F., *Tracing the Economic Transformation of Turkey from the 1920 to EU Accession*, Martinus Njihoff Publishers, Leiden-Boston, 2008

Platsas, A. E., *The Functional and the Dysfunctional in the Comparative Method of Law: Some Critical Remarks*, in *Electronic Journal of Comparative Law*, 2008, pp. 1–15

Rabel, E., *The Conflict of Laws*, vol. 1, University of Michigan Press, Ann Arbor, 1945

Riles A. (dir.), *Rethinking the Masters of Comparative Law*, Hart, Oxford, 2001

Ruggie, J.G. *Territoriality and Beyond: Problematizing Modernity in International Relations*, in *International Organization*, 1993, pp. 140–168

Ruskola, T., *Legal Orientalism: China, the United States, and Modern Law*, Cambridge, MA, Harvard University Press, 2013

Salomon, C., *L'occupation des territoires sans maître. Étude de droit international*, Giard, Paris, 1889

Sacco, R., *Legal Formants: A Dynamic Approach to Comparative Law (Instalment II of II)*, in *Am J Comp. L.* 1991, pp. 343–401

Sacco, R., *Introduzione al diritto comparato*, Utet, Torino, 1995

Sacco, R., *Circolazione e mutazione dei modelli*, in *Digesto delle discipline privatistiche—Sezione civile*, vol. 2, Torino, 1988, pp. 365–387

Sacco, R., *Antropologia giuridica. Contributo a una macrostoria del diritto*, Il Mulino, Bologna, 2007

Scarciglia, R., *Introduzione al diritto pubblico comparato*, Il Mulino, Bologna, 2006

Somma, A., *Introduzione al diritto comparato*, 3ª ed., Torino, Giappichelli, 2025

Tomuschat, C., *Obligations for States*, in *Recueil des Cours de l'Académie de droit international*, 1993

C. Tomuschat, *International Law: Ensuring The Survival Of Mankind On The Eve Of A New Century. General Course On Public International Law*, in *Recueil des Cours de la Académie de Droit International*, vol. 281, 2001

Triepel, H., *Völkerrecht und Landesrecht*, Scientia Antiquariat, Aalen, 1958; orig. pub. 1899.

Twining, W., *General Jurisprudence: Understanding Law from a Global Perspective*, Cambridge University Press, Cambridge, 2009

Twiss, T., *The Law of Nations Considered as Independent Political Communities*, Oxford University Press, Oxford, 1861

Yu-Hao Tseng, *The Termination of Unequal Treaties in International Law: Studies in Comparative Jurisprudence and Conventional Law of Nations*, The Commercial Press, Shanghai, 1931, pp. 51–80.

Watson, A., *Legal transplants: An approach to Comparative Law*, 2 ed., University of Georgia Press, Athens, GA, 1993

Wheaton, H., *Elements of International Law*, Carnegie Endowment for International Peace / Clarendon Press / Oxford University Press, Washington, 1936

Westlake, J., *International Law*, Cambridge University Press, Cambridge, 1910

Zweigert, K., *Des solutions identiques par des voies différentes*, in *Revue internationale de droit comparé*, 18, 1966, pp. 5–34

Zweigert, K.-Kötz, H., *Einführung in die Rechtsvergleichung auf dem Gebiete des Privatrechts*, 3.ª ed., Mohr Siebeck, Tübingen, 1996

Judgments

In Re Ross, 140 U.S. 453 (1891) ('In Re Ross').

S.S. Wimbledon, Permanent Court of International Justice, Series A, no. 1, 1923.

SS Lotus Case: France v. Turkey (1927) PCIJ Rep Ser. A No. 10, 18.

Chapter 6: Comparative Law and International Law in the Twenty-First Century

Abi-Saab, G., *The Portrait of the Jurist as an international Judge*, in Peck C. - Lee R.S. (eds), *Increasing the Effectiveness of the International Court of Justice: Proceedings of the ICJ/UNITAR Colloquium to Celebrate the 50th Anniversary of the Court*, 1997, pp. 166–187

Becker Lorca, A., *Universal International Law: Nineteenth-Century Histories of Imposition and Appropriation*', in *Harvard International Law Journal*, 2010, pp. 475–552

Bermann G. –Glenn P.– Lane-Scheppele K.–Shalakany A. –Snyder D. V. –Zoller E., *Comparative Law: Problems and Prospects*, in *American University International Law Review*, 201

Brownlie, I., *Discussion*, in *Change and Stability In International Law-Making*, Cassese A.- Weiler J.H.H. (eds.), Walter de Gruyteer, Berlín /Nueva York, 1988, pp. 98–128

Cartabia, M., *Editorial. Courts' Relations*, in *Intern. Rev. Const. Law*, 2020, pp. 1–4

Cassese, S., *Il diritto globale*, Einaudi, Torino, 2009

Cassese, S., *I tribunali di Babele. I giudici alla ricerca di un nuovo ordine globale*, Roma, 2009

Chimni, B.S., *International Law and World Order: A Critique of Contemporary Approaches*, Cambridge University Press, Cambridge, 2017

Comparative International Law, Roberts A. - Stephan P. B.-Hugues Verdier P.-Versteeg M. (eds.), Oxford University Press, Oxford, 2017

D'Amato, A., *It's a Bird, It's a Plane, It's Jus Cogens*, in *Conn. J. Int'l L. 1*, 1990, pp. 1–6.

Darian-Smith, E., *Postcolonial Theories of Law*, in *Law and Social Theory*, Banakar R. - Travers M. (eds.), Hart Publishing, Oxford, 2017, pp. 247–264

de Wet, E., *The International Constitutional Order*, in *Intern. Compar. Law Quart.*, 2006, pp. 51–76

de Wet, *The emergence of International and Regional Value System as a Manifestation of the Emerging International Constitutional Order*, in *Leiden Journal of International Law*, 2006, pp. 611–632

Di Martino, A., *Circolazione delle soluzioni giuridiche e delle idee costituzionali. Questioni di metodo comparativo e prassi tra culture costituzionali e spazi globali*, in *DPCE online*, 2021

Di Martino, A., *Comparare le identità costituzionali: circolazione degli argomenti giuridici e contesti storico-politici*, in *Esperienze giuridiche in dialog*o. *IL ruolo della comparazione*, Graziadei M. - Somma A. (eds.), Sapienza Università Editrice, Rome, 2024, p. 199.

Dupuy, P.M., *The Constitutional Dimension of the Charter of the United Nations Revisited*, in *Max-Planck Yearbook of International Law*, vol. I, 1997, pp. 1–33.

Elster, J., *Ulysses Unbound: Studies in Rationality, Precommitment, and Constraints*, Cambridge University Press, Cambridge, 2000

Ferrarese, M.R., *Diritto sconfinato. Inventiva giuridica e spazi nel mondo globale*, Laterza, Roma-Bari, 2006

Forteau, M., *Comparative International Law. Within, not against, International Law: lessons from the International Law Commission*, in *American Journ. Intern. Law*, 2015, pp. 651–666

Frankenberg, G., *Comparative Law as Critique*, Edgar, London, 2014

Glendon, A.M., *Comparative Law in the Age of Globalization*, in *Duquesne Law* Review, pp. 1–24

Habermas, J., *The Theory of Communicative Action. Volume 1: Reason and the Rationalization of Society*, Beacon, London, 1985

Habermas, J., *The Divided West*, Polity Press, Cambridge, 2006

Hakimi, M., *Making Sense of Customary International Law*, in *Michigan Law Review*, 2020, pp. 1487–1537

Hanna, M. P., *The Substantive/Procedural Distinction: Law's Solution to the Problem of Jus Cogens in a World of Sovereign States*, in *Germ. Law Journ*, 2022, pp. 21–241

Kennedy, David W., *The Disciplines of International Law and Policy*, in *Leiden J. Int'l L. 9*, 1999, p. 12–39

Kennedy, David W., *The Dark Side of Virtue: Reassessing International Humanitarism*, Princeton University Press, Princeton, 2004

Klabber, J., *Constitutionalism Lite*, in *IOLR*, 2004, pp. 31–58

Klabbers J. –Peters A. –Ulfstein G., *The Constitutionalization of International Law*, Oxford University Press, Oxford, 2009

Klabbers J.- Palombella, G., *The Challenge of Inter-Legality*, Cambridge University Press, Cambridge, 2019

Koskenniemi, M., *The Case for Comparative International Law*, in *Finnish Yearbook of International Law*, 2011, pp. 1–8

Jouannet E., *La Communauté Internationale Vue Par Les Juristes*, in *Annuaire français des relations internationales*, 2005, Vol. VI, pp. 3–25.

Jullien, F., *Il n'y a pas d'identité culturelle*, Éditions de l'Herne, Paris, 2016

Lazari, A., *Modelli e paradigmi della responsabilità dello Stato*, Giappichelli, Torino, 2005

Lazari, A., *Dialogo judicial y resolución de controversias internacionales*, in E.M. Vázquez Gómez, M.D. Adam Muñoz, N. Cornago Prieto (eds.) *El arreglo pacífico de las controversias internacionales*, XXIV Jornadas de la Asociación Española de Profesores de Derecho internacional y Relaciones internacionales (AEPDIRI), Córdoba, 20–22 October, Tirant lo Blanch, 2013, pp. 169–184.

Luhmann, N., *Soziale Systeme. Grundriss einer allgerneinen Theorie*, Suhrkamp, Francfort, 1984

Lupoi M. - Graziadei M., *The Historical Context of Saunders v Vautier* in *Edinburgh Law Review*, 2025, pp. 1–21

Lustig, D.-Weiler, J.H.H., *Judicial review in the contemporary world—Retrospective and prospective*, in *International journal of constitutional law*, 2018, pp. 315–372

McDonald R.- Johnston D.M., *Towards World Constitutionalism: Issues in the Legal Ordering of the World Community*, Martinus Nijhoff, The Hague, 2005

Muir Watt, H., *Globalization and Comparative Law*, in AA.VV., *The Oxford Handbook of Comparative Law*, edited by M. Reimann–R. Zimmermann, Hart, Oxford, 2006

Mutua, M., *What Is TWAIL?* in the *Proceedings of the ASIL Ann. Meeting*, 2000, pp. 31–40

Obrégon, L., *Completing Civilization: Creole Consciousness and International Law in Nineteenth-Century Latin America*, in *International Law and its Others*, A. Orford (ed.), Cambridge University Press, 2006, pp. 247–264

Peters, A., *Compensatory Constitutionalism: The Functions and Potential of Fundamental International Norms and Structures*, in *Leiden Journal of International Law*, 2006, pp. 579–610

Prost, M., *The Concept of Unity in Public International Law*, Hart, Oxford, 2012

Rasulov, A., *International Law and the Poststructuralist Challenge*, in *Leiden Journal of International Law*, 2006, pp. 799–827

Reimann, M., *Comparative Law and neighbouring disciplines*, in *The Cambridge Companion to Comparative Law (Cambridge Companions to Law)*, Bussani M. –Mattei U., Cambridge University Press, Cambridge, 2012

Remiro Brotóns A. –Riquelme Cortado R. - Orihuela Catalayud E.- Diez-Hochleitner J.– Pérez-Prat Durbán L., *Derecho Internacional. Curso General*, Tirant Lo Blanch, Valencia, 2010

Roberts, A., *Is International Law International?* Oxford University Press, Oxford, 2017

Roughan, N., *Democratic Custom V. International Customary Law*, in *Vict. Univ. Wellin. Law Rev*, 2007, pp. 403–424

Simma, B., *The Contribution of Alfred Verdross to the Theory of International Law*, in *Europ. Journ. Intern. Law*, vol. 6, 1995, pp. 33–59

Tomuschat, C. –Thouvenin, J.M., *The Fundamental Rules of the International Legal Order: Jus Cogens and Obligation Erga Omnes*, Martinus Nihjoff, Leiden, 2006

Tomuschat, C., *Obligations Arising for the States without or against Their Will*, in *Recueil des Cours de l'Académie de Droit International de la Haye*, vol, 241, 1993

Tomuschat, C., *International Law: Ensuring the Survival of Mankind on the eve of a New Century*, in *Recueil des Cours de l'Académie de Droit International de la Haye*, vol. 281, 2001

Thuo Gathii, J., *Economic Integration and the Question of the Third World*, Cambridge University Press, Cambridge, 2015

Tuori, K., *European Constitutionalism*, Cambridge University Press, Cambridge, 2015

Tuori, K., *The Properties of Law. Modern Law and After*, Cambridge University Press, Cambridge, 2021

Vogliotti, M., *La fine del "grande stile" e la ricerca di una nuova identità per la scienza giuridica*, in *L'identità delle scienze giuridiche in ordinamenti multilivello*, Barsotti V. (ed.), Maggioli, Santarcangelo di Romagna, 2014, pp. 41–64

Yasuaki, O. *When was the Law of International Society Born? An Inquiry of the History of International Law from an Intercivilizational Perspective*', in *Journal of the History of International Law*, 2000, pp. 1–64

Weiler, J.H.H., *The Constitution of Europe: "Do the New Clothes Have an Emperor?" and Other Essays on European Integration*, Cambridge University Press, Cambridge, 1999

Weiler, J.H.H. *The Transformation of Europe*, in *Yale Law Journal*, 1991, pp. 2403–2483
Weiler, J.H.H., *The Political and Legal Culture of European Integration: An Exploratory Essay*, in *Int'l J. Const. L.*, 2011, pp. 551–567
Werner, W., *The Never-ending Closure: Constitutionalism and International Law*, in *Transnational Constitutionalism: International and European Perspective*, Tsagourias N. (ed.), Cambridge University Press, Cambridge, 2007

Judgements

PCIJ, *Case of S.S. Wimblendon* (United Kingdom and others. V. Germany), Judgement, 1923 P.C.I.J. Series A-No. 01, p. 25.
PCIJ, *The Case of S.S. Lotus* (France. v. Turkey.), Judgement, 1927 P.C.I.J. Series A-No. 10
ICJ, *Reparation for injuries suffered in the service of the United Nations*, Advisory Opinion of 11 April 1949, I.C. J. Reports 1949, p. 185.
ICJ, *Corfu Channel case*, Judgment of 9 April 1949, ICJ Reports, 1949
ICJ, *United States Diplomatic and Consular Staff in Tehran* (United States of America v. Iran), Judgment of 24 May 1980: I.C.J. Reports 1980
ICJ, *Barcelona Traction, Light and Power Company, Limited* (Belgium v. Spain), Judgment, I.C.J. Reports 1970
ICJ, *Legality of the Use of Nuclear Weapons*, Advisory Opinion of 9 July 1996, ICJ Reports 1996, p. 66
ICJ, *Armed Activities on the Territory of the Congo*, Judgment of 3 February 2006, ICJ Reports, 2005, p. 168
ICJ, *Jurisdictional Immunities of the State (Germany v. Italy: Greece intervening)*, Judgment, I.C.J. Reports 2012, p. 99
CJEU, 3 September 2008, joined cases C-402/05 P and C-415/05 P, Yassin Abdullah Kadi and Al Barakaat International Foundation v. Council and Commission, EU:C:2008:461
CJUE, 5 December 2017, C-42/17, MAS and MB, EU:C:2017:936
TIHU, Moiwana Village v. Suriname, Ruling of 15 June 2005, IACHR, (Ser. C) No. 145 (2005); YakeAxa vs. Paraguay, 17 June 2005. Series C No. 125, paras. 124, 131

Chapter 7: The Relational Identity of Inclusion

Antoniolli, L., *L'identità delle scienze giuridiche in ordinamenti multilivello: il diritto comparato*, in *L'identità delle scienze giuridiche in ordinamenti mrtyuultilivello*, V. Barsotti (ed.), Maggioli, Santarcangelo di Romagna, 2014, pp. 65–85

Ballin, E.H., *Constitutional identity in the Netherlands: Sailing with others*, in *Constitutional identity in a Europe of multilevel constitutionalism*, Calliess C.-van der Schyff G. (eds.), Cambridge University Press, Cambridge, 2019, pp. 222–242

Barber, N., *Legal pluralism and the EU*, in *European Law Journal*, 12, 2006, pp. 306–332

Beck, U., *Der Kosmopolitische Blick oder: Krieg ist Frieden*, Suhrkamp Verlag, Frankfut am Main, 2004

Brownlie, I., *Recognition in Theory and Practice*, in *British Yearbook of International Law*, 1982, pp. 197–211

Burgorgue-Larsen, L., *Sobre un acercamiento dialógico al Derecho Constitucional Europeo*, in *Revista de Derecho Constitucional Europeo*, 2016, pp. 13–38

Cannizzaro, E., *La sovranità oltre lo Stato*, Il Mulino, Bologna, 2020

Carrillo Salcedo, J.A., *Droit international et souveraineté des états: cours général de droit international public*, in *Recueil des Cours, Collected courses of the Hague Academy of International Law*, 1996

Cartabia, M., *Principi fondamentali e integrazione europea*, Giuffré, Milan, 1995

Cassese, S., *Fine della solitudine delle corti costituzionali, ovvero il dilemma del porcospino*, in *Atti Sc. Mor.*, 2015, pp. 15–25

Constitutionalism Identity, Difference and Legitimacy (Rosenfeld M. ed.), Duke University Press, Durham, 2004

Crawford, J. *The Current Political Discourse Concerning International Law*, in *Common Mar. Law Rev.*, 2018, pp. 1381–1398

Faraguna, P., *Taking Constitutional Identity away from the Courts*, in *Brooklyn Journal of International Law*, n. 41/2016, pp. 491–577

Fernández Arribas, G., *Contemporary Challenges to the Fundamental Principles of International Law and EU Interaction*, Springer, Cham, 2024

Glenn, H.P., *Com-paring*, in *Comparative Law. A Handbook*, Örücü E. - Nelken D. (eds.), Hart Publishing, Oxford, 2010, pp. 91–108

Glenn, H.P., *Doin' the Transsystemic: Legal Systems and Legal Traditions*, in *McGill L.J.*, 2005, pp. 853–874

Glenn, H.P., *The Cosmopolitan State*, Oxford University Press, Oxford, 2013

Glenn, H.P., *Aims of Comparative Law*, in *Elgar Encyclopedia of Comparative Law*, J.M. Smits (ed.), 2015, p. 53–76.

Hart, H.L.A., *The Concept of Law*, 2nd ed., Clarendon Press, Oxford, 1994

Huntington, S.P., *The Clash of Civilizations and the Remaking of World Order*, Simon & Schuster, New York, 1996

Kallis, A., *Populism, Sovereigntism, and the Unlikely Re-Emergence of the Territorial Nation-State*, in *Fudan J. Hum. Soc. Sci.*, 2018, 11, pp. 285–302

Kelsen, H., *Pure Theory of Law*, University of California Press, Berkeley, 1967

Krieger, H., *Populist Governments and International Law*, in *Europ. Journ. Intern. Law*, 2019, pp. 971–996

Jacobsohn, G.J., *Constitutional Identity*, Harvard University Press, Harvard, 2010

Jullien, F., *Il n'y a pas d'identité culturelle*, Éditions de l'Herne, Paris, 2016

Lauterpacht, H., *Recognition in International Law*, Cambridge University Press, Cambridge, 2012

Martinico, G., *The Tangled Complexity of the EU Constitutional Process. The Frustrating Knot of Europe*, Routledge, London, Second Edition, 2023

MacCormick, N., *Beyond the Sovereign State*, in *Modern Law Review*, 1993, pp. 1–18

Michaels, R., *Law and Recognition—Towards a Relational Concept of Law*, in *In Pursuit of Pluralist Jurisprudence*, Roughan N. - Halpin A. (eds.), Cambridge University Press, Cambridge, 2017, pp. 90–115

Oliete, E. – Aldea, E., *The Porosity of Identity Boundaries*, in *Hybrid Heritage on Screen*, Palgrave Macmillan, London, 2015

Oppenheim, L., *International Law*, H. Lauterpacht (ed.), 8th ed., Longmans, Green and Co., London/New York, 1955

Palombella G., *Theory, Realities, and Promises of Inter-Legality. A* Manifesto, in Klabber J.- Palombella G. (eds.), *The Challenge of Inter-Legality*, Cambridge University Press, Cambridge, 2019, pp. 363–390

Pellet, A., *Guest Editorial—The Proper Use of Sovereignty*, in https://esil-sedi.eu/esil-newsletter-autumn2021/#guest_editorial

Poiares Maduro, M., *Contrapunctual Law: Europe's constitutional pluralism in action*, in N. Walker (ed.), *Sovereignty in transition (Essays in European Law)*, Hart Publishing, Oxford, 2003, pp. 501–537

Raz, J., *The Authority of Law: Essays on Law and Morality*, Clarendon Press, Oxford, 1979

Ricouer, P., *Soi-même comme un autre*, Éditions du seuil, Paris, 1990

Rodotà, S., *Il pensiero debole dell'Europa che s'accontenta*, in *MicroMega*, 10 January 2014, p. 1–13

Roughan, N., *Authorities. Conflicts, Cooperation, and Transnational Legal Theory*, Oxford University Press, Oxford, 2013

Sacco, R., *Il diritto muto. Neuroscienze, conoscenza tacita, valori condivisi*, Il Mulino, Bologna, 2015

Schiemann, K., *Europe and the loss of sovereignty*, in *Int Comp Law Q.*, 2007, p. 470–490

Scoditti, E., *Legalità al plurale*, in *Quaderni costituzionali*, 2013, p. 307–328

Tomuschat, C., *Obligations arising for states without or against their will*, in *Recueil des Cours. Collected courses of the Hague Academy of International Law*, vol 241, 1993

von Daniels, D., *The Concept of Law from a Transnational Perspective*, Ashgate Publishing, Farnham / Burlington, 2010, p. 161

Wajner, D.F., *Populism in power and regional (dis-)integration: charting paths of populist regionalism in Europe and Latin America*, in *Journal Europ. Integr.*, 2025, pp. 1–24

Weiler, J.H.H., *Federalism without Constitutionalism: Europe's Sonderweg'*, in Nicolaidis K. - Howse R. (eds), *The Federal Vision*, Oxford University Press, Oxford, 2001, pp. 54–70

Wessel, R.A., *Studying International and European Law: confronting perspectives and combining interests*, in *Grotius Centre Working Paper Series*, No. 2018/071-PIL2018

Judgments

Island of Palmas case, (Netherlands, USA), 4 April 1928, Reports of International Arbitral Awards, Vol. II, p. 838

UKSC, R. (on the application of Miller and another) (Respondents) v Secretary of State or Exiting the European Union (Appellant) [2017] UKSC 5

High Court of South Africa (Guateng Division), *Democratic Alliance* v *Minister of International Relations and Cooperation and Others*, Ruling of 22 February 2017, Case No 83145/2016

CJEU judgement, C-42/17, MAS and MB, 5 December 2017, EU:C:2017:936

Documents

CIJ, *Legal Consequences for States of the Continued Presence of South Africa in Namibia*, Advisory Opinion of 21 June 1971, dissenting opinion of Sir Gerald Fitzmaurice, par. 115

Declaration of the Russian Federation and the People's Republic of China on the promotion of International Law, signed in Beijing on 25 June 2016 at http://www.mid.ru/en/foreign_policy/news/-/asset_publisher/cKNonkJE02Bw/content/id/2331698

White House Press Secretary, 'Statement by President Trump on the Paris Climate Accord', 1 June 2017 at https://www.whitehouse.gov/the-press-office/2017/06/01/statementpresident-trump-paris-climate-accord

AGNU, Speech by Mr. Donald Trump, President of the United States of America (President Trump's 2017 Speech), UN Doc. A/72/PV.3, 19th September 2017.

AGNU, Speech by Mr. Donald Trump, President of the United States of America (President Trump's 2018 Speech), UN Doc. A/73/PV.6, 25 September 2018.

Conclusions of the Advocate General Ćapeta's, C-769/22, *Commission/Hungary*, presented on 5 June 2025, C-769/22, ECLI:EU:C:2025:408

Chapter 8: The First Encounter with the Other: The Origin of the First European Communities

Alter, K., *The European Court's Political Power: the Emergence of an Authoritative International Court in the European Union*, in *West Eur. Pol.*, 1996, pp. 458–487

Bon, P., *L'identité nationale ou constitutionnelle, une nouvelle notion juridique*, in *Mélanges en l'honneur du Professeur Jean-Arnaud Mazères*, Éditions l'Épitoge, Toulouse, 2013

Bonet Navarro, J., *El estatuto especial del monte Athos ante la tradición religiosa. El derecho eclesiástico griego y el derecho comunitario europeo*, in *Boletín de la Facultad de Derecho de la UNED*, issue 27, 2005, pp. 93–113

Burgorgue-Larsen, L., *Pour une approche dialogique du Droit constitutionnel européen*, in *Annuaire de droit européen 2012*, vol. X, Bruylant, Brussels, 2014, pp. 29–53

Burley, A.M.- Mattli W., *Europe before the Court: A Political Theory of Legal Integration*, in *International Organization*, 1993, pp. 41–76

Cartabia, M., *L'ora dei diritti fondamentali in Europa*, in M. Cartabia (ed.), *I diritti in azione*, Il Mulino, Bologna, 2007

Ceruti, M. – Bellusci, F., *Abitare la complessità*, Mimesis, Milan – Udine, 2020

Cortina, A., *Ética cosmopolita. Una apuesta por la cordura en tiempos de pandemia*, Paidós, Madrid, 2021

Constantinesco, V., *La confrontation entre identité constitutionnelle européenne et identités constitutionnelles nationales: Convergences ou contradictions? contrepoint ou hiérarchie?*, in *Mélanges en l'honneur de Philippe Manin*, LGDJ, Paris, 2010, pp. 70–91.

Craig, P., *The Nature of the Community: Integration, Democracy and Legitimacy*, in P. Craig & G. De Búrca (eds.), *The Evolution of EU Law*, Oxford University Press, Oxford, 1999, p. 24–45.

Davies, B., *Integrity or Openness? Reassessing the History of the CJEU's Human Rights Jurisprudence*, in *American Journal of Comparative Law*, 2016, pp. 801–834

Davies, B., *The Internationale Handelsgesellschaft Case: The Source of the European Court of Justice's Human Rights* Jurisprudence, in EU *Law Stories: Contextual and Critical Histories of European Jurisprudence,* Nicola, F. - Davies, B. (eds.), Cambridge University Press, Cambridge, 2017, pp. 153–178.

Derrida, J., *Points de suspension. Entretiens*, Galilée, Paris, 1992

de Witte, B., *Direct Effect, Primacy and the Nature of the European Legal Order*, in *The Evolution of Eu Law*, G. de Búrca & P.P. Craig (eds.), 2021, pp. 187–212

Diez Picazo, L., *Observaciones sobre la cláusula de identidad nacional,* in *Constitución europea y constituciones nacionales*, Cartabia M., De Witte B., Pérez Tremps P., (eds.) Tirant lo Blanch, Valencia, 2005, pp. 437–448

Eco, U., *Il fascismo eterno*, La nave di Teseo, Milan, 2018

Elster, J., *Ulysses Unbound: Studies in Rationality, Precommitment, and Constraints*, Cambridge University Press, Cambridge, 2000

Faraguna, P., *Taking Constitutional Identities Away from the Courts*, en *Brook. J. Int'l L.*, 2016, pp. 41–68

Faraguna, P., *The Constitutional Identity of the EU as a Counterbalance for Unconstitutional Constitutional Identities of the Member States*, in *European Yearbook of Constitutional Law*, 2023, pp. 342–351

V. Ferreres Comella, *La Constitución española ante la cláusula de primacía del Derecho de la Unión europea. Un comentario a la Declaración 1/2004 del Tribunal Constitucional 1/2004*, in A. Lopez Castillo, A. Saiz Arnaiz & V. Ferreres Comella, *Constitución española y constitución europea*, Centro de Estudios Políticos y Constitucionales, Madrid 2005, pp. 77–90

Glenn, H.P., *Com-paring*, in *Comparative Law. A Handbook*, Örücü E. - Nelken D. (eds.), Hart Publishing, Oxford, 2010, pp. 91–108

Habermas, J., *Between Facts and Norms: contributions to a discourse theory of law and democracy*, MIT Press, Cambridge, 1998

Habermas, J., *Postnational Constellation*, MIT Press, Cambridge 2001

Halberstam, D., *Systems Pluralism and Institutional Pluralism in Constitutional Law: National, Supranational, and Global Governance*, in *Univ. of Michigan Public Law WorkingPaper* No. 229, 2011

Hartley, T., *The Foundations of European Union* Law, Oxford University Press, Oxford, 2010.

Integration Through Law: Europe and the American Federal Experience. A General Introduction, M. Cappelletti, J. Weiler, M. Soccombe (eds.), De Gruyter, Brussels, 1986

L'identité constitutionnelle saisie par les juges, L. Burgorgue-Larsen (ed.), Pedone, Paris, 2011

Merleau-Ponty, M., *Le visible et l'invisible*, Les Éditions Gallimard, Paris, 1964

Morin, E., *Changeons de voie: Les leçons du coronavirus*, Éditions Denoël, Paris, 2020

Perju, V., *Identity Federalism in Europe and the United States*, in *Vanderbilt Journal of Transnational Law*, 2020, pp. 443–504

Pescatore, P., *The Law of Integration* Sijthoff, Leiden, 1974

Pescatore, P., *L'ordre juridique des Communautés européennes: étude des sources du droit communautaire*, Presses universitaires de Liège, Liège, 1973,

Pescatore, P., *The Doctrine of Direct Effects: An Infant Disease of Community Law*, in *European Law Review*, vol. 8, 1984, pp. 155–177

Polimeni, S., *L'identità costituzionale come controlimite*, in *Ianus*, 2017, pp. 133–161

Pollicino, O., *Corte di giustizia e giudici nazionali: il moto "ascendente", ovverosia l'incidenza delle "tradizioni costituzionali comuni" nella tutela apprestata ai diritti dalla Corte dell'Unione*, in, *Crisi dello Stato nazionale, dialogo intergi-*

urisprudenziale, tutela dei diritti fondamentali, Ruggeri, A. *et al.* (eds.) Giappichelli, Torino, 2015, pp. 263–281

Ragone, S., *European Comparative Law: Reasons for «Enhanced Comparison» and Role of the CJEU*, en *Revista de Derecho Político*, 2021, pp. 157–187

Rodin, S., *Constitutional Relevance of Foreign Court Decisions*, in *Am J Comp Law* 2016, pp. 815–840

Rubio Llorente, F., *Derechos fundamentales, principios estructurales y respeto por la identidad nacional de los Estados miembros de la Unión Europea*, in *Anuario de la Facultad de Derecho de la Universidad Autónoma de Madrid*, 2013, pp. 515–531

Stein, E., *Lawyers, Judges and the Making of a Transnational Constitution*, in *Am. J. Int'l Law*, 1981, pp. 1–27

Von Bogdandy, A.- Grabenwarter, C., - Huber, P. M., *Constitutional Science in the European Legal Space*, in *The Max Planck Handbooks in European Public Law, Volume I: The Analysis of Public Law*, A. von Bogdandy, P. M. Huber y P. Cassese (eds.), Oxford University Press, Oxford, 2017, pp. 581–609.

Weber, F., *The Identity of Union Law in Primacy: Piercing Through Euro Box Promotion and Others*, in *European Papers* 2022, 2, pp. 761–786

Weiler, J.H.H., *The Community System: the Dual Character of Supranationalism*, in *Y.B. EUR. L.*, 1982, pp. 275–276

Weiler, J.H.H., *The Constitution of Europe. Do the New Clothes Have an Emperor?" and Other Essays on European Integration*, Cambridge University Press, Cambridge, 1999

Weiler, J.H.H., *Federalism without Constitutionalism: Europe's Sonderweg'*, in K. Nicolaidis and R Howse (eds), *The Federal* Vision, Oxford University Press, 2001, esp. pp. 54–68

Weiler, J.H.H., *Rewriting Van Gend & Loos*, in *Judicial Discretion in European Perspective*, O. Wiklund (ed.), 2003, pp. 150–163

Weiler, J.H.H., *Deciphering the Political and Legal DNA of European Integration: An Exploratory Essay*, in *Philosophical Foundations of European Union Law*, J. Dickson & P. Eleftheriadis (eds.), Oxford University Press, Oxford, 2012, pp. 137–158

Zagrebelsky, G., *L'identità europea*, in *Religione e spazio pubblico in Europa*, Donzelli Editore, Roma, 2007, pp. 3–14

Judgments

CJUE, 4 February 1959, *Friedrich Storck & Co. v High Authority of the European Coal and Steel Community*, Case 1/58, ECLI:EU:C:1959:1

CJUE, 12 July 1957, *Dinecke Algera and others v European Parliament*, Joined Cases C-7/56 and C-3/57 to C-7/57, ECLI:EU:C:1957:7

CJUE, 15 July 1964, *Costa vs ENEL*, C-6/64, ECLI:EU:C:1964:66

CJUE, 5 July 1960, *Präsidenten der Ruhrkohlen-Verkaufsgesellschaft mbH and Others v High Authority of the European Coal and Steel Community*, Joined Cases 36, 37, 38/59 and 40/59, ECLI:EU:C:1960:36

CJUE, 12 November 1969, *Erich Stauder v City of Ulm - Sozialamt*, Case 29-69, ECLI:EU:C:1969:52

CJUE, 17 December 1970, *Internationale Handelsgesellschaft mbH v Einfuhr- und Vorratsstelle für Getreide und Futtermittel*, Case 11/70, ECLI:EU:C:1970:114

CJUE, 14 May 1974, *J. Nold, Kohlen- und Baustoffgroßhandlung v Commission of the European Communities*, Case 4/73, ECLI:EU:C:1974:51

CJUE, 20 February 1979, *Rewe-Zentral AG v Bundesmonopolverwaltung für Branntwein*, C-120/78, ECLI:EU:C:1979:42.

CJUE, 13 December 1979, *Liselotte Hauer v Land Rheinland-Pfalz*, Case 44/79, ECLI:EU:C:1979:290

CJEU, 11 January 2000, *Netherlands and Gerard van der Wal v Commission*, C-174-189/98 P, EU:C:2000:1

CJUE, 26 February 2013, *Melloni*, C-399/11, EU:C:2013:107

Italian Constitutional Court, Judgment No. 14 of 7 March 1964, *Costa v. ENEL*, IT:COST:1964:14

Italian Constitutional Court, Judgment No. 183 of 27 December 1973, *Frontini v. Ministero delle Finanze*, IT:COST:1973:183

Italian Constitutional Court, Judgment No. 170 of 8 June 1984, *S.p.a. Fragd v. Amministrazione delle finanze dello Stato* (Granital), IT:COST:1984:170

Italian Constitutional Court, Judgment of 17 December 1973, *Frontini v. Ministero delle Finanze*, [1974] 2 C.M.L.R. 372.

German Federal Court[BVerfG] 29 May, 1974, 37 Entscheidungen Des Bundesverfassungsgerichts [BVerfGE] 271, 285

French Council of State, *Syndicat général de fabricants de semoules de France*, [1970] C.M.L.R. 395.

French Council of State, Judgment of 22 December 1978, *Minister of the Interior v. Cohn-Bendit*, [1980] 1 C.M.L.R. 543

Chapter 9: Second Encounter: Tempering Exclusive Identities Through Ponderation—The *Fin de Siècle* Ponderation of Interests

Cassese, S., *Fine della solitudine delle corti costituzionali, ovvero il dilemma del porcospino*, in *Atti Sc. Mor.*, 2015, pp. 15–25

Cruz Villalón, P., *La identidad constitucional de los Estados miembros: dos relatos europeos*, in *Anuario de la Facultad de Derecho de la Universidad Autónoma de Madrid*, 2013, 2013, pp. 501–514

Favoreu, L., *Cours constitutionnelles nationales et Cour européenne des droits de l'homme*, en *Revue universelle des droits de l'homme*, 2003, pp. 1–6
Favoreu, L., *Avertissement - article n. 2*, in *Revue internationale de droit comparé*, 1981, pp. 251–253
Menéndez Menéndez, A. J., *Una concepción alternativa de la identidad constitucional en el derecho comunitario: de las excepciones idiosincráticas a la resistencia constitucional colectiva*, in *Anuario de la Facultad de Derecho de la Universidad Autónoma de Madrid*, 2013, pp. 561–580
Ferrarese, M.R., *Dal "verbo" legislativo a chi dice l' ultima parola": Le Corti costituzionale e la rete giudiziaria*, in *Annuario di diritto comparato e di studi legislativi*, 2011, pp. 63–87.
Rodin, S., *Constitutional Relevance of Foreign Court Decisions*, in *Am J Comp Law* 2016, pp. 815–840
Wendel, M., *Lisbon before the courts. Comparative perspectives*, in J. M. Beneyto &I. Pernice (eds.), *Europe's constitutional challenges in the light of the recent case law of national constitutional courts*, Nomos, Baden-Baden, 2011, p. 65–104

JUDGMENTS

CJUE, 23 April 1986, *Parti écologiste "Les Verts" v European Parliament*, Case 294/83, ECLI:EU:C:1986:166
CJUE, 13 July 1989, *Hubert Wachauf v Bundesamt für Ernährung und Forstwirtschaft*, C- 5/88, ECLI:EU:C:1989:321
CJUE, 7 de septiembre de 2006, *Mariano Cordero Alonso contra Fondo de Garantía Salarial (Fogasa)*, C-81/05, ECLI:EU:C:2006:529.
European Court of Human Rights (Fifth Section), 6 December 2012, *Michaud v. France*, Application no. 12323/11, ECLI:CE:ECHR:2012:1206 JUD001232311
European Court of Human Rights (Grand Chamber) of 30 June 2005, *Bosphorus Hava Yolları Turizm ve Ticaret Anonim Şirketi v. Ireland*, Application no. 45036/98, ECLI:CE:ECHR:2005:0630JUD004503698.
German Federal Constitutional Court, 7 June 2000, BVerfGE 102
German Federal Constitutional Court, 29 May 1974, *Solange I*, 37 BVerfGE 271.
French Constitutional Council, Decision No. 2004-496 DC of 10 June 2004, *Act to confidence in the digital economy*, FR:CC:2004:2004.496.DC.

Chapter 10 Second Encounter: Tempering Exclusive Identities Through Ponderation—The Mechanisms of Relational Identity in the Twenty-First Century

Aboudrar-Ravanel, S., *Responsabilité et primauté, ou la question de l'efficience de l'outil*, in *Revue de l'Union européenne*, 1999, pp. 544–558

Allison, J.W.F., *Transplantation and Cross-fertilisation in European Public Law*, in *New Directions in European Public Law, Law*, J. Beatson & T. Tridimas (eds), Hart Publishing, Oxford, 1998, pp. 169–182

Alonso García, R., *La responsabilidad de los Estados miembros por infracción del Derecho Comunitario*, Civitas, Madrid, 1997

Alter, K.. *Explaining National Court Acceptance of European Court Jurisprudence: A Critical Evaluation of Theories of Legal Integration*, in *The European Courts and National Courts: Doctrine and Jurisprudence*, A.M. Slaughter, A. Stone Sweet, J.H.H. Weiler (eds.), Hart Publishing, Oxford, 1999, pp. 227–252

Andenas, M. - Fairgrieve, D., *Sufficiently Serious? Judicial Restraint in Tortious Liability for Public Authorities and the European Influence*, in M. Andenas (ed.), *English Public Law and the Common Law of Europe*, London, Key Haven Publications, 1998, pp. 285–321.

Antoniolli Deflorian, L., *La struttura istituzionale del nuovo diritto comune europeo: competizione e circolazione dei modelli giuridici*, Università degli Studi di Trento, Trento, 1996

Bell, J., *Mechanism for Cross-fertilisation of Administrative Law in Europe*, in *New Directions in European Public Law*, Beatson J.- Tridimas T. (eds.), Hart Publishing, Oxford, 1998, pp. 147–167

Benacchio, G., *L'Unione Europea e il diritto provato. Fenomenologia di un'evoluzione*, Cedam, Milano, 2024

Caranta, R., *Learning from the Neighbours: Public Law Remedies and Homogenization from Bottom Up*, in *Maastricht Journ. Europ. Comp. Law*, 1997, pp. 220–244

Cartabia, M., *'Unità nella diversità': il rapporto tra la Costituzione europea e le costituzioni nazionali, in Sul trattato che istituisce una costituzione per l'Unione Europea*, in *Giornata di studio in ricordo di A. Predieri*, Florence, 2005 available at http://www.giustamm.it/new_2005/Cartabia.pdf18

Caruso, D., *The Missing View of the Cathedral: The Private Law Paradigm of European Legal Integration*, in *European Law Journal*, 1997, pp. 3–32

Cassese, S., *L'arena pubblica. Nuovi paradigmi per lo Stato*, in *Riv. trim. dir. pubbl.*, 2001, pp. 601–650

Cassese, S., *The European Common Constitutional Traditions*, in E. Calzolaio, R. Torino y L. Vagni (eds.), *Liber Amicorum Luigi Moccia*, Roma, Roma TrE-Press, 2021, pp. 245–254

Chalmers, D., *Judicial Preferences and the Community Legal Order*, in *Modern Law Review*, 1997, pp. 164–199

Conant, L., *Justice Contained: Law and Politics in the European Union*, Cornell University Press, Ithaca/London, 2002

Constantinesco, V., *La Conciliation Entre la Primauté du Droit de l'Union Européenne et l'Identité Nationale des Etats Membres: Mission Impossible ou Espoir Raisonné?*, in H.-J. Blanke, P. Cruz Villalón, T. Klein y J. Ziller (eds.), *Common European Legal Thinking: Essays in Honour of Albrecht Weber*, Cham/ Berlín, Springer, 2015, pp. 467–483

Craig, P., *The Domestic Liability of Public Authorities in Damages: Lessons from the European Community?*, in *New Directions in European Public Law*, Beatson J.- Tridimas T. (eds.), Hart Publishing, Oxford, 1998, pp. 75–91

De Witte, B., *The role of the ECHR in the evolution of EU law*, in *Maastricht Journal of European and Comparative Law*, 2025, pp. 111–119

Eeckhout, P., *The European Court of Justice and the Legislature*, in *Yearbook of European Law*, 1998, pp. 544–558

Fines, F., *Quelle obligation de réparer pour la violation du droit communautaire ? Nouveaux développements jurisprudentiels sur la responsabilité de l'État normateur*, in *Revue de l'Union européenne*, 1997, pp. 583–600

Glenn, H.P., *Legal Traditions of the World*, Oxford University Press, Oxford, 2014

Graziadei, M. - Decaria, R., *The 'Constitutional Traditions Common to the Member States' in the Case-law of the European Court of Justice: Judicial Dialogue at its Finest*, in *Rivista trimestrale di diritto pubblico*, 2017, pp. 67–108

Graziadei, M., *Comparative Law, Legal History and the Holistic Approach to Legal Cultures*, in *Zeitschrift für Europäisches Privatrecht*, 1999, pp. 531–554

Harlow, C., *Francovich and the Problem of the Disobedient State*, citin *European Law Journal*, 1996, pp. 199–225

Harlow, C., *Voices of Difference in a Plural Community*, in *The American Journal of Comparative Law*, 2002, pp. 339–367

Harlow, C., *European Administrative Law and the Global Challenge*, European University Institute, Working Paper CSR n. 98/23

Jacobs, F. G., *Judicial Dialogue and the Cross-Fertilization of Legal Systems: The European Court of Justice*, in *Texas International Law Journal*, 2003, pp. 547–556

Jones, J., *'Common Constitutional Traditions': Can the Meaning of Human Dignity under German Law Guide the European Court of Justice?*, in *Public Law*, 2004, pp. 167–187

Lacché, L., *Crossing Boundaries: Comparative Constitutional History as a Space of Communication*, in *Glossae: European Journal of Legal History*, 2018, pp. 132–153

Lazari, A., *Modelli e paradigmi della responsabilità dello Stato*, Giappichelli, Torino, 2005

Lazari, A., *Últimas tendencias en la jurisprudencia del Tribunal de Justicia de la Unión Europea*, 2008–2011, J. Díez-Hochleitner Rodríguez, C. Martínez Capdevila, I. Blázquez Navarro, J. Frutos Miranda (eds.), 2012, pp. 209–236

Lazari, A., *La aplicación judicial del Derecho de la Unión Europea en España: el diálogo entre jueces tejedores*, in *Tratado de derecho y políticas de la Unión Europea*, J. Maillo González-Orús, B. Becerril Atienza (ed.); José María Beneyto Pérez (dir.), pp. 665–748.

Legrand, P., *European Legal Systems Are Not Converging*, in *International and Comparative Law Quarterly*, 1996, pp. 52–81

Lazari, A., *Paradeigma e Logos: la responsabilità del legislatore ed i destini dell'Europa*, in *Rivista Diritto Civile*, 2002, pp. 109–168

Lazari, A., *La cross-fertilisation y la formación del paradigma comunitario de responsabilidad del Estado: «el esquema de la crisis»*, in *Revista de Derecho Comunitario Europeo*, 2005, pp. 177–225

Lenaerts, K., *The constitutional traditions common to the Member States: the comparative law method*, in *EUnited in diversity: between common constitutional traditions and national identities*, Riga, Latvia—2-3 September 2021, Conference proceedings, pp. 21–38

Lenaerts, K. - Gutman, K., *The Comparative Law Method and the European Court of Justice: Echoes Across the Atlantic*, in *The American Journal of Comparative Law*, 2016, pp. 841-864

Martinico, G., *The tangled complexity of the EU constitutional process. The frustrating knot of Europe*, Routledge, London, Second Edition, 2023

Nicola, F. G., *National Legal Traditions at Work in the Jurisprudence of the Court of Justice of the European Union*, in *The American Journal of Comparative Law*, 2016, pp. 865–889

Pfander, J.E., *Member state liability and constitutional change in the United States and Europe*, in *Amer. J. Compar. Law*, 2003, pp. 237–274

Pollicino, O., *Common Constitutional Traditions in the Age of the European Bill(s) of Rights: Chronicle of a (Somewhat Prematurely) Foretold Death?*, in *Italian Journal of Public Law*, vol. 2, n° 1, 2010, pp. 57–108

Ragone, S., *Constitutional identities and traditions: a conundrum for comparative lawyers*, in *Revista de Direito Administrativo & Constitucional*, 2022, p. 11–36

Roughan, N., *Authorities. Conflicts, Cooperation, and Transnational Legal Theory*, Oxford University Press, Oxford, 2013

Ruggeri, A., *Tradizioni costituzionali comuni" e "controlimiti", tra teoria delle fonti e teoria dell'interpretazione*, in *Diritto pubblico comparato ed europeo*, 2003, p. 115–136

Sacco, R., *Introduzione al diritto comparato*, Utet, Torino, 1992

Sacco, R., *L'interpretazione: dato oggettivo e spirito dell'interprete*, en Derrida, J. - Vattimo, G. (eds.), *Diritto, giustizia e interpretazione*, Laterza, Bari, 1998

Scarciglia, R., *The Silent Language: From Chthonic Law to Global Legal Pluralism*, in R. Scarciglia - W. Menski (eds.), *Normative Pluralism and Religious Diversity: Challenges and Methodological Approaches*, Wolters Kluwer/CEDAM, Milano, 2018, pp. 39–56

Scholtes, J., *The Abuse of Constitutional Identity in the European Union*, Oxford University Press, Oxford, 2023

Tallberg, J., *European Governance and Supranational Institutions: Making States Comply (Routledge Advances in European Politics)*, Routledge, London, 2003

Tridimas, T., *Liability for Breach of Community Law: Growing up and Mellowing down?*, in *Common Market Law Review*, 2001, pp. 301–332

Van Gerven, W., *Bridging the unbridgeable: Community and national tort laws after Francovich and Brasserie*, in *Int. Comp. Law Quart.*, 1996, pp. 507–544

Weiler, J.H.H., *Bread and Circus: the State of European Union*, in *Columbia Journal of European Law*, 1998, pp. 223–248

Judgments

CJEU, 19 November 1991, C-6 and C-9/90, *Francovich* et al. v *Italian Republic*, ECLI:EU:C:1991:428

CJEU, 16 December 1993, Teodoro Wagner Miret v Fondo de garantía salarial, Case C-334/92, ECLI:EU:C:1993:945

CJEU, 5 March 1996, C-48/93, *Brasserie du Pêcheur SA v. Bundesrepublik Deutschland and The Queen v. Secretary of State for Transport, ex parte: Factortame Ltd et al.*, ECLI:EU:C:1996:79

CJEU, 26 March 1996, Regina v H. M. Treasury, ex parte British Telecommunications plc, Case C-392/93, ECR I-1631, ECLI:EU:C:1996:131.

CJEU, 8 October 1996, Erich Dillenkofer and Others v Bundesrepublik Deutschland, Joined Cases C-178/94, C-179/94, C-188/94, C-189/94 and C-190/94, ECLI:EU:C:1996:375

Documents

Conclusions of Advocate General Giuseppe Tesauro, presented on 28 November 1995, Joined Cases C-46/93 And C-48/93, ECLI:EU:C:1995:412

Conclusions of Advocate General Léger, presented on 8 April 2003, Gerhard Köbler v Republik Österreich, Case C-224/01, ECR I-10239, ECLI:EU:C:2003:207

Conclusions of Advocate General M. Poiares Maduro, presented on 20 February 2008, Joined Cases C-120/06 P and C-121/06 P, ECLI:EU:C:2008:98.

Conclusions of Advocate General Verica Trstenjak, presented 30 June 2009, Case C-101/08 Audiolux et al., ECLI:EU:C:2009:410. ECLI:EU:C:2011:559

Conclusions of Advocate General Kokott, presented on 29 April 2010, *Akzo Nobel Chemicals Ltd and Akcros Chemicals Ltd v European Commission*, C-550/07 P, ECLI:EU:C:2010:229

Conclusions of Advocate General Cruz Villalón, presented on 14 January 2015, Peter Gauweiler and Others v Deutscher Bundestag, Case C-62/14, ECLI:EU:C:2015:7.

Conclusions of Advocate General Ćapeta, presented on 5 June 2025, Commission v. Hungary, C-769/22, ECLI:EU:C:2025:408

European Commission, *Initial Contributions by the Commission to the Intergovernmental Conference on Political Union: Composite Working Paper*, SEC (91) 500. 15 May 1991

Chapter 11: Second Encounter: Tempering Exclusive Identities Through Ponderation—The Écart Between Common Constitutional Traditions, Constitutional Identity and Values of the European Union

Bartole, S., *Comparative Constitutional Law an Indispensable Tool for the Creation of Transnational Law*, in *European Constitutional Law Review*, 2017, pp. 601–610

Blanke, H.J., *Article 4 [The Relations Between the EU and the Member States]*, in *The Treaty on European Union (TEU). A Commentary*, H.-J. Blanke & S. Mangiameli (eds.), Springer, 2010, Berlin, Heidelberg, pp. 185–253

Cannizzaro, E., *La sovranità oltre lo Stato*, Il Mulino, Bologna, 2020

Cappelletti, M., - Golay, D., *The Judicial Branch in the Federal and Transnational Union: Its Impact on Integration*", in M. Cappelletti, M. Seccombe y J.H.H. Weiler (eds.), *Integration Through Law: Europe and the American Federal Experience,* Vol. 1 (Methods, Tools and Institutions), Book 2 (Political Organs, Integration Techniques and Judicial Process), Berlín/Nueva York, De Gruyter, 1986, pp. 261–313

Cloots, E., "National Identity, Constitutional Identity, and Sovereignty in the EU", in *Netherlands Journal of Legal Philosophy*, vol. 45, n° 2, 2016, pp. 82–102

Di Martino, A., *Comparare le identità costituzionali: circolazione degli argomenti giuridici e contesti storico-politici*, in M. Graziadei y A. Somma (eds.), *Esperienze giuridiche en diálogo: Il ruolo della comparazione*, Roma, Sapienza Università Editrice, 2024, pp. 119–138

E. Di Salvatore, *L'identità costituzionale dell'Unione europea e degli Stati membri*, Giappichelli, Torino, 2008

Dixon, R.-Landau, D., *Abusive Constitutional Borrowing*, in *Oxford Journal of Legal Studies*, 2017, pp. 69–95

Fabbrini, F. - Sajó, A., *The Dangers of Constitutional Identity*, in *European Law Journal*, 2019, pp. 457–473

Halmai, G., *Abuse of Constitutional Identity: The Hungarian Constitutional Court on Interpretation of Article E) (2) of the Fundamental Law*, in *Review of Central and East European Law*, 2018, pp. 23–42

Kelemen, R. D. - Pech, L., *The Uses and Abuses of Constitutional Pluralism: Assessing the 'Arguments of Resistance' of the Polish and Hungarian Constitutional Courts*, in *Common Market Law Review*, 2019, pp. 59–96

Kortvelyesi, Z. – Majtényi, B., *Game of Values: The Threat of Exclusive Constitutional Identity, the EU and Hungary*, in *German Law Journal* 18(7), December 2017, pp. 1721–1744

Kovács, K., *The Rise of an Ethnocultural Constitutional Identity in the Jurisprudence of the East Central European Courts*, in *German Law Journal*, 2017, pp. 1703–1720.

Faraguna, P. - Drinóczi, T., "Constitutional Identity in and on EU Terms", in *Verfassungsblog*, 21 de February de 2022

Komárek, J., *It's a Stupid Autonomy*, 2014, in http://verfassungsblog.de/its-a-stupid-autonomy-2/

Lenaerts, K., *Interlocking Legal Orders in the European Union and Comparative Law*, in *International and Comparative Law Quarterly*, vol. 52, n° 4, octubre 2003, pp. 873–906

Maduro, M. P., *Three Claims of Constitutional Pluralism*, in M. Avbelj y J. Komárek (eds.), *Constitutional Pluralism in the European Union and Beyond*, Oxford, Hart Publishing, 2012, pp. 67–84

Marcuse, H., *Eros and Civilization: A Philosophical Inquiry into Freud*, Boston, Beacon Press, 1955

Martinico, G., *Between Mimetism and Parasitism: Italian Populism in a Comparative Perspective*, in *European Public Law*, 2020, p. 23–36

Martinico, G. y Pollicino, O., *The National Judicial Resistance Against the European Court of Justice and the EU Charter of Fundamental Rights: Use and Abuse of a Promising Concept*, in F. Fontanelli, G. Martinico y P. Carrozza (eds.), *Shaping Rule of Law Through Dialogue: International and National Courts*, Groningen, Europa Law Publishing, 2010, pp. 243–270

Martinico, G., *The Tangled Complexity of the EU Constitutional Process. The Frustrating Knot of Europe*, Routledge, London, Second Edition, 2023

Pernice, I., *Der Schutz nationaler Identität in der Europäischen Union*, in *Archiv des öffentlichen Rechts*, 2011, pp. 185–221

Polimeni, S., *L'identità costituzionale come controlimite*, in *Ianus*, 2017, pp. 133–161

Pollicino, O., *Common Constitutional Traditions in the Age of the European Bill(s) of Rights: Chronicle of a (Somewhat Prematurely) Foretold Death?*, in *Italian Journal of Public Law*, vol. 2, n° 1, 2010, pp. 57–108

Rodotà, S., *Il diritto di avere diritti*, Laterza, Bari, 2012
Ruggieri, A., *Struttura e dinamica delle tradizioni costituzionali nella prospettiva dell'integrazione europea*, in *Anuario Iberoamericano de Justicia Constitucional*, n. 7, 2003, pp. 373–339
Salese, V., *The EU Integration through the Lenses of Domestic Constitutional/ Supreme Courts: the Material Scope of Constitutional Clashes*, in *Rivista di Diritti comparati*, 2022, p. 896–1013
Sarmiento, D., *What Schrems, Delvigne and Celaj Tell us about the State of Fundamental Rights in the EU*, 2015, http://verfassungsblog.de/author/daniel-sarmiento/
Scheppele, K. L., Kochenov, D. V., Grabowska-Moroz, B., *EU Values Are Law, after All: Enforcing EU Values through Systemic Infringement Actions by the European Commission and the Member States of the European Union*, in *Yearbook of European Law*, 2020, pp. 3–121.
Scholtes, J., *The Abuse of Constitutional Identity in the European Union*, Oxford University Press, Oxford, 2023
Schütze, R., *From Dual to Cooperative Federalism. The Changing Structure of European* Law, Oxford University Press, Oxford, 2009
Tripković, B., *The Metaethics of Constitutional Adjudication*, Oxford, Oxford University Press, 2017
von Bogdandy, A., & Schill, S. W., *Overcoming Absolute Primacy; Respect for National Identity under the Lisbon Treaty*, in *Common Market Law Review*, 2011, pp. 1417–1453
Weber, F., *The Identity of Union Law in Primacy: Piercing Through Euro Box Promotion and Others*, in *European Papers* 2022, 2, pp. 761–786
Zoteeva, A. & Kragh, M. *From constitutional identity to the identity of the Constitution*, in *Communist and Post-Communist Studies,* 2021, pp. 176–195

Judgments

CJEU, (Grand Chamber), 6 September 2017, Slovak Republic and Hungary v Council of the European Union, Joined Cases C-643/15 and C-647/15, ECLI:EU:C:2017:631
CJEU, (Grand Chamber), 5 December 2017, Case C-42/17, M.A.S., M.B., ECLI:EU:C:2017:936
CJEU, (Grand Chamber) of 6 March, 2018, *Slowakische Republik v. Achmea BV*, Case C-284/16, ECLI:EU:C:2018:234
CJEU, (plenary), 10 December 2018, *Andy Wightman and Others v. Secretary of State for Exiting the European Union, Case C-621/18,* ECLI:EU:C:2018:999
CJEU, (Grand Chamber), 3 September 2008, *Yassin Abdullah Kadi and Al Barakaat International Foundation v. Council of the European Union*, Joined

Cases C-402/05 P and C-415/05 P, Case Law 2008 I-06351, ECLI:EU:C:2008:461

CJEU, (Grand Chamber), 8 April 2014, *Digital Rights Ireland Ltd. v. Minister for Communications, Marine and Natural Resources and Others and Kärntner Landesregierung and Others*, Joined Cases C-293/12 and C-594/12, ECLI:EU:C:2014:238

CJEU, (Grand Chamber), 13 May 2014, *Google Spain, S.L. and Google Inc. v. Agencia Española de Protección de Datos (AEPD) and Mario Costeja González*, Case C-131/12, ECLI:EU:C:2014:317

CJEU, AK and others, 19 November 2019, C-585/18, C-624/18 and C-625/18, ECLI:EU:C:2019:982

CJEU, (Grand Chamber), 17 December 2020, European Commission v Hungary, Case C-808/18, ECLI:EU:C:2020:1029

CJEU (Grand Chamber), 2 April 2020, European Commission v Republic of Poland, Hungary and Czech Republic, Joined Cases C-715/17, C-718/17 and C-719/17, ECLI:EU:C:2020:25

CJEU, (Grand Chamber), 16 July 2020, Data Protection Commissioner v Facebook Ireland Ltd and Maximillian Schrems, Case C-311/18, ECLI:EU:C:2020:559

CJEU, 22 February 2022, C-156/21, *Hungary v European Parliament and Council of the European Union*; ECLI:EU:C:2022:97

CJEU, 22 February 2022, C-157/21, *Poland v European Parliament and Council of the European Union*, ECLI:EU:C:2022:98

ICJ, *Jurisdictional Immunities of the State (Germany v. Italy: Greece intervening)*, Judgment, I.C.J. Reports 2012, p. 99

Italian Constitutional Court, Order No. 24/2017, 26 January 2017, ECLI:IT:COST:2017:24

BVerfG, Judgment of the Second Senate of 05 May 2020 - 2 BvR 859/15, 2 BvR 980/15, 2 BvR 2006/15, 2 BvR 1651/15, ECLI:DE:BVerfG:2020:rs20200505.2bvr085915

BVerfG, Order of the Second Senate of 15 April 2021 - 2 BvR 547/21, ECLI:DE:BVerfG:2021:rs20210415.2bvr054721

Constitutional Tribunal of Poland, Judgment of 14 July 2021, Case P 7/20, ECLI:PL:TK:2021:P.7.20, paras. 109, 116 et seq., 204, 230.

Constitutional Tribunal of Poland, Judgment of 24 November 2021, Case K 6/21, ECLI:PL:TK:2021:K.6.21, paras. 68, 111

Constitutional Tribunal of Poland, Judgment of 10 March 2022, Case K 7/21, ECLI:PL:TK:2022:K.7.21, paras. 157, 312, 373, 393.

Constitutional Tribunal of Poland, Judgment of 7 October 2021, Case K 3/21, ECLI:PL:TK:2021:K.3.21, paras. III. 1.3, 4.1, 4.2, 4.4, 4.5.

Constitutional Tribunal of Poland, Judgment of 24 November 2021, Case K 6/21, ECLI:PL:TK:2021:K.6.21, paras. 68, 111

Constitutional Court of Hungary (Alkotmánybíróság), Decision 22/2016 (XII.5.) AB on the Interpretation of Article E(2) of the Fundamental Law, 30 November 2016, ECLI:HU:CC:2016:22

Constitutional Court of Hungary, Decision 32/2021 (XII. 20.) AB of 7 December 2021, ECLI:HU:CC:2021:32, para. 70

Documents

Conclusions of the Advocate General Ćapeta's, C-769/22, *Commission/Hungary*, presented on 5 June 2025; C-769/22, ECLI:EU:C:2025:408

Chapter 12: The Third Encounter with the Other: The European Union as a 'Community of Values'—Article 2 TEU as a Limit, Standard of Conduct and System of Values

Blanke, H.J., *Article 4 [The Relations Between the EU and the Member States]*, in *The Treaty on European Union (TEU). A Commentary*, H.-J. Blanke & S. Mangiameli (eds.), Springer, Berlin, Heidelberg, 2010, pp. 185–253

Ballin, E. H., *Constitutional Identity in the Netherlands: Sailing with Others*', in C. Calliess y G. van der Schyff (eds), *Constitutional Identity in a Europe of Multilevel Constitutionalism*, Cambridge University Press, 2020, pp. 234–251

Bonelli, M., *National Identity and European Integration Beyond 'Limited Fields'*, in *European Public Law* 27, no. 3, 2021, pp. 537–558

Calliess, C. – Schnettger, A., *Comparative Constitutional Identity and Multilevel constitutionalism*, in C. Calliess and G. van der Schyff (eds), *Constitutional Identity in a Europe of Multilevel Constitutionalism*, Cambridge University Press, Cambridge, 2020, pp. 372–392

Cloots, E., *National Identity, Constitutional Identity, and Sovereignty in the EU*, in *Netherlands Journal of Legal Philosophy*, 2016, pp. 82–98

Di Federico, G., *L'identità nazionale degli stati membri nel diritto dell'Unione europea. Natura e portata dell'art.* 4, *par. 2, TUE*, Editoriale Scientifica, Napoli, 2017

F. Fabbrini - O. Pollicino, *Constitutional Identity in Italy. Institutional Disagreements at a Time of Political Change*, in *Constitutional Identity in a Europe of Multilevel Constitutionalism*, cit., pp. 201–221

Lenaerts, K., *On Checks and Balances: The Rule of Law within the* EU, in *Columbia Journal of European Law*, 2023, pp. 25–63

Lenaerts, K.- Gutiérrez-Fons, J.A., *High Hopes: Autonomy and the Identity of the EU*, in *European Papers* 2021, p. 1500

L'identité constitutionnelle saisie par les juges en Europe, L. Burgorgue-Larsen (dir.), Editions Pedone, Paris, 2011

Lindahl, H., *The Purposiveness of Law: Two Concepts of Representation in the European Union*, in Law *and Philosophy*, 1998, pp. 481–507

Martinico, G., *Judging in the Multilevel Legal Order: Exploring the Techniques of 'Hidden Dialogue'*, in *King's Law Journal*, 2010, pp. 257–281

Millet, F.X., *Successfully Articulating National Constitutional Identity Claims: Strait Is the Gate and Narrow Is the Way*', in *European Public Law*, 2021, pp. 571–596

Poiares Maduro, M., *Three Claims of Constitutional Pluralism*, in M. Avbelj & J. Komárek, (eds), *Constitutional Pluralism in the European Union and Beyond*, Bloomsbury Publishing, London, 2012, pp. 67–84

Rideau, J., *The Case-law of the Polish, Hungarian and Czech Constitutional Courts on national Identity and the 'German Model'*, in *National Constitutional Identity and European Integration*, cit., pp. 243–263.

Rorty, R., *Contingency, Irony, and Solidarity*, Cambridge University Press, Cambridge, 1989

Rossi, L.S., '*Concretised', 'Flanked', or 'Standalone'? Some Reflections on the Application of Article 2 TEU*, in *European Papers—A Journal on Law and Integration*, 2025, pp. 1–24.

Rossi, L.S., '*2, 4, 6 (TUE)… l'interpretazione dell'"Identity Clause" alla luce dei valori fondamentali dell'UE, en Liber Amicorum in Onore Di Antonio Tizzano: De la CECA à la Cour de l'Union: Le Long Parcours de la Justice Européenne*, R. Adam, et al. (eds.), Giappichelli, Torino, 2018, pp. 40–65.

Rossi, L.S., *How to resolve the "Taricco question" … without relying on Art. 4, para. 2 TEU, SIDIBlog*, 17 May 2017, www.sidiblog.org

Rossi, L.S., *Il valore giuridico dei valori. L'Articolo 2 TUE: relazioni con altre disposizioni del diritto primario dell'UE e rimedi giurisdizionali*, in Federalismi.it, 2020, pp. iv–34

Safjan, M., *Between Mangold and Omega: Fundamental rights* versus *constitutional identity*, in *Dir. Un. eur.*, 2012, p. 437–461

Schnettger, A., *Article 4(2) TEU as a Vehicle for National Constitutional Identity in the Shared European Legal System*, in *Identity In A Europe of Multilevel Constitutionalism*, C. Calliess & G. van der Schyff (eds.), Cambridge University Press, Cambridge, 2020, pp. 9–38

Scholtes, J., *The Abuse of Constitutional Identity in the European Union*, Oxford University Press, 2023

Śledzińska-Simon, A., *Constitutional Identity in 3D: A Model of Individual, Relational, and Collective Self and Its Application in Poland*, in *Int'l J. Const. L.*, 2015, pp. 124–155

Spieker, L.D., *Transformative Constitutionalism in Luxembourg: How the Court Can Support Democratic Transitions*, in *Columbia Journal of European Law* 2023, pp. 65–92

Tomuschat, C., *The Defence of National Identity by the German Constitutional Court*, in A. Saiz Arnaiz y C. Alcoberro Llivina (eds), *National Constitutional Identity and European Integration*, Intersentia, Antwerp, 2013, pp. 205–225.

Tuori, K., *European Constitutionalism,* Cambridge University Press, Cambridge, 2015

Weiler, J. H. H., *In Defence of the Status Quo: Europe's Constitutional Sonderweg*, in M. Wind – J.H. H. Weiler (eds.), *European Constitutionalism Beyond the State*, Cambridge University Press, Cambridge, 2003, pp. 7–23.

Judgments

CJEU, 7 February 1973, *Commission v Italy*, C-39/72, ECLI:EU:C:1973:13

CJEU, 22 December 2010, Sayn-Wittgenstein, C-208/09, ECLI:EU:C:2010:80

CJUE, 26 February 2013, case C-399/11, Stefano Melloni and Ministerio Fiscal, ECLI:EU:C:2013:107

CJEU, 2 June 2016, Nabiel Peter Bogendorff von Wolffersdorff and Standesamt der Stadt Karlsruhe, Case C-438/14, ECLI:EU:C:2016:40

CJEU, 6 March 2018, C-284/16, *Slovak Republic v Achmea BV,* ECLI:EU:C:2018:158

ECLI:EU:C:2021:311

CJEU, (plenary), 10 December 2018, *Andy Wightman and Others v. Secretary of State for Exiting the European Union,* Case C-621/18, ECLI:EU:C:2018:999

CJEU, 20 April 2021, *Repubblika v Il-Prim Ministru,* C-896/19, ECLI:EU:C:2021:311

CJEU, 16 February 2022, *Hungary v Parliament and Council,* C-156/21, ECLI:EU:C:2022:97

CJEU, 22 February 2022, *RS (Effect of the decisions of a constitutional court),* C-430/21, ECLI:EU:C:2022:99

CJEU, 19 November 2024, European Commission v. Czech Republic, C-808/21

ECLI:EU:C:2024:962

Polish Constitutional Tribunal, Judgment of 24 November 2010, Case K 32/09 (Treaty of Lisbon).

Czech Constitutional Court, Judgment of 31 January 2012, Pl. ÚS 5/12 (*Slovak Pensions XVII / Landtová*)

Portuguese Constitutional Court, 5 April 2013, 5 april 2013, Acórdão n.° 187/2013

Documents

Conclusion of Advocate General Poiares Maduro, presented in C-160/03 *Spain v. Eurojust*, ECLI:EU: C:2005:168, para. 31.

Opinion 1/17 on the CETA EU-Canada (EU:C:2019:341), paragraph 110.

Conclusions of the Advocate General Ćapeta's, presented in C-769/22, *Commission/Hungary*, presented on 5 June 2025, C-769/22, ECLI:EU:C:2025:408

Chapter 13 Epilogue. The Relational Identity: Openness and Limits

Abi-Saab, G., *The Portrait of the Jurist as an international Judge*, in C. Peck & R.S. Lee (eds.), *Increasing the Effectiveness of the International Court of Justice: Proceedings of the ICJ/UNITAR Colloquium to Celebrate the 50th Anniversary of the Court*, La Haya, Martinus Nijhoff Publishers, 1997, pp. 166–172

Al Tamimi, Y., *Human Rights and the Excess of Identity: A Legal and Theoretical Inquiry into the Notion of Identity in Strasbourg Case Law*, in *Social & Legal Studies*, 2018, pp. 278–298

É. Balibar, *Le renversement de l'individualisme possessif*, in H. Guineret and A. Milanese, *La propriété: le propre, l'appropriation*, Ellipses, París, 2004, pp. 131–156

Sánchez Barrilao, J.F., *Tra identità: il futuro dell'integrazione europea nel contesto globale*, in *Nomos*, 2019, pp. 1–14.

Bennett, T. W., *Comparative Law and African Customary Law*, in M. Reimann – R. Zimmermann (eds), *The Oxford Handbook of Comparative Law*, Oxford University Press, Oxford, 2006, pp. 641–672

Bianchi, A., '*Epistemic Communities*', in Jean d'Aspremont and Sahib Singh (eds.), *Concepts for International Law Contributions to Disciplinary Thought*, Edward Elgar, London, 2019, pp. 251–266

Boaventura De Sousa, *A Gramática do tempo: para unha nova cultura política*, Porto, Edições Afrontamento, 2006

Boaventura De Sousa, *Towards a New Legal Common Sense: Law, Globalization and Emancipation*, 2nd edition, Butterworths, London, 2002

Bonelli, M., Has the Court of Justice embraced the language of constitutional identity?, in Diritti Comparati 2022, available in https://www.diritticomparati.it/has-the-court-of-justice-embraced-the-language-of-constitutional-identity/

Bradford, A., *The Brussels Effect – How the European Union rules the world*, Oxford University Press, Oxford, 2020

Butler, J., *Precarious Life: The Powers of Mourning and Violence*, Verso, London, 2004

Cartabia, M., Principi inviolabili e integrazione euro pea, Giuffré, Milan, 1995

Chevallier, J., *Les interprètes du droit*, in P. Amselek (ed.), *Interprétation et droit*, Bruylant, Bruselles, 1995

Casolari, F., *Il processo di europeizzazione delle identità nazionali degli Stati membri*, in *Quaderni AISDUE - Rivista quadrimestrale*, 2024, pp. 41–65

de Boer, N., *Judging European Democracy. The Role and Legitimacy of National Constitutional Courts in the EU*, Oxford University Press, Oxford, 2023

Duve, T., *History of Global Law: A Methodological Approach*, in *Max Planck Institute for the History of European Law, Research Paper Series*, No. 2016-04, available at: ssrn.com/abstract=2781104

Elster, J., *Ulysses Unbound: Studies in Rationality, Precommitment, and Constraints*, Cambridge University Press, 2000

Fabbrini F. - Sajó, A., *The dangers of constitutional identity*, in *European Law Journal*, 2019, pp. 457–473

Foucault, M., *The Order of Discourse*, in R. Young (ed.), *Untying the Text: A Post-Structuralist Reader*, Routledge & Kegan Paul, London, 1981

Fichera M. –Pollicino, O., *The Dialectics Between Constitutional Identity and Common Constitutional Traditions. Which Language for Cooperative Constitutionalism in Europe?*, in *German Law Journal*, 2019, pp. 1097–1118

Glenn, H.P., *The National Tradition*, vol. 11.3 Electronic Journal Of Comparative Law, (December 2007)

Goodman, N., *Ways of Worldmaking*, Hackett Publishing Company, London, 1978

Grossi, P., *Assolutismo giuridico e diritto privato*, Giuffré, Milano, 1998

Habermas, J., *The Inclusion of the Other: Studies in Political Theory*, Polity Press, Cambridge, 1998

Korhonen, O., *International. Law Situated: An Analysis of the Lawyer's Stance towards Culture, History and Community*, Kluwer, 2000

Koskienniemi, M., *The Gentle Civilizer of Nations. The Rise and Fall of International Law 1870–1960*, Cambridge University Press, Cambridge, 2001

Innerarity, D., *¿Quiénes somos 'nosotros'? Preliminares para una política de la identidad*, in *Doxa*, 2005, pp. 33–54

Jullien, F., *L'écart et l'entre. Leçon inaugurale de la Chaire sur l'altérité*, Galilée, Paris, 2012.

Lazari, A., *El diálogo entre jueces como paradigma comparativo europeo, in Diálogos judiciales en el sistema europeo de protección de derechos: una perspectiva interdisciplinaria*, Tirant Lo Blanch, Valencia, 2018, pp. 41–71

Legrand, P., *Le droit comparé*, PUF, Paris, 1999

Lenaerts, K., *Celebrating 20 Years Together, Opening Speech of the Conference "20 Years since the Accession of 10 States to the European Union: A New Constitutional Moment for Europe*, Court of Justice of the European Union, Luxembourg, 3 May 2024, p. 16, www.curia.europa.eu.

Lenaerts, K., *National Identity, The Equality of Member States before the Treaties and the Primacy of EU Law*, in B. Carotti (ed.), *Identità nazionale degli Stati membri, primato del diritto dell'Unione europea, Stato di diritto e indipendenza dei giudici nazionali*, Roma, Corte Costituzionale / Editoriale Scientifica, 2022, pp. 11–28

Levinas, E., *Totalité et Infini: Essai sur l'extériorité*, La Haya, Martinus Nijhoff, 1961

Levinas, E., *Autrement qu'être ou au-delà de l'essence*, Martinus Nijhoff, La Haye, 1974

Lustig, D.-Weiler, J.H.H., *Judicial review in the contemporary world—Retrospective and prospective*, in *International journal of constitutional law*, 2018, pp. 315–372

Mac Amhlaigh, C., *Taking Identity Seriously: On the Politics of the Individuation of Legal Systems*, in *Oxford Journal of Legal Studies*, 2022, pp. 521–547.

Martinico, G., *Conflictos constitucionales y pluralismo agónico: ¿Qué podemos apren der de la teoría política?*, in *Diálogos judiciales en el sistema europeo de protección de derechos: Una mirada interdisciplinar*, G. Fernández Arribas, M. Hermosín Álvarez, A. Lazari (ed.), 2018, pp. 21–40

Martinico, G., *Constitutions, openness and comparative law*, in *Estudios de Deusto: Revista de Derecho Público*, 2019, pp. 111–124

Martinico, G., *The asymmetric turn of the new European economic governance: some remarks on the treaty on stability, coordination and governance in the economic and monetary Union*, in *Revista catalana de dret public*, 2013, pp. 128–139

Menski, W.F., *Comparative Law in a Global Context: The Legal Systems of Asia and Africa*, Cambridge University Press, Cambridge, 2009

Muir Watt, H., *Alterity in the Conflict of Laws: An Ontology of the In-Between*, in *Rabels Zeitschrift für Auslandisches und Internationales Privatrecht*, 2023, pp. 2–32

Nancy, J.L., *Être singulier pluriel*, Éditions Galilée, Paris, 1996

Patrignani, E., *Alterity according to Emmanuel Levinas and Comparison of Laws*, in *Philosophy*, 2016, p. 40–65

Perju, V., *Identity Federalism in Europe and the United States*, in *Vanderbilt Journal of Transnational Law*, 2020, pp. 207–273

Pauwelyn, J., *Is it International Law or Not, and Does It Even Matter?*, in J. Pauwelyn, R. A. Wessel y J. Wouters (eds.), *Informal International Lawmaking*, Oxford, Oxford University Press, 2012, pp. 125–161

Petersen, N., *International Law, Cultural Diversity, and Democratic Rule: Beyond the Divide Between Universalism and Relativism*, in *Asian Journ. Intern. Law.*, 2011, pp. 149–163.

Pizzorusso, A., Il *patrimonio costituzionale europeo*, Il Mulino, Bologna, 2002

Popper, K. *The Open Society and Its Enemies*, Princeton University Press, Princeton, 2013

Resta, G., *L'albero e l'onda: il discorso della comparazione al crocevia delle discipline*, in V. Zeno-Zencovich y R. Onesti (eds.), *Comparare. Una riflessione tra le discipline*, Roma, RomaTrE-Press, 2011, pp. 13–46

Roughan, N., *Authorities. Conflicts, Cooperation, and Transnational Legal Theory*, Oxford University Press, Oxford, 2013

Ruskola, T., *China in the Age of the World Picture*, in *Oxford Handbook of the Theory of International Law*, in A. Orford y F. Hoffmann (eds.), *The Oxford Handbook of the Theory of International Law*, Oxford, Oxford University Press, 2016, pp. 151–168.

Sacco, R., *Il diritto muto. Neuroscienze, conoscenza tacita, valori condivisi*, Il Mulino, Bologna, 2015

P. Sands, *Sustainable Development: Treaty, Custom, and the Cross-Fertilization of International Law*', in A. Boyle and D. Freestone (eds.), *International Law and Sustainable Development: Past Achievements and Future Challenges*, Oxford University Press, New York, 1999

Scarciglia, R., *The Silent Language: From Chthonic Law to Global Legal Pluralism*, in R. Scarciglia - W. Menski (eds.), *Normative Pluralism and Religious Diversity: Challenges and Methodological Approaches*, Wolters Kluwer/CEDAM, Milano, 2018, pp. 39–56

Scholtes, J., *The Abuse of Constitutional Identity in the European Union*, Oxford University Press, 2023

Scicluna, N., *European Union Constitutionalism in Crisis*, Routledge, London, 2015

Sikkink, K., The Hidden Face of the Right: towards a Politics of Responsibility, Yale University Press, 2020

Tushnet, M., *Comment, What Then Is the American?*, in *Ariz. L. Rev.* 1996, pp. 625–634

Uitz, R., *National Constitutional Identity in the European Constitutional Project: A Recipe for Exposing Cover Ups and Masquerades*, in VerfBlog, 2016/11/11, https://verfassungsblog.de/national-constitutional-identity-in-the-european-constitutional-project-a-recipe-for-exposing-cover-ups-and-masquerades/

von Bogdandy, A., *The Transformation of European Law: The Reformed Concept and its Quest for Comparison*, in *European Law Journal*, 2016, pp. 519–538

Yusuf, A., *Diversity of Legal Traditions And International Law: Keynote Address*, in *Cambridge Journal of International and Comparative Law*, pp. 3–16

Weiler, J.H.H., *The Constitution of Europe*, Cambridge University Press, Cambridge, 1999

Weiler, J.H.H., *Federalism without Constitutionalism: Europe's Sonderweg*', in K. Nicolaidis and R Howse (eds), *The Federal* Vision, Oxford University Press, 2001, esp. pp. 54–68

Zagrebelsky, G., *La virtù del dubbio. Intervista su etica e diritto*, Roma-Bari, Laterza, 2007

Judgments

CJEU, 14 March 2017, *Achbita v G4S Secure Solutions*, C-157/15, ECLI:EU:C:2017:203

CJEU, 14 March 2017, *Bougnaoui v Micropole*, C-188/15, ECLI:EU:C:2017:204

CJEU, 27 June 2017, *Congregación de Escuelas Pías Provincia Betania v Ayuntamiento de Getafe*, C-74/16, ECLI:EU:C:2017:496

CJEU, 17 April 2018, *Egenberger*, C-414/16, ECLI:EU:C:2018:257

CJEU, 29 May 2018, *Liga van Moskeeën en Islamitische Organisaties Provincie Antwerpen v Vlaams Gewest*, C-426/16, ECLI:EU:C:2018:335

CJEU, 11 September 2018, *IR v JQ*, C-68/17, ECLI:EU:C:2018:696

CJEU, 22 January 2019, *Cresco Investigation v Achatzi*, C-193/17, ECLI:EU:C:2019:43

CJEU, 17 December 2020, *Centraal Israëlitisch Consistorie van België v Vlaamse Regering*, C-336/19, ECLI:EU:C:2020:1031.

ICJ, Gabčíkovo-Nagymaros Project (Hungary/Slovakia), Judgment, I.C.J. Reports 1997, p. 7

ECHR, 30 January 1998, *United Communist Party of Turkey and Others v. Turkey* [GC], App. No. 19392/92, ECHR 1998-I

ECHR, 18 March 2011, *Lautsi and Others v. Italy* [GC], App. No. 30814/06, ECHR 2011

ECHR, 1 July 2014, *S.A.S. v. France* [GC], App. No. 43835/11, ECHR 2014.

Documents

Conclusions of the Advocate General Ćapeta's, C-769/22, *Commission/Hungary*, presented on 5 June 2025, C-769/22, ECLI:EU:C:2025:408

The manufacturer's authorised representative in the EU is Springer Nature Customer Service Centre GmbH, Europaplatz 3, 69115 Heidelberg, Germany. If you have any concerns regarding our products, please contact ProductSafety@springernature.com

Printed and bound by CPI Group (UK) Ltd, Croydon, CR0 4YY
21/09/2026
02219945-0013